WHO IS JESUS CHRIST

WHO IS JESUS CHRIST

THE COMPLETE STORY

I am Alpha and Omega
The beginning and the ending
saith the Lord Which is, and which was
and which is to come The Almighty
—Revelation 1:8

2nd Edition

ABRAHAM HOWARD JR.

Who is Jesus Christ

This book is written to provide information and motivation to readers. Its purpose is not to render any type of psychological, legal, or professional advice of any kind. The content is the sole opinion and expression of the author, and not necessarily that of the publisher.

Copyright © 2020 by Abraham Howard Jr.

All rights reserved. No part of this book may be reproduced, transmitted, or distributed in any form by any means, including, but not limited to, recording, photocopying, or taking screenshots of parts of the book, without prior written permission from the author or the publisher. Brief quotations for noncommercial purposes, such as book reviews, permitted by Fair Use of the U.S. Copyright Law, are allowed without written permissions, as long as such quotations do not cause damage to the book's commercial value. For permissions, write to the publisher, whose address is stated below.

Unless otherwise indicated, Bible Scripture quotations and passages are taken from the King James Version of The New Open Bible, copyright © 1990 by Thomas Nelson, Inc.

Also by Rev Abraham Howard Jr.

Searching for Jesus, A Bible Study Book, copyright (c) 2010 by Xulon Press
Paperback: ISBN-13 9781609576677/hardcover: ISBN-13 9781612155340

"Who is Jesus Christ? The Complete Story, copyright (c) 2014 by Westbow Press
ISBN: 978-1-4908-3565-5 (sc)/ ISBN: 978-1-4908-3567-9 (hc)/ISBN: 978-1-4908-3566-2(e)

Printed in the United States of America.

ISBN   978-1-951913-45-8   (Paperback)
ISBN   978-1-951913-46-5   (Digital)

Lettra Press books may be ordered through booksellers or by contacting:

Lettra Press LLC
30 N Gould St. Suite 4753
Sheridan, WY 82801, USA
1 307-200-4314 | info@lettrapress.com
www.lettrapress.com

Contents

PREFACE XIX
INTRODUCTION XXI

CHAPTER 1   CHRIST NAME'S 1
Jesus is Called the Word of God 1
Jesus is Called the Son of God 2
Jesus is Called Christ / Messiah 3
Jesus is Called the Son of David 4
Jesus is Called the Lamb of God 5
Conclusion 5

CHAPTER 2   CREATION OF HEAVEN AND EARTH 8
First Day of Creation 8
   The Darkness 9
   The Spirit of God 10
   The Eternal Light 11
   Separation of Light and Darkness 13
   God's Day 13
   First Day Conclusion 14
The Gap Theory 14

CHAPTER 3   CREATION ON THE EARTH 16
Second Day of Creation 18
Third Day of Creation 21
Fourth Day of Creation 22
Fifth Day of Creation 26
Sixth Day of Creation 26

Creation of Mankind 28
   Creation of the Male 29
The Garden of Eden 31
   Creation of the Female 32
   Conditions in the Garden of Eden 33
The Seventh Day 34

CHAPTER 4   ANGELS 36
Creation of the Angels 36
God's Angelic Army 37
Human Protectors 38
Workers of the Kingdom 38
Angel Society and Environment 41
Messengers of God 42
Characteristic Features 43
Celestial Hierarchy 44
Conclusion 48

CHAPTER 5   SIN AND DEATH 49
The Sin Story 50
Everlasting Judgment 52
Death of Human Beings 53
The Beginning of Life on Earth 54
Death of Adam 57

CHAPTER 6   THE GREAT FLOOD 63
The Whole Earth is Flooded 65
A New Start 66
The Rainbow Sign 67

CHAPTER 7   SATAN ON THE EARTH 69
The War in Heaven 69
O Lucifer Confined to Live on Earth 70
Job Chapter 1 71
Job Chapter 2 74
Satan's Influence 77

David and Census Taking 77
King of Tyrus 78
King of Persia 79
The Last Days 80

CHAPTER 8   SPIRIT BEING AMONG US 82
What Happens When the Unclean Spirit Takes over a Human Body? 82
Authority to Cast out Devils 83
What Happens after an Unclean Spirit Is Cast Out of the Human Body? 85
What Are Satan and His Demons Up To? 86
How Do We Fight Against Him? 87
Inhabitants on the Earth 89

CHAPTER 9   ABRAHAM AND CHRIST 91
Jesus Proclaims His Friendship with Abraham 91
Abraham's Ancestry 94
God Calls Abraham (Genesis Chapter 12) 97
God's Second Appearance to Abraham 98
God's Third Appearance to Abraham 100
God's Fourth Appearance (Genesis Chapter 15) 102
Christ & Abraham during Fifth Appearance 102
Sarah's Intervention (Genesis Chapter 16) 104
Gods Sixth Appearance to Abraham 106
The New Circumcision 111
God's Seventh Appearance to Abraham (Genesis Chapter 18) .. 112
The Prophet Abraham and King Abimelech (Genesis Chapter 20) 115
The Birth of Isaac (Genesis Chapter 21) 117
God's Eighth Appearance to Abraham (Genesis Chapter 22) 119
The Death and Burial of Sarah 122
Isaac Marries His Cousin Rebekah227 128
Death of Abraham 130

CHAPTER 10 HEBREW NATION GENEALOGY 132

- Jacobs Seven Year Contract with Laban 132
- Jacobs second Seven Year Contract with Laban 133
- Death of Shem 134
- Jacobs Six Year Contract with Laban 135
- Jacob Leaves Laban 136
- Simeon and Levi Commit Murder (Genesis Chapter 34) 138
- Jacob's Name is Changed to Israel (Genesis Chapter 35) 139
- Rachel Gives Birth to Benjamin 139
- Reuben Sins Against His Father 140
- Death of Ishmael 140
- Joseph is Carried to Egypt (Genesis Chapter 37) 141
- Judah Fathers Twin Boys (Genesis Chapter 38) 141
- Joseph is Sold to Potiphar (Genesis Chapter 39) 142
- Joseph, the butler, and the Baker (Genesis Chapter 40) 143
- Joseph Stands before Pharaoh (Genesis Chapter 41) 144
- Death of Isaac 147
- The Seven Years of Plenty (Genesis 41: 47-53) 151
- Seven Years of Drought 152
- Israel Sends His Son's to Egypt (Genesis Chapter 42-45) 152

CHAPTER 11 THE HEBREWS IN EGYPT 154

- Beginning of the 400 Years in Egypt (Genesis Chapter 46 -47) 154
- Death of Jacob (Genesis Chapter 48-49) 155
- Joseph Treats His Brothers Kindly (Genesis Chapter 50) 157
- Death of Joseph 158
- The Hebrews are Enslaved (Exodus Chapter 1) 158
- Moses is Born (Exodus 2: 1-10) 160
- Moses Leaves Egypt (Exodus 2:11-25) 161
- Moses settles in Midian 162
- God Calls Moses (Exodus Chapter 3 – 4) 162
- Moses Requests Proof from God 166
- Moses Son is Circumcised 168
- Aaron Meets Moses in the Desert 169
- Conclusion 169

Moses and Aaron Stand Before Pharaoh 170

CHAPTER 12 THE TEN PLAGUE'S 173
1. The Plague of Blood 173
2. The Plague of Frogs: 175
3. The Plague of Lice 176
4. The Plague of Flies 177
5. The Plague of Animal Disease 179
6. The Plague of Boils 180
7. The Plague of Hail 181
8. The Plague of Locusts 183
9. The Plague of Darkness 185
10. The Plague of Death 186

CHAPTER 13 THE PASSOVER 189
The Time of the Passover 189
Passover Rules 193

CHAPTER 14 CHRIST AND THE CHILDREN OF ISRAEL 194
The Children of Israel Passes through the Red Sea (Exodus Chapters 12–14) 196
God Provides Manna [bread] from Heaven (Exodus 16:1-35) ... 198
  The Narrow Way 200
  The Broad Way 201
Christ Provides Water from a Rock (Exodus 17:1–7) 202
Christ is the Spiritual Rock (Exodus 23:20–24 / 32:34 / 33:1-3) 204
Israel Worships a Golden Calf (Exodus Chapter 32) 208
Lusting is Evil (Numbers Chapters 9–11) 211
  Moses Request That God Kill Him 212
  God Pours Out His Spirit 214
  Christ Administers the Spirit of God 215
  God Provides Meat for a Month 217
Israel is Prevented from entering the Promised Land (Numbers Chapter's 13, 14) 217

Beware of the Destroyer (Numbers Chapter 16) 219
   Korah Challenges Moses 220
   The Congregation Rail Against Moses and Aaron 222
Christ Will Save Us from the Serpents Bite (Numbers 21:4–9) .224
Fornication is a Deadly Sin (Numbers 25:1–9) 226
Israel's Suffering Revealed 229
The Death of Moses (Deuteronomy 34:5–6) 229

CHAPTER 15 THE PROMISED LAND 231
The Leadership of Joshua..231
The Twelve Tribes Transgress Against God 233
Judgement of The Angel of God..234
Othniel Defeats the Arameans and Rules Israel (Judges 3:8-11) 237
King Eglon of Moab Subjects the Israelites (Judges 3:14) 238
Ehud Assassinates Eglon and Begins an Era of Peace for Israel (Judges 3:14-30)..238
King Jabin of Hazor Oppresses Israel (Judges 4:2)...................239
Deborah Leads an Uprising Against Jabin, and Rules Israel (Judges 4-5) 239
Midianites Take Over Israel (Judges 6:1)371................................ 241
Gideon Defeats the Midianites Israel (Judges 6-8) 243
Abimelech Declares Himself King and Murders His Brothers (Judges 9)...244
Tola, Jair, Jephthah, Elon, and Abdon rule Israel (Judges 10-12)374
....244
Philistines Oppress Israel (Judges 13:1)375............................246

CHAPTER 16 THE WORD AND THE KINGS............255
Samson the Judge (Judges Chapters 13-16)...........................255
Samuel the Prophet / Judge 260
God calls Samuel into Service 263
Samuel Anoints Saul King of Israel.....................................265
Saul is Confirmed by God...267
Saul's First Disobedience...268
Saul's Second Disobedience...269
Samuel Anoints David King of Israel..................................273

God Takes His Holy Spirit from Saul 274
King David 275
Death of David 279
King Solomon 279
God's first Appearance unto Solomon406 280
Solomon Starts to Build the Temple of God 281
Christ Appears unto Solomon 281
The Temple of God is Finished 282
Solomon's Prayer 283
God's Answer to Solomon's Prayer 286
   The Sign 286
   God's Second visit to Solomon 287
Solomon's Disobedience (1 Kings 11:1-13) 289
Death of Solomon 293
The United Kingdom of Israel is Split in Two 293
Jeroboam's Sin (1 Kings 12:25-33) 293

CHAPTER 17 THE WORD AND THE PROPHETS ...298
The Prophet Obadiah 298
The Prophet Joel 299
The Prophet Jonah 300
The Prophet Amos 301
The Prophet Hosea 303
The Prophet Micah 304
The Prophet Isaiah 305
Isaiah Sees the Throne of God427 308
The Captivity of the Ten Tribes of Israel (2 Kings 17:1-6 / 18:9-11)
.... 309
Causes of the Ten Tribes Captivity (2 Kings 17:7-22) 311
Foreigners Repopulate Northern Israel (2 Kings 17:24-41) 313
Jesus and the Woman at the Well (John 4:1-9) 315
Death of Isaiah 316

CHAPTER 18 THE END OF KINGS 317
King Manasseh (2 Kings 21:1-18 / 2 Chronicles 33:1-24) 317

 God Judges Manasseh 318
 God Hears Manasseh's Prayer 319
 Manasseh Repents of His Past Ways 319
The Prophet Nahum 320
 Death of Manasseh 321
King Amon 321
King Josiah (2 Kings 22 – 23:1-30 / 2 Chronicles Chapters 34-35) 322
The Prophet Zephaniah 322
The Prophet Jeremiah 325
Christ Calls Jeremiah into Service 325
Josiah hears the Word God 327
The Prophetess Huldah 328
Josiah's Reform (2 Kings 23: 1-30) 329
Death of Josiah 336
Jehoahaz rules Judah 336
The Prophet Habakkuk 336

CHAPTER 19 THE SEVENTY YEAR CAPTIVITY 338
Jehoiakim is Made King 338
The Prophet Daniel 340
Jehoiachin rules Judah 341
The Prophet Ezekiel (593 -570 BC) 342
King Zedekiah (597-586) 344
Destruction of Jerusalem 348
Cyrus the Great 351
God Names Cyrus 351
God Gives Cyrus His Mission Assignment 351
Cyrus Completes His Mission Assignment 353
Cyrus Historical Record 355
Zerubbabel Rebuilds the Temple of God 356
The Prophet Haggai (520 – 505 BC) 356
The Prophet Zechariah (520 – 470 BC) 357
The Book of Esther459 358
Ezra the Scribe / High Priest (Chapters 7-10) 361

Nehemiah 362
The Prophet Malachi (437 -417 BC) 364
Old Testament Summary 372

CHAPTER 20 THE NEW TESTAMENT 374
John the Baptist 376
Jesus the Christ 383
The Birth of John the Baptist 389
The Birth of Jesus Christ 392
The Magi Worship the Baby Jesus 396
Jesus is dedicated in the Temple 399
Joseph Escapes to Egypt with His Family 400
Herod The Great 400
Death of Herod the Great 401
Joseph and Mary's Other Children 402
Joseph and Family Celebrate the Passover 403
Christ Starts His Earthly Ministry 404

CHAPTER 21 JESUS, MOSES, AND ELIJAH 407
God and Moses 408
Christ and Moses 410
   Moses and Fasting 411
   The Death of Moses 413
Elijah and Christ Jesus [Year 850 BC] 413
   An Angel Provides for Elijah 415
   Elijah and Christ 416
   Elijah and God 416
   Death of Elijah 418
The Commonality of Moses, Elijah, and Christ 419
   Forty-Day Fast 419
   Looking Upon God 419
Daniel's Fast 422

CHAPTER 22 CHRIST IS THE SAVIOR 423

CHAPTER 23 JESUS CHRIST IS THE MESSIAH 431
The Prophecy 431
The Commandment to Build Jerusalem 433
The Birth of the Messiah 433
Six Days Before the Passover 434
Five Days Before the Passover 435
Two Days Before the Passover 435
Judas is Determined to Betray Christ 436
The Death of Christ 438

CHAPTER 24 JESUS CHRIST IS OUR PASSOVER 439
The First Passover 446
Jewish Calendar 446
   Jewish Months 447
   Jewish Days 448
Jesus Celebrates the Passover 448
   The First Watch (6 p.m. to 9p.m.) 449
   The Second Watch (9 p.m. to Midnight) 452
   The Third Watch (Midnight to 3 a.m.) 453
   The Fourth Watch (3 a.m. to Sunrise) 454
   The First Hour (Sunrise to 9 a.m.) 455
   The Third Hour (9 a.m. to Noon) 456
   The Sixth Hour (Noon to 3 p.m.) 456
   The Ninth Hour (3 p.m. to Sunset) 457
First Day of the Resurrection 458
Second Day of The Resurrection 459
Third Day of The Resurrection 460
The Resurrection of Christ 461

CHAPTER 25 JESUS CHRIST IS OUR RESSURECTION 464
The Sanhedrin Council Membership 466
Christ Is Coming on the Clouds of Glory 467
The Resurrection of the Believers 469

CHAPTER 26 JESUS CHRIST THE SPIRIT OF GOD BAPTIZER 474
John the Baptist Identified Christ Jesus as the Holy Ghost Baptizer 474
Why Did John Baptize in Water? 475
The People Believe John's Witness Concerning Christ Jesus 476
John Questions Whether Jesus Is the Christ 478
John the Baptist Is Slain by Herod the Tetrarch 479
Christ Explains the Holy Ghost 480
Water Baptism 482
Born Again (Water and Spirit) 482
   Spirit Baptism 483
   Fruits of the Holy Ghost 488
Church Leadership 488
Christ the Holy Ghost Baptizer 489
The Day of Pentecost 490
The Witnesses of the Holy Ghost Baptism 492
Peter Explains the Holy Ghost Baptism 493
The Samarians Are Baptized with the Holy Ghost 493
   Water Baptism 493
   Holy Ghost Baptism 494
The Apostle Paul Is Baptized with the Holy Ghost (Acts Chapter 9) 494
   Saul is Baptized in the Spirit and then in Water 496
The Roman Cornelius 496
   Baptized in the Holy Ghost 498
   Baptized in Water 498
Apollos Preaches in the Power of the Holy Ghost 499
Have You Heard of the Holy Ghost? 502
The Holy Ghost Movement in the United States of America 503

CHAPTER 27 JESUS CHRIST IS THE JUDGE 504
The Will of the Father 508
The Judgment of Corporate Works 511
Judgment of Church Members' Performances 515

Judas Iscariot: He Preached and Cast Out Devils 516
   Wonderful Works in the Church 519
Conclusion 520
Judgment of Church Organizations 520
   Judgment of the Church of Ephesus (Revelation 2:1-7) 522
   Judgment of the Church of Smyrna (Revelation 2:8-11) 524
   Judgment of the Church of Pergamos (Revelation 2:12-17) 527
   Judgment of the Church of Thyatira (Revelation 2:18-29) 529
   Judgment of the Church of Sardis (Revelation 3:1-16) 532
   Judgment of the Church of Philadelphia (Revelation 3:7-13) 534
   Judgment of the Church of Laodicea (Revelation 3:14-22) 537
Summary Thoughts of the Seven Churches 538

CHAPTER 28 THE FINAL JUDGMENTS OF GOD .. 540
Spirit Beings' Control of Earth 540
The Wrath of God Will Fall on the Followers of the Beast 543
Judgment of Spirit Beings 547
Judgment of Human and Spirit Beings 548
The Lake of Fire Judgment 550
   The Fearful 552
   And Unbelieving 553
   The Abominable 556
   Uncleanness (Leviticus 15:1–33) 556
   Incest, Pornography, Fornication, and Adultery (Leviticus 18:1–20)
   558
   Homosexuality and Sodomy 561
   Prostitution (prostitute) 564
   Wearing Opposite Gender Clothing 565
   Bestiality 566
   Killing of Babies 567
   Eating Blood 568
   Cursing Father or Mother 570
   God's Judgment against Abominations 571
   And Murderers 571
   And Whoremongers 573

After the Law Was Given to Moses 576
And Sorcerers 577
And Idolaters 579
And All Liars 579

CHAPTER 29 CHRIST MESSAGE TO THE WORLD 582
The Parable of The Wheat and The Tares 582
Christ Jesus Explains the Parable of the Wheat and Tares 583
The Parable of The Householder 584
Parable of the Marriage feast 586

CHAPTER 30 THE END IS THE BEGINNING 589
The Beginning (Genesis Chapters 1 – 3) 590
The End (Revelation Chapters 21 – 22) 591
RESEARCH NOTES **599**
BIBLIOGRAPHY **625**

Preface

Many authors have written concerning the authenticity of the Lord Jesus Christ as the Messiah. The Hebrew writers of the Old Testament foretold of his impeding coming to the earth. New Testament writers sustained the Old Testament writing, and implied Jesus Christ is God: The Son of God.

So, thousands of books have been published, countless articles written, numerous movies produced, and hundreds of Christian religious denominations formed to try to get at the truth of Jesus Christ. But I believe that it all boils down to what's written in the Holy Bible. For this is the only informational source about the mystery surrounding the man Jesus Christ. Foretold prophesies, his birth by a virgin woman, his fulfilling of ancient prophesies, his powerful miracles, and awe-inspiring teaching, the circumstances surrounding his death (on or around the time of the Hebrew Passover), his burial in an unmarked grave, and his resurrection from the dead are all contained in this one book.

In my first book, *"Searching for Jesus—A Bible Study Book"* (ISBN 9781609576677), published in 2010 by Xulon Press, I presented scripture (Old and New Testament) as a basis for examination, study, and discussion to explain my research in finding the physical presence of Christ Jesus throughout the Bible.

However, feedback indicated the book was a bit over the top for those who have not really studied the Scriptures, and more explanation was needed. In this book, after much thought and input from fellow Christians, I decided to concentrate on what the New

Testament writers wrote about Christ concerning the past (the Old Testament), the present (the four Gospels and the Epistles), and the future (the book of Revelation).

This book is a compilation of over twenty years of my personal Bible study notes: garnered from teaching Sunday school, writing sermons, studying authors, reviewing other bibles, compiling newspaper clippings, critiquing movies, listening to televangelists, reading magazines, keeping up with tabloids, and the like. So if at times I step out of the traditional box or seem to be reaching or stretching to get at an answer to a certain scripture; remember I'm trying to explain a difficult subject concerning the Lord Jesus Christ—the Alpha and Omega, the beginning and the ending, the first and the last, the King of Kings and Lord of Lords, which is and which was, and which is to come.

My hope is that it will reach the eyes, ears, and minds of those who are hungry for the truth concerning Christ Jesus: and those who like to debate this subject. Therefore, I ask that you please be patient with me and not take my research as fact. Conduct your own study to verify or debunk what I have written.

Introduction

This is a concise, thorough, and theological research on the complete story of the Lord Jesus Christ (aka the Word of God). Presented are proofs in the bible that he was with God (the Father) when the heaven and earth were created. That he is the eternal light of the heaven(s). That he created all things on and under the earth. That the sun, moon, and planets were created after the earth was established. That humankind is his special creation: for humanity is a spirit contained in a fleshly spacesuit. However, angels are created spirits watching over the welfare of humankind.

That it was O Lucifer—the great Dragon, that old Serpent called the Devil and Satan—who brought sin, death, and destruction to the earth. He lied to Eve and Adam, and caused their sure deaths. That angel's left their home in heaven to live on the earth during Noah's time. That O Lucifer started war in heaven, and in defeat, was confined to the earth until judgment day; when he will be thrown into the lake of fire.

That Christ Jesus physically visited with the prophet Abraham, and knew him as a friend. That he was with Moses and the children of Israel as they traveled through the Sinai wilderness for forty years. That he was a close friend of Moses and Elijah. That he visited with the prophets of the Old Testament.

That he is truly the Savior of humankind, the only begotten Son of the true and living God. That he is the Great Prophet: for he revealed to us the past, present, and future. That he came and left this earth on a prophetic timetable. That he is our Passover from death into everlasting life. That he is the resurrection of the dead (both good and evil). That he is the baptizer of the Holy Ghost - the Spirit of God. That he is the one who will judge humankind's works, deeds, righteousness, and unrighteousness.

Therefore, I say to you, if you lack knowledge of the Lord Jesus Christ, and desire to know more, this book is for you. However, I beg you not to ignore the message I am delivering to all of humankind—the good, the bad, the ugly, the saved, and the lost—for your very soul is at stake.

The 2nd Edition

This book is an upgrade to my original finding, and is presented to help the unlearned and the scholar to better understand the Holy Bible writings concerning the Lord Jesus Christ, and his relationship to God (the Father) and mankind.

The difficulty in this task is trying to find a method that will not only give the needed information, but also enhance knowledge of the subject; not straying too deep into prophecy, works, or theology. Therefore, I have decided to give scripture, were needed, to stress and prove certain points, and write my commentary in between as a book; and add the study scriptures at the end of the book as "Research Notes:" therefore, please pay attention to these end of book notes. All scripture presented are from the King James Version of the Holy Bible.

I realize that this is a tough subject, but the truth and belief in Christ must be proven by the scriptures. When the Apostle Paul spoke to the Jews at the Berea Synagogue, "They received the word with all readiness of mind, and searched the scriptures daily, whether those things were so." And just like those people it is incombered upon the followers of Jesus to build up confidence in Christ by research, and meditation on the Holy Bible scriptures. In other words, know what you are talking about. Someone wrote a wise saying that I learned a long time ago:

"He that think he knows, and knows not is a fool. He that knows, but don't know that he knows is also, a fool. But he that knows, and know that he knows, is a wise man that is able to help others."

CHAPTER 1

CHRIST NAME'S

A name could mean everything, or a name could mean nothing; it all depends on who knows your name. At a very early age my brother and I were called by our nick-name. Nobody ever addressed us by our birth name. And for some unknown reason nick-names were used throughout the community: in the home, on the street, and when conducting business transactions. If you were looking for someone, and used their birth name, you would end up on a dead-end street. However, if you knew, and used their nick-name, you would find them with accuracy, and they would be pointed out, and described in detail.

Therefore, in order to understand and stabilize our search, we are going to first explore the different names that Christ Jesus was called (is called) throughout the bible.

Jesus is Called the Word of God

Of all the New Testament writers, John is the only one that called Jesus "The Word of God." He first used this term as an introduction to his gospel, "In the beginning was the Word, and the Word was with God, and the Word was God, the same was in the beginning with God."[1] John wrote this information around 66 AD and could have only gotten it from the lips of Jesus Christ.

He used it again when he wrote "For there are three that bear record in heaven, the Father, the Word, and the Holy Ghost: and these three are one."[2]

Then on the Isle of Patmos (around A.D. 95) he was given a snap shot of heaven, and wrote down what he saw and heard: confirming the heavenly name of Jesus Christ, "And I saw heaven opened, and behold a white horse; and he that sat upon him was called Faithful and True, and in righteousness he doth judge and make war. His eyes were as a flame of fire, and on his head were many crowns; and he had a name written, that no man knew, but he himself. And he was clothed with a vesture dipped in blood: and his name is called The Word of God."[3]

Jesus is Called the Son of God

When Matthew expressed the Triune God head (The Trinity), he did not call Jesus "The Word of God [for he only knew him as the only begotten Son of God]; "Go ye therefore, and teach all nations, baptizing them in the name of the Father, and of the Son, and of the Holy Ghost."[4]

However, there are more than twenty-seven scriptures[5] that indicate that Jesus Christ is the Son of God. But the most prominent is declared by God the Father. First when he was baptized by John the Baptist; "And lo a voice from heaven, saying, This is my beloved Son, in whom I am well pleased." (Matthew 3:17) And again, when He was up on the mountain with Peter, James and John, "While he yet spoke, behold a bright cloud overshadowed them: and behold a voice out of the cloud, which said, This is my beloved Son, in whom I am well pleased; hear ye him." (Matthew 17:5) Lastly, when Jesus knew that his hour had come to die, He said, "Father glorify thy name. Then came a voice from heaven, saying, I have both glorified it, and will glorify it again. The people therefore, that stood by, and heard it, said that it thundered: others said, An angel spake to him."[6]

Peter on the other hand was quick to acknowledge who Jesus was: "When Jesus came into the coasts of Caesarea Philippi, he asked his disciples, saying, Whom do men say that I the Son of man am? And they said, Some say that thou art John the Baptist: some, Elias; and others, Jeremias, or one of the prophets. He saith unto them, But whom say ye that I am? And Simon Peter answered and said, Thou art the Christ, the Son of the living God. And Jesus answered and said unto him, Blessed art thou, Simon Barjona: for flesh and blood hath not revealed it unto thee, but my Father which is in heaven."[7]

The Pharisees, the scribes, and the elders were the main Jews that did not believe that Jesus was the son of God, and did "persecute Jesus and sought to slay him, because he had done these things (*healing*) on the sabbath day." When asked why he healed on the sabbath day, Jesus answered and said, "My Father worketh hitherto, and I work. Therefore, the Jews sought the more to kill him, because he had broken the sabbath (*law*), but said also that God was his Father, making himself equal with God."[8]

Jesus is Called Christ / Messiah

The name Christ and Messiah are joined together as one, but expressed differently according on how you identify the savior. At seven different times was this method used:

The angels in heaven said on the day of his birth, "For unto you is born this day in the city of David a Saviour, which is Christ the Lord." (Luke 2:11)

When John the Baptist pointed Jesus out as the Lamb of God, Andrew his disciple "findeth his own brother Simon, and saith unto him, We have found the Messias, which is, being interpreted, the Christ." (John 1: 41)

The woman at the well said, "I know that Messias cometh, which is called Christ: when he is come, he will tell us all things. Jesus saith unto her, I that speak unto thee am he." (John 4:25-26)

Before he was crucified Jesus announced to his disciples who he was, "And this is life eternal, that they might know thee the only true God, and Jesus Christ, whom thou hast sent." (John 17: 3)

Jesus warned his disciples that there was only one Christ; "And call no man your father upon the earth: for one is your Father, which is in heaven. Neither be ye called masters: for one is your Master, even Christ." (Matthew 23: 9-10)

When the Jews were gathered in the Judgment hall to hear the sentence of Jesus, "Pilate said unto them, Whom will ye that I release unto you? Barabbas, or Jesus which is called Christ? (Matthew 27: 17)

When the prophet Daniel was praying, the angel Gabriel brought him a message concerning the seventy years of Jewish captivity by the Babylonian Empire, and the time line of the Messiah which was accomplished in Jesus Christ.[9]

Jesus is Called the Son of David

> "And the angel said unto her, Fear not, Mary: for thou hast found favour with God. And, behold, thou shalt conceive in thy womb, and bring forth a son, and shalt call his name Jesus. He shall be great, and shall be called the Son of the Highest: and the Lord God shall give unto him the throne of his father David: And he shall reign over the house of Jacob for ever; and of his kingdom there shall be no end." (Luke 2: 30-33)

This announcement by the angel Gabriel confirmed to Mary that she would borne a baby not fashioned by the seed of man; and his name would be called Jesus, the son of the Highest of the house of King David; which is to be accomplished through her tribe of Judah lineage; which is generally felt to be the genealogy list ascribed in Luke 3:23-38. However, the genealogy of Christ, in relationship to his earthy father Joseph is listed in Matthew 1: 1-16.

> "And when Jesus departed thence, two blind men followed him, crying, and saying, Thou Son of David, have mercy on us." (Matthew 9: 27)

"And one of the elders saith unto me, Weep not: behold, the Lion of the tribe of Juda, the Root of David, hath prevailed to open the book, and to loose the seven seals thereof." (Revelation 5:5)

The reference to him being the Lion of Judah comes from a prophecy given by Jacob in Genesis 49:8-12, and God's promise to David that his house, kingdom, and throne would be established forever. (2 Samuel 7: 1-17).

Jesus is Called the Lamb of God

I found that this is the name, most preferred when addressing Christ in the book of Revelation. Since Christ was sacrificed for mankind, it stands to reason that his new title is "The Lamb of God;" for he is no longer referred to as "The Word of God or even Christ." Once again, I will provide you with the scriptures that relate to Christ as the Lamb of God. Why? Because there are so many interpretations of the Holy Bible, and I want to keep your train of thought concentrated in one language and one direction. My other reasoning is that it will save you the time of looking up the scriptures.

"The next day John seeth Jesus coming unto him, and saith, Behold the Lamb of God, which taketh away the sin of the world. This is he of whom I said, After me cometh a man which is preferred before me: for he was before me. And I knew him not: but that he should be made manifest to Israel, therefore am I come baptizing with water." (John 1:29-31)

The Lamb is the only one authorized to take the book out of the one who sets on the throne in heaven; and loose the seven seals upon the earth. When He does this deed, the entire heavenly host began to shout, cry and sing praises unto the Father and the Lamb.[10]

Conclusion

From Genesis to Revelation there are a lot of references concerning

Christ, but no clear description is ever given of him. Different names are used to substantiate his visits to the earth, but there aren't any known physical records that he ever existed except for what's written in the Holy Bible. And even at that, without tedious research and study, you will not see or identify him at all, except for Old Testament prophecy that was fulfilled in the New Testament.

This is a mystery, because no one really knows him except God the Father, and no one really knows God the Father except him.[11] His disciples walked with him for over three years, but they still didn't know him. When Phillip asked him to show them the Father Jesus gave them a strange answer; which is a direct reference to the ONE-NESS of Christ and the Father:

John 14: 8. Philip saith unto him, Lord, shew us the Father, and it sufficeth us.

> **9. Jesus saith unto him, have I been so long time with you, and yet hast thou not known me, Philip? he that hath seen me hath seen the Father; and how sayest thou then, Shew us the Father?**
>
> **10. Believest thou not that I am in the Father, and the Father in me? the words that I speak unto you I speak not of myself: but the Father that dwelleth in me, he doeth the works.**
>
> **11. Believe me that I am in the Father, and the Father in me: or else believe me for the very works' sake.**

In his sermon "How the Father, the Son, & Holy Ghost are one" Bishop T.D. Jakes used water to explain this mystery. He said, if you have a glass of liquid water, and put ice in it, you will notice the ice is in the water. However, ice is frozen water. Therefore, the water and the ice look separate in the glass; but the ice is in the water, and the water is in the ice: and they are one of the same. Yet, if you heat the glass of water and ice together you will get a mist that we call steam, but it is still water. Final conclusion is that the water, the ice, and the steam are all three separates but one of the same.

Therefore, water has three characteristics (liquid, ice, steam) but never loses its basic chemical formula called H20: which is "a clear, colorless, odorless, and tasteless compound of hydrogen and oxygen, occurring as a liquid that covers about three-quarters of the earth's surface, and also in solid form as ice, and in a gaseous form which we call clouds.[12]

Liquid water is the basic life-giving fluid that everything on the earth has to have in order to sustain live within, and without its structure. Ice on the other hand is used to preserve the things of the earth for long periods of time; and is able to hold back aging. But steam comes from both liquid water and ice, and is the vehicle that carries water up into the heaven to form clouds of mist, which returns to the earth as rain.

It can be surmised that God is like liquid water, because everything on earth needs him to live. The Son is like ice, because he saves and preserves the soul until it is ready to return to the Father. The Holy Ghost is likened to steam, because it is through his power that the souls are carried up into the heaven. And so, it is that the Father, the Word, and the Holy Ghost are three, but also one within each other.[13]

Therefore, all the names above are used throughout the Holy Bible to describe one person during different dispensations, times of history, and interactions with prophets, peoples, and events.

Yet, after more than two-thousand years, since the cross, the mystery of Christ and God are still debated to the point of contention. Some recognize the God Jehovah. Others seem to think that God is one entity with three personalities. Still, others believe that Jesus is God manifested in different dispensations of time. And this is why we are searching the scriptures to find if what is written about him is true.

CHAPTER 2

CREATION OF HEAVEN AND EARTH

**Genesis 1: 1 In the beginning God created the heaven and the earth.
2. And the earth was without form, and void; and darkness was upon the face of the deep. And the Spirit of God moved upon the face of the waters.
3. And God said, Let there be light: and there was light.
4. And God saw the light, that it was good: and God divided the light from the darkness.
5. And God called the light Day, and the darkness he called Night. And the evening and the morning were the first day."**

First Day of Creation

On the first day of creation the Father created the heaven and the earth. The heaven is the home of God, and earth is his resting place; for it is written, "Thus saith the Lord, The heaven is my throne, and the earth is my footstool"[14]

Mankind has a name for the different sections of heaven; such as the universe, the cosmos, star systems, galaxies, constellations, solar systems, and interstellar space to name a few. But to God the heaven is one singular unit; the same as He, the Son, and the Holy Ghost are one.

However, God knows the thoughts of mankind, and left us with this word of wisdom, "The heaven, even the heavens, are the Lords; but the earth hath he given to the children of men."[15]

So, then it is plain to see that the earth is a spinning water ball (without form or life) that is suspended in darkness; and that the Holy Ghost (living water)[16] is preparing the water for life upon the earth.

The Darkness

Why is the heaven and the earth created in total darkness? The only explanation is referenced in the Holy Bible which states that God the Father is shrouded in darkness; thereby keeping his identity a secret.

When Moses went up on the mountain to meet with God, he heard a voice that said, "Lo, I come unto thee in a thick cloud, that the people may hear when I speak with thee, and believe thee for ever. And Moses told the words of the people unto the Lord."[17]

From this meeting God told Moses to gather the people at the foot of the mountain, on the third day, so that he could speak with them. As the people gathered together, on the morning of the third day, they were witness to the grand entrance of God; for there were "thunders, and lighting, and a thick cloud upon the mount, and the voice of the trumpet exceeding loud; so that the people that was in the camp trembled. And when the voice of the trumpet sounded long, and waxed louder, and louder, Moses spake, and God answered him by a voice."[18]

It was during this time that God gave Moses the Ten Commandments; and gave him instructions to bring his brother Aaron up to the top of the mountain; but restrain the priests and the people from coming up on the mountain lest they die.

Moses didn't have to worry about the people trying to break

through to see God; for when they "saw the thundering, and the lightings, and the noise of the trumpet, and the mountain smoking," they hurriedly removed themselves to a safe place a far off from the mountain.

When Moses came down from the mountain, and told them about the Ten Commandments, they said, "Moses speak thou with us, and we will hear; but let not God speak with us, lest we die. And Moses said unto the people, Fear not: for God is come to prove you, and that his fear may be before your faces, that you sin not."

With that being said, Moses went back up on the mountain and "drew near unto the thick darkness where God was.[19]

There are other times when God operated in darkness; but you will have to conduct your own research to find them, for example: when God caused darkness to fall on the nation of Egypt and all the first born died; or when Adam and Eve heard his voice walking in the Garden of Eden but did not see him.

The Spirit of God

There is not a lot written about the Spirit of God; except that Jesus said his name is called the Holy Ghost.[20] And the un-fallible fact is that the Holy Ghost is always a presence where God the Father is; and is his vehicle of power: "Not by might, nor by power, but by my spirit, saith the Lord of hosts."[21]

We see the spirit of God in action when he came upon the Benjamite Saul: and he became a new man and began to prophesy.[22] Again, when John the Baptist Father Zacharias was filled with the Holy Ghost he began to prophesy about the goodness and wonders of God.[23]

Yet, Jesus said that when he is on the earth the Holy Ghost is in heaven with the Father; and when he returns to heaven (after his visit is finished on the earth) the Holy Ghost will return to the earth: "Nevertheless, I tell you the truth: it is expedient for you that I go away: for if I go not away, the comforter will not come unto you; but if I depart I will send him unto you."[24]

Therefore, the Holy Ghost will be down on the earth until the return of Christ.

The Eternal Light

Then God said, "Let there be light: and there was light." But this light was not like the light of the sun or the moon because they were not created until the fourth day of creation. This light is alive, and is the one called <u>the Word of God:</u> whom God commanded to step out of the darkness. Also bear in mind that this light is not created, but is a part of the Father that was hidden in the darkness. This fact is confirmed by the Apostle Paul who wrote, "Who being the brightness of his glory, and the express image of his person, and upholding all things by the word of his power, when he had by himself purged our sins, sat down on the right hand of the Majesty on high."[25] Those that believe that Jesus was the first created being are dead wrong in their belief, and are heading for same destruction as the unbelieving Jews: "I said therefore unto you, that you shall die in your sins: for if ye believe not that I am he, ye shall die in your sins."[26]

John's gospel bare witness when he said, "And the light shineth in darkness, and the darkness comprehended it not."[27] The meaning is that no amount of darkness can distinguish this light.

This is the light that Peter, James and John saw when they witnessed Jesus being transformed into his heavenly form; so that he could talk to Moses and Elijah. Matthew recorded that Jesus "was transfigured before them: and his face did shine as the sun, and his raiment was white as the light." And that above them "a bright cloud overshadowed them: and behold a voice out of the cloud, which said, This is my beloved Son, in whom I am well pleased; hear ye him." Take note that the light of Jesus is above brightness, but the Father was there watching from within a near dark cloud.[28]

After the crucifixion of Jesus, when the church was in its early stage, it was persecuted by Saul of Tarsu: a priest of the Pharisee sect.[29] After Saul had witnessed the stoning of Stephen, he started on a journey to Damascus with papers to bring back bound any and all followers of Jesus Christ. But to his surprise <u>the Word of God</u> met him as he drew near to Damascus, and his light was so bright that it blinded his party, and knocked them from their horses. When Saul retold his story, he said that the event happened around noon time, and the light was brighter than the sun, and as he fell to the ground, a voice from out of the light said, "Saul, Saul, why persecutest me?" And Saul answered saying, "Who art thou Lord?" And the voice said, "I am Jesus of Nazareth whom thou persecutest."[30]

When John was exiled on the Isle of Patmos God chose him to write the last prophetic book of the bible: "The Revelation of Jesus Christ, which God gave unto him, to shew unto his servants things which must shortly come to pass; and he sent and signified it by his angel unto his servant John: Who bare record of the word of God, and of the testimony of Jesus Christ, and of all things that he saw."[31]

He saw many things concerning the earth and the last days, but he was also showed the future new heaven and new earth, and the city called the New Jerusalem. The city measures four square by 1377 miles. It has twelve pearly gates; with three facing, north, south, east and west: inscribed with the names of the twelve tribes of Israel. There is an angel assigned to each gate. "And the wall of the city had twelve foundations, and in them the names of the twelve apostles of the Lamb. And the street of the city was pure gold, as it were transparent glass. And I saw no temple therein: for the Lord God Almighty and the Lamb are the temple of it. And the city had no need of the sun, neither of the moon, to shine in it: for the glory of God did lighten it, and the Lamb *(Jesus Christ)* is the light thereof."[32]

Note that the same light that is present on the first day of creation is also manifested before and after the crucifixion of the Lord Jesus Christ; and will be the light in the new heaven and new earth: in a city four square of over a quarter mile. This proves that the light that is in the beginning is not a created light but the light from God *(the Word of God)* that shines out of darkness.

Separation of Light and Darkness

On this day God separated light from darkness, and he called the light Day, and the darkness he called it Night. This seems to be the point where God begins the separation of all things, e.g. right from wrong, righteousness from un-righteousness, good from evil, salvation from damnation, everlasting life from death eternal, the wide gate from the narrow gate, the church from the world, the spirit of flesh from the Holy Ghost, mankind from angels, the Son God from the son of the morning, the sheep from the goats, the Shepard from the hireling, the preacher from the false prophet, and etc.

Yet, how strange it is indeed that on the fourth day of creation there is also a light for the day (the sun) and a light for the night (the moon); with a twenty-four-hour rotation to regulate days, weeks, months, and years.

God's Day

Further, note that the day of God starts in darkness and ends in the light; "the evening and the morning was the first day." This brings up the question, "Since there is no Sun or Moon, how long was the first day?" In the Old testament it is written, "For a thousand years in thy sight are but as yesterday when it is past, and as a watch in the night."[33] Peter backs this up when he wrote, "But, beloved, be not ignorant of this one thing, that one day is with the Lord as a thousand years, and a thousand years as one day."[34]

A great mystery that mankind cannot solve. However, we can look at something that Jesus said that may shed some light on the subject; "For as Jonas was three days and three nights in the whale's belly; so shall the Son of man be three days and three nights in the heart of the earth."[35] Looking at what he said, I noticed that he expressed Day and Night as on the first day of creation: evening and the morning = 6 pm until 6 am / and the day time = 6 am to 6 pm. In the modern way of thinking we would say three days which would include both day and night: from midnight to midnight [24 hours].

Yet, looking at the expression "evening and morning were the first day" brings into question that it really is only twelve hours. Other twelve-hours will have to happen before it can be called a full day

Mathematically, if an event happened at ten o'clock PM on the 13th day of the month we would count it as the 13th day. But if you use bible logic, the event would be counted as starting on the 12th day, and ending on the 13th day. Well, all I can say is, "Learn Gods way and you'll do fine!

First Day Conclusion

- That God the Father is the creator of heaven and earth.
- That the earth is one big ball of water (without form and void).
- That the earth is suspended in place, and spinning in darkness.
- That the Spirit of God {the Holy Ghost} is there; moving upon the face of the waters (solid water).
- That there is total darkness until God said "Let there be light."
- That the light was before the fourth day creation of the Sun, Moon and Stars.
- That God was well pleased with the light that came forth from darkness.
- That <u>the Word of God</u> *[Christ Jesus]* is not clearly seen, but he is the light called out of darkness.
- That there is a separation of light and darkness, and the beginning of Day and Night.
- That God's day begins in the evening (night), and ends at the beginning of day (morning).

The Gap Theory

The Gap theory reasons that there is a lost period of time between the first, and second verse of Genesis chapter one; that the earth was ruled by Satan and destroyed by a flood when he and some angels rebelled against God; that all the previous animals (dinosaurs) and water-borne life-forms were also destroyed; and that God re-created the earth in six days, thereby justifying the evening and the morning as twenty-four hour periods for the entire six days of creation.

In the twenty-first century, this theory is presented (and believed as a truth) by some preachers of the gospel of the Lord Jesus Christ, taught in theological classrooms, and are part of the oral doctrine of numerous church denominations. One of the main sources of information on this theory is (Finis Jennings) Dake's Annotated Reference Bible. Dake backs up his theory with numerous scriptures, and copious commentary notes.[36]

The question remains: "If the theory is the truth, where is the factual proof?" The only answer I can give is that you must research all available data and judge the results yourself, because belief in God and scriptural writing is encumbered on each individual.

CHAPTER 3

CREATION ON THE EARTH

John 1: 1 In the beginning was the Word, and the Word was with God, and the Word was God.
2. The same was in the beginning with God.
3. All things were made by him: and without him was not any thing made that was made.
4. In him was life; and the life was the light of men.
5. And the light shineth in darkness, and the darkness comprehended it not.

John states, as an introduction to his gospel, that the <u>Word of God *(Jesus Christ)*</u> was with the Father [God] in the beginning, and was also an equal with God. John wrote this statement before any of his other writing. John further quoted Jesus as saying, "My Father is greater than I." (John 14: 28) John also, wrote down other startling statements about Jesus being in the beginning with the Father:

> "And now, O Father, glorify thou me with thine own self with the glory which I had with thee before the world was." (John 17:5)

"Father, I will that they also, whom thou hast given me, be with me where I am; that they may behold my glory, which thou hast given me: for thou lovedst me before the foundation of the world." (John 17:24)

"For I came down from heaven, not to do mine own will, but the will of him that sent me. (John 6:38)

"And the Father himself, which hath sent me, hath borne witness of me. Ye have neither heard his voice at any time, nor seen his shape. (John 5:37)

"Not that any man hath seen the Father, save he which is of God, he hath seen the Father. (John 6:46)

The Old Testament, in the book of Proverbs, also gave witness to the beginning, before the earth was created; which helps to substantiate the writing of John:

"The Lord possessed me in the beginning of his way, before his works of old. I was set up from everlasting, from the beginning, or ever the earth was. When there were no depths, I was brought forth; when there were no fountains abounding with water. Before the mountains were settled, before the hills was I brought forth: While as yet he had not made the earth, nor the fields, nor the highest part of the dust of the world. When he prepared the heavens, I was there: when he set a compass upon the face Of the depth: When he established the clouds above: when he strengthened the fountains of the deep: When he gave to the sea his decree, that the waters should not pass his commandment: when he appointed the foundations of the earth: Then I was by him, as one brought up with him: and I was daily his delight, rejoicing always before him; Rejoicing in the habitable

part of his earth; and my delights were with the sons of men."[37]

From these writings there is no doubt that living entities existed before the earth was created: and that these entities were responsible to each other, and their actions. Added to this is the fact that this heaven is what we call outer space, where there is no breathable oxygen: but there is a gaseous atmosphere that only God, The Word, and the Holy is cognize of. For mankind to live and breathe in outer space he must resort to space ships and space suits.

Now does that make God, the Word, and the Holy Ghost aliens? Or space creatures from another world? Or even a super race controlling the earth through some type of sophisticated computer design? According to the science fiction world all these statements could be true. This can be proved with movies like the Matrix, Life Force, Star Trek, Thor, West World, Star Wars, and etc.

To believe that Jesus was with the Father before the creation of heaven and earth, and was sent from heaven to dwell among men as a human being, and to suffer and die on a cross for all mankind, and then rise from the dead and return to the heaven from whence he came is within itself mind blowing, and hard to comprehend; however, this is exactly what the scriptures are hinting at for us to believe. And make no bones about it, when your mind is renewed to this line of thinking you will be free of all earthly and worldly thinking.

For the Lord Jesus Christ saith to those that believe in him, "If ye continue in my word, then ye are my disciples indeed; and ye shall know the truth, and the truth shall make you free. If thee son therefore shall make you free, ye shall be free indeed."[38]

Second Day of Creation

The song says, "For this is the day that the Lord has made, we will rejoice and be glad in it."[39] The Father rejoiced in this day, because this is when <u>the Word of God</u> began to carry out the creation orders of the Father.

The truism is when John wrote, "<u>In the beginning was the Word, and the Word was with God, and the Word was God. The same was in the beginning with God. All things were made by him; and without him was not anything made that was made.</u>"

There is no question that when God created the heaven and the earth that <u>the Word of God</u> and the Holy Ghost were right there with him. It is stated that all the things of, and on the earth were created by the <u>Word of God</u>; and this is what I will be closely scrutinizing. First let's look at the second day scripture:

> **Genesis 1: 6 And God said, Let there be a firmament in the midst of the waters, and let it divide the waters from the waters.**
> **7 And God made the firmament, and divided the waters which were under the firmament from the waters which were above the firmament: and it was so.**
> **8 And God called the firmament Heaven. And the evening and the morning were the second day.**

When looking at the scripture it doesn't jump out at you that <u>the Word of God</u> is creating anything! But a closer look begs the question, "Why would God say let there be, and then create what he declared to come into existence? Do you agree that this makes no since! But what does make since is that the Father told the Word what he wanted done, and the Word (God) carried out his wishes. What! Sounds a little crazy? But let's look at what's recorded in the book of gospel of John.

> **John 5: 17. But Jesus answered them, My Father worketh hitherto, and I work.**
> **18. Therefore the Jews sought the more to kill him, because he not only had broken the sabbath, but**

said also that God was his Father, making himself equal with God.

19. Then answered Jesus and said unto them, Verily, verily, I say unto you, The Son can do nothing of himself, but what he seeth the Father do: for what things soever he doeth, these also doeth the Son likewise.

20. For the Father loveth the Son, and sheweth him all things that himself doeth: and he will shew him greater works than these, that ye may marvel.

21. For as the Father raiseth up the dead, and quickeneth them; even so the Son quickeneth whom he will.

22. For the Father judgeth no man, but hath committed all judgment unto the Son:

23. That all men should honour the Son, even as they honour the Father. He that honoureth not the Son honoureth not the Father which hath sent him."

So then, Jesus verified that he did nothing without the consent of the Father, and that if there was a question the Father stepped in and showed him exactly what, how, and where he wanted it accomplished. Jesus put an explanation on this point when he said, "Believest thou not that I am in the Father, and the Father in me? The words that I speak unto you I speak not of myself: but the Father that dwelleh in me, he doeth the works. Believe me that I am in the father, and the Father in me: or else believe me for the very works sake."[40]

This method of communicating between God and the <u>Word of God</u> is testified in the gospel of Luke. Before Jesus was crucified on the cross, he went up on a mountain to talk things over with his father. He took Peter, James and John with him. When the father appeared, Jesus was transfigured into his heavenly appearance which to the three witnesses was a white light. Then the Word of God two friends Moses and Elijah appeared in glorified bodies and talked with him about his death and what must be accomplished at Jerusalem. When the talk was over Moses and Elijah disappeared, and Jesus reverted back to his earthly form. Suddenly the father appeared over head in a bright cloud and said, "This is my beloved Son: hear him."[41]

Not convinced? Well maybe you need to step outside of the traditional religious box and renew your mind; for the Apostle Paul wrote, "And be not conformed to this world: but be ye transformed by the renewing of your mind, that ye may prove what is that good, acceptable, and perfect, will of God."[42]

Second Day Conclusion
That God said, "let there be."

That God (the Word of God) carried out the Father's order.

That a permanent force field (firmament) called heaven was placed between the waters above (clouds) and the waters below (seas, rivers, streams, etc.) so that they are not able to touch one another.

That this is another evening and morning day without a twenty-four-hour clock; Keeping in mind that the earth is suspended and spinning in place.

Third Day of Creation

> **Genesis 1:9 And God said, Let the waters under the heaven be gathered together unto one place, and let the dry land appear: and it was so.**
> **10 And God called the dry land Earth; and the gathering together of the waters called he Seas: and God saw that it was good.**
> **11 And God said, Let the earth bring forth grass, the herb yielding seed, and the fruit tree yielding fruit after his kind, whose seed is in itself, upon the earth: and it was so.**

> **12 And the earth brought forth grass, and herb yielding seed after his kind, and the tree yielding fruit, whose seed was in itself, after his kind: and God saw that it was good.**
> **13 And the evening and the morning were the third day."**

The third day of creation reveals yet another strange thing that is different from the second day of creation. On the second day God said, and then God made. But on this day God said and it was so.

- Which means that on the first day God the Father spoke, and created the heaven and the earth.

- On the second day God the Father spoke, and God (the Word) carried out the order and separated the waters above from the waters below.

- And on the third day God (the Word) spoke into existence land, seas, vegetation, trees, and grass.

Now I want to point out here that the vegetation began to produce reproduction seed, not from sun light, but from the light coming from <u>the Word of God</u>; for this is the same life-giving light in the New Jerusalem.[43] All this while the earth is suspended and spinning in place. Therefore, the length of the evening and morning cannot be determined according to human logic.

Fourth Day of Creation

> **Genesis 1: 14 And God said, Let there be lights in the firmament of the heaven to divide the day from the night; and let them be for signs, and for seasons, and for days, and years:**
> **15 and let them be for lights in the firmament of the heaven to give light upon the earth: and it was so.**

16 And God made two great lights; the greater light to rule the day, and the lesser light to rule the night: he made the stars also.
17 And God set them in the firmament of the heaven to give light upon the earth,
18 and to rule over the day and over the night, and to divide the light from the darkness: and God saw that it was good.
19 And the evening and the morning were the fourth day.

On this fourth day of creation we are back to God said, and God made. Properly because we're dealing with things that will affect the heaven, and the Father wants to make sure that there is no mistake.

This is just my human mind thinking out loud; because with this back and forth jargon it can be confusing trying to tell who is saying or doing what. For example, when Phillip came upon the eunuch from Ethiopia, he was reading a passage from the book of Isaiah concerning the messiah. He didn't understand what he was reading and asked Phillip to explain to him what the scripture meant and who was the prophet talking about? Was he talking about himself or someone else!

"HE WAS LED AS A SHEEP TO THE SLAUGHTER; AND HE LIKE A DUMB LAMB BEFORE HIS SHEARER, SO OPENED NOT HIS MOUTH: IN HIS HUMILIATION HIS JUDGMENT WAS TAKEN AWAY: AND WHO SHALL DECLARE HIS GENERATION? FOR HIS LIFE IS TAKEN FROM THE EARTH."[44]

Phillip explained that the verses of scripture was taking about the Lord Jesus Christ, who was crucified on a cross outside the gates of Jerusalem. Upon hearing this news, the eunuch said, "See here is water; what doth hinder me to be baptized? And Phillip said, If thou believest with all thine heart, thou mayest. And he answered and said, I believe that Jesus Christ is the Son of God."⁴⁵

Therefore, from this point on you need to make sure of your understanding, and review all of my scripture references, and end note references.

On this day the Sun is created to give light to the earth: which in turn will be the power for life to all things of the earth. It is also the vehicle in which the earth will rotate around to regulate time (hours, days, weeks, and years), and the four seasons (spring, summer, fall and winter).

The Moon on the other hand is the separator of day and night: and is a force to balance the rotation of the earth around the Sun.

The stars are the other worlds God made in the heaven; that are used as signs for navigation, astrology, mythology, and astronomical constellations in the belt of the Zodiac. This is confirmed in the book of Job, who mentions the stars in the constellations of heaven:[46]

- **Arcturus** is the brightest star in the constellation Bootes; which means herdsman or plowman, and is seen in the northern sky, located between 0 degrees and +60 degrees declination, and 13 and 16 hours of right ascension on the celestial sphere.
  Constellation Ursa Major (the Great Bear), referred to in Job 9:9 and 38:32 (KJV) in connection with the constellation Orion and the Pleiades.[47]

- **Orion** is a prominent constellation located on the celestial equator and is visible throughout the world. It is one of the most conspicuous and recognizable constellations in the night sky.
  Septuagint name for a constellation widely believed to resemble a giant hunter, belted or fettered. Various legends grew about this hunter—in Greece, that he had been banished to the sky for foolish boasting; in Semitic lands, for foolishly asserting his strength against God (the Hebrew means both

"sturdy" and "fool"). Job 9:9 mentions the "making" of Orion among the great, unsearchable things God does in nature (cf. Amos 5:8). God challenged Job to attempt what only God could do—loose Orion's fetters (Job 38:31-32). The real significance of the question lies in the fact that the appearance of the Pleiades ushers in the spring and Orion ushers in the winter, both under the direction of God.[48]

- **The Pleiades**, also known as the Seven Sisters and Messier 45, are an open star cluster containing middle-aged, hot B-type stars located in the constellation of Taurus the Bull. It is among the nearest star clusters to Earth, and is the cluster most obvious to the naked eye in the night sky. It is well known as the Halloween cluster, because it's almost overhead in the sky at midnight on October 31, Halloween day.
Name of a constellation in the eastern sky composed of six bright and many other less visible stars. Telescopic photography has captured the appearance of these stars as being strung together by currents of matter. Job is asked a question that reflects this phenomenon: "Can you hold back the movements of the stars? Are you able to restrain the Pleiades or Orion?" (Job 38:31, NLT).[49]

Someone once said that the earth is the center of the universe, and he was laughed to scorn. But if we take a look at the big picture, we find that first it was the heaven and the earth; then the Sun, moon and stars. The earth was not placed among the worlds, but just the opposite, the worlds were created to support the earth.

Now God (the Word) is the one that God (the Father) put in charge of all this creation. This is confirmed by the Apostle Paul when he wrote, "God…..hath in these last days spoken unto us by his Son, Whom he hath appointed heir of all things, by whom he also made the worlds: Who being the brightness of his glory, and the express image of his person, and upholding all things by the word of his power.[50]

Remember that the evening and the morning of this day is the first day of the twenty-four-hour clock, and will be used to govern all time (seconds, minutes, and hours) on the earth.

Fifth Day of Creation

> **Genesis 1:20 And God said, Let the waters bring forth abundantly the moving creature that hath life, and fowl that may fly above the earth in the open firmament of heaven.**
> **21 And God created great whales, and every living creature that moveth, which the waters brought forth abundantly, after their kind, and every winged fowl after his kind: and God saw that it was good.**
> **22 And God blessed them, saying, Be fruitful, and multiply, and fill the waters in the seas, and let fowl multiply in the earth.**
> **23 And the evening and the morning were the fifth day.**

On this day God said, and God created from the water fish, and birds that "fly above the earth in the open firmament of the heaven (*sky*). God commanded the fish to multiply in the water; but the birds to multiply on the earth: and it is still so that no birds that fly make nests in or near water.

And yes, the evening and the morning is a twenty-four-hour day; because the earth is rotating around the Sun.

Sixth Day of Creation

> **Genesis 1:24 And God said, Let the earth bring forth the living creature after his kind, cattle, and creeping thing, and beast of the earth after his kind: and it was so.**

25 And God made the beast of the earth after his kind, and cattle after their kind, and every thing that creepeth upon the earth after his kind: and God saw that it was good.

26 And God said, Let us make man in our image, after our likeness: and let them have dominion over the fish of the sea, and over the fowl of the air, and over the cattle, and over all the earth, and over every creeping thing that creepeth upon the earth.

27 So God created man in his own image, in the image of God created he him; male and female created he them.

28 And God blessed them, and God said unto them, Be fruitful, and multiply, and replenish the earth, and subdue it: and have dominion over the fish of the sea, and over the fowl of the air, and over every living thing that moveth upon the earth.

29 And God said, Behold, I have given you every herb bearing seed, which is upon the face of all the earth, and every tree, in the which is the fruit of a tree yielding seed; to you it shall be for meat.

30 And to every beast of the earth, and to every fowl of the air, and to every thing that creepeth upon the earth, wherein there is life, I have given every green herb for meat: and it was so.

31 And God saw every thing that he had made, and, behold, it was very good. And the evening and the morning were the sixth day.

On this day God created all the creatures of the earth (male & female) that must breathe air to live: living creatures, animals, insects, beast of the earth (dinosaurs?), and mankind. Included in this bunch are birds that cannot fly in the firmament of heavenly air: chickens, etc.

God also made it plain that he wanted mankind to be the

caretaker of the earth, and have "dominion over the fish of the sea, over the fowl of the air, and over every living thing that moveth upon the earth." Based upon Gods command, there is no reason why the inhabitants of the earth should give ownership credence to Satan: for if they do; they, like Jacobs son Esau, are giving away their inheritance, and are being deceived by a terrible lie.

Creation of Mankind

The creation of mankind is unique because he is the express projection of the Father, the Word, and the Holy Ghost. This fact is substantiated when God said, "Let us make man in our image, after our likeness." There is no record of any other creation that is formed after the image of God; not even the angels!

So, does mankind look exactly like God? No! Does mankind resemble God in any way? Maybe! Even the angels questioned God about his relationship toward mankind:

- "What is man, that thou art mindful of him? and the son of man, that thou visitest him? For thou hast made him a little lower than the angels, and hast crowned him with glory and honour. Thou madest him to have dominion over the works of thy hands; thou hast put all things under his feet:" (Psalm 8:4-6)

- "Lord, what is man, that thou takest knowledge of him! or the son of man, that thou makest account of him! Man is like to vanity: his days are as a shadow that passeth away." (Psalm 144:3-4)

The angels were mystified that God would pay so much attention to a creature that was formed from the dust of the ground, and whose life span was as a shadow on the ground: here for a moment, and gone in a second. And that God would put so much personal time and effort into grooming, and caring for mankind. God didn't give them an answer right away; but did leave an answer in the following scriptures:

- "Even everyone that is called by my name: for I have created him for my glory, I have formed him; yea I have made him." (Isaiah 43:7)

- "The Lord have made all things for himself: yea, even the wicked for the day of evil." (Proverbs 16:4)

- "Thou art worthy, O Lord, to receive glory, and honor and power: for thou hast created all things, and for thy pleasure they are, and were created." (Revelation 4:11)

Creation of the Male

Genesis 2:7 "And the Lord God formed man of the dust of the ground, and breathed into his nostrils the breath of life; and man became a living soul."

So right here I want to point out it was God the Father who said, "Let us make man in our image, after our likeness." But it was the Lord God (Jesus Christ) who formed him from the dust of the ground. Is this believable? Yes, because the truth is in the wording of the Scriptures.

Now when the Lord God made man, he did not just scoop up the dust, make a big mud pile, and then shape it into an image. Rather, he put man together by using reproducing mud balls we call cells.

I can best explain it by telling you a story of my experience. While taking an art class at Colombia College, the art teacher took us on a field trip to the Art Institute of Chicago, Illinois. She told us to stand back and look at a particular picture hanging on the gallery wall. It looked like all the other pictures hanging there, and as a class, we couldn't figure out why that one was so important. After much debate, she took us closer to the picture, to where our faces almost touched the painting. To our surprise and amazement, we found the whole picture was comprised of nothing but a lot of little dots. But from a distance, it looked smooth as a photograph. The title of the picture was A Sunday on La Grande Jatte, painted in 1884 by Georges Pierre Seurat.

We know from the study of anatomy that the flesh of the body is nothing more than a lot of little living cells (dots), wrapped in skin (dirt), and growing on a frame we call a skeleton. But in order for this flesh (dirt) to function on this skeleton, it must have constant water to hold it together and blood (which is manufactured from inside the bone) to keep the cells supplied with nourishment for reproduction.

So, the picture that is developing is that God made a frame (a bone structure), and meticulously placed sophisticated mud balls (cells) on the frame. These cells are programmed to produce functioning organs, and an image and likeness of God. Now God is ready to give this form life; to live and reproduce (after his kind) like the plants and animals. However, the difference between the life inside humans, and that inside animals is the fact that the Lord God (the word of God), "breathed into his nostrils (*the breath of life*); and man became a living soul."

Right here I want say that what the Lord God (the Word of God) breathed into the nostrils of man was a portion of the Light from himself. The apostle John bears this out when he wrote, "in him (the Word of God) was life, and the life was the light of men."[51] This Light of men is talking about the soul of man, which is housed inside the flesh of the body, but is separate from the flesh, water, and bone/blood. The body needs all these ingredients working together in order to be active on the earth.[52] When the elements work together, the brain creates an electrical charge that pulsates throughout the body. It is a known scientific fact that water mixed with salt (which is present in human and animal body tissues and fluids) creates an electrical charge.[53] For this reason, static electricity is ever present in the body, and is one of the main reasons the body of clay has movement. Without the replenishment of salt, the body would die. Christ Jesus made a comparison to the human race when he told his disciples "Ye are the salt of the earth: but if the salt have lost his savour, wherewith shall it be salted? It is thenceforth good for nothing, but to be cast out, and to be trodden under foot of men."[54]

But on the other hand, we can think of the body as a living space suit. When inside this space suit, we are able to feel, eat, procreate, and develop civilizations. Yet outside the body, we are nothing more than light (which we call a ghost, spirit, or an apparition), roaming around in space until the Father calls us home (heaven or hell). Am I reaching here, grasping at thin air? Or have I read too many scientific books, or seen too many science fiction movies? Maybe! But it is something to think about.

So, coming outside the box, it is plain to see that the breath, that was breathed into the created male, was the light of Christ, and that this light inside mankind is called the soul of man. Therefore, it stands to reason that we live and we die by the will of God the Father and His son Christ Jesus. This can be concluded the reason why the story of Christ Jesus has a numbing and joyous effect on the soul of man: for this story causes the soul to morn, grown, weep, and cry and grieve over how they beat, whipped, and crucified the Lord Jesus on a cross. No other human story has this cause effect on mankind (no not Buddha, or Muhammad). But not to worry soul, because the Lord will bring us back to him, and we will dwell in the New Jerusalem forever more.

The Garden of Eden

After God created the male, he placed him in his garden which was east of Eden. In the garden was every kind of tree, to include those that were good to eat from. In the mist (center) of the garden was <u>the tree of life</u>; also planted there was <u>the tree of the knowledge of good and evil</u>. The male's job was care keeper of the garden. However, God gave him specific instructions to follow while in the garden:

> *"And the Lord God commanded the man, saying, Of every tree of the garden thou mayest freely eat: but of the tree of the knowledge of good and evil, thou shalt not eat of it: for in the day that thou eatest thereof thou shalt surely die."*[55]

Now it is plain to see that God intended his human creation to be vegetarians, and to eat from the fruit of the trees. And take note that eating fruit from the tree of life was not restricted; only eating from <u>the tree of the knowledge of good and evil</u>: which seems to be the basis of conscious awareness.

After this, God said that it was not a good thing that man should be alone; "and out of the ground God formed every beast of the field, (*sheep, goat, cattle, and etc.*) and every fowl (*bird*) of the air (*doves, pigeons, and etc.*) take note that this is not the same type of fowl that God called from the water on the fifth day: for there are no aggression, or prey for food in the garden.[56]

Creation of the Female

Then God brought all the animals and birds before the man and he named them. Take note that it took a high intelligence to perform this task. However, a suitable mate was not found for the male. Therefore, God took action to correct this default:

> *"And the Lord God caused a deep sleep to fall upon Adam, and he slept: and he took one of his ribs, and closed up the flesh instead thereof; and the rib, which the Lord God had taken from man, made he a woman, and brought her unto the man. And Adam said, This is now bone of my bones, and flesh of my flesh: she shall be called Woman, because she was taken out of Man. Therefore shall a man leave his father and his mother, and shall cleave unto his wife: and they shall be one*

Who is Jesus Christ

flesh. And they were both naked, the man and his wife, and were not ashamed.[57]

God wanted a companion for the male that would be compatible in oneness as he is with the Word, and the Holy Ghost. Therefore, instead of creating the female from the dust of the ground, he created her from out of the man. That's why the male stated that the female was part of his flesh and bone: which resulted in him calling her woman. And that the male would forsake his father and mother for this gift of God. "And they were both naked, the man and his wife, and were not ashamed."

Now the man called the female woman; but God called them both Adam.[58] This is another proof that God is very adamite about the male and female joining together as one identity.

Conditions in the Garden of Eden

Being in the garden naked, the human beings had to be in a humidity controlled environment, and encased under a force field bubble: for the temperature had to be constant around 70-75 degrees Fahrenheit in order for them to survive; and you have to consider that the four seasons (spring, summer, fall and winter) would not be a factor in their lives. Also, you have to realize that the earth was not affected by the bubble, and continued on its daily, weekly, monthly, and yearly rotation cycle.

So then, it can be clearly seen that inside the bubble there were two naked human beings with plants and animals; and outside the bubble there were other plants, and animals [dinosaurs, etc.].

Therefore, God gave them every kind of herb and food tree to eat from. He also allowed them to eat the fruit from the <u>Tree of Life</u> (where upon they could live forever); but forbid them to eat from the <u>Tree of the knowledge of Good and Evil</u>: for upon eating from this tree they would lose eternal life, and their body would begin to die.[59]

So, the question is formulated, "How long was Adam and Eve in the Garden of Eden? First of all, they were eating from the tree of life, and that in itself gave them longevity and extended their years of life (hundreds, thousands and/or even millions). Second, they remained in the garden until they listened to O Lucifer (the great dragon, that old serpent, called the Devil, and Satan),[60] and sinned against God by eating from the tree of the knowledge of good and evil.

Again, how long were Adam and Eve in the Garden of Eden? Nobody knows! But what is known are two facts:

- From the six day of creation until the day they sinned they were in the Garden of Eden, and unrestricted from all of its contents.

- However, from the day they were put out of the Garden, until this very day: nearly six thousand years have come to completion (according to the Jewish calendar A.D. 2013 marks the 5774 year since Adam and Eve stepped out of the garden).

So, were all the questions satisfactorily answered concerning "the Word of God" (Christ) being in the beginning with God (the Father); and the creator of all things? If not, just remember that I tried my best to convince you, and I gave it my best shot! You say you want more research, explanation and/or data! Sorry, that's another research book. So, let's move on?

The Seventh Day

After everything was created to his satisfaction, God took a rest. Like a good constructionist, he took time to observe the work of his hands.

So, was God exhausted and needed rest after everything was created? To the contrary. I believe that at the end of creation, there is no more to do, and it is time to develop and prepare the angels, and humankind for the future new heaven and new earth. The Holy Bible and history have determined this to some degree. Also, God created a day of rest, because he knew the workaholic attitude of humans would wear out the fleshly body. He created a law to this effect:

> *"Remember the sabbath day, to keep it holy. Six days shalt thou labour, and do all thy work: But the seventh day is the sabbath of the Lord thy God: in it thou shalt not do any work, thou, nor thy son, nor thy daughter, thy manservant, nor thy maidservant, nor thy cattle, nor thy stranger that is within thy gates: For in six days the Lord made heaven and earth, the sea, and all that in them is, and rested the seventh day: wherefore the Lord blessed the sabbath day, and hallowed it."* (Exodus 20:8–11)

CHAPTER 4

ANGELS

Creation of the Angels

Research in the bible does not reveal when, where, or how the Angels were created; but it does state that angels were created by God (the Father) as ministering spirits like flaming fire.[61]

Looking at the totality of creation we find that the Father created the heaven and the earth, and the angels: and was the author and director of God (the Word) creating everything on the earth. Yet, the Apostle Paul explained that the Father gave orders that the angels would worship his only begotten Son (the Word of the Lord): and give due diligence to his scepter.[62]

Christ revealed to the world that God is a spirit, and the only way to worship him (*have communication*) is in spirit and in truth.[63] Logic dictates that God would create beings liken unto himself: which are invisible to the human eye, but are made manifest to complete heavenly missions on the earth.

One such a time is when the Lord (the Word) and two angels stopped to visited with Abraham on their journey to Sodom. These three looked and talked like humans, and did eat the food that Abraham had prepared for them.[64] While the Lord stayed a while with Abraham the two angels continued on toward Sodom. When the reached the gates of Sodom they were greeted by Lot, Abrahams nephew, and he invited them to his house. They must have been very beautiful to look at because all the males of the city surrounded lots house, and demanded that Lot turn the two men over to them for the purpose of sexual gratification. Lot refused to release them to the raging mob; and as they stormed the house, the angels put forth their hands and blinded them from entering the home. This depravity by the city males was one of the major activities that caused the total destruction of Sodom, Gomorra, and the surrounding cities: by fire raining down from heaven.[65]

God's Angelic Army

Psalm 34:7 The angel of the Lord encampeth round about them that fear him, and delivereth them.

Are angels' aliens from another planet in the solar system? No! Do angels live on the earth in parallel life with humans? No! So then, where do angels live? Not an easy question to answer, but all indications point to them being in the heaven with God; and is his kingdom workers and military army. This is not an easy concept to gasp, but let me give you a few examples:

When Christ was being questioned by Pontus Pilate, he stated that if he wanted to escape the punishment against him, he could have called out to the Father, and twelve legions of angels[66] would come to his rescue: a Roman legion was equal to 5 companies of 1100 soldiers; however, the Old Testament states that God's army of chariots consist of "twenty thousand, even thousands of angels."[67] Further, these chariots of God are seen in action during the days of King Jehoshaphat of Judah, and the prophet Elisha, when the land of Judah was invaded by the Syrian army. As Elisha and his servant approached the battlefield, the servant cried out that the Syrian army was vast and mighty. Elisha quickly said, "Fear not: for they that be with us are more than they that be with them. And Elisha prayed, and said, Lord, I pray thee, open his eyes, that he may see. And the Lord opened the eyes of the young man; and he saw: and, behold, the mountain was full of horses and chariots of fire round about Elisha."

Of course, the Syrian army lost the battle because they were blind to the army that surrounded and out numbered them.

During one campaign against the Philistines King David asked God to deliver the enemy into his hands. David wanted to attack right away, but God told him to wait until he heard a rustling noise "in the tops of the mulberry trees:" this was a sign that the army of God was in the forefront of the battle, and would ensure the victory.[68]

Human Protectors

> **Psalm 91: 11 For he shall give his angels charge over thee, to keep thee in all thy ways.**
> **12 They shall bear thee up in their hands, lest thou dash thy foot against a stone.**

The above Psalm was used by Satan to temp Christ into jumping off a mountain top: for he knew that the angels would catch him before he hit the ground.[69]

As the time grew near for Christ to endure the cross, he removed himself from his disciples and kneeling down in prayer he said, "Father, if thou be willing, remove this cup from me: nevertheless not my will, but thine, be done. And (*immediately*) there appeared an angel unto him from heaven, strengthening him."[70] This was the prayer of a celestial being who would have to face the agony of death; but was promised by the Father to rise up from the grip of the grave.[71] Also, great compassion is shown by the angel that came down from heaven to comfort him in his hour of tremendous pressure: "And being in an agony he prayed more earnestly: and his sweat was as it were great drops of blood falling down to the ground." Then he arose from prayer, and followed the path to the cross.

Workers of the Kingdom

Jesus often spoke in parables to the multitudes, and in private told his disciples the meaning of the parable. Such was the case when he discussed his mission on earth and the coming of the end times concerning the human race; this he did with the parable of the Wheat and the Tares:

- *Matthew 13:24 Another parable put he forth unto them, saying, The kingdom of heaven is likened unto a man which sowed good seed in his field:*
25 but while men slept, his enemy came and sowed tares among the wheat, and went his way.
26 But when the blade was sprung up, and brought forth fruit, then appeared the tares also.
27 So the servants of the householder came and said unto him, Sir, didst not thou sow good seed in thy field? from whence then hath it tares?
28 He said unto them, An enemy hath done this. The servants said unto him, Wilt thou then that we go and gather them up?
29 But he said, Nay; lest while ye gather up the tares, ye root up also the wheat with them.
30 Let both grow together until the harvest: and in the time of harvest I will say to the reapers, Gather ye together first the tares, and bind them in bundles to burn them: but gather the wheat into my barn.

A good imagination, with simple logic, could probably come up with a solution to this parable; but on all accounts would be dead wrong. A genius mind may come close, but still would not be able to figure out its true meaning. Why? Because nowhere in this parable can you fit in actions from the angels of God. Now let's look at how Jesus explained this parable:

- *Matthew 13:36 Then Jesus sent the multitude away, and went into the house: and his disciples came unto him, saying, Declare unto us the parable of the tares of the field.*
- *37 He answered and said unto them, He that soweth the good seed is the Son of man;*

> *38 the field is the world; the good seed are the children of the kingdom; but the tares are the children of the wicked one;*
> *39 the enemy that sowed them is the devil; the harvest is the end of the world; and the reapers are the angels.*
> *40 As therefore the tares are gathered and burned in the fire; so shall it be in the end of this world.*
> *41 <u>The Son of man shall send forth his angels, and they shall gather out of his kingdom all things that offend, and them which do iniquity;</u>*
> *42 <u>and shall cast them into a furnace of fire:</u> there shall be wailing and gnashing of teeth. 43 <u>Then shall the righteous shine forth as the sun in the kingdom of their Father.</u> Who hath ears to hear, let him hear.*

Now what I want to point out, and dwell on, is the fact that the angels are employed by Christ to gather the souls in the last days, and to separate them for heaven or hell. This is not isolated verbiage but is stated by Christ as fact:

- *Matthew 25:29 Immediately after the tribulation of those days shall the sun be darkened, and the moon shall not give her light, and the stars shall fall from heaven, and the powers of the heavens shall be shaken: 30 and then shall appear the sign of the Son of man in heaven: and then shall all the tribes of the earth mourn, <u>and they shall see the Son of man coming in the clouds of heaven with power and great glory. 31 And he shall send his angels with a great sound of a trumpet, and they shall gather together his elect from the four winds, from one end of heaven to the other.</u>*

- *Matthew 25: 31 <u>When the Son of man shall come in his glory, and all the holy angels with him,</u> then shall he sit upon the throne of his glory: 32 and before him shall be gathered all nations: and he shall separate them one from another, as a* *shepherd divideth his sheep from the goats: 33 and he shall set the sheep on his right hand, but the goats on the left.*

- *Revelation 13: 9 And the third angel followed them, saying with a loud voice, If any man worship the beast and his image, and receive his mark in his forehead, or in his **hand**, 10 the same shall drink of the wine of the wrath of God, which is poured out without mixture into the cup of his indignation; <u>and he shall be tormented with fire and brimstone in the presence of the holy angels, and in the presence of the Lamb:</u>*

Angel Society and Environment

Luke 20: 34 And Jesus answering said unto them, The children of this world marry, and are given in marriage:
35 but they which shall be accounted worthy to obtain that world, and the resurrection from the dead, neither marry, nor are given in marriage:
36 neither can they die any more: for they are equal unto the angels; and are the children of God, being the children of the resurrection.
37 Now that the dead are raised, even Moses shewed at the bush, when he calleth the Lord the God of Abraham, and the God of Isaac, and the God of Jacob.
38 For he is not a God of the dead, but of the living: for all live unto him.

A great mystery is cloaked around the question of angels and sexual intercourse. However, it is plain to see that Jesus explained the difference of this world society and that of the angels. Human beings were created male and female, and are given the option to marry and bring forth children after their kind through the bonding of copulation. But the angels were created to do the work of God, and do not marry among themselves, nor are they given in marriage to each other.

Some preach heavily that this means angels are incapable of having sexual intercourse. Yet, the scripture above didn't say that they couldn't have sexual intercourse: just that they don't; and when we / you are risen from the grave there will be no sexual marriage activity among the eternal souls.

Are the angels capable of sexual activity? The answer is yes! Are they capable of falling in love, and marrying, and having children? The answer again is yes! Are any of these things recorded in the Holy Bible? Yes indeed!

In the year 1556 Noah was five hundred years old, and he had three sons, Shem, Ham, and Japheth. The sons of God (the angels) looked upon the earth and saw that the female human was very beautiful and fair. So, they left their home in heaven and took the earthly women to themselves as wives. From this union were produced giants and mighty men of mythical tales.[72] God was not pleased with what the angels did, and for their sin he "casted them down to hell, and delivered them into chains of darkness, to be reserved unto judgment."[73]

Messengers of God

God at certain times used the angels to parlay his messages to human kind. These messengers were sometimes visible, but often times invisible with only a voice being heard, for example:

Abrahams wife Sarah surrogated her Egyptian hand maid to Abraham so that they could have children: preferably a son. When the girl knew that she was impregnated, she began to openly despise Sarah. This did not go well with Sarah and she complained to Abraham; who gave Sarah lead way to deal with the situation. Therefore, Sarah began to treat the girl so harshly that she took flight into the desert. However God sent an angel to fetch her back to Abrahams camp and told her that she would bear a son whose name is to be called Ishmael: "and he will be a wild man: his hand will be against every man, and every man's hand will be against him; and he shall dwell in the presence of his brethren." Abraham was 86 years old when the baby Ishmael was born.[74]

When Abraham was 100 years old, his wife Sarah, who was 90, gave birth to his son Isaac. When Ishmael made fun of the birth, Sarah took offense to him and demanded that Abraham send him and his mother out of their camp. Abraham was saddened by Sarah's request, but God told him to honor Sarah's demand because Isaac was the son of promise: and because Ishmael was Abrahams son, he would make from him a nation. With a heavy heart Abraham sent Hagar and Ishmael into the Beersheba desert with bread and a bottle of water. When both items were spent, Hagar and Ishmael laid down to die. But God heard their cry for help and dispatched an angel to rescue them. Hagar heard the voice of the angel of God from heaven say into her, "Arise, lift up the lad, and hold him in thine hand; for I will make him a great nation."[75] God kept his promise, and Ishmael had twelve son's which formed the Arab nations: for Ishmael is called the father of the Arabs.[76]

Characteristic Features

There is no true description of an angel, or of God for that matter. But tidbits are sown throughout the bible that may (or may not) quell our curiosity. An example is given by the prophet Daniel:

> *"In those days I Daniel was mourning three full weeks. I ate no pleasant bread, neither came flesh nor wine in my mouth, neither did I anoint myself at all, till three whole weeks were fulfilled. And in the four and twentieth day of the first month, as I was by the side of the great river, which is Hiddekel; then I lifted up mine eyes, and looked, and behold a certain man clothed in linen, whose loins were girded with fine gold of Uphaz: his body also was like the beryl, and his face as the appearance of lightning, and his eyes as*

> *lamps of fire, and his arms and his feet like in colour to polished brass, and the voice of his words like the voice of a multitude."*[77]

Right here I want to stress that Daniel did not see the celestial being under normal circumstances: for he had been fasting without food or drink for twenty-one days. Now what he saw in a vision was a man dressed in white linen, with a gold cord around his waist. His body was like the beryl stone (light-blueish green), and his face like that of lightning flashing when there is a storm. His eyes were red as fire, with arms and feet like polished brass. His voice was like many voices speaking; but Ezekiel explained that the voice was more like "a noise of many waters."[78]

Celestial Hierarchy

God is the master of organization and order. He set this world in rhythm with him by establishing laws, precepts, instructions, and commands. But on a higher plain he also set a rank and file among the angels. Therefore, the order goes something like this, God, then the Word and Holy Ghost, then the angels, and lastly mankind. Apostle Paul addressed this concept when he wrote his epistle to the Colossians:

> *(Christ) "who is the image of the invisible God, the firstborn of every creature: for by him were all things created, that are in heaven, and that are in earth, visible and invisible, whether they be thrones, or dominions, or principalities, or powers: all things were created by him, and for him: and he is before all things, and by him all things consist."*[79]

Now I want to pause right here and reflect on the fact that in past days God had an anointed cherup that was in charge of all the heavenly beings. His name was O Lucifer: he was the one that sinned against God and was booted out of heaven; him I will discuss in length in a later chapter. But for our purpose, Christ is (now) the head of everything in heaven, on the earth, and under the earth.[80]

Many have tackled this subject, "but the mot influential Christian angelic hierarchy was that put forward by Pseudo-Dionysius the Areopagite in the 4th or 5th century in his book de Coelesti Hierachia (On the Celestial Hierarchy)" (Wikipedia – Christian angelology)

Men who studied this subject list nine orders of angels; which are based on their interpretation of the scriptures. Are there more? Who knows! But God! The following is a list that I retrieved from the dictionary, and the Holy Bible:[81]

- **Seraphim** – these are the four guards around the throne of God. Each of them has a set of three wings: one set to cover their face, one set to fly with, and one set to cover their feet. Each one of them had eyes that seem to be all over their body. One beast had the face of a man, another the face of a lion, the third the face of an ox, and the fourth the face of an eagle. As they fly around the throne of God they are heard to say, "Holy, holy, holy is the Lord of hosts: the whole earth is full of his glory."[82]

- **Cherubim's** – these are creatures that have four faces on each side of their head (a man, a lion, an ox, and an eagle). The also, have two sets of wings (one pair to fly with, and the other pair covered their bodies); with hands under their wings. They transport the throne of God throughout the heaven.[83] God also placed these same Cherubim's at the entrance of the Garden of Eden, to include a flaming sword that turned in a complete circle, to guard against anyone entering into it.[84]

- **Thrones** – these are described as the wheels that carry Gods throne and are an in harmony with the Cherubim's.[85]

- **Dominions** – the root of this word means control, rule, and sovereignty.[86]

The disciples of Jesus Christ were always debating who was the greatest among them; and they asked Jesus, "Who is the greatest in the kingdom of heaven?" Jesus drew a little child to himself and replied, "Verily I say unto you, Except ye be converted, and become as little children, ye shall not enter into the kingdom of heaven. Whosoever therefore shall humble himself as this little child, the same is greatest in the kingdom of heaven. And whoso shall receive one such little child in my name receiveth me. But whoso shall offend one of these little ones which believe in me, it were better for him that a millstone were hanged about his neck, and that he were drowned in the depth of the sea."

Then he warned his disciples that an angel is assigned to all believers, and "That in heaven their angels do always behold the face of my Father which is in heaven. For the Son of man is come to save that which was lost."[87]

During the days of the prophet Daniel, king Nebuchadnezzar of Babylon was judged by the watchers and the holy one's to serve seven years of walking around in the fields like a wild animal. Within the hour of hearing this prophesy from Daniel, "he was driven from men, and did eat grass as oxen, and his body was wet with the dew of heaven, till his hairs were grown like eagles' feathers, and his nails like birds' claws."[88]

- **Virtue** – Moral excellence and righteousness: goodness; effective force or power: ability to produce a definite result.[89]

When Jesus was passing by a thong of people, a woman who had an issue of blood for twelve long years reached down and touched the hem of his garment; for she said to herself "If I may touch but his clothes, I shall be whole." When Jesus felt virtue leave his body he looked around and cried out, "who touched my clothes?" In confusion the disciples said, "thou seest the multitude thronging thee, and sayest thou, Who touched me? And when he saw the woman who had touched him he said, "daughter, thy faith made the whole; go in peace, and be whole of thy plague."[90]

- **Powers** – A person, group, or nation having great influence or control over others.[91]

When Jesus had crossed over into the country of the Gadarenes, he encountered a man who was possessed with a group of demons called Legion. When Jesus ordered them to come out of the man, they begged him to let them enter into a herd of nearby swine. "And forth with Jesus gave them leave. And the unclean spirits went out, and entered into the swine: and the herd ran violently down a steep place into the sea, (they were about two thousand;) and were chocked in the sea."[92]

- **Principalities** – A territory ruled by a prince or from which a prince derives his title. The position or jurisdiction of a prince.[93]

Jesus told his disciples that he would send the Holy Ghost down to the earth after his mission was completed on the cross. And that the Holy Ghost would convict the world of sin, righteousness, and judgment; of sin because of non-belief in him, of righteousness because he had to endure the cross to go back to the Father, and of judgment because the prince of this world (the great dragon, that old serpent, called the Devil and Satan) is judged;[94] for God has prepared the everlasting fire of hell for him and his angels.[95]

The Apostle Paul entered the fray when he reminded the Ephesians that the real fight was not against humans but against the evil forces of Satan.[96]

- **Archangel** – These seem to be the top warriors in God's army, with the power to defeat the Devil.[97]

- **Angels** – the workers of God which are mentioned throughout the book of Revelation: "This is a revelation from* Jesus Christ, which God gave him to show his servants the events that must soon* take place. <u>He sent an angel to present this revelation to his servant John,</u> who faithfully reported everything he saw."[98]

Conclusion

The whole Hebrew Bible is one story concerning two types of beings: one a spirit, and the other a spirit encased in a fleshly shell (a human being).

The spirit being is invisible, and cannot be seen by the fleshly being. However, the spirit being may reveal itself to the fleshly being via dreams, visions, and by entering in and joining the human being in his or her fleshly shell. The spirit being lives primarily in space above and beyond planet earth; the fleshly being is confined to planet earth, and must use spaceships to travel into outer space.

Both beings were created by the same God, and are living parallel on planet earth {here I'm talking about "the great dragon, that old serpent, called the Devil and Satan;" and his angels which are called demons and evil spirits}. However, the human beings are headed to either heaven or hell, but the Devil and his angels have already been judged to be thrown into the eternal lake of fire.[99] Now to unravel this puzzle may take a bit of dipping, dodging, twisting, and turning. But stay with me, and we'll get there.

CHAPTER 5

SIN AND DEATH

The story of how sin and death entered the lives of human beings has its start in the peaceful Garden of Eden. When God created a male and female human being, he put them in a place called the Garden of Eden. There, the two fleshly beings roamed around naked (they did not know they were naked) and enjoyed frequent meetings with God. They also had free rein of the garden, and could eat from every food tree, including the Tree of Life. But God forbade them to eat from the Tree of the Knowledge of Good and Evil. Why? Because God said, "The day they eat from that tree they would surely die." And being innocent creatures that they were, they followed God's instruction to the letter.

Now it seemed this commune in the garden would last forever. However, things would soon change when a spirit being named O Lucifer (the great Dragon, that old Serpent called the Devil and Satan) is brought to the garden.

Why is O Lucifer in the Garden of Eden? We find the answer in the books of Isaiah and Ezekiel;[100] where it is written that he was created perfect in beauty, was highly intelligent, full of wisdom, wore a covering of precious stones, and had a beautiful singing voice. He was in the Garden of Eden because he was God's anointed cherub over all of God's affairs, and he walked with God upon the holy mountain. Further, he was perfect in all his ways until the day he sinned against God, and was thrown out of heaven: down to the earth.[101] This was confirmed by the Lord Jesus Christ when he said, "I beheld Satan as lighting fall from heaven."[102]

What sin did he commit? The story of how he sinned is told in the third chapter of the book of Genesis. So, you may ask what motivated a perfect creation like O Lucifer to sin against God. It is not clear what drove him to sin, but I'll retell the story of his sin. Maybe you can come to a more-focused conclusion on why.

It is not known how many trips O Lucifer made to the Garden of Eden, but his last trip is the one recorded in the book of Genesis: chapter three.[103]

The Sin Story

Satan: While God was away, he entered the body of the Serpent. The Serpent was like O Lucifer, full of wisdom and deceptive, elusive, crafty, and cunning. Through the Serpent, O Lucifer asked the woman, "Listen, did God say that you cannot eat from every tree in the garden?"

Eve: The woman, quick to answer, told him they could eat from every tree except the Tree of the Knowledge of Good and Evil. And if they touched or ate the fruit from the tree, they would die.

Satan: "And the serpent (O Lucifer) said unto the woman, Ye shall not surely die: For God doth know that in the day ye eat thereof, then your eyes shall be opened, and ye shall be as gods, knowing good and evil."

Eve: "And when the woman saw that the tree was good for food, and that it was pleasant to the eyes, and a tree to be desired to make one wise, she took of the fruit thereof, and did eat, and gave also unto her husband (Adam) with her; and he did eat."

Adam and Eve: "And the eyes of them both were opened, and they knew that they were naked; and they sewed fig leaves together, and made themselves aprons."

So, we see here that O Lucifer's first sin was lying on God, and his second sin was murder (for his lying tongue would bring death to both the woman and the man). The conclusion is that O Lucifer committed the first two sins in this world, and the woman and the man committed the third sin by disobeying God.

Is any of what I'm saying true? Yes, because Jesus confirmed it when he told the Jews, "Ye are of your father the devil, and the lusts of your father ye will do. He was a murderer from the beginning, and abode not in the truth, because there is no truth in him. When he speaketh a lie, he speaketh of his own: for he is a liar, and the father of it"[104]

And just as he trapped Eve and Adam into sin, he is still walking up and down in the earth, using an age-old proven tactic to bait and snare human beings into sin. James (the brother of Jesus) brought this process to light when he wrote,

> *"Blessed is the man that endureth temptation: for when he is tried, he shall receive the crown of life, which the Lord hath promised to them that love him. Let no man say when he is tempted, I am tempted of God: for God cannot be tempted with evil, neither tempteth he any man: But every man is tempted, when he is drawn away of his own lust, and enticed. Then when lust hath conceived, it bringeth forth sin: and sin, when it is finished, bringeth forth death."*[105]

The apostle John added to what James said: "For all that is in the world, the lust of the flesh, and the lust of the eyes, and the pride of life, is not of the Father, but is of the world"[106] For you see, it was lying and lust that brought sin and death into this world.

When the man and the woman heard God walking in the garden,

they hid among the trees: "And the Lord God called unto Adam: (for God called both of them Adam[107]) and said unto them. Where art thou?" The man spoke saying, "I heard thy voice in the garden, and I was afraid, because I was naked, and I hid myself."

God demanded to know who told him he was naked, and if he had eaten from the Tree of the Knowledge of Good and Evil. When God questioned Adam about why he sinned, he put the blame on Eve: "The woman whom thou gavest to be with me, she gave me of the tree [*fruit*], and I did eat." The woman likewise put the blame on the Serpent. God didn't question the Serpent but instead judged him.

Everlasting Judgment

God started his judgment with the Serpent; (1) he would be cursed to crawl on his belly throughout his life, and (2) there would be enmity between the woman's seed and his seed; her seed would bruise (*crush*) his head, while the Serpent seed would bruise (*strike*) at his heel.

Interestingly, a woman does not produce a seed, but an egg: upon which the seed of a man penetrates to form a baby. However, when Jesus was born, he was considered the seed of the virgin Mary. During the time he walked upon this earth, he crushed sin and death; even while his enemies nipped had his heels (the elders, the scribes, the Pharisees, the Herodians, the Sanhedrin council, and the Romans). After his death, the established church is considered the woman of Christ: and her seed are the believers; which are being persecuted by the workers of iniquity.[108]

Next, God told the woman she would bear children with great pain and sorrow, and that her husband would rule over her.

Further, God told Adam that since he had disobeyed his commandment, by listening to his wife, he would till the ground in sorrow for his food all the days of his life, and would sweat for his daily bread until he returned to the dust of the ground.

Then God made Adam and his wife clothing from the skin of animals (this is the first recorded bloodshed on earth to protect mankind), and put them out of the Garden of Eden This is when Adam named his wife Eve, because she would become the mother of all living human being.

And to make sure they did reenter the garden, God placed cherubim's (angels) to seal the entrance; lest they would reenter and eat from the Tree of Life in their sinful state and live forever.

Death of Human Beings

This is when the actual physical process of dying began for Adam and Eve. They could no longer sustain eternal life by eating the fruit from the Tree of Life. Fresh out of the Garden of Eden, Adam and Eve produced two sons (Cain and Abel). However, Cain slew Abel and God cursed him to be a fugitive, and a vagabond for the rest of his life. At the age of 130 Adam brought forth a son named Seth. After Seth was born, Adam lived another eight hundred years: "and he begat sons and daughters." Adams total life span was 930 years.[109] There is no record of how long Eve lived.

Nothing is said about what happened to O Lucifer. Logical reason says God put all four out of the garden: the man, the woman, the Serpent, and O Lucifer. Therefore, it would be wise to heed the words of James, and seek answers from God; lest you be thrown into hell for ignorance sake.

> *James 1: 5 If any of you lack wisdom, let him ask of God, that giveth to all men liberally, and upbraideth not; and it shall be given him.*
> *6 But let him ask in faith, nothing wavering. For he that wavereth is like a wave of the sea driven with the wind and tossed.*
> *7 For let not that man think that he shall receive any thing of the Lord.*
> *8 A double minded man is unstable in all his ways.*

YEAR – O

The Beginning of Life on Earth

This is the beginning of sin and death in the lives of human beings; and the introduction of corrupt angels on the earth. There is no substantial time line before O Lucifer, Adam, and Eve sinned against God: only eternal living. Therefore, mankind's life span has been physically shortened to around 85 years,[110] but his eternal soul has been extended to enter either heaven or hell. However, the corrupt spirit beings that sinned against God were created eternal, and remain that way until they are thrown into the lake of fire.[111] To ease the cost of mankind's transgressions, God instituted the system of love, grace, and mercy through his only begotten Son, The Lord Jesus Christ: aka The Word.[112]

After Adam and Eve were put out of the Garden of Eden, they started a life of planting, harvesting, and domesticating animals. They had two sons. The first was Cain, and the younger was Abel. However, because of sin, Cain slew Abel, and was questioned by God concerning his deed:

Cain – "was a tiller of the ground. And in process of time it came to pass, that Cain brought of the fruit of the ground an offering unto the Lord. but unto Cain and to his offering he had not respect. And Cain was very wroth, and his countenance fell."

Abel – "was a keeper of sheep And Abel, he also brought of the firstlings of his flock and of the fat thereof. And the Lord had respect unto Abel and to his offering:"

God – "And the Lord said unto Cain, Why art thou wroth? and why is thy countenance fallen? If thou doest well, shalt thou not be accepted? and if thou doest not well, sin lieth at the door. And unto thee shall be his desire, and thou shalt rule over him."

Cain - "talked with Abel his brother: and it came to pass, when they were in the field, that Cain rose up against Abel his brother, and slew him."

God - "And the Lord said unto Cain, Where is Abel thy brother?"

Cain - "And he said, I know not: Am I my brother's keeper?"

God - "And he said, What hast thou done? the voice of thy brother's blood crieth unto me from the ground. And now art thou cursed from the earth, which hath opened her mouth to receive thy brother's blood from thy hand. When thou tillest the ground, it shall not henceforth yield unto thee her strength; a fugitive and a vagabond shalt thou be in the earth."[113]

Cain - "said unto the Lord, My punishment is greater than I can bear. Behold, thou hast driven me out this day from the face of the earth; and from thy face shall I be hid; and I shall be a fugitive and a vagabond in the earth; and it shall come to pass, that every one that findeth me shall slay me."

God – "And the Lord said unto him, Therefore whosoever slayeth Cain, vengeance shall be taken on him sevenfold. And the Lord set a mark upon Cain, lest any finding him should kill him."

Cain - "went out from the presence of the Lord, and dwelt in the land of Nod, on the east of Eden. And Cain knew his wife; and she conceived, and bare Enoch: and he builded a city, and called the name of the city, after the name of his son, Enoch. And unto Enoch was born Irad: and Irad begat Mehujael: and Mehujael begat Methusael: and Methusael begat Lamech."[114]

> **LAMECH** - a descendant of Cain, and the husband of Adah and Zillah. Lamech's sons by Adah were Jabal, "the father of those who dwell in tents and have livestock," and

Jubal, "the father of all those who play the lyre and pipe." A son, Tubal-cain, "the forger of all instruments of bronze and iron," and a daughter, Naamah, were Lamech's children by Zillah (Genesis 4:18-22). In the account of beginnings given in the early chapters of Genesis, the sons of Lamech are the first herdsmen, musicians, and metalworkers. His song of vengeance (verses 23-24) is an example of early Hebrew poetry. In the song Lamech declares that he has killed a man for wounding him and compares the act to his forebear Cain's slaying of Abel (cf. verses 8-12). He asserts that "if anyone who kills Cain is to be punished seven times, anyone who takes revenge against me will be punished seventy-seven times!" Lamech's song indicates that, as civilization became more complex, pride and the propensity for violence increased. Jesus' word about forgiving "seventy times seven" (Matthew 18:22) stands in sharp contrast to Lamech's example.[115]

My first observation from the scriptures above is that God showed grace and mercy toward Cain when he didn't sentence him to death for killing his brother Abel. God gave Noah two ordnances concerning the shedding of blood:

- "And surely your blood of your lives will I require; at the hand of every beast will I require it, and at the hand of man; at the hand of every man's brother will I require the life of man."

- "Whoso sheddeth man's blood, by man shall his blood be shed: for in the image of God made he man."[116]

YEAR 130 - 235

At the age of one-hundred-thirty Adam brought forth another son named Seth. Then Seth brought forth his son Enos when he was one-hundred-five years old. At the birth of Enos men began to call upon the name of the Lord. I will stretch here and say that it was probably during the dedication of the child to God. In any case God is now entering into the human religious atmosphere: which will be carried to the birth of Jesus Christ.

> **History of Seth:** "This third son of Adam and Eve replaced Abel, whom Cain murdered (Genesis 4:25). He appears as the firstborn son of Adam in the genealogy of Jesus Christ as well as other genealogies Genesis 5:3-8, 1Chronicles 1:1 (KJV "Sheth"), and Luke 3:38. It was through Seth's line that Jesus was born. Seth was the father of Enosh and lived 912 years."[117]

> **History of Enosh:** "Seth's son and the grandson of Adam (Genesis 4:26; 1 Chronicles 1:1). He became the father of Kenan at 90 years of age, after which he fathered other sons and daughters, dying at the age of 905 (Genesis 5:6-11). He is mentioned as Jesus' ancestor in Luke's genealogy (Luke 3:38; KJV, RSV "Enos")."[118]

YEAR 930

Death of Adam

So then, God protected Cain, and allowed him to live out his remaining days on the earth. But the puzzling question has always been, "of whom did Cain marry?"

- First, I want to say that Adam lived nine-hundred and thirty years, and tradition says that he had thirty-three sons, and twenty-three daughters[119]

- In conclusion, Cain had to have married his sister since no other women were available; and incest was prevalent until God gave Moses the law against it.[120]

Historic Adam: "Adam was the first man. He was also the father of the human race. Adam's role in the Bible is helpful in understanding the Old Testament. A study of Adam also helps in understanding the meaning of salvation and the person and work of Jesus Christ.

The creation of Adam and the first woman, Eve, is recited in two accounts in the book of Genesis. The first account (Genesis 1:26-31) presents the pair in relationship to God and to the rest of the created order. God said the first humans were created male and female in God's image. He gave them a specific command to populate and rule over the earth. In relation to creation the first humans were, on one hand, part of it. They were created on the same day as other land animals. But they were also distinctly above it. They were the highest point of the creation process and the only animals to bear God's image.

The second account is much more specific (Genesis 2:4–3:24). It explains the origin of the present human condition of sin and death. It sets the stage for the drama of redemption, that Christ paid the price for our sins. The second account treats in detail aspects of Adam's creation. It tells of the formation of Adam from the dust of the ground and of his receiving the breath of life from God (2:7). It recounts the planting of the Garden and the responsibility given to Adam to cultivate it (2:8-15). God instructed Adam that the fruit of every tree in the Garden was his for food, except one. It also records the solemn warning that the fruit of the "tree of the knowledge of good and evil" was never to be eaten, under the pain of death (2:16-17). Adam's loneliness after naming the animals and not finding a suitable companion is also described. The creation of the first woman is introduced (2:18-22). The creation of Eve from Adam's rib portrays the essential unity of spirit and purpose of the sexes intended by God.

The story does not end on such a positive note, however. It records the great deception Satan played upon Eve through the serpent. By distorting God's original commandment (compare Genesis 3:1 with 2:16-17), the serpent tricked Eve into eating the forbidden fruit and sharing it with Adam. Eve seems to have eaten because she was deceived (1 Timothy 2:14); Adam ate out of a willful and conscious rebellion. Ironically, the two beings originally created in God's image and likeness believed that they could become like God by disobeying him (Genesis 3:5).

The effects of their disobedience were immediate. For the first time a barrier of shame disrupted the unity of man and woman (Genesis 3:7). More important, a barrier of real moral guilt came between the first couple and God. The story relates that when God came looking for Adam after his rebellion, he was hiding among the trees. He was already aware of his separation from God (3:8). When God questioned him, Adam blamed Eve and then God: "It was the woman you gave me who brought me the fruit" (3:12). Eve, in turn, blamed the serpent (3:13).

According to the story in Genesis, God held all three responsible. Each one was informed of the consequences of their rebellion (Genesis 3:14-19). The two great commands, originally signs of pure blessing, became mixed with curse and pain. The earth could now be populated only through the woman's birth pangs. It could be conquered only by the man's labor and perspiration (3:16-18). Further, the unity of man and woman would be strained by a struggle for dominance between them. Finally, God pronounced the ultimate consequence. As he had originally warned, Adam and Eve were to die. Someday the breath of life would be taken from them, and their bodies would return to the dust from which they were made (3:19). That very day they also experienced a "spiritual" death. In other words, they were separated from God, the giver of life, and from the tree of life, the symbol of eternal life (3:22). God sent them out of Eden, and there was no way back. The entrance to paradise was blocked (3:23-24). Only God could restore what they had lost.

Adam's story is not devoid of hope. God was merciful even then. He made Adam and Eve garments of skin to cover their bodies. He promised that someday the serpent Satan would be crushed by the woman's "seed" (Genesis 3:15; see Romans 16:20). Many scholars consider that promise to be the first biblical mention of redemption.

THE SIGNIFICANCE OF ADAM

Adam's significance is based upon the fact that he was a historical individual. That assumption was made by many Old Testament writers (Genesis 4:25; 5:1-5; 1 Chronicles 1; Hosea 6:7). The New Testament writers agreed (Luke 3:38; Romans 5:14; 1 Corinthians 15:22, 45; 1 Timothy 2:13-14; Jude 1:14). But he was more than an individual. To begin with, the Hebrew word adam is not merely a proper name. Even in the Genesis story it is not used as a name until Genesis 4:25. The word is one of several Hebrew words meaning "man." It is the generic term for the human race. In the vast majority of cases it refers either to a male individual (Leviticus 1:2; Joshua 14:15; Nehemiah 9:29; Isaiah 56:2) or to humanity in general (Exodus 4:11; Numbers 12:3; 16:29; Deuteronomy 4:28; 1 Kings 4:31; Job 7:20; 14:1). The sense of the word adam is also behind the phrase "children (or sons) of men" (2 Samuel 7:14; Psalms 11:4; 12:1; 14:2; 53:2; 90:3; Ecclesiastes 1:13; 2:3). That phrase, literally "sons of adam," simply means "men" or "human beings." When it is used, the entire human race is in view. Indeed, the word adam indicates a concern in the Old Testament that extends to all the earth's people and the Lord of all nations (Genesis 9:5-7; Deuteronomy 5:24; 8:3; 1 Kings 8:38-39; Psalms 8:4; 89:48; 107:8-31; Proverbs 12:14; Micah 6:8).

It is no accident, then, that the first man was named Adam, or "Man." To speak about Adam is to speak about the entire human race. This usage can perhaps best be understood using an ancient Hebrew mind-set. Modern thinking emphasizes the individual. Other social relationships are seen as secondary. The Hebrew understanding was quite different. The separate personality of the individual was appreciated (Jeremiah 31:29-30; Ezekiel 18:4). But there was a strong tendency to see the social group (family, tribe, nation) as a single living body with a corporate identity of its own. A group representative displayed the corporate personality of the group. The actions and decisions of the representative were reflected on the entire group. If the group was a family, the father was usually considered the corporate representative. For good or for ill, his family received the results of his actions (Genesis 17:1-8; compare with 20:1-9, 18; Exodus 20:5-6; Joshua 7:24-25; Romans 11:28; Hebrews 7:1-10).

Adam was the original man and father of humankind, in whose image all succeeding generations would be born (Genesis 5:3). Thus, he was the corporate representative of humanity. The creation accounts themselves give the impression that the commands of 1:26-30 (compare with Genesis 9:1, 7; Psalms 8:5-7; 104:14) as well as the curses of Genesis 3:16-19 (compare with Psalm 90:3; Ecclesiastes 12:7; Isaiah 13:8; 21:3) were meant not only for Adam (and Eve) but for the entire race.

In Romans 5:12-21 the apostle Paul made this contrast: death and condemnation came upon humanity by Adam's disobedience. But life and righteousness was given to humanity through Christ's obedience.

For Paul, the human race was divided into two groups in the persons of Adam and Christ. Those who remain a part of Adam are the "old" humanity. They bear the image of the "man of dust" and partake of his sin and alienation from God and creation (Romans 5:12-19; 8:20-22). But those who are a part of Christ by faith become Christ's "body" (Romans 12:4-5; 1 Corinthians 12:12-13, 27; Ephesians 1:22-23; Colossians 1:18). They are re-created in Christ's image (Romans 8:29; 1 Corinthians 15:49; 2 Corinthians 3:18). They become one "new man" (Ephesians 2:15; 4:24; Colossians 3:9-10, KJV). They also partake of the new creation (2 Corinthians 5:17; Galatians 6:15). The old barriers raised by Adam are removed by Christ (Romans 5:1; 2 Corinthians 5:19; Galatians 3:27-28; Ephesians 2:14-16). For Paul, the similarity of Adam and Christ as human representatives meant that Christ had restored what Adam had lost."[121]

CHAPTER 6

THE GREAT FLOOD

I touched on this before, but now I want to go into more detail because I want you to fully realize that mankind is not alone on this earth; and it's not aliens from outer space: but Satan and his fallen angels; which are called devils, demons, and unclean spirits.

> **YEAR – 1556**
> (Methuselah is 869, his son Lamech is 682)

<u>METHUSELAH</u> – 'Methuselah was the son of Enoch. He was Lamech's father, and he was the grandfather of Noah through Seth's line (Genesis 5:21-27 and 1 Chronicles 1:3). Methuselah lived for 969 years, which makes him the oldest person recorded in the Bible. His lineage is included in Luke's genealogy of Christ (Luke 3:37)."[122]

God Calls Noah

In this year a man named Noah was five-hundred years old, and three sons were born of him: Shem, Ham, and Japheth. Noah's father was Lamech, whose father was Methuselah, whose father was Enoch: who walked with God for over three-hundred years and God took him alive into the heaven.[123]

Again, as afore mentioned, when the population of the earth

began to expand, some of the angels (the sons of God) left their heavenly abode and decided to live on the earth. This was after they saw how beautiful the human women were to look upon. The children of these copulations are indirectly responsible for myths, fairy tales, and stories of black magic. They are directly responsible for the total corruption of all fleshly beings.

God was watching as the spirit beings and the fleshly beings joined together. He took note that "the wickedness of man was great in the earth, and that every imagination of the thoughts of his heart was only evil continually." Further, "The earth also was corrupt before God, and the earth was filled with violence. And God looked upon the earth, and behold, it was corrupt, for all flesh had corrupted his way upon the earth."[124] Therefore, God put forth two judgments.

- He rounded up all the angels who had sinned, with the fleshly beings and, "cast them down to hell, and delivered them into chains of darkness, to be reserved unto judgment" day.[125] Jude confirmed this when he wrote, "And the angels which kept not their first estate, but left their own habitation, he hath reserved in everlasting chains under darkness unto the judgment of the great day"[126].

- The state of the world that God had created broke his heart: "And it repented the Lord that he had made man on the earth, and it grieved him at his heart. And the Lord said, I will destroy man whom I have created from the face of the earth; both man, and beast, and the creeping thing, and the fowls of the air; for it repenteth me that I have made them."[127]

However, God found favor in Noah. And God said unto Noah, "The end of all flesh is come before me; for the earth is filled with violence through them; and, behold, I will destroy them with the earth; And, behold, I, even I, do bring a flood of waters upon the earth, to destroy all flesh, wherein is the breath of life, from under heaven; and every thing that is in the earth shall die."[128]

God had a plan to save some of his creation that lived on the land of the earth. He commanded Noah to build a boat of gopher wood that would house and protect the saved creation from the impending rain, flood, thunderstorms, and wind.

Noah started building the ark when he was around five hundred years old. During this time, he had a wife and three sons: Shem, Ham, and Japheth.

> **YEAR – 1651**
> (Lamech, Noah's father died at the age of 777 [874-1651]

LAMECH – "Methuselah's son, and the father of Noah (Genesis 5:25-31; 1 Chronicles 1:3). When Noah was born, Lamech expressed his hope that the child would bring relief to humanity from the curse placed upon Adam (Genesis 5:29; cf. 3:17). His life span—777 years—is one of the longest in the listing of those who lived before the Flood. Fanciful conversations in old age between Lamech and his father, Methuselah, are recorded in the Dead Sea Scrolls. Lamech is listed as an ancestor of Jesus in the genealogy recorded in Luke 3:36."[129]

> **YEAR – 1656**
> (Methuselah died at age 969 / Noah is 600, Shem is 100)

The Whole Earth is Flooded

In the same year that Methuselah died, and at the close of Noah's six hundredth birthday, he stocked the ark with food and water. Then God said unto Noah, "Of every clean beast thou shalt take to thee by sevens, the male and his female: and of beasts that are not clean by two, the male and his female. Of fowls also of the air by sevens, the male and the female; to keep seed alive upon the face of all the earth."[130]

After everything was aboard the ark, Noah, his wife, and his three sons (and their wives) entered the Ark; and God closed and locked the door: and let loose the waters from below the earth, and the rain from above the earth. This lasted forty days and forty nights. The waters were fifteen cubits (about twenty-three feet) above the mountaintops. The floodwaters prevailed upon the earth a total of 150 days (five months) before they began to recede. By the seventh month, the ark came to rest upon the mountains of Ararat, which is in the nation now known as Turkey.

Three months later, Noah, his wife, and his three sons, and their wives, and all the saved creatures left the ark. "And Noah built an altar unto the Lord: and took of every clean beast, and of every clean fowl, and offered burnt offering on the altar." This act of thanksgiving by Noah pleased God: "And the Lord smelled a sweet savour; and the Lord said in his heart, I will not again curse the ground any more for man's sake; for the imagination of man's heart is evil from his youth; neither will I again smite any more every thing living, as I have done. While the earth remaineth, seedtime and harvest, and cold and heat, and summer and winter, and day and night shall not cease."[131]

> **YEAR - 1657**
> Noah is 601, Shem is 101

A New Start

However, since the land dwellers were starting over from scratch, God gave them some new instructions, which were different from those given to Adam and Eve.[132]

> (1) "And God blessed Noah and his sons, and said unto them, Be fruitful, and multiply, and replenish the earth."

> (2) "And the fear of you and the dread of you shall be upon every beast of the earth, and upon every fowl of the air, upon all that moveth upon the earth, and upon all the fishes of the sea; into your hand are they delivered."

(3) "Every moving thing that liveth shall be meat for you; even as the green herb have I given you all things."

(4) "But flesh with the life thereof, which is the blood thereof, shall ye not eat."

(5) "And surely your blood of your lives will I require; at the hand of every beast will I require it, and at the hand of man; at the hand of every man's brother will I require the life of man. Whoso sheddeth man's blood, by man shall his blood be shed: for in the image of God made he man."

(6) "And you, be ye fruitful, and multiply; bring forth abundantly in the earth, and multiply therein."

(7) "And God spake unto Noah, and to his sons with him, saying, And I, behold, I establish my covenant with you, and with your seed after you; And with every living creature that is with you, of the fowl, of the cattle, and of every beast of the earth with you; from all that go out of the ark, to every beast of the earth. And I will establish my covenant with you, neither shall all flesh be cut off any more by the waters of a flood; neither shall there any more be a flood to destroy the earth."[133]

The Rainbow Sign

"And God said, This is the token of the covenant which I make between me and you and every living creature that is with you, for perpetual generations: I do set my bow in the cloud, and it shall be for a token of a covenant between me and the earth. And it shall come to pass, when I bring a cloud over the earth, that the bow shall be seen in the cloud: And I will remember my covenant, which is between me and you and every

living creature of all flesh; and the waters shall no more become a flood to destroy all flesh. And the bow shall be in the cloud; and I will look upon it, that I may remember the everlasting covenant between God and every living creature of all flesh that is upon the earth. And God said unto Noah, This is the token of the covenant, which I have established between me and all flesh that is upon the earth."[134]

CHAPTER 7

SATAN ON THE EARTH

The War in Heaven

What I'm about to say here cannot be established by a time line, but I suspect the war in heaven happened sometime after Adam and Eve left the Garden of Eden, and prior to the calling of Abraham. Mainly, I'm basing my theory on what happened during the time of Job; who lived in the city of Uz: which was named after the oldest son of Aram; who was the youngest son of Shem; who was the oldest son of Noah.[135]

After the incident in the Garden of Eden, O Lucifer tried to take God's throne. He said in his heart, "I will ascend into heaven, I will exalt my throne above the stars of God: I will sit also upon the mount of the congregation, in the sides of the north: I will ascend above the heights of the clouds; I will be like the most High." But God answered him with a solemn vow, "Yet thou shalt be brought down to hell, to the sides of the pit."[136]

Therefore, there was a war in heaven. On one side was O Lucifer: with one-third of the angels.[137] On the other side was Michael the archangel, with the remaining angels. The Apostle John was allowed to see the war, and recorded the results.

> *"And there was war in heaven: Michael and his angels fought against the dragon; and the dragon fought and his angels, and prevailed not; neither was their place found any more in heaven. And the great dragon was cast out, that old serpent, called the Devil, and Satan, which deceiveth the whole world: he was cast out into the earth, and his angels were cast out with him."*[138]

O Lucifer Confined to Live on Earth

Not only was O Lucifer defeated in battle; he also acquired a new name—the Devil and Satan. Likewise, his fallen angels are now called devils, demons and unclean spirits. Christ Jesus was a witness to O Lucifer being cast out of heaven. He said, "I beheld Satan as lightning fall from heaven."[139]

When O Lucifer was cast out of heaven, the angels that remained in heaven rejoiced but also cried out with grief that he was full of wrath, and like a roaring lion, walking up and down on the earth, seeking whom he may devour (possess).[140]

In Genesis 10:21, it states that Shem (Noah's oldest son) was the father of five sons: Elam, Asshur, Arphaxad, Lud, and Aram (who was the father of Uz). Arphaxad was born two years after the flood, when Shem was 102 years old. Uz was Aram's oldest son, which puts Job approximately four hundred years before the birth of Abraham. But what I want to focus on is the fact that Satan is walking up and down on the earth during the time of Job. And he shows his contempt and wrath toward human beings when he is questioned by God.

So then, if Arphaxad was born two years after the flood, and he was thirty when his son Salah was born, and the succeeding son line was between thirty and forty years. Therefore, it can be estimated that the time line for from Shem to Job would look something like this:

- 1659 - Elam is born
- 1660 – his brother Asshur is born
- 1661 – his brother Arphaxed is born.
- 1662 - his brother Lud is born.
- 1663 - his brother Aram is born.
- 1691 - his son UZ is born.
- 1741 – Job is living in the land of UZ with his wife, ten sons and three daughters.

UZ - Uz was the homeland of Job (Job 1). The name appears in parallels with Edom and is associated with the Uz in the family tree of the original Horites in Seir (Lamentations 4:21). The book of Job does not give the location of Uz, but it does say that the sons of the East lived there (Job 1:3). Uz is also said to be close to the desert (1:15) and to the Chasdim (1:17). This indicates that it was located to the east of the land of Israel.

The associations with Edom strongly suggest that the land of Uz was populated by descendants of the Horites of Seir. Further support for this view is a verse in the Greek version at the end of the book of Job: "since he had lived in the land of Uz on the borders of Edom and Arabia."[141]

YEAR – 1741

Job Chapter 1

The book of Job opens with the story of how he was from the land of Uz. And that he was a man who was, "perfect and upright, and one that feared God, and eschewded *(avoided)* evil." Further, God had blessed Job with riches, and ten children (seven sons and three daughters). Job's sons enjoyed the riches of their father, and feasted every day of the week. Each son had a day of feasting, "and sent and called for their sisters to eat and drink with them."

While the feasting was going on, "Job sent and sanctified them, and rose up early in the morning, and offered burnt offerings according to the number of them all: for Job said, It may be that my sons have sinned, and cursed God in their hearts. Thus, did Job continually."

Nevertheless, for all his efforts to stay the hand of trouble by sending up prayers, and worship praises to God, the test of his faith in God was about to be revealed. Tribulation came into Job's life when God called his angels to a meeting in heaven. Satan also came to the meeting. It seems he may have been an uninvited guest, because God immediately began to question him.

God: "Whence comest thou?"

Satan: "From going to and fro in the earth, and from walking up and down in it."

God: "Ast thou considered my servant Job, that there is none like him in the earth, a perfect and an upright man, one that feareth God, and escheweth evil?"

Satan: "Doth Job fear God for nought? Hast not thou made an hedge about him, and about his house, and about all that he hath on every side? thou hast blessed the work of his hands, and his substance is increased in the land. But put forth thine hand now, and touch all that he hath, and he will curse thee to thy face."

God: "Behold, all that he hath is in thy power; only upon himself put not forth thine hand."

The Devil: "So Satan went forth from the presence of the Lord."

When Satan went out from the presence of God, he unleashed his wrath and unmerciful fury—his hatred of God—on all that Job owned. The record of his destruction is thus.

- And there came a messenger unto Job, and said, The oxen were plowing, and the asses feeding beside them: And the Sabeans fell upon them, and took them away; yea, they have slain the servants with the edge of the sword; and I only am escaped alone to tell thee.

- While he was yet speaking, there came also another, and said, The fire of God is fallen from heaven, and hath burned up the sheep, and the servants, and consumed them; and I only am escaped alone to tell thee.

- While he was yet speaking, there came also another, and said, The Chaldeans made out three bands, and fell upon the camels, and have carried them away, yea, and slain the servants with the edge of the sword; and I only am escaped alone to tell thee.

- While he was yet speaking, there came also another, and said, Thy sons and thy daughters were eating and drinking wine in their eldest brother's house: And, behold, there came a great wind from the wilderness, and smote the four corners of the house, and it fell upon the young men, and they are dead; and I only am escaped alone to tell thee.

I know Job was in disbelief and great pain when he heard the three messenger's state that he had lost all his possessions. What grieved him the most was the fourth messenger; with news that his seven sons and three daughters were dead. But Job, true to God's brag on him, "arose, and rent his mantle, and shaved his head, and fell down upon the ground, and worshipped, And said, Naked came I out of my mother's womb, and naked shall I return thither: the Lord gave, and the Lord hath taken away; blessed be the name of the Lord. In all this Job sinned not, nor charged God foolishly."

Just like in suspenseful movies, you get the feeling this is the end of Job's story. But put on your thinking cap, because God and Satan are not through yet. Again, God convenes a meeting in heaven with the angels; and again, Satan comes.

Job Chapter 2

The second chapter of job gives us the foot print of Satan relentless attack on human beings. It seems that he lives by an old established saying that I heard from my mother, "If at first you don't succeed, try, try again." Therefore, don't be alarmed that he will attack you head on; and come back at a later time if he didn't get to you the first time, or the third time, or the fourth time!

God: "And the Lord said unto Satan, From whence comest thou?"

The Devil: "And Satan answered the Lord, and said, From going to and fro in the earth, and from walking up and down in it."

God: "And the Lord said unto Satan, Hast thou considered my servant Job, that there is none like him in the earth, a perfect and an upright man, one that feareth God, and escheweth evil? and still he holdeth fast his integrity, although thou movedst me against him, to destroy him without cause."

The Devil: "And Satan answered the Lord, and said, Skin for skin, yea, all that a man hath will he give for his life. But put forth thine hand now, and touch his bone and his flesh, and he will curse thee to thy face."

God: "And the Lord said unto Satan, Behold, he is in thine hand; but save his life."

The Devil: "So went Satan forth from the presence of the Lord, and smote Job with sore boils from the sole of his foot unto his crown."

Job: "And he took him a potsherd to scrape [the sore boils] himself withal; and he sat down among the ashes."

Job's Wife: "Then said his wife unto him, Dost thou still retain thine integrity? curse God, and die."

Job: "But he said unto her, Thou speakest as one of the foolish women speaketh. What? shall we receive good at the hand of God, and shall we not receive evil? In all this did not Job sin with his lips."

More than anything else, the story of Job gives us a view of how the spirits being (the Devil and his demons) are given authority to test humankind by using lies, temptation, and deceit. Why does God condone this procedure? There is no clear-cut answer, but I found satisfaction hidden in the book of Deuteronomy.

> *"If there arise among you a prophet, or a dreamer of dreams, and giveth thee a sign or a wonder, And the sign or the wonder come to pass, whereof he spake unto thee, saying, Let us go after other gods, which thou hast not known, and let us serve them; Thou shalt not hearken unto the words of that prophet, or that dreamer of dreams: for the Lord your God proveth you, to know whether ye love the Lord your God with all your heart and with all your soul."*[142]

So it is that God will allow false prophets to roam among his people to prove whether they will hold onto their faith, and love their God with all their heart, soul, mind, and strength. Or will they follow after beautiful flattery and sensational, supernatural, spiritual wickedness.

The apostle Peter wrote that we should not be surprised when we are tested ("as though some strange thing has come upon us"), but that the trial of your faith in Christ is like gold going through fire to burn away all impurities).[143] He goes on to say we should rejoice in suffering as Job and Christ did.

Christ put the cap on testing when he said, "Blessed are ye, when men shall revile you, and persecute you, and shall say all manner of evil against you falsely, for my sake. Rejoice, and be exceeding glad: for great is your reward in heaven: for so persecuted they the prophets which were before you."[144]

After all this explanation, some will still be in doubt about the spirit beings' role in testing of the fleshly beings to see if they are worthy to go with Christ into heaven. But lest we forget, Christ—who came down from heaven and was born of a woman—also had to be tested once he put on a fleshly body shell. And the only spirit being capable of testing him was Satan. We know Christ defeated him by quoting the written Word and overcoming the challenge of the cross by defeating death.[145]

So, we see that Satan has been walking up and down on the earth since the days of Job, and he has been developing his skills to deceive humankind for well over five thousand years. I don't think these facts can be denied, but it will be up to those who read my analysis to judge for themselves. Who knows what revelation you will receive after reading this?

Further, the door to heaven has been closed to Satan because the Word is now the doorway into the heavenly kingdom. For Christ has said, "I am the way, the truth, and the life; no man cometh to the father, but by me."[146] And to put icing on the cake, John recorded that the angels in heaven are rejoicing that Christ completed his mission on the earth: through the cross.

> *"And I heard a loud voice saying in heaven, Now is come salvation, and strength, and the kingdom of our God, and the power of his Christ: for the accuser of our brethren is cast down, which accused them before our God day and night. And they overcame him by the*

blood of the Lamb, and by the word of their testimony; and they loved not their lives unto the death. Therefore rejoice, ye heavens, and ye that dwell in them. Woe to the inhabiters of the earth and of the sea! for the devil is come down unto you, having great wrath, because he knoweth that he hath but a short time."[147]

Satan's Influence

In the Old Testament, there is not a lot mentioned about the influence of spirit beings on the lives of humankind. Yet in the spots that are there, we can see Satan's suggestive powers and control in high places.

David and Census Taking

In the book of Numbers, God told Moses to go through the twelve tribes and number all the men, "from twenty years old and upward, all that are able to go forth to war in Israel: thou and Aaron shall number them by their armies; Only thou shalt not number the tribe of Levi, neither take the sum of them among the children of Israel; But thou shalt appoint the Levites over the tabernacle of testimony, and over all the vessels thereof, and over all things that belong to it: they shall bear the tabernacle, and all the vessels thereof; and they shall minister unto it, and shall encamp round about the tabernacle.[148]

David: In 1 Chronicles Chapter 21, it states that David was influenced by Satan to take a census, and he told his general, Joab, to go and number all of Israel. Joab protested this decision and numbered all of Israel except the tribes of Levi and Benjamin. David's breaking of God's commandment brought forth swift judgment.

God: "And the Lord spake unto Gad, David's seer, saying, Go and tell David, saying, Thus saith the Lord, I offer thee three things: choose thee one of them, that I may do it unto thee."

The Prophet Gad*:* "So Gad came to David, and said unto him, Thus saith the Lord, Choose thee (1) Either three years' famine; (2) or three months to be destroyed before thy foes, while that the sword of thine enemies overtaketh thee; (3) or else three days the sword of the Lord, even the pestilence, in the land, and the angel of the Lord destroying throughout all the coasts of Israel. Now therefore advise thyself what word I shall bring again to him that sent me."

David: "And David said unto Gad, I am in a great strait: let me fall now into the hand of the Lord; for very great are his mercies: but let me not fall into the hand of man."

God: "So the Lord sent pestilence upon Israel: and there fell of Israel seventy thousand men.'

King of Tyrus

In Ezekiel Chapter 28, God reveals to Ezekiel how the king of Tyrus was influenced by O Lucifer (the great Dragon, that old Serpent called the Devil and Satan). The first thing that Satan did was to convince the king of Tyrus in his heart that he was a god, and to sit in the seat of God over his people. The Devil used this same tactic when he told the woman in the Garden of Eden, "Ye shall not surely die: for God doth know that in the day ye eat thereof, then your eyes shall be opened and ye shall be as gods, knowing good and evil"[149]

Satan also bestowed wisdom and riches (gold and silver) on the king of Tyrus. God said his heart was lifted up by the craftiness of the Devil. During the temptation of Christ, "The devil taketh him up into an exceeding high mountain, and sheweth him all the kingdoms of the world, and the glory of them; And saith unto him,

All these things will I give thee, if thou wilt fall down and worship me;" but "Then saith Jesus unto him, Get thee hence, Satan: for it is written, Thou shalt worship the Lord thy God, and him only shalt thou serve"[150] For his disobedience with Satan, God pronounced judgment on the king of Tyrus.

> *"Therefore thus saith the Lord God; Because thou hast set thine heart as the heart of God; Behold, therefore I will bring strangers upon thee, the terrible of the nations: and they shall draw their swords against the beauty of thy wisdom, and they shall defile thy brightness. They shall bring thee down to the pit, and thou shalt die the deaths of them that are slain in the midst of the seas. Wilt thou yet say before him that slayeth thee, I am God? but thou shalt be a man, and no God, in the hand of him that slayeth thee. Thou shalt die the deaths of the uncircumcised by the hand of strangers: for I have spoken it, saith the Lord God."*

King of Persia

During the first year of the reign of Darius, king of the Chaldeans, Daniel was reading the book of Jeremiah, and came to the realization that the seventy-year captivity was coming to a close. "For thus saith the Lord, That after seventy years be accomplished at Babylon I will visit you, and perform my good word toward you, in causing you to return to this place. For I know the thoughts that I think toward you, saith the Lord, thoughts of peace, and not of evil, to give you an expected end. Then shall ye call upon me, and ye shall go and pray unto me, and I will hearken unto you. And ye shall seek me, and find me, when ye shall search for me with all your heart."[151]

With this knowledge in his grasp, Daniel humbled himself down to pray, confessing before God his sin, and the sins of Israel. God heard Daniel's prayer, and sent the angel Gabriel to give Daniel his answer; which was news that the seventy-year captivity would soon be over, and the Messiah would be released to come to the earth.[152]

In the third year of the reign of Cyrus, king of Persia, Daniel was again praying about the seventy-year captivity. But he did not get a quick answer from God, like he had the first time he prayed about the subject. So, he decided to fast and pray, which lasted twenty-one days. Then in a vision, Daniel saw and spoke to the messenger from God, who told him that the prince of the kingdom of Persia had prevented him from coming to Daniel, and that Michael, the archangel, had to use force to break him free from the clutches of Satan.[153]

The apostle Paul warned us of evil in the hierarchy of governments when he wrote, "For we wrestle not against flesh and blood, but against principalities, against powers, against the rulers of the darkness of this world, against spiritual wickedness in high places"[154]

The Last Days

The last days began after Christ had risen from the grave, and the Holy Ghost was released upon the earth. For thus saith the Lord God almighty from the book of Joel, "And it shall come to pass in the last days, saith God, I will pour out of my Spirit upon all flesh: and your sons and your daughters shall prophesy, and your young men shall see visions, and your old men shall dream dreams: and on my servants and on my handmaidens I will pour out in those days of my Spirit; and they shall prophesy: and I will shew wonders in heaven above, and signs in the earth beneath; blood, and fire, and vapour of smoke: the sun shall be turned into darkness, and the moon into blood, before that great and notable day of the Lord come: and it shall come to pass, that whosoever shall call on the name of the Lord shall be saved."[155]

A great deal of the signs of the times are revealed in the book of Revelation; more importantly it gives us two important events. First, the beast (who gets his power from Satan) will be given power to make war against the saints of God, and will prevail against them.[156]

Second, John recorded a great evil that will be unleashed upon the word in the name of religion; "And I saw three unclean spirits like frogs come out of the mouth of the dragon, and out of the mouth of the beast, and out of the mouth of the false prophet. For they are the spirits of devils, working miracles, which go forth unto the kings of the earth and of the whole world, to gather them to the battle of that great day of God Almighty."[157]

To this end Christ gave this warning concerning the last days, "Then if any man shall say unto you, Lo, here is Christ, or there; believe it not. For there shall arise false Christs, and false prophets, and shall shew great signs and wonders; insomuch that, if it were possible, they shall deceive the very elect."[158]

Yet, to this very day people are still following sensational religious spiritualism where men, and women, are blowing on crowds of congregations: and the people in them all seem to fall down by an invisible power. Or, the people are made to form a line to be touched by the religious leader for the purpose of being healed: and are seemingly knocked to the floor by an invisible power force. Better still, cancer and other diseases being openly pulled from their bodies by a preacher. In all these things, reports are surfacing that hardly any healing is taking place, only crowd showboating.

CHAPTER 8

SPIRIT BEING AMONG US

Humankind has convinced itself that it is necessary to look into outer space to find other living beings, and/or a planet like earth. Yet, the Bible is clear that spirit beings are living among fleshly beings on planet earth, and have been since the Garden of Eden. But they have so greatly camouflaged themselves with illusionary magic that humankind is not fully conscious of them. The New Testament is saturated with information concerning them. Therefore, I want to point out the Scriptures that, like a Labrador retriever, flush them into the open.

What Happens When the Unclean Spirit Takes over a Human Body?

When God created males and females, they were innocent of sin. They came to know sin when they ate from the Tree of the Knowledge of Good and Evil. Even after God put them out of the garden, humankind was good natured until Cain slew his brother Abel. Since that first murder between human beings, humankind has been on a collision course of constant war and mayhem. However, according to the words of the Lord Jesus Christ, humankind has been helped by spirit beings entering the body to commit wicked and evil deeds. Let's look at an example outlined in the Bible.

> *"When Jesus came to the country of the Gadarenes, he met a man that was overtaken by unclean spirits (demons). This man had been possessed by them a long time, and walked around naked in the grave yard. The people tried to bound him with chains and fetters, but he was so strong that he broke them like they were paper. He could be heard crying night and day as he walked in the mountains, and among the tombs: being tormented by the demons. As a last resort he tried to cut them out of his body with the use of stones."*[159]

So, it's plain to see that when the spirit being enters the human body, there is a violent reaction when the body tries to reject it. Why? Because the body was made to cohabit with only the Holy Spirit of God: "Know ye not that your body is the temple of the Holy Ghost?"[160]

Despite his efforts, the man could not drive the unclean spirits from his body. But one word from the Lord Jesus Christ, and they were vanquished: but before they left the man's body and entered into about two-thousand swine:[161] which ran over a cliff and drowned in the sea; they said, "What have we to do with thee, Jesus, thou Son of God? art thou come hither to torment us before the time?"[162] It seems that the demons were not afraid to be tossed out of the body of the man, or even to go into the bodies of the swine, but were frightened to the core that the Word of God had come to throw them down into the pit of hell, and everlasting fire.

Authority to Cast out Devils

The authority to cast out devils has been extended to all believers of Christ. This authority is not for public display, but must be used according to the rules outlined and given by the Lord Jesus Christ. The penalty for misuse is death and destruction; see Matthew 7:21–23.

> *"And he said unto them, Go ye into all the world, and preach the gospel to every creature. He that believeth and is baptized shall be saved; but he that believeth not shall be damned. And these signs shall follow them that believe; In my name shall they cast out devils; they shall speak with new tongues; They shall take up serpents; and if they drink any deadly thing, it shall not hurt them; they shall lay hands on the sick, and they shall recover. So then after the Lord had spoken unto them, he was received up into heaven, and sat on the right hand of God."*[163]

The power to cast out devils is nothing to gloat about, but it is essential to a believer's walk of faith in the Lord Jesus Christ. When Jesus sent the twelve disciples out among the people, he gave them the power to "heal the sick, cleanse the lepers, raise the dead, and cast out devils. He further charged them not to charge for their service when he said, "freely you have received, freely give."[164] After this he sent another seventy disciples with some of the same instructions.[165]

This is totally different then what is happening in the modern church; for after the Spirit of God moves in a worship service there seems to always be a call to collect a monetary offering to offset the free gift from God. Usually, a person of leadership will get up an say, "now that you have heard or witnessed the power of God, it is now time to dig deep into you pocket books and wallets for a blessed offering of thanks giving; for God loves a cheerful giver, and holding back will lessen your ability to enter into his kingdom.

When the disciples reported back to Jesus they said, "Lord, even the devils are subject unto us through thy name." Jesus replied them," I beheld Satan as lightning fall from heaven. Behold, I give unto you power to tread on serpents and scorpions, and over all the power of the enemy: and nothing shall by any means hurt you.

Notwithstanding in this rejoice not, that the spirits are subject unto you; but rather rejoice, because your names are written in heaven."[166]

What Happens after an Unclean Spirit Is Cast Out of the Human Body?

Keep in mind that the Devil and his demons are continually walking up and down on / in the earth, seeking whom they may devour (possess). So, when the rite of exorcism is performed, the individual falsely believes the demon is gone for good, and is surprised when the demon reenters the victim. Human beings had no idea how or why this happened until Christ Jesus revealed this knowledge from heaven.

> *"When the unclean spirit is gone out of a man, he walketh through dry places, seeking rest, and findeth none. Then he saith, I will return into my house from whence I came out; and when he is come, he findeth it empty, swept, and garnished. Then goeth he, and taketh with himself seven other spirits more wicked than himself, and they enter in and dwell there: and the last state of that man is worse than the first. Even so shall it be also unto this wicked generation."*[167]

So then, the only protection from the unclean spirit is to embrace the Lord Jesus Christ, and receive the gift of the Holy Ghost. Without Christ, the body and soul are condemned to eternal damnation, and destruction in the eternal lake of fire.

Since the human body was made to receive the Holy Spirit of God,[168] it stands to reason that a created spirit being cannot peacefully enter into another created being; whether it be visible or invisible. Therefore, those that call themselves devil hunters, and go around throughout the religious establishments calling out demons, and casting out devils, should be cognizant that they are doing more damage than good. Because, if the unclean spirit is cast out, and the

Spirit of God does not come to dwell within that person, then it is true that the persons body is sweep clean, but no one is in the house to prevent a return of the unclean spirit.

To prevent this problem, God requires that a person who has been relieved of an unclean spirit be given a chance to be saved; by openly confessing Jesus Christ with their mouth, and believing in their heart that God have raised him from the dead.[169]

Unfortunately, there is no other religious path to escape the clutches of Satan's evil demonic influence. And those who hear the gospel of the Lord Jesus, and reject it throughout their life time will no doubt end up in hell and everlasting fire.[170]

What Are Satan and His Demons Up To?

Satan's strategy is very simple: feed people with beautiful lies, and use magic and craftiness to deceive them. It seems humankind gets excited when supernatural powers are displayed. This always helps Satan catch us in his snare. The New Testament is full of warning about the workings of Satan; for example:

- <u>Like a thief he is trying to steal our bodies, kill us if we don't submit to his will, and destroy us by getting us to believe his lies</u>. Jesus said it this way, "I am the door: by me if any man enter in, he shall be saved, and shall go in and out, and find pasture. The thief cometh not, but for to steal, and to kill, and to destroy: I am come that they might have life, and that they might have it more abundantly."[171]

- <u>He is always trying to temp us into committing fornication and adultery.</u> "The wife hath not power of her own body, but the husband: and likewise also the husband hath not power of his own body, but the wife. Defraud ye not one the other, except it be with consent for a time, that ye may give yourselves to fasting and prayer; and come together again, that Satan tempt you not for your incontinency."[172]

- He hangs around the church in an attempt to take the word of God out of our hearts. "The seed is the word of God. Those by the way side are they that hear; then cometh the devil, and taketh away the word out of their hearts, lest they should believe and be saved."[173]

- He puts a lot of effort in trying to stop the spread of the gospel: of the Lord Jesus Christ. "Wherefore we would have come unto you, even I Paul, once and again; but Satan hindered us."[174]

- He calls forth false prophets. "For such are false apostles, deceitful workers, transforming themselves into the apostles of Christ. And no marvel; for Satan himself is transformed into an angel of light. Therefore, it is no great thing if his ministers also be transformed as the ministers of righteousness; whose end shall be according to their works."[175]

- Roaming around the earth seeking out weak minded individuals. "Be sober, be vigilant; because your adversary the devil, as a roaring lion, walketh about, seeking whom he may devour: whom resist stedfast in the faith, knowing that the same afflictions are accomplished in your brethren that are in the world."[176]

How Do We Fight Against Him?

Does Christ Jesus want his followers to publicly and openly display signs from heaven? The obvious answer is no! But what he does want us to do is follow an ancient proverb written by king Solomon (the wisest man on planet earth), "Trust in the Lord with all thine heart; and lean not unto thine own understanding. In all thy ways acknowledge him, and he shall direct thy paths."[177] Therefore, there are certain rules to follow, for example:

- Claim the Lord Jesus Christ as your savior. "Submit yourselves therefore to God. Resist the devil, and he will flee from you. Draw nigh to God, and he will draw nigh to you."[178]

- Learn all you can about the enemy. "lest Satan should get an advantage of us: for we are not ignorant of his devices."[179]

- Keep in mind who the real enemy is. "For we wrestle not against flesh and blood, but against principalities, against powers, against the rulers of the darkness of this world, against spiritual wickedness in high places. Wherefore take unto you the whole armour of God, that ye may be able to withstand in the evil day, and having done all, to stand. Stand therefore, having your loins girt about with truth, and having on the breastplate of righteousness; and your feet shod with the preparation of the gospel of peace; above all, taking the shield of faith, wherewith ye shall be able to quench all the fiery darts of the wicked. And take the helmet of salvation, and the sword of the Spirit, which is the word of God: praying always with all prayer and supplication in the Spirit, and watching thereunto with all perseverance and supplication for all saints;"[180]

- Love your human enemies. "But I say unto you which hear, Love your enemies, do good to them which hate you, bless them that curse you, and pray for them which despitefully use you. And unto him that smiteth thee on the one cheek offer also the other; and him that taketh away thy cloke forbid not to take thy coat also. Give to every man that asketh of thee; and of him that taketh away thy goods ask them not again. And as ye would that men should do to you, do."[181]

- Remember the steps of temptation. "Blessed is the man that endureth temptation: for when he is tried, he shall receive the crown of life, which the Lord hath promised to them that love him. Let no man say when he is tempted, I am tempted of God: for God cannot be tempted with evil, neither tempteth he any man: but every man is tempted, when he is drawn away of his own lust, and enticed. Then when lust hath conceived, it bringeth forth sin: and sin, when it is finished, bringeth forth death. Do not err, my beloved brethren."[182]

- <u>Don't fear death</u>. "And fear not them which kill the body, but are not able to kill the soul: but rather fear him which is able to destroy both soul and body in hell."[183]

- <u>Always be ready to restore a believer back to the fold</u>. "Brethren, if a man be overtaken in a fault, ye which are spiritual, restore such an one in the spirit of meekness; considering thyself, lest thou also be tempted. Bear ye one another's burdens, and so fulfil the law of Christ."[184]

Inhabitants on the Earth

In these last days there is a great effort to find other life forms in the solar system. Great concentration has been given to Unidentified flying Objects (alien space craft). But the bible, and strong recorded incidents are quite specific on the inhabitants living on the earth. Based on this knowledge I made a short list of my finding.

- **God** – The creator of heaven and earth. (Genesis 1:1-5; Psalm 24:1-10)

- **The Word** - The Lord Jesus Christ, who is the creator of all things on the earth, to include the sun, the moon, the stars, and the worlds. (John 1:1-5 & 14 / Hebrews 1:1-3 / Colossians 1:15-17)

- **The Holy Ghost** - The Spirit of God which is released upon the earth in these last days. (John 7:37-39; 14:16-17; 26; 15:26-27; 16:7-14 / Acts 1:5-8; 2:1-4 / 1 Corinthians 3:16-17; 6:19)

- **The Holy Angels** - God's heavenly workers. (Psalm 148:2-5 / Luke 20:36 & 15:10 / Matthew 25:31 / Hebrews 1:13-14 & 12:22)

- **The Watchers** – The holy ones that watch over mankind with direct links. (Daniel 4:3-17 & 31-33)

- **Lucifer** - The great dragon, that old serpent, called the Devil and Satan. (Revelation 12:7-12)

- **Demons** - Fallen angels of Satan called unclean spirits. (Revelation 12:1-6 / Matthew 25:41)

- **Mankind** - Male and female human beings. (Genesis 1:26-27 & 2:7 {18} [21-25])
  Animals, Fowl that fly, and insects - Creatures that live on dry land. (Genesis 1:24-25 & 2:19-20)

- **Fish** - Creatures that live in water. (Genesis 1:20-22)

- **Vegetation** - Food and protection for all creatures of the earth. (Genesis 1: 11-12)

- **Aliens** - Some seem to think that some aliens got loose on the earth when a space ship crashed in Roswell Nevada area 51 in 1947.

CHAPTER 9

ABRAHAM AND CHRIST

Jesus Proclaims His Friendship with Abraham

The eighth chapter of the gospel John starts with the Jewish scribes (lawyers or interpreters of the Pentateuch) and the Pharisees (appointed priests) bringing to Jesus a woman caught in "the very act of" adultery. They wanted Jesus to condemn the woman according to the Law of Moses. However, they themselves broke the law by not bringing forth both the man and the woman: "And the man that committeth adultery with another man's wife, even that committeth adultery with his neighbours wife, the adulterer and the adulteress shall surely be put to death."[185]

Jesus simply ignored them. And when they continued to press him for an answer, he said, "He that is without sin among you, let him first cast a stone at her" Being guilty of the same sin, they walked away, leaving Jesus alone with the woman. Jesus told the woman that her accusers had all walked away, and she was free to go her way. But he warned her "to go and sin no more."

Then Jesus said to the Pharisees, "I am the light of the world: he that followeth me shall not walk in darkness, but shall have the light of life." This statement started a contentious and heated argument between the Pharisees and Jesus, that got down right dirty and personal; to the point that they both accused the other of lying.

Jesus: "I am one that bear witness of myself, and the Father that sent me bearth witness of me. Ye are from beneath; I am from above: ye are of this world; I am not of this world."

Pharisees: "Thou bearest record of thyself; thy record is not true."

Jesus: "I am one that bear witness of myself, and the Father that sent me beareth witness of me."

Pharisees: "Where is thy Father? We be Abraham's seed, and Abraham is our father. We be not born of fornication; we have one Father, even God."

The Pharisees not only disavowed his claim as being from the Father; but they also took a personal dig in implying he was a child of fornication, and a bastard child. His mother was three months pregnant when she returned to Joseph from visiting her cousin Elisabeth, the mother of John the Baptist.[186]

The argument brought both sides to calling the other the devil. Yet what finally brought the Pharisees to take up stones against Jesus were two astonishing startling statements.

Jesus: "Your father Abraham rejoiced to see my day: and he saw it, and was glad."

Pharisees: "Thou art not yet fifty years old, and hast thou seen Abraham?"

Jesus: "Verily, verily, I say unto you, Before Abraham was, I am."

Now I know that some would wonder why I went through the dialogue between the Pharisees and the Lord Jesus Christ. First, I wanted to establish how Christ was goaded into revealing his personal relationship with Abraham. And second, can it be true that Christ was with Abraham? The Pharisees clearly understood he claimed to not only have seen Abraham, but knew him personally.

I also wanted to portray a character of Christ that is often overlooked and not considered, because we want him to be mild mannered, humble, and in a state of piety. Yet in his debate with the Pharisees, he showed that he was a man of strong temperance, because he held back the power to destroy them. He could have called down fire from heaven, judged them into everlasting damnation, or called for an army of angels. However, Christ gave his followers an example of how to face opposition, and trust God, through the Holy Ghost, to control our emotions, for it is written, "Be ye angry, and sin not: let not the sun go down upon your wrath" [Ephesians 4:26].

Is Christ telling the truth about his relationship with Abraham? Let's go back to Genesis and examine some Scriptures.

From this point on we are going to be talking about "the word of the Lord," and how he interacted with mankind on this earthly world. Keep in mind that the Word (the light – aka Jesus Christ) was made flesh, and dwelt among human kind; "He was in the world, and the world was made by him, and the world knew him not."[187] Yet, he was a friend to everyone who had a chance to see and meet him. And a true fried was a man called Abraham.

> **YEAR – 1878**
> (Nahor (1849-1997) begat Terah)[188]

NAHOR - Abraham's grandfather (Genesis 11:22-25; 1 Chronicles 1:26); also an ancestor of Jesus according to Luke's genealogy (Luke 3:34, where some English translations follow the Greek spelling, Nachor). The Genesis and 1 Chronicles passages show that Nahor is from Shem's line. Hence, Abraham and his descendants are part of the Semitic family of nations.[189]

> **YEAR – 1948**
> (Terah begat Abraham, Nahor, and Haran / Shem is 392, Noah is 892)[190]

Abraham's Ancestry

During the year 1948, Terah, a descendant of Noah's son Shem, was seventy years old when Abraham was born in Ur of the Chaldees: and after him came two brothers: Nahor and Haran.

> "**UR** - Ur was the home town of the father of Abraham, whose name was Terah. Ur was the birthplace of Abraham and Sarah. It is mentioned by name only four times in the Bible (Genesis 11:28, 31; 15:7; Nehemiah 9:7). The full name was "Ur of the Chaldeans."
>
> The modern site is known as "The Mound of Bitumen." The results of archaeological investigations demonstrate that Abraham came from a great city. Ur was cultured, sophisticated, and powerful. The landscape was dominated by the ziggurat, or temple tower. The life of the city was controlled by a religion with a multiplicity of gods. The chief deity was Nannar, or Sin, the moon god, who was also worshiped at Haran. Near his ziggurat was a temple dedicated to his companion, the moon goddess, Ningal.
>
> Many clay tablets found at Ur tell of the business life of the city, which focused on the temples and their income. There were factories here, such as the weaving establishment for the manufacture of woolen cloth. Some tablets dealt with religion, history, law, and education. Students were instructed in reading and writing in cuneiform, the characters used for the script of that time. They were taught multiplication and division. Some were even able to extract square roots and cube roots.

Domestic architecture was highly developed. Houses had two stories and ten to twenty rooms, sometimes with a private chapel. Small clay religious figures were discovered. Many art objects made of precious metals and other costly materials have been excavated, especially in the royal tombs. These tombs also contained the remains of a number of servants. They must have been put to death at the time of the royal burials in order to accompany their masters in the afterlife."[191]

Haran fathered a son named Lot, and two daughters: Milcah, and Iscah; soon after he died. Abraham married his half-sister Sarah,[192] and his brother Nahor married his niece Milcah.[193] Abraham and Sarah did not have any children; but Nahor and Milcah would have a son named Bethuel, who was the father of Rebekah, who married Abraham's son Isaac.[194]

Terah moved the family to Haran, Syria: located in the Canaan land; and there he died at the ripe old age of two-hundred and five years old.[195]

"HARAN (PLACE): Haran is a city of northern Mesopotamia. It is first mentioned in Genesis 11:31 as the destination of Terah, Abraham's father, when he migrated from Ur. It was Terah's home until his death. At age seventy-five, Abraham was commanded by God to move from Haran to a land that God had for him (12:1-4).

There were relatives who remained in Haran, however. It was to them that Jacob, Abraham's grandson, fled in fear of Esau (Genesis 27:42-43). Jacob stayed in Haran many years while serving his Uncle Laban and acquiring Leah and Rachel as wives, as well as many sheep and goats, servants, camels, and donkeys (30:43)."[196]

YEAR - 2006
(Noah dies at 950 [1056-2006], Shem is 450, Terah 128, Abraham 58)

NOAH'S HISTORY - Noah was a righteous man who protected his faithful family from God's judgment. He was the son of Lamech and the grandson of Methuselah, a descendant of Seth, the third son of Adam (Genesis 5:3-20). Lamech named his son Noah, a name that sounds like a Hebrew term that can mean "relief" or "comfort." When Lamech gave him this name, he said, "He will bring us relief from the painful labor of farming this ground that the LORD has cursed" (Genesis 5:29).

God was determined to destroy creation because of widespread wickedness (compare Matthew 24:37-39; Luke 17:26-27). But God made an exception with Noah, a man righteous in God's sight and blameless before people (Genesis 6:3-9). Following God's precise instructions, Noah constructed an ark. Only eight people entered the ark: Noah and his wife and his three sons and their wives. Also entering the ark were all kinds of creatures in pairs. They were all protected from the deluge in which all other living things perished (Genesis 6:14-8:19). When they emerged from the ark, Noah built an altar and sacrificed burnt offerings that pleased God. God promised that the Flood would never be repeated or the sequence of the seasons disrupted, despite man's sin (Genesis 8:20-9:17).

Noah had withstood mighty temptations. However, later, whether through carelessness or old age, he became drunk. Family members reacted differently and were judged accordingly. Shem and Japheth received blessing. Ham received no blessing, but his son Canaan was cursed (Genesis 9:20-27). Noah was 950 years old when he died (1056-2006), 350 years after the Flood.

Noah, Daniel, and Job are specifically cited for "their righteousness" in Ezekiel 14:12-14, 19-20. The Letter to the Hebrews commends Noah, who by faith, holy fear, and rejection of the world became the heir of righteousness (Ezekiel 11:7). In 2 Peter 2:5 Peter calls him "a preacher of righteousness."[197]

> **YEAR 2023**
> Abraham is 75, Sarah is 65, Terah is 145,
> Shem is 467, Arphaxad 365, Salah 330, Eber 300, Reu 236, Serug 204

God Calls Abraham (Genesis Chapter 12)

Abraham was seventy-five when God called him into service. God laid out a plan for Abraham to follow:

- Get thee out of thy country, and from thy kindred, and from thy father's house
- unto a land that I will shew thee:
- and I will make of thee a great nation, and I will bless thee,
- and make thy name great; and thou shalt be a blessing:
- and I will bless them that bless thee,
- and curse him that curseth thee:
- and in thee shall all families of the earth be blessed.

Abraham's Greatness

God promised to make Abraham's name great; and stated that he would be a blessing to all humans on the earth. The Jews claim the greatness of Abraham to the kingship of David. The Muslims, on the other hand, revere Abraham, Ishmael [the first son of Abraham], and the prophet Mohammad. However, the birth of Christ ushered in the King of Kings, and the Lord of Lords and the only name whereby a human being can be saved from the wrath of God (which is the lake of fire).

This was accomplished when the angel Gabriel announced to the Virgin Mary "And, behold, thou shalt conceive in thy womb, and bring forth a son, and shalt call his name Jesus. He shall be great, and shall be called the Son of the Highest: and the Lord God shall give unto him the throne of his father David: And he shall reign over the house of Jacob for ever; and of his kingdom there shall be no end."[198]

Without the faith of Abraham, this birth may never have happened. The apostle Paul alluded to this when he wrote "Therefore it is of faith, that it might be by grace; to the end the promise might be sure to all the seed; not to that only which is of the law, but to that also which is of the faith of Abraham; who is the father of us all."[199] Further, "That at the name of Jesus every knee should bow, of things in heaven, and things in earth, and things under the earth; And that every tongue should confess that Jesus Christ is Lord, to the glory of God the Father."[200]

God didn't go into a lot of detail, and it is not recorded how long Abraham and God had been in communication; but is true is that Abraham believed in God, and trusted him enough to follow him from Haran, south through the land of Canaan, to a place called Sichem, "unto the plain of Moreh." With Abraham was his wife Sarah, his nephew Lot, and the servants he had obtained in Haran.[201]

God's Second Appearance to Abraham

Once there, God appeared unto Abraham and said, "unto thy seed will I give this land." Upon hearing this news, Abraham traveled to a place that was between Bethel on the west, and Hai on the East; here he builds an altar to worship God.[202]

> "BETHEL(PLACE), BETHELITE: 1. Bethel was an important Old Testament city located about 11 miles (17.7 kilometers) north of Jerusalem on the north-south ridge road at the tribal borders of Benjamin and Ephraim (Joshua 16:1-2 ; 18:13). Hiel, a resident of the city, is referred to as a Bethelite in 1 Kings 16:34 (KJV). As a trading center, Bethel attracted merchandise both from the Mediterranean coast and from Transjordan by way of Jericho. Although the site was located in dry hill country, several springs supplied ample water for

its inhabitants (the oldest artifact recovered from the site is a water jar dating from about 3500 BC).

The name Bethel, meaning "house of El (god)," may have been used as early as the fourth millennium BC by Canaanites in the area. Archaeological excavations at levels between the Stone Age and the Bronze Age indicate that pagan worship of the Canaanite deity El was already taking place on top of the hill. The patriarch Jacob named the place Bethel, or gave the old name new significance, after having a dream from God there (Genesis 28:10-22). The site was said to be known as Bethel to the patriarch Abraham (Genesis 12:8). That, however, could be an update of a more ancient local name, since Bethel had earlier been known as Luz (Genesis 28:19). Possibly the sanctuary was known as Bethel, the nearby settlement as Luz. No doubt the name Bethel was firmly established by around 2200 BC and remained throughout its history. An Old Testament passage mentioning both names records that a man from Luz founded another city of that name in Hittite territory (Judges 1:26)."[203]

There was famine in the land, and Abraham was forced to go into the land of Egypt for relief. As he drew near to the Egyptian border, he told his wife to tell the Egyptians that she was his sister: because she was so beautiful, and he feared that they would kill him for her.

Many a sermon has been preached of how Abraham lied to save his own skin. But the truth of the bible revealed that Abraham quibbled; in that he told the truth, but not the whole truth; for his wife was the daughter of his father, but not by his mother.[204]

When the Egyptian's saw Sarah, and her beauty, they took her to Pharaohs house; who was so taken by her, that he gave Abraham "sheep, oxen, donkeys (male & female), manservants, maidservants, and camels.

God was not pleased with the arrangement between Abraham, Pharaoh, and Sarah; "And the Lord plagued Pharaoh and his house with great plagues because of Sarai Abraham's wife." Interestingly, Pharaoh confronted Abraham, but did not order him to death for his deception:

Pharaoh - "And Pharaoh called Abram, and said, What is this that thou hast done unto me? why didst thou not tell me that she was thy wife? Why saidst thou, She is my sister? so I might have taken her to me to wife: now therefore behold thy wife, take her, and go thy way. And Pharaoh commanded his men concerning him: and they sent him away, and his wife, and all that he had."[205]

Abraham – "And Abram went up out of Egypt, he, and his wife, and all that he had, and Lot with him, into the south. And Abram was very rich in cattle, in silver, and in gold. And he went on his journeys from the south even to Bethel, unto the place where his tent had been at the beginning, between Bethel and Hai; unto the place of the altar, which he had made there at the first: and there Abram called on the name of the Lord."[206]

When Abraham went into the land of Egypt, he was wealthy, and you could say a little above middle class; but he came out of Egypt rich on a level of a millionaire.

By and by there came strife between the herdsmen of Abraham and Lot. To quill the trouble, Abraham told Lot to pick a spot out of the land and pitch his tent's. Lot choose the land toward Sodom, which was well watered liken unto the Garden of Eden, but also had a reputation being wicked and highly sinful.

God's Third Appearance to Abraham

Now after Lot had departed, God made another promise to Abraham; that would stretch up and down the channels of history to form a nation known as Israel: which is located in the land of Canaan, whose capital is Jerusalem: the past city of the Jebusites.[207]

> **Genesis 13: 14 And the Lord said unto Abram, after that Lot was separated from him, Lift up now thine eyes, and look from the place where thou art northward, and southward, and eastward, and westward:**
> **15 for all the land which thou seest, to thee will I give it, and to thy seed for ever. 16 And I will make thy seed as the dust of the earth: so that if a man can number the dust of the earth, then shall thy seed also be numbered.**
> **17 Arise, walk through the land in the length of it and in the breadth of it; for I will give it unto thee. 18 Then Abram removed his tent, and came and dwelt in the plain of Mamre, which is in Hebron, and built there an altar unto the Lord.**

Take note that this promise of God is bound up in the word, "forever." This means that no matter how the world changes, or nations arise and fall, or the power of geography shifts, or military might be granted, the land given to Abraham and his descendants (through Isaac and Jacob) will never be brokered to any other.

Ishmael, by being the first-born son of Abraham, is bound by tradition as the "son of inheritance." But Isaac is the "son of promise," and therefore the inheritor of God's promise to Abraham.

Right here, take note that there is no direct wording that identifies Christ in the initial calling of Abraham. Sentence structure suggests it is God alone who called to Abraham. Further, Abraham only listened, and then followed the instructions of God. There was no open dialogue between them.

Although God appeared to Abraham a second, and a third time, we still don't see any wording that directly identifies the Lord Jesus Christ or proves his claim that he personally knew Abraham. Again, notice Abraham had no conversation with God.

God's Fourth Appearance (Genesis Chapter 15)

Christ: "After these things **the word of the Lord - came unto Abram in a vision**, **saying**, Fear not, Abram: I am thy shield, and thy exceeding great reward."

Abraham: "And Abram said, Lord God, what wilt thou give me, seeing I go childless, and the steward of my house is this Eliezer of Damascus?"

Abraham: "And Abram said, Behold, to me thou hast given no seed: and, lo, one born in my house is mine heir."

In this exchange with God, we see that it is not the Father, but <u>the word of God</u> (Christ) that engages in a conversation with Abraham via a vision. During the conversation Abraham complains that he has not been blessed to have his own man child.

Christ & Abraham during Fifth Appearance

Christ: "And, behold, **the word of the Lord came unto him**, **saying**, This shall not be thine heir; but he that shall come forth out of thine own bowels shall be thine heir. And he brought him forth abroad, and said, Look now toward heaven, and tell the stars, if thou be able to number them: and he said unto him, So shall thy seed be."

Abraham: "**And he believed in the Lord; and he counted it to him for righteousness.**"

God: "And he said unto him, I am the Lord that brought thee out of Ur of the Chaldees, to give thee this land to inherit it."

Abraham: "And he said, Lord God, whereby shall I know that I shall inherit it?"

Who is Jesus Christ

Note: *Even though Abraham believed Christ he wanted a sign to justify his belief.*

God: "And he said unto him, Take me an heifer of three years old, and a she goat of three years old, and a ram of three years old, and a turtledove, and a young pigeon. And he took unto him all these, and divided them in the midst, and laid each piece one against another: but the birds divided he not. And when the fowls came down upon the carcases, Abram drove them away.

And when the sun was going down, a deep sleep fell upon Abram; and, lo, an horror of great darkness fell upon him."

- And he said unto Abram, Know of a surety that thy seed shall be a stranger in a land that is not theirs, and shall serve them;
- and they shall afflict them four hundred years;
- and also that nation, whom they shall serve, will I judge:
- and afterward shall they come out with great substance.
- And thou shalt go to thy fathers in peace; thou shalt be buried in a good old age.
- But in the fourth generation they shall come hither again: for the iniquity of the Amorites is not yet full.
- And it came to pass, that, when the sun went down, and it was dark, behold a smoking furnace, and a burning lamp that passed between those pieces. In the same day the Lord made a covenant with Abram, saying, Unto thy seed have I given this land, from the river of Egypt unto the great river, the river Euphrates: the Kenites, and the Kenizzites, and the Kadmonites, and the Hittites, and the Perizzites, and the Rephaims, and the Amorites, and the Canaanites, and the Girgashites, and the Jebusites.

In this fifth meeting, the gloves are taken off, and Christ talks with Abraham face to face. He tells Abraham not to fret or worry because his heir will come from his loins, and will be a great number as the stars of heaven. He also tells, and shows Abraham the future of his offspring which will be fulfilled in the prophet Moses.[208]

This is the juncture in Abraham's life where a friendship with the word of God (Christ) began, and was spoken of by Christ when he was in a heated debate with the Jews. This was a deep friendship that was spoken of throughout the history of the bible, and into the era of Christianity.

> **2 Chronicles 20: 7** Art not thou our God, who didst drive out the inhabitants of this land before thy people Israel, and gavest it to the seed of Abraham thy friend for ever?
>
> **Isaiah 41: 8** But thou, Israel, art my servant, Jacob whom I have chosen, the seed of Abraham my friend.
>
> **Romans 4: 1** What shall we say then that Abraham our father, as pertaining to the flesh, hath found? 2 For if Abraham were justified by works, he hath whereof to glory; but not before God. 3 For what saith the scripture? Abraham believed God, and it was counted unto him for righteousness.
>
> **Galatians 3: 6** Even as Abraham believed God, and it was accounted to him for righteousness.
>
> **James 2: 23** "And the scripture was fulfilled which saith, Abraham believed God, and it was imputed unto him for righteousness: and he was called the Friend of God."

YEAR – 2033
(Abraham is 85, Sarah 75, Terah 155, Shem 477)

Sarah's Intervention (Genesis Chapter 16)

When Sarah realized that she was not going to have a child, she begged Abraham to take her Egyptian handmaid as his concubine;

Who is Jesus Christ

in this way a child would be born from the loins of Abraham as promised by God.

Abraham consented to the wishes of Sarah, and impregnated Hagar: the Egyptian handmaid. However, the younger woman and Sarah had some friction between them, and Sarah told Abraham to send her away. Reluctantly, Abraham sent the pregnant Hagar out of the camp.

But God dispatched an angel to return her back to the safety of Abraham, with instructions to submit to the whims of Sarah. He also made some promises about the unborn child.

- "And the angel of the Lord said unto her, I will multiply thy seed exceedingly, that it shall not be numbered for multitude."
- "And the angel of the Lord said unto her, Behold, thou art with child, and shalt bear a son, and shalt call his name Ishmael; because the Lord hath heard thy affliction."
- "And he will be a wild man; his hand will be against every man, and every man's hand against him;"
- "and he shall dwell in the presence of all his brethren."

YEAR – 2034
(Abraham is 86, Sarah 76, Terah 156, Shem 478

And Hagar bare Abram a son: and Abram called his son's name, which Hagar bare, Ishmael.

"And Abram was fourscore and six years old, when Hagar bare Ishmael to Abram."[209]

YEAR – 2047
(Abraham is 99; Sarah is 89, Ishmael is 13, Terah is 169, Shem is 491

Gods Sixth Appearance to Abraham

Genesis 17: 1-27
1. And when Abram was ninety years old and nine, the Lord appeared to Abram, and said unto him, I am the Almighty God; walk before me, and be thou perfect.

You will multiply exceedingly
2. And I will make my covenant between me and thee, and will multiply thee exceedingly.
3. And Abram fell on his face: and God talked with him, saying,

You will be the father of many nations and your name will be called Abraham
4. As for me, behold, my covenant is with thee, and thou shalt be a father of many nations.
5. <u>Neither shall thy name any more be called Abram, but thy name shall be Abraham</u>; for a father of many nations have I made thee.

Kings will come from your seed
6. And I will make thee exceeding fruitful, and I will make nations of thee, and kings shall come out of thee. (**Saul, David, Solomon, etc**)

An everlasting covenant between God, Abraham, and Abraham seed, and their generations
7. And I will establish my covenant between me and thee and thy seed after thee in their generations for an everlasting covenant, to be a God unto thee, and to thy seed after thee.

God will give the land of Canaan to Abraham's seed for an everlasting blessing
8. And I will give unto thee, and to thy seed after thee, the land wherein thou art a stranger, all the land of Canaan, for an everlasting possession; and I will be their God.

The commandment of circumcision

Who is Jesus Christ

9. And God said unto Abraham, Thou shalt keep my covenant therefore, thou, and thy seed after thee in their generations.
10. This is my covenant, which ye shall keep, between me and you and thy seed after thee; Every man child among you shall be circumcised.
11. And ye shall circumcise the flesh of your foreskin; and it shall be a token of the covenant betwixt me and you.
12. <u>And he that is eight days old shall be circumcised among you</u>, every man child in your generations, he that is born in the house, or bought with money of any stranger, which is not of thy seed.
13. He that is born in thy house, and he that is bought with thy money, must needs be circumcised: and my covenant shall be in your flesh for an everlasting covenant.

- **Luke 1: 59-60**; performed on 8th day and child is named. **(Luke 2:21)**
- **Exodus 12: 43-50**; Allowed right to the Passover.

Punishment for disobedience

14. And the uncircumcised man child whose flesh of his foreskin is not circumcised, that soul shall be cut off from his people; he hath broken my covenant.

- <u>**Exodus 4:**</u> 24. And it came to pass by the way in the inn, that the Lord met him, and sought to kill him.
  25. Then Zipporah took a sharp stone, and cut off the foreskin of her son, and cast it at his feet, and said, Surely a bloody husband art thou to me.
  26. So he let him go: then she said, A bloody husband thou art, because of the circumcision.

- <u>**Joshua 5:**</u> 1. And it came to pass, when all the kings of the Amorites, which were on the side of Jordan westward, and all the kings of the Canaanites, which were by the sea, heard that the Lord had dried up the waters of Jordan from before the children of Israel, until we were passed over, that their heart melted, neither was there spirit in them any more, because of the children of Israel.

2. <u>At that time the Lord said unto Joshua, Make thee sharp knives, **and circumcise again the children of Israel the second time.**</u> (Numbers 9: 1-5)

3. <u>And Joshua made him sharp knives, and circumcised the children of Israel at the hill of the foreskins.</u>

4. <u>And this is the cause why Joshua did circumcise: All the people that came out of Egypt, that were males, even all the men of war, died in the wilderness by the way, after they came out of Egypt.</u>

5. Now all the people that came out were circumcised: but all the people that were born in the wilderness by the way as they came forth out of Egypt, them they had not circumcised.

6. For the children of Israel walked forty years in the wilderness, till all the people that were men of war, which came out of Egypt, were consumed, because they obeyed not the voice of the Lord: unto whom the Lord sware that he would not shew them the land, which the Lord sware unto their fathers that he would give us, a land that floweth with milk and honey.

7. And their children, whom he raised up in their stead, them Joshua circumcised: for they were uncircumcised, because they had not circumcised them by the way.

8. And it came to pass, when they had done circumcising all the people, that they abode in their places in the camp, till they were whole.

9. And the Lord said unto Joshua, This day have I rolled away the reproach of Egypt from off you. Wherefore the name of the place is called Gilgal unto this day.

10. <u>And the children of Israel encamped in Gilgal, and kept the passover on the fourteenth day of the month at even in the plains of Jericho.</u>

God changes Sarai name to Sarah
15. And God said unto Abraham, As for Sarai thy wife, thou shalt not call her name Sarai, but Sarah shall her name be.

She will bear a child in her old age
16. And I will bless her, and give thee a son also of her: yea, I will bless her, and she shall be a mother of nations; kings of people shall be of her.

Abraham is astonished in unbelief
17. Then Abraham fell upon his face, and laughed, and said in his heart, Shall a child be born unto him that is an hundred years old? and shall Sarah, that is ninety years old, bear?

Abraham ask god to let Ishmael fulfill the promised child prophecy
18. And Abraham said unto God, O that Ishmael might live before thee!

God restates that Sarah will have the promised child Isaac
19. And God said, Sarah thy wife shall bear thee a son indeed; and thou shalt call his name Isaac: and I will establish my covenant with him for an everlasting covenant, and with his seed after him.

Ishmael will be blessed with 12 princes
20. And as for Ishmael, I have heard thee: behold, I have blessed him, and will make him fruitful, and will multiply him exceedingly; twelve princes shall he beget, and I will make him a great nation.

> **Genesis 25: 12. Now these are the generations of Ishmael, Abraham's son, whom Hagar the Egyptian, Sarah's handmaid, bare unto Abraham: 13. And these are the names of the sons of Ishmael, by their names, according to their generations: the firstborn of Ishmael, Nebajoth; and Kedar, and Adbeel, and Mibsam,**

14. And Mishma, and Dumah, and Massa,
15. Hadar, and Tema, Jetur, Naphish, and Kedemah:
16. These are the sons of Ishmael, and these are their names, by their towns, and by their castles; twelve princes according to their nations.
17. And these are the years of the life of Ishmael, an hundred and thirty and seven years: *(2033-2170)* and he gave up the Ghost and died; and was gathered unto his people.
18. And they dwelt from Havilah unto Shur, that is before Egypt, as thou goest toward Assyria: and he died in the presence of all his brethren.

God will establish his covenant with Isaac
21. But my covenant will I establish with Isaac, which Sarah shall bear unto thee at this set time in the next year.
22. And he left off talking with him, and God went up from Abraham.

Abraham performs the rite of circumcision
23. And Abraham took Ishmael his son, and all that were born in his house, and all that were bought with his money, every male among the men of Abraham's house; and circumcised the flesh of their foreskin in the selfsame day, as God had said unto him.
24. And Abraham was ninety years old and nine, when he was circumcised in the flesh of his foreskin.
25. And Ishmael his son was thirteen years old, when he was circumcised in the flesh of his foreskin.
26. In the selfsame day was Abraham circumcised, and Ishmael his son.
27. And all the men of his house, born in the house, and bought with money of the stranger, were circumcised with him.

The New Circumcision

There has been a lot of debate about circumcision: concerning cleanliness, and science. And even though circumcising is a physical act, Apostle Paul hinted that the belief in God is a spiritual act in which the heart must be circumcised by cutting away the sinful skin. Yet, this type of thinking was not new to the New Testament but was a grave concern in the Old Testament.

Deuteronomy 10: 16. Circumcise therefore the foreskin of your heart, and be no more stiffnecked.
17. For the Lord your God is God of Gods, and Lord of Lords, a great God, a mighty, and a terrible, which regardeth not persons, nor taketh reward:
18. He doth execute the judgment of the fatherless and widow, and loveth the stranger, in giving him food and raiment.
19. Love ye therefore the stranger: for ye were strangers in the land of Egypt.
20. Thou shalt fear the Lord thy God; him shalt thou serve, and to him shalt thou cleave, and swear by his name.
21. He is thy praise, and he is thy God, that hath done for thee these great and terrible things, which thine eyes have seen.
22. Thy fathers went down into Egypt with threescore and ten persons; and now the Lord thy God hath made thee as the stars of heaven for multitude.

Deuteronomy 30: 6. And the Lord thy God will circumcise thine heart, and the heart of thy seed, to love the Lord thy God with all thine heart, and with all thy soul, that thou mayest live.

Jeremiah 4: 4. Circumcise yourselves to the Lord, and take away the foreskins of your heart, ye men of Judah and inhabitants of Jerusalem: lest my fury come forth like fire, and burn that none can quench it, because of the evil of your doings.

Romans 2: 25. For circumcision verily profiteth, if thou keep the law: but if thou be a breaker of the law, thy circumcision is made uncircumcision.
26. Therefore if the uncircumcision keep the righteousness of the law, shall not his uncircumcision be counted for circumcision?
27. And shall not uncircumcision which is by nature, if it fulfil the law, judge thee, who by the letter and circumcision dost transgress the law?
28. For he is not a Jew, which is one outwardly; neither is that circumcision, which is outward in the flesh:
29. But he is a Jew, which is one inwardly; and circumcision is that of the heart, in the spirit, and not in the letter; whose praise is not of men, but of God. (Matthew 4:12-17)

Philippians 3: 3 For we who worship by the Spirit of God* are the ones who are truly circumcised. We rely on what Christ Jesus has done for us.

<u>**Colossians 2:**</u> 11 When you came to Christ, you were "circumcised," but not by a physical procedure. Christ performed a spiritual circumcision—the cutting away of your sinful nature.

<u>**Matthew 15: 18**</u>. But those things which proceed out of the mouth come forth from the heart; and they defile the man. (Matthew 12:34; Proverbs 4:23; Romans 10: 8-10)
19. For out of the heart proceed evil thoughts, murders, adulteries, fornications, thefts, false witness, blasphemies: (Mark 7:20-23)

God's Seventh Appearance to Abraham (Genesis Chapter 18)

A seventh visit is recorded in Genesis chapter eighteen, and takes place when Abraham sees Christ and two angels walking across the desert sands. By this time, Abraham and "the word of the Lord" had forged a close bond. This friendship caused Christ to stop by Abraham's home on the way to Sodom and Gomorrah.[210]

Abraham begged them to stay and eat with him. This was a happy meeting but also one of sadness. Christ brought Abraham the good news it was nearing time for his wife, Sarah, to conceive and bring forth Isaac, the son of promise.

Christ: "Where is Sarah, your wife?"

Abraham: "She's inside the tent,"

Christ: Then one of them said, "I will return to you about this time next year, and your wife, Sarah, will have a son!"

Sarah: Sarah was listening to this conversation from the tent. Abraham was 99, and Sarah was 89, and Sarah was long past the age of having children. So, she laughed silently to herself and said, "How could a worn-out woman like me enjoy such pleasure, especially when my master—my husband—is also so old?"

Christ: Then the Lord said to Abraham, "Why did Sarah laugh? Why did she say, 'Can an old woman like me have a baby?' Is anything too hard for the Lord? I will return about this time next year, and Sarah will have a son."

Sarah: Sarah was afraid, so she denied it, saying, "I didn't laugh."

Christ: But the Lord said, "No, you did laugh."

Abraham's Plea Bargain

The sad news concerned the destruction of Sodom and Gomorrah. The Lord knew Abraham's nephew Lot was in Sodom.

Because of Christ's friendship with Abraham, he said this within himself, "Shall I hide from Abraham that thing which I do; Seeing that Abraham shall surely become a great and mighty nation, and all the nations of the earth shall be blessed in him? For I know him, that he will command his children and his household after him, and they shall keep the way of the Lord, to do justice and judgment; that the Lord may bring upon Abraham that which he hath spoken of him."

Then Christ said unto Abraham, "Because the cry of Sodom and Gomorrah is great, and because their sin is very grievous; I will go down now, and see whether they have done altogether according to the cry of it, which is come unto me; and if not, I will know."

So, Christ sent the two angels on ahead of him to Sodom and Gomorrah, while he lingered to talk with Abraham. When Abraham heard what was going to happen to Sodom and Gomorrah, he began to plead for mercy.

> *"Wilt thou also destroy the righteous with the wicked? Peradventure there be fifty righteous within the city: wilt thou also destroy and not spare the place for the fifty righteous that are therein? That be far from thee to do after this manner, to slay the righteous with the wicked: and that the righteous should be as the wicked, that be far from thee: shall not the Judge of all the earth do right?"*

When pleading with Christ about the destruction of Sodom and Gomorrah, Abraham makes the point that it is not within the nature of God to destroy the righteous along with wicked, sinful evildoers. Abraham is on target with his deduction. In the parable of the wheat and tares, Christ implied he would let the wheat and tares grow to maturity, and then gather the tares for destruction. But the wheat would go into his barn (Matthew 13:24-30 / 36-43).

Abraham proceeded to plead with Christ down to ten righteous, and Christ agreed to this number.[211] This proves Christ has great compassion for the souls of humankind, and will do whatever it takes to save a soul. On the other hand, human beings must grasp the opportunity to turn from their wickedness to be saved. The citizens of Sodom and Gomorrah did not, and they were destroyed.[212]

The Prophet Abraham and King Abimelech (Genesis Chapter 20)

After the destruction of Sodom and Gomorrah Abraham traveled south to Gerar: which was between Kadesh and Shur. The King of Gerar was Abimelech the Philistine.

Abraham told Abimelech that Sarah was his sister, and Abimelech added her to his harem. This is the same tactic Abraham used against the Pharaoh of Egypt. This led God to again take matter into his hands.

God: "But God came to Abimelech in a dream by night, and said to him, Behold, thou art but a dead man, for the woman which thou hast taken; for she is a man's wife."

Abimelech: "But Abimelech had not come near her: and he said, Lord, wilt thou slay also a righteous nation? Said he not unto me, She is my sister? and she, even she herself said, He is my brother: in the integrity of my heart and innocency of my hands have I done this."

God: "And God said unto him in a dream, Yea, I know that thou didst this in the integrity of thy heart; for I also withheld thee from sinning against me: therefore suffered I thee not to touch her. Now therefore restore <u>the man</u> his wife; for he <u>is a prophet</u>, and he shall pray for thee, and thou shalt live: and if thou restore her not, know thou that thou shalt surely die, thou, and all that are thine."

Abimelech: "Therefore Abimelech rose early in the morning, and called all his servants, and told all these things in their ears: and the men were sore afraid."

Abimelech confronts Abraham: "Then Abimelech called Abraham, and said unto him, What hast thou done unto us? and what have I offended thee, that thou hast brought on me and on my kingdom a great sin? thou hast done deeds unto me that ought not to be done.

And Abimelech said unto Abraham, What sawest thou, that thou hast done this thing?"

Abraham: "And Abraham said, Because I thought, Surely the fear of God is not in this place; and they will slay me for my wife's sake. And yet indeed she is my sister; she is the daughter of my father, but not the daughter of my mother; and she became my wife."

Note: I want to note here the Josephus writes that Abraham's brother Haran had a son Lot, and two daughters, Sarai, and Milcha. Abraham married his niece Sarai, and Nahor married his niece Milcha. Well, there seems to be a controversy, but that's history.[213]

Abraham's reasoning: "And it came to pass, when God caused me to wander from my father's house, that I said unto her, This is thy kindness which thou shalt shew unto me; at every place whither we shall come, say of me, He is my brother."

Abimelech: "And Abimelech took sheep, and oxen, and menservants, and women servants, and gave them unto Abraham, and restored him Sarah his wife."

Abimelech's concession: "And Abimelech said, Behold, my land is before thee: dwell where it pleaseth thee."

Abimelech's gift to Sarah: "And unto Sarah he said, Behold, I have given thy brother a thousand pieces of silver: behold, he is to thee a covering of the eyes, unto all that are with thee, and with all other: thus she was reproved."

Abraham: "So Abraham prayed unto God: and God healed Abimelech, and his wife, and his maidservants; and they bare children. For the Lord had fast closed up all the wombs of the house of Abimelech, because of Sarah Abraham's wife."

What a beautiful story of how God protected his promise with close scrutiny of Abraham and Sarah. Those who believe in God, and follow the Lord Jesus Christ, have the same scrutiny and love shown toward these two patriarchs.

- **Psalm 55: 22** Cast thy burden upon the Lord, and he shall sustain thee: he shall never suffer the righteous to be moved.

- **1 Peter 5:** 6 Humble yourselves therefore under the mighty hand of God, that he may exalt you in due time: 7 casting all your care upon him; for he careth for you.

> **YEAR - 2048**
> (Abraham is 100, Sarah 90, Ishmael 14, Isaac is born, Terah 170, Shem 492

The Birth of Isaac (Genesis Chapter 21)

As God had promised, Sarah conceived and brought forth a son for Abraham whom they named Isaac. The miracle of the birth hinges on the fact that Abraham is 100 and his wife Sarah is 90. In all my research I have not come across any other historical record of a woman giving birth at 90 years old.

When the child was eight days old, Abraham circumcised him. Keep in mind that this was done with a knife, in a tent, in the middle of the desert, where the temperature can rise, at ten o'clock in the morning, to 130 degrees Fahrenheit. Not only did the baby have to protected from the elements, but also infection and disease.

However, Isaac grew to be a healthy boy, and was weaned from his mother. Abraham was excitedly happy and threw a great feast to celebrate the event. Not every one was happy, and Sarah took action to ensure future happiness.

Sarah: "And Sarah saw the son of Hagar the Egyptian, which she had born unto Abraham, mocking. Wherefore she said unto

Abraham, Cast out this bondwoman and her son: for the son of this bondwoman shall not be heir with my son, even with Isaac."

Abraham: "And the thing was very grievous in Abraham's sight because of his son."

God: "And God said unto Abraham, Let it not be grievous in thy sight because of the lad, and because of thy bondwoman; in all that Sarah hath said unto thee, hearken unto her voice; for in Isaac shall thy seed be called. And also of the son of the bondwoman will I make a nation, because he is thy seed."

Abraham: "And Abraham rose up early in the morning, and took bread, and a bottle of water, and gave it unto Hagar, putting it on her shoulder, and the child, and sent her away: and she departed, and wandered in the wilderness of Beer-sheba."

Hagar: "And the water was spent in the bottle, and she cast the child under one of the shrubs. And she went, and sat her down over against him a good way off, as it were a bowshot: for she said, Let me not see the death of the child. And she sat over against him, and lift up her voice, and wept."

God: "And God heard the voice of the lad; and the angel of God called to Hagar out of heaven, and said unto her, What aileth thee, Hagar? fear not; for God hath heard the voice of the lad where he is. Arise, lift up the lad, and hold him in thine hand; for I will make him a great nation."

Hagar: "And God opened her eyes, and she saw a well of water; and she went, and filled the bottle with water, and gave the lad drink."

God: "And God was with the lad; and he grew, and dwelt in the wilderness, and became an archer."

Ishmael: "And he dwelt in the wilderness of Paran: and his mother took him a wife out of the land of Egypt."[214]

The above story shows how much God cares about the human race; and even though Ishmael was not the son of promise, God looked after him just because he was the seed of his prophet Abraham. Jesus took this concept a little further when he said: "Ye have heard that it hath been said, Thou shalt love thy neighbour, and hate thine enemy. But I say unto you, Love your enemies, bless them that curse you, do good to them that hate you, and pray for them which despitefully use you, and persecute you; that ye may be the children of your Father which is in heaven: for he maketh his sun to rise on the evil and on the good, and sendeth rain on the just and on the unjust." (Matthew 5:43-45)

God's Eighth Appearance to Abraham (Genesis Chapter 22)

During Abraham's walk with God, and his friendship with "the word of God," he went through quite a number of life's stumbling blocks. But now comes the time of ultimate testing. Unlike Job, he will not be tested by the Devil, but by his faith in God; for he is asked to take his son Isaac and sacrifice him. The place of sacrifice is in the land of Moriah.

> "In 2 Chronicles 3:1, **Mt Moriah** is the place of Solomon's temple, specifically identified with the threshing floor of Ornan the Jebusite (cf. 2 Samuel 24; 1 Chronicles 21), but not explicitly with the place of Abraham's sacrifice. Some, however, see in the description of the Lord's appearing to David a reminder of his appearing to Abraham there. The Jewish historian Josephus (Antiquities 1.13.2; 7.13.4) clearly connects the place of the temple with the place where Isaac was offered up, as does the

second-century BC book of Jubilees (Jubilees 18:13). Samaritan tradition linked Moriah with Mt Gerizim. Muslim tradition connects the Dome of the Rock that stands today on the site of the Jerusalem temple with Abraham's sacrifice of Isaac on the great rock under the dome of the mosque."[215]

Abraham followed God's orders to sacrifice Isaac, but before he could execute the deed God provided a ram, which was stuck in a bush by his horns, as a substitute for Isaac. In the book of Hebrews, the Apostle Paul wrote:

- **Hebrews 11: 17** "By faith Abraham, when he was tried, offered up Isaac: and he that received the promises offered up his only begotten son

After this, Abraham, Isaac, and his servants returned to his home in Beersheba.

- "**BEERSHEBA** - Beersheba was the scriptural name for the southern edge of the Promised Land, located twenty-eight miles (45.1 kilometers) southwest of Hebron. Abraham's concubine Hagar wandered with Ishmael in this area, as did Abraham himself. Later Isaac (Genesis 26:23) and Jacob (Genesis 46:1) both had significant spiritual experiences there, and later yet it was important in the lives of numerous other Hebrews."[216]

Upon his arrival back home Abraham was greeted with news concerning his family in Haran. By the following report his father was very old, and his brother Nahor was dead.

Genesis 22: 19 Then they returned to the servants and traveled back to Beersheba, where Abraham continued to live.

20 Soon after this, Abraham heard that Milcah, his brother Nahor's wife, had borne Nahor eight sons.
21 The oldest was named Uz, the next oldest was Buz, followed by Kemuel (the ancestor of the Arameans),
22 Kesed, Hazo, Pildash, Jidlaph, and Bethuel.
23 (Bethuel became the father of Rebekah.) In addition to these eight sons from Milcah, 24 Nahor had four other children from his concubine Reumah. Their names were Tebah, Gaham, Tahash, and Maacah.

YEAR – 2083
Terah dies at age 205 in Haran, Syria (1878-2083) (he is the father of Abraham and Sarah)

TERAH's HISTORY - Father of Abram (Abraham), Nahor, and Haran (Genesis 11:26, 1 Chronicles 1:26; Luke 3:34). Though Abram is listed first among his sons, it is likely that Abram was not the oldest. After Terah lived 70 years, he fathered Abram, Nahor, and Haran (Genesis 11:26). Stephen reports in the New Testament, however, that Abram left Haran after the death of his father, at which time Abram was 75 years old (Genesis 12:4; Acts 7:4). Terah died at the age of 205, which suggests that Terah was at least 130 when Abram was born. Terah initiated the trip to Canaan, though he failed to go beyond Haran (Genesis 11:31-32). Abram was commanded there to leave his family and proceed to Canaan (Genesis 12:1).[217]

Josephus confirms that Terah was 205 when he died, and was buried in Haran, Syria.[218] Therefore, even though there seems to be a conflict of his death in the book of Acts,[219] it does not change the fact of his birth and death date.

> **YEAR - 2085**
> Sarah dies at 127 (1958-2085), Abraham 137, Ishmael 52, Isaac 37, Shem 529

The Death and Burial of Sarah

Genesis 23: 1-24
1. And Sarah was an hundred and seven and twenty years old: these were the years of the life of Sarah.
2. And Sarah died in Kirjatharba; the same is Hebron in the land of Canaan: and Abraham came to mourn for Sarah, and to weep for her.

> **Kirjatharba** - Topics: Kir'jath-ar'ba Text: city of Arba, the original name of Hebron (q.v.), so called from the name of its founder, one of the Anakim (Gen. 23:2; 35:27; Josh. 15:13). It was given to Caleb by Joshua as his portion. The Jews interpret the name as meaning "the city of the four", i.e., of Abraham, Isaac, Jacob, and Adam, who were all, as they allege, buried there.[220]
>
> **Hebron** - Topics: He'bron Text: a community; alliance.
> (1.) A city in the south end of the valley of Eshcol, about midway between Jerusalem and Beersheba, from which it is distant about 20 miles in a straight line. It was built "seven years before Zoan in Egypt" (Gen. 13:18; Num. 13:22).

It still exists under the same name, and is one of the most ancient cities in the world. Its earlier name was Kirjath-arba (Gen. 23:2; Josh. 14:15; 15:3). But "Hebron would appear to have been the original name of the city, and it was not till after Abraham's stay there that it received the name Kirjath-arba, who [i.e., Arba] was not the founder but the conqueror of the city, having led thither the tribe of the Anakim, to which he belonged. It retained this name till it came into the possession of Caleb, when the Israelites restored the original name Hebron" (Keil, Com.).

The name of this city does not occur in any of the prophets or in the New Testament. It is found about forty times in the Old. It was the favorite home of Abraham. Here he pitched his tent under the oaks of Mamre, by which name it came afterwards to be known; and here Sarah died, and was buried in the cave of Machpelah (Gen. 23:17-20), which he bought from Ephron the Hittite.

From this place the patriarch departed for Egypt by way of Beersheba (37:14; 46:1). It was taken by Joshua and given to Caleb (Josh. 10:36, 37; 12:10; 14:13). It became a Levitical city and a city of refuge (20:7; 21:11). When David became king of Judah this was his royal residence, and he resided here for seven and a half years (2 Sam. 5:5); and here he was anointed as king over all Israel (2 Sam. 2:1-4, 11; 1 Kings 2:11).

It became the residence also of the rebellious Absalom (2 Sam. 15:10), who probably expected to find his chief support in the tribe of Judah, now called el-Khulil. <u>In one part of the modern city is a great mosque, which is built over the grave of Machpelah.</u> The first European who was permitted to enter this mosque was the Prince of Wales in 1862. It was also visited by the Marquis of Bute in 1866, and by the late Emperor Frederick of Germany (then Crown-Prince of Prussia) in 1869. One of the largest oaks in Palestine is found in the valley of Eshcol, about 3 miles north of the town. It is supposed by some to be the tree under which Abraham pitched his tent, and is called "Abraham's oak."[221]

Abraham buys a burial plot

3. And Abraham stood up from before his dead, and spake unto the sons of Heth, saying,

> **Heth** - Topics: Heth Text: dread, a descendant of Canaan, and the ancestor of the Hittites (Gen. 10:18; Deut. 7:1), who dwelt in the vicinity of Hebron (Gen. 23:3, 7). The Hittites

were a Hamitic race. They are called "the sons of Heth" (Gen. 23:3, 5, 7, 10, 16, 18, 20).[222]

4. I am a stranger and a sojourner with you: give me a possession of a buryingplace with you, that I may bury my dead out of my sight.
5. And the children of Heth answered Abraham, saying unto him,
6. Hear us, my lord: thou art a mighty prince among us: in the choice of our sepulchres bury thy dead; none of us shall withhold from thee his sepulchre, but that thou mayest bury thy dead.

Sepulchre - Topics: Sep'ulchre   Text: first mentioned as purchased by Abraham for Sarah from Ephron the Hittite (Gen. 23:20). This was the "cave of the field of Machpelah," where also Abraham and Rebekah and Jacob and Leah were burried (Genesis 49:29-33). In Acts 7:16 it is said that Jacob was "laid in the sepulchre that Abraham bought for a sum of money of the sons of Emmor the father of Sychem."

It has been proposed, as a mode of reconciling the apparent discrepancy between this verse an Gen. 23:20, to read Acts 7:16 thus: "And they [i.e., our fathers] were carried over into Sychem, and laid in the sepulchre that Abraham bought for a sum of money of the sons of Emmor [the son] of Sychem." In this way the purchase made by Abraham is not to be confounded with the purchase made by Jacob subsequently in the same district. Of this purchase by Abraham there is not direct record in the Old Testament.[223]

7. And Abraham stood up, and bowed himself to the people of the land, even to the children of Heth.
8. And he communed with them, saying, If it be your mind that I should bury my dead out of my sight; hear me, and intreat for me to Ephron the son of Zohar,

Abraham bargains for the cave of Machpelah
9. That he may give me the cave of Machpelah, which he hath, which is in the end of his field; for as much money as it is worth he shall give it me for a possession of a buryingplace amongst you.

10. And Ephron dwelt among the children of Heth: and Ephron the Hittite answered Abraham in the audience of the children of Heth, even of all that went in at the gate of his city, saying,

11. Nay, my lord, hear me: the field give I thee, and the cave that is therein, I give it thee; in the presence of the sons of my people give I it thee: bury thy dead.

12. And Abraham bowed down himself before the people of the land.

13. And he spake unto Ephron in the audience of the people of the land, saying, But if thou wilt give it, I pray thee, hear me: I will give thee money for the field; take it of me, and I will bury my dead there.

14. And Ephron answered Abraham, saying unto him,

15. My lord, hearken unto me: the land is worth four hundred shekels of silver; what is that betwixt me and thee? bury therefore thy dead.

> **Shekel** - Topics: She'kel Text: weight, the common standard both of weight and value among the Hebrews. It is estimated at 220 English grains, or a little more than half an ounce avoirdupois. The "shekel of the sanctuary" (Ex. 30:13; Num. 3:47) was equal to twenty gerahs (Ezek. 45:12).

There were shekels of gold (1 Chr. 21:25), of silver (1 Sam. 9:8), of brass (17:5), and of iron (7). When it became a coined piece of money, the shekel of gold was equivalent to about 2 pound of our money. Six gold shekels, according to the later Jewish system, were equal in value to fifty silver ones.

The temple contribution, with which the public sacrifices were bought (Ex. 30:13; 2 Chr. 24:6), consisted of one common shekel, or a sanctuary half-shekel, equal to two Attic drachmas.

The coin, a stater (q.v.), which Peter found in the fish's mouth paid this contribution for both him and Christ (Matt. 17:24, 27). A zuza, or quarter of a shekel, was given by Saul to Samuel (1 Sam. 9:8).[224]

> **Gerah** - Topics: Ge'rah Text: a bean, probably of the carob tree, the smallest weight, and also the smallest piece of money, among the Hebrews, equal to the twentieth part of a shekel

(Ex. 30:13; Lev. 27:25; Num. 3:47). This word came into use in the same way as our word "grain," from a grain of wheat.[225]

16. And Abraham hearkened unto Ephron; and Abraham weighed to Ephron the silver, which he had named in the audience of the sons of Heth, four hundred shekels of silver, current money with the merchant. ($51,200)

Abraham buries Sarah in the cave of Machpelah

17. And the field of Ephron which was in Machpelah, which was before Mamre, the field, and the cave which was therein, and all the trees that were in the field, that were in all the borders round about, were made sure
18. Unto Abraham for a possession in the presence of the children of Heth, before all that went in at the gate of his city.
19. And after this, Abraham buried Sarah his wife in the cave of the field of Machpelah before Mamre: the same is Hebron in the land of Canaan.
20. And the field, and the cave that is therein, were made sure unto Abraham for a possession of a buryingplace by the sons of Heth.

Cave of Machpelah - Topics: Cave. Text: There are numerous natural caves among the limestone rocks of Syria, many of which have been artificially enlarged for various purposes. The first notice of a cave occurs in the history of Lot (Gen. 19:30). The next we read of is the cave of Machpelah (q.v.), which Abraham purchased from the sons of Heth (Gen. 25:9, 10). It was the burying-place of Sarah and of Abraham himself, also of Isaac, Rebekah, Leah, and Jacob (Gen. 49:31; 50:13).

Machpelah - Topics: Machpe'lah Text: portion; double cave, the cave which Abraham bought, together with the field in which it stood, from Ephron the Hittite, for a family burying-place (Gen. 23). It is one of those Bible localities about the identification of which there can be no doubt. It was on the slope of a hill on the east of Hebron, "before Mamre." Here were laid the bodies of Abraham and Sarah, Isaac and Rebekah, Jacob and Leah (Gen. 23:19; 25:9; 49:31; 50:13).

Over the cave an ancient Christian church was erected, probably in the time of Justinian, the Roman emperor. <u>This church has been converted into a Mohammedan mosque.</u> The whole is surrounded by the el-Haram i.e., "the sacred enclosure," about 200 feet long, 115 broad, and of an average height of about 50. This building, from the immense size of some of its stones, and the manner in which they are fitted together, is supposed by some to have been erected in the days of David or of Solomon, while others ascribe it to the time of Herod.

It is looked upon as the most ancient and finest relic of Jewish architecture. On the floor of the mosque are erected six large cenotaphs as monuments to the dead who are buried in the cave beneath. Between the cenotaphs of Isaac and Rebekah there is a circular opening in the floor into the cavern below, the cave of Machpelah. Here it may be that the body of Jacob, which was embalmed in Egypt, is still preserved (much older embalmed bodies have recently been found in the cave of Deir elBahari in Egypt, see PHARAOH), though those of the others there buried may have long ago mouldered into dust.

The interior of the mosque was visited by the Prince of Wales in 1862 by a special favour of the Mohammedan authorities. An interesting account of this visit is given in Dean Stanley's Lectures on the Jewish Church. It was also visited in 1866 by the Marquis of Bute, and in 1869 by the late Emperor (Frederick) of Germany, then the Crown Prince of Prussia. In 1881 it was visited by the two sons of the Prince of Wales, accompanied by Sir C. Wilson and others. (See Palestine Quarterly Statement, October 1882).[226]

> **YEAR – 2088**
> (Abraham 140, Ishmael 55, Isaac 40, Shem 532)

Isaac Marries His Cousin Rebekah[227]

After Sarah died Abraham sought a wife for Isaac from among his people in Haran. He sent his servant on the mission to bring back the bride. The servant was successful, and brought back Rebekah, the daughter of Abraham's nephew Bethuel, and the sister of her brother Laban.[228]

In the year 2088 Isaac was forty years old when he married Rebekah. This union would produce twin brothers Esau and Jacob. Of the two, Jacob would be the one to shoulder the responsibility of starting the Jewish nation with twelve sons.

Abraham Marries Keturah[229]

Once Isaac was married, Abraham also remarried a woman named Keturah. Abraham was around one-hundred forty; and the woman had to be very young for she produced six sons. In this case age didn't matter, only love.

> **Zimran** - One of the sons of Abraham by Keturah (Genesis 25:2; 1 Chronicles 1:32). Unlike the other sons of Abraham by Keturah, there is little evidence that Zimran is associated with a later tribal group.
>
> **Jokshan** - Son of Abraham and Keturah, and the father of Sheba and Dedan (Genesis 25:2-3; 1 Chronicles 1:32).
>
> **Medan** - Third son of Abraham by his second wife, Keturah (Genesis 25:2; 1 Chronicles 1:32).
>
> **Midian** - Midian was a son of Abraham by Abraham's second marriage. His land was called Midian and the people that

lived there were called Midianites, though there were few, if any, permanent settlements. Midian was on the eastern edge of Gilead, Moab, and Edom south into northwest Arabia.

Midian and his descendants figure prominently only in the early history of Israel, in connection with Abraham (Genesis 25:1-6), Joseph (Genesis 37:25-36), Moses (Exodus 2:15-3:1), Balaam (Numbers 22:1-6; 25), and Gideon (Judges 6:1-8:28).

Midian was Isaac's younger half brother, the fourth of six sons born to Keturah, whom Abraham married as an old man (Genesis 25:1-2). By calling Midian and his full brothers "the sons of Keturah" (Genesis 25:4), the Bible carefully distinguishes them from Isaac, the son of Sarah, who was the one through whom God's promise to Abraham would be fulfilled (Genesis 12:1-3). In fact, Abraham and the Israelites regarded these other sons as having no more inheritance rights than a concubine's sons (Genesis 25:5-6).

Expelled from Abraham's family, for Isaac's sake, they became partially nomadic peoples of the deserts east and south of Palestine (Genesis 25:5-6).

Ishbak - One of the sons of Abraham by Keturah (Genesis 25:2; 1 Chronicles 1:32)

Shuah - 1. One of six sons borne to Abraham by Keturah (Genesis 25:2; 1 Chronicles 1:32). He was perhaps the forefather of the Shuhite Arab tribe that dwelt near the land of Uz (Job 2:11)

YEAR – 2108
(Isaac 60, Abraham 160, Ishmael 75, Shem 552)[230]

Birth of Esau & Jacob (Genesis 25: 19-34)

The twin boys Esau and Jacob are born twenty years after Isaac and Rebekah are married. While still in their mother's womb they fought so fiercely that Rebekah went to God with the problem. God told Rebekah that two nations would be the product of the boys; Esau the nation of Edom, and Jacob the nation of Israel.

Upon birth, Esau came out hairy and red all over, and Jacob came out smooth skinned but holding the heel of Esau.

Esau developed into a skillful hunter, while Jacob became a domestic living in tents. Isaac loved his son Esau for his ruggedness and the venison he brought home; but Rebekah loved Jacob.

One day Jacob made a pot of stew. When Esau came into the camp from a long day of hunting, he asked Jacob for some of the stew. Jacob agreed to give him the stew if he would give of up his eldership birthright. Hunger had completely taken over Esau's train of thought and he gave Jacob his birthright, and swore not to retreat on his promise.

> ### YEAR – 2123
> (Ishmael 90, Isaac 75, Esau & Jacob 15, Shem 567)[231]

Death of Abraham

Abraham died at the age of 175 (1948-2123) and was buried with his wife, Sarah, by his two sons, Isaac and Ishmael.[232] The future of things concerning the seed of Abraham came to pass during the days of Jacob, Joseph, and Moses. However, to verify Christ's statement ("Your father Abraham rejoiced to see my day: and he saw it, and was glad"), I believe we have to look at the story he told about the poor man Lazarus and the rich man (Luke 16:19-31).

The strangeness of this story is their deaths: "And it came to pass that the beggar died, and was carried by the angels into Abraham's bosom: the rich man also died, and was buried, and in hell he lifted up his eyes, being in torments, and seeth Abraham afar off, and Lazarus in his bosom."

Reading on, we find both men were in a place called Sheol (hell), but separated by a force field; they could see each other but could not physically touch one another. Lazarus and Abraham were enjoying eternal life, while the rich man was being tormented in eternal fire.

I strongly believe this is the place Christ showed Abraham, and that Abraham rejoiced to know his soul would be saved from the second death (the lake of fire); more importantly, that Christ himself would come and take him from there into paradise. This same promise is given to all who believe in Christ Jesus. (John 5:24-30)[233]

CHAPTER 10

HEBREW NATION GENEALOGY

> **YEAR – 2148**
> (Ishmael 115, Isaac 100, Jacob 40,[234] Shem 592)

Jacobs Seven Year Contract with Laban

When Esau turned forty years old, he married two Hittite women of Canaanite ethnicity. His father Isaac, and his mother Rebekah grieved heavily over his wife selection.

When it came time for the boys to receive the blessing of their father, Rebekah urged Jacob to dress up in animal skins and pretend to be his brother Esau. Isaac wasn't completely fooled, but he eventually gave the inheritance blessing to Jacob.

Esau was infuriated with anger, and vowed to kill Jacob when Isaac was dead. Rebekah was sure that Esau meant business and sent Jacob to stay with her brother Laban in Syria.

After Jacob and Laban exchanged greeting Jacob agrees to work seven years for Laben in order to marry his youngest daughter Rachel.

> **YEAR – 2155**
> (Ishmael 122, Isaac 107, Jacob 47,[235] Shem 599)

Jacobs second Seven Year Contract with Laban

When the seven-year contract was completed Laban held a marriage feast, and got Jacob drunk on wine. Then he switched brides, and sent his oldest daughter Leah into the bridal chamber. Jacob consummated the marriage and was astonished to find Leah in his bed instead of Rachel.

Laban assured Jacob that everything would be fine if he agreed to work an additional seven years after marrying Rachel. Jacob confirmed this new arrangement and immediately consummated his marriage to Rachel.

During this period of time leach had four sons and Rachel had no children. So, to have children Rachel gave Jacob her handmaid Bilhah as a concubine. Not to be outdone, Leah then gave Jacob her handmaid Zilpah. Between the four-women Jacob fathered eleven sons and one daughter. And after he left the service of Laben he fathered his last son Benjamin by his wife Rachel. Herein is the order in which they were born:

- By Leah – (1) Reuben, (2) Simeon, (3) Levi, (4) Judah, (9) Issachar, (10) Zebulun.
  (11) Diniah
- By Bilhah – (5) Dan, (6) Naphtali.
- By Zilpah – (7) Gad, (8) Asher
- By Rachel – (12) Joseph, (13) Benjamin [*Rachel dies during birth.][236]

> **YEAR – 2158**
> (Ishmael 125, Isaac 110, Jacob 50)

Death of Shem

Shem died at the age of six-hundred and two years old (1556-2158 = 602). [237] He was the elder son of Noah, and was born one-hundred years before the flood. He fathered his first son Arphaxad two years after the flood. He out lived all of his off spring, and thirty-five years past the prophet Abraham. And in keeping with how the bible keep record of deaths, there is no mention of when, where or how he died. But we have to be satisfied with how long he lived. And if I may stretch a little a say that he probably had some of Adams genes locked up in his body. Therefore, God made sure that no modern scientist will dig up his body, and discover the secret of the tree of life, and longevity life: by probing his DNA – deoxyribonucleic acid, a self-replicating material which is present in nearly all living organisms as the main constituent of chromosomes. It is the carrier of genic information.

> **SHEMS HISTORY** - Shem was the oldest son of Noah (Genesis 5:32, 6:10, 7:13, 9:18, 23, 26-27, 11:10, 1 Chronicles 1:4, 1:17-27 and Luke 3:36) and the ancestor of the Jewish peoples (Genesis 10:1, 21-21). Shem lived six hundred years (11:10-11). In Hebrew, Shem means "name," perhaps implying that Noah expected this son's name to become great.
> After their deliverance from the great Flood, Shem and Japheth acted with respect and dignity toward their drunken father on an occasion when their brother Ham dishonored him (Genesis 9:20-29). Because of this act, Noah later pronounced a curse on Canaan, who was the son of Ham, and a blessing on both Shem and Japheth.
> In Genesis 11:10-27, the line of descent for the promised seed, which was to crush the power of Satan (3:15 and 5:1-32), is traced through Shem to Abraham, and ultimately through Judah and David to Jesus Christ (Luke 3:36). The blessing of Noah on Shem is taken as an indication that the line of Shem will be the line that will produce the seed that is described

in Genesis 3:15. This is the first time in the Bible that God is called the God of some particular individual or group of people. The statement that Canaan would be a servant to Shem was fulfilled centuries later when the Israelites, who descended from Shem, entered the land of Canaan and conquered the inhabitants of the land (1 Kings 9:20-21).

Noah also said that Japheth's descendants would be great and would dwell in the tents of Shem (Genesis 9:27). After Japheth's descendants would be greatly increased in numbers, the Japhethites would be brought into contact with Shem and would share in the blessings and promises of the Jewish faith. Many scholars see fulfillment of this prophecy in the opening of the gospel to the Gentiles during the time of the New Testament when the Christian Church was established. In the "table of nations" recorded in Genesis 10, five descendants of Shem are mentioned (Elam, Asshur, Arphaxad, Lud, and Aram). Eber, from the line of Arphaxad, receives particular emphasis among these descendants, when his line is traced to Abraham in 11:16-27.[238]

YEAR – 2162
(Ishmael 129, Isaac 114, Jacob 54)[239]

Jacobs Six Year Contract with Laban

Just as Jacobs second seven-year contract with Laban ends, Rachel gives birth to Joseph. Jacob decides to leave Laban and go back home to his mother and father. But Laban entices him to stay longer and gives him the overseer work of his flock. Jacob continues with Laban for another six years and then is forced to leave because of internal family strife over his management of the flocks.

> **YEAR - 2168**
> (Ishmael 135, Isaac 120, Jacob 60, Joseph 6)[240]

Jacob Leaves Laban

After twenty-years of service, Jacob packs up his family, and leaves Laban's household under the cover of darkness. Laban discovers that his golden god statures are missing, and forms a band of men to chase after Jacob. Upon reaching Jacobs camp his search did not reveal his beloved gods. He didn't know that his daughter Rachel had stolen the gods, and was sitting on them during the search. Laban and Jacob reconciled their differences, and departed in peace; with these everlasting words, "The Lord watch me and thee, when we are absent one from another."[241]

Jacob was so afraid that Esau would exact revenge upon him that he divided his camp in half. He reasoned, that if Esau attacked one group, the other could escape the slaughter. He also prayed heavily to God to bring peace between him and his brother, and protection too his family.

When Jacob was alone, and bedded down for the night, an angel visited him and they tussled all night long until the morning. Jacob released the angel when he was struck a blow to his hip: which caused him to have a permanent limp. During their conversation the angel changed Jacobs name to Israel.[242]

Soon Jacob and his brother Esau reconciled their differences and joined together in friendship. When they departed Esau went to Seir, and Jacob pitched his tents near the city of Shalem in Shechem. While there Jacob brought a parcel of land from the Canaanite Hamor.[243]

> **Seir** - This mountain range of Edom extends from the Dead Sea southward to the Gulf of Aqaba. Bordered by the great valley of Arabah on the west and by desert on the east, Mount Seir is the modern Jebel esh-Shera.

Seir was formerly inhabited by the Horites, whose defeat to King Kedorlaomer is recorded in Genesis 14:4-6. The Horites were later dispossessed from this region by Esau (Deuteronomy 2:12); however, a remnant of Horite chiefs was listed among the descendants of Esau living in Seir (Genesis 36:20-30). As this area was given by the Lord as an inheritance to Esau (Joshua 24:4), the Israelites were warned not to provoke the sons of Esau to war as they passed through Seir on their wilderness travels (Deuteronomy 2:1-8). During Israel's occupation of Palestine, they were drawn into a number of battles against the people of Seir. A band of Simeonites destroyed the Amalekites dwelling in Seir and resettled it with their own people (1 Chronicles 4:42). Jehoshaphat, king of Judah (872-848 BC), gained an incredible victory over the allied armies of Ammon, Moab, and Seir (2 Chronicles 20:10-23). King Amaziah of Judah (796-767 BC) routed an army from Seir in the valley of Salt (25:11-14). And finally, the prophet Ezekiel pronounced a curse of destruction on the inhabitants of Seir for their antagonism against Israel (Ezekiel 35:1-15).[244]

Esau History: (Genesis Chapter 36) Esau was Isaac's son, and the older twin brother of Jacob (Genesis 25:24-26). He was given his name because of the hair on his body at birth. Because the baby Esau had a reddish color, and because the color red was to play an important role in his life, he also became known by the name Edom, or "red." The race of people known as the Edomites claimed to be Esau's descendants, and even the name of their land, "Seir," may come from the word sair, meaning "hairy."
A good hunter, Esau brought tasty wild meat to his father, who enjoyed its strong flavor much more than he enjoyed the milder-tasting meat that Jacob brought him from the family's flocks. One day Esau came home very hungry from an unsuccessful hunting trip. Jacob talked Esau into selling

Jacob his birthright (the special blessing he would receive from his father) in return for food (Genesis 25:29-34).

Archaeological information from Nuzi shows us that birthrights were indeed sometimes sold or given to another member of the family. Esau's marriage to two local women who were not descendants of Abraham made life extremely difficult for his parents (Genesis 26:34-35). This may have been the reason why his mother, Rebekah, decided to help Jacob get the blessing from his father that should have gone to his brother Esau (27). After this, Esau was so angry that Jacob left for Haran, though twenty years later Esau generously forgave his brother and the brothers were reunited (33:4-16). Just as the younger, weaker Jacob was able to outwit his older, stronger brother, the Edomite descendants of Esau went to war (and lost) with the offspring of Jacob. They were subservient to the Israelites from the time of David (2 Samuel 8:11-15; 1 Chronicles 18:13) until the time of Jehoram (2 Kings 8:20-22; 2 Chronicles 21:8-10). After a rebellion in 845 BC, the Edomites gained their independence for a while but were conquered again by Amaziah (796-767 BC). They regained their freedom in 735 BC.[245]

Simeon and Levi Commit Murder (Genesis Chapter 34)

One day Jacobs daughter Dinah went among the women of Shechem. When Hamor's son Shechem saw her, he took her by force. Then he sent his father Hamor to ask for the hand of Dinah in marriage. After much debate, Jacob agreed to the marriage with the stipulation that all the males of Hamor's clan would summit to being circumcised. Hamor consented to this arrangement. And while they were healing Dinah's brothers Simeon and Levi went to the camp and slew all the males, and brought the women, children, and possessions to Jacob.[246]

Jacob's Name is Changed to Israel (Genesis Chapter 35)

While Jacob was in a fit of fear and confusion, God told Jacob to move to Bethel, and build an altar to God. While at Bethel God appeared to Jacob, and confirmed all the promises he made to Abraham; and changes his name to Israel.

Rachel Gives Birth to Benjamin

At this time Rachel was pregnant with Benjamin, and died in the city of Ephrath; which is later called Bethlehem. After burying Rachel Jacob moved his camp to Edar.

> **Ephrath:** 1. Town in the Judean hill country later named Bethlehem. It was on the road to Ephrath that Rachel died while giving birth to Benjamin (Genesis 35:16-19). This town was the home of Naomi's family, who identified themselves as Ephrathites (Ruth 1:2). Ephrath was the dwelling place of Ruth and Boaz (Ruth 4:11), the childhood home of David (1 Samuel 17:12), and the announced birthplace of the Messiah (Micah 5:2).
> 2. District in which the city of Kiriath-jearim was situated and where the ark of the covenant was kept (Psalm 132:6).[247]
>
> **Edar** (Eder): 1. First camping place of Jacob between Ephrath (Bethlehem) and Hebron, following Rachel's death. The tower of Eder, meaning "the tower of the flock," was perhaps a watchtower constructed for shepherds to guard their flocks (Genesis 35:21). It was located a short distance from Bethlehem.
> 2. One of the 29 cities located near the border of Edom in the southern extremity of the land allotted to Judah's tribe for an inheritance. It is listed between Kabzeel and Jagur in Joshua 15:21. Its site is unknown.[248]

Reuben Sins Against His Father

It was here that Reuben, Jacobs elder son, had sexual relations with Jacob's concubine Bilhah. Strangely, Jacob heard about the sexual encounters, but did not confront Reuben.[249]

- **SHECHEM** – (JACOB'S WELL) This place is mentioned only in John's Gospel (John 4:5-29). It was here that Jesus sat and talked with the unnamed woman of Samaria, who readily accepted Jesus' words. This well is located in a plot of ground acquired by the patriarch Jacob, about 300 yards (274 meters) southeast of the traditional tomb of Joseph (Genesis 33:19; Joshua 24:32; John 4:5-6).

- **HAMOR** - Hamor was a Hivite or Horite prince of the country about Shechem (Genesis 34:2), from whom Jacob bought land when returning with his family from Paddan-aram.

YEAR – 2170

Death of Ishmael

Ishmael died at the age of one-hundred thirty-seven years old (2033-2170 = 137).[250] As I stated before, Ishmael is the son of inheritance, and Isaac is the son of promise. As the oldest son, Ishmael by tradition is the first in line to receive his father's blessing, and all his possessions. By contrast, God let Ishmael be born from the loins of Abraham, but the promise of a nation to inherit the Canaan land was on the son of promise, through his wife Sarah.

Ishmael had twelve sons, and is called the father of the Arabs. Jacobs name was changed to Israel by God, and he had twelve sons that formed the twelve tribes of the Hebrew nation.

Now you may ask what does all this mean? Well, for one thing it means that in the year 2019 A.D. the son of inheritance and the son of promise are still fighting over the birthright to the Canaan land known as Palestine.

> **YEAR – 2179**
> (Isaac 131, Jacob 71, Joseph 17)[251]

Joseph is Carried to Egypt (Genesis Chapter 37)

When Joseph was around seventeen, he was known as his father Jacob's favorite son. His brothers hated him because he also had a reputation of being a tell-tale. On top of that his farther made him a coat of many colors. But the thing that infuriated them the most was his two dreams that indicated he would rule over them, and his whole household.

One day Jacob sent Joseph to look for his brothers. When he found them, they conspired to kill him, but Reuben, after they stripped him of his coat, convinced them to throw him in a deep pit. While they were away a caravan of Midianites (merchantmen) came by and rescued Joseph, and took him to Egypt. When Joseph's brothers discovered that he was not in the pit, they killed a goat, and dipped Joseph's coat in the blood; they reported back to Jacob that Joseph had been killed by a wild beast.

Judah Fathers Twin Boys (Genesis Chapter 38)

Meanwhile Josephs brother Judah had sexual relations with a Canaanite woman, and they produced three sons: Er, Onan, and Shelah.

Judah gave to his son Er a wife named Tamar. But Er was evil in the sight of God, and died at an early age; and did not produce any children.

Therefore, Judah gave Tamar to his second son Onan, but he would pull away from her during copulation, and spew his semen on the ground. This act displeased God, and he was slain.

Then Judah promised Tamar that she could live in his house, and wait until his youngest son Shelah, was old enough to marry her, and produce children. But when Shelah was grown Judah did not keep his promise to Tamar. Also, around this time Judah's wife died, and he went about his business of sheepshearing.

Therefore, Tamar took things into her own hands, and dressed up like a harlot, and waited along the roadside for Judah to pass by. When Judah saw her, he went in her tent and had sexual relations with her; but he did not know it was Tamar. He left her his signet ring, his staff, and his bracelets to keep until he returned with her promised payment of a kid from the flock. When Judah sent the payment, she was nowhere to be found.

Three months later Judah was told that his daughter in law Tamar was pregnant with child because she had had played the harlot, and was having a child as a result of whoredom. With this news Judah demanded that Tamar be brought the town council, and burnt before the people. When they asked Tamar who was the father, she produced the items that belonged to Judah. In shame, Judah acknowledged that he was the father, and that he had wronged Tamar by not giving her his youngest son.

Tamar gave birth to twin boys. The first boys hand came out, and the midwives tied a ribbon around his hand, but he drew the hand back into the womb. Then the second boy came out and they called his name Pharez. Seconds later, the second twin came out with the ribbon wrapped around his hand, and they called his name Zarah.[252] Both boys are mentioned in the "Genealogy of Christ."[253]

Joseph is Sold to Potiphar (Genesis Chapter 39)

When the Midianite caravan reached Egypt, they sold Joseph to Potiphar, the captain of Pharaoh's guard. Potiphar saw that Joseph was very intelligent, and put him in charge of his whole household; and told him that he had access to everything he owned. With Joseph in charge Potiphar's house was blessed by God, and Joseph saw great favor in the eyes of Potiphar.

Potiphar's wife took an exception to Joseph, and tried to induce him to her bed. When he wouldn't come voluntarily, she grabbed him and tried to force herself upon him. Joseph rejected her advances, and pulled away as she ripped of his coat. With Joseph coat as proof, she convinced Potiphar that Joseph tried to rape her. Reluctantly, Potiphar had Joseph put in jail. Again, Joseph was well liked by the warden of the prison, and was put in charge of all the prison personnel duties. [254]

YEAR – 2190
(Isaac 142, Jacob 82, Joseph 28)[255]

Joseph, the butler, and the Baker (Genesis Chapter 40)

During Joseph's stay in prison he met Pharaoh's chief butler and baker: both had offended Pharaoh. During one of their conversations, both men told Joseph of a weird dream they had. Joseph told them to tell him their dream and he would God to give him the interpretation:

The Butler – "And the chief butler told his dream to Joseph, and said to him, In my dream, behold, a vine was before me; and in the vine were three branches: and it was as though it budded, and her blossoms shot forth; and the clusters thereof brought forth ripe grapes: and Pharaoh's cup was in my hand: and I took the grapes, and pressed them into Pharaoh's cup, and I gave the cup into Pharaoh's hand."

Joseph's Interpretation – "And Joseph said unto him, This is the interpretation of it: The three branches are three days: yet within three days shall Pharaoh lift up thine head, and restore thee unto thy place: and thou shalt deliver Pharaoh's cup into his hand, after the former manner when thou wast his butler.'

Joseph's Request – "But think on me when it shall be well with thee, and shew kindness, I pray thee, unto me, and make mention of me unto Pharaoh, and bring me out of this house: for indeed I was stolen away out of the land of the Hebrews: and here also have I done nothing that they should put me into the dungeon."

The Baker - When the chief baker saw that the interpretation was good, he said unto Joseph, I also was in my dream, and, behold, I had three white baskets on my head: and in the uppermost basket there was of all manner of bake-meats for Pharaoh; and the birds did eat them out of the basket upon my head.

Joseph's Interpretation – "And Joseph answered and said, This is the interpretation thereof: The three baskets are three days: yet within three days shall Pharaoh lift up thy head from off thee, and shall hang thee on a tree; and the birds shall eat thy flesh from off thee."

Pharaoh – "And it came to pass the third day, which was Pharaoh's birthday, that he made a feast unto all his servants: and he lifted up the head of the chief butler and of the chief baker among his servants. And he restored the chief butler unto his butlership again; and he gave the cup into Pharaoh's hand: but he hanged the chief baker: as Joseph had interpreted to them."

The Butler – "Yet did not the chief butler remember Joseph, but forgat him."

> ### YEAR – 2192
> (Isaac 144, Jacob 84, Joseph 30)[256]

Joseph Stands before Pharaoh (Genesis Chapter 41)

After Pharaoh restored the butler back to his position, he had two disturbing dreams. They were so freighting that he called for all his magicians and wise men to interpret the dreams; but they could not interpret Pharaoh's dreams.

Then the chief butler told Pharaoh how a young Hebrew prisoner had truly interpreted his dream, and the chief baker's dream. Pharaoh immediately sent for Joseph and told him the dreams. Interestedly, is how Pharaoh and Joseph were quickly becoming friends because of the dream's interpretation.

Joseph Meets Pharaoh – "Then Pharaoh sent and called Joseph, and they brought him hastily out of the dungeon: and he shaved himself, and changed his raiment, and came in unto Pharaoh."

Pharaoh – "And Pharaoh said unto Joseph, I have dreamed a dream, and there is none that can interpret it: and I have heard say of thee, that thou canst understand a dream to interpret it."

Joseph – "And Joseph answered Pharaoh, saying, It is not in me: God shall give Pharaoh an answer of peace."

Pharaoh' 1st Dream – "And Pharaoh said unto Joseph, In my dream, behold, I stood upon the bank of the river: and, behold, there came up out of the river seven kine, fatfleshed and well favoured; and they fed in a meadow: and, behold, seven other kine came up after them, poor and very ill favoured and leanfleshed, such as I never saw in all the land of Egypt for badness: and the lean and the ill favoured kine did eat up the first seven fat kine: and when they had eaten them up, it could not be known that they had eaten them; but they were still ill favoured, as at the beginning.'

Pharaoh's 2nd Dream – "So I awoke. And I saw in my dream, and, behold, seven ears came up in one stalk, full and good: and, behold, seven ears, withered, thin, and blasted with the east wind, sprung up after them: and the thin ears devoured the seven good ears: and I told this unto the magicians; but there was none that could declare it to me."

Joseph – "And Joseph said unto Pharaoh, <u>The dream of Pharaoh is one:</u> God hath shewed Pharaoh what he is about to do. The seven good kine are seven years; and the seven good ears are seven years: the dream is one. And the seven thin and ill favoured kine that came up after them are seven years; and the seven empty ears blasted with the east wind shall be seven years of famine. This is the thing which I have spoken unto Pharaoh: What God is about to do he sheweth unto Pharaoh."

The Interpretation of the Dreams – "Behold, there come seven years of great plenty throughout all the land of Egypt: and there shall arise after them seven years of famine; and all the plenty shall be forgotten in the land of Egypt; and the famine shall consume the land; and the plenty shall not be known in the land by reason of that famine following; for it shall be very grievous. And for that the dream was doubled unto Pharaoh twice; it is because the thing is established by God, and God will shortly bring it to pass."

Joseph Solution – "Now therefore let Pharaoh look out a man discreet and wise, and set him over the land of Egypt. Let Pharaoh do this, and let him appoint officers over the land, and take up the fifth part of the land of Egypt in the seven plenteous years. And let them gather all the food of those good years that come, and lay up corn under the hand of Pharaoh, and let them keep food in the cities. And that food shall be for store to the land against the seven years of famine, which shall be in the land of Egypt; that the land perish not through the famine."

Pharaoh – "And the thing was good in the eyes of Pharaoh, and in the eyes of all his servants. And Pharaoh said unto his servants, Can we find such a one as this is, a man in whom the Spirit of God is?"

Joseph is Elevated with Pharaoh – "And Pharaoh said unto Joseph, Forasmuch as God hath shewed thee all this, there is none so discreet and wise as thou art: Thou shalt be over my house, and according unto thy word shall all my people be ruled: only in the throne will I be greater than thou."

Joseph is Ruler of Egypt – "And Pharaoh said unto Joseph, See, I have set thee over all the land of Egypt. And Pharaoh took off his ring from his hand, and put it upon Joseph's hand, and arrayed him in vestures of fine linen, and put a gold chain about his neck; and he made him to ride in the second chariot which he had; and they cried before him, Bow the knee: and he made him ruler over all the land of Egypt."

Pharaoh gives Joseph a Wife – "And Pharaoh said unto Joseph, I am Pharaoh, and without thee shall no man lift up his hand or foot in all the land of Egypt. And Pharaoh called Joseph's name Zaphnath-paaneah; and he gave him to wife Asenath the daughter of Poti-pherah priest of On."

Joseph – "And Joseph was thirty years old when he stood before Pharaoh king of Egypt. And Joseph went out from the presence of Pharaoh, and went throughout all the land of Egypt."

YEAR – 2228
Isaac dies at 180 [2048 – 2228] (Jacob 120, Joseph 66)

Death of Isaac

While Joseph is in Egypt, Isaac died at the age of one-hundred eighty years old (2048-2228 = 180). [257] His twin boys, Esau and Jacob, buried him in the cave of Machpelah, where lay the bodies of Abraham and Sarah.

Historic Isaac

"Isaac was the son of Abraham and Sarah. He was the father of Jacob and Esau. The name Isaac means "he laughs" or "he laughed." Scholars have debated these meanings. If God is implied, the name could indicate divine amusement at an aged couple ridiculing the prospect of having a child (Genesis 17:17; 18:12). But Abraham and Sarah did become parents, as God had promised.

Isaac's lineage is also interesting. Sarah was not only the wife of Abraham but also his half sister (Genesis 20:12). This fact alone may have interfered with conception in their earlier years. Because of this relationship, Isaac belonged to both sides of the family of Terah (Abraham's father). According to the custom of the age, the son of the legal wife ranked above the male offspring of a secondary wife. Isaac had priority of inheritance over Ishmael, his half brother (child of Abraham and Hagar, the slave woman). The gifts that Abraham later gave to the sons of his secondary wives (25:6) were without prejudice to the inheritance of Isaac.

Following God's instructions (Genesis 17:10-14), Isaac was circumcised on the eighth day. That was customary in the covenant community. The next ceremony came when he was old enough for weaning, probably around three years old. In some eastern countries this procedure is still observed. The child's transition from milk to solid protein and carbohydrates is normally celebrated in the context of a feast. During the celebration the mother chews a mouthful of solid food and then pushes it into the baby's mouth with her tongue. The infant is often so shocked by this treatment that it promptly expels the food. Then the mother repeats the process. For an observer the procedure can be hilarious. Ishmael may have been laughing at such a spectacle when he incurred Sarah's wrath (21:8-10).

During the years of Isaac's adolescence, Abraham was living in Philistine territory (Genesis 21:34). The supreme test of the father's faith and obedience came in this period. Abraham had watched this son of God's promise grow up into a healthy young man. But Abraham is asked by God to offer him as a sacrifice. Isaac was familiar with sacrificial rituals and helped with the preparations. He probably had some misgivings, though. He would have also been familiar with the traditions that gave the head of the family power of life or death over everyone and everything in the family. If he voiced any protest as he lay bound on the sacrificial altar, it is not recorded. When Abraham's faith did not waver, God intervened at the crucial moment and provided another offering in the form of a ram. Because of his obedience, God promised Abraham great blessing. Isaac also participated in this blessing (22; 25:11). Paul honored this act of faith and obedience centuries later. He called Abraham the forefather of the Christian church (Romans 4).

After Sarah's death (Genesis 23), Abraham set about securing a bride for Isaac. It was the custom for parents to arrange marriages for their children. Abraham didn't want his son to marry a local pagan woman. He sent his household steward to Nahor in Mesopotamia to seek a bride for his son from among his relatives. Genesis 24 describes how the servant met Rebekah and betrothed her to Isaac. This is an account that emphasizes faith, perseverance, and divine blessing. Bethuel, Rebekah's father, and Laban, her brother, agreed to this arrangement. She left with the family's blessing to take up her new responsibilities in Palestine as Isaac's wife.

When Abraham died at a ripe old age, Isaac and Ishmael buried him in the cave of Machpelah (Genesis 25:8-9). Isaac was now patriarch of the family. He pleaded with God that his wife, Rebekah, might bear children. As a result, she bore twin sons, Esau ("the hairy one") and Jacob ("supplanter"). Esau became a hunter, and Isaac favored him. Jacob was more of a settler and farmer and was favored by his mother. Jacob was also crafty and took advantage of Esau's extreme hunger one day. He bargained with his older brother to exchange his birthright for some lentil stew. Possession of the birthright secured for Jacob a double portion of the inheritance (Deuteronomy 21:17).

When famine gripped the land, God instructed Isaac not to visit Egypt (Genesis 26:2). If he would stay in Palestine, he would enjoy great prosperity. When the men of the area asked about Rebekah, Isaac became fearful and said she was his sister. When the deception was uncovered, Abimelech the king scolded Isaac and forbade anyone to interfere with him. Isaac prospered so greatly that Abimelech finally asked him to relocate. He moved to Beersheba, where there was sufficient water for his flocks, and his fortune increased.

Although Esau was Isaac's favorite son, he displeased his father by marrying two Hittite women. Near the end of his life, Isaac wanted to bless his firstborn in the traditional patriarchal manner (Genesis 27). Rebekah overheard his instructions to Esau. She encouraged Jacob to deceive the blind old man by disguising himself as Esau and taking his brother's blessing. The deception succeeded, and Isaac gave Jacob the blessing of the firstborn. When Esau appeared to receive his blessing he was too late. He was very bitter against Jacob because of what had happened. Rebekah sent Jacob away to her brother Laban in Mesopotamia. The purpose was to escape Esau's anger and also to obtain a wife. Esau did receive a blessing from Isaac, but a lesser one. Two decades later a rich and prosperous Jacob returned with his family. He made peace with Esau before Isaac died, and the brothers buried Isaac in Hebron (35:27-29).

Isaac is given less prominence in the narratives than the other patriarchs, Abraham and Jacob. But his importance for faith was recognized in such New Testament passages as Acts 7:8, Romans 9:7, Galatians 4:21-31, and Hebrews 11:9-20."[258]

> **YEAR - 2229**
> (Jacob 121, Joseph 67)[259] Benjamin 52, Dan 73, Naphtali 72, Gad 72, Asher 70
> Reuben 74, Simeon 73, Levi 72, Judah 71, Dinah 68 Issachar 70, Zebulun 71)
> Manasseh and Ephraim (children of Joseph and Egyptian woman)

The Seven Years of Plenty (Genesis 41: 47-53)

After years of building silos, and warehouses Joseph was now ready to store food garnished during the coming years of prosperity: "And in the seven plenteous years the earth brought forth by handfuls. And he gathered up all the food of the seven years, which were in the land of Egypt, and laid up the food in the cities: the food of the field, which was round about every city, laid he up in the same. "And Joseph gathered corn as the sand of the sea, very much, until he left numbering; for it was without number."

Joseph Two Son's are Born

> "And unto Joseph were born two sons before the years of famine came, which Asenath the daughter of Poti-pherah priest of On bare unto him. And Joseph called the name of the firstborn <u>Manasseh</u>: For God, said he, hath made me forget all my toil, and all my father's house. And the name of the second called he <u>Ephraim</u>: For God hath caused me to be fruitful in the land of my affliction. And the seven years of

plenteousness, that was in the land of Egypt, were ended."

> **YEAR – 2236**
> (Jacob 128, Joseph 74)[260]

Seven Years of Drought

"And the seven years of dearth began to come, according as Joseph had said: and the dearth was in all lands; but in all the land of Egypt there was bread. And when all the land of Egypt was famished, the people cried to Pharaoh for bread: and Pharaoh said unto all the Egyptians, Go unto Joseph; what he saith to you, do. And the famine was over all the face of the earth: And Joseph opened all the storehouses, and sold unto the Egyptians; and the famine waxed sore in the land of Egypt. And all countries came into Egypt to Joseph for to buy corn; because that the famine was so sore in all lands."[261]

Israel Sends His Son's to Egypt (Genesis Chapter 42-45)

At the beginning of the seven-year drought Jacob sent his ten sons to buy food from Egypt; but he kept Benjamin at home with him. While there, they encountered the Egyptian ruler of all the store houses. When Joseph saw his brothers, he was over joyed, but they did not know him. And as they talked among themselves, he didn't let on that he understood the Hebrew language.

After several meetings, Joseph revealed himself to them, and demanded that they persuade Jacob to move the family to Egypt where they could be cared for by him. Joseph assured them that it was God's doing to bring him into Egypt. And admonished them to remember that five-years of drought still remained to fulfill God's plan.

When the boys told Jacob, that Joseph was not only alive, but one of the rulers of Egypt, he was filled with tears of joy, and said, "Joseph my son is yet alive: I will go and see him before I die.

Jacob – "And Israel took his journey with all that he had, and came to Beer-sheba, and offered sacrifices unto the God of his father Isaac."

God – "And God spake unto Israel in the visions of the night, and said, Jacob, Jacob."

Jacob – "And he said, Here am I."

God – "And he said, I am God, the God of thy father: fear not to go down into Egypt; for I will there make of thee a great nation: I will go down with thee into Egypt; and I will also surely bring thee up again: and Joseph shall put his hand upon thine eyes."

Jacob – "And Jacob rose up from Beer-sheba: and the sons of Israel carried Jacob their father, and their little ones, and their wives, in the wagons which Pharaoh had sent to carry him. And they took their cattle, and their goods, which they had gotten in the land of Canaan, and came into Egypt, Jacob, and all his seed with him: his sons, and his sons' sons with him, his daughters, and his sons' daughters, and all his seed brought he with him into Egypt."

CHAPTER 11

THE HEBREWS IN EGYPT

> **YEAR – 2238**
> (Jacob is 130, Joseph is 76)

Beginning of the 400 Years in Egypt (Genesis Chapter 46 -47)

When Jacob brings his whole family, and all of his possessions to Egypt, he fulfilled the four-hundred-year prophecy given to Abraham by <u>the word of the Lord</u> (Christ Jesus). [262]

At the age of one-hundred-thirty, with the blessing of Pharaoh, Jacob relocated to the land of Goshen Egypt [263] with his family, and all that he owned. The total number of Hebrews was seventy: to include Joseph, his wife, and two boys.

After this, Jacob spend seventeen-years in Goshen before he died of natural causes.

> **YEAR – 2243**
> Drought Ends (Jacob 135, Joseph 81, Manasseh 7, Ephraim 6)[264]

True to the word of God, Joseph had brought Egypt through the hardship of a seven-year drought. Not only that, but he also full filled his dreams of ruling over his total family; his two dreams happened when he was seventeen years old.

YEAR – 2255
Jacob Prophecies to his sons, and dies at 147 [2108-2255]
- Joseph is 93, Manasseh is 20, Ephraim 19
- Reuben is 100

Death of Jacob (Genesis Chapter 48-49)

Jacob died at the age of one-hundred forty-seven. [265] But before Jacob died, he gave each of his son's their father's blessing. This was sought of like the last rites; but more on the order of how the father evaluated their life with him. I'm going to list the first four sons blessing; because they are the ones that affect the Messianic blood line.

Reuben – "Reuben, thou art my firstborn, my might, and the beginning of my strength, the excellency of dignity, and the excellency of power: Unstable as water, thou shalt not excel; because thou wentest up to thy father's bed; then defiledst thou it: he went up to my couch."

*Because Reuben had sexual relations with Jacobs concubine Bilhah, he could not receive the elder son inheritance. Later when God gives Moses the law, this type of sexual behavior is outlawed. (Leviticus 18:7-8)

Simeon and Levi – "Simeon and Levi are brethren; instruments of cruelty are in their habitations. O my soul, come not thou into their secret; unto their assembly, mine honour, be not thou united: for in their anger they slew a man, and in their selfwill they digged down a wall.

Cursed be their anger, for it was fierce; and their wrath, for it was cruel: I will divide them in Jacob, and scatter them in Israel."

Being second and third in line to receive the elder son inheritance, Simeon and Levi were rejected because they deceived the people of Hamor, and his son Shechem, with the promise of marriage to their sister Dinah, only to murder all the males as they recovered from the wounds of circumcision.

<u>Judah</u> – "Judah, thou art he whom thy brethren shall praise: thy hand shall be in the neck of thine enemies;'

- "thy father's children shall bow down before thee.'

- "Judah is a lion's whelp: from the prey, my son, thou art gone up: he stooped down, he couched as a lion, and as an old lion; who shall rouse him up?"

- "The sceptre shall not depart from Judah, nor a lawgiver from between his feet, until Shiloh come; and unto him shall the gathering of the people be."

- "Binding his foal unto the vine, and his ass's colt unto the choice vine; he washed his garments in wine, and his clothes in the blood of grapes:'

- "His eyes shall be red with wine, and his teeth white with milk."

Judah, the fourth son of Jacob, received the blessing of the elder son, and the title as the chief tribe. Through Judah would come the crown of the Jews, and the King of Kings and the Lord of Lords: who is called the lion of Judah. (Revelation 5:1-7)

After Jacob died, Joseph and all his people mourned for forty days. And then they took Jacobs body up to the Canaan land and buried him with Abraham, Sarah, and Isaac.[266]

Joseph Treats His Brothers Kindly (Genesis Chapter 50)

Upon returning to Goshen, Josephs brother said, "Joseph will peradventure hate us, and will certainly requite us all the evil which we did unto him. And they sent a messenger unto Joseph, saying, Thy father did command before he died, saying, So shall ye say unto Joseph, Forgive, I pray thee now, the trespass of thy brethren, and their sin; for they did unto thee evil: and now, we pray thee, forgive the trespass of the servants of the God of thy father."

> "And Joseph wept when they spake unto him. And his brethren also went and fell down before his face; and they said, Behold, we be thy servants. And Joseph said unto them, Fear not: for am I in the place of God? But as for you, ye thought evil against me; but God meant it unto good, to bring to pass, as it is this day, to save much people alive. Now therefore fear ye not: I will nourish you, and your little ones. And he comforted them, and spake kindly unto them."

The kindness that Joseph showed toward his brothers (that harmed him) demonstrates the doctrine Christ taught about forgiveness:

> **Matthew 18:** 15 Moreover if thy brother shall trespass against thee, go and tell him his fault between thee and him alone: if he shall hear thee, thou hast gained thy brother. 16 But if he will not hear thee, then take with thee one or two more, that in the mouth of two or three witnesses every word may be established.
> 17 And if he shall neglect to hear them, tell it unto the church: but if he neglect to hear the church, let him be unto thee as a heathen man and a publican.

18 Verily I say unto you, Whatsoever ye shall bind on earth shall be bound in heaven: and whatsoever ye shall loose on earth shall be loosed in heaven.

19 Again I say unto you, That if two of you shall agree on earth as touching any thing that they shall ask, it shall be done for them of my Father which is in heaven.

20 For where two or three are gathered together in my name, there am I in the midst of them.

Jesus tells the parable of the unforgiving debtor

21 Then came Peter to him, and said, Lord, how oft shall my brother sin against me, and I forgive him? till seven times?

22 Jesus saith unto him, I say not unto thee, Until seven times: but, Until seventy times seven.

YEAR – 2272

Death of Joseph

Joseph lived seventeen years after Jacob died, and he expired at the age of one-hundred-ten years old (2162-2272 = 110).[267], and is buried in Egypt. But he made a request before he died, that his bones be taken out of the Egypt, and buried in Canaan, when the Hebrews four-hundred-year occupation comes to an end.

The Hebrews are Enslaved (Exodus Chapter 1)

After the death of Joseph and his brothers, and all memory had been forgotten of how he saved Egypt from famine, a new Pharaoh came to power who said unto his people, "Look, the people of Israel now outnumber us and are stronger than we are. We must make a plan to keep them from growing even more. If we don't, and if war breaks out, they will join our enemies and fight against us. Then they will escape from the country."

- So the Egyptians made the Israelites their slaves.

- They appointed brutal slave drivers over them, hoping to wear them down with crushing labor.

- They forced them to build the cities of Pithom and Rameses as supply centers for the king.

- But the more the Egyptians oppressed them, the more the Israelites multiplied and spread, and the more alarmed the Egyptians became.

- So the Egyptians worked the people of Israel without mercy. They made their lives bitter, forcing them to mix mortar and make bricks and do all the work in the fields.

When Pharaoh saw that his efforts to deplete the population of Israel was not working through slavery, he gave the order that all new born baby boys would be killed at birth: the command was given to the Hebrew mid-wives.

But the mid-wives disobeyed Pharaohs command and saved all the boy babies. In a fit of rage Pharaoh brought the mid-wives in for questioning:

Pharaoh: Then Pharaoh, the king of Egypt, gave this order to the Hebrew midwives, Shiphrah and Puah: "When you help the Hebrew women as they give birth, watch as they deliver. If the baby is a boy, kill him; if it is a girl, let her live."

Mid-wives: But because the midwives feared God, they refused to obey the king's orders. They allowed the boys to live, too.

Pharaoh: So the king of Egypt called for the midwives. "Why have you done this?" he demanded. "Why have you allowed the boys to live?"

Mid-wives: "The Hebrew women are not like the Egyptian women," the midwives replied. "They are more vigorous and have their babies so quickly that we cannot get there in time."

God: So God was good to the midwives, and the Israelites continued to multiply, growing more and more powerful.

Mid-wives: And because the midwives feared God, he gave them families of their own.

Pharaoh: Then Pharaoh gave this order to all his people: "Throw every newborn Hebrew boy into the Nile River. But you may let the girls live."[268]

YEAR - 2588

Moses is Born (Exodus 2: 1-10)

At this time a Levite named Amram took Jochebed, his fathers' sister, to be his wife.[269] They produced three children: Miriam, Aaron, and Moses; Aaron was three years older than Moses.[270]

When Moses was born his mother hid him for three months. Not being able to keep him concealed, she placed him in a basket made of weeds, and put the baby in a safe place along the river bank. His sister Miriam kept watch where he was lain.

But out of nowhere the daughter of Pharaoh came down to the river bank to take a bath; while her handmaidens walked along the rivers edge. As she waded in the water, she spotted the basket, and told her handmaiden to bring it to her. To her surprise, a beautiful baby boy was wrapped up inside; "and, behold, the babe wept. And she had compassion on him, and said, This is one of the Hebrews' children."

Miriam: Then said his sister to Pharaoh's daughter, Shall I go and call to thee a nurse of the Hebrew women, that she may nurse the child for thee?

Pharaoh daughter: And Pharaoh's daughter said to her, Go.

Miriam: And the maid went and called the child's mother.

Jochebed: And Pharaoh's daughter said unto her, Take this child away, and nurse it for me, and I will give thee thy wages. And the woman took the child, and nursed it.

Moses: And the child grew, and she brought him unto Pharaoh's daughter, and he became her son. And she called his name Moses: and she said, Because I drew him out of the water.[271]

YEAR – 2628

Moses Leaves Egypt (Exodus 2:11-25)

When Moses was around forty-years old he saw an Egyptian abusing one of his Hebrew brethren. Moses took action, and killed the Egyptian; and hid his body in the sand.

Two days later Moses was out strolling when he saw two Hebrew men fighting.

Moses: he said to him that did the wrong, Wherefore smitest thou thy fellow?

The Hebrew: And he said, Who made thee a prince and a judge over us? intendest thou to kill me, as thou killedst the Egyptian?

Moses: And Moses feared, and said, Surely this thing is known.

Pharaoh: Now when Pharaoh heard this thing, he sought to slay Moses.

Moses settles in Midian

Moses fled for his life to the land of Midian. While there he met a priest named Jethro, who had seven daughters. Moses fell in love with Zipporah, and married her: they had a son named Gershom.[272]

> *Exodus 2: 23 And it came to pass in process of time, that the king of Egypt died: and the children of Israel sighed by reason of the bondage, and they cried, and their cry came up unto God by reason of the bondage.*
> *24 And God heard their groaning, and God remembered his covenant with Abraham, with Isaac, and with Jacob.*
> *25 And God looked upon the children of Israel, and God had respect unto them.*

God Calls Moses (Exodus Chapter 3 – 4)

Now I want to pause right here and say that this is when Moses meets "the word of the Lord." And I want you to follow some of the dialogue between them.

The Word: "And the angel of the Lord appeared unto him in a flame of fire out of the midst of a bush: and he looked, and, behold, the bush burned with fire, and the bush was not consumed.

Moses: And Moses said, I will now turn aside, and see this great sight, why the bush is not burnt.

God: And <u>when the Lord saw that he turned aside to see,</u> <u>God called unto him</u> out of the midst of the bush, and said, Moses, Moses.

Moses: And he said, Here am I.

God: And he said, Draw not nigh hither: put off thy shoes from off thy feet, for the place whereon thou standest is holy ground. Moreover he said, I am the God of thy father, the God of Abraham, the God of Isaac, and the God of Jacob.

Moses: And Moses hid his face; for he was afraid to look upon God.

The Word: And the Lord said, I have surely seen the affliction of my people which are in Egypt, and have heard their cry by reason of their taskmasters; for I know their sorrows; and I am come down to deliver them out of the hand of the Egyptians, and to bring them up out of that land unto a good land and a large, unto a land flowing with milk and honey; unto the place of the Canaanites, and the Hittites, and the Amorites, and the Perizzites, and the Hivites, and the Jebusites. Now therefore, behold, the cry of the children of Israel is come unto me: and I have also seen the oppression wherewith the Egyptians oppress them. Come now therefore, and I will send thee unto Pharaoh, that thou mayest bring forth my people the children of Israel out of Egypt.

Moses: And Moses said unto God, Who am I, that I should go unto Pharaoh, and that I should bring forth the children of Israel out of Egypt?

God: And he said, Certainly I will be with thee; and this shall be a token unto thee, that I have sent thee: When thou hast brought forth the people out of Egypt, ye shall serve God upon this mountain.

Moses: And Moses said unto God, Behold, when I come unto the children of Israel, and shall say unto them, The God of your fathers hath sent me unto you; and they shall say to me, What is his name? what shall I say unto them?

God: And God said unto Moses, I AM THAT I AM: and he said, Thus shalt thou say unto the children of Israel, **I AM** hath sent me unto you.

Now this name "I AM" is significant in that it identifies God. Thus, it can only be used by God; it is considered blasphemy if used by anyone else. Yet, when Jesus was debating with the Jews, he flatly stated that he knew Abraham, and that Abraham believed what he said: to the point that Abraham was shown the future of Christ coming to save the world of sin.

The Jews were astonished, and said, "You aren't even fifty years old. How can you say you have seen Abraham?" Jesus answered, "I tell you the truth, before Abraham was even born, I Am!" At that point they picked up stones to throw at him. But Jesus was hidden from them and left the Temple.[273]

What I'm saying here is that "the angel of the Lord," whom appeared to Moses in the flaming bush, is none other than "The Word" identified in the fist chapter of the gospel of John. When Moses turned to look at the flame that's when the Father spoke to him. I don't stand alone in my belief; for there are two others that came to the same conclusion:

- "the angel of the Lord who appeared to Moses is none other than the pre-incarnate Christ. Some people would debate this conclusion, but this is my conviction after years of studying the word of God." (Dr. J. Vernon McGee)[274]

- (*I AM*) "This is one of the eternal names of God, proving that he existed before Abraham. The Jews understood that He (*Jesus*) applied this name to Himself, thus declaring his deity. (Finis Jennings Dake's)[275]

God told Moses that he was to gather the Elders of Israel, and go to the court of Pharaoh. The message he was commanded to deliver was very simple, "The Lord God of the Hebrews hath met with us: and now let us go, we beseech ye, three days journey into the wilderness, that we may sacrifice to the Lord our God."

God then told Moses that, "I am sure that the king of Egypt will not let you go, no, not by a mighty hand (even by the force of a mighty army). Why would the Pharaoh feel this way?

- First, he would lose all his free labor; and his people would have to finish building his cities, and temples.

- Second, a three-day trip into the Sinai desert would be about sixty miles (20 miles per day). And to complete a sacrifice to God would take about three months or more.

- Third, the Hebrews would get a taste of freedom and not return back to Egypt.

- Fourth, in a military fight, the tribes of the desert, which were akin to Abraham, would side with the Hebrews against the Egyptians; like the Midianites, Moabites, Ammonites, and Ishmaelites.

Moreover, God said that he was going to perform some miracles beyond the imagination of mankind, and that when they were finished Pharaoh would let his people go as he commanded. He also stated that he would at the time fulfill his promise to Abraham the people in bondage would leave Egypt rich in monetary substance:

> "Then at last he will let you go. And I will cause the Egyptians to look favorably on you. They will give you gifts when you go so you will not leave empty-handed. Every Israelite woman will ask for articles of silver and gold and fine clothing from her Egyptian neighbors

and from the foreign women in their houses. You will dress your sons and daughters with these, stripping the Egyptians of their wealth."[276]

Moses Requests Proof from God

Moses had doubt whether or not the Hebrews would believe he was sent from God, or whether Pharaoh would even listen to him. Moses fear caused him and God to get into a long conversation:

Moses: And Moses answered and said, But, behold, they will not believe me, nor hearken unto my voice: for they will say, The Lord hath not appeared unto thee.

God: And the Lord said unto him, What is that in thine hand?

Moses: And he said, A rod.

God: And he said, Cast it on the ground. And he cast it on the ground, and it became a serpent;

Moses: and Moses fled from before it.

God: And the Lord said unto Moses, Put forth thine hand, and take it by the tail.

Moses: And he put forth his hand, and caught it, and it became a rod in his hand:

God: that they may believe that the Lord God of their fathers, the God of Abraham, the God of Isaac, and the God of Jacob, hath appeared unto thee.

God: And the Lord said furthermore unto him, Put now thine hand into thy bosom.

Moses: And he put his hand into his bosom: and when he took it out, behold, his hand was leprous as snow.

God: And he said, Put thine hand into thy bosom again.

Moses: And he put his hand into his bosom again; and plucked it out of his bosom, and, behold, it was turned again as his other flesh.

God: And it shall come to pass, if they will not believe thee, neither hearken to the voice of the first sign, that they will believe the voice of the latter sign. And it shall come to pass, if they will not believe also these two signs, neither hearken unto thy voice, that thou shalt take of the water of the river, and pour it upon the dry land: and the water which thou takest out of the river shall become blood upon the dry land.

Moses: And Moses said unto the Lord, O my Lord, I am not eloquent, neither heretofore, nor since thou hast spoken unto thy servant: but I am slow of speech, and of a slow tongue.

God: And the Lord said unto him, Who hath made man's mouth? or who maketh the dumb, or deaf, or the seeing, or the blind? have not I the Lord? Now therefore go, and I will be with thy mouth, and teach thee what thou shalt say.

Moses: And he said, O my Lord, send, I pray thee, by the hand of him whom thou wilt send.

God: And the anger of the Lord was kindled against Moses, and he said, Is not Aaron the Levite thy brother? I know that he can speak well. And also, behold, he cometh forth to meet thee: and when he seeth thee, he will be glad in his heart. And thou shalt speak unto him, and put words in his mouth: and I will be with thy mouth, and with his mouth, and will teach you what ye shall do. And he shall be thy spokesman unto the people: and he shall be, even he shall be to thee instead of a mouth, and thou shalt be to him instead of God. And thou shalt take this rod in thine hand, wherewith thou shalt do signs.

Jethro: And Moses went and returned to Jethro his father in law, and said unto him, Let me go, I pray thee, and return unto my brethren which are in Egypt, and see whether they be yet alive.

And Jethro said to Moses, Go in peace.

God: And the Lord said unto Moses in Midian, Go, return into Egypt: for all the men are dead which sought thy life.

Moses: And Moses took his wife and his sons, and set them upon an ass, and he returned to the land of Egypt: and Moses took the rod of God in his hand.

God: And the Lord said unto Moses, When thou goest to return into Egypt, see that thou do all those wonders before Pharaoh, which I have put in thine hand: but I will harden his heart, that he shall not let the people go. And thou shalt say unto Pharaoh, Thus saith the Lord, Israel is my son, even my firstborn: 23 and I say unto thee, Let my son go, that he may serve me: and if thou refuse to let him go, behold, I will slay thy son, even thy firstborn.

Moses Son is Circumcised

> "And it came to pass by the way in the inn, that the Lord met him, and sought to kill him. Then Zipporah took a sharp stone, and cut off the foreskin of her son, and cast it at his feet, and said, Surely a bloody husband art thou to me. So, he let him go: then she said, A bloody husband thou art, because of the circumcision."[277]

Aaron Meets Moses in the Desert

God: And the Lord said to Aaron, Go into the wilderness to meet Moses.

Aaron: And he went, and met him in the mount of God, and kissed him.

Moses: And Moses told Aaron all the words of the Lord who had sent him, and all the signs which he had commanded him.

Moses and Aaron Meet with the Elders

Moses and Aaron: And Moses and Aaron went and gathered together all the elders of the children of Israel:

Aaron: and Aaron spake all the words which the Lord had spoken unto Moses, and did the signs in the sight of the people.

The Hebrew People: And the people believed: and when they heard that the Lord had visited the children of Israel, and that he had looked upon their affliction, then they bowed their heads and worshipped.

Conclusion

When God sends you on a mission, he expects you to be faithful to the cause. Yet, if you have doubts, or questions, or feel that you don't measure up to the task he will:

- Listen to all your questions; for it is written, "Come now, and let us reason together, saith the Lord: though your sins be as scarlet, they shall be as white as snow; though they be red like crimson, they shall be as wool."[278]
- Second, if you lack the skills to complete his commandment, he will provide you a friend. He did this for the Apostle Paul

by giving him Barnabas; and after they split up, he gave him Silas.[279]

- And if you don't have an elegant speech pattern, he will give you the gift of the Holy Ghost: who will speak for you.[280]
- Lastly, he will equip you with his body armor, so that you will be protected from the fiery darts of the Devil.[281]

YEAR – 2668

Moses and Aaron Stand Before Pharaoh

Moses is 80 years old, and Aaron is 83 when they went to Pharaoh's court.[282] They gave Pharaoh God's message; and Pharaoh said, "Who is the Lord, that I should obey his voice to let Israel go? I know not the Lord, neither will I let Israel go."

Pharaoh's answer to God's request to let his people go into the desert, on a three-day journey, to worship him, was met with a commandment to work the Hebrews harder, and force them to gather straw from the wilderness to make bricks.

This edict by Pharaoh caused the Hebrews to confront and question Moses and Aaron's authority to represent God. Why? Because instead of being freed, their over life was made harder. In confusion, Moses presented the problem before God.

Moses: And Moses returned unto the Lord, and said, Lord, wherefore hast thou so evil entreated this people? why is it that thou hast sent me? For since I came to Pharaoh to speak in thy name, he hath done evil to this people; neither hast thou delivered thy people at all.

God: Then the Lord said unto Moses, Now shalt thou see what I will do to Pharaoh: for with a strong hand shall he let them go, and with a strong hand shall he drive them out of his land.

God reassures Moses of his name and power; and gives him

instruction to tell the children of Israel not worry, because he has heard their groaning, and will deliver them out of bondage. Moses did as God commanded but the people "hearkened not unto Moses for anguish of spirit, and for cruel bondage." Strangely, the fear of going back to confront Pharaoh brought on a long discussion between God and Moses.

God: And the Lord spake unto Moses, saying, Go in, speak unto Pharaoh king of Egypt, that he let the children of Israel go out of his land.

Moses: And Moses spake before the Lord, saying, Behold, the children of Israel have not hearkened unto me; how then shall Pharaoh hear me, who am of uncircumcised lips?

Moses and Aaron: And the Lord spake unto Moses and unto Aaron, and gave them a charge unto the children of Israel, and unto Pharaoh king of Egypt, to bring the children of Israel out of the land of Egypt.

God: "the Lord spake unto Moses, saying, I am the Lord: speak thou unto Pharaoh king of Egypt all that I say unto thee.

Moses: And Moses said before the Lord, Behold, I am of uncircumcised lips, and how shall Pharaoh hearken unto me?

God: And the Lord said unto <u>Moses, See, I have made thee a god to Pharaoh</u>: and <u>Aaron thy brother shall be thy prophet</u>. Thou shalt speak all that I command thee: and Aaron thy brother shall speak unto Pharaoh, that he send the children of Israel out of his land. And I will harden Pharaoh's heart, and multiply my signs and my wonders in the land of Egypt. But Pharaoh shall not hearken unto you, that I may lay my hand upon Egypt, and bring forth mine armies, and my people the children of Israel, out of the land of Egypt by great judgments. And the Egyptians shall know that I am the Lord, when

I stretch forth mine hand upon Egypt, and bring out the children of Israel from among them.

Moses and Aaron: And Moses and Aaron did as the Lord commanded them, so did they. And Moses was fourscore years old, and Aaron fourscore and three years old, when they spake unto Pharaoh.

Aaron's Staff Becomes a Serpent

God: And the Lord spake unto Moses and unto Aaron, saying, When Pharaoh shall speak unto you, saying, Shew a miracle for you: then thou shalt say unto Aaron, Take thy rod, and cast it before Pharaoh, and it shall become a serpent.

Moses and Aaron: And Moses and Aaron went in unto Pharaoh, and they did so as the Lord had commanded:

Aaron: and Aaron cast down his rod before Pharaoh, and before his servants, and it became a serpent.

Pharaoh: Then Pharaoh also called the wise men and the sorcerers: now the magicians of Egypt, they also did in like manner with their enchantments. For they cast down every man his rod, and they became serpents: but Aaron's rod swallowed up their rods. And he hardened Pharaoh's heart, that he hearkened not unto them; as the Lord had said.

CHAPTER 12

THE TEN PLAGUE'S

Once God showed his power to the Egyptians, he was now ready to demonstrate his might and dominance over the elements of the earth.[283] To accomplish this feat, God would use both Moses and Aaron. Further, God did not let his people suffer the plague's like the Egyptians, but he took them through the plague's liken unto Daniels three friends: Shadrach, Meshach, and Abednego in the fiery furnace.[284] Further, pay close attention to the dialogue between God, Moses, and Pharaoh; for God's simple request to let his people come out into the desert to worship him was rejected, and strongly resisted by Pharaoh.

1. The Plague of Blood

God to Moses: And the Lord said unto Moses, Pharaoh's heart is hardened, he refuseth to let the people go. Get thee unto Pharaoh in the morning; lo, he goeth out unto the water; and thou shalt stand by the river's brink against he come; and the rod which was turned to a serpent shalt thou take in thine hand. And thou shalt say unto him, The Lord God of the Hebrews hath sent me unto thee, saying, Let my people go, that they may serve me in the wilderness: and, behold, hitherto thou wouldest not hear.

The Sign: Thus saith the Lord, In this thou shalt know that I am the Lord: behold, I will smite with the rod that is in mine hand upon the waters which are in the river, and they shall be turned to blood. And the fish that is in the river shall die, and the river shall stink; and the Egyptians shall lothe to drink of the water of the river.

God to Aaron: And the Lord spake unto Moses, Say unto Aaron, Take thy rod, and stretch out thine hand upon the waters of Egypt, upon their streams, upon their rivers, and upon their ponds, and upon all their pools of water, that they may become blood; and that there may be blood throughout all the land of Egypt, both in vessels of wood, and in vessels of stone.

Moses and Aaron: And Moses and Aaron did so, as the Lord commanded; and he lifted up the rod, and smote the waters that were in the river, in the sight of Pharaoh, and in the sight of his servants; and all the waters that were in the river were turned to blood. And the fish that was in the river died; and the river stank, and the Egyptians could not drink of the water of the river; and there was blood throughout all the land of Egypt.

Pharaoh's Magicians: And the magicians of Egypt did so with their enchantments:

Pharaoh: and Pharaoh's heart was hardened, neither did he hearken unto them; as the Lord had said. And Pharaoh turned and went into his house, neither did he set his heart to this also.

The Egyptian People: And all the Egyptians digged round about the river for water to drink; for they could not drink of the water of the river.

The Length of the Plague: And seven days were fulfilled, after that the Lord had smitten the river.

2. The Plague of Frogs:

God to Moses:: And the Lord spake unto Moses, Go unto Pharaoh, and say unto him, Thus saith the Lord, Let my people go, that they may serve me. And if thou refuse to let them go, behold, I will smite all thy borders with frogs: and the river shall bring forth frogs abundantly, which shall go up and come into thine house, and into thy bedchamber, and upon thy bed, and into the house of thy servants, and upon thy people, and into thine ovens, and into thy kneading troughs: and the frogs shall come up both on thee, and upon thy people, and upon all thy servants.

God to Aaron: And the Lord spake unto Moses, Say unto Aaron, Stretch forth thine hand with thy rod over the streams, over the rivers, and over the ponds, and cause frogs to come up upon the land of Egypt. And Aaron stretched out his hand over the waters of Egypt; and the frogs came up, and covered the land of Egypt.

Pharaoh's Magicians: And the magicians did so with their enchantments, and brought up frogs upon the land of Egypt.

Pharaoh: Then Pharaoh called for Moses and Aaron, and said, Intreat the Lord, that he may take away the frogs from me, and from my people; and I will let the people go, that they may do sacrifice unto the Lord.

Moses: And Moses said unto Pharaoh, Glory over me: when shall I intreat for thee, and for thy servants, and for thy people, to destroy the frogs from thee and thy houses, that they may remain in the river only?

Pharaoh: And he said, Tomorrow.

Moses: And he said, Be it according to thy word: that thou mayest know that there is none like unto the Lord our God. And the frogs shall depart from thee, and from thy houses, and from thy servants, and from thy people; they shall remain in the river only.

Moses Prayer: And Moses and Aaron went out from Pharaoh: and Moses cried unto the Lord because of the frogs which he had brought against Pharaoh. And the Lord did according to the word of Moses; and the frogs died out of the houses, out of the villages, and out of the fields.

Egyptians: And they gathered them together upon heaps: and the land stank.

Pharaoh: But when Pharaoh saw that there was respite, he hardened his heart, and hearkened not unto them; as the Lord had said.

3. The Plague of Lice

God: And the Lord said unto Moses, Say unto Aaron, Stretch out thy rod, and smite the dust of the land, that it may become lice throughout all the land of Egypt.

Aaron: And they did so; for Aaron stretched out his hand with his rod, and smote the dust of the earth, and it became lice in man, and in beast; all the dust of the land became lice throughout all the land of Egypt.

Pharaoh's Magicians: And the magicians did so with their enchantments to bring forth lice, but they could not: so there were lice upon man, and upon beast. Then the magicians said unto Pharaoh, This is the finger of God: and Pharaoh's heart was hardened, and he hearkened not unto them; as the Lord had said.

4. The Plague of Flies

God: And the Lord said unto Moses, Rise up early in the morning, and stand before Pharaoh; lo, he cometh forth to the water; and say unto him, Thus saith the Lord, Let my people go, that they may serve me. Else, if thou wilt not let my people go, behold, I will send swarms of flies upon thee, and upon thy servants, and upon thy people, and into thy houses: and the houses of the Egyptians shall be full of swarms of flies, and also the ground whereon they are.

The Hebrew People: <u>And I will sever in that day the land of Goshen, in which my people dwell, that no swarms of flies shall be there; to the end thou mayest know that I am the Lord in the midst of the earth. And I will put a division between my people and thy people: tomorrow shall this sign be.</u>

The Flies: And the Lord did so; and there came a grievous swarm of flies into the house of Pharaoh, and into his servants' houses, and into all the land of Egypt: the land was corrupted by reason of the swarm of flies.

**Now there is no fence or wall separating the land of Goshen from the rest of Egypt. As a matter of record the land of Goshen is a wet land where you would expect a lot of flies, and other water breeding insects. Yet, God said that he would not allow the Hebrews to suffer "the plague of the flies" or any of the forwarding plagues. Similarly, Christ Jesus brought a great multitude out of the "Great Tribulation." (Revelation 7:9-17)

> **Goshen** - 1. Goshen was a region in Egypt. It was occupied by the Israelites during their journey in Egypt from the time of Joseph to the Exodus. Genesis 46-47 gives us several pieces of information concerning Goshen. It was a definite part of Egypt. It was the place where Joseph met his father after their

years of separation, when Jacob moved his family to Egypt. It was an area good for grazing flocks. Goshen has been associated with Egyptian bull cults and was important for the care and raising of domesticated animals. At one period the princes of Thebes sent their cattle to the Delta for pasture, even though it was controlled by the Hyksos. Sacred cattle were probably pastured there by Egyptians also. Goshen is called "the best of the land" in two different verses (Genesis 47:6, 11) and is identified as the "land of Rameses." In addition, Goshen probably had a military outpost on its eastern border.

2. Goshen was a region of about 900 square miles, consisting of two districts. The western half ran from Zoan to Bubastis, a distance of about 35 miles from north to south. This district was an irrigated plain, containing some of the most fertile land in Egypt. It is about 15 miles wide at the Mediterranean Sea and narrows to about 10 miles between Zagazig and Tell el-Kebir on the south. The eastern sector contains a large desert area between the Nile Plain and the Suez. As it stretches to the south from Daphnai to the Wadi Tumilat, it increases in width to about 40 miles from east to west. South of this section more desert area stretches to the Suez on the south and from the Bitter Lakes on the east to Heliopolis on the west. The physical arrangement of Goshen is important in determining the route of the Exodus. Given the above description, the Wadi Tumilat would have been the most logical route to the Red Sea for people who were driving flocks and herds. The route would have led from the south side of the field of Zoan near Bubastis, east of the edge of the wilderness and the head of the Bitter Lakes.[285]

Pharaoh: And Pharaoh called for Moses and for Aaron, and said, Go ye, sacrifice to your God in the land.

Moses: And Moses said, It is not meet so to do; for we shall sacrifice the abomination of the Egyptians to the Lord our God: lo, shall we sacrifice the abomination of the Egyptians before their eyes, and will they not stone us? We will go three days' journey into the wilderness, and sacrifice to the Lord our God, as he shall command us.

Pharaoh: And Pharaoh said, I will let you go, that ye may sacrifice to the Lord your God in the wilderness; only ye shall not go very far away: intreat for me.

Moses: And Moses said, Behold, I go out from thee, and I will intreat the Lord that the swarms of flies may depart from Pharaoh, from his servants, and from his people, tomorrow: but let not Pharaoh deal deceitfully any more in not letting the people go to sacrifice to the Lord.

Moses Prayer: And Moses went out from Pharaoh, and intreated the Lord. And the Lord did according to the word of Moses; and he removed the swarms of flies from Pharaoh, from his servants, and from his people; there remained not one.

Pharaoh: And Pharaoh hardened his heart at this time also, neither would he let the people go.

5. The Plague of Animal Disease

God: Then the Lord said unto Moses, Go in unto Pharaoh, and tell him, Thus saith the Lord God of the Hebrews, Let my people go, that they may serve me. For if thou refuse to let them go, and wilt hold them still, behold, the hand of the Lord is upon thy cattle which is in the field, upon the horses, upon the asses, upon the camels, upon the oxen, and upon the sheep: there shall be a very grievous murrain.

The Hebrews: And the Lord shall sever between the cattle of Israel and the cattle of Egypt: and there shall nothing die of all that is the children's of Israel.

The Time of the Plague: And the Lord appointed a set time, saying, Tomorrow the Lord shall do this thing in the land.

The Plague: And the Lord did that thing on the morrow, and all the cattle of Egypt died: but of the cattle of the children of Israel died not one.

Pharaoh: And Pharaoh sent, and, behold, there was not one of the cattle of the Israelites dead. And the heart of Pharaoh was hardened, and he did not let the people go.

**Take note that physical evidence of God's power would not sway Pharaoh's hardened heart.

6. The Plague of Boils

God: And the Lord said unto Moses and unto Aaron, Take to you handfuls of ashes of the furnace, and let Moses sprinkle it toward the heaven in the sight of Pharaoh. And it shall become small dust in all the land of Egypt, and shall be a boil breaking forth with blains upon man, and upon beast, throughout all the land of Egypt.

Moses and Aaron: And they took ashes of the furnace, and stood before Pharaoh; and Moses sprinkled it up toward heaven; and it became a boil breaking forth with blains upon man, and upon beast.

Pharaoh's Magicians: And the magicians could not stand before Moses because of the boils; for the boil was upon the magicians, and upon all the Egyptians.

Pharaoh: And the Lord hardened the heart of Pharaoh, and he hearkened not unto them; as the Lord had spoken unto Moses.

7. The Plague of Hail

God: And the Lord said unto Moses, Rise up early in the morning, and stand before Pharaoh, and say unto him, Thus saith the Lord God of the Hebrews, Let my people go, that they may serve me. For I will at this time send all my plagues upon thine heart, and upon thy servants, and upon thy people; that thou mayest know that there is none like me in all the earth.

- For now I will stretch out my hand, that I may smite thee and thy people with pestilence; and thou shalt be cut off from the earth.
- And in very deed for this cause have I raised thee up, for to shew in thee my power; and that my name may be declared throughout all the earth.
- As yet exaltest thou thyself against my people, that thou wilt not let them go?
- Behold, tomorrow about this time I will cause it to rain a very grievous hail, such as hath not been in Egypt since the foundation thereof even until now.
- Send therefore now, and gather thy cattle, and all that thou hast in the field; for upon every man and beast which shall be found in the field, and shall not be brought home, the hail shall come down upon them, and they shall die.

The Egyptians: He that feared the word of the Lord among the servants of Pharaoh made his servants and his cattle flee into the houses: and he that regarded not the word of the Lord left his servants and his cattle in the field.

God: And the Lord said unto Moses, Stretch forth thine hand toward heaven, that there may be hail in all the land of Egypt, upon man, and upon beast, and upon every herb of the field, throughout the land of Egypt.

Moses: And Moses stretched forth his rod toward heaven: and the Lord sent thunder and hail, and the fire ran along upon the ground; and the Lord rained hail upon the land of Egypt. So there was hail, and fire mingled with the hail, very grievous, such as there was none like it in all the land of Egypt since it became a nation. And the hail smote throughout all the land of Egypt all that was in the field, both man and beast; and the hail smote every herb of the field, and brake every tree of the field.

The Hebrews: <u>Only in the land of Goshen, where the children of Israel were, was there no hail.</u>

Pharaoh: And Pharaoh sent, and called for Moses and Aaron, and said unto them, I have sinned this time: the Lord is righteous, and I and my people are wicked. Intreat the Lord (for it is enough) that there be no more mighty thundering's and hail; and I will let you go, and ye shall stay no longer.

Moses: And Moses said unto him, As soon as I am gone out of the city, I will spread abroad my hands unto the Lord; and the thunder shall cease, neither shall there be any more hail; that thou mayest know how that the earth is the Lord's. But as for thee and thy servants, I know that ye will not yet fear the Lord God.

The Damage of the Hail: And the flax and the barley was smitten: for the barley was in the ear, and the flax was bolled. But the wheat and the rie were not smitten: for they were not grown up.

Moses Prayer: And Moses went out of the city from Pharaoh, and spread abroad his hands unto the Lord: and the thunders and hail ceased, and the rain was not poured upon the earth.

Pharaoh: And when Pharaoh saw that the rain and the hail and the thunders were ceased, he sinned yet more, and hardened his heart, he and his servants. And the heart of Pharaoh was hardened, neither would he let the children of Israel go; as the Lord had spoken by Moses.

8. The Plague of Locusts

God: And the Lord said unto Moses, Go in unto Pharaoh: for I have hardened his heart, and the heart of his servants, that I might shew these my signs before him:

Reason for the Plague's: and that thou mayest tell in the ears of thy son, and of thy son's son, what things I have wrought in Egypt, and my signs which I have done among them; that ye may know how that I am the Lord.

Moses and Aaron: And Moses and Aaron came in unto Pharaoh, and said unto him, Thus saith the Lord God of the Hebrews, How long wilt thou refuse to humble thyself before me? let my people go, that they may serve me. Else, if thou refuse to let my people go, behold, tomorrow will I bring the locusts into thy coast: and they shall cover the face of the earth, that one cannot be able to see the earth: and they shall eat the residue of that which is escaped, which remaineth unto you from the hail, and shall eat every tree which groweth for you out of the field: and they shall fill thy houses, and the houses of all thy servants, and the houses of all the Egyptians; which neither thy fathers, nor thy fathers' fathers have seen, since the day that they were upon the earth unto this day. And he turned himself, and went out from Pharaoh.

Pharaoh's Staff: And Pharaoh's servants said unto him, How long shall this man be a snare unto us? let the men go, that they may serve the Lord their God: knowest thou not yet that Egypt is destroyed?

Pharaoh: And Moses and Aaron were brought again unto Pharaoh: and he said unto them, Go, serve the Lord your God: but who are they that shall go?

Moses: And Moses said, We will go with our young and with our old, with our sons and with our daughters, with our flocks and with our herds will we go; for we must hold a feast unto the Lord.

Pharaoh: And he said unto them, Let the Lord be so with you, as I will let you go, and your little ones: look to it; for evil is before you. Not so: go now ye that are men, and serve the Lord; for that ye did desire. And they were driven out from Pharaoh's presence.

God: <u>And the Lord said unto Moses, Stretch out thine hand over the land of Egypt for the locusts, that they may come up upon the land of Egypt, and eat every herb of the land, even all that the hail hath left.</u>

Moses: And Moses stretched forth his rod over the land of Egypt, and the Lord brought an east wind upon the land all that day, and all that night; and when it was morning, the east wind brought the locusts. And the locusts went up over all the land of Egypt, and rested in all the coasts of Egypt: very grievous were they; before them there were no such locusts as they, neither after them shall be such. For they covered the face of the whole earth, so that the land was darkened; and they did eat every herb of the land, and all the fruit of the trees which the hail had left: and there remained not any green thing in the trees, or in the herbs of the field, through all the land of Egypt.

Pharaoh: Then Pharaoh called for Moses and Aaron in haste; and he said, I have sinned against the Lord your God, and against you. Now therefore forgive, I pray thee, my sin only this once, and intreat the Lord your God, that he may take away from me this death only.

Moses Prayer: And he went out from Pharaoh, and intreated the Lord. And the Lord turned a mighty strong west wind, which took away the locusts, and cast them into the Red sea; there remained not one locust in all the coasts of Egypt.

Pharaoh: But the Lord hardened Pharaoh's heart, so that he would not let the children of Israel go.

9. The Plague of Darkness

God: And the Lord said unto Moses, <u>Stretch out thine hand toward heaven, that there may be darkness over the land of Egypt, even darkness which may be felt.</u>

Moses: And Moses stretched forth his hand toward heaven; <u>and there was a thick darkness in all the land of Egypt three days:</u> they saw not one another, neither rose any from his place for three days:

The Hebrews: <u>but all the children of Israel had light in their dwellings.</u>

Pharaoh: And Pharaoh called unto Moses, and said, Go ye, serve the Lord; only let your flocks and your herds be stayed: let your little ones also go with you.

Moses: And Moses said, Thou must give us also sacrifices and burnt offerings, that we may sacrifice unto the Lord our God. Our cattle also shall go with us; there shall not an hoof be left behind; for thereof must we take to serve the Lord our God; and we know not with what we must serve the Lord, until we come thither.

Pharaoh: But the Lord hardened Pharaoh's heart, and he would not let them go. And Pharaoh said unto him, Get thee from me, take heed to thyself, see my face no more; for in that day thou seest my face thou shalt die.

Moses: And Moses said, Thou hast spoken well, I will see thy face again no more.

10. The Plague of Death

God: And the Lord said unto Moses, Yet will I bring one plague more upon Pharaoh, and upon Egypt; afterwards he will let you go hence: when he shall let you go, he shall surely thrust you out hence altogether.

- Speak now in the ears of the people, and let every man borrow of his neighbour, and every woman of her neighbour, jewels of silver, and jewels of gold.

- And the Lord gave the people favour in the sight of the Egyptians.

Moreover the man Moses was very great in the land of Egypt, in the sight of Pharaoh's servants, and in the sight of the people.

Moses: And Moses said, Thus saith the Lord,

- About midnight will I go out into the midst of Egypt: and all the firstborn in the land of Egypt shall die, from the firstborn of Pharaoh that sitteth upon his throne, even unto the firstborn of the maidservant that is behind the mill; and all the firstborn of beasts. And there shall be a great cry throughout all the land of Egypt, such as there was none like it, nor shall be like it any more.

- But against any of the children of Israel shall not a dog move his tongue, against man or beast: that ye may know how that the Lord doth put a difference between the Egyptians and Israel. *God protected the Hebrews with the blood of the "Passover Lamb."*

- And all these thy servants shall come down unto me, and bow down themselves unto me, saying, Get thee out, and all the people that follow thee: and after that I will go out. And he went out from Pharaoh in a great anger.

God: And the Lord said unto Moses, Pharaoh shall not hearken unto you; that my wonders may be multiplied in the land of Egypt. And Moses and Aaron did all these wonders before Pharaoh: and the Lord hardened Pharaoh's heart, so that he would not let the children of Israel go out of his land.

***Death came upon the first born of all those not protected by the blood of the Passover Lamb. In the New Testament this protection is granted to all those who believe in Jesus Christ, and the blood he shed on the cross.*

The Plague: And it came to pass, that at midnight the Lord smote all the firstborn in the land of Egypt, from the firstborn of Pharaoh that sat on his throne unto the firstborn of the captive that was in the dungeon; and all the firstborn of cattle.

Pharaoh: And Pharaoh rose up in the night, he, and all his servants, and all the Egyptians; and there was a great cry in Egypt; for there was not a house where there was not one dead.

Pharaoh calls for Moses and Aaron: And he called for Moses and Aaron by night, and said, Rise up, and get you forth from among my people, both ye and the children of Israel; and go, serve the Lord, as ye have said. Also take your flocks and your herds, as ye have said, and be gone; and bless me also.

The Egyptians: And the Egyptians were urgent upon the people, that they might send them out of the land in haste; for they said, We be all dead men.

The Hebrews: And the people took their dough before it was leavened, their kneading troughs being bound up in their clothes upon their shoulders. And the children of Israel did according to the word of Moses; and they borrowed of the Egyptians jewels of silver, and jewels of gold, and raiment: and the Lord gave the people favour in the sight of the Egyptians, so that they lent unto them such things as they required. And they spoiled the Egyptians.

Note: <u>Question:</u> *Would God keep his word to bring the children of Israel back to Egypt if Pharaoh had let them go into the desert, on a three-day journey, to worship him? The answer is yes; based on Moses confession of truth: "God is not a man, that he should lie; neither the son of man, that he should repent: hath he said, and shall he not do it? or hath he spoken, and shall he not make it good"*[286]

However, Pharaoh was quick to realize that a three-day journey, into the Sinai desert would cover over a sixty-mile trek. In Pharaohs mind (as it is with all slave masters,) once the slaves leave, and take all their possessions, to include women and children, they will not be in a hurry to return to their slavery duties. Therefore, Pharaoh resisted the request of God.

And let's not forget that God asked Pharaoh to let them go to worship him; but he could have forced Pharaoh with fire from heaven (as he did at Sodom and Gomorra); if he wanted too. Yet, God chose to demonstrate / show his power over the elements of the earth as a means to gain the confidence of his people Israel. Jesus Christ also used this method to gain the confidence of his followers, i.e. turning water into wine, walking on water, multiplying two fish and seven loves of bread to feed over five thousand hungry souls, and etc.

CHAPTER 13

THE PASSOVER

There is no other ordinance in the bible that is greater than the Passover decree. For it is this set of instructions that is locked into the Hebrew time line of 'forever." And is the root of passing from physical death into eternal life with God. It is also the bridge in which God set in motion that Christ would be the doorway to heaven.

Therefore, it would behoove us to fully understand the whole concept of the Passover, and the conduct concerning its rules. Right here I'm going to give you the full scope of instructions God gave Moses and the children of Israel; this is in direct correlation with the Lord Jesus Christ and the cross. Make no mistake, if there is no "Passover," there is no cross, or resurrection of the dead.

The Time of the Passover

God: And the Lord spake unto Moses and Aaron in the land of Egypt, saying,

The First Month of the Hebrew Year

- This month shall be unto you the beginning of months: it shall be the first month of the year to you.

> ***Nisan*** – *The first month of the Hebrew Sacred Calendar Year, which is based on the new moon in March and ends in April (a thirty-day period)*[287]

The Ten day of the month Nisan

- Speak ye unto all the congregation of Israel, saying, In the tenth day of this month they shall take to them every man a lamb, according to the house of their fathers, a lamb for an house: and if the household be too little for the lamb, let him and his neighbour next unto his house take it according to the number of the souls; every man according to his eating shall make your count for the lamb.

- Your lamb shall be without blemish, a male of the first year: ye shall take it out from the sheep, or from the goats:

The Fourteenth day of the month Nisan

- and ye shall keep it up until the fourteenth day of the same month: and the whole assembly of the congregation of Israel shall kill it in the evening.

- And they shall take of the blood, and strike it on the two side posts and on the upper door post of the houses, wherein they shall eat it.

- And they shall eat the flesh in that night, roast with fire, and unleavened bread; and with bitter herbs they shall eat it.

- Eat not of it raw, nor sodden at all with water, but roast with fire; his head with his legs, and with the purtenance thereof.

- And ye shall let nothing of it remain until the morning; and that which remaineth of it until the morning ye shall burn with fire.

- And thus shall ye eat it; with your loins girded, your shoes on your feet, and your staff in your hand; and ye shall eat it in haste: it is the Lord's passover.

- For I will pass through the land of Egypt this night, and will smite all the firstborn in the land of Egypt, both man and beast; and against all the gods of Egypt I will execute judgment: I am the Lord.

- And the blood shall be to you for a token upon the houses where ye are: and when I see the blood, I will pass over you, and the plague shall not be upon you to destroy you, when I smite the land of Egypt.

- <u>And this day shall be unto you for a memorial; and ye shall keep it a feast to the Lord throughout your generations; ye shall keep it a feast by an ordinance for ever.</u>

The Feast of Unleavened Bread

Seven days shall ye eat unleavened bread; even the first day ye shall put away leaven out of your houses: for whosoever eateth leavened bread from the first day until the seventh day, that soul shall be cut off from Israel.

The Fifteenth Day of the month Nisan (a high sabbath day){John 19:31}

  ◦ And in the first day there shall be an holy convocation,

The Twenty-first Day of the month Nisan **(a high sabbath day)**

  ◦ and in the seventh day there shall be an holy convocation to you; no manner of work shall be done in them, save that which every man must eat, that only may be done of you.

- And ye shall observe the feast of unleavened bread; for in this selfsame day have I brought your armies out of the land of Egypt: therefore shall ye observe this day in your generations by an ordinance for ever.

The Passover is An Eight Day Observance

- In the first month, on the fourteenth day of the month at even, ye shall eat unleavened bread, until the one and twentieth day of the month at even.
- Seven days shall there be no leaven found in your houses: for whosoever eateth that which is leavened, even that soul shall be cut off from the congregation of Israel, whether he be a stranger, or born in the land. Ye shall eat nothing leavened; in all your habitations shall ye eat unleavened bread.

Moses: Then Moses called for all the elders of Israel, and said unto them, Draw out and take you a lamb according to your families, and kill the passover.

- And ye shall take a bunch of hyssop, and dip it in the blood that is in the basin, and strike the lintel and the two side posts with the blood that is in the basin;
- and none of you shall go out at the door of his house until the morning.
- For the Lord will pass through to smite the Egyptians; and when he seeth the blood upon the lintel, and on the two side posts, the Lord will pass over the door, and will not suffer the destroyer to come in unto your houses to smite you.
- And ye shall observe this thing for an ordinance to thee and to thy sons for ever.
- And it shall come to pass, when ye be come to the land which the Lord will give you, according as he hath promised, that ye shall keep this service.

- And it shall come to pass, when your children shall say unto you, What mean ye by this service? That ye shall say, It is the sacrifice of the Lord's passover, who passed over the houses of the children of Israel in Egypt, when he smote the Egyptians, and delivered our houses.

The Hebrews: And the people bowed the head and worshipped. And the children of Israel went away, and did as the Lord had commanded Moses and Aaron, so did they.

Passover Rules

God: And the Lord said unto Moses and Aaron, This is the ordinance of the passover:

<u>There shall no stranger eat thereof</u>:

- but every man's servant that is bought for money, when thou hast circumcised him, then shall he eat thereof.
- <u>A foreigner and an hired servant shall not eat thereof.</u>
- In one house shall it be eaten; thou shalt not carry forth ought of the flesh abroad out of the house; <u>neither shall ye break a bone thereof.</u>
- All the congregation of Israel shall keep it.
- And when a stranger shall sojourn with thee, and will keep the passover to the Lord, let all his males be circumcised, and then let him come near and keep it; and he shall be as one that is born in the land: for no uncircumcised person shall eat thereof.
- <u>One law shall be to him that is homeborn, and unto the stranger that sojourneth among you.</u>
- Thus did all the children of Israel; as the Lord commanded Moses and Aaron, so did they.
- And it came to pass the selfsame day, that the Lord did bring the children of Israel out of the land of Egypt by their armies.

CHAPTER 14

CHRIST AND THE CHILDREN OF ISRAEL

The apostle Paul wrote the epistle of 1 Corinthians to the Corinth Church around 56 AD. He talked about faith, love, unity, grace, marriage, social relationships between believers and unbelievers, righteousness and unrighteousness, who will enter into God's kingdom and who will not, keeping the body pure for the Holy Ghost, the principles of liberty in Christ and the effect on weaker believers, and the rights and wrongs of ministry.

But in chapter ten he switches the thought, and tells his readers that Christ was in the desert with Moses and the children of Israel. Is this true? Can we really believe Christ Jesus was with Moses and the children of Israel when they traveled across the Sinai Desert for forty years? There is only one way to find out, and that is to examine the Scriptures. Let's look at what Paul wrote (**1 Corinthians 10: 1-11**):

- Moreover, brethren, I would not that ye should be ignorant, how that all our fathers were under the cloud, and all passed through the sea; (See Exodus 12-14:22)

- And were all baptized unto Moses in the cloud and in the sea; (See Exodus 14: 23-31)

- And did all eat the same spiritual meat; (See Exodus 16:1–35)

- And did all drink the same spiritual drink: for they drank of that spiritual Rock that followed them: and that Rock was Christ. (See Exodus 17:1–7; 23:20–24)

- But with many of them God was not well pleased: for they were overthrown in the wilderness. (See Numbers 13–14)

- Now these things were our examples, to the intent we should not lust after evil things, as they also lusted. (See Numbers 9–11)

- Neither be ye idolaters, as were some of them; as it is written, The people sat down to eat and drink, and rose up to play. (See Exodus 32)

- Neither let us commit fornication, as some of them committed, and fell in one day three and twenty thousand. (See Numbers 25:1–9)

- Neither let us tempt Christ, as some of them also tempted, and were destroyed of serpents. (See Numbers 21:4–9)

- Neither murmur ye, as some of them also murmured, and were destroyed of the destroyer. (See Numbers 16)

- Now all these things happened unto them for ensamples: and they are written for our admonition, upon whom the ends of the world are come.

I'm going to cross-reference each verse with its corresponding event, and dwell heavily on the storyline of the Scriptures to flush out what Paul wrote. So, let's get to the truth!

The Children of Israel Passes through the Red Sea (Exodus Chapters 12–14)

God used Moses to deliver the children of Israel out of the land of Egypt under the sign of ten devastating plagues. The children of Israel spent 430 years in Egypt [Year 2238 to 2668]; many of them under bondage and slavery. In my estimation, the number that came out of Egypt was close to two million people:[288]

- Seed of Abraham: 600 thousand men, 700 thousand women, and 300 thousand children
- A mixed multitude: 100 thousand.

I hope you noticed that not everyone who came out with Moses were from the loins of Jacob (Israel). Yet God called the whole group "the children of Israel." This means God has no respect of person, and that he keeps his promise. He promised Abraham he would keep covenant with any family whose male(s) accepted the rite of circumcision. He would be their God, and they would be his son(s)[289]

This invitation was extended to all humankind by Christ when he said, "For God so loved the world that he gave his only begotten Son, that whosoever believeth in him should not perish, but have everlasting life. For God sent not his Son into the world to condemn the world; but that the world through him might be saved."[290]

To follow Christ the heart must be circumcised and not the flesh of man; for the foreskin of sin must be cut away from the heart (and destroyed), and replaced by the Spirit of God (the Holy Ghost) so that we can bring praise unto God through worshiping him.[291]

The children of Israel didn't just walk out into the desert. They were led by God in a pillar of cloud by day, and a pillar of fire by night.

For whatever the reason, Pharaoh decided to follow after them with his entire army of chariots (six hundred chosen chariots and all the chariots of Egypt).

The children of Israel became frightened when they saw the army behind them, and the Red Sea to their front; and they first cried out to God: then they lashed out against Moses, because they thought he brought them into the desert to die. God heard their cry, and informed Moses he was going to destroy Pharaoh's army. And that is when a strange thing happened. Experience the words with me:

- And <u>the angel of God, which went before the camp of Israel, removed and went behind them;</u>

- and <u>the pillar of the cloud went from before their face, and stood behind them</u>:

- And it came between the camp of the Egyptians and the camp of Israel;

- and <u>it was a cloud and darkness to them,</u> (*Egyptians*)

- <u>but it gave light by night to these</u>: (*Hebrews*)

- so that the one came not near the other all the night.[292]

Now "<u>the angel of God, which went before the camp of Israel</u>" is further explained in Exodus Chapter 23:20-23. But what I want you to notice with great observance is the fact that there are now two celestial beings hovering over the camp of Israel. Yet, previously the author only mentioned the pillar of cloud by day, and the same cloud turning into a pillar of fire by night.

However, now there are two up in the sky. The first one goes and gets between the Hebrews and the Egyptians. Then the pillar of cloud joins the first one: one is a bright light, while the other one is deep darkness (or you could say blacker than black). This ensured that the two opposing people could not see, or come near each other.

Earlier, in Genesis chapter one, verses one thru five, we explored the idea that the light was Christ, and the darkness was the cloak of God.[293] Here I want to say that my bible experience and research concludes that the Father, Word, and Holy Ghost always travel together, and work together as one: and are one indeed.[294]

So, I'm going to stretch a little here by saying this is a good demonstration of the Father (God), and the Son (Christ, the Word of God) working together for the people called by their name. The Holy Ghost is not mentioned, but we know he is there; because the triune Godhead is never separated.

When Moses saw the light and the darkness unfold, he stretched his rod out toward the Red Sea, "and the Lord caused the sea to go back by a strong east wind all that night, and made the sea dry land, and the waters were divided. And the children of Israel went into the midst of the sea upon the dry ground: and the waters were a wall unto them on their right hand, and on their left."[295]

Now the question begs itself, "how wide would the pathway across the Red Sea have to be for around two million people to pass safely to the other side? Not easily answered. But looking at when Joshua led the children of Israel across the flooded Jordon river; God backed the river uphill for approximately eighteen miles: from Jericho to Adam.[296]

Surely you can see that Moses and the children of Israel passed through the Red Sea (below the water surface line) on dry land; looking up at water on both their left and right sides. Therefore, Paul correctly said they were under the cloud, in the presence of God the Father, and they all passed through the Red Sea—passed from death unto life. They were all baptized unto Moses (the lawgiver) in the cloud, in the presence of Christ, and in the sea: a symbol of water baptism.[297]

God Provides Manna [bread] from Heaven (Exodus 16:1-35)

As the children of Israel traveled across the Sinai Desert, they began to complain to Moses and Aaron about the shortage of food: "would to God we had died by the hand of the Lord in the land of

Egypt, when we sat by the flesh pots, and when we did eat bread to the full; for ye have brought us forth into this wilderness, to kill this whole assembly with hunger." I experienced this same type of anger during the time of war in the military, and when my wife felt her hunger pains. The dread of hunger can cause the sweetest lips to spew out anger and curses.

As always, God heard their cry. He told Moses he was going to bring quail for them to eat in the evening, and would rain down bread from heaven for them to eat each morning. The bread would be available each morning for six days. On the sixth day, twice as much would be gathered to carry over to the seventh day, because gathering on the Sabbath was forbidden.

The children of Israel called this bread from heaven "manna," because it was "a small round thing, as small as the hoar frost on the ground." They ate this manna for forty years; until they finally reached the Jordan River and crossed into the promised Canaan land.

In the gospel of John, Christ told the Jews they sought after him not because of the miracles he performed, but because they did eat of the "five barley loaves and two small fishes" that fed well over five thousand men. And if you count women and children, this number could increase to approximately ten thousand. They took up twelve baskets of fragments after everyone ate.

Further, Christ said unto them, "Labour not for the meat which perisheth, but for that meat which endureth unto everlasting life, which the Son of man shall give unto you: for him hath God the Father sealed."

In their answer to him, the Jews wanted to know what would be required to obtain the power of God to work the miracles. Jesus replied, "This is the work of God that ye believe on him whom he hath sent." The Jews then put forth a twofold question: (1) they wanted him to show them a sign from God, so they could believe in him, and what he was saying; (2) and how was believing in him going to increase their bread? They went on to say that history revealed, "Our fathers did eat manna in the desert; as it is written, He gave them bread from heaven to eat."

Christ agreed with them that God did provide manna for Moses and the children of Israel, but God was now giving them the true bread from heaven: "For the bread of God is he which cometh down from heaven, and giveth life unto the world." With gladness they cried out, "Lord, evermore give us this bread." Jesus answer to them simply said, "I am the bread of life: he that cometh to me shall never hunger; and he that believeth on me shall never thirst."[298]

Just as God provided manna to Moses and the children of Israel as they traveled toward the promised Canaan land, Christ has promised to sustain his believers for eternity with bread and water from heaven as we strive to reach the New Jerusalem in the new heaven and new earth.

So, God (the Father) sent the true bread down from heaven, to the earth for humankind to eat. A small number ate of this bread and were saved. But a very large number rejected this bread and were destroyed. Therefore, there seems to be two paths for humankind to walk while on this earth. One leads to eternal life, and the other to eternal damnation. The choice between the two can be taken until the last breath.

Christ Jesus explained these two paths when he said, "Enter ye in at the strait gate: for wide is the gate, and broad is the way, that leadeth to destruction, and many there be which go in thereat: because strait is the gate, and narrow is the way, which leadeth unto life, and few there be that find it."[299]

The Narrow Way

When a person gives his or her life over to Christ, the individual enters into the holiness of God; for He saith, "Be ye holy because I am holy."[300] The apostle Paul said it this way: "Therefore if any man be in Christ, he is a new creature: old things are passed away; behold all things are become new."[301] This means you must put away the things of the world, and learn how to live within the statures, ordinances, and precepts of God. An example of this is given in Ephesians, and Colossians.[302] And make no mistake, God intends for those who follow him to study and adhere to his every word; this is stated in the Old and New Testaments.[303]

The Broad Way

The broad-way is the path every living soul starts his journey of life on. They are going about their daily routines of eating, drinking, marrying, giving in marriage [arranged marriages], planting, harvesting, and so on. They live in misery according to the flesh of their bodies, and don't realize a great and terrible war is being fought within their bodies. Plus, they ignorant of the eternal destruction that awaits them if they continue in this mold.

And why is all this fighting going on in the body of mankind? The answer is found in the Garden of Eden where Satan convinced two innocent people to disobey God, and eat from the "Tree of the Knowledge of Good and Evil." The Bible tells us exactly how this war is being conducted, and what the end result is for those who lose the battle. Victory can only be achieved through Christ Jesus. Now don't take the Scripture[304] I'm going to present lightly. Study it very carefully.

- *Lifelong campaign of war:* This I say then, Walk in the Spirit, and ye shall not fulfil the lust of the flesh. For the flesh lusteth against the Spirit, and the Spirit against the flesh: and these are contrary the one to the other: so that ye cannot do the things that ye would. But if ye be led of the Spirit, ye are not under the law.

- *Those who lose the battle:* Now the works of the flesh are manifest, which are these; Adultery, fornication, uncleanness, lasciviousness. Idolatry, witchcraft, hatred, variance, emulations, wrath, strife, seditions, heresies, Envyings, murders, drunkenness, revellings, and such like: of the which I tell you before, as I have also told you in time past, that they which do such things shall not inherit the kingdom of God.

- ***Those who gain victory through Christ Jesus:*** But the fruit of the Spirit is love, joy, peace, longsuffering, gentleness, goodness, faith, Meekness, temperance: against such there is no law. And they that are Christ's have crucified the flesh with the affections and lusts. If we live in the Spirit, let us also walk in the Spirit. Let us not be desirous of vain glory, provoking one another, envying one another.

I have heard, and know for a fact that some do not want to be a follower of Christ—become a Christian—because they have to give up the things of the world. A man once told me he wanted to go to hell, because that's where all the hot women were. I agreed with him that yes, the women there will be hot, and just right for his hotness. But the truth of the whole matter is that you must give up sinful ways, which the world loves, to be with God in the New Jerusalem. John made this concept plain when he wrote:

- **1 John** 15 Love not the world, neither the things that are in the world. If any man love the world, the love of the Father is not in him.
  16 For all that is in the world, the lust of the flesh, and the lust of the eyes, and the pride of life, is not of the Father, but is of the world.
  17 And the world passeth away, and the lust thereof: but he that doeth the will of God abideth for ever.

What the world doesn't realize is that the Bible is true, and that God stands on all his promises. But you have to hold onto your faith in the Lord Jesus Christ until you take your last breath of life. Are you convinced about the Lord Jesus Christ yet? Let's explore on.

Christ Provides Water from a Rock (Exodus 17:1–7)

As the children of Israel traveled further and further into the Sinai Desert, they found water increasingly difficult to find. So, they began to grumble, complain, groan, murmur, and argue with Moses, saying, "Wherefore is this that thou hast brought us up out of Egypt, to kill us and our children and our cattle with thirst?" Behind these words came a threat to stone Moses to death. This crisis caused Moses to cry out to the Lord about the people's partition and threats. Christ intervened and provided water for Moses and the people. But how it was done is what Paul wrote about.

- And the Lord said unto Moses, Go on before the people, and take with thee of the elders of Israel; and thy rod, wherewith thou smotest the river, take in thine hand, and go.

- <u>Behold, I will stand before thee there upon the rock in Horeb; and thou shalt smite the rock, and there shall come water out of it,</u> that the people may drink.

Christ's instructions to Moses were very simple and easy to follow. But did you notice he told Moses to strike the rock when Moses saw him standing on it? This implies that Christ changed the elements of the rock to form water when Moses struck the rock. He demonstrated this when he changed water into wine at the wedding banquet in Cana of Galilee.[305]

Some years later, we find Moses and the children of Israel in a similar situation. They are out of water and complaining, "Would God that we had died when our brethren died before the Lord! And why have ye brought up the congregation of the Lord into this wilderness, that we and our cattle should die there? And wherefore have ye made us to come up out of Egypt, to bring us in unto this evil place? it is no place of seed, or of figs, or of vines, or of pomegranates; neither is there any water to drink."[306]

However, instead of standing on the rock as before, "the glory of the Lord appeared unto them. And the Lord spake unto Moses, saying, Take the rod, and gather thou the assembly together, thou, and Aaron thy brother, and speak ye unto the rock before their eyes; and it shall give forth his water, and thou shalt bring forth to them water out of the rock: so thou shalt give the congregation and their beasts drink."

Moses was so furious at the children of Israel that he took his rod and struck the rock until water came out. This act of disobedience displeased God. He said to Moses and Aaron, "Because ye believed me not, to sanctify me in the eyes of the children of Israel, therefore ye shall not bring this congregation into the land which I have given them."

Aaron died right after this event, but Moses was allowed to travel to the borders of the Promised Land and look upon its beauty. However, he was restricted from entering the Promised Land with the children of Israel. But Christ still allowed water to come from the rock to quench the people's thirst.

Christ has put the same kind of restriction on those who won't have a change of heart and believe in him. For he told the Pharisees, "I go my way, and ye shall seek me, and shall die in your sins: whither I go, ye cannot come. Ye are from beneath; I am from above: ye are of this world; I am not of this world. I said therefore unto you, that ye shall die in your sins: for if ye believe not that I am he, ye shall die in your sins."[307]

And just as Christ gave the children of Israel spiritual water to drink, he has also provided and invited us to drink of the living water (the Holy Ghost), whereby we will never thirst.[308]

Christ is the Spiritual Rock (Exodus 23:20–24 / 32:34 / 33:1–3)

This is where we see Christ and the fullness of the authority given unto him by God the Father. I'm giving you the Scripture so that you can examine it for yourself.

> **Exodus 23**: 20 <u>Behold, I send an Angel before thee</u>, to keep thee in the way, and to bring thee into the place which I have prepared.

21 Beware of him, and <u>obey his voice</u>, provoke him not; <u>for he will not pardon your transgressions</u>: <u>for my name is in him</u>.
22 But if thou shalt indeed obey his voice, and do all that I speak; then I will be an enemy unto thine enemies, and an adversary unto thine adversaries.
23 <u>For mine Angel shall go before thee</u>, and bring thee in unto the Amorites, and the Hittites, and the Perizzites, and the Canaanites, the Hivites, and the Jebusites: and I will cut them off.
24 Thou shalt not bow down to their gods, nor serve them, nor do after their works: but thou shalt utterly overthrow them, and quite break down their images.
25 And ye shall serve the Lord your God, and he shall bless thy bread, and thy water; and I will take sickness away from the midst of thee.
26 There shall nothing cast their young, nor be barren, in thy land: the number of thy days I will fulfil.

On examination of the above Scripture, it is plain to see that God the Father has placed the children of Israel into the hands of his angel (Christ), and has given specific instructions that allow Christ to judge and bless them.

But there are some who don't believe that this Angel is the Lord Jesus Christ. But the Apostle Paul was convinced, and so are some modern theologian bible teachers.

- Finis Jennings Dake wrote, "This Angel was none other than the second person of the divine Trinity in His pre-incarnate state as God. And an equal member with the other two of the Godhead."[309]

- In his bible commentary Jimmy Swaggart wrote, "The Angel" mentioned here is the "Son of God."[310]

- Dr J. Vernon McGee wrote, "Who is this Angel?........It is the Lord Jesus that they were to obey. He is definitely the one in view here."[311]

How then can we know that this angel is Christ? Well, there are some distinct things that stand out in this passage.

- He is given the authority to judge their transgressions; "Whosoever committeth sin, transgresseth also the law: for sin is the transgression of the law."[312]

- The Father's name is in him. In the history of the bible, no one on earth, in heaven, or under the earth, has every had the Father's name in him except Jesus Christ. To this end Jesus had a few things to say concerning him and his Father.

    (1) *"I am come in my Father's name, and ye receive me not: if another shall come in his own name, him ye will receive. How can ye believe, which receive honour one of another, and seek not the honour that cometh from God only?*

    (2) *Do not think that I will accuse you to the Father: there is one that accuseth you, even Moses, in whom ye trust.* <u>*For had ye believed Moses, ye would have believed me: for he wrote of me*</u>*. But if ye believe not his writings, how shall ye believe my words?"*[313]

    (3) <u>The Father is greater than the Son</u>: *"Ye have heard how I said unto you, I go away, and come again unto you. If ye loved me, ye would rejoice, because I said, I go unto the Father: for my Father is greater than I."*[314]

    (4) <u>Jesus Christ and the Father are one</u>: *"And now I am no more in the world, but these are in the world, and*

> *I come to thee. Holy Father, keep through thine own name those whom thou hast given me, that they may be one, as we are one."*³¹⁵ *"And the glory which thou gavest me I have given them; that they may be one, even as we are one."*³¹⁶ *"<u>I and my Father are one</u>."*³¹⁷

Yet still, in bible authority, only God the Father and God the Son has the authority to forgive sins; however, the Holy Ghost is the one that convicts a person of sin. This is demonstrated in the gospel of Mark chapter two.³¹⁸

They brought to Jesus a man who was sick with the palsy. Before Jesus healed the man, he said, "Son, thy sins be forgiven thee." When the scribes heard this they said in their hearts, "Why doth this man thus speak blasphemies? Who can forgive sins but God only?"

When Jesus, by the Spirit, heard their reasoning, he replied, "Why reason ye these things in your hearts? Whether is it easier to say to the sick of the palsy, Thy sins be forgiven thee; or to say, Arise, and take up thy bed, and walk? But that ye may know that the Son of man hath power on earth to forgive sins, (he saith to the sick of the palsy) I say unto thee, Arise, and take up thy bed, and go thy way into thine house."

When God sent Christ to lead the children of Israel to the Promised Land, he also said that through Christ, he would bless their bread and water, and not let sickness run rampart over them. This promise was confirmed by Moses during his last address to the children of Israel.

> **"All the commandments which I command thee this day shall ye observe to do, that ye may live, and multiply, and go in and possess the land which the Lord sware unto your fathers. And thou shalt remember all the way which the Lord thy God led thee these forty years in the wilderness, to humble thee, and to prove thee, to know what was in thine heart, whether thou wouldest keep his**

> commandments, or no. And he humbled thee, and suffered thee to hunger, and fed thee with manna, which thou knewest not, neither did thy fathers know; that he might make thee know that man doth not live by bread only, but by every word that proceedeth out of the mouth of the Lord doth man live. Thy raiment waxed not old upon thee, neither did thy foot swell, these forty years."[319]

When God sent his son to dwell on the earth, he made the same promise to the world. Jesus confirmed this when he said, "The Spirit of the Lord is upon me, because He hath anointed me to preach the gospel to the poor; he hath sent me to heal the brokenhearted, to preach deliverance to the captives, and recovering of sight to the blind, to set at liberty them that are bruised, to preach the acceptable year of the Lord."[320] The proof of what Christ said is recorded in the book of Matthew.

> "And Jesus went about all Galilee, teaching in their synagogues, and preaching the gospel of the kingdom, and healing all manner of sickness and all manner of disease among the people. And his fame went throughout all Syria: and they brought unto him all sick people that were taken with divers diseases and torments, and those which were possessed with devils, and those which were lunatick, and those that had the palsy; and he healed them. And there followed him great multitudes of people from Galilee, and from Decapolis, and from Jerusalem, and from Judaea, and from beyond Jordan."[321]

Israel Worships a Golden Calf (Exodus Chapter 32)

While Moses was up on the mountain, receiving instructions from God, the children of Israel threatened Aaron into making an idol in the image of a golden calf: fashioned from the earrings of their wives, and from their sons, and daughters. When the idol was finished, the children of Israel began to sing and dance naked before the idol; chanting, "this is the god that brought us up out of the land of Egypt."

God told Moses to get from among the people, because he was going to destroy the lot of them. But Moses begged God to stay his hand; and the Lord listened to Moses and spared them. However, their disobedience and sin caused God's judgment to fall on three thousand of their men and women: "Thus saith the Lord God of Israel (*to the Levites*), Put every man his sword by his side, and go in and out from gate to gate throughout the camp, and slay every man his brother, and every man his companion, and every man his neighbour."

Moses then went to the Lord with a partition of mercy for the people and for himself. Yet it was a strange request that he made.

Moses to the people*:* And it came to pass on the morrow, that Moses said unto the people, Ye have sinned a great sin: and now I will go up unto the Lord; peradventure I shall make an atonement for your sin.

Moses to God the Father: And Moses returned unto the Lord, and said, Oh, this people have sinned a great sin, and have made them gods of gold. Yet now, if thou wilt forgive their sin; and if not, blot me, I pray thee, out of thy book which thou hast written.

God's answer: (1) And the Lord said unto Moses, "Whosoever hath sinned against me, him will I blot out of my book. (2) "Therefore, now go, lead the people unto the place of which I have spoken unto thee: <u>behold, mine Angel shall go before thee</u>: nevertheless, in the day when I visit, I will visit their sin upon them."

God's Book of Life

*Did you notice this is the first mention of God keeping a "book of life," containing the names of his people? And that he reserves the right to erase a name he considers no longer worthy to be in his book.

Christ alluded to this when he told his disciples, "I am the true vine, and my Father is the husbandman. Every branch in me that beareth not fruit he taketh away: and every branch that beareth fruit, he purgeth it, that it may bring forth more fruit."[322]

In these last days, God has given complete authority of the earth over to the Lord Jesus Christ; for he controls the "books of works" and the Lamb's Book of Life.[323]

When addressing the seven churches in the book of Revelation, Christ stressed that he would blot out any name from the Book of Life that did not turn away from sinful ways.[324]

Some would argue against what I just said, and hold onto "Once you're saved, you are always saved." But I want to draw your attention to a few Scriptures that show the seriousness God places on the books he keeps.

- But I say unto you, That every idle word that men shall speak, they shall give account thereof in the day of judgment (Revelation 20:11–15) For by thy words thou shalt be justified, and by thy words thou shalt be condemned.[325]

- For there are three that bear record in heaven, the Father, the Word, and the Holy Ghost (here on earth): and these three are one.[326] (1 John 5:7)

- Many will say to me in that day (*Day of Judgment*), Lord, Lord, have we not prophesied in thy name? and in thy name have cast out devils? and in thy name done many wonderful works? And then will I profess unto them, I never knew you: depart from me, ye that work iniquity.[327]

Therefore, it is with great urgency that I plead through this book for every person who reads what I have written to get an understanding of who Jesus Christ is. For to turn to him is everlasting life, but to reject him is eternal damnation: "in the lake which burneth with fire and brimstone: which is the second death."[328]

Lusting is Evil (Numbers Chapters 9–11)

In the eighth chapter of the book of Romans, the apostle Paul said, "And we know that all things work together for good for them that love God, to them who are called according to his purpose."[329] I believe this very thought is presented in this chapter of the book of Numbers.

As the children of Israel traveled across the Sinai Desert, they followed the pillar of cloud during the day, and the pillar of fire at night. Sometimes the cloud would stop for a day, and then move, or two days, or a week, or a month, or even a year, but the cloud was always moving. This caused them to get hardly any rest in their tents while waiting for the cloud to move. So, whether it was by night or by day, and regardless of weather conditions, the people journeyed only when the cloud moved.

This constant moving seemed to aggravate the people, and they began to vehemently complain. This so angered the Lord that he rained down fire upon them and burned up many of them. The people cried unto Moses for relief, and, "when Moses prayed unto the Lord, the fire was quenched."

You'd think this would have stopped their constant complaining, but it did not. The children of Jacob put the blame on the mixed multitude, (those who came out of Egypt with the Hebrews) and said they started a ruckus; because they were tired of eating manna every day, and that there was a scarcity of meat to eat: "We remember the fish, which we did eat in Egypt freely; the cucumbers, and the melons, and the leeks, and the onions, and garlic: but now our soul is dried away: there is nothing at all, beside this manna, before our eyes."

Again, God was ready to destroy his people for their constant murmuring and complaining, but stayed his hand because of Moses' compassionate mercy pleas.

Moses Request That God Kill Him

Yet, Moses was so affected by the people's actions that he begged God to kill him. At this juncture of his service with the Lord, he showed signs of complete and total burnout.

This proves constant bickering, complaining, badgering, in fighting, reveling, arguments, strife, and the like (especially in the church) can cause even a strong warrior to give up. And don't believe you can escape what Moses felt. But there is hope, because other prophets (even the Lord Jesus Christ) in the Bible went through the same thing Moses experienced.

> **The Prophet Elijah:** "And Ahab told Jezebel all that Elijah had done, and withal how he had slain all the prophets with the sword." Then Jezebel sent a messenger to tell Elijah that she would take his life as he took the lives of her prophets. Upon hearing this Elijah went to Beersheba, and onward into the desert until he found a juniper tree to rest under: "and he requested for himself that he might die; and said, it is enough; now, O Lord, take away my life; for I am not better than my fathers."[330]

> **The Prophet Jeremiah:** "Cursed be the day wherein I was born: let not the day wherein my mother bare me be blessed. Cursed be the man who brought tidings to my father, saying, A man child is born unto thee; making him very glad. And let that man be as the cities which the Lord overthrew, and repented not: and let him hear the cry in the morning, and the shouting at noontide; Because he slew me not from the womb; or that my mother might have been my grave, and her womb to be always great with me. Wherefore came I forth out of the womb to see labour and sorrow, that my days

should be consumed with shame? O Lord, thou hast deceived me, and I was deceived; thou art stronger than I, and hast prevailed: I am in derision daily, every one mocketh me. For since I spake, I cried out, I cried violence and spoil; because the word of the Lord was made a reproach unto me, and a derision, daily. Then I said, I will not make mention of him, nor speak any more in his name. But his word was in mine heart as a burning fire shut up in my bones, and I was weary with forbearing, and I could not stay."[331]

Jesus Christ: "And a certain scribe came, and said unto him, Master, I will follow thee whithersoever thou goest. And Jesus saith unto him, The foxes have holes, and the birds of the air have nests; but the Son of man hath not where to lay his head."[332]

The Author of this book: In 1980 AD I was ordered, by the Army, to report to Germany. Dutifully I applied for transportation to move my family and household goods to Germany. However, my wife, for the fear of flying, refused to go with me to my next assignment.

On my way to Germany I stopped off to see my Mother, Brother and sister. While there, my sister told an old girlfriend of mine that I was in town. When the woman called me, all the past flames of passion began to stir up. It was then that I realized the weakness of my flesh. I quickly prayed to God to lift me out of this sinful situation. Upon arrival at my mothers house the woman notified me that she had rented a van that had a mattress in the back; and there we could spend some copulation time together. He announcement tore at my body like a hot flame, and I knew that if I gave in, she would lead me away "like a bull to the slaughter." (Proverbs 7: 6-27)

Yet, the power of the Holy Ghost kept me in my mother's house until she gave up and left. At that movement, I came to the conclusion that I was going to fail God in my flesh; because I reasoned, how could a man used to visit with his wife every night be able to resist the wiles of a woman's sexual appeal?

Like Moses, and the prophets I begged God to "just kill me and get it over with." Why wait until I fail in the flesh? Within in my self I knew that I had not the physical strength to resist the call of human desire.

Yet God didn't honor my request for death, but instead sustained me by taking that desire away. And because I didn't indulge in womenfolk, some began to say that I was gay or a homosexual. I did not challenge their claim, but was determined to serve God with all my heart, soul, mind, and strength. To this end God blessed me with knowledge, and a little wisdom. Amen.

Even though Moses wanted to resign from his leadership position, God would not accept his resignation. Instead, he fixed the problem in a twofold way. First, he would personally come down and take the Spirit that was upon Moses, and split it among seventy handpicked elders: "and they shall bear the burden of the people with thee, that thou bear it not thyself alone."

> Number 11: 16 Then the Lord said to Moses, "Gather before me seventy men who are recognized as elders and leaders of Israel. Bring them to the Tabernacle* to stand there with you.
>
> 17 I will come down and talk to you there. I will take some of the Spirit that is upon you, and I will put the Spirit upon them also. They will bear the burden of the people along with you, so you will not have to carry it alone.

Second, God told Moses he was going to provide meat for them eat for a period of thirty days, and it would be so much meat they would tire of eating it.

God Pours Out His Spirit

The splitting of the Spirit of God among the seventy elders is a prerequisite to what happened on the day of Pentecost: when God poured out his Spirit (the Holy Ghost) on a hundred-twenty men and women.[333] * Did you notice this event required God to physically touch Moses?

On hearing this news, Moses didn't have any questions concerning the Holy Spirit of God. Instead, he dwelled on the miracle of God providing meat for thirty days: "And Moses said, The people among whom I am, are six hundred thousand footmen; and thou hast said, I will give them flesh, that they may eat a whole month."

Puzzled by what God said, Moses asked him, "Shall the flocks and the herds be slain for them, to suffice them? Or shall all the fish of the sea be gathered together for them, to suffice them? This whole miracle of meat had Moses totally confused.

Christ Administers the Spirit of God

Then a strange thing happened concerning the seventy elders who were to receive the Holy Spirit of God.

- "And the Lord came down in a cloud, and spake unto him, and took of the spirit that was upon him, and gave it unto the seventy elders: and it came to pass, that, when the spirit rested upon them, they prophesied, and did not cease."

- "But there remained two of the men in the camp, the name of the one was Eldad, and the name of the other Medad: and the spirit rested upon them; and they were of them that were written, but went not out unto the tabernacle: and they prophesied in the camp."

Now the Lord that came down in a cloud was none other than the Lord Jesus Christ, because he is the one God has authorized to baptize humankind with the Holy Ghost. John the Baptist restated this authority when he said, "I indeed baptize you with water unto repentance: but he that cometh after me is mightier than I, whose shoes I am not worthy to bear: he shall baptize you with the Holy Ghost, and with fire."[334]

Did you notice that there were only sixty-eight elders gathered with Moses at the tabernacle? For some reason, two of them were delayed, and still in the camp. But when the Lord poured out his Spirit, all seventy (whose names were on the list) were baptized into the Spirit of God (the Holy Ghost), and prophesied (in the Hebrew tongue) without ceasing. This is the same thing that happened when Zacharias, father of John the Baptist, was filled with the Holy Ghost; he immediately prophesied in his native tongue.[335]

However, on the Day of Pentecost the hundred-twenty men and women were filled with the Holy Ghost and spoke in tongues [not their native language], in a language unknown to them, as the Spirit gave them utterance. This happened because God had said that in the last days; he would speak through his people with stammering lips and another tongue.[336]

When Joshua heard Eldad and Medad prophesy in the camp, he requested that Moses forbid them from speaking. Moses in turn told Joshua, "Enviest thou for my sake? would God that all the Lord's people were prophets, and that the Lord would put his spirit upon them!"

Joshua's position is the same mistake made in the modern church, where there is a strong movement to prevent the speaking out in tongues. How is it possible that a human being can prevent the Holy Ghost of God from speaking?

The apostle Paul faced this same dilemma in the Corinthian church, and addressed it in the fourteenth chapter of his epistle to them: "If any man think himself to be a prophet, or spiritual, let him acknowledge that the things that I write unto you are the commandments of the Lord. But if any man be ignorant, let him be ignorant. Wherefore, brethren, covet to prophesy, and forbid not to speak with tongues."[337]

God Provides Meat for a Month

After the Holy Spirit baptism of the seventy elders, God provided meat for the children of Israel to eat. But God's fulfillment of their request carried a destructive price: "And while the flesh was yet between their teeth, ere it was chewed, the wrath of the Lord was kindled against the people, and the Lord smote the people with a very great plague. And he called the name of that place Kibrothhattaavah: because there they buried the people that lusted"

In the end, all things did work out for the good for the children of Israel, but this was not achieved without judgment falling on those who committed the sin of lust.

Why were they destroyed with death? James put it this way: "But every man is tempted, when he is drawn away of his own lust, and enticed. Then when lust hath conceived, it bringeth forth sin: and sin, when it is finished, bringeth forth death."[338]

Israel is Prevented from entering the Promised Land (Numbers Chapter's 13, 14)

God brought the children of Israel to the border of the Promised Land (Canaan). He told Moses to pick out twelve men (a leader from each tribe, which included Caleb and Joshua), and send them to spy out the land: check out the people, their houses, their fortifications and battlements, and the fruit trees and crops. After forty days elapsed, the twelve spies returned and gave their report.

They stated that the land was plenteous, as the Lord had said, but, "the people be strong that dwell in the land, and the cities are walled, and very great: and moreover we saw the children of Anak there." Anak is a short name for a race of Giants called the Anakim who lived at Hebron[339]

- After the children of Israel crossed over the Jordan river into the Canaan land Caleb drew the task of fighting against the giants of Anak.[340]

- David became a great man in Israel when he defeated the Anak giant Goliath who was close to ten feet tall.[341] Goliath's brothers, and other members of his clan were also slain by David's men.[342]

Caleb seized on this opportunity and said, "Let us go up at once, and possess it; for we are well able to overcome it."

But ten of the other spies stood against him and caused the people to fear: "We be not able to go up against the people; for they are stronger than we. The land, through which we have gone to search it, is a land that eateth up the inhabitants thereof; and all the people that we saw in it are men of a great stature. And there we saw the giants, the sons of Anak, which come of the giants: and we were in our own sight as grasshoppers, and so we were in their sight."

Hearing this, all the people were moved to a state of panic and began to weep and cry, which lasted all night. Then they turned their fear and anger against Moses and Aaron with venomous threats and complaints: "Would God that we had died in the land of Egypt! or would God we had died in this wilderness! And wherefore hath the Lord brought us unto this land, to fall by the sword, that our wives and our children should be a prey? were it not better for us to return into Egypt? And they said one to another, Let us make a captain, and let us return into Egypt."

In humbleness, Moses and Aaron fell on their knees to plead with the people. But Joshua and Caleb were so infuriated with the people that they tore the clothes off their bodies, and along with Moses and Aaron, pleaded with the people to go into the Promised Land as ordered by God. They argued that no matter the circumstances, God would overcome any obstacle before them: "The Lord is with us, fear them not."

But the people wouldn't listen, and took up stones to stone them to death. Suddenly, "The glory of the Lord appeared in the tabernacle of the congregation before all the children of Israel. And the Lord said unto Moses, How long will this people provoke me? and how long will it be ere they believe me, for all the signs which I have

Who is Jesus Christ

shewed among them? I will smite them with the pestilence, and disinherit them, and will make of thee a greater nation and mightier than they."

God was so moved with anger that he was ready to destroy the whole nation of Israel and start all over again. But Moses, full of compassion for the people, pleaded with God to spare them. God listened to Moses but decreed that everyone over the age of twenty—except Caleb and Joshua—would roam the desert for forty years, until they were all dead. So it was that it took them forty years to travel six hundred miles to the Promised Land of Canaan.

Moses relayed to the people God's judgments, and they "mourned greatly." Early the next morning the people decided to venture into the Promised Land. Moses warned them not to go, but they went anyway and were defeated in battle, and driven back into the Sinai desert by the Amalekites: descendants of Esau; and the Canaanites, descendants of Ham's youngest son, Canaan.[343]

Just as the children of Israel did not make it into the Promised Land because of disobedience, but wandered around in the Sinai Desert for forty years, we, too, will not inherit the New Jerusalem if we disobey the will of God. And what is the will of God? Glad you asked! Here is the self-explanatory Scripture that depicts God's will.

> "For I came down from heaven, not to do mine own will, but the will of him that sent me. And this is the Father's will which hath sent me, that of all which he hath given me I should lose nothing, but should raise it up again at the last day. And this is the will of him that sent me, that every one which seeth the Son, and believeth on him, may have everlasting life: and I will raise him up at the last day."[344]

Beware of the Destroyer (Numbers Chapter 16)

The apostle Paul gives us a warning about the "destroyer." The question that comes to my mind is "who and what the destroyer is."

I found Christ gave the only feasible answer when he sent his twelve disciples (two by two) out on the mission field: "And fear not them which kill the body, but are not able to kill the soul: but rather fear him which is able to destroy both soul and body in hell."[345]

So the destroyer is the one that ejected Adam and Eve from the garden of Eden; that put a permanent curse on the Serpent; that kicked O Lucifer (the great Dragon, that old Serpent called the Devil and Satan) and his angels out of heaven; that destroyed the earth with a flood; that saved Noah and his family (to include animals, birds, and insects) from the flood; that formed a nation from the loins of Abraham; that called Moses from a burning bush; that judged Egypt with ten devastating plagues; that delivered the children of Israel out of bondage; that made a passageway across the Red Sea; that destroyed Pharaoh's chariot army; that caused water to flow from a rock; that rained down bread (manna) from heaven; that poured out his Spirit on seventy elders of Jacob's loins; that brought quail across the sea for a whole month to feed the children of Israel; and is the one who judged the children of Israel in the desert for forty years.

Korah Challenges Moses

In this story, we find a Levite named Korah (with the help of Dathan and Abiram, the sons of Reuben, and fifty-two tribal leaders) in opposition to the authority of Moses.

> "And they gathered themselves together against Moses and against Aaron, and said unto them, Ye take too much upon you, seeing all the congregation are holy, every one of them, and the Lord is among them: wherefore then lift ye up yourselves above the congregation of the Lord?"

When reconciliation failed, Moses told Korah to meet him in front of the tabernacle, and let God choose the true leader of the people. They both agreed that Aaron and Korah, with his two hundred tribal leaders, would bring censers filled with incense before the Lord.

In a final plea, Moses reminded Korah how God had separated the Levites out from the nation of Israel to be his ministers. He warned him not to seek this foolish insurrection: "For which cause both thou and all thy company are gathered together against the Lord: and what is Aaron, that ye murmur against him?" Then Moses tried to make amends with Dathan and Abiram, but they were stubborn and fixed in their position against Moses.

- Is it a small thing that thou hast brought us up out of a land that floweth with milk and honey, to kill us in the wilderness, except thou make thyself altogether a prince over us?

- Moreover thou hast not brought us into a land that floweth with milk and honey, or given us inheritance of fields and vineyards: wilt thou put out the eyes of these men? we will not come up.

Their attitude drove Moses to bring his petition before the Lord, and in humbleness, "said unto the Lord, Respect not thou their offering: I have not taken one ass from them, neither have I hurt one of them."

Reluctantly, Moses told Korah to gather his followers before the Lord (in front of the door of the tabernacle) with censers filled with incense; and God would confirm the leader.

When everyone was in place, God appeared in his glory, and ordered Moses to separate the camp into two groups—those who were with Moses, and those who were with Korah.

Moses warned the people to stay clear of Korah and his followers; because God was going to give them a sign that would confirm Moses as his chosen leader: "But if the Lord make a new thing, and the earth open her mouth, and swallow them up, with all that appertain unto them, and they go down quick into the pit; then ye shall understand that these men have provoked the Lord."

As soon as Moses finished speaking, the ground opened up beneath Korah and his followers, and they were all drawn down into the earth: "They, and all that appertained to them, went down alive into the pit, and the earth closed upon them: and they perished from among the congregation."

When the people witnessed the works of the destroyer, and heard the wailing cries of Korah and his followers, they scattered in panic. They cried out as they ran, "Lest the earth swallow us up also."

Then fire came down from heaven and burned up the two-hundred-fifty leaders who sided with Korah, and offered incense.

The Congregation Rail Against Moses and Aaron

The next day, the children of Israel gathered together and, "murmured against Moses and against Aaron, saying, Ye have killed the people of the Lord." What an accusation to make when it was Korah who started an insurrection against Moses. It was God who brought judgment to end the crisis. Yet common sense would say leave the chosen leaders of God alone. To this end, God left a word to the wise: "Touch not mine anointed, and do my prophet no harm"[346]

Once again this brought God into the fray. He announced to Moses that he was going to destroy the people. But Moses told Aaron to fill a censer with hot coals from the altar, and burn incense upon them. Then he was to stand in the gap between God and the people, "to make an atonement for them: for there is wrath gone out from the Lord; the plague is begun" (the death cloud had fallen upon the children of Israel).

And Aaron did as Moses commanded, "and stood between the dead and the living." Aaron's actions caused God to remove the death angel, but not before fourteen-thousand -seven-hundred people perished. This was in addition to those who went down into the earth with Korah, and the two-hundred-fifty who were burned up with fire from heaven.

Just as Korah buffeted up against Moses, the followers of Jesus will also be persecuted.[347] But the will of God is that we seek reconciliation and peace with our fellow human beings so that he will not have to destroy disobedient souls; for Christ's sake he will hold back destruction. Therefore, in this walk with the Lord, we are given specific instructions on how to settle disputes.

In the church: "Moreover if thy brother shall trespass against thee, go and tell him his fault between thee and him alone: if he shall hear thee, thou hast gained thy brother. But if he will not hear thee, then take with thee one or two more, that in the mouth of two or three witnesses every word may be established. And if he shall neglect to hear them, tell it unto the church: but if he neglect to hear the church, let him be unto thee as a heathen man and a publican."[348]

In the world: "But I say unto you which hear, Love your enemies, do good to them which hate you. Bless them that curse you, and pray for them which despitefully use you. And unto him that smiteth thee on the one cheek offer also the other; and him that taketh away thy cloak forbid not to take thy coat also. Give to every man that asketh of thee; and of him that taketh away thy goods ask them not again. And as ye would that men should do to you, do ye also to them likewise. For if ye love them which love you, what thank have ye? for sinners also love those that love them. And if ye do good to them which do good to you, what thank have ye? for sinners also do even the same. And if ye lend to them of whom ye hope to receive, what thank have ye? for sinners also lend to sinners, to receive as much again. But love ye your enemies, and do good, and lend, hoping for nothing again; and your reward shall be great, and ye shall be the children of the Highest: for he is kind unto the unthankful and to the evil. Be ye therefore merciful, as your Father also is merciful. Judge not, and ye shall not be judged: condemn not, and ye shall not be condemned: forgive, and ye shall be forgiven:"[349]

As you can see, the Lord Jesus Christ has laid down some tough rules of engagements for his followers, and he expects them to be carried out to the full letter! The reasoning for this is found in the book of Ezekiel, where it is written, "Say unto them, As I live, saith the Lord God, I have no pleasure in the death of the wicked; but that the wicked turn from his way and live: turn ye, turn ye from your evil ways; for why will ye die, O house of Israel?"[350]

Further, the apostle Paul reminds us that "if God be for us, who can be against us?" (Romans 8:31) And in the book of Isaiah, God promised protection to his people Israel, which is extended to the followers of Christ: "No weapon that is formed against thee shall prosper; and every tongue that shall rise against thee in judgment thou shalt condemn. This is the heritage of the servants of the Lord, and their righteousness is of me, saith the Lord" (Isaiah 54:17).

Christ Will Save Us from the Serpents Bite (Numbers 21:4–9)

The Apostle Paul flat out tells the Corinthian Church that it was Christ who judged the children of Israel when they were in the Sinai Desert for forty years, and that it was him who saved them from the deadly serpent's bite.

This story is very short but reaches across time to the cross of Jesus Christ. To understand how is to examine every Scripture, and their direct and indirect references to Christ.

First, the people became weary and discouraged as they traveled across the Sinai Desert, going around in circles, and getting nowhere. They had forgotten this was God's judgment against them for disobeying his order to enter the Promised Land. For God had decreed that only Joshua and Caleb, and those under twenty-one years of age would enter into the Promised Land.

Second, they began to bitterly complain, murmur, and speak out openly against God and Moses: "Wherefore have ye brought us up out of Egypt to die in the wilderness? for there is no bread, neither is there any water; and our soul loatheth this light bread." Even manna experienced their anger.

Third, God's judgment sent poisonous serpents to bite the people, and many of them died.

Fourth, the people had no recourse but to beg Moses for relief and help: "We have sinned, for we have spoken against the Lord, and against thee; pray unto the Lord, that he take away the serpents from us." In his compassion Moses prayed to God for the people to be saved from the serpents' bite.

Fifth, God heard Moses prayer and told him to "Make thee a fiery serpent, and set it upon a pole: and it shall come to pass, that every one that is bitten, when he looketh upon it, shall live."

Sixth, Moses followed God's instructions to the letter and, "made a serpent of brass, and put it upon a pole; and it came to pass, that if a serpent had bitten any man, when he beheld the serpent of brass, he lived."

**Between 715 – 686 BC King Hezekiah destroyed this brazen serpent because the people had begun to worship and burn incense to it.[351]

But the saving power of the Serpent on the hill did not prevent their continued grumbling, murmuring, and complaining. In the same way, the people of this world are set upon by the "wicked one" (the great Dragon, that old Serpent called the Devil and Satan): "who as a roaring lion, walks up and down the in the earth, seeking all that he may devour." He is out to steal, kill, and destroy the human body, and capture souls to join him in hell—the lake of fire.[352]

And why are devils so viciously attacking the people of this world? The answer is twofold: (1) because of the sin of Eve and Adam, and (2) because of the unbelief in the God of Abraham, Isaac, and Jacob.

Yet God, in his wisdom, sent his only begotten Son, Jesus Christ, to save us from the Serpent's bite. All we have to do is believe in Christ, and look up at the cross of Christ to be forever healed. This is a promise spewed forth by Christ himself: "And as Moses lifted up the serpent in the wilderness, even so must the Son of man be lifted up: That whosoever believeth in him should not perish, but have eternal life."³⁵³

But like the people in Moses day, the people are still grumbling, growling, complaining, murmuring, and living in disbelief that a look to the cross can save them. However, Christ has promised that, And I, if I be lifted up from the earth, will draw all men unto me." (John 12:32)

Fornication is a Deadly Sin (Numbers 25:1–9)

This chapter further explains how God views sexual immorality. He first showed us his temperament toward this type of sin when he completely destroyed Sodom and Gomorrah, and the surrounding towns and villages.

So, we should glean from this how serious sexual sin is, and that fornication and adultery are high on the list of judgments. Again, let's walk down the Scriptures to find the meaning of the judgment pointed out by the Apostle Paul.

The children of Israel stopped to rest in a place called Shittim, in the land of Moab. This land is named after the son of the incestuous relationship between Lot and his oldest daughter after they escaped the destruction of Sodom and Gomorrah.³⁵⁴ While at this resting place, they began having sexual activity with the women of Moab, and committed to bowing their knee in worship and sacrifice to their god Baalpeor.

This caused God's wrath to fall upon them: "And the Lord said unto Moses, Take all the heads of the people, and hang them up before the Lord against the sun, that the fierce anger of the Lord may be turned away from Israel."

Moses carried out the order by mustering the Levites and saying to them, "Slay ye every one his men that were joined unto Baalpeor."

This judgment brought the children of Israel to their knees in front of the tabernacle door with weeping, moaning, and grievous groans.

However, one man refused to put away his sexual sin, and without shame brought a Midianitish woman into his tent in the sight of Moses, and the whole congregation. He began to have intimate relations with her. Seeing this, Phinehas (the son of Eleazar, the son of Aaron, the high priest) took a javelin and rammed it through the man's back: and it went clear through into the belly of the woman. Thus, both were slain with one blow.

This act of violence by Phinehas caused God to lift his hand of judgment, but not before twenty-four thousand heads were severed, and hung up on sticks.

- During the day, temperatures in the Sinai Desert can go over 120 degrees Fahrenheit. So, you know these heads created a putrid smell, and a gruesome sight.

- Also, the stench was probably in the air for several miles. In my mind I can see thousands of insects (ants, flies, and maggots) and scavengers of the animal world (buzzards, etc.) being drawn to the rotting flesh and blood.

- Just the thought of those 24,000 heads on sticks in the hot sun brought me to the point of nausea and pain. So, I can visualize and imagine the heartache, and hysteria Moses and the children of Israel went through.

One thing is clear, this judgment of God, though it may seem harsh, stopped all fornication from happening again during their journey through the Sinai Desert.

Just as he pointed out the judgment of sexual sin among the children of Israel as they crossed the Sinai Desert with Moses; the apostle Paul warns us several times that sin will not enter the kingdom of God. And for our benefit, he names some we are familiar with.

> *"Know ye not that the unrighteous shall not inherit the kingdom of God? Be not deceived: neither fornicators, nor idolaters, nor adulterers, nor effeminate, nor abusers of themselves*

> *with mankind, Nor thieves, nor covetous, nor drunkards, nor revilers, nor extortioners, shall inherit the kingdom of God."*[355]

> *"But fornication, and all uncleanness, or covetousness, let it not be once named among you, as becometh saints; Neither filthiness, nor foolish talking, nor jesting, which are not convenient: but rather giving of thanks. For this ye know, that no whoremonger, nor unclean person, nor covetous man, who is an idolater, hath any inheritance in the kingdom of Christ and of God. Let no man deceive you with vain words: for because of these things cometh the wrath of God upon the children of disobedience. Be not ye therefore partakers with them."*[356]

I know some will argue that Paul was a devout Jew, and therefore, his writings are geared toward Hebrew Old Testament law. This may have some truth in it, but remember, he is trying to warn the followers of Christ (the church) about sexual immorality by pointing out the judgment that fell on the children of Israel for sexual sin, and disobedience toward God. Because of fornication, they began to worship other gods. Therefore, Paul explains the reason God gave the law to Moses to deliver to the children of Israel; who were supposed to carry His word (law) to the world.

> *"Knowing this, that the law is not made for a righteous man, but for the lawless and disobedient, for the ungodly and for sinners, for unholy and profane, for murderers of fathers and murderers of mothers, for manslayers, For whoremongers, for them that defile themselves with mankind, for menstealers, for liars, for perjured persons, and if there be any other thing that is contrary to sound doctrine; According to the glorious gospel of the blessed God, which was committed to my trust."*[357]

Israel's Suffering Revealed

> **1 Corinthians 10:11 "Now all these things happened unto them for ensamples: and they are written for our admonition, upon whom the ends of the world are come"**

Here Paul explains that what the children of Israel experienced with God in the desert is an example of how he will deal with the whole world concerning Jesus Christ, his only begotten Son). Since this subject will roll over into the "Judgments of Christ," I will address this issue in a later chapter in the book.

YEAR- 2708

The Death of Moses (Deuteronomy 34:5-6)

We know from Scripture that God forbade Moses from entering the Promised Canaan Land, because of his disobedience when ordered to call water from the rock (Numbers 20:7–13). Yet God let Moses go into the mountains of Nebo and view the Promised Land from the top of Mount Pisgah (Deuteronomy 34:1–4).

At this juncture of life, Moses was a hundred-twenty years old: "his eye was not dim, nor his natural force abated." He was still walking upright, and in complete control of his physical and mental faculties. When Moses didn't come back from his trip to Mount Pisgah, the people wept and moaned for thirty days, "for he was much beloved." Now this is where the strange part of the death of Moses comes in.

- "So, Moses the servant of the Lord died there in the land of Moab, according to <u>the word of the Lord.</u>"

- "And he (*Christ*) buried him in a valley in the land of Moab, over against Bethpeor: but no man knoweth of his sepulcher unto this day."

If you read between the lines you may be able to see that the angel of the Lord (Christ) told the twelve tribes that Moses was dead, and that he buried him in the land of Moab.

CHAPTER 15

THE PROMISED LAND

The Leadership of Joshua

After Moses died Joshua became the leader of the twelve tribes of Israel. When God pushed back the waters of the flooded Jordon river, Joshua and the twelve tribes crossed near the town of Jericho. After crossing the Jordon river into the promised land of Canaan he circumcised every male in the camps: "at the hill of foreskins."[358]

Then at the direction of God he defeated the city of Jericho, and Ai. These two victories caused the people of the land to tremble with fear and loathing.

To ensure that the lives of their people would be spared, the Gibeonites (of the Hivites nation) dressed up as ambassadors from a faraway foreign country, and tricked Joshua into signing an agreement of peace. When their deceit was found out Joshua made them servants of the twelve tribes.[359]

What Joshua did was a direct disobedience to the commandment of God given to the children of Israel when God appointed his Angel to overseer them across the Sinai desert.[360]

- <u>For mine Angel shall go before thee</u>, and bring thee in unto the Amorites, and the Hittites, and the Perizzites, and the Canaanites, the Hivites, and the Jebusites: and I will cut them off.

- Thou shalt not bow down to their gods, nor serve them, nor do after their works: <u>but thou shalt utterly overthrow them,</u> and quite break down their images.

- I will send my fear before thee, and will destroy all the people to whom thou shalt come, and I will make all thine enemies turn their backs unto thee.

- And I will send hornets before thee, which shall drive out the Hivite, the Canaanite, and the Hittite, from before thee.

- I will not drive them out from before thee in one year; lest the land become desolate, and the beast of the field multiply against thee.

- By little and little I will drive them out from before thee, until thou be increased, and inherit the land.

- And I will set thy bounds from the Red sea even unto the sea of the Philistines, and from the desert unto the river: for I will deliver the inhabitants of the land into your hand; and thou shalt drive them out before thee.

- <u>Thou shalt make no covenant with them</u>, nor with their gods.

- <u>They shall not dwell in thy land</u>, <u>lest they make thee sin against me</u>: for if thou serve their gods, it will surely be a snare unto thee.

After the pact with the Gibeonites, Joshua divided the land among the twelve tribes, and each tribe went about to conquer the Canaanites in their district.[361]

> **YEAR - 2738**
> *This is the end of the time count from Adam to Joshua using the bible listed years of births, deaths, and events.

Joshua was around forty-years old when God delivered Israel from Egyptian bondage, and died at the age of one-hundred-ten years old.[362]

The Twelve Tribes Transgress Against God

After the death of Joshua, and all the elders that came out of Egypt with Moses, the twelve tribes were not able to completely conquer the Canaan people.

- Judges 1: 18 Also <u>Judah</u> took Gaza with the coast thereof, and Askelon with the coast thereof, and Ekron with the coast thereof.
  19 And the Lord was with Judah; and he drave out the inhabitants of the mountain; but could not drive out the inhabitants of the valley, because they had chariots of iron.

- Judges 1: 21 And the children of <u>Benjamin</u> did not drive out the Jebusites that inhabited Jerusalem; but the Jebusites dwell with the children of Benjamin in Jerusalem unto this day.

- Judges 1: 27 Neither did <u>Manasseh</u> drive out the inhabitants of Beth-shean and her towns, nor Taanach and her towns, nor the inhabitants of Dor and her towns, nor the inhabitants of Ibleam and her towns, nor the inhabitants of Megiddo and her towns: but the Canaanites would dwell in that land.
  28 And it came to pass, when Israel was strong, that they put the Canaanites to tribute, and did not utterly drive them out.

- Judges 1: 29 Neither did <u>Ephraim</u> drive out the Canaanites that dwelt in Gezer; but the Canaanites dwelt in Gezer among them.

- Judges 1: 30 Neither did <u>Zebulun</u> drive out the inhabitants of Kitron, nor the inhabitants of Nahalol; but the Canaanites dwelt among them, and became tributaries.

- Judges 1: 31 Neither did <u>Asher</u> drive out the inhabitants of Accho, nor the inhabitants of Zidon, nor of Ahlab, nor of Achzib, nor of Helbah, nor of Aphik, nor of Rehob: 32 but the Asherites dwelt among the Canaanites, the inhabitants of the land: for they did not drive them out.

- Judges 1: 33 Neither did <u>Naphtali</u> drive out the inhabitants of Beth-shemesh, nor the inhabitants of Beth-anath; but he dwelt among the Canaanites, the inhabitants of the land: nevertheless the inhabitants of Beth-shemesh and of Beth-anath became tributaries unto them.

- Judges 1: 34 And the Amorites forced the children of <u>Dan</u> into the mountain: for they would not suffer them to come down to the valley:
  35 but the Amorites would dwell in mount Heres in Aijalon, and in Shaalbim: yet the hand of the house of Joseph prevailed, so that they became tributaries.
  36 And the coast of the Amorites was from the going up to Akrabbim, from the rock, and upward.

Judgement of The Angel of God

Here I want to remind you, that God not only put his Angel (*Christ*) in charge of the Twelve Tribes, but also told them that he would judge their transgressions: "Behold, I send an Angel before thee, to keep thee in the way, and to bring thee into the place which

I have prepared. Beware of him, and obey his voice, provoke him not; for he will not pardon your transgressions: for my name is in him."

After the dust settles, and the twelve tribes are living in harmony with the Canaanite people, <u>the Angel of God</u> (*Christ*) shows up to pronounce judgement on them.[363]

Christ: "And an angel of the Lord came up from Gilgal to Bochim, and said, I made you to go up out of Egypt, and have brought you unto the land which I sware unto your fathers; and I said, I will never break my covenant with you. And ye shall make no league with the inhabitants of this land; ye shall throw down their altars: but ye have not obeyed my voice: why have ye done this? Wherefore I also said, I will not drive them out from before you; but they shall be as thorns in your sides, and their gods shall be a snare unto you.

The People: And it came to pass, when the angel of the Lord spake these words unto all the children of Israel, that the people lifted up their voice, and wept.

Yes, the people wept and cried, and had sorrow in their hearts, but they did not turn from their wicked ways, nor did they stop mingling with the Canaanites; but took up worshipping their gods.[364]

- And the children of Israel did evil in the sight of the Lord, and served Baalim:

- and they forsook the Lord God of their fathers, which brought them out of the land of Egypt, and followed other gods, of the gods of the people that were round about them, and bowed themselves unto them, and provoked the Lord to anger.

- And they forsook the Lord, and served Baal and Ashtaroth.[365]

    BAAL (IDOL) - Baal was the most prominent Canaanite deity. As the fertility god of the Canaanite pantheon (roster of gods), Baal's sphere of influence included agriculture, animal husbandry, and human sexuality. Places for worship of Baal were often high places in the hills consisting of an altar and a sacred tree, stone, or pillar.

ASHTAROTH (Ashterathite) Ashtaroth is the plural form of Ashtoreth, the name of the Canaanite fertility goddess who was worshiped there.

- And the anger of the Lord was hot against Israel, and he delivered them into the hands of spoilers that spoiled them, and he sold them into the hands of their enemies round about, so that they could not any longer stand before their enemies.

- Whithersoever they went out, the hand of the Lord was against them for evil, as the Lord had said, and as the Lord had sworn unto them: and they were greatly distressed.

- Nevertheless the Lord raised up judges, which delivered them out of the hand of those that spoiled them.

- And yet they would not hearken unto their judges, but they went a whoring after other gods, and bowed themselves unto them: they turned quickly out of the way which their fathers walked in, obeying the commandments of the Lord; but they did not so.

- And when the Lord raised them up judges, then the Lord was with the judge, and delivered them out of the hand of their enemies all the days of the judge: for it repented the Lord because of their groanings by reason of them that oppressed them and vexed them.

- And it came to pass, when the judge was dead, that they returned, and corrupted themselves more than their fathers, in following other gods to serve them, and to bow down unto them; they ceased not from their own doings, nor from their stubborn way.

Christ: And the anger of the Lord was hot against Israel; and he said, Because that this people hath transgressed my covenant which I commanded their fathers, and have not hearkened unto my voice;

- I also will not henceforth drive out any from before them of the nations which Joshua left when he died:

- that through them I may prove Israel, whether they will keep the way of the Lord to walk therein, as their fathers did keep it, or not.

- Therefore the Lord left those nations, without driving them out hastily; neither delivered he them into the hand of Joshua.

> **YEAR 1367-1327 BC**
> *From herein this time count is taken from the historic time table of BC & AD

Othniel Defeats the Arameans and Rules Israel (Judges 3:8-11)

"This judge of Israel is mentioned as the son of Kenaz and Caleb's nephew (or perhaps brother), who delivered Israel from the tyranny of Cushan-rishathaim, king of Mesopotamia. He earlier distinguished himself by capturing Debir (Joshua 15:15-17; Judges 1:11-13; 3:8-11).

When Caleb promised his daughter Achsah to anyone who could conquer Debir, Othniel took Debir and received Achsah for his wife. When Caleb gave her and her land as a present, Achsah asked for a water source and was given the upper springs and the lower springs (Joshua 15:19; Judges 1:15).

Later, Othniel delivered the Israelites from the oppressive Cushan-rishathaim, whom the Israelites had served for eight years on account of their sin (Judges 3:7). When the people cried for relief, the Lord raised up Othniel. He was described as someone that the "Spirit of the Lord came upon" (3:10). The impact of his work as judge lasted for a generation (3:9-11)."[366]

YEAR 1327-1309 BC

King Eglon of Moab Subjects the Israelites (Judges 3:14)

"Eglon was the Moabite king who captured Jericho and held it for eighteen years, exacting a tribute from Israel. Ehud, an Israelite judge pretending to bring tribute, killed Eglon (Judges 3:12-30)."[367]

YEAR 1309 – 1229 BC

Ehud Assassinates Eglon and Begins an Era of Peace for Israel (Judges 3:14-30)

"Ehud was one of the judges of Israel. From the tribe of Benjamin, he delivered Israel from Eglon, the king of the Moabites (Judges 3:12-30). Ehud was notable because he was left-handed. Before taking Israelite taxes to Eglon, he made an iron dagger, and he used it to assassinate the unsuspecting Eglon during a private meeting. He then rallied the Israelites west of the Jordan River to encircle the Moabite troops before they could return south to Moab. When the eighteen-year rule of Eglon over the Israelites ended, an eighty-year period of peace began."[368]

> **YEAR 1229-1209 BC**

King Jabin of Hazor Oppresses Israel (Judges 4:2)

1. King of Hazor who led a coalition against Joshua at Merom. Jabin and his allies were destroyed in the battle, and Hazor was burned to the ground (Joshua 11:1-14).

2. King of Hazor during the period of the judges (Judges 4:1). God allowed him to oppress Israel for 20 years because of their wickedness. His army included 900 chariots of iron. Eventually, God delivered Israel through the prophetess Deborah and her captain, Barak, who defeated Sisera, the captain of Jabin's army. While resting after his flight from battle, Sisera was killed by a woman. Jabin was no longer a threat after Sisera's death and was soon killed (4:24; Psalm 83:9).[369]

> **YEAR 1209-1169 BC**

Deborah Leads an Uprising Against Jabin, and Rules Israel (Judges 4-5)

> "Deborah was the name of two Old Testament women. The word in Hebrew means "honeybee" (Psalm 118:12; Isaiah 7:18).

1. Deborah was Rebekah's nurse (Genesis 35:8). This Deborah died as she was traveling to Bethel with her master Jacob's household. She was buried in a spot called Allon-bacuth ("the oak of weeping"). That

probably indicates that she had been well loved. She was probably Rebekah's longtime companion (24:59-61).

2. Deborah was also a prophetess and judge (Judges 4-5). Deborah's position as a prophetess shows that her message was from God. That was not unique in the Bible, but it was unusual. Other prophetesses included Miriam (Exodus 15:20), Huldah (2 Kings 22:14), and Anna (Luke 2:36). Deborah, however, was unique. Only she is said to have "judged Israel" before the major event that marks her story (Judges 4:4). Her husband, Lappidoth, is otherwise unknown.

Deborah, known as a "mother in Israel" (Judges 5:7), remained in one location and the people came to her for guidance. Evidently over two hundred years later, when the book of Judges was compiled, a giant palm tree still marked the spot. Though she lived within the boundary of Benjamin (4:5; compare Joshua 16:2; 18:13), Deborah was probably from the tribe of Ephraim. That was the most prominent tribe of northern Israel. Some feel she came from the tribe of Issachar (Judges 5:14-15).

Under Deborah's inspired leadership, the poorly equipped Israelites defeated the Canaanites in the plain of Esdraelon (Judges 4:15). The flooding of the Kishon River evidently interfered with the enemy's impressive chariots (5:21-22). The Canaanites retreated to the north, perhaps to Taanach near Megiddo (5:19). They never reappeared as an enemy within Israel. The Song of Deborah (chapter 5) is a poetic version of the account recorded in Judges 4.[370]

> **Note:** *Deborah is the second named woman prophetess in the bible. Moses sister Miriam is the first (Exodus 15:20-21). Also take heed that Deborah was liken unto a king, and a prophet, but she was not allowed any priestly duties in the Tabernacle of God; which was restricted to the tribe of Levy.*

> **YEAR 1169-1162 BC**

Midianites Take Over Israel (Judges 6:1)371

"Midian was a son of Abraham by Abraham's second marriage. His land was called Midian and the people that lived there were called Midianites, though there were few, if any, permanent settlements. Midian was on the eastern edge of Gilead, Moab, and Edom south into northwest Arabia.

Midian and his descendants figure prominently only in the early history of Israel, in connection with Abraham (Genesis 25:1-6), Joseph (Genesis 37:25-36), Moses (Exodus 2:15-3:1), Balaam (Numbers 22:1-6; 25), and Gideon (Judges 6:1-8:28).

Midian was Isaac's younger half brother, the fourth of six sons born to Keturah, whom Abraham married as an old man (Genesis 25:1-2). By calling Midian and his full brothers "the sons of Keturah" (Genesis 25:4), the Bible carefully distinguishes them from Isaac, the son of Sarah, who was the one through whom God's promise to Abraham would be fulfilled (Genesis 12:1-3). In fact, Abraham and the Israelites regarded these other sons as having no more inheritance rights than a concubine's sons (Genesis 25:5-6).

Expelled from Abraham's family, for Isaac's sake, they became partially nomadic peoples of the deserts east and south of Palestine (Genesis 25:5-6).

THE LAND OF MIDIAN: Midian was probably far south of Edom on the eastern side of what is today called the Gulf of Aqaba. The Alexandrian geographer Ptolemy (second century AD) mentions a city named Modiana on the coast, and a Madiana twenty-six miles inland (modern el-Bed') in this region. This identification is supported by the Jewish historian Josephus (first century AD) and the Christian church historian Eusebius (early fourth century).

In early Old Testament times Midian seems to have been the land on the edge of the deserts bordering Gilead, Moab, and Edom south even into eastern Sinai.

In Joseph's day, some Midianite clans must have lived in the northern Transjordanian desert adjacent to Gilead or Bashan, because they were part of an Ishmaelite caravan traveling the trade route from Damascus across Gilead past Dothan to Egypt (Genesis 37:17, 25-28, 36).

When Moses fled from Pharaoh, he settled in Midian and eventually married Zipporah, the daughter of a Midianite priest (Exodus 2:15-22). Moses asked his Midianite relative Hobab to act as a guide from Horeb to Kadesh-barnea (Deuteronomy 1:19); Hobab was familiar with the wilderness of Paran (Numbers 10:11-12, 29-31), even though his own land and relatives were elsewhere (Numbers 10:30).

In the Balaam episode (the prophet Balaam being hired to curse Israel) and its bloody aftermath (Numbers 22:31), a substantial group of Midianites appears to have been living on the eastern frontier of Moab. The Moabite king Balak, who was subject to the Amorite king named Sihon (Numbers 21:26-30), discussed the Israelite threat with the elders of Midian, and a joint delegation was sent to Balaam (Numbers 22:2-7). At Acacia in the plains of Moab, an Israelite met and married a Midianite princess (Numbers 25:6-18; Numbers 31:8). The Midianite kings were considered puppet kings of King Sihon (Joshua 13:21). All the indications are that Midianite clans lived nearby, on the borders of Moab. Since Moab is north of Edom, the reference to an Edomite victory over Midian (Genesis 36:35) might indicate a northern encroachment by the Midianites on Edomite territory.

The Midianite invasion that Gideon (a judge or leader of Israel) repulsed had all the appearances of an invasion from the east. It would therefore seem that while "the land of Midian" is a term that may refer to a territory south of Edom, Midianites were living over a much wider area-on marginal land-east of Moab and Edom and south of Edom into east Sinai and northwest Arabia.

YEAR 1162-1122 BC

Gideon Defeats the Midianites Israel (Judges 6-8)

OPHRAH: 1. City in Benjamin, probably identical with Ephraim (2 Samuel 13:23; 2 Chronicles 13:19, "Ephron"; John 11:54). Ophrah is usually identified with the modern et-Taiyibeh, five miles (8 kilometers) north of Michmash and four miles (6.5 kilometers) northeast of Bethel.

2. City in Manasseh owned by Gideon's father, Joash the Abiezrite, and Gideon's home (Judges 6:11). There the angel appeared to Gideon, commissioning him as God's agent of relief from the Midianites (verses 12-24). Following his spectacular victory, Gideon was nominated for kingship, but he refused. Strangely, he constructed an ephod from the spoils of battle (8:22-28), which Israel worshiped. The idol at Ophrah became a snare to Gideon and his family. Gideon died at Ophrah, an old man (verses 29-32). His son Abimelech, ambitious for power, slaughtered his sibling rivals at Ophrah; only one of the 70, Jotham, escaped (9:1-6).[372]

YEAR 1122-1119 BC

Abimelech Declares Himself King and Murders His Brothers (Judges 9)

> "Abimelech was also Gideon's son by a concubine in Shechem (Judges 8:31). After his father's death, Abimelech conspired with his mother's family to assassinate his seventy half brothers. Only one of them, Jotham, escaped (9:1-5). In Abimelech's third year of rule, he cruelly suppressed a rebellion (9:22-49). Eventually his skull was crushed by a millstone thrown down by a woman on a tower. Abimelech ordered his armor bearer to kill him with a sword so that no one could say he had been killed by a woman (9:53-57)."[373]

YEAR 1119 – 1095 BC

Tola, Jair, Jephthah, Elon, and Abdon rule Israel (Judges 10-12)[374]

<u>**TOLA**</u>: "One of the judges of Israel, the son of Puah and the grandson of Dodo (Judges 10:1), of Issachar's tribe. Shamir, his home and burial place, was in the hill country of Ephraim. There he judged Israel for 23 years.

Although he "delivered" Israel after the debacle of Abimelech's abortive attempt to establish a monarchy at Shechem, his accomplishment is covered in just two verses (Judges 10:1-2). Like other "minor judges," mentioned only briefly (e.g., 12:8-15), he actually functioned in the judicial role—some more prominent "judges" (e.g., Gideon and Jephthah) were first, and perhaps solely, military heroes."

JAIR: "1. Descendant of Manasseh (Numbers 32:41), who at the time of the Conquest took several villages in the Argob region of Bashan and Gilead and called them after his own name, Haversesoth-jair, meaning "Towns of Jair" (Deuteronomy 3:14; cf. Joshua 13:30; 1 Kings 4:13; 1 Chronicles 2:23).

2. One of the judges of Israel. He judged Israel 22 years. His being a Gileadite makes it probable that he was a descendant of #1 above (Judges 10:3-5)."

JEPHTHAH: "Jephthah was the illegitimate son of Gilead (Judges 11:1) and a leader in the period of the judges. The son of a harlot, Jephthah was dispossessed by his father's other sons and refused a share in their father's home. He moved to the land of Tob, a small Aramean state east of the Jordan River (Judges 11:3-5), and became leader of a band of malcontents and adventurers who went raiding with him.

When war broke out between the Israelites and the Ammonites, the leaders of Gilead begged Jephthah to return and lead their army. At first he refused because of their previous mistreatment of him. When they promised to make him Gilead's ruler, he accepted and became commander in chief and ruler (Judges 11:4-10). The agreement was ratified before the Lord at a general assembly of the people at Mizpah (Judges 11:11) in Gilead, probably just south of the Jabbok River.

After diplomatic negotiations with the king of Ammon failed, Jephthah waged war against the Ammonites. Before the fighting started, he vowed to the Lord that if he was victorious, on his return home he would sacrifice to God whoever met him at the door of his house. Then he successfully led his army against the Ammonites, destroying them with a terrible slaughter (Judges 11:29-33).

When Jephthah returned home, he was shocked to find that the first person to meet him was his only child, his daughter, playing a tambourine and dancing for joy. When he saw her, he tore his clothes and said, "Alas, my daughter! You have brought me very low, and you have become the cause of great trouble to me; for I have opened my mouth to the LORD, and I cannot take back my vow" (Judges 11:35, RSV). She submitted to her destiny but begged that it might be postponed for two months so that she and her companions could retreat to the mountains and lament that she must die a virgin (Judges 11:34-38). A woman in ancient Israel could suffer no greater disgrace than to die unmarried and childless. When she returned, her father fulfilled his vow (Judges 11:38-39).

Jephthah also led Gilead against the Ephraimites, who were resentful that they had not been included in the fight against Ammon. They had been given a previous chance to ally with Gilead but had refused. Jephthah captured the fords of the Jordan behind the Ephraimites and prevented their escape by an ingenious strategy. Gileadite guards put fugitives to a test, demanding that they say "Shibboleth." If they could not pronounce the "sh," they were revealed as Ephraimites and killed. The account says that 42,000 Ephraimites died at that time (Judges 12:1-6).

Jephthah was judge over Gilead for six years (Judges 12:7), and when he died, he was buried in one of the cities of Gilead. In the Letter to the Hebrews, Jephthah is named with Gideon, Barak, and others as a hero of faith (Hebrews 11:32)."

ELON: "Judge from Zebulun who judged Israel for 10 years. He was buried in Aijalon (Judges 12:11-12)."

ABDON: "Hillel's son who judged Israel for eight years (Judges 12:13-15). Abdon was a very wealthy man, as indicated by reference to the 70 donkeys he owned."

YEAR 1095 – 1055 BC

Philistines Oppress Israel (Judges 13:1)375

Note: The Philistines are descendants of Ham's second son

Mizraim. And all of the other tribes in the Middle East came mostly from Ham's youngest son Canaan.

- **Genesis 10:6** - The descendants of Ham were Cush, **Mizraim**, Put, and Canaan.

- **Genesis 10: 13** And <u>Mizraim</u> begat Ludim, and Anamim, and Lehabim, and Naphtuhim, **14** and Pathrusim, and Casluhim, (**out of whom came Philistim**,) and Caphtorim.

- **I Chronicles 1: 11** And **Mizraim** begat Ludim, and Anamim, and Lehabim, and Naphtuhim, **12** and Pathrusim, and Casluhim, (**of whom came the Philistines**,) and Caphthorim.

CUSH: Eldest of Ham's four sons (Genesis 10:6; 1 Chronicles 1:8). Because the other three (Egypt, Put, and Canaan) are place-names, it is likely that Cush also is a place. It is usually identified with Ethiopia.

MIZRAIM: <u>Hebrew word for the land of Egypt and/or its people</u>, though some scholars suggest that Mizraim refers to a site either on the Edomite border or in northern Syria. In Genesis 10:6, Mizraim (Egypt) is identified as one of the sons of Ham who settled south of Canaan. Genesis 10:14 and Isaiah 11:11 distinguish Mizraim from Pathrushim, that is, Upper Egypt (the southern half of the United Kingdom of Egypt), but in the majority of the nearly 700 known references to Mizraim, there is no distinction between the two parts of the kingdom, and the term refers simply to the Egyptian territory.

PUT: Third of Ham's four sons, who most likely settled in northern Africa and is perhaps the forefather of the peoples of Egypt and Libya (Genesis 10:6; 1 Chronicles 1:8).

Ancient nation, descended from a man of the same name. It is commonly identified as Libya, although it has been argued that it was the Punt of Egyptian records, somewhere along the northeast coast of Africa, perhaps Somalia. Its association with Egypt, Cush, and Canaan, and the usage of the name in the OT, make the Libyan location probable. In the OT the Libyan people are called Lubim, a name that always appears in the plural.

PHUT

1. KJV spelling of Put, Ham's third son, in Genesis 10:6.
2. KJV spelling of Put, a region close to Egypt along the Mediterranean Sea, in Ezekiel 27:10.

CANAAN: Ham's youngest son whose descendants are under the curse of Noah.[376]

Philistine Cities[377]

ASHDOD: Ashdod was one of the Philistines' five main cities (the "pentapolis") along with Gaza, Ashkelon, Gath, and Ekron (Joshua 13:3). Ashdod was located midway between Joppa and Gaza, about three miles (4.8 kilometers) from the coast. The ancient tell has been excavated extensively since 1962. The earliest level found was Canaanite, dating to the 17th century B.C. When the Israelites arrived in the Promised Land, the city was inhabited by the giant Anakim (Joshua 11:21-22). Though unconquered, it was assigned to Judah's tribe (Joshua 15:46-47). Its people were referred to as Ashdodites (Joshua 13:4; Nehemiah 4:7). During the 12th century BC the coast of Palestine was invaded by the Sea Peoples, a group of tribes from the Aegean area. Ashdod was destroyed and reoccupied by one of these peoples, the Philistines. Excavations at Ashdod have uncovered three levels of Philistine occupation and have furnished a glimpse of the material culture of these traditional enemies of Israel.

GAZA: Gaza is a city near the Palestinian coast, about 50 miles (80.5 kilometers) west-southwest of Jerusalem. It has been occupied almost continuously since ancient times; modern Gaza has played an important part in the conflict between Arabs and Israelis. Gazite and Gazathite are biblical names for the residents of the town.

Set about midpoint of the length of the plain of Philistia, Gaza was a rich agricultural area where wheat and similar grains flourished. Situated some three miles (4.8 kilometers) from the Mediterranean, Gaza's position as the greatest trading center of ancient Palestine did not come from the sea but from the highways, which brought caravans from all parts of the Fertile Crescent. This accessibility was also a handicap, for the roadways along the coast were the easiest route for the armies of Egypt, Assyria, Babylonia, Persia, Greece, and Rome. Often Gaza was the victim of their passage.

GATH: Gath was a walled city (2 Chronicles 26:6) and one of the five chief cities of the Philistines, which also included Gaza, Ashdod, Ashkelon, and Ekron (Joshua 13:3 and 1 Samuel 6:17). All of these cities were situated on or near the southern coast of Palestine. Although frequently involved in conflict with the Israelites, the city was apparently not conquered until the time of King David (1 Chronicles 18:1). It was a Canaanite city, the home of the giant Goliath (1 Samuel 17:4) and other men of great height (2 Samuel 21:18-22). A remnant of the Anakim was left in the city even after the extensive military campaigns of Joshua (Joshua 10:36-39 and 11:21-22).

When the Philistines captured the ark of God, they carried it from Ebenezer to Ashdod, from there to Gath (1 Samuel 5:8), and then to Ekron. After many of the Philistines died or were stricken with tumors, the ark was returned to Israel, first to Beth-shemesh and then to Kiriath-jearim (6:14 and 7:1). When David fled from Saul, he came to Gath and faked insanity before Achish, who was the king of the city (21:10-15). During the rebellion of Absalom, six hundred soldiers from Gath served in King David's military (2 Samuel 15:18). According to 2 Chronicles 11:8, Rehoboam fortified the city of Gath, and 2 Kings 12:17 relates that it was taken by Hazael, king of Syria, in the ninth century (2 Chronicles and 2 Kings 12:17). However, it was apparently again under Philistine control when Uzziah broke down its walls (2 Chronicles 26:6). The city disappeared after being besieged and conquered by Sargon II in the eighth century BC (Amos 6:2).

The Canaanites[378]

- **Genesis 10: 15** And Canaan begat Sidon his firstborn, and Heth,
  16 and the Jebusite, and the Amorite, and the Girgasite,
  17 and the Hivite, and the Arkite, and the Sinite,
  18 and the Arvadite, and the Zemarite, and the Hamathite: and afterward were the families of the Canaanites spread abroad.
  19 And the border of the Canaanites was from Sidon, as thou comest to Gerar, unto Gaza; as thou goest, unto Sodom, and Gomorrah, and Admah, and Zeboim, even unto Lasha

HETH: Progenitor of the Hittite people and a descendant of Canaan, in Ham's line (Genesis 10:15; 1 Chronicles 1:13).

JEBUSITE: This walled city lay on the boundary between Judah and Benjamin.

After being conquered by David, it was known as the "city of David," or ancient Jerusalem. Its occupants were Jebusites (Joshua 18:16). They were one of the several clans or tribes collectively known as Canaanites (Genesis 10:15-16). Their land, along with that of their neighbors, was repeatedly promised to the Israelites (Exodus 3:8; 13:5; Deuteronomy 7:1; 20:17). This promise was partially fulfilled early in the campaign under Joshua (Joshua 3:10; 12:8; 18:16). It is said that the men of Judah fought against Jerusalem and took it (18:28). "The Benjamites, however, failed to dislodge the Jebusites, who were living in Jerusalem; to this day the Jebusites live there with the Benjamites" (Judges 1:21, NIV). Apparently the city was captured by the men of Judah, but its inhabitants were not destroyed, and they later reoccupied the site.

Jebus (or Jerusalem) lay on the borderline between two tribes, and this may account for its survival until the time of David. The borders of Judah and Benjamin are thus defined: "The boundary then passed through the valley of the son of Hinnom, along the southern slopes of the Jebusites, where the city of Jerusalem is located. Then it went west to the top of the mountain above the valley of Hinnom, and on up to the northern end of the valley of Rephaim" (Joshua 15:8). This account indicates that Jebus lay on the southern slope of the "mountain" north of the valley of Hinnom, the site of East Jerusalem today.

The city's survival was assured by a constant supply of water, the spring of Gihon, and by strong natural defenses. It was easily defended by steep valleys on three sides: the Kidron on the east, the Hinnom on the south and west. The Jebusites therefore considered their city impregnable. This gave them a certain arrogance and complacency. After the death of Saul, when David was seeking to consolidate the kingdom, the Jebusites scornfully challenged David to capture their stronghold (2 Samuel 5:6). As the last remaining Canaanite stronghold in the area, it presented a unique challenge. Joab apparently led the attack up the water shaft and succeeded where previous attempts had failed (5:8).

For political as well as strategic reasons, David decided to move his capital from Hebron to Jebus. Politically, it lay in neutral territory between Judah and Benjamin and thus aroused no jealousy. Strategically, it was easily defended and more centrally located. The choice proved a wise one. In spite of the fact that Jebus-Jerusalem lies on no waterway or major highway, it has become through the centuries the spiritual capital of the world. Under David and Solomon, it became Israel's religious center, and today it is of prime importance to the three major monotheistic religions of mankind: Judaism, Islam, and Christianity.

AMORITE: The Amorites were Semitic people found throughout the Fertile Crescent of the Near East at the beginning of the second millennium B.C. Amorites are first mentioned in the Bible as descendants of Canaan in a list of ancient peoples (Genesis 10:16, compare 1 Chronicles 1:13-16). Some of these nomadic people seem to have migrated from the Syrian Desert into Mesopotamia, others into Palestine.

Farther to the west, Amorites had been in Palestine and Syria as early as the third millennium B.C. Egyptian texts of the early part of the 19th century BC show that additional waves of Amorite nomads were entering Canaan at that time. Many of their names are similar to the Amorite names from upper Mesopotamia. In fact, many names from the Mari tablets are identical with or similar to names in the patriarchal accounts in Genesis. People named Jacob, Abraham, Levi, and Ishmael were known at Mari, and names similar to Gad and Dan have been found there. Benjamin was known as the name of a tribe. Nahor was found to be the name of a city near Haran. According to Genesis, Abraham lived in Haran many years before going to Canaan. Jacob spent 20 years there and married two women from Haran.

Amorites appear prominently in the Old Testament as major obstacles to the occupation of Canaan (the Promised Land) by the Israelites after the Exodus. Calling Moses to lead Israel out of Egypt, the Lord spoke of Canaan, then occupied by Amorites and others, as a good land (Exodus 3:8, 17). When the Israelites were in the wilderness, God promised to destroy those nations (23:23) and drive them out of the land (33:2). The Hebrew people were warned not to make covenants with any of them, to intermarry with them, or to tolerate their idol worship (34:11-17).

GIRGASHITE: Canaanite tribe (Genesis 10:16; 1 Chronicles 1:14) whose land was promised to Abraham (Genesis 15:21; Deuteronomy 7:1; Joshua 3:10) and was ultimately acquired (Joshua 24:11; Nehemiah 9:8). The tribe's location is unknown, though they may have lived in Karkisha, a city mentioned in Hittite texts, or in Kirkishati, an area east of the Tigris. The name Gresh appeared in 13th century BC Ugaritic texts and might indicate a tribe. In Matthew 8:28; Mark 5:1; and Luke 8:26, a name variously translated as "Gergesenes"

(KJV), "Gerasenes," and "Gadarenes" may preserve the tradition of Girgashite occupation of Palestine.

HIVITES: Name of a pre-Israelite group living in Canaan. Though not yet discovered/rated archaeologically or from secular history as a people, they were regarded as emerging from a son of Canaan (Genesis 10:17) and as inhabiting areas of the Lebanon Mountains (Judges 3:3) and Mt Hermon (Joshua 11:3). They are referred to frequently as a group dispossessed by Israel (Joshua 12:8; 24:11; 1 Kings 9:20) but who managed to survive into the kingdom period (2 Samuel 24:7) and lived at that time near Tyre as well as in other possible areas. Some scholars think that an error in copying, involving the changing of the letters r (resh) to w (waw) was responsible for the origin of the name Hivite from Horite.

ARKITE: Name of a clan descended from Ham's son Canaan (Genesis 10:17; 1 Chronicles 1:15). The Arkites were probably residents of Arqa, a Phoenician town north of Tripolis in Syria. According to an early inscription, Arqa was captured by the Assyrian Tiglath-pileser III in 738 BC. Possibly another branch of the tribe settled near Ataroth, a town on the border between Ephraim and Benjamin (Joshua 16:2).

SINITE: Canaanite tribe, possibly located in northern Lebanon, whose ancestry is traced to Canaan, Ham's son (Genesis 10:17; 1 Chronicles 1:15).

ARVADITE: Small fortified island about 2 miles (3.2 kilometers) off the coast of Syria (ancient Phoenicia) and 30 miles (48 kilometers) north of Tripolis. Arvad developed a large trading and fighting fleet, and the fame of its sailors was referred to in a description of the naval power of Tyre (Ezekiel 27:8, 11). Egyptian records recount Arvad's fall to Thutmose III about 1472 BC. Assyrian records indicate the importance of Arvad and its recurrent conquest by foreign powers from the 11th to the 7th centuries BC.

Arvad was later known as Aradus or Arados, and is referred to as such in 1 Maccabees 15:23. During the Persian and Hellenistic periods it was once again an important Mediterranean seaport, only to decline again. The Canaanite tribe of Arvadites (Genesis 10:18; 1 Chronicles 1:16) possibly had an ethnic connection with the island Arvad. Today Arvad is known as Ruad.

ZEMARITE: One of the families of the Canaanites in the ethnological lists of Genesis 10 (verse 18) and 1 Chronicles 1 (verse 16). The Zemarites were a Hamitic tribe mentioned in connection with the Arvadites and the Hamathites. They were probably located near the Mediterranean in the vicinity of Tripoli.

HAMATHITE: City and district located about 125 miles (201 kilometers) north of Damascus (Syria), on the Orontes River. The early residents apparently were of the Hamitic race from the descendants of Canaan (Genesis 10:18), but later inhabitants were Semitic. It was to be the northern boundary of the nation of Israel, described as the "entrance of Hamath" (Numbers 34:7-8; Joshua 13:5; Hebrew, Lebo Hamath), but actually it was such only in the early monarchy and under Jeroboam II (793–753 BC). The location is uncertain but was between the Lebanon and Anti-Lebanon Mountains. Some scholars have thought of it as an actual place-name, Lebo-hamath, and have identified it with modern Lebweh on the Orontes. Others have located it elsewhere in Syria.

Hamath was established during the Neolithic period and destroyed about 1750 BC, perhaps by the Hyksos. It was later rebuilt and conquered by Thutmose III (1502–1448 BC), and while Egypt controlled Syria, Hamath prospered. Several Hittite inscriptions have been discovered that disclose that Hamath had become the capital of a small Hittite kingdom prior to 900 BC.

CHAPTER 16

THE WORD AND THE KINGS

John 5: 39 "Search the scriptures, for in them ye think ye have eternal life: and they are they which testify of me."

If you search for him, Christ Jesus can be seen throughout the Old Testament, bringing messages from the Father to the prophets, kings, and the people. I will get you started by showing you a few of the persons he visited. After that, you will be able to find him again, and again, and again; Keep in mind when examining these examples that Christ is known as **the word of the Lord**, **the word of God**, and also **the angel of the Lord**. Therefore, I will be dealing with history, and prophesies, and with the Lord Jesus Christ, and his appearances in the Old Testament: from Samson to the book of Malachi.

YEAR - 1127 BC

Samson the Judge (Judges Chapters 13-16)

After Joshua died, to include all the elders that came through the forty-year Sinai crossing, the children of Israel did evil in the sight of God by mingling with the people of the promised land, and worshiping the gods of the Canaanites. Therefore, God gave them "Judges" to rule over them, and to be his representative among them. One such judge was a man named Samson whose birth was announced by <u>the angel of the Lord</u>.[379]

God: "And the children of Israel did evil again in the sight of the Lord; and the Lord delivered them into the hand of the Philistines forty years.

Samson's Father: And there was a certain man of Zorah, of the family of the Danites, whose name was Manoah; and his wife was barren, and bare not.

Samson Mother: And <u>the angel of the Lord</u> appeared unto the woman, and said unto her, Behold now, thou art barren, and bearest not: but thou shalt conceive, and bear a son.

Samson Father: And Manoah said unto <u>the angel of the Lord,</u> I pray thee, let us detain thee, until we shall have made ready a kid for thee.

The Angel: And <u>the angel of the Lord</u> said unto Manoah, Though thou detain me, I will not eat of thy bread: and if thou wilt offer a burnt offering, thou must offer it unto the Lord. For Manoah knew not that he was an <u>angel of the Lord</u>.

Samson Father: And Manoah said unto <u>the angel of the Lord</u>, <u>What is thy name, that when thy sayings come to pass we may do thee honour?</u>

The Angel: <u>And the angel of the Lord said unto him,</u> "<u>Why askest thou thus after my name, seeing it is secret?</u>"

Now right here I want to pause for a second, and take a deep breath. <u>The angel of the Lord</u>, by saying his name is a secret, reveals two things:

- That this is the same <u>angel of the Lord</u> that led Moses and the children of Israel across the Sinai desert, and is in fact Christ himself before he was manifested in the flesh.

- That the only scripture in the bible that identifies a celestial being with a secret name is in the book of Revelation; when Christ returns to the earth: "And I saw heaven opened, and behold a white horse; and he that sat upon him was called Faithful and True, and in righteousness he doth judge and make war. His eyes were as a flame of fire, and on his head were many crowns; and <u>he had a name written</u>, <u>that no man knew</u>, <u>but he himself</u>. And he was clothed with a vesture dipped in blood: <u>and his name is called</u> <u>The Word of God.</u>

Samson's History: "Samson was Manoah's son, from Dan's tribe. His mother, whose name is not given in the Bible, had been barren. The angel of the Lord announced to her that she would have a son who was to be a Nazirite all of his life (i.e., he was not to drink wine or strong drink, not to eat anything ceremonially unclean, and not to allow a razor to touch his head, Numbers 6:1-6). She was also told that he would begin to deliver Israel from the Philistines, who had controlled them for 40 years (Judges 13:1-5). She reported this to her husband, Manoah, and Manoah prayed concerning this angelic visit (13:8). The angel of the Lord appeared again and gave instructions about the child who was to be born. Manoah made a burnt offering, and the angel of the Lord ascended to heaven in the smoke. Manoah feared that they would die, for he now realized that they had seen God (13:22). The child was born and the Lord blessed him as he grew. The Spirit of the Lord moved upon him in Mahaneh-dan (13:25).

Samson went to Timnah and saw a Philistine woman whom he wished to marry. The Lord was seeking an opportunity against the Philistines, and in Samson's case these occasions came through Philistine women. When he and his parents went to Timnah to arrange the marriage, a lion came out of the vineyards, and Samson, upon whom the Spirit of the Lord came mightily, tore the lion in half. Later he found that a swarm of bees had made honey in the carcass of the lion (Judges 14:2-9).

Samson made a feast at Timnah, as was the custom, and told the Philistine men a riddle that involved the lion and the honey. A wager was made on the riddle and the Philistines prevailed upon his wife to learn the answer and disclose it to them. When they came up with the answer, Samson knew what had happened, so he went out and killed 30 Philistine men to pay for his bet (14:19). Samson went home, and his father-in-law gave Samson's wife to Samson's best man.

When Samson returned to see his wife, he was not allowed to visit her, so he took 300 foxes, tied them in pairs tail to tail, fixed a torch to each pair, and turned them loose in the grainfields of the Philistines, so that the shocks and standing grain were burned. Consequently, the Philistines came and burned his wife and her father. In revenge, Samson went out and slaughtered many of them (Judges 15:1-8).

During these days, the Philistines came against Judah, and the people of Judah bound Samson with new ropes to turn him over to the Philistines. When they came to Lehi, where the Philistines were camped, the Spirit of the Lord came on him mightily again. He snapped the ropes, seized the jawbone of a donkey, and killed 1,000 Philistines. Being very thirsty, he cried to the Lord, so God opened a spring of water at Lehi (Judges 15:9-20).

Samson's weakness for Philistine women continued to create trouble for both him and the Philistines. He went down to Gaza, where he became involved with a prostitute (Judges 16:1). The men of the city learned that he was there and plotted to kill him at dawn, but he arose at midnight and walked off with the doors, posts, and bar of the city gate and put them on top of the hill before Hebron.

Then he found Delilah, from the valley of Sorek. The Philistines enlisted her by bribery to find out the source of his strength (Judges 16:4-5). She kept pestering him, so he told her that if they bound him with seven fresh bowstrings he would be as weak as other men. So

Who is Jesus Christ

she bound him and cried, "The Philistines are upon you." He easily broke the bowstrings. In response to her continued questions, he kept lying to her about the secret of his strength. In succession, she bound him with new ropes and seven locks of his hair woven together and attached to a loom. Finally, she wore him down and he told her the truth. If someone shaved his head and broke his Nazirite vow, his strength would be gone. While Samson slept with his head on her knees, she called a barber, who shaved off his hair. This time when she cried, "The Philistines are upon you," the Philistines seized him, gouged out his eyes, and took him to Gaza (16:21).

At Gaza, Samson was bound with bronze fetters and forced to grind at a mill. During the weeks he was doing this, his hair began to grow again. At a time when the Philistines were having a great festival at the temple of their god, Dagon, they celebrated their victory over Samson and asked that he be brought so they could mock him. Some 3,000 people watched while Samson entertained them. At his request, Samson was placed between the two pillars (that were supporting the temple). He asked the Lord for strength and pushed against the pillars, so that the entire building collapsed. Samson died with the Philistines as he had requested, but he killed more Philistines in this final act than he had previously (Judges 16:1-30).

Samson's family came to retrieve his body, and they buried him between Zorah and Eshtaol in the tomb of his father, Manoah. He had served as "judge," or leader, of Israel for 20 years (Judges 16:31)."[380]

DELILAH: Delilah was Samson's mistress. She betrayed him to his Philistine enemies (Judges 16). Philistia held southern Israel as servants at the time (around 1070 BC). Samson was the judge chosen by God to begin the delivery of Israel. His success prompted the five Philistine rulers to offer Delilah a bribe if she would help capture him by discovering the secret of his enormous strength.

Delilah was from the valley of Sorek, in the southeast corner of Dan's territory. That was only a few miles from Samson's home in Zorah. It is clear from Judges 14:1 that she was a Philistine. The large reward she accepted (5,500 pieces of silver) implies that her motivations were other than Philistine loyalty. Her other contacts with men probably indicate that she was a prostitute.

On her fourth attempt Delilah finally tricked Samson into revealing his secret. His strength was from God. His long hair was part of his Nazirite vow (see Numbers 6:1-8). Thus, he was "set apart" by God for special service (Judges 13:5), and his hair was never to be cut. Delilah lulled him to sleep, shaved his head, and delivered him (still unsuspecting) into the hands of his enemies.[381]

YEAR - 1105 BC

Samuel the Prophet / Judge

The prophet Samuel was born under peculiar circumstances. His father was a Levite named Elkanah: who had two wives; one was named Hannah, and the other Peninnah. Hannah was barren, but Penninnah gave birth to sons and daughters.[382]

It sorely grieved Hannah that she bore no children, and the fact that Peninnah mocked her greatly because she was barren. Therefore, when they were at the yearly feast before the tabernacle of the Lord in Shiloh, she put forth her plea to God for help.[383]

After Hannah's prayer it came to pass that she conceived, and had a son: and called his name Samuel. Once Samuel was weaned, she took him up to Shiloh, and gave him over to the high priest Eli. Samuel was lodged in a room down the hall from Eli, and served out his duties, girded with a linen ephod."

> **EPHOD** (Garment) -A vest worn over a blue robe that ancient Hebrew priests would put on during religious services in the tabernacle or temple (Exodus 28:31). Urim and Thummim, the two lots or dice that the priests would cast to determine the will of God, were attached to the ephod. Sometimes the word "ephod" also meant the complete dress of the high priest

(1 Samuel 2:28; 23:6, 9; 30:7) or similar garments worn by less-important priests.

Made of dyed material and fine linen, the ephod was embroidered in blue, purple, scarlet, and gold. Two shoulder straps were attached at the top, and each had an onyx stone inscribed with the names of Israel's 12 tribes. The breastplate, which also had the tribal names written upon it, was bound to the ephod by cords and chains (Exodus 28:22-29).

Jewish writers give us several different ideas of <u>how the ephod may have looked</u>:

1. like an apron, covering the body from the chest to the heels; or

2. a covering for the body from the waist down, with the upper body being covered **by** the breastplate; or

3. a jacket with sleeves with the middle of the breast uncovered so the breastplate could be inserted easily.[384]

Eli had two sons: Hophni and Phinehas who was in charge of the tithe and offering brought to the tabernacle of God. Their duty as Levite priest were to accept the tithe and offering, and make distribution in accordance to the law God gave to Moses and to Aaron (the High Priest).[385] But instead of keeping the law they did wickedly before the Lord:

- **1 Samuel 2**: 12 Now the sons of Eli were scoundrels who had no respect for the Lord 13 or for their duties as priests. Whenever anyone offered a sacrifice, Eli's sons would send over a servant with a three-pronged fork. While the meat of the sacrificed animal was still boiling,

14 the servant would stick the fork into the pot and demand that whatever it brought up be given to Eli's sons. All the Israelites who came to worship at Shiloh were treated this way.

15 Sometimes the servant would come even before the animal's fat had been burned on the altar. He would demand raw meat before it had been boiled so that it could be used for roasting.

16 The man offering the sacrifice might reply, "Take as much as you want, but the fat must be burned first." Then the servant would demand, "No, give it to me now, or I'll take it by force." 17 So the sin of these young men was very serious in the Lord's sight, for they treated the Lord's offerings with contempt.

- **1 Samuel 2**: 22 Now Eli was very old, and heard all that his sons did unto all Israel; and how they lay with the women that assembled at the door of the tabernacle of the congregation.
23 And he said unto them, Why do ye such things? for I hear of your evil dealings by all this people.
24 Nay, my sons; for it is no good report that I hear: ye make the Lord's people to transgress.
25 If one man sin against another, the judge shall judge him: but if a man sin against the Lord, who shall intreat for him? Notwithstanding they hearkened not unto the voice of their father, because the Lord would slay them.

Because Eli didn't stop his sons from abusing the law of God, or from having sexual relations with the women that ministered unto the tabernacle, God sent a prophet to tell Eli that he was going to remove him, and his sons by the reason of death. And that he was going to raise up a faithful priest instead. The sign of this charge to Eli would be the death of both his sons: in one day.[386]

God calls Samuel into Service

Some will not believe that God will speak to you in an audible voice, in your language, accordance to your understanding. His calling of Samuel is a classic case of why we sometimes miss the boat when he calls us and we fail to react to his call.[387]

Samuel's duties: And the child Samuel ministered unto the Lord before Eli. And the word of the Lord was precious in those days; there was no open vision.

Eli: And it came to pass at that time, when Eli was laid down in his place, and his eyes began to wax dim, that he could not see; and ere the lamp of God went out in the temple of the Lord, where the ark of God was,

God calls Samuel: and Samuel was laid down to sleep; that the Lord called Samuel: and he answered, Here am I.

Samuel: And he ran unto Eli, and said, Here am I; for thou calledst me.

Eli: And he said, I called not; lie down again.

God calls Samuel again: And he went and lay down. And the Lord called yet again, Samuel.

Samuel: And Samuel arose and went to Eli, and said, Here am I; for thou didst call me.

Eli: And he answered, I called not, my son; lie down again.

> **Note:** Now Samuel did not yet know the Lord, neither was the word of the Lord yet revealed unto him.

God calls Samuel the third time: And the Lord called Samuel again the third time.

Samuel: And he arose and went to Eli, and said, Here am I; for thou didst call me.

Eli: And Eli perceived that the Lord had called the child. Therefore Eli said unto Samuel, Go, lie down: and it shall be, if he call thee, that thou shalt say, Speak, Lord; for thy servant heareth.

Samuel: So Samuel went and lay down in his place.

God: And the Lord came, and stood, and called as at other times, Samuel, Samuel.

Samuel: Then Samuel answered, Speak; for thy servant heareth.

God: And the Lord said to Samuel, Behold, I will do a thing in Israel, at which both the ears of every one that heareth it shall tingle.

- In that day I will perform against Eli all things which I have spoken concerning his house: when I begin, I will also make an end.

- For I have told him that I will judge his house for ever for the iniquity which he knoweth; because his sons made themselves vile, and he restrained them not.

- And therefore I have sworn unto the house of Eli, that the iniquity of Eli's house shall not be purged with sacrifice nor offering for ever.

Samuel: And Samuel lay until the morning, and opened the doors of the house of the Lord. And Samuel feared to shew Eli the vision.

Eli: Then Eli called Samuel, and said, Samuel, my son.

Samuel: And he answered, Here am I.

Eli: And he said, What is the thing that the Lord hath said unto thee? I pray thee hide it not from me: God do so to thee, and more also, if thou hide any thing from me of all the things that he said unto thee.

Samuel: And Samuel told him every whit, and hid nothing from him.

Eli: And he said, It is the Lord: let him do what seemeth him good.

Samuel: And Samuel grew, and the Lord was with him, and did let none of his words fall to the ground.

The People: And all Israel from Dan even to Beer-sheba knew that Samuel was established to be a prophet of the Lord.

God: And the Lord appeared again in Shiloh: **for the Lord revealed himself to Samuel in Shiloh by the word of the Lord.**

*Now don't go any further until you let it sink in that (Christ), the word of the Lord, was the one that communicated with Samuel, and guided him how to deal with the Hebrew people. I say this in a whole heartily way because this is not just simply reading, but studying to enhance knowledge about God and his interaction with human kind. More importantly, Christ in the Old Testament.

When Eli was eighty-eight years old, he received word that his two sons were dead, and the ark of the covenant had been captured by the Philistines. Upon hearing the news, he fell off of a perch on the wall, and broke his neck. Eli served as the high priest of Israel for forty-years.[388]

Samuel Anoints Saul King of Israel

After the death of Eli and his two sons, Samuel became the

religious spokesman of God. He was a Levite priest, but he was not a blood relative of the family of Aaron, and therefore could not inherit the job of High Priest: for only those in Aaron's genealogy, by law, could be high priest.[389]

When Samuel was getting to be too old for the judge's job, he appointed his two sons as judges. However, his sons were wicked like Eli's sons, "And his sons walked not in his ways, but turned aside after lucre, and took bribes, and perverted judgment."[390]

Their behavior forced the twelve tribes to partition Samuel to give them a king like all the other nations surrounding them. Samuel grieved over this request before God, but was given permission to choose the Benjamite Saul as king. When Samuel meet Saul, he gave him specific instructions concerning the kingship and serving God.[391]

- Then Samuel took a vial of oil, and poured it upon his head, and kissed him, and said, Is it not because the Lord hath anointed thee to be captain over his inheritance?

- When thou art departed from me today, then thou shalt find two men by Rachel's sepulchre in the border of Benjamin at Zelzah; and they will say unto thee, The asses which thou wentest to seek are found: and, lo, thy father hath left the care of the asses, and sorroweth for you, saying, What shall I do for my son?

- Then shalt thou go on forward from thence, and thou shalt come to the plain of Tabor, and there shall meet thee three men going up to God to Bethel, one carrying three kids, and another carrying three loaves of bread, and another carrying a bottle of wine:

- and they will salute thee, and give thee two loaves of bread; which thou shalt receive of their hands.

- After that thou shalt come to the hill of God, where is the garrison of the Philistines: and it shall come to pass, when thou art come thither to the city, that thou shalt meet a company of prophets coming down from the high place with a psaltery, and a tabret, and a pipe, and a harp, before them; and they shall prophesy:

- and the Spirit of the Lord will come upon thee, and thou shalt prophesy with them, and shalt be turned into another man.

- And let it be, when these signs are come unto thee, that thou do as occasion serve thee; for God is with thee.

- <u>And thou shalt go down before me to Gilgal; and, behold, I will come down unto thee, to offer burnt offerings, and to sacrifice sacrifices of peace offerings</u>: <u>seven days shalt thou tarry, till I come to thee, and shew thee what thou shalt do.</u>

YEAR - 1065 BC (1 Samuel 8 – 16:1-15)

Saul is Confirmed by God

God: And it was so, that when he had turned his back to go from Samuel, God gave him {*Saul*}another heart: and all those signs came to pass that day.

Saul: And when they came thither to the hill, behold, a company of prophets met him; and the Spirit of God came upon him, and he prophesied among them.

The People: And it came to pass, when all that knew him beforetime saw that, behold, he prophesied among the prophets, then the people said one to another, What is this that is come unto the son of Kish? Is Saul also among the prophets? And one of the same place answered and said, But who is their father? Therefore it became a proverb, Is Saul also among the prophets?

Saul: And when he had made an end of prophesying, he came to the high place.

Saul's First Disobedience

While waiting for Samuel at Gilgal Saul defeated the Philistines with the help of his son Jonathan. When the seventh day had passed Saul took it upon himself to offer up to God the burnt offering and the peace offering; he was the king, but he broke the law of God, because only a Levite priest could make the offering to God.[392]

Samuel: And he tarried seven days, according to the set time that Samuel had appointed: but Samuel came not to Gilgal; and the people were scattered from him.

Saul: And Saul said, Bring hither a burnt offering to me, and peace offerings. And he offered the burnt offering.

Samuel: And it came to pass, that as soon as he had made an end of offering the burnt offering, behold, Samuel came;

Saul: and Saul went out to meet him, that he might salute him.

Samuel: And Samuel said, What hast thou done?

Saul: And Saul said, Because I saw that the people were scattered from me, and that thou camest not within the days appointed, and that the Philistines gathered themselves together at Michmash; therefore said I, The Philistines will come down now upon me to Gilgal, and I have not made supplication unto the Lord: <u>I forced myself therefore</u>, <u>and offered a burnt offering</u>.

Samuel: And Samuel said to Saul, Thou hast done foolishly: thou hast not kept the commandment of the Lord thy God, which he commanded thee: for now would the Lord have established thy kingdom upon Israel for ever. But now thy kingdom shall not continue: the Lord hath sought him a man after his own heart, and the Lord hath commanded him to be captain over his people, because thou hast not kept that which the Lord commanded thee.

Saul's Second Disobedience

Even though Saul did not follow Samuels instructions to the letter, and was told that the kingship would be pulled from him, God gave Saul another chance to prove himself by fighting against the Amalekites. Again, "One day Samuel said to Saul, "It was the Lord who told me to anoint you as king of his people, Israel. Now listen to this message from the Lord! This is what the Lord of Heaven's Armies has declared: I have decided to settle accounts with the nation of Amalek for opposing Israel when they came from Egypt. Now go and completely destroy the entire Amalekite nation—men, women, children, babies, cattle, sheep, goats, camels, and donkeys."[393]

> **AMALEK, AMALEKITES** - Amalek was the son of Eliphaz (Esau's son) by his concubine, Timna (Genesis 36:12; 1 Chronicles 1:36). Descendants of this tribal chief of Edom were known as Amalekites. They settled in the Negev Desert and became allies of the Edomites, Ammonites, Moabites, Ishmaelites, and Midianites. The Amalekites were notable enemies of Israel. Amalek inherited the feud between his grandfather Esau and Esau's brother Jacob. Since Jacob was one of the ancestors of Israel, the conflict between Amalek and Israel was both religious and political.
>
> The territory of the nomadic Amalekites (in the Negev) ranged from south of Beersheba to the southeast as far as Elath and Ezion-geber. They undoubtedly raided westward

into the coastal plain, eastward into the Arabah wastelands, and possibly over into Arabia. In the Negev, they blocked the path of the Israelites during the Exodus (Exodus 17:8-16).

Israel's first encounter with the warriors of Amalek came at Rephidim, near Sinai. Moses stood on top of a hill and held up the rod of God until Israel won the battle. He then built an altar and named it "The Lord Is My Banner" (Exodus 17:1, 8-16). The Amalekites attacked stragglers during Israel's desert wanderings (Deuteronomy 25:17-18). After reaching the boundary of the Promised Land, the disheartened Israelites attacked the Amalekites and were defeated. (Numbers 14:39-45)[394]

Saul: Then Saul slaughtered the Amalekites from Havilah all the way to Shur, east of Egypt.

- He captured Agag, the Amalekite king, but completely destroyed everyone else.

- Saul and his men spared Agag's life and kept the best of the sheep and goats, the cattle, the fat calves, and the lambs—everything, in fact, that appealed to them. They destroyed only what was worthless or of poor quality.

God: Then the Lord said to Samuel, "I am sorry that I ever made Saul king, for he has not been loyal to me and has refused to obey my command."

Samuel: Samuel was so deeply moved when he heard this that he cried out to the Lord all night.

Samuel & Saul: Early the next morning Samuel went to find Saul. Someone told him, "Saul went to the town of Carmel to set up a monument to himself; then he went on to Gilgal."

Saul: When Samuel finally found him, Saul greeted him cheerfully. "May the Lord bless you," he said. "I have carried out the Lord's command!"

Samuel: "Then what is all the bleating of sheep and goats and the lowing of cattle I hear?" Samuel demanded.

Saul: "It's true that the army spared the best of the sheep, goats, and cattle," Saul admitted. "But they are going to sacrifice them to the Lord your God. We have destroyed everything else."

Samuel: Then Samuel said to Saul, "Stop! Listen to what the Lord told me last night!"

Saul: "What did he tell you?" Saul asked.

Samuel: And Samuel told him, "Although you may think little of yourself, are you not the leader of the tribes of Israel? The Lord has anointed you king of Israel. And the Lord sent you on a mission and told you, 'Go and completely destroy the sinners, the Amalekites, until they are all dead.' Why haven't you obeyed the Lord? Why did you rush for the plunder and do what was evil in the Lord's sight?"

Saul: "But I did obey the Lord," Saul insisted. "I carried out the mission he gave me. I brought back King Agag, but I destroyed everyone else. Then my troops brought in the best of the sheep, goats, cattle, and plunder to sacrifice to the Lord your God in Gilgal."

Samuel: But Samuel replied, What is more pleasing to the Lord: your burnt offerings and sacrifices or your obedience to his voice? Listen! Obedience is better than sacrifice, and submission is better than offering the fat of rams. Rebellion is as sinful as witchcraft,

and stubbornness as bad as worshiping idols. So because you have rejected the command of the Lord,he has rejected you as king."

Saul: Then Saul admitted to Samuel, "Yes, I have sinned. I have disobeyed your instructions and the Lord's command, for I was afraid of the people and did what they demanded. But now, please forgive my sin and come back with me so that I may worship the Lord."

Samuel: But Samuel replied, "I will not go back with you! Since you have rejected the Lord's command, he has rejected you as king of Israel."

Saul: As Samuel turned to go, Saul tried to hold him back and tore the hem of his robe.

Samuel: And Samuel said to him, "The Lord has torn the kingdom of Israel from you today and has given it to someone else—one who is better than you. And he who is the Glory of Israel will not lie, nor will he change his mind, for he is not human that he should change his mind!"

Saul: Then Saul pleaded again, "I know I have sinned. But please, at least honor me before the elders of my people and before Israel by coming back with me so that I may worship the Lord your God."

Samuel: So Samuel finally agreed and went back with him, and Saul worshiped the Lord.

- Then Samuel said, "Bring King Agag to me." Agag arrived full of hope, for he thought, "Surely the worst is over, and I have been spared!" But Samuel said, "As your sword has killed the sons of many mothers, now your mother will be childless." And Samuel cut Agag to pieces before the Lord at Gilgal.

- Then Samuel went home to Ramah, and Saul returned to his house at Gibeah of Saul.

- Samuel never went to meet with Saul again, but he mourned constantly for him. And the Lord was sorry he had ever made Saul king of Israel.

Samuel Anoints David King of Israel

God was not pleased with Samuel grieving over Saul being rejected as King of Israel. Therefore, God told him, "fill thine horn with oil, and go, I will send thee to Jesse the Bethlehemite: for I have provided me a king among his sons."395

When Samuel arrived at Jesse's house, and told him why he had come, Jesse paraded his seven sons before Samuel for his approval of one of them. But God stepped in and changed the plans of all that was there.

Jesse: Again, Jesse made seven of his sons to pass before Samuel.

Samuel: And Samuel said unto Jesse, The Lord hath not chosen these. And Samuel said unto Jesse, Are here all thy children?

Jesse: And he said, There remaineth yet the youngest, and, behold, he keepeth the sheep.

Samuel: And Samuel said unto Jesse, Send and fetch him: for we will not sit down till he come hither.

David: And he sent, and brought him in. Now he was ruddy, and withal of a beautiful countenance, and goodly to look to.

God: And the Lord said, Arise, anoint him: for this is he.

Samuel: Then Samuel took the horn of oil, and anointed him in the midst of his brethren: and the Spirit of the Lord came upon David from that day forward. So Samuel rose up, and went to Ramah.

Abraham Howard Jr.

God Takes His Holy Spirit from Saul

Saul: But the spirit of the Lord departed from Saul, and an evil spirit from the Lord troubled him.

Saul's Servants: And Saul's servants said unto him, Behold now, an evil spirit from God troubleth thee. Let our lord now command thy servants, which are before thee, to seek out a man, who is a cunning player on an harp: and it shall come to pass, when the evil spirit from God is upon thee, that he shall play with his hand, and thou shalt be well.

There is a lot of talk about what God will do, and what he won't do. A lot of it has to do with the theory of "once you are saved, you are always saved." Still some claim that God will not pull his Holy Spirit from you. Why? They argue that it's God's nature to love, forgive, and execute mercy.

But we see here that he did pull his Holy Spirit from Saul, and replaced it with an evil spirit. His servants noticed a change in his character, and told him that the Spirit of God had left him. They also, told him that music would soothe the troubling evil spirits.

In my experience of worldly music, and church hymns, gospel songs, and harmonic rhythm preaching, it seems that these are the tools that people use to soothe their troubling minds. Some go to bed at night playing music; while others play music as they travel back and forth to work. No matter what the music is, it seems to work as a soothing ointment.

But the question remains in these modern times, after the death, burial, and resurrection of Jesus Christ, whether or not God will let his Holy Ghost come upon you, and then take it back because of disobedience? The answer may be found in what the Lord Jesus Christ said about the call to discipleship in three scriptures:

- "For many are called, but few are chosen."[396]

- "Enter ye in at the strait gate: for wide is the gate, and broad is the way, that leadeth to destruction, and many there be which go in thereat: because strait is the gate, and narrow is the way, which leadeth unto life, and few there be that find it."[397]

- "He that overcometh, the same shall be clothed in white raiment; and I will not blot out his name out of the book of life, but I will confess his name before my Father, and before his angels."[398]

YEAR – 1015 BC

Samuel died at the ripe old age of ninety-years old:[399] "And Samuel died; and all the Israelites were gathered together, and lamented him, and buried him in his house at Ramah." But before he died, he lived to see David get the victory over the giant Goliath, and take his rightful place in the palace of king Saul.

YEAR – 1011 BC

King David

After the death of Saul, David was made king over the land of Judah, in Hebron, for seven-years and six months.[400]

However, Saul's son Ishbosheth ruled over the ten-tribes of Israel. After he was in office for two years, two of his body guards murdered him while he slept at noon.

YEAR - 1004 BC

Then all the elders came to David and agreed to made him king of all Israel. David was thirty-years old when he began to reign and he reigned for forty-years [1011-971 BC]: "In Hebron he reigned over

Judah seven years and six months: and in Jerusalem he reigned thirty and three years over all Israel and Judah."⁴⁰¹

As king, David decided to bring the Ark of God to Jerusalem with the idea of building a permanent structure to worship God. But God had other plans and sent his prophet Nathan to express his feeling to David.⁴⁰²

David: And it came to pass, when the king sat in his house, and the Lord had given him rest round about from all his enemies; that the king said unto Nathan the prophet, See now, I dwell in an house of cedar, but the ark of God dwelleth within curtains.

Nathan: And Nathan said to the king, Go, do all that is in thine heart; for the Lord is with thee.

God: And it came to pass that night, that the word of the Lord came unto Nathan, saying, Go and tell my servant David, Thus saith the Lord,

- Shalt thou build me an house for me to dwell in?

- Whereas I have not dwelt in any house since the time that I brought up the children of Israel out of Egypt, even to this day, but have walked in a tent and in a tabernacle.

- In all the places wherein I have walked with all the children of Israel spake I a word with any of the tribes of Israel, whom I commanded to feed my people Israel, saying, Why build ye not me an house of cedar?

- Now therefore so shalt thou say unto my servant David, Thus saith the Lord of hosts, I took thee from the sheepcote, from following the sheep, to be ruler over my people, over Israel:

- and I was with thee whithersoever thou wentest, and have cut off all thine enemies out of thy sight, and have made thee a great name, like unto the name of the great men that are in the earth.

- Moreover I will appoint a place for my people Israel, and will plant them, that they may dwell in a place of their own, and move no more; neither shall the children of wickedness afflict them any more, as beforetime,

- and as since the time that I commanded judges to be over my people Israel, and have caused thee to rest from all thine enemies.

- Also the Lord telleth thee that he will make thee an house.

- <u>And when thy days be fulfilled</u>, and thou shalt sleep with thy fathers, <u>I will set up thy seed after thee</u>, <u>which shall proceed out of thy bowels</u>, <u>and I will establish his kingdom.</u>

- <u>He shall build an house for my name</u>, <u>and I will stablish the throne of his kingdom for ever.</u>

- I will be his father, and he shall be my son.

- <u>If he commit iniquity, I will chasten him with the rod of men, and with the stripes of the children of men:</u>

- <u>but my mercy shall not depart away from him</u>, <u>as I took it from Saul</u>, whom I put away before thee.

- **<u>And thine house and thy kingdom shall be established for ever before thee: thy throne shall be established for ever.</u>**

- According to all these words, and according to all this vision, so did Nathan speak unto David.

After hearing the good news from Nathan; David lived a prosperous life that had a lot of ups and downs. But the one thing he did that greatly affected his life, and his relationship with God, was when he committed adultery with Bathsheba, and had her husband Uriah (the Hittite) killed in battle. Solomon was born to David and Bathsheba, and was the youngest son.[403]

God, disciplined David, and caused his family to turn against him. But he kept his promise not to treat David as he did Saul. David was thankful unto God and wrote a Psalm of his gratefulness.

> **Psalm 51: 1 Have mercy upon me, O God, according to thy lovingkindness: according unto the multitude of thy tender mercies blot out my transgressions.**
> **2 Wash me throughly from mine iniquity, and cleanse me from my sin.**
> **3 <u>For I acknowledge my transgressions</u>: <u>and my sin is ever before me</u>.**
> **4 <u>Against thee</u>, <u>thee only</u>, <u>have I sinned</u>, <u>and done this evil in thy sight</u>: that thou mightest be justified when thou speakest, and be clear when thou judgest.**
> **5 Behold, I was shapen in iniquity, and in sin did my mother conceive me.**
> **6 Behold, thou desirest truth in the inward parts: and in the hidden part thou shalt make me to know wisdom.**
> **7 Purge me with hyssop, and I shall be clean: wash me, and I shall be whiter than snow.**
> **8 Make me to hear joy and gladness; that the bones which thou hast broken may rejoice.**
> **9 Hide thy face from my sins, and blot out all mine iniquities.**
> **10 Create in me a clean heart, O God; and renew a right spirit within me.**
> **11 <u>Cast me not away from thy presence</u>; <u>and take not thy holy spirit from me</u>.**
> **12 Restore unto me the joy of thy salvation; and uphold me with thy free spirit.**

13 Then will I teach transgressors thy ways; and sinners shall be converted unto thee.
14 Deliver me from bloodguiltiness, O God, thou God of my salvation: and my tongue shall sing aloud of thy righteousness.
15 O Lord, open thou my lips; and my mouth shall shew forth thy praise.
16 For thou desirest not sacrifice; else would I give it: thou delightest not in burnt offering.
17 The sacrifices of God are a broken spirit: a broken and a contrite heart, O God, thou wilt not despise.
18 Do good in thy good pleasure unto Zion: build thou the walls of Jerusalem.
19 Then shalt thou be pleased with the sacrifices of righteousness, with burnt offering and whole burnt offering: then shall they offer bullocks upon thine altar.

Death of David

David was around seventy-years old when he died[404] (1041 - 971 BC). "Then he called for Solomon his son, and charged him to build a house for the Lord God of Israel. And David said to Solomon, "My son, as for me, it was in my mind to build an house unto the name of the Lord my God: But **the word of the Lord came to me, saying**, Thou hast shed blood abundantly, and hast made great wars: thou shalt not build an house unto my name, because thou hast shed much blood upon the earth in my sight."[405]

> **YEAR - 971 BC**

King Solomon

Solomon was the youngest of king David's twenty sons. His

mother was Bathsheba with whom David had committed adultery. And Bathsheba, with the help of the prophet Nathan, convinced David to make Solomon King.

In desperation of how to rule as king, Solomon went up to the high place in Gibeon, where the Tabernacle of God was, and offered up a thousand burnt sacrifices on the altar. He did this in order to seek the help of God.

God's first Appearance unto Solomon[406]

God: "In that night did God appear unto Solomon, and said unto him, Ask what I shall give thee."

Solomon: "And Solomon said unto God, Thou hast shewed great mercy unto David my father, and hast made me to reign in his stead. Now, O Lord God, let thy promise unto David my father be established: for thou hast made me king over a people like the dust of the earth in multitude. Give me now wisdom and knowledge, that I may go out and come in before this people: for who can judge this thy people, that is so great?"

God: "And God said to Solomon, Because this was in thine heart, and thou hast not asked riches, wealth, or honour, nor the life of thine enemies, neither yet hast asked long life; but hast asked wisdom and knowledge for thyself, that thou mayest judge my people, over whom I have made thee king: wisdom and knowledge is granted unto thee; and I will give thee riches, and wealth,

and honour, such as none of the kings have had that have been before thee, neither shall there any after thee have the like. And if thou wilt walk in my ways, to keep my statutes and my commandments, as thy father David did walk, then I will lengthen thy days."

Solomon: "And Solomon awoke; and, behold, it was a dream. And he came to Jerusalem, and stood before the ark of the covenant of the

Lord, and offered up burnt offerings, and offered peace offerings, and made a feast to all his servants."

> **YEAR - 967 BC**

Solomon Starts to Build the Temple of God

Solomon became known for his astounding wisdom, and he gained a large cache of wealth. Then Solomon set his heart upon fulling his promise, to his father David, to build a house for God, "And it came to pass in the four hundred and eightieth year after the children of Israel were come out of the land of Egypt, in the fourth year of Solomon's reign over Israel, in the month Zif, which is the second month, that he began to build the house of the Lord."[407]

Christ Appears unto Solomon

Before the Temple of God was finished, Solomon received another visit by God, "And **the word of the Lord came to Solomon, saying**, "Concerning this house which thou art in building, if thou wilt walk in my statutes, and execute my judgments, and keep all my commandments to walk in them; then will I perform my word with thee, which I spake unto David thy father: And I will dwell among the children of Israel, and will not forsake my people Israel."[408]

> ****Note:** First, Solomon was visited by God (the Father) in a dream, after king David died, and was given gifts of wisdom and wealth because of his unselfish request to serve the children of Israel, instead of his kingship.
>
> Secondly, the next visit to Solomon by God was Christ, who revealed himself in a physical form, and talked directly with Solomon.

YEAR – 960 BC

The Temple of God is Finished

"In the fourth year was the foundation of the house of the Lord laid, in the month Zif: and in the eleventh year, in the month Bul, which is the eighth month, was the house finished throughout all the parts thereof, and according to all the fashion of it. So was he seven years in building it."[409] / [410]

Solomon: "Then Solomon assembled the elders of Israel, and all the heads of the tribes, the chief of the fathers of the children of Israel, unto king Solomon in Jerusalem, that they might bring up the ark of the covenant of the Lord out of the city of David, which is Zion.'

The Men: "And all the men of Israel assembled themselves unto king Solomon at the feast in the month Ethanim, which is the seventh month."

The Elders: "And all the elders of Israel came, and the priests took up the ark. And they brought up the ark of the Lord, and the tabernacle of the congregation, and all the holy vessels that were in the tabernacle, even those did the priests and the Levites bring up."

Solomon: "And king Solomon, and all the congregation of Israel, that were assembled unto him, were with him before the ark, sacrificing sheep and oxen, that could not be told nor numbered for multitude."

The Ark: "There was nothing in the ark save the two tables of stone, which Moses put there at Horeb, when the Lord made a covenant with the children of Israel, when they came out of the land of Egypt."

The Congregation: "And it came to pass, when the priests were come out of the holy place: (for all the priests that were present were sanctified, and did not then wait by course:

- also the Levites which were the singers, all of them of Asaph, of Heman, of Jeduthun, with their sons and their brethren, being arrayed in white linen, having cymbals and psalteries and harps, stood at the east end of the altar,
- and with them an hundred and twenty priests sounding with trumpets:
  - it came even to pass, as the trumpeters and singers were as one, to make one sound to be heard in praising and thanking the Lord; and when they lifted up their voice with the trumpets and cymbals and instruments of musick, and praised the Lord, saying, For he is good; for his mercy endureth for ever: that then the house was filled with a cloud, even the house of the Lord;
  - so that the priests could not stand to minister by reason of the cloud: for the glory of the Lord had filled the house of God.

Now when there is a great celebration to God, then it stands to reason that God will show up to join in. This is often time seen in the church when the Holy Ghost comes upon the congregation during singing or preaching. The truth of this is when Jesus said, "For where two or three are gathered in my name, there am I in the mist of them."[411]

After the dedication of the temple, Solomon stood before the altar and preached praises unto the greatness of God. Then he lifted up his hands toward heaven and prayed to God for forgiveness and mercy.[412]

Solomon's Prayer

Solomon: "But will God in very deed dwell with men on the earth? behold, heaven and the heaven of heavens cannot contain thee; how much less this house which I have built! Have respect therefore to the prayer of thy servant, and to his supplication, O Lord my God, to hearken unto the cry and the prayer which thy servant prayeth before thee: that thine eyes may be open upon this house day and night, upon the place whereof thou hast said that thou wouldest put thy name there; to hearken unto the prayer which thy servant prayeth toward this place. Hearken therefore unto the supplications of thy servant, and of thy people Israel, which they shall make toward this place: hear thou from thy dwelling place, even from heaven; and when thou hearest, forgive."

- "<u>If a man sin against his neighbour</u>, and an oath be laid upon him to make him swear, and the oath come before thine altar in this house; then hear thou from heaven, and do, and judge thy servants, by requiting the wicked, by recompensing his way upon his own head; and by justifying the righteous, by giving him according to his righteousness."

- "<u>And if thy people Israel be put to the worse before the enemy</u>, because they have sinned against thee; and shall return and confess thy name, and pray and make supplication before thee in this house; then hear thou from the heavens, and forgive the sin of thy people Israel, and bring them again unto the land which thou gavest to them and to their fathers."

- "<u>When the heaven is shut up</u>, and there is no rain, because they have sinned against thee; yet if they pray toward this place, and confess thy name, and turn from their sin, when thou dost afflict them; then hear thou from heaven, and forgive the sin of thy servants, and of thy people Israel, when thou hast taught them the good way, wherein they should walk; and send rain upon thy land, which thou hast given unto thy people for an inheritance."

- "<u>If there be dearth in the land</u>, if there be pestilence, if there be blasting, or mildew, locusts, or caterpillers; if their enemies besiege them in the cities of their land; whatsoever sore or whatsoever sickness there be: then what prayer or what supplication soever shall be made of any man, or of all thy people Israel, when every one shall know his own sore and his own grief, and shall spread forth his hands in this house: then hear thou from heaven thy dwelling place, and forgive, and render unto every man according unto all his ways, whose heart thou knowest; (for thou only knowest the hearts of the children of men:) 31 that they may fear thee, to walk in thy ways, so long as they live in the land which thou gavest unto our fathers."

- "Moreover concerning the stranger, which is not of thy people Israel, but is come from a far country for thy great name's sake, and thy mighty hand, and thy stretched out arm; if they come and pray in this house; then hear thou from the heavens, even from thy dwelling place, and do according to all that the stranger calleth to thee for; that all people of the earth may know thy name, and fear thee, as doth thy people Israel, and may know that this house which I have built is called by thy name."

- "If thy people go out to war against their enemies by the way that thou shalt send them, and they pray unto thee toward this city which thou hast chosen, and the house which I have built for thy name; 35 then hear thou from the heavens their prayer and their supplication, and maintain their cause."

- "If they sin against thee, (for there is no man which sinneth not,) and thou be angry with them, and deliver them over before their enemies, and they carry them away captives unto a land far off or near; yet if they bethink themselves in the land whither they are carried captive, and turn and pray unto thee in the land of their captivity, saying, We have sinned, we have done amiss, and have dealt wickedly; if they return to thee with all their heart and with all their soul in the land of their captivity, whither they have carried them captives, and pray toward their land, which thou gavest unto their fathers, and toward the city which thou hast chosen, and toward the house which I have built for thy name: then hear thou from the heavens, even from thy dwelling place, their prayer and their supplications, and maintain their cause, and forgive thy people which have sinned against thee."

Solomon's conclusion: "Now, my God, let, I beseech thee, thine eyes be open, and let thine ears be attent unto the prayer that is made in this place. Now therefore arise, O Lord God, into thy resting place, thou, and the ark of thy strength: let thy priests, O Lord God, be clothed with salvation, and let thy saints rejoice in goodness. O Lord God, turn not away the face of thine anointed: remember the mercies of David thy servant."

God's Answer to Solomon's Prayer

Sometimes God answers prayers right away; but then again, he will delay his answer. The church has an old established saying, "he may not come when you call him, but he's always on time." First God gave Solomon a sign that he heard his prayer, and then he visited him.[413]

The Sign

- "Now when Solomon had made an end of praying, the fire came down from heaven, and consumed the burnt offering and the sacrifices; and the glory of the Lord filled the house."

- "And the priests could not enter into the house of the Lord, because the glory of the Lord had filled the Lord's house."

- "And when all the children of Israel saw how the fire came down, and the glory of the Lord upon the house, they bowed themselves with their faces to the ground upon the pavement, and worshipped, and praised the Lord, saying, For he is good; for his mercy endureth for ever."

God's Second visit to Solomon

- <u>And the Lord appeared to Solomon by night</u>, and said unto him, I have heard thy prayer, and have chosen this place to myself for an house of sacrifice.

- If I shut up heaven that there be no rain, or if I command the locusts to devour the land, or if I send pestilence among my people;

- <u>if my people, which are called by my name, shall humble themselves, and pray, and seek my face, and turn from their wicked ways; then will I hear from heaven, and will forgive their sin, and will heal their land.</u>

- "Now mine eyes shall be open, and mine ears attent unto the prayer that is made in this place."

- "For now have I chosen and sanctified this house, that my name may be there for ever: and mine eyes and mine heart shall be there perpetually."

- "And as for thee, if thou wilt walk before me, as David thy father walked, and do according to all that I have commanded thee, and shalt observe my statutes and my judgments; then will I stablish the throne of thy kingdom, according as I have covenanted with David thy father, saying, There shall not fail thee a man to be ruler in Israel."

- "But if ye turn away, and forsake my statutes and my commandments, which I have set before you, and shall go and serve other gods, and worship them;"

- "then will I pluck them up by the roots out of my land which I have given them; and this house, which I have sanctified for my name, will I cast out of my sight, and will make it to be a proverb and a byword among all nations."

- "And this house, which is high, shall be an astonishment to every one that passeth by it; so that he shall say, Why hath the Lord done thus unto this land, and unto this house?"

- "And it shall be answered, Because they forsook the Lord God of their fathers, which brought them forth out of the land of Egypt, and laid hold on other gods, and worshipped them, and served them: therefore hath he brought all this evil upon them."

Solomon went on to become the wisest, and richest man on earth. His fame brought the Queen of Sheba to visit his kingdom. And she was so impressed with Solomon that she said, "It was a true report that I heard in mine own land of thy acts and of thy wisdom. Howbeit I believed not the words, until I came, and mine eyes had seen it: and, behold, the half was not told me: thy wisdom and prosperity exceedeth the fame which I heard."[414]

Now with all this fame and fortune given to Solomon, by the hand of God, you'd think that he would keep his promise to walk in the statures and ordonnances of God. But as it always happens: power, money, and women will bring a good man to his knees.

Solomon's Disobedience (1 Kings 11:1-13)

Solomon Love of Many Women

1 But king Solomon loved many strange women, together with the daughter of Pharaoh, women of the Moabites, Ammonites, Edomites, Zidonians, and Hittites;

- **Moabites** - According to Genesis 19:37, the Moabites descended from Moab, the son of Lot and his oldest daughter (Genesis 19:34-37)

- **Ammonites** - The Ammonites traced their ancestry to the younger daughter of Lot (Genesis 19:38). Their name in Hebrew originally meant "son of my paternal clan," which suggests the family relationship between the Ammonites and Israelites (Lot was Abraham's nephew, making the Ammonites and the Israelites distant relatives). The Ammonites were a powerful people who occupied a portion of the land of Canaan. They lived in a fertile area northeast of Moab in the area east of the Jordan between the Arnon and Jabbok Rivers and extending eastward to the Syrian Desert. The main city was Rabbah (Rabbath-ammon), which today is known as Amman, the capital of Jordan.

- **Edomites** - Esau was Isaac's son, and the older twin brother of Jacob (Genesis 25:24-26). He was given his name because of the hair on his body at birth. Because the baby Esau had a reddish color, and because the color red was to play an important role in his life, he also became known by the name Edom, or "red." The race of people known as the Edomites claimed to be Esau's descendants, and even the name of their land, "Seir," may come from the word sair, meaning "hairy."

- **Zidonians** - Sidon was a city on the Phoenician coast between Beirut and Tyre. Phoenicia was an ancient land on the eastern end of the Mediterranean Sea. Sidon is frequently called Zidon in the King James Version. The names Sidon and Sidonian appear thirty-eight times in the Old Testament, and Sidon occurs twelve times in the New Testament.

- The age of such cities as Tyre and Sidon may be determined by the "table of nations" (Genesis 10). Sidon is named as the firstborn son of Canaan, who was a son of Ham. The territory of the Canaanites extended from Sidon to Gaza and east to the Cities of the Plain.

- **Hittites** – (Hivites) Name of a pre-Israelite group living in Canaan. Though not yet discovered/rated archaeologically or from secular history as a people, they were regarded as emerging from a son of Canaan (Genesis 10:17) and as inhabiting areas of the Lebanon Mountains (Judges 3:3) and Mt Hermon (Joshua 11:3)

Solomon broke the marriage law of God

2 of the nations concerning which the Lord said unto the children of Israel, Ye shall not go in to them, neither shall they come in unto you: for surely they will turn away your heart after their gods: Solomon clave unto these in love.

- **Exodus 34:** 12 Take heed to thyself, lest thou make a covenant with the inhabitants of the land whither thou goest, lest it be for a snare in the midst of thee:
  13 but ye shall destroy their altars, break their images, and cut down their groves:
  14 for thou shalt worship no other god: for the Lord, whose name is Jealous, is a jealous God: 15 lest thou make a covenant with the inhabitants of the land, and they go a whoring after their gods, and do sacrifice unto their gods, and one call thee, and thou eat of his sacrifice;

16 and thou take of their daughters unto thy sons, and their daughters go a whoring after their gods, and make thy sons go a whoring after their gods.
17 Thou shalt make thee no molten gods.

Solomon wives turn his heart against God
3 And he had seven hundred wives, princesses, and three hundred concubines: and his wives turned away his heart.

- **Deuteronomy 17:17** The king must not take many wives for himself, because they will turn his heart away from the Lord.

4 For it came to pass, when Solomon was old, that his wives turned away his heart after other gods: and his heart was not perfect with the Lord his God, as was the heart of David his father. 5 For Solomon went after Ashtoreth the goddess of the Zidonians, and after Milcom the abomination of the Ammonites.

- **Ashtoreth** - Pagan mother-goddess widely worshiped throughout the ancient Near East (1 Kings 11:5, 33; 2 Kings 23:13); also known as Astarte.

- **Milcom** - Milcom, the national god of the Ammonites, was better known as Molech or Moloch. Worship of this deity, which was accompanied by sacrificing children in the fire, was strictly prohibited to Israel (Leviticus 18:21; Jeremiah 32:35). Solomon built Milcom a worship site (1 Kings 11:5, 33), which Josiah later tore down (2 Kings 23:13)

Solomon built temples to pagan gods
6 And Solomon did evil in the sight of the Lord, and went not fully after the Lord, as did David his father.
7 Then did Solomon build an high place for Chemosh, the abomination of Moab, in the hill that is before Jerusalem, and for Molech, the abomination of the children of Ammon.

- **Chemosh** - Chemosh was the name of the national god of Moab (Numbers 21:29) and was also associated with the Ammonites (Judges 11:24).

- **Molech** - Ammonite god worshiped with human sacrifice (Leviticus 18:21; Jeremiah 32:35).

Solomon turns to worshipping other gods

8 And likewise did he for all his strange wives, which burnt incense and sacrificed unto their gods.

9 <u>And the Lord was angry with Solomon, because his heart was turned from the Lord God of Israel, which had appeared unto him twice,</u> (1 Kings 3:1-15 / 2 Chronicles 7: 12-22)

10 and had commanded him concerning this thing, that he should not go after other gods: but he kept not that which the Lord commanded.

- **Exodus 20:** 3 Thou shalt have no other gods before me.

- 4 Thou shalt not make unto thee any graven image, or any likeness of any thing that is in heaven above, or that is in the earth beneath, or that is in the water under the earth: 5 thou shalt not bow down thyself to them, nor serve them: for I the Lord thy God am a jealous God, visiting the iniquity of the fathers upon the children unto the third and fourth generation of them that hate me; 6 and shewing mercy unto thousands of them that love me, and keep my commandments.

God's fourth visit to Solomon

11 Wherefore the Lord said unto Solomon, Forasmuch as this is done of thee, and thou hast not kept my covenant and my statutes, which I have commanded thee, I will surely rend the kingdom from thee, and will give it to thy servant.

12 Notwithstanding in thy days I will not do it for David thy father's sake: but I will rend it out of the hand of thy son.

13 Howbeit I will not rend away all the kingdom; but will give one tribe to thy son for David my servant's sake, and for Jerusalem's sake which I have chosen.

> **YEAR – 931 BC**

Death of Solomon

Solomon reigned as king over united Israel for forty-years [971-931 BC]. When he died the people buried him in Jerusalem with his father: which is called the city of David.[415]

The United Kingdom of Israel is Split in Two

After the death of Solomon, his son Rehoboam became king. But he would not listen to the council of the tribal elders, and this caused the United Kingdom to be split into a Southern and Northern kingdom.

- o Rehoboam was left with being king of the Southern Kingdom of Israel: over the tribes of Judah, and Benjamin; and the capital city was Jerusalem. He reigned from 930-913 BC.

- o Jeroboam, an adversary of Solomon, was chosen by the ten tribes of Israel to be the king of the Northern Kingdom: with Samaria as its capital.

Jeroboam's Sin (1 Kings 12:25-33)

25 Then Jeroboam built Shechem in mount Ephraim, and dwelt therein; and went out from thence, and built Penuel.
26 And Jeroboam said in his heart, Now shall the kingdom return to the house of David:
27 if this people go up to do sacrifice in the house of the Lord at Jerusalem, then shall the heart of this people turn again unto their

lord, even unto Rehoboam king of Judah, and they shall kill me, and go again to Rehoboam king of Judah.

28 Whereupon the king took counsel, <u>and made two calves of gold</u>, and said unto them, It is too much for you to go up to Jerusalem: <u>behold thy gods, O Israel, which brought thee up out of the land of Egypt.</u> (Exodus Chapter 32)

29 And he set the one in Bethel, and the other put he in Dan.

- **BETHEL:** "When Israel and Judah became separate entities in the time of Jeroboam I (930–909 BC), Bethel became the capital of the northern kingdom of Israel and the counterpart of Judah's capital, Jerusalem. Bethel was one of two northern cities where golden calves were worshiped (1 Kings 12:28-33); the sanctuary area for that cultic practice has not been discovered. The city was the home of an elderly prophet (13:11) who may have been connected with the prophetic colony existing there in the time of Elijah and Elisha (2 Kings 2:2-3). During the reign of Judah's King Abijah (913–910 BC), Bethel fell under Judah's control (2 Chronicles 13:19) but later was returned to Israel. The prophet Amos went to Bethel to deliver scathing denunciations about contemporary social and religious life in Israel, for which the priest Amaziah had him expelled" (Amos 7:10-13).[416]

- **DAN:** "Eventually Israel separated into two kingdoms. When Jeroboam I became king of the northern kingdom of Israel, Dan housed one of two shrines where golden calves were worshiped. The cultic worship of Baal at Dan survived even Jehu's drastic purge. During Ben-hadad's reign, the city fell under Syrian control (2 Kings 10:28-32). Later, when the Syrians were attempting to ward off Assyrian attacks during the time of Jeroboam II (793-753 BC), Dan was reconquered by the northern kingdom. Ultimately, its inhabitants were deported to Assyria (2 Kings 17:6) by Tiglath-pileser III (745-727 BC). Nevertheless, the site continued to be inhabited

> (see Jeremiah 4:15; 8:16), and its high place, or acropolis, at the northern peak of the mound was used for worship. This particular area was enlarged periodically in both Greek and Roman times. In the New Testament period, Dan was eclipsed by Caesarea, which was only a few miles away."[417]

30 And this thing became a sin: for the people went to worship before the one, even unto Dan.
31 <u>And he made an house of high places,</u> and made priests of the lowest of the people, which were not of the sons of Levi.
32 And Jeroboam ordained a feast in the eighth month, on the fifteenth day of the month, like unto the feast that is in Judah, and he offered upon the altar. So did he in Bethel, sacrificing unto the calves that he had made: and he placed in Bethel the priests of the high places which he had made.
33 So he offered upon the altar which he had made in Bethel the fifteenth day of the eighth month, even in the month which he had devised of his own heart; and ordained a feast unto the children of Israel: and he offered upon the altar, and burnt incense.

- **SHECHEM** -Fortress erected on the acropolis of Shechem, housing the temple of Baal-berith and situated inside the city walls. The city of Shechem was located in the hill country of the tribe of Ephraim near Mt Gerizim. The remnants of the tower of Shechem have been found within the ancient town of Shechem at Tell Bala'ta, a short distance northeast of modern Nablus in central Palestine. Modern excavations show that the tower of Shechem was used as a temple and a fortress.[418]

- **PENUEL** - Penuel is the name given to the place near the Jabbok River where Jacob wrestled all night with God (Genesis 32:31). It is alternately called Peniel in Genesis 32:30. During the period of the judges, Gideon destroyed the tower of Penuel and killed the men of the city for refusing to join him in war against the Midianites (Judges 8:8-9, 17).

Later, King Jeroboam rebuilt the town (1 Kings 12:25). It was positioned near Succoth east of the Jordan River, though its exact location remains uncertain.

God Gives Jeroboam a Sign (1 Kings Chapter 13)

Because of Jeroboams disobedience, a prophet of God, instructed by **the word of the Lord** (Christ) was sent to Bethel during the time that Jeroboam burned incense on the altar. And as instructed the prophet cried out against the alter and said:

The Prophet: "O altar, altar, thus saith the Lord; Behold, <u>a child shall be born unto the house of David, Josiah by name</u>; and upon thee shall he offer the priests of the high places that burn incense upon thee, and men's bones shall be burnt upon thee." (2 Kings 22 – 23:1-30)

The Sign: "This is the sign which the Lord hath spoken; Behold, the altar shall be rent, and the ashes that are upon it shall be poured out."

Jeroboam: "And it came to pass, when king Jeroboam heard the saying of the man of God, which had cried against the altar in Bethel, that he put forth his hand from the altar, saying, Lay hold on him. And his hand, which he put forth against him, dried up, so that he could not pull it in again to him."

The Sign Enacted: "The altar also was rent, and the ashes poured out from the altar, according to the sign which the man of God had given by the word of the Lord."

Jeroboam: "And the king answered and said unto the man of God, Intreat now the face of the Lord thy God, and pray for me, that my hand may be restored me again."

Prophet: "And the man of God besought the Lord, and the king's hand was restored him again, and became as it was before."

Jeroboam: "And the king said unto the man of God, Come home with me, and refresh thyself, and I will give thee a reward."

The Prophet: "And the man of God said unto the king, If thou wilt give me half thine house, I will not go in with thee, neither will I eat bread nor drink water in this place: <u>for so was it charged me by</u> **the word of the Lord** (*Christ*), saying, Eat no bread, nor drink water, nor turn again by the same way that thou camest. So he went another way, and returned not by the way that he came to Bethel."

"After this thing Jeroboam returned not from his evil way, but made again of the lowest of the people priests of the high places: whosoever would, he consecrated him, and he became one of the priests of the high places. And this thing became sin unto the house of Jeroboam, even to cut it off, and to destroy it from off the face of the earth."

Sorry to say that the prophet of God was waylaid by another prophet, who lied and said, "an angel spake unto me by <u>the word of the Lord</u>, saying, Bring him back with thee into thine house, that he may eat bread and drink water." This lie caused the prophet of God to disobey the instructions of <u>the word of the Lord</u> (Christ), and he was killed by a lion; and was buried by the prophet who had lied to him.[419]

Thus, Jeroboams evil quest to stay in power caused the northern Kingdom of Israel to continue in his sin for over two-hundred years; through eighteen kings: and countless wars until they were carried off the land in 722 BC to the land of the Assyrians during the time of the prophet Isaiah and Hezekiah – king of the southern kingdom.

CHAPTER 17

THE WORD AND THE PROPHETS

> YEAR 850-840 BC

The Prophet Obadiah

Prophecy Against Esau
Obadiah "8 Shall I not in that day, saith the Lord, even destroy the wise men out of Edom, and understanding out of the mount of Esau?
9 And thy mighty men, O Teman, shall be dismayed, to the end that every one of the mount of Esau may be cut off by slaughter.
10 For thy violence against thy brother Jacob shame shall cover thee, and thou shalt be cut off for ever.
11 In the day that thou stoodest on the other side, in the day that the strangers carried away captive his forces, and foreigners entered into his gates, and cast lots upon Jerusalem, even thou wast as one of them.
12 But thou shouldest not have looked on the day of thy brother in the day that he became a stranger; neither shouldest thou have rejoiced over the children of Judah in the day of their destruction; neither shouldest thou have spoken proudly in the day of distress.

13 Thou shouldest not have entered into the gate of my people in the day of their calamity; yea, thou shouldest not have looked on their affliction in the day of their calamity, nor have laid hands on their substance in the day of their calamity;
14 Neither shouldest thou have stood in the crossway, to cut off those of his that did escape; neither shouldest thou have delivered up those of his that did remain in the day of distress."

- o   2 Chronicles 21: 16-17
- o   2 Kings 8:20-22 2 Chronicles 21:8-11

Prophecy Concerning Jacob
"17 But upon mount Zion shall be deliverance, and there shall be holiness; and the house of Jacob shall possess their possessions.
18 And the house of Jacob shall be a fire, and the house of Joseph a flame, and the house of Esau for stubble, and they shall kindle in them, and devour them; and there shall not be any remaining of the house of Esau; for the Lord hath spoken it."[420]

YEAR 835-796 BC

The Prophet Joel

- o   Joel was a prophet during of Joash king of Judah.

- o   **JOASH** -Joash was an alternate name for Jehoash, Ahaziah's son (1 Chronicles 3:11), and king of Judah (835-796 BC), 2 Kings 11:1-21 / 12: 1-21 and 2Chronicles 22 -24:1-27 3:11.

The prophet Joel is credited with giving the prophecy concerning the pouring out of God's Holy Spirit during the last days; which began with the birth of Christ.

Joel 2: 28 And it shall come to pass afterward, that I will pour out my spirit upon all flesh; and your sons and your daughters shall prophesy, your old men shall dream dreams, your young men shall see visions:

29 And also upon the servants and upon the handmaids in those days will I pour out my spirit.
30 And I will shew wonders in the heavens and in the earth, blood, and fire, and pillars of smoke.
31 The sun shall be turned into darkness, and the moon into blood, before the great and the terrible day of the Lord come.
32 And it shall come to pass, that whosoever shall call on the name of the Lord shall be delivered: for in mount Zion and in Jerusalem shall be deliverance, as the Lord hath said, and in the remnant whom the Lord shall call. (Acts 2:16-21)

> **YEAR – 782 -753 BC**

The Prophet Jonah

Historic Record: A prophet of Israel, Jonah was Amittai's son (Jonah 1:1) of the city of Gath-hepher (2 Kings 14:25). The historian who wrote 2 Kings recorded that Jonah had a major prophetic role in the reign of King Jeroboam II (793-753 BC). Jonah had conveyed a message encouraging expansion to the king of Israel, whose reign was marked by prosperity, expansion, and unfortunately, moral decline. In the midst of all the political corruption of Israel, Jonah remained a zealous patriot. His reluctance to go to Nineveh probably stemmed partially from his knowledge that the Assyrians would be used as God's instrument for punishing Israel. The prophet, who had been sent to Jeroboam to assure him that his kingdom would prosper, was the same prophet God chose to send to Nineveh to forestall that city's (and thus that nation's) destruction until Assyria could be used to punish Israel in 722 BC. It is no wonder that the prophet reacted emotionally to his commission.

No other prophet was so strongly Jewish (compare his classic confession, Jonah 1:9), yet no other prophet's ministry was so strongly directed to a non-Jewish nation. Jonah's writing is also unusual among the prophets. The book is primarily historical narrative. His actual preaching is recorded in only five words in the Hebrew-eight words in most English translations (3:4).[421]

- **2 Kings 14:** 23 In the fifteenth year of Amaziah the son of Joash king of Judah Jeroboam the son of Joash king of Israel began to reign in Samaria, and reigned forty and one years. 24 And he did that which was evil in the sight of the Lord: he departed not from all the sins of Jeroboam the son of Nebat, who made Israel to sin.
  25 He restored the coast of Israel from the entering of Hamath unto the sea of the plain, according to <u>the word of the Lord</u> God of Israel, which he spake by the hand of <u>his servant Jonah</u>, the son of Amittai, the prophet, which was of Gathhepher.

- **Jonah 1:**1-3 1 Now the word of the Lord came unto Jonah the son of Amittai, saying, 2 Arise, go to Nineveh, that great city, and cry against it; for their wickedness is come up before me.

- 3 But Jonah rose up to flee unto Tarshish from the presence of the Lord, and went down to Joppa; and he found a ship going to Tarshish: so he paid the fare thereof, and went down into it, to go with them unto Tarshish from the presence of the Lord.

YEAR – 763 -755 BC

The Prophet Amos

Amos 1: 1 The words of Amos, who was among the herdmen of Tekoa, which he saw concerning Israel in the days of Uzziah king of Judah, and in the days of Jeroboam the son of Joash king of Israel, two years before the earthquake.

2 And he said, The Lord will roar from Zion, and utter his voice from Jerusalem; and the habitations of the shepherds shall mourn, and the top of Carmel shall wither.

Historic Record: Amos was a Hebrew prophet of the eighth century B.C. Nothing is known about Amos apart from the book that bears his name. He was a shepherd living in Tekoa, a village about ten miles south of Jerusalem, when God spoke to him in a vision (Amos 1:1-2). The kingdom was then divided, with Uzziah king of Judah in the south and Jeroboam II king of Israel in the north. In Amos's vision, the Lord appeared like a lion, roaring out his judgment against injustice and idolatry, especially the idolatry of God's own people.

In his book, Amos is shown preaching only at Bethel, in Israel, about twelve miles north of Jerusalem and just over the border. King Jeroboam I had made Bethel the royal religious sanctuary of Israel, in an attempt to rival Jerusalem, and here Amos prophesied that Israel would be overrun and its king killed. The priest of Bethel, Amaziah, called Amos a traitor and told him to go back to Judah and do his prophesying there. Amos replied, "I'm not one of your professional prophets. I certainly never trained to be one. I'm just a shepherd, and I take care of fig trees." But the Lord told him, "Go and prophesy to my people in Israel" (Amos 7:10-15). Evidently, Amos was a God-fearing man who deeply felt the mistreatment of the poor by the rich. He did not want to be identified with an elite group of professional prophets. His writings reflect his earthy, shepherd's background (3:12). But he spoke a message given him by the Lord God of Hosts: "I want to see a mighty flood of justice, a river of righteous living that will never run dry" (5:24). Amos called Israel to repent of personal and social sins and return to the worship of the one true God.[422]

YEAR - 755 -710 BC

The Prophet Hosea

The prophet Hosea ministered during the reigns of Uzziah [767-739 BC], Jotham 739-731 BC], Ahaz 731-715 BC, and Hezekiah [715-686 BC].

> **Hosea 1:1** The word of the Lord that came unto Hosea, the son of Beeri, in the days of Uzziah, Jotham, Ahaz, and Hezekiah, kings of Judah, and in the days of Jeroboam the son of Joash, king of Israel.
> 2 The beginning of the word of the Lord by Hosea. And the Lord said to Hosea, Go, take unto thee a wife of whoredoms and children of whoredoms: for the land hath committed great whoredom, departing from the Lord.

Historic record: "Hosea was a prophet of ancient Israel in the northern kingdom. Little is known of him outside of the book that bears his name. His prophetic ministry is best placed in the third quarter of the eighth century B.C. His name means "help" or "helper," and is based on the Hebrew word for salvation.

Hosea is placed in the northern kingdom because the book is concerned mainly with the northern tribes. Hosea frequently identifies them as "Ephraim," a common title for the northern kingdom. And the dialect of Hebrew in which the book was written also seems to point this way.

The circumstances surrounding the marriage of Hosea form the basis for his prophetic message. He was commanded by God to marry Gomer, who apparently was a harlot. His marriage provided an analogy with Israel, who was guilty of spiritual adultery.

Scholars differ as to the interpretation of this controversial account. However, there is little reason for doubting that it was a literal event. The act of sacrifice involved in Hosea's obedience to God forms a marvelous picture of God's sacrificial love for man."[423]

YEAR – 739 BC

The Prophet Micah

Micah 1:1 The word of the Lord that came to Micah the Morasthite in the days of Jotham, Ahaz, and Hezekiah, kings of Judah, which he saw concerning Samaria and Jerusalem.
2 Hear, all ye people; hearken, O earth, and all that therein is: and let the Lord God be witness against you, the Lord from his holy temple.
3 For, behold, the Lord cometh forth out of his place, and will come down, and tread upon the high places of the earth.
4 And the mountains shall be molten under him, and the valleys shall be cleft, as wax before the fire, and as the waters that are poured down a steep place.
5 For the transgression of Jacob is all this, and for the sins of the house of Israel. What is the transgression of Jacob? is it not Samaria? and what are the high places of Judah? are they not Jerusalem?

Historic Record: Micah was also a prophet and author of the Old Testament book of Micah that bears his name (Micah 1). A native of Moresheth, a town about twenty-one miles southwest of Jerusalem, Micah prophesied to both the northern kingdom of Israel and the southern kingdom of Judah during the reigns of Jotham, Ahaz, and Hezekiah (750-686 BC). According to 1:9, he was still prophesying in 701 BC when the Assyrian armies under Sennacherib (compare Isaiah 36-37) besieged Jerusalem. About one hundred years later, Micah is used as an example of an early prophet who predicted the destruction of Jerusalem (compare Jeremiah 26:16-19).[424]

YEAR – 740 BC

The Prophet Isaiah

Historic Record: "This prophet lived in the eighth century BC during the reigns of the Judean kings Uzziah, Jotham, Ahaz, and Hezekiah. He was also the author of the Bible book of Isaiah. Isaiah was the son of Amoz (Isaiah 1:1) and may have been a relative of King Amaziah. Growing up in Jerusalem, Isaiah received the best education the capital of Judah could supply. He was deeply knowledgeable about people, and he became the political and religious conscience of the nation. He was able to communicate with the kings of Judah easily and may have been the historiographer (official history-writer) at the Judean court for several reigns (2 Chronicles 26:22; 2 Chronicles 32:32).

Isaiah's wife is referred to as a prophetess (Isaiah 8:3) and they had at least two sons, Shear-jashub (Isaiah 7:3) and Maher-shalal-hash-baz (Isaiah 8:3). Isaiah wore a prophet's clothing: sandals and a garment of goat's hair or sackcloth. At one point during his ministry, the Lord commanded Isaiah to go naked and bare-foot for a period of three years (wearing only a loincloth, Isaiah 20:2-6). This must have been humiliating in a society that measured a person's social status through clothing.

Isaiah worked to reform social and political evils. He berated soothsayers (fortune-tellers) and denounced wealthy, influential people who ignored the responsibilities that come with wealth. He exhorted the common people to obedience, and rebuked kings for their sin.

Isaiah's writings express his deep awareness of God's majesty and holiness. The prophet denounced not only Canaanite idolatry but also his own people's religious worship, when this was insincere (Isaiah 1:10-17; Isaiah 29:13). He prophesied that the idolatrous Judeans would soon be judged, declaring that only a righteous few would survive (Isaiah 6:13).

Isaiah also foretold the coming of the Messiah, the "peaceful prince," and the ruler of God's kingdom-Jesus Christ (Isaiah 11:1-11; see also Isaiah 9:6-7). He depicted this Messiah as a suffering, obedient servant (Isaiah 53:3-12). Isaiah's images and metaphors were grand and powerful; his imagination produced forceful, brilliant figures of speech.

Isaiah prophesied during the last three decades of the northern kingdom of Israel, but because he lived in Jerusalem, in Judah, he rarely talked directly about Israel. When that kingdom fell, Judah lay open to conquest by Assyria. Isaiah advised King Ahaz to avoid getting entangled with foreign countries, and to depend on God to protect his people. Ahaz ignored this advice.

It was Hezekiah, Ahaz's pious son, who tried to remove Judah from this dangerous situation. When the Assyrians under Sennacherib approached Jerusalem, Isaiah inspired Hezekiah and the Judeans to rely on the Lord for the city's defense, and "the angel of the Lord" destroyed Sennacherib's army (Isaiah 37:36-38), giving Hezekiah and the Judeans a short period of peace.

Hebrew prophecy reached its peak with Isaiah, who was greatly respected in both Old Testament and New Testament times. One indication of his fame is the large amount of apocryphal literature associated with his name."[425]

The ministry of the prophet Isaiah lasted approximately sixty-years (740 – 680 BC). "He began his ministry near the end of Uzziah's reign (790 – 739 BC), and continued through the reign's of Jotham (739 – 731 BC), Ahaz (731 – 715 BC), and Hezekiah (715 – 686 BC); and into the reign of Manasseh (686 – 642 BC)

"The word of the Lord spoke with the prophet Isaiah well over thirty times. Why so many visits? Here are my thoughts on the matter.

- The people Christ brought messages too had to commit them to memory, and recite them word for word as they received them, with no addition of their own thoughts. Therefore, frequent short visits were made, so the concentration of passages was not overwhelming.

- What was said between the word of the Lord and the prophet had to be written down as a record of proof that it was from God on high, so it had to be exact and clear.

- The word of the Lord had to increase the faith of those he visited, because they would have to endure constant physical threats when delivering the word of God.

During Isiah's ministry he received the word of God through vision, dreams, and direct visits. The Lord of Hosts (God the Father) came to him in in visions and dreams,[426] while the word of the Lord (Christ) came to him directly, and in human form.

The book of Isaiah is dived into two sections. The first section contains thirty-nine chapter's outlining God's concern towards the sinful and wicked ways of Israel, and the neighboring nations. The second section of twenty-seven chapters are prophesies of the Messiah, and his relationship with mankind.

Abraham Howard Jr.

Isaiah Sees the Throne of God[427]

Isaiah's Vision: "In the year that king Uzziah died I saw also the Lord sitting upon a throne, high and lifted up, and his train filled the temple. Above it stood the seraphims: each one had six wings; with twain he covered his face, and with twain he covered his feet, and with twain he did fly. And one cried unto another, and said, Holy, holy, holy, is the Lord of hosts: the whole earth is full of his glory. And the posts of the door moved at the voice of him that cried, and the house was filled with smoke."

Isaiah: "Then said I, Woe is me! for I am undone; because I am a man of unclean lips, and I dwell in the midst of a people of unclean lips: for mine eyes have seen the King, the Lord of hosts."

The Angel: "Then flew one of the seraphims unto me, having a live coal in his hand, which he had taken with the tongs from off the altar: and he laid it upon my mouth, and said, Lo, this hath touched thy lips; and thine iniquity is taken away, and thy sin purged."

God: "Also I heard the voice of the Lord, saying, Whom shall I send, and who will go for us?"

Isaiah: "Then said I, Here am I; send me."

God: "And he said, Go, and tell this people, Hear ye indeed, but understand not; and see ye indeed, but perceive not. Make the heart of this people fat, and make their ears heavy, and shut their eyes; lest they see with their eyes, and hear with their ears, and understand with their heart, and convert, and be healed."

Isaiah: "Then said I, Lord, how long?"

God: "And he answered, Until the cities be wasted without inhabitant, and the houses without man, and the land be utterly desolate, and the Lord have removed men far away, and there be a great forsaking in the midst of the land. But yet in it shall be a tenth, and it shall return, and shall be eaten: as a teil tree, and as an oak, whose substance is in them, when they cast their leaves: so the holy seed shall be the substance thereof.

YEAR – 722 BC

The ten-tribes of Northern Israel had sinned to the point that God's judgement was moved to remove them from the land permanently. This happened when Hezekiah was king of the Southern kingdom (729-700 BC), and Isaiah was his prophet.

The Captivity of the Ten Tribes of Israel (2 Kings 17:1-6 / 18:9-11)

"And it came to pass in the fourth year of king Hezekiah, which was the seventh year of Hoshea son of Elah king of Israel, that Shalmaneser king of Assyria came up against Samaria, and besieged it.[428]

"And at the end of three years they took it: even in the sixth year of Hezekiah, that is the ninth year of Hoshea king of Israel, Samaria was taken."

Hoshea was the son of Elah and the last of the nineteen of the Northern Kingdom of Israel (2 Kings 17:1-6). He reigned for nine years, from 732 BC to 723 BC, before being taken captive by the Assyrians.

"And the king of Assyria did carry away Israel unto Assyria, and put them in Halah and in Habor by the river of Gozan, and in the cities of the Medes: because they obeyed not the voice of the Lord their God, but transgressed his covenant, and all that Moses the servant of the Lord commanded, and would not hear them, nor do them.

Assyria was the symbol of terror and tyranny in the Near East for more than three centuries. The Assyrians were ruthless warriors who conquered city after city, nation after nation. They gobbled up territory like candy, finally ruling over all of Syria and Babylonia. They even tried to overrun Egypt. However, for all their earthly power, they refused to recognize the heavenly power of God. In fact, they conquered the northern kingdom of Israel and took God's people captive.

- **Habor:** Modern Habur (Chaboras) River. The Habor River runs from the mountains in north-central Assyria, in Gozan, into the Euphrates River at a junction about 250 miles (402 kilometers) south and west of Nineveh. Numerous tributaries feed the Habor farther to the north. The OT names the river as the site to which King Shalmaneser carried the captive Israelites (2 Kings 17:6; 18:11; 1 Chronicles 5:26).

- **Gozan:** City and district near the Euphrates River. The Habor River (modern Khabur) flowed through it. The Assyrians conquered it sometime before Sennacherib's invasion of Judah (701 BC). This fact is mentioned by Sennacherib, king of Assyria, in a blasphemous letter sent to Hezekiah, king of Judah (2 Kings 19:12; Isaiah 37:12). Later it became one of the places in Assyria where conquered Israelites were deported.

- **SYRIA, SYRIANS**: These terms are used in some English translations to express the names Aram, Arameans.

- **HISTORY OF THE ARAMEANS:**

1. According to the "table of nations" in Genesis 10:22-23, the Arameans were a Semitic group, descendants of Shem. Another genealogy in Genesis 22:20-21 makes Aram a descendant of Nahor. According to Amos 9:7, the Arameans (Syrians) came from Kir, which is linked with Elam in Isaiah 22:6. The exile of the Arameans to Kir (2 Kings 16:9; Amos 1:5) may suggest they were to go back to their original home. The precise origins of this group of people are unknown.

When they emerged clearly into history, they were settled around the central Euphrates. From there, they were spread out east, west, and north.

2. The Arameans were thought to have been established in upper Mesopotamia in the first part of the second millennium B.C. Bethuel and Laban were known as Arameans (Genesis 25:20; Genesis 28:1-7). The home of Bethuel was in Paddan-aram (Genesis 25:20). The prophet Hosea recalls the tradition by noting that Jacob fled to "the field of Aram" (Hosea 12:12) or "Aram-naharaim" (Aram of the two rivers). That was the northern part of Mesopotamia between the Euphrates and Tigris Rivers. In Deuteronomy 26:5, the Israelite who brought his firstfruits confessed, "My father [probably Jacob] was a wandering Aramean."

3. Probably the best early evidence of an Aramean presence in this area comes from Tiglath-pileser I. In his accounts of his fourth year (1112 BC), he speaks of a campaign among the "Akhlama, Arameans" in the Middle Euphrates area and the sacking of six Aramean villages in the Mount Bishri area.

Causes of the Ten Tribes Captivity (2 Kings 17:7-22)

For so it was, that the children of Israel had sinned against the Lord their God, which had brought them up out of the land of Egypt, from under the hand of Pharaoh king of Egypt, and had feared other gods, and walked in the statutes of the heathen, whom the Lord cast out from before the children of Israel, and of the kings of Israel, which they had made.

<u>Northern Kingdom</u>

- And the children of Israel did secretly those things that were not right against the Lord their God,

- and they built them high places in all their cities, from the tower of the watchmen to the fenced city.
- And they set them up images and groves in every high hill, and under every green tree:
- and there they burnt incense in all the high places, as did the heathen whom the Lord carried away before them; and wrought wicked things to provoke the Lord to anger:
- for they served idols, whereof the Lord had said unto them, Ye shall not do this thing.

Northern & Southern Kingdom

- Yet the Lord testified against Israel, and against Judah, by all the prophets, and by all the seers, saying, Turn ye from your evil ways, and keep my commandments and my statutes, according to all the law which I commanded your fathers, and which I sent to you by my servants the prophets.
- Notwithstanding they would not hear, but hardened their necks, like to the neck of their fathers, that did not believe in the Lord their God.
- And they rejected his statutes, and his covenant that he made with their fathers, and his testimonies which he testified against them; and they followed vanity, and became vain, and went after the heathen that were round about them, concerning whom the Lord had charged them, that they should not do like them.
- And they left all the commandments of the Lord their God, and made them molten images, even two calves, and made a grove, and worshipped all the host of heaven, and served Baal.
- And they caused their sons and their daughters to pass through the fire, and used divination and enchantments, and sold themselves to do evil in the sight of the Lord, to provoke him to anger.

- Therefore the Lord was very angry with Israel, and removed them out of his sight: there was none left but the tribe of Judah only.

<u>Southern Kingdom</u>

- Also Judah kept not the commandments of the Lord their God, but walked in the statutes of Israel which they made.
- And the Lord rejected all the seed of Israel, and afflicted them, and delivered them into the hand of spoilers, until he had cast them out of his sight.
- For he rent Israel from the house of David; and they made Jeroboam the son of Nebat king: and Jeroboam drave Israel from following the Lord, and made them sin a great sin.

<u>Northern Kingdom</u> (the 10 lost Tribes of Israel)

- For the children of Israel walked in all the sins of Jeroboam which he did; they departed not from them;
- until the Lord removed Israel out of his sight, as he had said by all his servants the prophets.
- So was Israel carried away out of their own land to Assyria unto this day."

Foreigners Repopulate Northern Israel (2 Kings 17:24-41)

- "And <u>the king of Assyria brought men from Babylon</u>, and from Cuthah, and from Ava, and from Hamath, and from Sepharvaim, <u>and placed them in the cities of Samaria</u> instead of the children of Israel: <u>and they possessed Samaria, and dwelt in the cities thereof</u>."

- "And so it was at the beginning of their dwelling there, that they feared not the Lord: therefore the Lord sent lions among them, which slew some of them."

- "Wherefore they spake to the king of Assyria, saying, The nations which thou hast removed, and placed in the cities of Samaria, know not the manner of the God of the land: therefore he hath sent lions among them, and, behold, they slay them, because they know not the manner of the God of the land."

- "Then the king of Assyria commanded, saying, Carry thither one of the priests whom ye brought from thence; and let them go and dwell there, and let him teach them the manner of the God of the land."

- "Then one of the priests whom they had carried away from Samaria came and dwelt in Bethel, and taught them how they should fear the Lord."

- "Howbeit every nation made gods of their own, and put them in the houses of the high places which the Samaritans had made, every nation in their cities wherein they dwelt."

- "And the men of Babylon made Succoth-benoth, and the men of Cuth made Nergal, and the men of Hamath made Ashima, and the Avites made Nibhaz and Tartak,"

- "and the Sepharvites burnt their children in fire to Adrammelech and Anammelech, the gods of Sepharvaim."

- "So they feared the Lord, and made unto themselves of the lowest of them priests of the high places, which sacrificed for them in the houses of the high places."

- "They feared the Lord, and served their own gods, after the manner of the nations whom they carried away from thence."

- "Unto this day they do after the former manners: they fear not the Lord, neither do they after their statutes, or after their ordinances, or after the law and commandment which the Lord commanded the children of Jacob, whom he named Israel;"

- "with whom the Lord had made a covenant, and charged them, saying, Ye shall not fear other gods, nor bow yourselves to them, nor serve them, nor sacrifice to them:"

- "but the Lord, who brought you up out of the land of Egypt with great power and a stretched out arm, him shall ye fear, and him shall ye worship, and to him shall ye do sacrifice."

- "And the statutes, and the ordinances, and the law, and the commandment, which he wrote for you, ye shall observe to do for evermore; and ye shall not fear other gods."

- "And the covenant that I have made with you ye shall not forget; neither shall ye fear other gods."

- "But the Lord your God ye shall fear; and he shall deliver you out of the hand of all your enemies."

- "Howbeit they did not hearken, but they did after their former manner."

- "So these nations feared the Lord, and served their graven images, both their children, and their children's children: as did their fathers, so do they unto this day."

Jesus and the Woman at the Well (John 4:1-9)

Seven-hundred years later Jesus meets a woman of Samaria at a well, and they began to converse on why he was there.

The Pharisees: "When therefore the Lord knew how the Pharisees had heard that Jesus made and baptized more disciples than John, (though Jesus himself baptized not, but his disciples,) he left Judaea, and departed again into Galilee."

Jesus: "And he must needs go through Samaria. Then cometh he to a city of Samaria, which is called Sychar, near to the parcel of ground that Jacob gave to his son Joseph."

Jacobs Well: "Now Jacob's well was there. Jesus therefore, being wearied with his journey, sat thus on the well: and it was about the sixth hour *(12 noon)*."

Jesus: "There cometh a woman of Samaria to draw water: Jesus saith unto her, Give me to drink. (For his disciples were gone away unto the city to buy meat.)"

The Woman: "Then saith the woman of Samaria unto him, How is it that thou, being a Jew, askest drink of me, which am a woman of Samaria? for the Jews have no dealings with the Samaritans."

Evidently the woman didn't know the history of Samaria, but Jesus did. She was not aware that her ancestry was not of the Jews, but of the Assyrians and Babylonians; with this knowledge she would know why the Jews shunned the Samarians.

Death of Isaiah

"It is recorded that in 681 BC[429] Isiah died by the hands of Hezekiah's son Manasseh (686 - 631 BC):[430] the most wicked, and evilest king in the history of the Hebrew nation.[431] "Talmudic tradition says his persecutors sawed him in two during the reign of Manasseh.[432]

CHAPTER 18

THE END OF KINGS

YEAR – 686 BC

King Manasseh (2 Kings 21:1-18 / 2 Chronicles 33:1-24)

"Manasseh was twelve years old when he began to reign, and he reigned fifty and five years in Jerusalem: but did that which was evil in the sight of the Lord, like unto the abominations of the heathen, whom the Lord had cast out before the children of Israel."

"For he built again the high places which Hezekiah his father had broken down, and he reared up altars for Baalim, and made groves, and worshipped all the host of heaven, and served them.
Also he built altars in the house of the Lord, whereof the Lord had said, In Jerusalem shall my name be for ever."

"And he built altars for all the host of heaven in the two courts of the house of the Lord.
And he caused his children to pass through the fire in the valley of the son of Hinnom:

also he observed times, and used enchantments, and used witchcraft, and dealt with a familiar spirit, and with wizards: he wrought much evil in the sight of the Lord, to provoke him to anger.

And he set a carved image, the idol which he had made, in the house of God, of which God had said to David and to Solomon his son, In this house, and in Jerusalem, which I have chosen before all the tribes of Israel, will I put my name for ever: neither will I any more remove the foot of Israel from out of the land which I have appointed for your fathers; so that they will take heed to do all that I have commanded them, according to the whole law and the statutes and the ordinances by the hand of Moses."

"So Manasseh made Judah and the inhabitants of Jerusalem to err, and to do worse than the heathen, whom the Lord had destroyed before the children of Israel."

"Moreover Manasseh shed innocent blood very much, till he had filled Jerusalem from one end to another; beside his sin wherewith he made Judah to sin, in doing that which was evil in the sight of the Lord."

God Judges Manasseh

"And the Lord spake by his servants the prophets, saying, Because Manasseh king of Judah hath done these abominations, and hath done wickedly above all that the Amorites did, which were before him, and hath made Judah also to sin with his idols: therefore thus saith the Lord God of Israel, Behold,

- o   I am bringing such evil upon Jerusalem and Judah, that whosoever heareth of it, both his ears shall tingle.

- And I will stretch over Jerusalem the line of Samaria, and the plummet of the house of Ahab:
- and I will wipe Jerusalem as a man wipeth a dish, wiping it, and turning it upside down.
- And I will forsake the remnant of mine inheritance, and deliver them into the hand of their enemies; and they shall become a prey and a spoil to all their enemies; because they have done that which was evil in my sight, and have provoked me to anger, since the day their fathers came forth out of Egypt, even unto this day.

"Wherefore the Lord brought upon them the captains of the host of the king of Assyria, which took Manasseh among the thorns, and bound him with fetters, and carried him to Babylon."

God Hears Manasseh's Prayer

"And when he was in affliction, he besought the Lord his God, and humbled himself greatly before the God of his fathers, and prayed unto him: and he was intreated of him, and heard his supplication, and brought him again to Jerusalem into his kingdom. Then Manasseh knew that the Lord he was God."

Manasseh Repents of His Past Ways

"Now after this he built a wall without the city of David, on the west side of Gihon, in the valley, even to the entering in at the fish gate, and compassed about Ophel, and raised it up a very great height, and put captains of war in all the fenced cities of Judah."

"And he took away the strange gods, and the idol out of the house of the Lord, and all the altars that he had built in the mount of the house of the Lord, and in Jerusalem, and cast them out of the city."

"And he repaired the altar of the Lord, and sacrificed thereon peace offerings and thank offerings, and commanded Judah to serve the Lord God of Israel. Nevertheless the people did sacrifice still in the high places, yet unto the Lord their God only."

YEAR – 663 – 612 BC

The Prophet Nahum

Nahum 2: 8 <u>But Nineveh</u> is of old like a pool of water: yet they shall flee away. Stand, stand, shall they cry; but none shall look back.

9 Take ye the spoil of silver, take the spoil of gold: for there is none end of the store and glory out of all the pleasant furniture.

10 She is empty, and void, and waste: and the heart melteth, and the knees smite together, and much pain is in all loins, and the faces of them all gather blackness.

11 Where is the dwelling of the lions, and the feedingplace of the young lions, where the lion, even the old lion, walked, and the lion's whelp, and none made them afraid?

12 The lion did tear in pieces enough for his whelps, and strangled for his lionesses, and filled his holes with prey, and his dens with ravin.

13 Behold, I am against thee, saith the Lord of hosts, and I will burn her chariots in the smoke, and the sword shall devour thy young lions: and I will cut off thy prey from the earth, and the voice of thy messengers shall no more be heard.

Historic Record: "A prophet of Judah, Nahum's name means "consolation" or "consoler." This name fits his message, as he wrote to encourage the people of Judah while they were being oppressed by the Assyrians (Nahum 1:1).

Other than his being the prophet who wrote the book of Nahum, nothing is known of him except that he came from the village of

Elkosh. Its exact location is unknown, but four suggestions have been made. First, it was the town of Alqush, near Mosul on the Tigris River just north of Nineveh. A tradition declares this to be the site of Nahum's tomb, but it is first mentioned by Masius in the 16th century. The tomb and its location have no archaeological confirmation, and its authenticity is highly suspect.

Nahum was also an ancestor of Jesus, according to Luke's genealogy of Jesus Christ (Luke 3:25)."[433]

**" Nahum predicted that that Nineveh would end "with an over running flood" (1:8), and this is precisely what occurred. The Tigris river overflowed its banks and the flood destroyed part of Nineveh's wall." Then the Babylonian army entered the city and set it on fire after they had finished plundering.[434]

YEAR – 642 BC

Death of Manasseh

"Now the rest of the acts of Manasseh, and his prayer unto his God, and the words of the seers that spake to him in the name of the Lord God of Israel, behold, they are written in the book of the kings of Israel. His prayer also, and how God was intreated of him, and all his sins, and his trespass, and the places wherein he built high places, and set up groves and graven images, before he was humbled: behold, they are written among the sayings of the seers. So Manasseh slept with his fathers, and they buried him in his own house: and Amon his son reigned in his stead."[435]

King Amon

Manasseh's son Amon was twenty-two when he reigned as king of Judaea. His kingship only lasted two-years. He was evil like his father, "for Amon sacrificed unto all the carved images which Manasseh his father had made, and served them."

Amon knew that his father had repented of his sins against God, and had humbled himself before the Lord in prayer, and had made reforms to turn the nation back to God. But Amon grew worse and worse in his evil ways. Therefore, "his servants conspired against him, and slew him in his own house. But the people of the land slew all them that had conspired against king Amon; and the people of the land made Josiah his son king in his stead."

YEAR – 640 BC

King Josiah (2 Kings 22 – 23:1-30 / 2 Chronicles Chapters 34-35)

Josiah was the son of Amon, who was the son of Manasseh. God named Josiah king approximately three-hundred years before he was born, "Behold a child shall be born unto the house of David, Josiah by name."[436] He was born in 648 BC, and died 609 BC during a battle with Pharaoh-necho of Egypt.

Josiah was eight-years old when he became king, and he reigned for thirty-one years in Jerusalem. "And he did that which was right in the sight of the Lord, and walked in all the way of David his father, and turned not aside to the right hand or to the left."

YEAR 635-625 BC

The Prophet Zephaniah

Zephaniah 1: 1 The word of the Lord which came unto Zephaniah the son of Cushi, the son of Gedaliah, the son of Amariah, the son of Hizkiah, in the days of Josiah the son of Amon, king of Judah. 2 I will utterly consume all things from off the land, saith the Lord.

3 I will consume man and beast; I will consume the fowls of the heaven, and the fishes of the sea, and the stumblingblocks with the wicked; and I will cut off man from off the land, saith the Lord.

4 I will also stretch out mine hand upon Judah, and upon all the inhabitants of Jerusalem; and I will cut off the remnant of Baal from this place, and the name of the Chemarims with the priests;

5 And them that worship the host of heaven upon the housetops; and them that worship and that swear by the Lord, and that swear by Malcham;

6 And them that are turned back from the Lord; and those that have not sought the Lord, nor enquired for him.

AUTHOR - According to the editorial heading (Zephaniah 1:1), Zephaniah prophesied during the reign of Josiah (640–609 BC). His family tree is given in an unusually full form. Some scholars have suggested that his great- great-grandfather was King Hezekiah (715–686 BC). But remarkably there is no Jewish or Christian tradition to support the suggestion, which there probably would have been if it had been true. His own name, meaning "he whom the Lord protects or hides," was not uncommon and was a testimony to the keeping power of God.

DATE, ORIGIN, AND DESTINATION - Zephaniah probably prophesied around 630 BC. The fall of Nineveh (612 BC) had not yet occurred (2:13-15). Josiah's reign falls into two periods, dividing at 622 BC. In that year, while the temple was being cleared of pagan articles, the Book of the Law was found, which gave momentum to Josiah's religious reforms (2 Kings 22). The unreformed state of affairs described by Zephaniah (Zephaniah 1:4-12; 3:1-4) points to a date before 622, at least for his denunciations. The prophet addressed Judah, the southern kingdom, and in particular the civil and religious authorities in Jerusalem. He most probably prophesied during the reign of Josiah, who came to the throne at the age of eight.

The negative parts of the book concerning the sin and punishment of Judah—now fulfilled—would serve as a serious warning against disobedience to God. Moreover, the fulfillment of Zephaniah's prophetic threats would serve to enhance the positive side of the book, confirming the hope of completion in the experience of a fresh generation of God's people.

BACKGROUND - Politically, the Assyrian Empire had spread westward and held Palestine in its grip. The long reign of Manasseh (696–642 BC) had been a period of total subservience to Assyria. Political subservience as an Assyrian vassal meant religious subservience to the gods of Assyria, especially worship of the heavenly bodies (2 Kings 21:5). Zephaniah complained of this sin (Zephaniah 1:5). When the door opened to one foreign religion, others naturally came in. Once the exclusiveness of the worship of the God of Israel was abandoned, Palestinian cults were openly accepted. The Canaanite Baal was blatantly worshiped (2 Kings 21:3), as Zephaniah attested (Zephaniah 1:4). Zephaniah condemned the worshipers of Molech (verse 5), who sacrificed children to the Ammonite god (1 Kings 11:7; 2 Kings 23:10). International imperialism meant a weakening of national culture, so that foreign customs were practiced, probably with religious overtones (Zephaniah 1:8-9).

The reign of Josiah brought changes, marking a political and religious turning point. Assyria, preoccupied with troubles on the eastern and northern frontiers and unable to consolidate its acquisitions, became unable to reinforce its authority in the west. This weakness induced Josiah to launch a national liberation movement. He threw off the yoke of Assyria and expanded his sphere of influence northward into the territory of the old northern kingdom. From a religious standpoint, he completely dissociated himself and his country from the religions that prevailed in Judah and recalled the nation to a pure and exclusive faith in the God of Israel. The book of Zephaniah shows that there was at least one person who shared his ideals. His prophetic ministry undoubtedly paved the way for Josiah's subsequent reformation. He was a contemporary of Jeremiah, at least for the early part of that prophet's career (Jeremiah began prophesying in 627 BC).[437]

YEAR – 627 BC

The Prophet Jeremiah

Jeremiah's ministry was from 627 – 570 BC. He was the contemporary of Zephaniah, Habakkuk, Daniel, and Ezekiel. He was a good friend of king Josiah: the reformer king. He was also known as the weeping prophet; he shed many tears because of Israel's sins against God. Further, he's known and called an end times preacher, because he prophesied the seventy-year captivity of Israel.

Christ Calls Jeremiah into Service

"<u>The words of Jeremiah</u> the son of Hilkiah, of the priests that were in Anathoth in the land of Benjamin: <u>To whom the word of the Lord came in the days of Josiah</u> the son of Amon king of Judah, <u>in the thirteenth year of his reign</u>. It came also in the days of Jehoiakim the son of Josiah king of Judah, unto the end of the eleventh year of Zedekiah the son of Josiah king of Judah, unto the carrying away of Jerusalem captive in the fifth month. Then <u>the word of the Lord came unto me, saying</u>,[438]

- Before I formed thee in the belly I knew thee;
- and before thou camest forth out of the womb I sanctified thee,
- and I ordained thee a prophet unto the nations."
- Then said I, Ah, Lord God! behold, I cannot speak: for I am a child.
- But the Lord said unto me, Say not, I am a child: for thou shalt go to all that I shall send thee, and whatsoever I command thee thou shalt speak.
- Be not afraid of their faces: for I am with thee to deliver thee, saith the Lord.
- Then the Lord put forth his hand, and touched my mouth.

- And the Lord said unto me, Behold, I have put my words in thy mouth.
- See, I have this day set thee over the nations and over the kingdoms, to root out, and to pull down, and to destroy, and to throw down, to build, and to plant.

ANATHOTH (PLACE), ANATHOTHITE -Town in Benjamin's territory set aside for the Levites (Joshua 21:18; 1 Chronicles 6:60). Anathoth may have been named by the Canaanites for their goddess Anath, or later by the Israelites for one of Benjamin's descendants (1 Chronicles 7:8). The town was probably located at Ras el-Karrubeh near the modern town of Anata three miles (4.8 kilometers) north of Jerusalem. Its residents were sometimes called Anethothites or Anetothites (2 Samuel 23:27; 1 Chronicles 27:12). Abiezer, one of David's military leaders, was from Anathoth (1 Chronicles 11:28, KJV "Antothite") as was the soldier Jehu (1 Chronicles 12:3) and the priest Abiathar (1 Kings 2:26). It was also the hometown of the prophet Jeremiah (Jeremiah 1:1), though some of its inhabitants violently opposed him (Jeremiah 11:21, 23). Just before Judah fell to Babylon, Jeremiah bought a field in Anathoth as a sign that Israel would be restored to her land (Jeremiah 32:7-9). Years later, 128 men of Anathoth returned from the exile, and the town was resettled (Nehemiah 11:32).[439]

Now I want to pause here a moment and reflect on Jerimiah. First, he is the son of Hilkiah the high priest, who is a direct descendent of Aaron the first High priest. Second this makes Jeremiah a high priest by heritage: for only those of Aaron's family line could be high priests.[440]

Therefore, God chose a high priest to start the nation of Israel religious order, and a high priest to end the religious rites by the seventy-year captivity; which destroyed the Temple of God, and forced the disappearance of the Ark of the Covenant.

The <u>word of the Lord came and spoke to Jeremiah close to one</u>

hundred times. Jeremiah was an end-time's preacher in the Southern kingdom of Judah, who pronounced the end of Israel as a nation;

- o because God had sentenced them to seventy years of captivity in the land of Babylon (Jeremiah 29:10–13).

- o Approximately one hundred years prior, the judgment of God removed the Northern kingdom of Israel (Samaria—the ten tribes) to the land of Assyria; later ruled by Babylon.[441]

Because the book of Jeremiah is not written in chronological order, I will now begin to insert reference scriptures so that those who wish further study can do so without frustration.

- o The Sign of Jeremiah's Calling (Jeremiah 1:11-14)
- o Jeremiah's Assurance (Jeremiah 1:17-19)
- o Jeremiah's first Sermon (Jeremiah 2:1-9)
- o Judah is Called to Repent (Jeremiah 3:11-25)
- o The Religious Condition (Jeremiah 5:30-31 / Isiah 30:8-13)
- o Disobedience cause God not to hear prayer (Jeremiah 11:1-14)
- o The priests of Anathoth seek the life of Jeremiah (Jeremiah 11:18-23 (12:6)
- o Jeremiah's Complaint (Jeremiah 12:1-17)

> **YEAR – 622 BC**
> 2 Kings 22 and 23:1-30 / 2 Chronicles 34 to 35:1-27

Josiah hears the Word God

During his eighteenth year as king, [Josiah, is twenty-six], he took on the task of repairing the Temple of God. Inside the temple was found the book of the law, and it was brought and read to Josiah. The words of the law so moved Josiah that he told Hilkiah, the high priest, "Go ye, inquire of the Lord for me, and for the people, and for all Judah, concerning the words of this book that is found: for great is the wrath of the Lord that is kindled against us, because our fathers have not hearkened unto the words of this book, to do according unto all that which is written concerning us."

The Prophetess Huldah

When Josiah sent Hilkiah to inquire of the Lord, it was assumed that he would go to the prophet Zephaniah, or the young prophet Jeremiah. But instead he inquired of the prophetess Huldah, " the wife of Shallum the son of Tikvah, the son of Harhas, keeper of the wardrobe; (now she dwelt in Jerusalem in the college;), and they communed with her."

> *"And she said unto them, Thus saith the Lord God of Israel, Tell the man that sent you to me. Thus saith the Lord, Behold, I will bring evil upon this place, and upon the inhabitants thereof, even all the words of the book which the king of Judah hath read: because they have forsaken me, and have burned incense unto other gods, that they might provoke me to anger with all the works of their hands; therefore my wrath shall be kindled against this place, and shall not be quenched. But to the king of Judah which sent you to inquire of the Lord, thus shall ye say to him, Thus saith the Lord God of Israel, As touching the words which thou hast heard; because thine heart was tender, and thou hast humbled thyself before the Lord, when thou heardest what I spake against this place, and against the inhabitants thereof, that they should become a desolation and a curse, and hast rent thy clothes, and wept before me; I also have heard thee, saith the Lord. Behold therefore, I will gather thee unto thy fathers, and thou shalt be gathered into thy grave in peace; and thine eyes shall not see all the evil which I will bring upon this place."*

Josiah's Reform (2 Kings 23: 1-30)

When Josiah heard the reply from God, given by the Prophetess Huldah, he went on a rampage to turn the nation back to God. He was determined to get rid of anything that resembled a transgression against God, and to bring back worship of God only.

Josiah gathers together all the elders of Israel
1 And the king sent, and they gathered unto him all the elders of Judah and of Jerusalem.
2 And the king went up into the house of the Lord, and all the men of Judah and all the inhabitants of Jerusalem with him, and the priests, and the prophets, and all the people, both small and great: and he read in their ears all the words of the book of the covenant which was found in the house of the Lord.

Josiah swears a covenant to God
3 And the king stood by a pillar, and made a covenant before the Lord, to walk after the Lord, and to keep his commandments and his testimonies and his statutes with all their heart and all their soul, to perform the words of this covenant that were written in this book. And all the people stood to the covenant.

Josiah cleanses the temple of idols
4 And the king commanded Hilkiah the high priest, and the priests of the second order, and the keepers of the door, to bring forth out of the temple of the Lord all the vessels that were made for Baal, and for the grove, and for all the host of heaven: and he burned them without Jerusalem in the fields of Kidron, and carried the ashes of them unto Bethel.

He took the false priests out of office
5 And he put down the idolatrous priests, whom the kings of Judah had ordained to burn incense in the high places in the cities of Judah, and in the places round about Jerusalem; them also that burned

incense unto Baal, to the sun, and to the moon, and to the planets, and to all the host of heaven.

He took the grove out of the temple
6 And he brought out the grove from the house of the Lord, without Jerusalem, unto the brook Kidron, and burned it at the brook Kidron, and stamped it small to powder, and cast the powder thereof upon the graves of the children of the people.

> <u>**GROVE**</u> – "Mistaken KJV translation of a Hebrew word that was the name of a Canaanite goddess, Asherah. Often sacred trees were designated as symbols of that fertility goddess; sometimes wooden poles were erected. God commanded the Israelites to destroy those symbols (called "Asherim," "Asheroth") by cutting them down (Exodus 34:13) and burning them (Deuteronomy 12:3). Because the poles were wooden, archaeologists have been unable to find any clear remains. In an early sanctuary at Ai, however, a large piece of carbonized wood was discovered lying between incense burners. It may have been a tree trunk from which the branches had been trimmed. Some researchers suggest it was an Asherah pole.
>
> God strictly forbade the Israelites to worship Asherah or to erect sacred symbols in her honor. From time to time Israel disobeyed God and engaged in false worship. One account of the downfall of the northern kingdom attributes its failure to the existence of groves and the worship of the pagan goddess and her male counterpart, Baal (2 Kings 17:7-18). Jezebel, a priestess of the Tyrian Baal, promoted the spread of such idolatry. The "grove" of Genesis 21:33 (KJV) was actually a tamarisk tree."[442]

He tore down the Homosexual houses
7 And he brake down the houses of the sodomites, that were by the house of the Lord, where the women wove hangings for the grove.

He tore down all the High Places
8 And he brought all the priests out of the cities of Judah, and defiled the high places where the priests had burned incense, from Geba to Beer-sheba, and brake down the high places of the gates that were in the entering in of the gate of Joshua the governor of the city, which were on a man's left hand at the gate of the city.
9 Nevertheless the priests of the high places came not up to the altar of the Lord in Jerusalem, but they did eat of the unleavened bread among their brethren.

He stopped the sacrifice of children
10 And he defiled Topheth, which is in the valley of the children of Hinnom, that no man might make his son or his daughter to pass through the fire to Molech. **(1 Kings 11:1-8)**

> **TOPHETH** - Location within the valley of Hinnom outside Jerusalem where Israel profaned the Lord by offering human sacrifices to Molech. As part of his religious reform, Josiah defiled Topheth and tore down its altars (2 Kings 23:10). Josiah's reforms appear to have had only temporary impact, for the practice recurred under Manasseh (2 Chronicles 33:6) and was later condemned by Jeremiah (Jeremiah 7:31-32). Jeremiah prophesied that the valley would be renamed the "Valley of Slaughter" because it would be the site where the Babylonians would rout Judah during their siege of Jerusalem. Jeremiah repeated the prophecy during his parable of the potter's flask, emphasizing the fact that Jerusalem would be destroyed so thoroughly that it would resemble Topheth (19:12). By this time, Topheth had evidently become a sort of city dump where broken pottery was thrown away and where

burials that could not be accommodated in any of the city cemeteries would take place (verse 11).

While Topheth is not mentioned in the NT, it is linked to Gehenna (Aramaic form of "valley of Hinnom"). Gehenna refers to the place of destruction and is typically translated "hell" in the NT (Matthew 5:22, 29-30; 10:28; 18:9; Mark 9:43-47; Luke 12:5).[443]

VALLEY OF HINNOM – "Valley on the south side of Jerusalem, called Gehenna in the Greek NT"

GEHENNA – "Gehenna is a word derived from the Hebrew phrase "the Valley of [the son(s) of] Hinnom." The name properly designates a deep valley marking the boundaries of the territories of the tribes of Benjamin and Judah (Joshua 15:8; 18:16). It is commonly identified with Wadi el-Rababi that runs from beneath the western wall of the Old City, forming a deep ravine south of Jerusalem.

The place became notorious because of the idol worship practices that were carried out there in the days of Judah's kings Ahaz and Manasseh, especially involving the heinous crime of infant sacrifices associated with the Molech (Milcom) ceremonies (2 Kings 16:3; 21:6). The spiritual reformation of King Josiah brought an end to these sinister proceedings (23:10). The prophet Jeremiah referred to the valley in picturing God's judgment upon his people (Jeremiah 2:23; 7:30-32).

Because of all that, the valley appears to have been used for the burning of the city's refuse and the dead bodies of criminals. Interestingly, a well-established tradition locates the scene of Judas's suicide and the consequent purchase of the Potter's Field on the south side of this valley.

The ravine's reputation for extreme wickedness gave rise, especially during the time period between the Old and New Testament, to use of its name as a term for the place of final punishment for the wicked (Isaiah 66:24). Jesus himself utilizes the term to designate the final abode of the unrepentant wicked (Matthew 10:28). Since Gehenna is considered a fiery abyss (Mark 9:43), it is also the lake of fire (Revelation 20:14-15) to which all the godless will ultimately be consigned (Matthew 23:15, 33), together with Satan and his devils (Revelation 19:20).

Gehenna must be carefully differentiated from other terms relative to the afterlife or final state. Whereas the Old Testament "Sheol" and New Testament "hades" uniformly designate the temporary abode of the dead (before the last Day of Judgment), "Gehenna" specifies the final place where the wicked will suffer everlasting punishment."[444]

He burned the idols of the sun god
11 And he took away the horses that the kings of Judah had given to the sun, at the entering in of the house of the Lord, by the chamber of Nathan-melech the chamberlain, which was in the suburbs, and burned the chariots of the sun with fire.

He tore down the false altars
12 And the altars that were on the top of the upper chamber of Ahaz, which the kings of Judah had made *(2 Kings 16:1-20)*, and the altars which Manasseh had made in the two courts of the house of the Lord, did the king beat down, and brake them down from thence, and cast the dust of them into the brook Kidron.

He tore down the high places in Jerusalem
13 And the high places that were before Jerusalem, which were on the right hand of the mount of corruption, which Solomon the king of Israel had builded for Ashtoreth the abomination of the Zidonians,

and for Chemosh the abomination of the Moabites, and for Milcom the abomination of the children of Ammon, did the king defile.

He transferred the grove site's into grave yards
14 And he brake in pieces the images, and cut down the groves, and filled their places with the bones of men.

He tore down the Bethel altar
15 Moreover the altar that was at Bethel, and the high place which Jeroboam the son of Nebat, who made Israel to sin, had made, both that altar and the high place he brake down, and burned the high place, and stamped it small to powder, and burned the grove. *(1 Kings 12:25-33)*

He burnt the bones of the dead
16 And as Josiah turned himself, he spied the sepulchres that were there in the mount, and sent, and took the bones out of the sepulchres, and burned them upon the altar, and polluted it, according to the word of the Lord which the man of God proclaimed, who proclaimed these words.

He preserved the bones of God's prophet
17 Then he said, What title is that that I see? And the men of the city told him, It is the sepulchre of the man of God, which came from Judah, and proclaimed these things that thou hast done against the altar of Bethel. *(1 Kings 13:1-32)*
18 And he said, Let him alone; let no man move his bones. So they let his bones alone, with the bones of the prophet that came out of Samaria.

He tore down the high places in Samaria
19 And all the houses also of the high places that were in the cities of Samaria, which the kings of Israel had made to provoke the Lord to anger, Josiah took away, and did to them according to all the acts that he had done in Bethel.

He slew all the false priests
20 And he slew all the priests of the high places that were there upon the altars, and burned men's bones upon them, and returned to Jerusalem.

He commanded the people keep the Passover
21 And the king commanded all the people, saying, Keep the passover unto the Lord your God, as it is written in the book of this covenant.
22 Surely there was not holden such a passover from the days of the judges that judged Israel, nor in all the days of the kings of Israel, nor of the kings of Judah;
23 but in the eighteenth year of king Josiah, wherein this passover was holden to the Lord in Jerusalem.

He got rid of black magic
24 Moreover the workers with familiar spirits, and the wizards, and the images, and the idols, and all the abominations that were spied in the land of Judah and in Jerusalem, did Josiah put away, that he might perform the words of the law which were written in the book that Hilkiah the priest found in the house of the Lord.

There was no king before or after like Josiah
25 And like unto him was there no king before him, that turned to the Lord with all his heart, and with all his soul, and with all his might, according to all the law of Moses; neither after him arose there any like him.

Even with reform God would not stay his hand from banishment
26 Notwithstanding the Lord turned not from the fierceness of his great wrath, wherewith his anger was kindled against Judah, because of all the provocations that Manasseh had provoked him withal.
27 And the Lord said, I will remove Judah also out of my sight, as I have removed Israel, and will cast off this city Jerusalem which I have chosen, and the house of which I said, My name shall be there.

> **YEAR – 609 BC**

Death of Josiah

28 Now the rest of the acts of Josiah, and all that he did, are they not written in the book of the chronicles of the kings of Judah?
29 In his days Pharaoh-nechoh king of Egypt went up against the king of Assyria to the river Euphrates: and king Josiah went against him; and he slew him at Megiddo, when he had seen him.

Jehoahaz rules Judah

After the death of king Josiah, his son Jehoahaz became king. "Jehoahaz was twenty and three years old when he began to reign; and he reigned three months in Jerusalem." "And he did that which was evil in the sight of the Lord, according to all that his fathers had done." "And Pharaoh-nechoh put him in bands at Riblah in the land of Hamath, that he might not reign in Jerusalem; and put the land to a tribute of an hundred talents of silver, and a talent of gold.

And Pharaoh-nechoh made Eliakim the son of Josiah king in the room of Josiah his father, and turned his name to Jehoiakim, and took Jehoahaz away: and he came to Egypt, and died there."[445]

> **YEAR 607 BC**

The Prophet Habakkuk

Habakkuk 1: 1 The burden which Habakkuk the prophet did see.
2 O Lord, how long shall I cry, and thou wilt not hear! even cry out unto thee of violence, and thou wilt not save!
3 Why dost thou shew me iniquity, and cause me to behold grievance? for spoiling and violence are before me: and there are that raise up strife and contention.

4 Therefore the law is slacked, and judgment doth never go forth: for the wicked doth compass about the righteous; therefore wrong judgment proceedeth.

The Lord's answer

5 Behold ye among the heathen, and regard, and wonder marvellously: for I will work a work in your days, which ye will not believe, though it be told you.

6 <u>For, lo, I raise up the Chaldeans</u> (*Babylonians*), that bitter and hasty nation, which shall march through the breadth of the land, to possess the dwellingplaces that are not theirs.

Historic Record: Habakkuk was the author of the eighth book of the Minor Prophets. The meaning of Habakkuk's name is uncertain. It was probably derived from a Hebrew word meaning "to embrace." Nothing is known about Habakkuk apart from what is mentioned in his book. Several legends attempt to give accounts of his life. However, they are generally regarded as untrustworthy. One writing describes a miraculous transporting of Habakkuk to Daniel while Daniel was in the den of lions. A Jewish legend makes Habakkuk the son of the Shunammite woman mentioned in 2 Kings 4:8-37. That legend apparently is based on the tradition that she would "embrace" a son. Chronological difficulties make both accounts unlikely.

Habakkuk lived in the period during the rise of the Chaldeans (Hebrews 1:6), that is, during the reigns of the Judean kings Josiah and Jehoiakim. <u>His prophetic activity probably took place between 612-589 B.C.</u>

The book of Habakkuk reveals a man of great sensitivity. His deep concern about injustice and his prayer (Hebrews 3:1) reveal his profound religious conviction and social awareness.[446]

CHAPTER 19

THE SEVENTY YEAR CAPTIVITY

Jehoiakim is Made King

"Jehoiakim was twenty and five years old when he began to reign; and he reigned eleven years in Jerusalem." "And he did that which was evil in the sight of the Lord, according to all that his fathers had done."

HISTORY - Jehoiakim was the second son of the Hebrew king Josiah, Jehoiakim was born to Josiah's wife Zebidah (2 Kings 23:36; 1 Chronicles 3:15; 2 Chronicles 36:4). Jehoiakim became king of Judah in 609 BC He replaced his younger brother Jehoahaz as king when Jehoahaz was taken from the throne and exiled by Pharaoh Neco after three months as king (2 Kings 23:31-35). Jehoiakim was made king at age twenty-five, and he ruled for eleven years in Jerusalem. His given name, Eliakim, means "God will establish." Neco changed his name to Jehoiakim, meaning "Yahweh will establish" (2 Kings 23:34), perhaps hoping that this would ensure Yahweh's support for his action.

Pharaoh Neco demanded a large amount of tribute money from

Judah, and Jehoiakim raised the money by taxing the whole land (2 Kings 23:35; also see Jeremiah 22:13-17, where the oracle against Jehoiakim implies that he used some of this money for himself). Jehoiakim served the Egyptians until the battle of Carchemish in 605 BC, when Nebuchadnezzar and the Babylonians beat Neco. Judah then became a property of Babylon for three years (2 Kings 24:1-2). After Nebuchadnezzar failed to completely destroy Neco in a second fierce battle in 601 BC, Jehoiakim tried to throw off Babylonian rule. Angered, Nebuchadnezzar invaded Judah in 598 BC to punish the rebellious king (2 Kings 24:3-7). Jehoiakim had expected help from Egypt, but this never came, and the Babylonians destroyed the important Judahite cities of Debir and Lachish, seized control of the Negev, and exiled several thousand of Judah's most important citizens. This crippled the economy and left Judah without leaders. Jehoiakim died during the Babylonian attack (probably late in 598 B.C.). His son Jehoiachin was placed on the throne.

Although the details of Jehoiakim's death are not reported, the Bible's authors pass judgment on him, saying that Jehoiakim was as evil as his fathers (2 Kings 23:37; 2 Chronicles 36:5, 8. Jeremiah 22:18-19 and Jeremiah 36:27-32 predict that Jehoiakim's dead body would be cast on the ground outside of Jerusalem without proper burial, and that he would have no children upon the throne. Jeremiah describes the evils that were common during Jehoiakim's rule: idolatry, social injustice, robbery of the poor worker, greed, murder, oppression, extortion, and forsaking of the covenant of the Lord (Jeremiah 22:1-17). Despite Jeremiah's thundering prophecies in chapters Jeremiah 25-26, and Jeremiah 36, Jehoiakim remained disobedient, unrepentant, and smug, living in stolen prosperity (Jeremiah 22:18-23).[447]

- 1st year of Jehoiakim. (Jeremiah 26 and 27: 1-11)
- Judah's religious sins (Jerimiah 7-10)
- Judah's judgment and resentment towards Jeremiah (Jeremiah 14-20)
- God's message to the Rechabites. (Jeremiah 35)

- 4th year of Jehoiakim, Message of the scroll. (Jeremiah 36-42)
- God's message to Jeremiah's secretary Baruch. (Jeremiah 45:1-5)
- Jeremiah pronounces the seventy-year captivity. (Jeremiah 25)
- Gentile nation prophesies (Jeremiah 46-49)
- Signs from God (Jeremiah 13)
- God's message to Jehoiakim (Jeremiah 22:1-23)

> **YEAR - 605 DC**
> 2 Kings 24:1-7 / 2 Chronicles 36:4-8 / Jeremiah 52:28

The Prophet Daniel

During the seventh year of Nebuchadnezzar's reign, he attacked Jehoiakim in the third year of his kingship, and took three-thousand-three-hundred -twenty captives to Babylon. Daniel and his three friends (Shadrach, Meshach, and Abednego) were of those taken.[448] "Nebuchadnezzar also carried of the vessels of the house of the Lord to Babylon, and put them in his temple at Babylon."[449] Daniel ministered from 605-536 BC; until the third year of Cyrus the great.

DANIEL - Daniel was a Jewish leader and prophet who lived in the court of the king of Babylon. The Old Testament book of Daniel tells his story. We know nothing about his parents or family, but he probably came from a long line of noble Jewish families (Daniel 1:3). According to one guess, Daniel was about 16 when he and his three friends-Hananiah, Mishael, and Azariah-were taken from Jerusalem to Babylon by King Nebuchadnezzar.

Daniel, renamed Belteshazzar (meaning "may Bel [god] protect his life"), was to serve the king as a member of his court. He earned a reputation for intelligence and for total faithfulness to his God. After three years of instruction, he began a career in court that lasted nearly seventy years (Daniel 1:21).[450]

Who is Jesus Christ

Daniel is one of those special prophets of God; for he was allowed, not only to see the Father and the Son, but to also feel the power of the Holy Ghost in visions of the future. Added to that was the prophecy of the coming Messiah.

The four kingdoms of the earth. (Daniel 7:1-8 / 15-21 / 23-28)
The Father and the Son. (Daniel 7:9-14)
The Messiah. (Daniel 9: 24-27) [see chapter 21]

> **YEAR – 597 BC**
> 2 Kings 24:8-16 / 2 Chronicles 36:9-10 / Jeremiah 52:29

Jehoiachin rules Judah

<u>**2 Kings 24:**</u> 8 Jehoiachin was eighteen years old when he began to reign, and he reigned in Jerusalem three months. And his mother's name was Nehushta, the daughter of Elnathan of Jerusalem.
9 And he did that which was evil in the sight of the Lord, according to all that his father had done.
10 At that time the servants of Nebuchadnezzar king of Babylon came up against Jerusalem, and the city was besieged.
11 And Nebuchadnezzar king of Babylon came against the city, and his servants did besiege it.
12 And Jehoiachin the king of Judah went out to the king of Babylon, he, and his mother, and his servants, and his princes, and his officers: and the king of Babylon took him in the eighth year of his reign.
13 And he carried out thence all the treasures of the house of the Lord, and the treasures of the king's house, and cut in pieces all the vessels of gold which Solomon king of Israel had made in the temple of the Lord, as the Lord had said.
14 And he carried away all Jerusalem, and all the princes, and all the mighty men of valour, even ten thousand captives, and all the craftsmen and smiths: none remained, save the poorest sort of the people of the land.

15 And he carried away Jehoiachin to Babylon, and the king's mother, and the king's wives, and his officers, and the mighty of the land, those carried he into captivity from Jerusalem to Babylon.
16 <u>And all the men of might, even seven thousand</u>, and craftsmen and smiths a thousand, all that were strong and apt for war, even them the king of Babylon brought captive to Babylon.

- o God's message to Jehoiachin. (Jeremiah 22:24-30)
- o God's message of the coming righteous king. (Jeremiah 23:1-40)
- o After thirty-seven years Jehoiachin is released from captivity. (Jeremiah 52:31-34)

The Prophet Ezekiel (593 -570 BC)

In the fifth year of Jehoiachin's captivity, the priest Ezekiel was among the captives, down by the river Chebar, in Babylon, when he saw a vision of God and <u>the word of the Lord</u> came and laid his hand on him, and he saw God coming with a great heavenly host. Thus, Ezekiel became God's prophet among the people during the seventy-year captivity.

So then, Jeremiah is in Israel, Daniel is a member of the Babylonian king staff, and Ezekiel is down among the captives. Therefore, I'm going to say that God's three prong prophets are in control of the whole nation of Israel (all twelve tribes to include the Levites) which are now represented in the land of Babylon. This can be clearly seen during the time of Esther.

> **History:** "Ezekiel was a priest and prophet during the time of Israel's exile in Babylon. Ezekiel came from the influential priestly family of Zadok (Ezekiel 1:3) and probably grew up in Jerusalem. He was familiar with the rituals of the temple, although it is unknown whether he served as a priest there. All that we know of his personal life comes from the Old Testament book of Ezekiel.

Ezekiel was married (Ezekiel 24:16-18). He was among the Judeans who were forced out of the country by an invading Babylonian army; he was about 25 years old at this time. After this, he lived at Tel-abib in Babylonia (Ezekiel 3:15), in his own house (Ezekiel 3:24; Ezekiel 8:1)-most of the other Judean captives had settled by the Kebar Canal (Ezekiel 1:3), which went from Babylon by Nippur to Erech. The elders of Israel who lived there sought out Ezekiel's counsel (Ezekiel 8:1; Ezekiel 14:1; Ezekiel 20:1). In the fifth year of the exile, when Ezekiel was between 25 and 30 years old, God called him to be a prophet (Ezekiel 1:1-3:11). During the exile, his wife died suddenly, but he was told not to mourn for her in public (Ezekiel 24:16-18). Her sudden death was meant as a warning-a striking and solemn warning of what would happen to Israel (Ezekiel 24:15-27).

Ezekiel prophesied during the same historical period as Jeremiah and Daniel-an unusual time in Israel's history. Judah experienced political and social turmoil, and its people turned to other gods, disobeying the laws that had been handed down to Moses. Israel and Judah fought repeatedly with the surrounding countries, and the balance of power constantly shifted throughout the Near East.

Ezekiel ministered between 592 BC and the 27th year of the exile (around 570 BC) (Ezekiel 29:17). His career falls into two main periods. During the first period (592-587 BC), he warned the exiled Judeans to repent and place their faith in God. After Nebuchadnezzar of Babylon destroyed Jerusalem and the temple, Ezekiel's career entered its second phase (586-570 B.C.). During this time, the prophet comforted the exiles and encouraged them to look to the future in hope (Ezekiel 33-48). He learned of the fall of Jerusalem while in Babylon (Ezekiel 33:21-22). There were 13 years, from 585

BC (Ezekiel 32:1, Ezekiel 17:1; Ezekiel 33:21) to 572 BC (Ezekiel 40:1), during which Ezekiel did not prophesy.

Ezekiel's main message was that Judah was ripe for judgment. At first Ezekiel's messages were not accepted, but time proved him right; his predictions came true, and Judeans began to repent.

Ezekiel has been called "the father of Judaism" because of his influence on the way post-exile Israel worshipped. According to tradition, he helped to create the synagogue-the place of worship for Jews living after the destruction of the temple-by meeting with Jewish elders in Babylon to worship. He stressed the ideas of personal immortality, resurrection, and keeping the ritual law.

Ezekiel carried out his messages with vivid and dramatic symbolic acts (e.g., Ezekiel 4:1-8; Ezekiel 5:1-17). Some readers find his writing style to be heavy and repetitious, but his metaphors and images are often powerful. For example, the image of eating a scroll with prophecy written upon it (Ezekiel 2:8-3) appears again in the book of Revelation.

We do not know where or how he died, and he is not mentioned again in the Old Testament."[451]

> **2 Kings 24:17-19 & 25:1-29 / 2 Chronicles 36:11-15**

King Zedekiah (597-586)

After Jehoiachin was dethroned, Nebuchadnezzar made his uncle[452] Mattaniah king, and changed his name to Zedekiah.

"Zedekiah was one and twenty years old when he began to reign, and reigned eleven years in Jerusalem. And he did that which was evil in the sight of the Lord his God, and humbled not himself before Jeremiah the prophet speaking from the mouth of the Lord."

"And he also rebelled against king Nebuchadnezzar, who had made him swear by God: but he stiffened his neck, and hardened his heart from turning unto the Lord God of Israel."

"Moreover all the chief of the priests, and the people, transgressed very much after all the abominations of the heathen; and polluted the house of the Lord which he had hallowed in Jerusalem."

"And the Lord God of their fathers sent to them by his messengers, rising up betimes, and sending; because he had compassion on his people, and on his dwelling place: but they mocked the messengers of God, and despised his words, and misused his prophets, until the wrath of the Lord arose against his people, till there was no remedy."

> **History:** "Zedekiah was the last king of Judah and a very important figure during the last days of the southern kingdom. He reigned from 597 BC to 586 BC During this time, King Nebuchadnezzar attacked Jerusalem twice. The first attack was because of the rebellion of Jehoiakim, who ruled Judah from 609 BC to 598 B.C. However, by the time this attack was over, Jehoiakim had died and his 18-year-old son, Jehoiachin, had become king. Nebuchadnezzar deported the young king to Babylon, along with other elite people in Judah. This included government officials, army officers, and craftsmen. Nebuchadnezzar appointed Jehoiachin's uncle, Mattaniah, to be the new ruler in Judah. Mattaniah was the third son of Josiah to rule the people of Judah. Nebuchadnezzar gave Mattaniah the name Zedekiah, which means "the Lord is my righteousness."
>
> Zedekiah found himself in a difficult position as the new king of Judah. Many people in Judah still thought Jehoiachin was the real king (Jeremiah 28:1-4). The Judeans deported to Babylonia dated events based on the reign of Jehoiachin (2 Kings 25:27 and Ezekiel 1:2). Though the Babylonians made

Zedekiah take an oath of loyalty (2 Chronicles 36:13 and Ezekiel 17:13-18), evidence suggests that they also thought Jehoiachin was the legitimate king of Judah. They may have been holding Jehoiachin in case they wanted to restore his power.

In addition, Judah was filled with a false optimism that could hardly have helped the new king. The Judeans confidently expected that the deportation of the leading citizens would only be a temporary situation. The prophets said that Babylon's power would be broken within two years (Jeremiah 28:2-4). These prophets were opposed by another group of prophets, led by Jeremiah, whose message was not very popular among the people of Judah.

Zedekiah felt pressure to change his political allegiance from within and from without the nation. In 593 BC, the neighboring states of Ammon, Moab, Tyre, and Sidon formed a coalition to fight for independence from Babylon. These nations sent envoys to Zedekiah (Jeremiah 27:1-3). However, Jeremiah advised the king not to get involved. In the same year, according to Jeremiah 51:59, Zedekiah visited Babylon. He may have been summoned to affirm his loyalty and to explain his role in the political alliance. The planned rebellion did not occur, perhaps because the aid these countries were expecting from Egypt did not come.

Within the Judean government, there was a large group of people who thought Egypt would be a helpful ally in trying to break away from the rule of Babylon. This was similar to the situation when Hezekiah was king a century before (Isaiah 31:1-3 and Isaiah 36:6). Zedekiah, who found it very difficult to resist this political pressure, eventually transferred his allegiance to Egypt.

Hophra, who reigned in Egypt from 589 BC to 570 BC, was the heir of Psammetichus. Hophra organized a joint rebellion in the west against Babylon. According to Ezekiel 21:18-32 and 25:12-17, Judah and Ammon supported him, while Edom and Philistia did not participate. Zedekiah was rebuked by the prophet Ezekiel (17:13-18) for breaking his oath to Nebuchadnezzar (2 Chronicles 36:13) and rebelling against him by sending envoys to Egypt to negotiate for military support.

In the face of this western uprising engineered by his Egyptian rival, Nebuchadnezzar was forced to march westward. Setting up headquarters at Riblah in northern Syria, he decided to make Jerusalem his prime target of attack (Ezekiel 21:18-23). The siege of Jerusalem was temporarily lifted because of an Egyptian attack, but it was later resumed until the city was conquered. Zedekiah, fleeing eastward with his troops, was caught near Jericho and taken north to King Nebuchadnezzar at Riblah. He was put on trial for breaking his oath of loyalty. As his punishment, his sons were killed before his eyes. This tragic sight was the last thing he ever saw, because his eyes were then put out. He was taken in chains to Babylon, where he eventually died in prison (2 Kings 25:5-7; Jeremiah 39:7; 52:8-11, and Ezekiel 12:13)."[453]

- o God's message to Zedekiah (Jeremiah 21)
- o Jeremiah's Two Basket of Figs vision (Jeremiah 24:1-10)
- o Jeremiah stands before Zedekiah (Jeremiah 27:12-22)
- o Judgment of Hananiah the prophet (Jeremiah 28)
- o Letter to the exiles (Jeremiah 29:1-32)
- o God's message to Babylon (Jeremiah 50-51)
- o Restoration of Israel (Jeremiah 30-33)
- o Message against Zedekiah (Jeremiah 21)
- o Message to the people (Jeremiah 34)
- o Jeremiah is imprisoned (Jeremiah 37-38:1-13 & 39:15-18)

o Jerusalem falls (Jeremiah 39: 1-14 / 52:1-334 / 40-44)

YEAR – 586

Destruction of Jerusalem

2 Kings 25: 1 And it came to pass in the ninth year of his reign, in the tenth month, in the tenth day of the month, that Nebuchadnezzar king of Babylon came, he, and all his host, against Jerusalem, and pitched against it: and they built forts against it round about.
2 <u>And the city was besieged unto the eleventh year of king Zedekiah.</u>
3 And on the ninth day of the fourth month the famine prevailed in the city, and there was no bread for the people of the land.

Zedekiah is Captured
4 And the city was broken up, and all the men of war fled by night by the way of the gate between two walls, which is by the king's garden: (now the Chaldees were against the city round about:) and the king went the way toward the plain.
5 And the army of the Chaldees pursued after the king, and overtook him in the plains of Jericho: and all his army were scattered from him.
6 So they took the king, and brought him up to the king of Babylon to Riblah; and they gave judgment upon him.
7 And they slew the sons of Zedekiah before his eyes, and put out the eyes of Zedekiah, and bound him with fetters of brass, and carried him to Babylon.

Jerusalem is demolished
8 And in the fifth month, on the seventh day of the month, which is the nineteenth year of king Nebuchadnezzar king of Babylon, came Nebuzaradan, captain of the guard, a servant of the king of Babylon, unto Jerusalem:
9 and he burnt the house of the Lord, and the king's house, and all the houses of Jerusalem, and every great man's house burnt he with fire.

The Walls of Jerusalem are Broken Down
10 And all the army of the Chaldees, that were with the captain of the guard, brake down the walls of Jerusalem round about.
11 Now the rest of the people that were left in the city, and the fugitives that fell away to the king of Babylon, with the remnant of the multitude, did Nebuzaradan the captain of the guard carry away.
12 But the captain of the guard left of the poor of the land to be vinedressers and husbandmen.

The Temple of God is Ransacked (2 Chronicles 36:17-21)
13 And the pillars of brass that were in the house of the Lord, and the bases, and the brasen sea that was in the house of the Lord, did the Chaldees break in pieces, and carried the brass of them to Babylon.
14 And the pots, and the shovels, and the snuffers, and the spoons, and all the vessels of brass wherewith they ministered, took they away.
15 And the firepans, and the bowls, and such things as were of gold, in gold, and of silver, in silver, the captain of the guard took away.
16 The two pillars, one sea, and the bases which Solomon had made for the house of the Lord; the brass of all these vessels was without weight.
17 The height of the one pillar was eighteen cubits, and the chapter upon it was brass: and the height of the chapter three cubits; and the wreathen work, and pomegranates upon the chapter round about, all of brass: and like unto these had the second pillar with wreathen work.

The Nobles are taken to Nebuchadnezzar
18 And the captain of the guard took Seraiah the chief priest, and Zephaniah the second priest, and the three keepers of the door:
19 and out of the city he took an officer that was set over the men of war, and five men of them that were in the king's presence, which were found in the city, and the principal scribe of the host, which mustered the people of the land, and threescore men of the people of the land that were found in the city:

20 and Nebuzaradan captain of the guard took these, and brought them to the king of Babylon to Riblah:
21 and the king of Babylon smote them, and slew them at Riblah in the land of Hamath. So Judah was carried away out of their land.

Leadership after the fall of Jerusalem
22 And as for the people that remained in the land of Judah, whom Nebuchadnezzar king of Babylon had left, even over them he made Gedaliah the son of Ahikam, the son of Shaphan, ruler.
23 And when all the captains of the armies, they and their men, heard that the king of Babylon had made Gedaliah governor, there came to Gedaliah to Mizpah, even Ishmael the son of Nethaniah, and Johanan the son of Careah, and Seraiah the son of Tanhumeth the Netophathite, and Jaazaniah the son of a Maachathite, they and their men.
24 And Gedaliah sware to them, and to their men, and said unto them, Fear not to be the servants of the Chaldees: dwell in the land, and serve the king of Babylon; and it shall be well with you.
25 But it came to pass in the seventh month, that Ishmael the son of Nethaniah, the son of Elishama, of the seed royal, came, and ten men with him, and smote Gedaliah, that he died, and the Jews and the Chaldees that were with him at Mizpah.
26 And all the people, both small and great, and the captains of the armies, arose, and came to Egypt: for they were afraid of the Chaldees.

Jehoiachin is released from Prison
27 And it came to pass in the seven and thirtieth year of the captivity of Jehoiachin king of Judah, in the twelfth month, on the seven and twentieth day of the month, that Evil-merodach king of Babylon in the year that he began to reign did lift up the head of Jehoiachin king of Judah out of prison;
28 and he spake kindly to him, and set his throne above the throne of the kings that were with him in Babylon;

29 and changed his prison garments: and he did eat bread continually before him all the days of his life.
30 And his allowance was a continual allowance given him of the king, a daily rate for every day, all the days of his life.

YEAR – 538 BC

Cyrus the Great

Cyrus was no ordinary king born of a woman. After the ten tribes were taken captive by the Assyrians (722 BC), and king Hezekiah was given a fifteen-year extension on his life, <u>the word of the Lord</u> named Cyrus as the deliverer of the Hebrews from captivity. This was approximately one-hundred-sixty-two years before Cyrus became king of the Medes-Persia.

Therefore, to excavate my research I will provide the following information for those who like to have proof of historical events.

God Names Cyrus

<u>Isaiah 44: 28</u> **That** saith of Cyrus, He is my shepherd, and shall perform all my pleasure: even saying to Jerusalem, Thou shalt be built; and to the temple, Thy foundation shall be laid.

God Gives Cyrus His Mission Assignment

<u>Isaiah 45:</u> 1 Thus saith the Lord to his anointed, to Cyrus, whose right hand I have holden, to subdue nations before him; and I will loose the loins of kings, to open before him the two leaved gates; and the gates shall not be shut;
2 I will go before thee, and make the crooked places straight: I will break in pieces the gates of brass, and cut in sunder the bars of iron:

3 And I will give thee the treasures of darkness, and hidden riches of secret places, that thou mayest know that I, the Lord, which call thee by thy name, am the God of Israel.
4 For Jacob my servant's sake, and Israel mine elect, I have even called thee by thy name: I have surnamed thee, though thou hast not known me.
5 I am the Lord, and there is none else, there is no God beside me: I girded thee, though thou hast not known me:
6 That they may know from the rising of the sun, and from the west, that there is none beside me. I am the Lord, and there is none else.
7 I form the light, and create darkness: I make peace, and create evil: I the Lord do all these things.
8 Drop down, ye heavens, from above, and let the skies pour down righteousness: let the earth open, and let them bring forth salvation, and let righteousness spring up together; I the Lord have created it.
9 Woe unto him that striveth with his Maker! Let the potsherd strive with the potsherds of the earth. Shall the clay say to him that fashioneth it, What makest thou? or thy work, He hath no hands?
10 Woe unto him that saith unto his father, What begettest thou? or to the woman, What hast thou brought forth?
11 Thus saith the Lord, the Holy One of Israel, and his Maker, Ask me of things to come concerning my sons, and concerning the work of my hands command ye me.
12 I have made the earth, and created man upon it: I, even my hands, have stretched out the heavens, and all their host have I commanded.
13 I have raised him up in righteousness, and I will direct all his ways: he shall build my city, and he shall let go my captives, not for price nor reward, saith the Lord of hosts.
14 Thus saith the Lord, The labour of Egypt, and merchandise of Ethiopia and of the Sabeans, men of stature, shall come over unto thee, and they shall be thine: they shall come after thee; in chains they shall come over, and they shall fall down unto thee, they shall make supplication unto thee, saying, Surely God is in thee; and there is none else, there is no God.

15 Verily thou art a God that hidest thyself, O God of Israel, the Saviour.
16 They shall be ashamed, and also confounded, all of them: they shall go to confusion together that are makers of idols.
17 But Israel shall be saved in the Lord with an everlasting salvation: ye shall not be ashamed nor confounded world without end.
18 For thus saith the Lord that created the heavens; God himself that formed the earth and made it; he hath established it, he created it not in vain, he formed it to be inhabited: I am the Lord; and there is none else.

Cyrus Completes His Mission Assignment

<u>2 Chronicles 36:</u> 22 Now in the first year of Cyrus king of Persia, that the word of the Lord spoken by the mouth of Jeremiah might be accomplished, the Lord stirred up the spirit of Cyrus king of Persia, that he made a proclamation throughout all his kingdom, and put it also in writing, saying,
23 Thus saith Cyrus king of Persia, All the kingdoms of the earth hath the Lord God of heaven given me; and he hath charged me to build him an house in Jerusalem, which is in Judah. Who is there among you of all his people? The Lord his God be with him, and let him go up.

<u>Ezra 1:</u> 1 Now in the first year of Cyrus king of Persia, that the word of the Lord by the mouth of Jeremiah might be fulfilled, the Lord stirred up the spirit of Cyrus king of Persia, that he made a proclamation throughout all his kingdom, and put it also in writing, saying,
2 Thus saith Cyrus king of Persia, The Lord God of heaven hath given me all the kingdoms of the earth; and he hath charged me to build him an house at Jerusalem, which is in Judah.
3 Who is there among you of all his people? his God be with him, and let him go up to Jerusalem, which is in Judah, and build the house of the Lord God of Israel, (he is the God,) which is in Jerusalem.

4 And whosoever remaineth in any place where he sojourneth, let the men of his place help him with silver, and with gold, and with goods, and with beasts, beside the freewill offering for the house of God that is in Jerusalem.

5 Then rose up the chief of the fathers of Judah and Benjamin, and the priests, and the Levites, with all them whose spirit God had raised, to go up to build the house of the Lord which is in Jerusalem.

6 And all they that were about them strengthened their hands with vessels of silver, with gold, with goods, and with beasts, and with precious things, beside all that was willingly offered.

7 Also Cyrus the king brought forth the vessels of the house of the Lord, which Nebuchadnezzar had brought forth out of Jerusalem, and had put them in the house of his gods;

8 even those did Cyrus king of Persia bring forth by the hand of Mithredath the treasurer, and numbered them unto Sheshbazzar, the prince of Judah.

9 And this is the number of them: thirty chargers of gold, a thousand chargers of silver, nine and twenty knives,

10 thirty basins of gold, silver basins of a second sort four hundred and ten, and other vessels a thousand.

11 All the vessels of gold and of silver were five thousand and four hundred. All these did Sheshbazzar bring up with them of the captivity that were brought up from Babylon unto Jerusalem.

> **Note:** The Ark of the Covenant is not among the temple items brought back to Jerusalem. The last recording of the ark is when Josiah had it brought to the temple during the Passover celebration in 622 BC. From 606 – 586 BC Nebuchadnezzar raided the temple of God and took its treasures to Babylon. However, the Ark of the Covenant was never mentioned as one of the artifacts taken. Therefore, it can be surmised that the ark never left Israel. What happened to it? No one knows. But the search has been going on for a long time. Yet, John said that he saw, in heaven, the Ark of the Testimony in the Temple of God.[454]

Cyrus Historical Record

"Cyrus was a Persian king (559–530 BC) who founded the Persian Empire. Cyrus (II) was the son of Cambyses I (600–599 BC) and Mandane, daughter of the Median king Astyages (585?–550 BC). Cyrus took over the kingship from his father and established himself as king about 559 BC He joined nearby peoples and tribes to his kingdom. Ambitious and gutsy, he made the area into a solid block of Persian power, then revolted against Astyages of Media. When it became clear that Cyrus would win, Astyages's troops mutinied and joined with Cyrus. When Cyrus conquered the Median kingdom, however, he came into conflict with Babylon, since the two kingdoms claimed much of the same territory.

Before fighting the Babylonians, Cyrus consolidated his power by conquering Asia Minor; wealthy King Croesus of Lydia and the Lydians then submitted to him; he overtook the mountainous northern region between the Caspian Sea and the northwest corner of India.

By 539 BC, Cyrus was ready to move against Babylon. The Babylonian governor of Elam joined Cyrus's army. The armies of Cyrus then entered the Babylonian capital in 539 BC, facing little resistance. Nabonidus was taken prisoner but was treated with respect and mercy. Sixteen days later Cyrus himself entered the city, to the praise of many of its inhabitants.

Isaiah's prophecy spoke of Cyrus as the Lord's anointed (Isaiah 45:1). Israel believed that Cyrus was called and anointed by God to free them. Under Cyrus, the Jews were allowed to rebuild Jerusalem and its temple (44:28). Documents reprinted in the Old Testament tell us that in his first year in Babylon, Cyrus decreed that the house of God at Jerusalem could be rebuilt (2 Chronicles 36:22-23; Ezra 1:1-3; 6:2-5). He also returned sacred vessels that Babylonian king Nebuchadnezzar had taken from the temple.

During excavations (1879–1882) at Babylon, archaeologist Hormuzd Rassam discovered an inscription telling of Cyrus's conquest of the city and of his policies. The books of Isaiah and

Chronicles agree with the content of the inscription, which says that captured peoples were allowed to return home and build sanctuaries to their own gods.

Nothing is known about the death of Cyrus. According to some accounts, he was killed in battle, but the statements are conflicting. The Greek historian Herodotus is probably right in suggesting that Cyrus died in a terrible disaster that destroyed the Persian army as they fought the Massagetae. The tomb of Cyrus can still be seen at Pasargadae in Iran."[455]

> **YEAR 536 – 516 BC**
> Ezra Chapters 1-6

Zerubbabel Rebuilds the Temple of God

When Cyrus issued his decree in 538 BC, to lift the Jews out of captivity, it ended the seventy-year prophecy of the Prophet Jeremiah.

Zerubbabel, a descendant of David, led 49,897 captives[456] from Babylon to Israel. This hoard consisted of the Northern Ten Tribes captured in 722 BC by the Assyrians, and Judah captured by Babylon between 606-586 BC.

After the Jews settled in, they began to rebuild the Temple of God, and finished the foundation in 534 BC. However, old adversaries of Judah and Benjamin put up a strong resistance, and was successful in halting the reconstruction of the temple until the year 520 BC.

To complete the temple, the word of the Lord sent the prophets Haggai and Zechariah to admonish the people of their neglect to finish the work of the temple. Because of their effort, the people got a new decree for king Darius and finished the temple in 516 BC.

The Prophet Haggai (520 – 505 BC)

"Haggai was a prophet whose book is included in the Old Testament. Haggai's name probably came from a word for "festival."

We have no information concerning his family or social background. He is referred to merely as Haggai the prophet (Haggai 1:1; Ezra 5:1; 6:14). According to Jewish tradition, he was known as a prophet in Babylon during the Exile. The major concern of his prophetic ministry was to encourage the people to rebuild the temple, which had been destroyed during the earlier years of the Exile."[457]

The Prophet Zechariah (520 – 470 BC)

"A prophet, Berechiah's son and the grandson of Iddo, Zechariah began prophesying as a young man in 520 BC during the reign of King Darius I of Persia (Zechariah 1:1; compare 2:4). Little is known about the prophet. He ministered with Haggai, his contemporary, in postexilic Jerusalem during the days of Zerubbabel, the governor, and Jeshua, the high priest (Ezra 5:1). He exhorted the Jews to finish building the second temple (Ezra 6:14) and headed Iddo's priestly family during Joiakim's term as high priest (Nehemiah 12:16). Like Jeremiah and Ezekiel, Zechariah served as both priest and prophet (Zechariah 1:1, 7:1, 8). Numerous suggestions have been offered to resolve the discrepancy of Zechariah's pedigree. In the Ezra and Nehemiah passages, Iddo is listed as his father, whereas in Zechariah, Berechiah is the father. Some conclude that Berechiah and Iddo were different names for the same person, or that Berechiah's name (Zechariah 1:1, 7) was a later scribal emendation that confused Jeberechiah's son with Iddo's son. A more plausible theory identifies Iddo as Zechariah's grandfather, the renowned head of his family, who returned to Jerusalem from exile in 538 B.C. Either by Berechiah's early death or by the precedence of his grandfather's name, Zechariah was considered Iddo's successor."[458]

> YEAR – 483-473 BC

The Book of Esther459

The book of Esther fits in between Ezra, Chapters 6-7; the first return led by Zerubbabel, and the second return led by Ezra. Esther is important, because she was the one that God designated to preserve the whole nation of Israel while they we recovering from captivity in Assyria, Babylon, and Persia. The Jews celebrate her remembrance with the annual Feast of Purim.

> **History:** "Esther is one of two names of the Jewish queen of Persia. Hadassah (Hebrew "Myrtle") apparently was her Jewish name (Esther 2:7), and Esther (Persian "Star") her name as queen of Persia. Some scholars speculate about a connection with the Babylonian goddess Ishtar, since exiled Jews were occasionally given pagan names (see Daniel 1:7).

Esther was an orphan from the tribe of Benjamin who lived with the Jewish exiles in Persia. She was reared by her cousin Mordecai, a minor government official and covert leader of the Jewish community (Esther 3:5-6) in Susa, capital of the Persian kingdom. Esther became queen after King Ahasuerus (Xerxes) became displeased with Queen Vashti when she refused to obey his command to attend a banquet (1:11-12).

After Esther's coronation, she discreetly won Xerxes' confidence by informing him of an assassination plot (Esther 2:21-23). The favor she won in the king's eyes enabled her to deliver her family and her people from a massacre by Haman, a high official to the king.

The Feast of Purim was instituted to celebrate God's deliverance of his people through Esther and Mordecai. This Jewish festival is still observed annually."

MORDECAI

1. Mordecai was a Jewish leader during the time of exile (when the Jews lived in captivity in Babylon). All that we know about Mordecai comes from the book of Esther, which, according to some Jewish rabbinic sources, Mordecai himself wrote. Mordecai's activities are set in the time when King Xerxes (Ahasuerus) reigned over ancient Persia, a vast empire stretching over 127 provinces. Mordecai was a Jew of the tribe of Benjamin, a descendant of Kish, who was the father of King Saul. His relatives were among those Jews who left Palestine for Babylon during the captivity of Nebuchadnezzar. While his name comes from the Babylonian language, his heart burned with love for his Jewish countrymen who had settled in Babylon to live, rather than face the hardships of resettling in Palestine (the Persian king, Cyrus, had permitted Jews to return to their homeland in 538 BC).

Mordecai's remarkable life is intertwined with Hadassah (Esther), his young cousin, who became his responsibility and ward following the death of her parents. Esther's sudden, unexpected rise to the position of queen following the prior queen Vashti's fall from grace was an essential link to the deliverance of her people; Mordecai's forceful influence upon this beautiful Jewess was another. Behind them both, however, moved their sovereign God, whose love for Israel provided protection against the evil plans of Haman, Xerxes' prime minister.

Haman, the very incarnation of evil, had determined to kill all the Jews of Persia, in angry reaction to Mordecai's unwillingness to honor Haman and pay him homage. Mordecai, learning of the plot, told Queen Esther by way of Hathach, one of the king's officers. Her hesitancy to intervene on behalf of her people was met with her cousin's concise and stern answer: "Do not think that because you are in the king's house you alone of all the Jews will escape. For if you remain silent at this time, relief and deliverance for the Jews will arise from another place, but you and your father's family will perish. And who knows but that you have come to royal position for such a time as this?" (Esther 4:13-14, NIV).

Several days passed during which Haman built enormous gallows upon which to hang Mordecai. On the evening of its completion, Xerxes, unable to sleep, ordered the book containing the record of his reign to be read to him. Upon hearing of the actions of Mordecai in stopping an earlier assassination attempt against him, the king asked what honors Mordecai had received in recognition of his service. Finding he had not been rewarded, Xerxes summoned Haman and asked him what fitting thing should be done for a man the king wanted to highly honor. Haman, thinking that he was the object of this honor, responded with three grand ideas (Esther 6:7-9). Ironically, Haman was chosen by the king to carry out his own grand recommendations toward Mordecai. A final touch of irony is seen in the execution of Haman on the very instrument he had prepared for Mordecai.

Following Haman's death, Mordecai and Esther had to act quickly to counteract the first edict directed against the Jews at Haman's request. Xerxes, now open to the Jews' well-being, issued another edict allowing the Jews the freedom both to defend themselves and to retaliate against any aggressors. Apparently, the Persian officials to whom Mordecai forwarded this follow-up decree cooperated fully in protecting the Jews from their enemies, thousands of whom were slain.

Consequently, Mordecai instructed all Jews to celebrate the time of their deliverance annually on the 14th and 15th days of Adar (roughly, March). The name of the festival, Purim, is derived from the word pur ("lot"), which was cast by Haman to determine the day for the Jews' annihilation.

2. Mordecai was the name of one of the 10 leaders who returned to Jerusalem and Judah with Zerubbabel after the exile (Ezra 2:2; Nehemiah 7:7).

- o Ahasuerus – Xerxes, king of Persia, (486-464 BC) [Ester 1:1-3]
- o Ester becomes Queen 479 BC [Ester 2]
- o Artaxerxes I (464-423 BC)

YEAR – 457 BC
Ezra chapters 7-10

Ezra the Scribe / High Priest (Chapters 7-10)

History "A reformer of Jewish religious worship who worked during Israel's return from exile, Ezra's genealogy (Ezra 7:1-5; compare 1 Chronicles 6:3-15) places him in the family line of Aaron-Zadok. He is called "priest" (Ezra 10:10, 16; Nehemiah 8:2), "scribe" (Ezra 7:6; Nehemiah 12:36), and "priest and scribe" (Ezra 7:11-12; Nehemiah 8:9; 12:26). In the Old Testament the scribe was not a mere copyist, as in Christ's time, but a great student of God's laws and commandments (Ezra 7:11-12; Jeremiah 8:8). The Persian king Artaxerxes described Ezra as "priest" and "scribe" (Ezra 7:6-11). It was Ezra who began the traditional view of the scribe as a religious leader, a "bookman"; this view lasted until 200 BC. Scribes were qualified to teach and preach the Scriptures as well as interpret them, but by the first century AD, the scribe's function was more limited.

As "Secretary of State for Jewish Affairs" in the Persian Empire, Ezra visited Jerusalem about 458 BC, and on his return reported his findings. Little was done, however, until Nehemiah went to Jerusalem in 445. Once the city walls had been rebuilt, Ezra started a religious reformation in which the ancient Torah (the Law) was made the rule for Jewish life. He also demanded that Jews who had married foreigners must divorce them to keep the Jewish purity that the Torah required. Ezra set an example of piety and dedication for his people by his prayer and fasting. He set the pattern for life in post-exile Jewish culture, making God's Word and worship central parts of life. The date and place of his death are unknown."[460]

YEAR – 444 BC

Nehemiah

Nehemiah is no ordinary man, but one that was called to do a specific job for God. The Temple of God had been rebuilt; now it was time to rebuild the walls of Jerusalem, and thus fulfill the prophesy of Daniel; which will begin the Messiah's earthly clock.

> **Daniel 9:** 24 Seventy weeks are determined upon thy people and upon thy holy city, to finish the transgression, and to make an end of sins, and to make reconciliation for iniquity, and to bring in everlasting righteousness, and to seal up the vision and prophecy, and to anoint the most Holy.
>
> 25 <u>Know therefore and understand, that from the going forth of the commandment to restore and to build Jerusalem unto the Messiah the Prince shall be seven weeks</u>, and threescore and two weeks: the street shall be built again, and the wall, even in troublous times.

26 And after threescore and two weeks shall Messiah be cut off, but not for himself: and the people of the prince that shall come shall destroy the city and the sanctuary; and the end thereof shall be with a flood, and unto the end of the war desolations are determined. 27 And he shall confirm the covenant with many for one week: and in the midst of the week he shall cause the sacrifice and the oblation to cease, and for the overspreading of abominations he shall make it desolate, even until the consummation, and that determined shall be poured upon the desolate.

The degree to rebuild the walls of Jerusalem was signed on March 4, 444 BC by king Artaxerxes I; Esther's stepson.[461] Therefore, those that question why the book of Nehemiah is included in the holy cannon, only have to look at the book's relation to the prophecy of Daniel. No wall, no Christ.

History "The best-known Nehemiah in the Bible was governor of Judah during the restoration. Originally cupbearer to the Persian king Artaxerxes I (464-424 BC), Nehemiah pleaded to be sent to Judah to aid his fellow Jews in their difficulties and in particular to rebuild Jerusalem (Nehemiah 1:1-2:8). He was appointed governor of Judah for twelve years.

After inspecting the walls upon his arrival, he realized that their repair was to be his prime task. This repair would guarantee the security of the city and could provide a focal point for the Jewish community scattered throughout Judah. That he was able to marshal support for this project and to complete it attests to his skills in management and administration. He also had a strong personal faith, as his prayers (Nehemiah 1:4-11-2:4) and conviction of divine guidance and help (Nehemiah 2:8, 18, 20) attest. He had to overcome hostility and intimidation from powerful authorities in neighboring

Samaria, Ammon, and Arabia (Nehemiah 4:1-9; Nehemiah 6:1-14). He also required economic justice (Nehemiah 5:1). A few rich Jews were exploiting a food shortage by exacting high interest from their poorer brothers.

Included in Nehemiah's concern for Jerusalem was a strong interest in the maintenance of temple worship. He was involved in the production of a document in which the Jewish community pledged themselves to support the temple personnel and to provide offerings (Nehemiah 10:1, 32, 39). Clearly, he realized that Judah needed at its heart a religious emphasis as well as political stability. These particular religious reforms are linked with those of his second period as governor. Other reforms of that period concerned the observance of the Sabbath (Nehemiah 13:15-22) and the problem of marriages to non-Jews (Nehemiah 13:23-27). Nehemiah was a forceful leader (Nehemiah 13:25) who used his imperial powers to restore to the settlers a national and religious identity in a period of political and economic weakness.[462]

The Prophet Malachi (437 -417 BC)

The burden of the word of the Lord to Israel by Malachi. (Malachi 1:1) Malachi is the last Old Testament prophet. He prophesied during the days of Nehemiah, approximately 444–425 BC.

Before Nehemiah, the children of Israel had returned to the land of Judah. They rebuilt the temple of God under the guidance of Zerubbabel, a son of the house of David (538–515 BC).[463]

Around 457 BC, Ezra the scribe returned to Judah, and began to rebuild the spiritual needs of the people. He daily read and taught the word of God.

Nehemiah, on the other hand, received a decree from Artaxerxes (king of Persia) to repair the streets of Jerusalem, and rebuild its walls (Nehemiah 1 and 2).

Significantly, Malachi (4:5–6), prophesied the coming of John the Baptist which was culminated four hundred years later.[464]

History: "Malachi was a prophet and author of the last book of the Old Testament (Malachi). He lived about 500-460 BC. His name means "my angel" or "my messenger" and is so translated in Malachi 3:1 and elsewhere. Apart from the book that bears his name, nothing else is known about him from the Bible. In the apocryphal book (an ancient manuscript not included in the Bible) of 2 Esdras 1:40 he is identified as "Malachi, who is also called a messenger of the Lord." Rabbinic tradition suggests that Malachi may be another name for Ezra the scribe, although there is no supporting evidence for this."[465]

MALACHI, BOOK OF: "Last prophetic book of the Jewish canon; last book of the Old Testament."

AUTHOR: "The name Malachi means "my messenger" or "messenger of the Lord." Since the word appears in 3:1, some scholars think that it is not a proper name at all and does not provide the name of the author of the book. According to one ancient tradition, the "messenger" was Ezra, the priest responsible for the books of Ezra and Nehemiah. Yet it would be most unusual for the Jews to preserve a prophetic book without explicitly attaching to it the name of the author. All of the other major and minor prophets—including Obadiah—are named after a particular prophet. Moreover, "messenger of the Lord" would be a most appropriate name for a prophet (cf. 2 Chronicles 36:15-16; Haggai 1:13)."

BACKGROUND: "During the fifth century BC, the struggling Jewish community in Judah was greatly assisted by the return of Ezra and Nehemiah. In 458 BC Ezra was encouraged by King Artaxerxes of Persia to lead a group of exiles back to Jerusalem and to institute religious reform. About 13 years later, in 445 BC, a high-ranking government official named Nehemiah was allowed to go to Jerusalem to rebuild the city walls, a task he accomplished in 52 days (Nehemiah 6:15). As governor, Nehemiah led the people in a financial reform that provided for the poor and encouraged tithing to support the priests and Levites (5:2-13; 10:35-39). Like Ezra, Nehemiah urged the people to keep the Sabbath and avoid intermarrying with pagan neighbors. After a 12-year term, Nehemiah returned to Persia and the spiritual condition of Judah deteriorated. Perhaps discouraged by their lack of political power, tithing became sporadic, the Sabbath was not kept, intermarriage was common, and even the priests could not be trusted. When Nehemiah came back to Jerusalem sometime later, he had to take firm action to straighten out the situation (13:6-31)."

DATE: Since Malachi had to deal with the same sins mentioned in Nehemiah 13 (see Malachi 1:6-14; 2:14-16; 3:8-11), it is likely that the prophet ministered either during Nehemiah's second term as governor or in the years just before his return. The reference to "the governor" in Malachi 1:8 implies that someone other than Nehemiah was in office, so it may be best to place Malachi just after 433 BC, the year Nehemiah had returned to Persia.

PURPOSE AND THEOLOGY: Malachi was written to shake the people of Judah from their spiritual lethargy and to warn them that judgment was coming unless they repented. The people doubted God's love (1:2) and justice (2:17) and did not take his commands seriously (1:6; 3:14-18). Yet God was "a great King" (1:14) with a great name that was to be feared even beyond the border of Israel (verses 5, 11). Malachi repeatedly urged both the priests and the people to revere God and give him the honor he deserved. God was Israel's

Father and Creator (2:10), but the nation showed contempt for his name (1:6; 3:5). In response to this contempt, God would send his messenger to announce the Day of the Lord (3:1). John the Baptist did call the nation to repentance, and Christ came to cleanse the temple (John 2:14-15) and to establish the covenant (Malachi 3:1-2). Most of the work of refining and purifying will take place at the Second Coming, when Christ returns to purify his people (cf. verses 2-4) and judge the wicked (4:1).

BOOK CONTENT

GOD'S GREAT LOVE FOR ISRAEL (1:1-5):

To introduce the book, Malachi presents a contrast between God's love for Israel and his hatred for Edom. Yet the assertion of God's love is greeted with a strange question: "How have you loved us?" God loved Israel by entering into a covenant with the nation at Mt Sinai, just after he had freed them from the prison of Egypt. He had chosen them as his special people (cf. Genesis 12:1-3; Exodus 19:5-6), whereas the descendants of Esau were not chosen (cf. Romans 9:10-13). Both Israel and Edom endured invasion and destruction, but only Israel was restored and rebuilt after the exile. The people of Edom were driven from their homeland by the Nabateans between 550 and 400 BC, and they never regained their territory. Through the judgment of Edom, God demonstrated that he is the great Ruler over the nations (Malachi 1:5) and that he will not forget Israel.

THE UNACCEPTABLE SACRIFICES OF THE PRIESTS (1:6-14):

Although God deserved the honor and reverence of the Israelites, both the people and the priests openly disdained his laws and regulations. Strangely, it was the priests who led the way into disobedience. Sacrifices and offerings were supposed to atone for sin, but the animals offered by the priests only served to pollute or defile the altar (1:7, 12). According to Leviticus, animals with defects were unacceptable as sacrifices, but Malachi mentions that the priests were offering to the Lord animals that were stolen and mutilated, crippled and sick (verse 13; cf. verse 8). To emphasize their contempt, the Lord challenged the priests to bring comparable presents to the governor. Would they dare to insult him in this fashion and face sure rejection? Rather than having the priests continue to bring unfit sacrifices to the altar, the Lord asked them to close the temple doors entirely (verse 10). Going through the motions never pleased God, either in ancient times (cf. Isaiah 1:12-13) or modern. By calling the altar and its sacrifices "contemptible" (Malachi 1:7, 12), the priests were no better than the wicked sons of Eli, whose disregard of the rules for sacrifices sent them to a premature death (cf. 1 Samuel 2:15-17).

In sharp contrast to the attitude of the priests stands the emphasis upon God's greatness in Malachi 1:11 and 14. God is more powerful than the gods of other nations, and even if Israel's priests and people dishonor the Lord, eventually pure offerings will be brought to God by believing Gentiles. Perhaps these offerings refer to prayer and praise (cf. Psalm 19:14; Hebrews 13:15; Revelation 5:8), but others interpret the reference more literally (cf. Isaiah 56:7; 60:7). Peter may be alluding to this verse in connection with the conversion of Cornelius (Acts 10:35).

THE PUNISHMENT OF THE PRIESTS (2:1-9): One of the functions of the priests was to pronounce blessings upon the people in the name of God, but their disgraceful behavior turned the blessings into curses (Malachi 2:2). Because of the priests' sinfulness and the poor condition of the animals, their sacrifices were also worthless, and the entrails of the animals will be spread on their faces as a sign that God holds them in contempt. The disgrace heaped upon the priests differs sharply from the honor enjoyed by Aaron and his descendants. Malachi refers to a covenant of life and peace (verse 5) made with Levi and more particularly with Aaron's grandson Phinehas, who courageously took action against the Jews involved in idolatry and immorality (Numbers 25:10-13). In those days the priests revered the Lord and turned many from sin (Malachi 2:6).

Another responsibility of the priests was to teach the nation the law handed down by Moses (cf. Leviticus 10:11). Like prophets, they were messengers of the Lord (Malachi 2:7) who were supposed to walk close to the Lord, but now the priests disregarded the law and were dishonest in handing down judicial decisions (Malachi 2:9; cf. Leviticus 19:15).

THE UNFAITHFULNESS OF THE PEOPLE (2:10-16): In light of the attitude of the priests, it is not surprising to discover that the people at large were unfaithful to the Lord. God had formed Israel to be his special people, but the people had broken faith with him. A major factor in their unfaithfulness was intermarriage with foreigners, a sin mentioned in Ezra 9:1-2 and Nehemiah 13:23-29. By marrying pagan women, the men of Israel invariably began to worship pagan gods and turn from the Lord. When such intermarriage occurred, it sometimes followed the divorce of an Israelite wife. In Malachi 2:14-15 God underscores the sacred commitment that he himself witnesses when two people marry. If that marriage covenant is shattered by divorce, God is deeply displeased. And it is even more tragic if divorce became an excuse to marry a more attractive or appealing foreigner.

THE COMING OF THE MESSENGER OF THE COVENANT (2:17–3:5): The sins of the priests and the people did not go unnoticed, even though the nation doubted that God would take action (2:17). But the third chapter opens with the announcement that the messenger of the covenant will indeed come to his temple. His way will be prepared by another messenger—a prophecy of John the Baptist, who prepared the way for the ministry of Christ (cf. Matthew 11:10; Mark 1:2-3). When Christ came, he revealed his anger when he cleansed the temple (cf. John 2:13-17) and denounced the scribes and Pharisees (cf. 9:39), but most of his purifying and refining work awaits the Second Coming. Someday the priests and Levites will bring acceptable sacrifices, as they did in the days of Moses and Phinehas (cf. Malachi 3:3-4 and 2:4-5). Verse 5 of chapter 3 broadens the scope of the judgment to include the whole nation, as sorcerers, adulterers, and those who oppress the poor are condemned.

THE BENEFITS OF FAITHFUL TITHING (3:6-12): Another specific weakness of postexilic Judah was the failure of the people to bring their tithes to the Lord. Encouraged by Nehemiah, the nation promised to tithe faithfully (cf. Nehemiah 10:37-39), but apparently their good intentions were short-lived (cf. 13:10-11). According to Malachi 3:8-9, the tithes of the nation were so dismal that the people were, in effect, robbing God and were therefore under a curse. In verses 10-12 Malachi challenges the nation to bring their tithes; then God would pour out his blessing upon them. Just as the opening of the "windows in heaven" meant the end of a famine in 2 Kings 7:2, 19, so God promises that their crops will be so abundant that they will run out of storage space. The hope of "blessing" in Malachi 3:10 and 12 provides welcome relief from the curses mentioned in 1:14, 2:2, 3:9, and 4:6.

THE DAY OF THE LORD (3:13–4:6): Faced with the challenge of Malachi 3:10-12, the people of Israel responded in two different ways. One group denied that serving God brought any benefit (3:13-15), while another segment of the nation bowed low before him with deep reverence (verses 16-18). The unbelievers argued that obeying the Lord was useless and that arrogant and evil people were the ones who prospered. In response to their charge, Malachi noted that God would remember who the righteous were in the Day of Judgment. Although all of Israel was included in the promise made to Abraham, only those who genuinely believed would be God's treasured possession (3:17; cf. Exodus 19:5), with their names written in the Book of Life (cf. Malachi 3:16). As for the arrogant and evildoers, the Day of the Lord will consume them and they will have no survivors (4:1). Those who revere the Lord will enjoy spiritual and physical health under the blessing and protection of God, who is called the "sun of righteousness" (verse 2). Like calves just released from confinement, the righteous will trample down the wicked and triumph over them (verse 3).

In view of the judgment associated with the Day of the Lord, Malachi urged the people to repent. To do this they needed to heed the law of Moses and take seriously the decrees and commands given at Mt Sinai (4:4; cf. 3:7). Just as Elijah called on Israel to turn back to God, so a new "Elijah" will preach repentance to a rebellious nation. When John the Baptist prepared the way for Christ (cf. Malachi 3:1), he ministered "in the spirit and power of Elijah" and begged the Jews to turn from their sin and humble themselves before God (Luke 1:17). If they refused to listen, the nation faced the prospect of total destruction, the curse placed upon the people of Canaan (cf. Joshua 6:17-19) and upon the nation of Edom, whose collapse was described in Malachi 1:2-5.

Old Testament Summary

In the above examples of Christ Jesus speaking to different people in the Old Testament, it should dawn on you that he is the invisible hand Churchill spoke of: shaping and directing human history. Look at Revelation 1:1–2.

It can also be surmised that from the beginning, God the Father has always ruled the universe through Christ - <u>the word of God</u>. Before moving on from here, make sure you have a good and clear understanding of the Lord Jesus Christ, and the ramifications of misunderstanding the totality of who he is. Your very soul is at stake if you stumble and fall away from him.

At this point in the book, you may still question the authenticity of Christ Jesus. Don't be ashamed, because the Jews—especially the Pharisee priest—were also warped in their thinking toward him. After Christ healed a man on the Sabbath day, the Jews were very angry and, "sought the more to kill him; because he not only had broken the sabbath, but said also that God was his Father; making himself equal with God" (John 5:18). Christ's reply to them was centered on several points designed to drive home his deity.

- He doesn't do anything without the approval of his Father.
- The Father has committed the total judgment of humankind into his hands.
- Upon his voice the dead (the good, the bad, and the ugly) will be called into judgment: "the good, unto the resurrection of life, and they that have done evil, into the resurrection of damnation" (John 5:19-30).
- John the Baptist was a shining light that bear witness to him.
- God is his true witness, because he knows his voice and has seen his shape.
- They need to "search the scriptures; for in them ye think ye have eternal life: and they are they which testify of me."[466]

Now that you know what the challenge is from Christ, I challenge you to dig through the Old Testament and see Christ Jesus in a new light. This is not a new revelation, nor is it a prophetic message. Rather, it is sharing knowledge that you will need to brace against the evil of these last days. You will need all your strength to combat the dark forces that are driving wickedness upon us, such as abortion, sexual immorality, sodomy as a lifestyle, outlawing prayer and the Holy Bible from the schools and workplace, and removal of the Ten Commandments from the courtroom and city/town public displays.

CHAPTER 20

THE NEW TESTAMENT

Luke 24: 44 Then he said, "When I was with you before, I told you that everything written about me in the law of Moses and the prophets and in the Psalms must be fulfilled."

45 Then he opened their minds to understand the Scriptures.

46 And he said, "Yes, it was written long ago that the Messiah would suffer and die and rise from the dead on the third day.

47 It was also written that this message would be proclaimed in the authority of his name to all the nations,* beginning in Jerusalem: 'There is forgiveness of sins for all who repent.'

48 You are witnesses of all these things.

49 "And now I will send the Holy Spirit, just as my Father promised. But stay here in the city until the

Holy Spirit comes and fills you with power from heaven."

The story of Jesus Christ is the thrust of the New Testament. His birth, his life on the earth, his death, his burial, and his resurrection, are all based on Old Testament scriptures. Even the way he talked in parables were guided by prophecy: "Give ear, O my people, to my law: incline your ears to the words of my mouth. I will open my mouth in a parable: I will utter dark sayings of old: Which we have heard and known, and our fathers have told us."[467]

Matthew attested to prophecy when he said, "Now the birth of Jesus Christ was on this wise."[468] The word "wise" is defined as, having wisdom, showing common sense, prudent, having great learning, having knowledge or information."

So then, Matthew tells us that the story of Jesus Christ is not just something that he heard, but is based on the knowledge, and proven evidence of the Old Testament; which was made manifest in the flesh: "And the Word was made flesh, and dwelt among us, (and we beheld his glory, the glory as of the only begotten of the Father,) full of grace and truth."[469]

Therefore, I will use scripture (with intertwining reference scriptures) too make convincing points about who Jesus Christ is. Why? Because my telling you, without your bible study approval serves no end.

When the Apostle Paul and Silas preached Jesus to the people of Berea, "They received the word with all readiness of mind, and searched the scriptures daily (*Old Testament*), whether these things were so. Therefore, many believed; also, of honorable women which were Greeks, and of men, not a few."[470] And just like the people of Berea, you need to be convinced of truth, of the Lord Jesus Christ, by studying the scriptures. The Apostle Paul adhered to this when he said:

- **1 Timothy 6**: 20 "O Timothy, keep that which is committed to thy trust, avoiding profane and vain babblings, and oppositions of science falsely so called:
  21 Which some professing have erred concerning the faith. Grace be with thee. Amen."

- **2 Timothy 2:** "15 Study to shew thyself approved unto God, a workman that needeth not to be ashamed, rightly dividing the word of truth.
  16 But shun profane and vain babblings: for they will increase unto more ungodliness."

YEAR – 7 BC

John the Baptist

The birth of John the Baptist is the beginning of the New Testament of the Holy Bible. He is the forerunner prophesied by Isaiah to usher in the promised Messiah: "The voice of him that crieth in the wilderness, Prepare ye the way of the Lord, make straight in the desert a highway for our God Every valley shall be exalted, and every mountain and hill shall be made low: and the crooked shall be made straight, and the rough places plain: And the glory of the Lord shall be revealed, and all flesh shall see it together: for the mouth of the Lord hath spoken it."[471]

Right here I want to inject that John the Baptist is no ordinary baby. First, he is the only person, anointed by God, that was filled with the Holy Spirit of God, while in his mother womb. Second, he is an inherited "High Priest" (a descendent of Moses brother Aaron the first High Priest), and a prophet of God. Therefore, lets look at the scripture verses that bear out these facts.

Zacharias Ministers in the Temple

Luke 1: 5-80
5. There was in the days of Herod, the king of Judaea, <u>a certain priest named Zacharias,</u> <u>of the course of Abia:</u> and his wife was of the daughters of Aaron, and her name was Elisabeth.

Now the scripture at a glance does not bear witness that John's father Zacharias is a son of Moses brother Aaron. But it does bear witness that he is a Levite: for only they could hold the rank and title of priest.

- **Numbers 18:** 1 And the Lord said unto Aaron, Thou and thy sons and thy father's house with thee shall bear the iniquity of the sanctuary: and thou and thy sons with thee shall bear the iniquity of your priesthood.
  2 And thy brethren also of the tribe of Levi, the tribe of thy father, bring thou with thee, that they may be joined unto thee, and minister unto thee: but thou and thy sons with thee shall minister before the tabernacle of witness.
  3 And they shall keep thy charge, and the charge of all the tabernacle: only they shall not come nigh the vessels of the sanctuary and the altar, that neither they, nor ye also, die.
  4 And they shall be joined unto thee, and keep the charge of the tabernacle of the congregation, for all the service of the tabernacle: and a stranger shall not come nigh unto you

- **Numbers 18**: 7 Therefore thou and thy sons with thee shall keep your priest's office for every thing of the altar, and within the vail; and ye shall serve: I have given your priest's office unto you as a service of gift: and the stranger that cometh nigh shall be put to death.

- 8 And the Lord spake unto Aaron, Behold, I also have given thee the charge of mine heave offerings of all the hallowed things of the children of Israel; unto thee have I given them by reason of the anointing, and to thy sons, by an ordinance for ever.

- **Chronicles 24:** 1 <u>Now these are the divisions of the sons of Aaron</u>. The sons of Aaron; Nadab, and Abihu, Eleazar, and Ithamar.
2 But Nadab and Abihu died before their father, and had no children: therefore Eleazar and Ithamar executed the priest's office.
3 And David distributed them, both Zadok of the sons of Eleazar, and Ahimelech of the sons of Ithamar, according to their offices in their service.
4 And there were more chief men found of the sons of Eleazar than of the sons of Ithamar; and thus were they divided. Among the sons of Eleazar there were sixteen chief men of the house of their fathers, and eight among the sons of Ithamar according to the house of their fathers.
5 Thus were they divided by lot, one sort with another; for the governors of the sanctuary, and governors of the house of God, were of the sons of Eleazar, and of the sons of Ithamar.
6 And Shemaiah the son of Nethaneel the scribe, one of the Levites, wrote them before the king, and the princes, and Zadok the priest, and Ahimelech the son of Abiathar, and before the chief of the fathers of the priests and Levites: one principal household being taken for Eleazar, and one taken for Ithamar.
7 Now the first lot came forth to Jehoiarib, the second to Jedaiah,
8 the third to Harim, the fourth to Seorim,
9 the fifth to Malchijah, the sixth to Mijamin,
10 the seventh to Hakkoz, <u>the eighth to Abijah,</u>

Now that you've had a chance to examine the reference scriptures for yourself you should come to the conclusion that yes, John the

Baptist was a "High Priest" after his father Zacharias, a son of Aaron. And also, that his mother Elisabeth is of high priest genealogy.

Zacharias and Elisabeth were old and barren of child

6. And they were both righteous before God, walking in all the commandments and ordinances of the Lord blameless.
7. And they had no child, because that Elisabeth was barren, and they both were now well stricken in years.
8. And it came to pass, that while he executed the priest's office before God in the order of his course,
9. According to the custom of the priest's office, his lot was to burn incense when he went into the temple of the Lord.
10. And the whole multitude of the people were praying without at the time of incense.

The angel Gabriel announces the birth of John the Baptist

11. And there appeared unto him an angel of the Lord standing on the right side of the altar of incense.
12. And when Zacharias saw him, he was troubled, and fear fell upon him.
13. But the angel said unto him, Fear not, Zacharias: for thy prayer is heard; and <u>thy wife Elisabeth shall bear thee a son, and thou shalt call his name John.</u>
14. And thou shalt have joy and gladness; and many shall rejoice at his birth.
15. <u>For he shall be great in the sight of the Lord, and shall drink neither wine nor strong drink; and he shall be filled with the Holy Ghost, even from his mother's womb.</u>

- **The law of the <u>Nazarite:</u> (Numbers 6: 1-27)**
  1 And the Lord spake unto Moses, saying,
  2 Speak unto the children of Israel, and say unto them, When either man or woman shall separate themselves to vow a vow of a Nazarite, to separate themselves unto the Lord:

3 he shall separate himself from wine and strong drink, and shall drink no vinegar of wine, or vinegar of strong drink, neither shall he drink any liquor of grapes, nor eat moist grapes, or dried.

4 All the days of his separation shall he eat nothing that is made of the vine tree, from the kernels even to the husk.

5 All the days of the vow of his separation there shall no razor come upon his head: until the days be fulfilled, in the which he separateth himself unto the Lord, he shall be holy, and shall let the locks of the hair of his head grow.

Note: John the Baptist is the only human being, born of a woman, that received God's Holy Spirit in his mother's womb. In the Old and New Testament, the Holy Spirit of God came upon people after they were born.

16. And many of the children of Israel shall he turn to the Lord their God.

- **John 3:** 27 John answered and said, A man can receive nothing, except it be given him from heaven.
  28 Ye yourselves bear me witness, that I said, I am not the Christ, but that I am sent before him.
  29 He that hath the bride is the bridegroom: but the friend of the bridegroom, which standeth and heareth him, rejoiceth greatly because of the bridegroom's voice: this my joy therefore is fulfilled.
  30 He must increase, but I must decrease.
  31 He that cometh from above is above all: he that is of the earth is earthly, and speaketh of the earth: he that cometh from heaven is above all.
  32 And what he hath seen and heard, that he testifieth; and no man receiveth his testimony. 33 He that hath received his testimony hath set to his seal that God is true.

34 For he whom God hath sent speaketh the words of God: for God giveth not the Spirit by measure unto him.
35 The Father loveth the Son, and hath given all things into his hand.
36 He that believeth on the Son hath everlasting life: and he that believeth not the Son shall not see life; but the wrath of God abideth on him.

17. <u>And he shall go before him in the spirit and power of Elias</u>, to turn the hearts of the fathers to the children, and the disobedient to the wisdom of the just; to make ready a people prepared for the Lord.

- **Malachi 4**: 5 Behold, I will send you Elijah the prophet before the coming of the great and dreadful day of the Lord: 6 and he shall turn the heart of the fathers to the children, and the heart of the children to their fathers, lest I come and smite the earth with a curse.

- **<u>Elijah the Tishbite</u> – 2 Kings 1: 8** And they answered him, He was an hairy man, and girt with a girdle of leather about his loins. And he said, It is Elijah the Tishbite.

- **<u>John the Baptist</u> - Mathew 3:** 1 In those days came John the Baptist, preaching in the wilderness of Judaea,
2 and saying, Repent ye: for the kingdom of heaven is at hand.
3 For this is he that was spoken of by the prophet Esaias, saying, The voice of one crying in the wilderness, Prepare ye the way of the Lord, make his paths straight.
4 And the same John had his raiment of camel's hair, and a leathern girdle about his loins; and his meat was locusts and wild honey.

Now the statement by the angel Gabriel that John the Baptist would come "in the spirit and power of Elijah" has caused a lot of friction and disbelief toward the Lord Jesus Christ. Why? Because, the world of unbelievers is looking for that Elijah, that was taken up into the heaven in a whirlwind.[472]

Yet, John is pointed too as the coming Elijah. Is this true? Well, according to the Lord Jesus Christ, John was that Elijah prophesied by the prophet Malachi: "Verily I say unto you, Among them that are born of women there hath not risen a greater than John the Baptist: notwithstanding he that is least in the kingdom of heaven is greater than he. And from the days of John the Baptist until now the kingdom of heaven suffereth violence, and the violent take it by force. For all the prophets and the law prophesied until John. <u>And if ye will receive it, this is Elias, which was for to come</u>. 15 He that hath ears to hear, let him hear."[473]

So then, what or who was John the Baptist? - if it is believed that he was not the prophesied Elijah? I submit to you that John is a clone of Elijah. And Elijah did come back to the earth with Moses to confer with the Lord Jesus Christ; the witness to this event was Peter, James, and John.[474]

Gabriel gives Zacharias a sign concerning the birth of John

18. And Zacharias said unto the angel, Whereby shall I know this? for I am an old man, and my wife well stricken in years.
19. And the angel answering said unto him, <u>I am Gabriel, that stand in the presence of God</u>; and am sent to speak unto thee, and to shew thee these glad tidings. **(Daniel 8:16 / 9:21)**
20. And, behold, thou shalt be dumb, and not able to speak, until the day that these things shall be performed, because thou believest not my words, which shall be fulfilled in their season.
21. And the people waited for Zacharias, and marvelled that he tarried so long in the temple.
22. And when he came out, he could not speak unto them: and they perceived that he had seen a vision in the temple: for he beckoned unto them, and remained speechless.

**Take note that the angel Gabriel is one that stands before God, and delivers messages from heaven. But "the angel of God," that was with

Moses and the children of Israel, came in the Fathers name, and the Fathers name was in him. (Exodus 23: 20-33)

Zacharias retires from the ministry
23. And it came to pass, that, as soon as the days of his ministration were accomplished, he departed to his own house.

- **Numbers 8:** 23 And the Lord spake unto Moses, saying,
  24 This is it that belongeth unto the Levites: from twenty and five years old and upward they shall go in to wait upon the service of the tabernacle of the congregation:
  25 and from the age of fifty years they shall cease waiting upon the service thereof, and shall serve no more:
  26 but shall minister with their brethren in the tabernacle of the congregation, to keep the charge, and shall do no service. Thus shalt thou do unto the Levites touching their charge.

So then, Zacharias was fifty-years old when he resigned his priestly duties in the temple. As a Levite he didn't have to work, because the law of God, through tithes, would sustain him and his family.[475]

Zacharias wife Elisabeth has conceived a child.
24. And after those days his wife Elisabeth conceived, and hid herself five months, saying,
25. Thus hath the Lord dealt with me in the days wherein he looked on me, to take away my reproach among men.

Jesus the Christ

The angel Gabriel visits Mary and announces the birth of Christ Jesus
26. And in the sixth month the angel Gabriel was sent from God unto a city of Galilee, named Nazareth,

"Nazareth is a village in the Roman province of Galilee, the home of Joseph, Mary, and Jesus. Always small and isolated, Nazareth is not mentioned in the Old Testament, the Apocrypha (ancient writings not included in the Bible), Jewish writings, or the histories of Josephus.

The town lies just north of the plain of Esdraelon in the limestone hills of the southern Lebanon range. It is situated on three sides of a hill. This location forms a sheltered valley with a moderate climate favorable to fruits and wildflowers. Trade routes and roads passed near Nazareth, but the village itself was not on any main road. Nazareth is about 15 miles west of the Sea of Galilee and 20 miles east of the Mediterranean. Jerusalem lies about 70 miles south. Archaeological remains indicate that the ancient town was higher on the western hill than the present village (compare Luke 4:29). In the time of Christ, Nazareth, along with the entire region of south Galilee, lay outside the mainstream of Jewish life, providing the background for Nathanael's wry remark to Philip, "Can anything good come out of Nazareth?" (John 1:46).

Nazareth is first mentioned in the New Testament as the home of Mary and Joseph (Luke 1:26-27). Sometime after Jesus was born at his parents' ancestral town of Bethlehem (about 80 miles to the south), Mary and Joseph returned to Nazareth (Matthew 2:23; Luke 2:39). Jesus grew up there (Luke 2:39-40, 51), leaving the village to be baptized by John in the Jordan River (Mark 1:9). When John was arrested, Jesus moved to Capernaum (Matthew 4:13). Though Jesus was often identified by his boyhood city as "Jesus of Nazareth" (John 18:5, 7), the New Testament records only one subsequent visit by Jesus to Nazareth. On this occasion, Jesus preached in the synagogue and was rejected by the townspeople (Luke 4:16-30). Jesus' followers were also derisively called "Nazarenes" (Acts 24:5).

Nazareth remained a Jewish city until the time of the emperor Constantine (AD 327), when it became a sacred place for Christian pilgrims. A large basilica was built in Nazareth about AD 600. Arabs and Crusaders alternately controlled the village until 1517, when it fell to the Turks, who forced all Christians to leave. Christians returned in 1620, and the town became an important Christian center."[476]

27. ***To a virgin espoused to a man whose name was Joseph***, of the house of David; **and the virgin's name was Mary.**
28. And the angel came in unto her, and said, Hail, thou that art highly favoured, the Lord is with thee: blessed art thou among women.
29. And when she saw him, she was troubled at his saying, and cast in her mind what manner of salutation this should be.
30. And the angel said unto her, Fear not, Mary: for thou hast found favour with God.
31. And, behold, thou shalt conceive in thy womb, and bring forth a son, and shalt call his name Jesus.
32. He shall be great, and shall be called the Son of the Highest: and the Lord God shall give unto him the throne of his father David: (**Matthew 21: 1-11**)
33. And he shall reign over the house of Jacob for ever; and of his kingdom there shall be no end. (**Daniel 7:13-14**)
34. Then said Mary unto the angel, How shall this be, seeing I know not a man?
35. And the angel answered and said unto her, The Holy Ghost shall come upon thee, and the power of the Highest shall overshadow thee: therefore also that holy thing which shall be born of thee shall be called the Son of God.

By His own words Christ said that God [the Father] sent him from the heaven; down to the earth. Does this make him an alien (?), or a being from another world (?), or even an ancient life force that has survived throughout the ages (?)! The world would say yes to all three;

but to the believer in God (the God of Abraham, Isaac, and Jacob), Christ is the loving creator that came down from the heaven to save his creation from total corruption, destruction, and damnation.

Yet we know from scripture that he was born of the virgin woman Mary. So how is it possible for him to have been with the Father before the creation of this world, but yet born of a woman in a fleshly human body?

The Apostle Paul weighed in on this same question when he said, "sacrifice and offering thou wouldest not, but a body hast thou prepared me."[477] From this we can deduct that God prepared the body of Mary to receive in her womb the Lord Jesus Christ; when the angel Gabriel told her, "The Holy Ghost shall come upon thee, and the power of the highest shall overshadow thee: therefore also that holy thing which shall be born of thee shall be called the Son of God."[478]

Often times while talking to the Jews, Christ Jesus told them that he came down from heaven, to the earth, and would return back to his Father (God); by means of the cross. Of course, as it was then, and is now, no one really paid attention to what he said, because the mind cannot comprehend how one could come down from heaven: yet be born of a woman; for it is the true mystery of Christ.

Some would make the argument that when the Holy Ghost came upon Mary, and the power of God overshadowed her, that she was impregnated by artificial insemination, or (even) that God had sexual intercourse with her. This may have some truth in it, but Jesus said that he came from above; which means that he came into the body of Mary, entered into her egg, and became a baby by divine design. I'm stretching a little here, but I'm trying to make the point that Christ Jesus was, and is, and has always been himself; no matter what form he chose or desired to take or appear in.

So then it wasn't sex that God had with Mary, but like the great doctor (that he is) he ensured that her body could adjust to the reception of the "light that shineth through darkness;" in other words, her body had to grow flesh around the light: "which were born, not of blood, nor of the will of flesh, nor of the will of man, but of God."[479]

Further, Mary had no complications during the delivery of the baby Jesus: because she was protected by the power of the Holy Ghost; which decreased her pain during the birth."[480]

Gabriel tells Mary about Elisabeth being with child

36. And, <u>behold, thy cousin Elisabeth, she hath also conceived a son in her old age: and this is the sixth month with her,</u> who was called barren.
37. For with God nothing shall be impossible.
38. And Mary said, Behold the handmaid of the Lord; be it unto me according to thy word. And the angel departed from her.

Mary goes to visit Elisabeth

39. And Mary arose in those days, and went into the hill country with haste, into a city of Juda;
40. And entered into the house of Zacharias, and saluted Elisabeth.
41. **And it came to pass, that, when Elisabeth heard the salutation of Mary, the babe leaped in her womb; and Elisabeth was filled with the Holy Ghost:**

> **Note:** John's mother was filled with the Holy Spirit of God from the baby within her womb. There are some who believe that this procedure is reversed when a pregnant woman, who is baptized with the Holy Ghost, and is moving in the spirit while praising God; that her jumping and shouting will cause the baby to filled with the Holy Ghost that is in her womb. Is this true? Only God knows if there is any truth to this belief.

Elisabeth's Prophecy

42. And she spake out with a loud voice, and said, Blessed art thou among women, and blessed is the fruit of thy womb.
43. And whence is this to me, that the mother of my Lord should come to me?
44. For, lo, as soon as the voice of thy salutation sounded in mine ears, the babe leaped in my womb for joy.

45. And blessed is she that believed: for there shall be a performance of those things which were told her from the Lord.

Mary's Proclamation of God
46. And Mary said, My soul doth magnify the Lord,
47. And my spirit hath rejoiced in God my Saviour.
48. For he hath regarded the low estate of his handmaiden: for, behold, from henceforth all generations shall call me blessed.
49. For he that is mighty hath done to me great things; and holy is his name.
50. And his mercy is on them that fear him from generation to generation.
51. He hath shewed strength with his arm; he hath scattered the proud in the imagination of their hearts.
52. He hath put down the mighty from their seats, and exalted them of low degree.
53. He hath filled the hungry with good things; and the rich he hath sent empty away.
54. He hath holpen his servant Israel, in remembrance of his mercy;
55. As he spake to our fathers, to Abraham, and to his seed for ever.

Mary goes back home
56. And Mary abode with her about three months, and returned to her own house.

- ## God prevents Joseph from divorcing Mary
  Matthew 1: 18. Now the birth of Jesus Christ was on this wise: When as his mother Mary was espoused to Joseph, before they came together, she was found with child of the Holy Ghost.
  19. Then Joseph her husband, being a just man, and not willing to make her a publick example, was minded to put her away privily.

Note: When Joseph found out that Mary was with child, he became suspicious that it happened when she visited her cousin Elisabeth for three months. And he didn't want her humiliated in public, so he planned to keep the matter privily, and not marry her. But God had other plans for him.

- **God comforts Joseph about Mary's conception.**
20. But while he thought on these things, behold, the angel of the Lord appeared unto him in a dream, saying, Joseph, thou son of David, fear not to take unto thee Mary thy wife: <u>for that which is conceived in her is of the Holy Ghost.</u>
21. And she shall bring forth a son, and thou shalt call his name JESUS: for he shall save his people from their sins.
22. Now all this was done, that it might be fulfilled which was spoken of the Lord by the prophet, saying,
23. Behold, a virgin shall be with child, and shall bring forth a son, and they shall call his name Emmanuel, which being interpreted is, God with us. **(Isaiah 7: 14)**

Joseph Marries Mary.
24. Then Joseph being raised from sleep did as the angel of the Lord had bidden him, and took unto him his wife:
25. And knew her not till she had brought forth her firstborn son: and he called his name JESUS.

YEAR – 6 BC

The Birth of John the Baptist

John the Baptist was born during the month of October 6 BC. He was six months older than his cousin Jesus, the son of Mary and Joseph.

John the Baptist is born

57. Now Elisabeth's full time came that she should be delivered; and she brought forth a son.
58. And her neighbours and her cousins heard how the Lord had shewed great mercy upon her; and they rejoiced with her.
59. And it came to pass, that on the eighth day they came to circumcise the child; and they called him Zacharias, after the name of his father.
60. And his mother answered and said, Not so; but he shall be called John.
61. And they said unto her, There is none of thy kindred that is called by this name.

Zacharias names his son John
62. And they made signs to his father, how he would have him called.
63. And he asked for a writing table, and wrote, saying, His name is John. And they marvelled all.
64. And his mouth was opened immediately, and his tongue loosed, and he spake, and praised God.
65. And fear came on all that dwelt round about them: and all these sayings were noised abroad throughout all the hill country of Judaea.
66. And all they that heard them laid them up in their hearts, saying, What manner of child shall this be! And the hand of the Lord was with him.

Zacharias Prophecy
67. **And his father Zacharias was filled with the Holy Ghost,** and prophesied, saying,
68. Blessed be the Lord God of Israel; for he hath visited and redeemed his people, (Isaiah 7: 10-16)
69. And hath raised up an horn of salvation for us in the house of his servant David; (2 Samuel 7: 12-16)
70. As he spake by the mouth of his holy prophets, which have been since the world began:
71. That we should be saved from our enemies, and from the hand of all that hate us;

Who is Jesus Christ

72. To perform the mercy promised to our fathers, and to remember his holy covenant;
73. The oath which he sware to our father Abraham,
74. That he would grant unto us, that we being delivered out of the hand of our enemies might serve him without fear, (Zechariah 12: 1-4)
75. In holiness and righteousness before him, all the days of our life. (John 1: 29-34)
76. And thou, child, shalt be called the prophet of the Highest: for thou shalt go before the face of the Lord to prepare his ways; (John 1: 6-8)
77. To give knowledge of salvation unto his people by the remission of their sins,
78. Through the tender mercy of our God; whereby the dayspring from on high hath visited us,
79. To give light to them that sit in darkness and in the shadow of death, to guide our feet into the way of peace. (John 1: 9-11 / 12-13 & Luke 21:24)

Zacharias moves his family into the desert

80. And the child grew, and waxed strong in spirit, and was in the deserts till the day of his shewing unto Israel.

> **Note:** The whole family of John is not only filled with the Holy Spirit of God, but also carry the title of High Priest. Yet, they did not speak with other tongues because the prophecy of Joel could only be brought forth through the Lord Jesus Christ. Yet, they did prophecy in their native Hebrew tongue. (Numbers 11:16-7 / 24-29)

YEAR – 5 BC

The Birth of Jesus Christ

LUKE 2: 1-20
1. And it came to pass in those days, that there went out a decree from Caesar Augustus that all the world should be taxed.
2. (And this taxing was first made when Cyrenius was governor of Syria.)
3. And all went to be taxed, every one into his own city.
4. And Joseph also went up from Galilee, out of the city of Nazareth, into Judaea, unto the city of David, which is called Bethlehem;* (because he was of the house and lineage of David:)
5. To be taxed with Mary his espoused wife, being great with child. (*about 80 miles from Nazareth)

> **Bethlehem:** 1. Bethlehem is the "City of David" and the place where Jesus Christ was born, five miles south of Jerusalem. This city is sometimes called Bethlehem-judah (KJV) or Ephrath (Genesis 35:19; Micah 5:2) to keep it from being confused with another city, Bethlehem of Zebulun.
>
> Bethlehem was first settled by the Canaanites and was associated with the earliest fathers (or "patriarchs") of Israel, because Rachel died and was buried near it (Genesis 35:16, 19; Genesis 48:7). The earliest mention of Bethlehem is in some ancient battle reports, written fourteen hundred years before Christ's birth, which refer to a city named bitil u-lahama south of Jerusalem. This name may have meant "house of (the goddess) Lahama." A branch of Caleb's family settled there, and Caleb's son Salma was known as "the father of Bethlehem" (1 Chronicles 2:51). Bethlehem was the home of a young Levite who served as priest to Micah (Judges 17:7-8),

and of Boaz, Ruth, Obed, and Jesse, the Bethlehemite, David's father (Ruth 4:11-17; 1 Samuel 16:18).

Bethlehem was the birthplace of David (1 Samuel 17:12) and the home of one of David's mighty men, Elhanan (2 Samuel 23:24; 1 Chronicles 11:26). Three of David's warriors performed a daring deed there by breaking through a chain of Philistine warriors who had taken over the city to bring David water from a well near the city gate of his hometown (2 Samuel 23:14-17). Much later, Bethlehem is mentioned as being next to the village of Geruth-kimham, where Jews running from the Babylonians stayed while they were on their way to Egypt (Jeremiah 41:17). People from Bethlehem were part of the group of Jews who returned to Israel after living in exile in Babylon (Ezra 2:21; Nehemiah 7:26; 1 Esdras 5:17).

When Jesus was born there, Bethlehem was only a small village (Matthew 2:1-16; Luke 2:4-6, 15; John 7:42). Under the law declared by Caesar Augustus, the emperor of Rome, Joseph had to go to Bethlehem because he was part of the family of David (Luke 2:4). The family may still have had property there. The birth of Jesus may have taken place in a cave in the rocks outside the town. The early Christian writer Justin Martyr thought so, as did another writer, Origen, some years later. Origen often lived in the Holy Land (the area where Jesus had lived) and wrote, "In Bethlehem you are shown the cave where he was born, and within the cave the manger where he was wrapped in swaddling clothes."

Jerome, another early Christian writer, later described the cave where the Roman Emperor Constantine had built a church. In 1934–35, some evidence was found near Bethlehem that suggested a second period of building in the time of a later emperor, Justinian (AD 527–565), during which Constantine's church was extended past its original boundaries. Steps led down to the cave, which seems to have been shaped artificially into a square, perhaps by Constantine's builders. But there is no description of the cave from before the construction of Constantine's church.

2. Bethlehem is also the name of a town in Zebulun (Joshua 19:15), probably the home of the judge Ibzan (Judges 12:8-10), an early ruler of Israel. Today it is considered to be the same place as the village of Beit Lahm, some seven miles northwest of Nazareth.[481]

Christ Jesus is born

6. And so it was, that, while they were there, the days were accomplished that she should be delivered.

7. And she brought forth her firstborn son, and <u>wrapped him in swaddling clothes</u>, and laid him in a manger; because there was no room for them in the inn.

> **Note:** Jesus birth date is confirmed as being 1 April 5 BC based upon the death of Herod the Great on March 13, 4 BC.[482] John the Baptist birth date is also calculated to be in October 6 BC; six months before the birth of Christ. Further, Jesus is born in the first month of the Jewish year (Abib), which is the time of the Passover and unleavened bread festival. Therefore, it is surmised that he was born and died during the Passover, and is the door of the Passover to the afterlife with God.

> **Swaddling Clothes**: "These were bandages tightly wrapped around a new-born child. The rank of the child was indicated by the splendor and costliness of the bands. Fine shawls or scarfs were used by the rich and common cloth by the poor. Babies so wrapped looked like mummies with no sign of arms or legs. Even the head was wrapped, the eyes only being

visible. This custom is referred to in Job 38:9; Lam 2:22; Ezek 16:4.[483]

The heavens acknowledge the birth of God's Christ

8. And there were in the same country shepherds abiding in the field, keeping watch over their flock by night.
9. And, lo, the angel of the Lord came upon them, and the glory of the Lord shone round about them: and they were sore afraid.
10. And the angel said unto them, Fear not: for, behold, I bring you good tidings of great joy, which shall be to all people.
11. For unto you is born this day in the city of David a Saviour, which is Christ the Lord.
12. And this shall be a sign unto you; Ye shall find the babe wrapped in swaddling clothes, lying in a manger.
13. And suddenly there was with the angel a multitude of the heavenly host praising God, and saying,
14. Glory to God in the highest, and on earth peace, good will toward men.

The shepherds acknowledge the birth of God's Christ.

15. And it came to pass, as the angels were gone away from them into heaven, the shepherds said one to another, Let us now go even unto Bethlehem, and see this thing which is come to pass, which the Lord hath made known unto us.
16. And they came with haste, and found Mary, and Joseph, and the babe lying in a manger.
17. And when they had seen it, they made known abroad the saying which was told them concerning this child.
18. And all they that heard it wondered at those things which were told them by the shepherds.
19. But Mary kept all these things, and pondered them in her heart.
20. And the shepherds returned, glorifying and praising God for all the things that they had heard and seen, as it was told unto them.

The Magi Worship the Baby Jesus

MATTHEW 2: 1-12

1. Now when Jesus was born in Bethlehem of Judaea in the days of Herod the king, behold, there came wise men from the east to Jerusalem,
2. Saying, Where is he that is born King of the Jews? for we have seen his star in the east, and are come to worship him. (**Numbers 24: 14-17 / Revelation 22: 16**)

- **MAGI** - these "wise men" (KVJ, NLT), appearing in Matthew 2:1-12, followed a star to Jerusalem and then to Bethlehem in order to pay homage to the newborn "king of the Jews." Matthew's account forms a significant introduction to his Gospel by drawing attention to the true identity of Jesus as King and by foreshadowing the homage paid by the Gentiles to Jesus throughout that Gospel.

- **THE MAGI OF THE ANCIENT WORLD** - Extra biblical evidence offers various clues that shed light on the place of origin and positions held by the magi of Matthew 2. The historian Herodotus mentioned magi as a priestly caste of Media, or Persia, and, as the religion in Persia at the time was Zoroastrianism, Herodotus's magi were probably Zoroastrian priests. Herodotus, together with Plutarch and Strabo, suggested that magi were partly responsible for ritual and cultic life (supervising sacrifices and prayers) and partly responsible as royal advisers to the courts of the East. Believing the affairs of history were reflected in the movements of the stars and other phenomena, Herodotus said, the rulers of the East commonly utilized the magi's knowledge of astrology and dream interpretation to determine affairs of state. The magi were, therefore, concerned with what the movement of the stars (as signs and portents) might signify for the future affairs of history. Such an interest could account not only for the magi's interest in the star in Matthew, but also their conclusion, shared with Herod, that the star's appearance signified the birth of a new ruler of great importance (2:2). Several centuries before Christ, a similar correlation was noted between a stellar phenomenon and the birth of Alexander the Great.[484]

The "wise men" that came to Jerusalem looking for the new born king, with an escort of 1000 strong, which were part of an army of 7000 who rested on the East banks of the Euphrates River; "their dress and appearance commanded respect, and their gifts for the king also indicated persons of no ordinary rank. The number was derived from the gifts that they had for the king:

- Gold – a symbol of a king.
- Myrrh – The bitterness of the passion, and the preparation of the tomb.
- Frankincense – Offered in adoration of the divinity of the Son of God.

The wise men told Herod the Great, that the star they followed was not an ordinary astrological sign, but a star that came down upon them and guided them across the terrain.

> "In the apocryphal book of Seth, it is said that this "star was a circle of light with a figure of a child and a cross over its head inside. They also said that they came on the expedition in obedience to a prophesy of Zoroaster, who said that in the latter days, there should be a Mighty One, a Redeemer, and that a star should announce his coming. And when the star appeared it was in the form of an infant with a cross, and a voice bade them to follow it to Judea, which they did travelling two years."[485]

King Herod would not believe the wise men followed a star to Jerusalem
3. When Herod the king had heard these things, he was troubled, and all Jerusalem with him.
4. And when he had gathered all the chief priests and scribes of the people together, he demanded of them where Christ should be born. (**Micah 5: 2**)

The wise men find out that Christ must be born in Bethlehem of Judea
5. And they said unto him, In Bethlehem of Judaea: for thus it is written by the prophet,
6. And thou Bethlehem, in the land of Juda, art not the least among the princes of Juda: for out of thee shall come a Governor, that shall rule my people Israel.
7. *Then Herod, when he had privily called the wise men, inquired of them diligently what time the star appeared.*
8. And he sent them to Bethlehem, and said, Go and search diligently for the young child; and when ye have found him, bring me word again, that I may come and worship him also.

The wise men acknowledge God's Christ
9. When they had heard the king, they departed; and, lo, the star, which they saw in the east, went before them, till it came and stood over where the young child was.
10. When they saw the star, they rejoiced with exceeding great joy.
11. And when they were come into the house, they saw the young child with Mary his mother, and fell down, and worshipped him: and when they had opened their treasures, they presented unto him gifts; gold, and frankincense, and myrrh. (**Psalm 72: 1-10**)

The wise men leave the country without telling King Herod
12 And being warned of God in a dream that they should not return to Herod, they departed into their own country another way.

Who is Jesus Christ

Jesus is dedicated in the Temple

Luke 2: 21-38
21. And when eight days were accomplished for the circumcising of the child, his name was called Jesus, which was so named of the angel before he was conceived in the womb.
22. And when the days of her purification according to the law of Moses were accomplished, they brought him to Jerusalem, to present him to the Lord;
23. (As it is written in the law of the Lord, Every male that openeth the womb shall be called holy to the Lord;)
24. And to offer a sacrifice according to that which is said in the law of the Lord, A pair of turtledoves, or two young pigeons.

Simeon Acknowledges God's Christ
25. And, behold, there was a man in Jerusalem, whose name was Simeon; and the same man was just and devout, waiting for the consolation of Israel: and the Holy Ghost was upon him.
26. And it was revealed unto him by the Holy Ghost, that he should not see death, before he had seen the Lord's Christ.
27. And he came by the Spirit into the temple: and when the parents brought in the child Jesus, to do for him after the custom of the law,
28. Then took he him up in his arms, and blessed God, and said,
29. Lord, now lettest thou thy servant depart in peace, according to thy word:
30. For mine eyes have seen thy salvation,
31. Which thou hast prepared before the face of all people;
32. A light to lighten the Gentiles, and the glory of thy people Israel.
33. And Joseph and his mother marvelled at those things which were spoken of him.
34. And Simeon blessed them, and said unto Mary his mother, Behold, this child is set for the fall and rising again of many in Israel; and for a sign which shall be spoken against;
35. (Yea, a sword shall pierce through thy own soul also,) that the thoughts of many hearts may be revealed.

The Prophetess Anna acknowledges God's Christ

36. And there was one Anna, a prophetess, the daughter of Phanuel, of the tribe of Aser: she was of a great age, and had lived with an husband seven years from her virginity;

37. And she was a widow of about fourscore and four years, which departed not from the temple, but served God with fastings and prayers night and day.

38. And she coming in that instant gave thanks likewise unto the Lord, and spake of him to all them that looked for redemption in Jerusalem.

Joseph Escapes to Egypt with His Family

<u>Mathew 2: 13-23</u>

13 And when they were departed, behold, the angel of the Lord appeareth to Joseph in a dream, saying, Arise, and take the young child and his mother, and flee into Egypt, and be thou there until I bring thee word: for Herod will seek the young child to destroy him. 14 When he arose, he took the young child and his mother by night, and departed into Egypt: 15 and was there until the death of Herod: that it might be fulfilled which was spoken of the Lord by the prophet, saying, Out of Egypt have I called my son.

YEAR – 4 BC

Herod The Great

16 Then Herod, when he saw that he was mocked of the wise men, was exceeding wroth, and sent forth, and slew all the children that were in Bethlehem, and in all the coasts thereof, from two years old and under, according to the time which he had diligently enquired of the wise men.

17 Then was fulfilled that which was spoken by Jeremy the prophet, saying,

18 In Rama was there a voice heard, lamentation, and weeping, and great mourning, Rachel weeping for her children, and would not be comforted, because they are not.

Herod the Great was born in 73 BC. His father was Antipater, a descendent of Jacobs brother Esau; which were called Edomites -Idumaeans. Antipater was appointed procurator of Judaea by Julius Caesar in 47 BC.

Antipater then appointed his son Herod military prefect of Galilee. After the death of Caesar, Herod was crowned "King of the Jews" by the Roman senate on advice of Antony and Octavian.[486] Herod reigned as king for 33 years.

Herod was the Great because of his building projects; he built many military fortifications, the city of Caesarea, monuments to the Roman gods, and restored God's Temple in Jerusalem: which began in 19 BC. On his death bed he willed his kingdom to his three sons; which was ratified by Augustus Caesar:[487]

- Judaea and Samaria – to Archelaus, Herod the Ethnarch.
- Galilee and Pereda – To Antipas, Herod the Tetrarch.
- His NE Territories – to Phillip

Death of Herod the Great

Yet, in 4 BC he ordered the death of all the babies in Bethlehem, two years and under, because he felt threaten by the news of the Magi, that the King of Israel was born. When Herod decreed that all the children two-years old and under be slain, Jesus was more than 1 year old, but less than two years old. Herod the Great died on March 13, 4 BC (the Hebrew month of Adar), in the year of Rome 750.[488]

- Herod gave the order to slay the children while he yet lived.
- Jesus was 23 ½ months old when Herod died.
- The time from April 1, 5 BC to March 13, 4 BC is 23 ½ months.

Josephus recorded that when Herod died, "that very night there was an eclipse of the moon. It happened March 13, in the year of the Julian period 4710, and the 4th year (of the Christian era AD)"[489]

Joseph and His Family Return to Israel

19 But when Herod was dead, behold, an angel of the Lord appeareth in a dream to Joseph in Egypt,

20 saying, Arise, and take the young child and his mother, and go into the land of Israel: for they are dead which sought the young child's life.

21 And he arose, and took the young child and his mother, and came into the land of Israel. 22 But when he heard that Archelaus did reign in Judaea in the room of his father Herod, he was afraid to go thither: notwithstanding, being warned of God in a dream, he turned aside into the parts of Galilee:

23 and he came and dwelt in a city called Nazareth: that it might be fulfilled which was spoken by the prophets, He shall be called a Nazarene.

Joseph and Mary's Other Children

Matthew 13: (Mark 6: 1-6 / John 7:1-4)

53. And it came to pass, that when Jesus had finished these parables, he departed thence.

54. And when he was come into his own country, he taught them in their synagogue, insomuch that they were astonished, and said, Whence hath this man this wisdom, and these mighty works?

55. **Is not this the carpenter's son? is not his mother called Mary? and his brethren, James, and Joses, and Simon, and Judas?**

56. And his sisters, are they not all with us? Whence then hath this man all these things?

57. And they were offended in him. But Jesus said unto them, A prophet is not without honour, save in his own country, and in his own house. (Mark 6:1-6)

58. And he did not many mighty works there because of their unbelief. (John 7:1-4)

> YEAR – March 20, 7 AD

Joseph and Family Celebrate the Passover

Luke 2: 41-52
41 Now his parents went to Jerusalem every year at the feast of the passover.
42 And **when he was twelve years old**, they went up to Jerusalem after the custom of the feast.

Jesus is separated from the Family
43 And when they had fulfilled the days, as they returned, the child Jesus tarried behind in Jerusalem; and Joseph and his mother knew not of it.
44 But they, supposing him to have been in the company, went a day's journey; and they sought him among their kinsfolk and acquaintance.
45 And when they found him not, they turned back again to Jerusalem, seeking him.

Jesus is Found Among the Religious Leaders
46 And it came to pass, that after three days they found him in the temple, sitting in the midst of the doctors, both hearing them, and asking them questions. 47 And all that heard him were astonished at his understanding and answers.

Mary Questions Jesus about his Separation
48 And when they saw him, they were amazed: and his mother said unto him, Son, why hast thou thus dealt with us? behold, thy father and I have sought thee sorrowing.

Jesus told Mary of His Mission on the Earth

49 And he said unto them, How is it that ye sought me? wist ye not that I must be about my Father's business?

50 And they understood not the saying which he spake unto them.

51 And he went down with them, and came to Nazareth, and was subject unto them: but his mother kept all these sayings in her heart.

52 And Jesus increased in wisdom and stature, and in favour with God and man.

YEAR – 25 AD

Christ Starts His Earthly Ministry

Jesus is around thirty years old when he began his ministry. He had been baptized in water by the High Priest John the Baptist, and anointed by God with the full power of the Holy Ghost. He had also endured the test of temptation by "the great dragon, that old serpent, called the Devil and Satan.

After John was put in prison by Herod the tetrarch, Jesus began to "preach and to say, Repent: for the kingdom of heaven is at hand.

- o Matthew 3:1-17, Jesus is baptized in water, and the full power of the Holy Ghost.
- o Mathew 4:1-11, Jesus is tempted by Satan.
- o Matthew 4:12-17, Jesus begins his ministry.

Before he assembled his twelve disciples, he first called individuals to follow him that had at one time followed John the Baptist. For John had confessed that Jesus was the son of God, and identified him when he said, "Behold, the Lamb of God, which taketh away the sin of the world."

- o John 1:29-42, Andrew and Peter.
- o John 1:43-51, Phillip and Nathanael.
- o Mathew 9:9-13, Matthew is called.

- Matthew 10: 1-4, The twelve disciples are formed and sent out on their first mission.

After John the Baptist is beheaded by Harold the tetrarch, Jesus announces that John was that Elijah spoken of by the prophet Malachi. And when we review the prophecy of the angel Gabriel, we find that John indeed was a replicate (clone) of the prophet Elijah. Yet, because of unbelief Jesus ended by saying, "And if you can receive it, this is the Elias, which was to come."

- Malachi 4:4-6, The coming of Elijah.
- Luke 1:11-17, Prophecy of John the Baptist.
- 2 Kings 1:8, The appearance of Elijah.
- Matthew 3:1-4, The appearance of John the Baptist.

During Christ walk on this earth he displayed the power of God, without measure, through the power of the Holy Ghost. The Pharisees were so amazed by his power to cast out evil spirits that they said, "This fellow doth not cast out devils, but by Beelzebub the prince of the devils." (Matthew 12:24)

Josephus, the Jewish historian said, "Now there was about this time, Jesus, a wise man, if it be lawful to call him a man, for he was a doer of wonderful works – a teacher of such men as receive the truth with pleasure. He drew over to him many of the Jews, and many of the Gentiles. He was [the] Christ; and when Pilate, at the suggestion of the principal men amongst us, had condemned him to the cross, those that loved him at the first did not forsake him, for he appeared to them alive again the third day, as the divine prophets had foretold these and ten thousand other wonderful things concerning him; and the tribe of Christians, so named from him, are not extinct at this day."[490]

The power of Jesus was awe struck when he changed water in to wine, and five thousand with two loaves of bread and five fish, and walked on water. But he bested all of that with his healing power.

- Matthew 4: 23 "And Jesus went about all Galilee, teaching in their synagogues, and preaching the gospel of the kingdom, and healing all manner of sickness and all manner of disease among the people.
  24 And his fame went throughout all Syria: and they brought unto him all sick people that were taken with divers diseases and torments, and those which were possessed with devils, and those which were lunatick, and those that had the palsy; and he healed them.
  25 And there followed him great multitudes of people from Galilee, and from Decapolis, and from Jerusalem, and from Judaea, and from beyond Jordan."

- Mark 6: 53 And when they had passed over, they came into the land of Gennesaret, and drew to the shore.
  54 And when they were come out of the ship, straightway they knew him,
  55 and ran through that whole region round about, and began to carry about in beds those that were sick, where they heard he was.
  56 And whithersoever he entered, into villages, or cities, or country, they laid the sick in the streets, and besought him that they might touch if it were but the border of his garment: and as many as touched him were made whole.

  - Matthew 9:20-22 – Healing a woman with an issue of blood. (Leviticus 15:20-30)
  - Matthew 14:34-36 – Touch Jesus garment hem to be healed.

CHAPTER 21

JESUS, MOSES, AND ELIJAH

Luke 9: 27 But I tell you of a truth, there be some standing here, which shall not taste of death, till they see the kingdom of God.

28 And it came to pass about an eight days after these sayings, he took Peter and John and James, and went up into a mountain to pray.

29 And as he prayed, the fashion of his countenance was altered, and his raiment was white and glistering.

30 And, behold, there talked with him two men, which were Moses and Elias:

31 who appeared in glory, and spake of his decease which he should accomplish at Jerusalem.

32 But Peter and they that were with him were heavy with sleep: and when they were awake, they saw his glory, and the two men that stood with him.

33 And it came to pass, as they departed from him, Peter said unto Jesus, Master, it is good for us to be here: and let us make three tabernacles; one for thee, and one for Moses, and one for Elias: not knowing what he said.

34 While he thus spake, there came a cloud, and overshadowed them: and they feared as they entered into the cloud.

35 And there came a voice out of the cloud, saying, This is my beloved Son: hear him. 36 And when the voice was past, Jesus was found alone. And they kept it close, and told no man in those days any of those things which they had seen.

The friendship of Christ Jesus, Moses, and Elijah is not easily defined, but can be explained through close scrutiny of the Scriptures. First, why did Jesus only meet with these two prophets? Second, why were none of the other prophets selected to appear and talk with Christ Jesus? For example, why not Enoch, who was taken by God when he was 365 years old?[491] Or the prophet Abraham, who was called a friend of God, for it, was he who God made an old ritual covenant and told how his seed would suffer for four hundred years. This was before Isaac, the child of promise, was born.[492] Or the prophet Daniel, who in a vision, saw Christ on the clouds of glory receiving instructions from God the Father about his everlasting dominion over the earth).[493]

God and Moses

All this is a great mystery, but I found a passage in Exodus chapter 33 that might explain how Moses and Christ formed a close relationship.

After Moses confronted Aaron and the children of Israel about the golden calf, he took the tabernacle of the congregation and pitched it outside the camp limits. The people watched in awe as Moses entered through the tent door, and the pillar of cloud descended and met him there. Then Moses began to speak to the cloud face-to-face, "as a man speaketh unto his friend."

During the conversation, Moses asked God to reveal himself to him, because he wanted to know God on a personal basis. God said he would honor Moses' request, "for thou hast found grace in my sight, and I know thee by name."

Not satisfied, Moses also requested to see God in all his glory. Again, God said he would grant Moses' request, but he added some stipulations.

- And he said, I will make all my goodness pass before thee, and I will proclaim the name of the Lord before thee; and will be gracious to whom I will be gracious, and will shew mercy on whom I will shew mercy.

- And he said, Thou canst not see my face: for there shall no man see me, and live.

- And the Lord said, Behold, there is a place by me, and thou shalt stand upon a rock: And it shall come to pass, while my glory passeth by, that I will put thee in a Clift of the rock, and will cover thee with my hand while I pass by: And I will take away mine hand, and thou shalt see my back parts: but my face shall not be seen. (Exodus 33:19–23)

From reading these writings, it is not too hard to imagine what is going to happen. God will put Moses between some rocks and cover him with his hand. When God passes by Moses will see his backside. Sound simple? Yet, what actually conspired, or happened, when God the Father passed by is not what was thought to be said! I'm talking about God covering Moses with his hand. So, let's look at the events as they are recorded.

Moses goes back up on Mount Sinai to receive a second set of Ten

Commandant tablets from God. God instructs Moses to not only come alone but warn the people to stay clear of the mountain with their flocks and their herds. After Moses fashioned the two tablets, he went up on the mountain.

Christ and Moses

This is where I want you to clearly see how the relationship develops between Moses and Christ Jesus.

- And the Lord [Christ] descended in the cloud, and stood with him [Moses] there, and proclaimed the name of the Lord (God).

- And the Lord [God the Father] passed by before him, and proclaimed, The Lord, The Lord God, merciful and gracious, longsuffering, and abundant in goodness and truth, keeping mercy for thousands, forgiving iniquity and transgression and sin, and that will by no means clear the guilty; visiting the iniquity of the fathers upon the children, and upon the children's children, unto the third and to the fourth generation.

- And Moses made haste, and bowed his head toward the earth, and worshipped. And he said, If now I have found grace in thy sight, O Lord [God the Father], let my Lord [Christ, the angel of God], I pray thee, go among us; for it is a stiffnecked people; and pardon our iniquity and our sin, and take us for thine inheritance. (Exodus 34:5–9)

Now the Lord who descended in a cloud and stood with Moses is none other than Christ Jesus (<u>the word of the Lord</u> / <u>the angel of God</u> /<u>the Rock identified by the apostle Paul</u>); for he is the hand of God that will protect Moses as God the Father passes by. Take note that Moses, after he had seen the Father, didn't ask for silver or gold, or fame or fortune, or even a healthy life. But he worshipped God in truth and in spirit, and asked the Father to allow the presence of Christ among his people, and forgiveness of their sins.

Reading on in Exodus 34, we find Moses was up on Mount Sinai for forty days and forty nights, without food or water. When he finally descended to the camp, his face was so bright it brought fear to all the people. Moses had to put a veil over his face when he talked with them. However, this brightness was not permanent, and eventually, the face of Moses returned to its natural features.

It can be summarized that Christ and Moses forged an everlasting friendship during his forty days and nights on Mount Sinai, and during the forty years the children of Israel traveled around, in, and through the Sinai Desert.

Moses and Fasting

It is recorded that Moses fasted three times for forty days and forty nights. This seems a bit odd, but why he did this is explained in the Scriptures.

- ***First time:*** "When I was gone up into the mount to receive the tables of stone, even the tables of the covenant which the Lord made with you, then I abode in the mount forty days and forty nights, I neither did eat bread nor drink water:" (Deuteronomy 9:9)

- ***Second time:*** "And the Lord said unto me, Arise, get thee down quickly from hence; for thy people which thou hast brought forth out of Egypt have corrupted themselves; they are quickly turned aside out of the way which I commanded them; they have made them a molten image. Furthermore the Lord spake unto me, saying, I have seen this people, and, behold, it is a stiffnecked people: Let me alone, that I may destroy them, and blot out their name from under heaven: and I will make of thee a nation mightier and greater than they. So I turned and came down from the mount, and the mount burned with fire: and the two tables of the covenant were in my two hands. And I looked, and, behold, ye had sinned against the Lord your God, and had made you a molten calf: ye had turned aside quickly out of the way which the Lord had commanded you. And I took the two tables, and cast them out of my two hands, and brake them before your eyes. And I fell down before the Lord, as at the first, forty days and forty nights: I did neither eat bread, nor drink water, because of all your sins which ye sinned, in doing wickedly in the sight of the Lord, to provoke him to anger." (Deuteronomy 9: 12–18)

- <u>*Third time*</u>*:* And at Taberah, and at Massah, and at Kibrothhattaavah, ye provoked the Lord to wrath. Likewise when the Lord sent you from Kadeshbarnea, saying, Go up and possess the land which I have given you; then ye rebelled against the commandment of the Lord your God, and ye believed him not, nor hearkened to his voice. Ye have been rebellious against the Lord from the day that I knew you. Thus I fell down before the Lord forty days and forty nights, as I fell down at the first; because the Lord had said he would destroy you." (Deuteronomy 9:22–25)

So, we see that Moses, as a representative of God, had good reason to fast and pray for God's people. This is an art that is lost in the modern church, but one that is commanded by the Lord Jesus Christ. In Matthew Chapter 6, he addresses how to pray, and then gives instructions on how to fast.

> "Moreover when ye fast, be not, as the hypocrites, of a sad countenance: for they disfigure their faces, that they may appear unto men to fast. Verily I say unto you, They have their reward. But thou, when thou fastest, anoint thine head, and wash thy face; That thou appear not unto men to fast, but unto thy Father which is in secret: and thy Father, which seeth in secret, shall reward thee openly." (Matthew 6:16–18)

The Death of Moses

We know from Scripture that God forbade Moses from entering the Promised Canaan Land because of his disobedience when ordered to call water from the rock (Numbers 20:7–13). Yet God let Moses go into the mountains of Nebo and view the Promised Land from the top of Mount Pisgah (Deuteronomy 34:1–4).

At this juncture of life, Moses was 120 years old: "his eye was not dim, nor his natural force abated." He was still walking upright and in complete control of his physical and mental faculties. When Moses didn't come back from his trip to Mount Pisgah, the people wept and moaned for thirty days, "for he was much beloved." Now this is where the strange part of the death of Moses comes in.

- "So Moses the servant of the Lord died there in the land of Moab, according to the word of the Lord."

- "And he buried him in a valley in the land of Moab, over against Bethpeor: but no man knoweth of his sepulchre unto this day." 9Deuteronomy 34:5–6)

So then Christ—the word of the Lord, the angel of God, the Rock that was with them—brought the people news that Moses died in the land of Moab, and that he had buried his body, and the whereabouts of his grave would not be known to humankind.

I'm going to go out on the limb and say Moses' body did die. But after that, he was resurrected, as Christ's body was resurrected (Luke 24:36–43), with a new, glorified, incorruptible, celestial, and terrestrial body. The body had no life-giving blood but was composed of flesh, bone, and Spirit (living water—the Holy Ghost). So, it's really not a marvel that this Moses came to visit Christ on the Mount of Transfiguration (Matthew 17:1-5).

Elijah and Christ Jesus [Year 850 BC]

The prophet Elijah represented God when Ahab was king of

Samaria (Northern Israel), and Jezebel was his queen. The Southern kingdom of Israel (Judah) was ruled by Asa: the house of David.

He was known as Elijah the tish'bite, an inhabitant of Tishbi in Gilead, a place in upper Galilee). It has been identified by some with el-Ishtib, a place twenty-two miles due south of the Sea of Galilee, among the mountains of Gilead.[494]

> "Tishbe was the native city of Elijah the prophet and its inhabitants (1 Kings 17:1; 1 Kings 21:17, 28; 2 Kings 1:3, 8; 2 Kings 9:36). The Hebrew form of Tishbe in 1 Kings 17,1 prompted the King James Version to translate the word as "of the inhabitants [of Gilead]." Most translations follow the Septuagint version, however, and consider Tishbe to be a proper noun. This reading is also supported by the fact that Elijah is elsewhere called a Tishbite. If Tishbe is considered a proper name, it is likely identified with Thisbe, a town in Naphtali that is mentioned in Tobit 1:2."[495]

The Prophet Elijah's walk on this earth was guided by <u>the word of the Lord</u> (Christ Jesus). There is no record of his birth, just that he appeared out of nowhere to confront Ahab and Jezebel. His full story starts in 1 Kings Chapter 17 and ends in 2 Kings 2:11.

Elijah was one prophet that followed "<u>the word of the Lord</u>, every instruction, and this finally led him to meet and talk with God the Father.

- Christ tells Elijah to tell Ahab, "As the Lord God of Israel liveth, before whom I stand, there shall not be dew nor rain these years, but according to my word." (1 Kings 17:1)

  James, the brother of Jesus, wrote that the drought lasted for three and a half years (James 5:17–18). This is where Christ began to visit Elijah and a long-lasting friendship is formed.

- Christ commands the ravens to feed Elijah. (1 Kings 17:2-7)

- "And <u>the word of the Lord</u> came unto him, saying, 9 Arise, get thee to Zarephath, which belongeth to Zidon, and dwell there: behold, I have commanded a widow woman there to sustain thee. (1 Kings 17:8-16) This visit of Elijah resulted in the miracle of an empty barrel of meal being replenished every time the widow dipped her cup in the barrel.

- Elijah raises the woman's son from the dead. (1 Kings 17:17-24)

- Elijah confronts Ahab on Mount Carmel and kills all the prophets of Jezebel: "Now therefore send, and gather to me all Israel unto mount Carmel, and the prophets of Baal four hundred and fifty, and the prophets of the groves four hundred, which eat at Jezebel's table." (1 Kings 18: 1-40)

- Christ sends rain to end the drought. (1 Kings 18:1-2 / 41-46)

An Angel Provides for Elijah

In fear for his life, Elijah went a day's journey into the desert. He did not take any food or water because Jezebel was hot on his heels. Tired, he sat under the shade of a juniper tree and had thoughts of death. He said to God, "It is enough; now O Lord, take away my life; for I am not better than my fathers." Then Elijah fell asleep.

How brave this man was when he faced the 850 prophets of Baal on Mount Carmel, only to be reduced to whimpering, hysteria, and anxiety when threatened with immediate [pending] death.

However, God in his wisdom dispatched an angel to cook a meal and provide water for Elijah. The angel shook Elijah awake and said, "Arise and eat." Elijah got up, ate, and went back to sleep.

After a little while, the angel came and woke him again, telling him to eat a second time; because the climb to the top of Mount Horeb would require all his strength: "and he arose, and did eat and drink, and went in the strength of that meat forty days and forty nights unto Horeb, the mount of God."

Abraham Howard Jr.

Elijah and Christ

Now we are going to examine the part of Elijah's life where he meets up with the Father (God), and the Son (Christ). Therefore, I want you to pay attention to what is said between Christ and Elijah, and Elijah and the Father. (1 Kings 19: 9-18)

Elijah: And he came thither unto a cave, and lodged there;

Christ: and, behold, <u>the word of the Lord</u> <u>came to him</u>, <u>and he said unto him</u>, What doest thou here, Elijah?

Elijah: And he said, I have been very jealous for the Lord God of hosts: for the children of Israel have forsaken thy covenant, thrown down thine altars, and slain thy prophets with the sword; and I, even I only, am left; and they seek my life, to take it away.

Christ: And he said, Go forth, and stand upon the mount before the Lord.

** On questioning, Elijah began to tell Christ about the iniquity of the children of Israel and how they had killed all God's prophets except for him. Christ then told Elijah to take up a position in the cave. And like he was with Moses, Christ was there to protect Elijah when God passed by.

Elijah and God

God: And, behold, the Lord passed by, and a great and strong wind rent the mountains, and brake in pieces the rocks before the Lord; but the Lord was not in the wind: and after the wind an earthquake; but the Lord was not in the earthquake: and after the earthquake a fire; but the Lord was not in the fire: and after the fire a still small voice.

Elijah: And it was so, when Elijah heard it that he wrapped his face in his mantle, and went out, and stood in the entering in of the cave.

God: And, behold, there came a voice unto him, and said, What doest thou here, Elijah?

Elijah: And he said, I have been very jealous for the Lord God of hosts: because the children of Israel have forsaken thy covenant, thrown down thine altars, and slain thy prophets with the sword; and I, even I only, am left; and they seek my life, to take it away.

God: And the Lord said unto him,
- Go, return on thy way to the wilderness of Damascus: and when thou comest, anoint Hazael to be king over Syria:
- and Jehu the son of Nimshi shalt thou anoint to be king over Israel:
- and Elisha the son of Shaphat of Abel-meholah shalt thou anoint to be prophet in thy room.
- And it shall come to pass, that him that escapeth the sword of Hazael shall Jehu slay:
- and him that escapeth from the sword of Jehu shall Elisha slay.
- Yet I have left me seven thousand in Israel, all the knees which have not bowed unto Baal, and every mouth which hath not kissed him.

When Moses saw God, he only looked on his backside as he passed by. However, Elijah would talk to God like Adam and Eve did after they had sinned: they heard the voice of God walking in the garden (Genesis 3:8).

God proceeded to give Elijah some instructions. First, he wanted him to return to Israel by way of Damascus and anoint Hazael to be the next king over Syria. Second, he wanted him to anoint Jehu, son of Nimshishalt, as the next king over Northern Israel. Third, he wanted him to anoint Elisha, son of Shaphat of Abelmeholah, as the next prophet after his death. Last, God told Elijah that he was not the only prophet left, because he had seven thousand loyal subjects in reserve who refused to bow down to other gods.

This message of God's reserve force is a joyous reminder for the followers of Christ, who at some point in time will feel like Elijah, that they are all alone. And like in the days of Elijah, the Lord Jesus Christ has a large reserve contingent in the church, and can quickly replace a fallen soldier when needed.

- o Elijah anoints Elisha to be a prophet of God. (1 Kings 19: 19-21)
- o Elijah announces judgement on Ahab and Jezebel (1 Kings 21:1-29)
- o Elijah pronounces judgement on Ahab's son Ahaziah. (2 Kings 1:1-18)
- o Elijah is taken up into the heaven by a whirl wind. (2 Kings 2:1-11)

Death of Elijah

Elijah did not ride the chariot up into heaven as some believe. Nor did he go up on a cloud. He left by the power of the Holy Spirit of God on the wings of the wind.

Elijah did not die a normal death; with a burial in the ground. Rather, he was transformed in a moment, in a twinkling of an eye, into a new celestial and terrestrial body. What truly happened is stated in 1 Corinthians 15:35–58. Keep in mind that the body God created on the sixth day of creation did die. But God brought forth a new body that will dwell and function in the new heaven and new earth (Revelation 21, 22).

On earth, the chemical body of Elijah was composed of light (human soul), water, flesh, and bone/blood. But when he was transformed, his body was changed into holy light—human spirit with living water (the Holy Ghost)—and with flesh and bone. His acquired the same type of body as the Lord Jesus Christ (Luke 24:36-43).

The Commonality of Moses, Elijah, and Christ

Now I want to get to the nitty-gritty of the friendship of Moses, Elijah, and Christ. So, brace yourself for some hard facts: for these facts cannot be disputed.

Forty-Day Fast

In the history of the world, as stated in the Holy Bible of Israel, only three men are recorded to have gone without food or drink for forty days and nights, and lived to tell about it—Moses, Elijah, and Jesus Christ.

If we go by scientific data, we would come to the conclusion that all three men should have died somewhere between the fifth and seventh day of the fast. This fact is substantiated in an article by Charles W. Bryant, "How Long Can You Go without Food and Water?" In it, Bryant states most humans can go up to eight weeks without food, as long they have water. But on an average, a human can live no longer than three to five days without water. He also states that "while most people may fast or try a body cleanse without food, you should absolutely never go without water more than a day." Further, the Mayo Clinic recommends drinking eight cups of water a day to maintain a healthy body. Based on Bryant's article, it is clear to me that Moses, Elijah, and Jesus Christ died out of their human body, but was kept alive by the power of the Holy Ghost. There is no other explanation of how they were able to live without food or drink for forty days and forty nights.

Looking Upon God

Christ Jesus, Moses, and Elijah (and Enoch—Genesis 5:23–24) are the only recorded human beings to have seen the form, or shape of God the Father. Further, Christ Jesus on this matter made two points clear to the Jews.

(b) And the Father himself, which hath sent me, hath borne witness of me. Ye have neither heard his voice at any time, nor seen his shape. ((John 5:37)

(b) Not that any man hath seen the Father, save he which is of God, he hath seen the Father. (John 6:46)

Here I must confess that in my research, I found that God the Father has allowed records to be made of his somewhat physical appearance. I present them for your viewing pleasure:

- "And above the firmament that was over their heads was the likeness of a throne, as the appearance of a sapphire stone: and upon the likeness of the throne was the likeness as the appearance of a man above upon it. And I saw as the colour of amber, as the appearance of fire round about within it, from the appearance of his loins even upward, and from the appearance of his loins even downward, I saw as it were the appearance of fire, and it had brightness round about. As the appearance of the bow that is in the cloud in the day of rain, so was the appearance of the brightness round about. This was the appearance of the likeness of the glory of the Lord. And when I saw it, I fell upon my face, and I heard a voice of one that spake."(Ezekiel 1:26–28)

- "And it came to pass in the sixth year, in the sixth month, in the fifth day of the month, as I sat in mine house, and the elders of Judah sat before me, that the hand of the Lord God fell there upon me. Then I beheld, and lo a likeness as the appearance of fire: from the appearance of his loins even downward, fire; and from his loins even upward, as the appearance of brightness, as the colour of amber. And he put forth the form of an hand, and took me by a lock of mine head; and the spirit lifted me up between the earth and the heaven, and brought me in the visions of God to Jerusalem, to the door of the inner gate that looketh toward the north; where was the seat of the image of jealousy, which provoketh to jealousy. And, behold, the glory of the God of Israel was there, according to the vision that I saw in the plain." (Ezekiel 8:1–4)

- "Afterward he brought me to the gate, even the gate that looketh toward the east: And, behold, the glory of the God of Israel came from the way of the east: and his voice was like a noise of many waters: and the earth shined with his glory. And it was according to the appearance of the vision which I saw, even according to the vision that I saw when I came to destroy the city: and the visions were like the vision that I saw by the river Chebar; and I fell upon my face. And the glory of the Lord came into the house by the way of the gate whose prospect is toward the east." (Ezekiel 43:1–4)

- "After this I looked, and, behold, a door was opened in heaven: and the first voice which I heard was as it were of a trumpet talking with me; which said, Come up hither, and I will shew thee things which must be hereafter. And immediately I was in the spirit: and, behold, a throne was set in heaven, and one sat on the throne. And he that sat was to look upon like a jasper and a sardine stone: and there was a rainbow round about the throne, in sight like unto an emerald." ([Revelation 4:1–3)

From the beginning of Genesis and throughout the Bible, God the Father always remained invisible; people heard his voice, but they saw no one. Yet he allowed Moses to have a glimpse of his backside as he passed by. And he let Ezekiel see him sitting upon his throne. And John had the privilege of seeing him on his throne in heaven. In the New Jerusalem, the redeemed will commune with God and Christ forever. Therefore, they will not only see him, but talk with him face-to-face.

ABRAHAM HOWARD JR.

Daniel's Fast

For the sake of argument, I want to inject the prophet Daniel into the mix. Some followers of Christ swear they are going on a Daniel fast, sublimated with a little food, water, or juice. I contend Daniel was a devout Jew and would not dishonor a fast with the Lord by taking any food or drink. Here is the Scripture.

> **Daniel 10:** 1 In the third year of Cyrus king of Persia a thing was revealed unto Daniel, whose name was called Belteshazzar; and the thing was true, but the time appointed was long: and he understood the thing, and had understanding of the vision.
> 2 In those days I Daniel was mourning three full weeks.
> 3 I ate no pleasant bread, neither came flesh nor wine in my mouth, neither did I anoint myself at all, till three whole weeks were fulfilled.

Now the truth of how Daniel fasted is in the above Scripture. The reason water is not mentioned is because wine is his water; in parts of the world where water is not palpable, wine is consumed instead. Again, it should be clear he did the same as Moses, Elijah, and Christ Jesus, for no food or drink entered his body during his twenty-one-day fast.

CHAPTER 22

CHRIST IS THE SAVIOR

In the Christian world, John 3:16 is one of the most quoted Scripture's in the Bible. However, I believe the true meaning is not truly understood by the church or the religious leaders of the world. Therefore, I will go line for line in John Chapter three and explain what I see in the Scripture base.

- **John 3: 13 And no man hath ascended up to heaven, but he that came down from heaven, even the Son of man which is in heaven.**

Christ said that no human being has gone up to heaven on their own accord, but he alone can go up or come down, even in his human form.

- **14 And as Moses lifted up the serpent in the wilderness, even so must the Son of man be lifted up:**
  15 that whosoever believeth in him should not perish, but have eternal life.

The first thing Christ did was put a heavy weight on believing in him hanging on the cross. He states that the same way people were saved during the days of Moses (by looking up on a hill and believing in the healing power of a brass serpent hanging on a pole), they would also be saved by receiving eternal life if they believed that he was crucified for them.

Throughout his ministry and in the epistles of the apostle Paul there are strong references to the importance of the cross.

- "He that loveth father or mother more than me is not worthy of me: and he that loveth son or daughter more than me is not worthy of me. And he that taketh not his cross, and followeth after me, is not worthy of me." (Matthew 10:37–38)

- ""Then said Jesus unto his disciples, If any man will come after me, let him deny himself, and take up his cross, and follow me. For whosoever will save his life shall lose it: and whosoever will lose his life for my sake shall find it. For what is a man profited, if he shall gain the whole world, and lose his own soul? or what shall a man give in exchange for his soul? For the Son of man shall come in the glory of his Father with his angels; and then he shall reward every man according to his works." (Matthew 16:24–27)

- "For the preaching of the cross is to them that perish foolishness; but unto us which are saved it is the power of God." (1 Corinthians 1:18)

- "Let this mind be in you, which was also in Christ Jesus: Who, being in the form of God, thought it not robbery to be equal with God: But made himself of no reputation, and took upon him the form of a servant, and was made in the likeness of men: And being found in fashion as a man, he humbled himself, and became obedient unto death, even the death of the cross. Wherefore God also hath highly exalted him, and given him a name which is above every name: That at the name of Jesus every knee should bow, of things in heaven, and

Who is Jesus Christ

things in earth, and things under the earth; And that every tongue should confess that Jesus Christ is Lord, to the glory of God the Father." ([Philippians 2:5–11)

- **16 For God so loved the world, that he gave his only begotten Son, that whosoever believeth in him should not perish, but have everlasting life.**

During the days of Noah, which start in Genesis chapter 6, God brought two judgments upon the inhabitants of the earth. The first judgment involved the angels, and the second humankind. The angels that sinned with women were cast down and chained in hell. Everything that lived on land was destroyed by a flood.

After the flood, God said water would not destroy the earth again; and he put a bow in the sky after each rain as a reminder of his eternal word. However, during the reign of Joash, king of Judah (835-796 BC), the prophet Joel prophesied that the earth will eventually be destroyed by fire.

> "And it shall come to pass afterward, that I will pour out my spirit upon all flesh; and your sons and your daughters shall prophesy, your old men shall dream dreams, your young men shall see visions: And also upon the servants and upon the handmaids in those days will I pour out my spirit. And I will shew wonders in the heavens and in the earth, blood, and fire, and pillars of smoke. The sun shall be turned into darkness, and the moon into blood, before the great and the terrible day of the Lord come. And it shall come to pass, that whosoever shall call on the name of the Lord shall be delivered: for in mount Zion and in Jerusalem shall be deliverance, as the Lord hath said, and in the remnant whom the Lord shall call." (Joel; 2:28–32)

So as stated in the book of Joel, the earth is on a scheduled collision course of total destruction by fire. And just like in the days of Noah, God is building an ark—the church of Jesus Christ—to take his people to safety. But this ship will only house the souls that believe in the Lord Jesus Christ as their Savior.

God has not only sent his only begotten Son to warn the world of the impeding danger, but he has also provided a space of time for souls to accept or reject Jesus Christ. The clock of Joel was put in motion on the day of Pentecost, and is quickly ticking toward judgment day. Where you will spend eternity rests solely on your shoulders and none other. You see, the New Testament is the last plea of God to the world, and the express compassion of his love toward his creation.

- **17 For God sent not his Son into the world to condemn the world; but that the world through him might be saved.**

As you can see, Christ said he was not sent to judge the world, as it was judged during the time of Noah, and Sodom and Gomorrah. But that the world come to know by his works that he is the messiah, who came down from heaven to save them for everlasting life in the new heaven and new earth, and from the wrath of God (being thrown into "the lake which burneth with fire and brimstone, which is the second death").[496] He also made other supporting statements toward this end during his ministry on the earth.

- "As Jesus was sitting and dining with his disciples may publicans and sinners came and sat down with him (and his disciples). When the Pharisees (religious leaders) saw this they remarked "Why eateth your Master with publicans and sinners?" Jesus flatly replied to them "They that be whole need not a physician, but they that are sick. But go ye and learn what that meaneth, I will have mercy, and not sacrifice: for I am not come to call the righteous, but sinners to repentance." (Matthew 9:10–13)

- "For the Father judgeth no man, but hath committed all judgment unto the Son: that all men should honour the Son, even as they honour the Father. He that honoureth not the Son honoureth not the Father which hath sent him. Verily, verily, I say unto you, He that heareth my word, and believeth on him that sent me, hath everlasting life, and shall not come into condemnation; but is passed from death unto life." (John 5:22-24)

- "Ye judge after the flesh; I judge no man. And yet if I judge, my judgment is true: for I am not alone, but I and the Father that sent me." (John 8:15-16)

  - **18 He that believeth on him is not condemned: but he that believeth not is condemned already, because he hath not believed in the name of the only begotten Son of God.**

What is Christ saying? Well, the fact of the matter is that the whole world is condemned based on the prophecy of Joel. And the only way to escape total destruction is to believe in Christ Jesus. The future of this world is outlined in the book of Revelation. Therefore, if you believe what he says is true, you will be saved. If not, you will meet the impeding scheduled destruction

  - **19 And this is the condemnation, that light is come into the world, and men loved darkness rather than light, because their deeds were evil.**

Before humankind sinned, pure light shone in the Garden of Eden; for there was no presence of evil there except for the Tree of the Knowledge of Good and Evil. But darkness came quickly when O Lucifer (the great dragon, that old serpent called the Devil and Satan) sinned by deceiving Eve and Adam to eat the forbidden fruit from the Tree of the Knowledge of Good and Evil. In this darkness, humankind has waged war, and spilled blood, by staining and straining the human body with vain immoralities, and destructive imaginations of the heart. And when eternal light came to blot out the darkness, it was rejected. Why? Because humankind had become accustomed to living with no light. This light not only opened their eyes, but also revealed the evil, corroded, and corrupted heart.

Therefore, God destroyed the world known to Noah, because no light was shining through the darkness of the heart. Then God created light in the world when he formed a nation that would carry his Word to the world; this from the bowels of the prophet Abraham. However, the children of Abraham (the Hebrews) were consumed by darkness, and began to murmur, complain, and grumble against the ordnances, statures, and precepts of God's law; and began to worship other gods. God had to reject them from his sight for seventy years, but he saved a remnant to be a launching pad for the light (Day who was in the beginning)[497] to enter the earth.

Yet, the prolonged period of darkness lasted from Noah until the birth of the Lord Jesus Christ, the Light of the World.

"Day" came with the good news that God had made a way to escape destruction from hell, and the lake of fire; for everyone who believed in him: the only begotten son of the Father.

> "There was a man sent from God, whose name was John. The same came for a witness, to bear witness of the Light, that all men through him might believe. He was not that Light, but was sent to bear witness of that Light. That was the true Light, which lighteth every man that cometh into the world. He was in the world, and the world was made by him, and the world knew him not. He came unto his own, and his own received him not. But as many as received him, to them gave he power to become the sons of God, even to them that believe on his name: which were born, not of blood, nor of the will of the flesh, nor of the will of man, but of God." (John 1:6-13)

Yet he was rejected and despised. His body was brutally broken, and hung a cross, on a hill outside the holy city of Jerusalem.

In my research, I found that money was the driving force behind evil toward the Lord Jesus Christ. The apostle Paul put it this way: "For the love of money is the root of all evil: which while some coveted after, they have erred from the faith, and pierced themselves through with many sorrows" (1 Timothy 6:10). And what is money? I found it was something people created to justify their evil and wicked ways.

Now we know that the tabernacle in the desert, and the temple Solomon built were holy unto God. Yet Christ found that the temple, which King Herod had improved on, was being defiled by the lust for money. This is recorded in the gospel of John chapter 2. However, I want to culminate what is written in the four gospels (Matthew, Mark, Luke, John[498]) so that you will get the full illustration of how the love of money will corrupt the mind into committing the sin of murder.

Christ: "And the Jews' Passover was at hand, and Jesus went up to Jerusalem. And found in the temple those that sold oxen and sheep and doves, and the changers of money (them that sold and bought in the temple). And when he had made a scourge of small cords, he drove them all out of the temple, and the sheep, and the oxen; and poured out the changers' money, and overthrew the tables; and would not suffer that any man should carry any vessel through the temple. And said unto them that sold doves, Take these things hence; make not my Father's house a house of merchandise. And he taught, saying unto them, Is it not written, My house shall be called of all nations the house of prayer? but ye have made it a den of thieves."

Pharisees: "And he taught daily in the temple. But the chief priests and the scribes and the chief of the people sought to destroy him, And could not find what they might do: for all the people were very attentive to hear him."

As you can, see the love of money drove the Jewish rulers toward hatred of the Lord Jesus Christ. But all of their schemes to kill him came to naught. Finally, they put a bounty on his head, which was accepted by Judas Iscariot, one of his twelve disciples.

The sad part of this whole story is that Christ had to tell them the truth of their final destination if they continued on the pathway of sin. He told them in John chapter 8, "Ye shall die in your sins: for if ye believe not that I am he, ye shall die in your sins."

- **20 For every one that doeth evil hateth the light, neither cometh to the light, lest his deeds should be reproved.
21 But he that doeth truth cometh to the light, that his deeds may be made manifest, that they are wrought in God.**

This world is in a sad state of sin. But God really loves this world, and it is true that he wants to save it without destroying it like in the days of Noah.

- So, God first build a religious nation that would substantiate his written word.

- Then he sent prophets to shore up his word with visions, and future predictions.

- Finally, he sent his Son (the word of the Lord) to proclaim how to escape the eternal death of darkness: "Then spake Jesus again unto them, saying, I am the light of the world: he that followeth me shall not walk in darkness, but shall have the light of life." (John 8:12)

CHAPTER 23

JESUS CHRIST IS THE MESSIAH

> Galatians 4: 4 but when the fulness of the time was come, God sent forth his Son, made of a woman, made under the law,
> 5 to redeem them that were under the law, that we might receive the adoption of sons.

I want to address the reason Christ's time on the earth was so short. He had a timetable that had to be fulfilled. Keep in mind I will discuss his timetable and not his life story. His time line on earth begins with the book of Daniel and ends in the four gospels.

The Prophecy

> **Daniel 9**: 24 Seventy weeks are determined upon thy people and upon thy holy city, to finish the transgression, and to make an end of sins, and to make reconciliation for iniquity, and to bring in everlasting righteousness, and to seal up the vision and prophecy, and to anoint the most Holy. *(Jeremiah 29: 10-14)*

25 Know therefore and understand, that from the going forth of the commandment to restore and to build Jerusalem unto the Messiah the Prince shall be seven weeks, and threescore and two weeks: the street shall be built again, and the wall, even in troublous times. (Nehemiah Chapters 1 – 6:1-15)

The Messiah's Time Line Formula

- 7 x 69 = 483 years (-) 7 years = 476 years[499]

- March 4, 444 BC (-) 3 Months
  <u>March 29, 33 AD (-) 9 Months</u>
  477 years (-) 1 year = 476 years

26 And after threescore and two weeks shall Messiah be cut off, but not for himself: and the people of the prince that shall come shall destroy the city and the sanctuary; and the end thereof shall be with a flood, and unto the end of the war desolations are determined.

27 And he shall confirm the covenant with many for one week: and in the midst of the week he shall cause the sacrifice and the oblation to cease, and for the overspreading of abominations he shall make it desolate, even until the consummation, and that determined shall be poured upon the desolate.

From the above scripture we learn that the seventy-year removal of the Hebrews from the Canaan land was a judgment of God to usher in the Messiah; to bring order back into the world, as it was in the beginning: with Adam and Eve.

Now the time line is strange, in that it starts when the edit is given to rebuild the walls of Jerusalem during the time of great stress. And that the Messiah would have seven years, times, sixty-nine years to appear upon the earth; but he would have to leave before the deadline: minus seven years. Further, that he could not simply die, but he had to sacrifice his life for others to live. Now the prophecy time line is thus:

The Commandment to Build Jerusalem

On or about **March 4, 444 BC**, Artaxerxes, the king of Persia, signed a decree for Nehemiah to rebuild the walls and streets of Jerusalem. Nehemiah did so under constant attack from enemies of the Jews.[500] This started the, seven, times, sixty-nine-week timetable for the Messiah's appearance.

The Birth of the Messiah

The Messiah was born April 1, 5 BC in the town of Bethlehem. This birth was unique, in that it was not the product of mankind; "And the Word was made flesh, and dwelt among us, (and we beheld his glory, the glory as of the only begotten of the Father,) full of grace and truth." (John 1:14)

YEAR - 33 AD

Jesus knew exactly when his time to leave this world would end. He often talked about it to the dismay of his disciples. They didn't understand that he was talking about fulfilling the prophecy of Daniel; not the threats by the ruling Jews to kill him. Herein are some of his statements.

- "From that time forth began Jesus to shew unto his disciples, how that he must go unto Jerusalem, and suffer many things of the elders and chief priests and scribes, and be killed, and be raised again the third day. Then Peter took him, and began to rebuke him, saying, Be it far from thee, Lord: this shall not be unto thee." (Matthew 16:13-21)

- "Then he took unto him the twelve, and said unto them, Behold, we go up to Jerusalem, and all things that are written by the prophets concerning the Son of man shall be accomplished. For he shall be delivered unto the Gentiles, and shall be mocked, and spitefully entreated, and spitted on: and they shall scourge him, and put him to death: and the third day he shall rise again. And they understood none of these things: and this saying was hid from them, neither knew they the things which were spoken." (Luke 18:31-34)

Six Days Before the Passover

On March 28, 33 AD Jesus was in the home of Lazarus, in the town of Bethany. "Then took Mary a pound of ointment of spikenard, very costly, and anointed the feet of Jesus, and wiped his feet with her hair: and the house was filled with the odour of the ointment."

- "But Judas Iscariot, one of the twelve disciples said, "Why was not this ointment sold for three hundred pence, and given to the poor? This he said, not that he cared for the poor; but because he was a thief, and had the bag, and bare what was put therein."

Note: Judas thought anointing Jesus was a waste of time because he was an unbeliever hiding among the believers. Jesus pointed out his disbelief in John 6: 60-71.

- "Then said Jesus, Let her alone: against the day of my burying hath she kept this. For the poor always ye have with you; but me ye have not always."

Note: This is the first time that Christ openly rebukes Judas.

- "Much people of the Jews therefore knew that he was there: and they came not for Jesus' sake only, but that they might see Lazarus also, whom he had raised from the dead."

- "But the chief priests consulted that they might put Lazarus also to death; because that by reason of him many of the Jews went away, and believed on Jesus." (John 12: 1-11)

Five Days Before the Passover

On March 29, 33 AD Christ made a "Triumphal Entry," into Jerusalem; riding on a donkey. The people began to praise him and "took branches of palm trees, and went forth to meet him, and cried, Hosanna: Blessed is the King of Israel that cometh in the name of the Lord." (John 12:12-22)

Two Days Before the Passover

On April 2, 33 AD, Christ was again in Bethany, in the home of Simon the leper. (Matthew 26:6-16)

- "Then "there came unto him a woman having an alabaster box of very precious ointment, and poured it on his head, as he sat at meat."

- " But when his disciples saw it, they had indignation, saying, To what purpose is this waste? For this ointment might have been sold for much, and given to the poor."

- "When Jesus understood it, he said unto them, Why trouble ye the woman? for she hath wrought a good work upon me. For ye have the poor always with you; but me ye have not always. For in that she hath poured this ointment on my body, she did it for my burial. Verily I say unto you, Wheresoever this gospel shall be preached in the whole world, there shall also this, that this woman hath done, be told for a memorial of her."

Note: This is the second time that Christ openly rebukes Judas.

Judas is Determined to Betray Christ

- "Then one of the twelve, called Judas Iscariot, went unto the chief priests, and said unto them, What will ye give me, and I will deliver him unto you? And they covenanted with him for thirty pieces of silver. And from that time he sought opportunity to betray him."

After being rebuked by Christ twice, Judas sought to get even by betraying him to the Pharisees, and collecting the bounty money. He already showed his love of money when he was known to have taken proceeds from the money bag of the disciples.

Now no one likes to be singled out and rebuked in public, but it is a necessary principle of the bible teachings. The power of rebuke is to harshly tell someone they are wrong. Therefore, here are some scriptures that bear out the reason for rebuke:

- Proverbs 27:5. Open rebuke is better than secret love. (***Don't hide your true feeling.***)
  6. Faithful are the wounds of a friend; but the kisses of an enemy are deceitful.

- Proverbs 9: 8. Reprove not a scorner, lest he hate thee: rebuke a wise man, and he will love thee.
  9. Give instruction to a wise man, and he will be yet wiser: teach a just man, and he will increase in learning.

- Proverbs 13: 1. A Wise son heareth his father's instruction: but a scorner heareth not rebuke.

- Luke 17: 3. Take heed to yourselves: If thy brother trespass against thee, **rebuke him**; and if he repent, forgive him.
  4. And if he trespass against thee seven times in a day, and seven times in a day turn again to thee, saying, I repent; **thou shalt forgive him**.

- I Timothy 5:20 Them that sin rebuke before all, that others also may fear.

  - *Galatians 2: 11 But when Peter was come to Antioch, I withstood him to the face, because he was to be blamed. 12 For before that certain came from James, he did eat with the Gentiles: but when they were come, he withdrew and separated himself, fearing them which were of the circumcision.*
    13 And the other Jews dissembled likewise with him; insomuch that Barnabas also was carried away with their dissimulation.
    14 But when I saw that they walked not uprightly according to the truth of the gospel, I said unto Peter before them all, If thou, being a Jew, livest after the manner of Gentiles, and not as do the Jews, why compellest thou the Gentiles to live as do the Jews?

- 2 Timothy 4:1. I charge thee therefore before God, and the Lord Jesus Christ, who shall judge the quick and the dead at his appearing and his kingdom;
  2. **Preach the word**; be instant in season, out of season; **reprove,** *rebuke,* **exhort with all longsuffering and doctrine.**
  3. For the time will come when they will not endure sound doctrine; but after their own lusts shall they heap to themselves teachers, having itching ears;
  4. And they shall turn away their ears from the truth, *and shall be turned unto fables.*

o Revelation 3:19 As many as I love, I rebuke and chasten: be zealous therefore, and repent.

The Death of Christ

Christ died on April 4, 33 AD - the evening of the Passover. This would put his age around thirty-eight years old. However, the Jews thought he was older when they said, "thou art not fifty years old, and hast thou seen Abraham?"[501]

The overall mission of the Messiah cannot be overlooked when comparing the life of Jesus with stated prophecy.

- "And in that day there shall be a root of Jesse, which shall stand for an ensign of the people; to it shall the Gentiles seek: and his rest shall be glorious." (Isaiah 11:10)

- "Behold my servant, whom I uphold; mine elect, in whom my soul delighteth; I have put my spirit upon him: he shall bring forth judgment to the Gentiles." (Isaiah 42:1)

- "I the Lord have called thee in righteousness, and will hold thine hand, and will keep thee, and give thee for a covenant of the people, for a light of the Gentiles." (Isaiah 42:6)

- "And he said, It is a light thing that thou shouldest be my servant to raise up the tribes of Jacob, and to restore the preserved of Israel: I will also give thee for a light to the Gentiles, that thou mayest be my salvation unto the end of the earth." (Isaiah 49:6)

CHAPTER 24

JESUS CHRIST IS OUR PASSOVER

One of the most controversial issues in the bible is the death, burial, and resurrection of the Lord Jesus Christ. At the root of the controversy are/is dates, times, and place of his demise and resurrection. Number one is the date he died. Number two is the place of his crucifixion. Number three is the place of his tomb. Number four is day of his resurrection. These are questions that cannot be answered; even with scrutinized study.

The first question surrounds the date of his crucifixion; the bible recorded that it was during the "Passover Holiday." But did not specify the date: however, the time and place are mentioned.

Now the first month of the Jewish calendar is Nisan, which is centered around the Passover (conducted on the fourteenth day of the month and ending on the twenty-first day of the month), and is based upon full moon to full moon. This is the month specified by God to Moses when he delivered them out of the land of Egypt. The time straddles the months of March and April, and has 29 or 30 days. Because of the moon as a measuring stick the Jewish calendar had only 354 days to a year;[502] which causes the Passover holiday to fluctuate between March and April: and never the same time each year, for example:

2014 – April 14 to April 22.
2015 – April 3 to April 11.
2016 – April 22 to April 30.
2017 – April 10 to April 18.
2018 – March 30 to April 7.
2019 – April 19 to April 27.

Secondly, the date, and time of his death, burial and resurrection is debated into contention because of what is recorded in the bible; which can be confusing due to the difference in the Jewish and Julian calendar.

The Jewish calendar counted a day as it is recorded in the Book of Genesis, "God called the light Day, and the darkness he called Night. And the evening and the morning were the first day." So, then the day started at 6 PM (Night), and ended at 6 AM in the morning: the rest of the day is finished up in the light (Day) which ends at 6 PM.

The Julian Calendar was "introduced by Julius Caesar in 46 B.C: it was eventually replaced by the Gregorian calendar:"[503] "the calendar in use throughout most of the world, introduced by Pope Gregory XIII in 1582."[504] (The American Heritage Dictionary, Gregorian Calendar)

The early Europeans and Egyptians said that a day started at midnight. They also divided the day into two 12-hour segments—from midnight to noon and from noon to midnight.

The Romans also had a two-part day, but they said that the first part began at sunrise and the second part at sunset.[505]

Therefore, if an event happened at ten o'clock on a Friday night, we would count it as true time. However, the Jewish calendar would count the event happening on Saturday (the sabbath day), simply because Friday ended at 6 P.M., and Saturday started at 6:01 P.M. A little confusing but you can see how difficult it is to nail down a bible date and time.

Thirdly, the place of crucifixion was called Golgotha (a place of a skull), and Calvary. This was an area outside of Jerusalem city: but its whereabouts are still unknown.

"Golgotha is the place near Jerusalem where Jesus and two thieves were crucified. Three of the Gospels use the name Golgotha, which is a Hebrew and Aramaic term meaning "skull" (Matthew 27:33; Mark 15:22; John 19:17), while Luke uses the Latin word "Calvary," which means the same thing (Luke 23:33).

The reason why this place was called "the skull" is unknown, although there are several guesses. According to the church father Jerome (AD 346-420), Golgotha was a common place for executions, and that the skulls of many who had been executed were lying around the site. But there is no evidence to back up this viewpoint. Some others have suggested that it was a place of execution and that "skull" was a figure of speech, a symbol of death. Early church theologian Origen (AD 185-253) mentioned an early, pre-Christian legend that the skull of Adam was buried in that place. Others have said that the place of the Crucifixion was a hill shaped like a skull, but again, there is no ancient evidence for this, and the New Testament does not directly describe the place as a hill.

No one is sure, either, where exactly Golgotha was. The biblical references give us only a general idea. It was outside the city (John 19:20; Hebrews 13:12), may have been on a hill or plateau since it could be seen from a distance (Mark 15:40), and was perhaps near a road since "passersby" are mentioned (Matthew 27:39; Mark 15:29). John describes it as being near a garden that contained the tomb in which Jesus was buried (John 19:41). The use of "the"-"the place of the skull"-indicates that it was a well-known place.

There seems to have been little interest in the site of Golgotha until the early part of the fourth century. Church historian Eusebius, who lived in Jerusalem for several years, said that the Roman Emperor Constantine instructed one of his bishops to find the place where Jesus was crucified and buried. Later legends said that the bishop was guided to the site by a ghostlike figure of the Queen Mother Helena. The site that he settled on contained a temple of Aphrodite, which the Emperor destroyed. There, according to legends, he found fragments of the cross of Christ. He built two churches, and this is the site of the Church of the Holy Sepulcher, which still stands today, although it has been destroyed and rebuilt several times.

In 1842 a scholar named Otto Thenius suggested that Golgotha was a rocky hill about 250 yards (228.5 meters) northeast of the Damascus Gate. The place Thenius mentioned had once been a Jewish place for stoning criminals, was outside of the city wall, and was shaped like a skull. Later General Charles Gordon also suggested this same spot, and it has come to be known as "Gordon's Calvary."[506]

Lastly, the day of his resurrection is not easily deciphered, but is problematic when you try to fit what is written into what you logically think is right. However, for this problem you have to study the scriptures and come outside the box, and into the Jewish calendar mathematics.

- Matthew 12: 38 Then certain of the scribes and of the Pharisees answered, saying, Master, we would see a sign from thee.
- 39 But he answered and said unto them, An evil and adulterous generation seeketh after a sign; and there shall no sign be given to it, but the sign of the prophet Jonas:
  40 for as Jonas was three days and three nights in the whale's belly; so shall the Son of man be three days and three nights in the heart of the earth.

Who is Jesus Christ

- Matthew 17: 22 After they gathered again in Galilee, Jesus told them, "The Son of Man is going to be betrayed into the hands of his enemies.
  23 He will be killed, but on the third day he will be raised from the dead." And the disciples were filled with grief.

- John 2: 18 Then answered the Jews and said unto him, What sign shewest thou unto us, seeing that thou doest these things?

- 19 Jesus answered and said unto them, Destroy this temple, and in three days I will raise it up.

- Hosea 6:2 After two days will he revive us: in the third day he will raise us up, and we shall live in his sight.

- 1 Corinthians 15:3 For I delivered unto you first of all that which I also received, how that Christ died for our sins according to the scriptures;
  4 and that he was buried, and that he rose again the third day according to the scriptures:

- Ephesians 4:7 But unto every one of us is given grace according to the measure of the gift of Christ.
  8 Wherefore he saith, When he ascended up on high, he led captivity captive, and gave gifts unto men.
  9 (Now that he ascended, what is it but that he also descended first into the lower parts of the earth?
  10 He that descended is the same also that ascended up far above all heavens, that he might fill all things.)

When you take in to account the above scriptures, you see that the third day is the most important factor. However, how you arrive at the third day conclusion is another problem within itself.

It is believed by the Christian world that Jesus rose from the grave on a Sunday morning (the first day of the week). Taking into account that Jesus died in the evening (during the ninth hour), and using the Jewish calendar to back track from the morning of the first day, you come up with the following formula to get three days and three nights:

DATE	NIGHT	DAY
Preparation	Tuesday 3 pm – 6 pm	
Passover	**Tue / Wed 6:01 pm – 6: am**	**Wed 6:01 A.M - 6 P.M. [Death & Burial]**
Day 15	Wed /Thur. 6:01 P.M – 6 A.M.	Thur. 6:01 A.M. – 6 P.M. 1st day
Day 16	Thur./Fri. 6:01 P.M. – 6 A.M.	Fri. 6:01 A.M. – 6 P.M. 2nd day
Day 17	Fri. / Sat. 6:01 P.M. – 6 A.M.	Sat. 6:01 A.M. – 6 P.M. 3rd day
Day 18	Sat / Sun 6:01 P.M. – 6 A.M.	Sun 6:01 AM [Empty tomb]

April 4, 33 AD

April 4, AD 33 is recorded as the Jewish Passover date compiled from US Navy astronomical data.[507] Now going into the next chapter, I want to address the Jewish Passover and the importance of Christ being our Passover. So, don't lose patience because of all the Scripture data. Keep in mind the Scripture is presented to convince you to believe in <u>the Word of God</u>.

The Passover is a feast God set in stone concerning the children of Israel, when he delivered them out of bondage in Egypt. This event is called the Passover because the dark death cloud physically passed over them, and they were saved by the blood of the sacrificial lamb. This same death cloud is hovering over the earth now, and those under the cloud can only be saved by believing in the blood of the Lamb (the Lord Jesus Christ), which was spilled on a cross outside the holy city of Jerusalem.

In Moses' day, the blood of the Passover lamb was put on the outside doorpost (top and two sides) of every believer's home. And when God saw the blood, he directed the death angel to pass over them. Christ identified himself as being the new Passover door: "I am the door: by me if any man enter in, he shall be saved, and shall go in and out, and find pasture." (John 10:9)

I'm going to stretch a little here, but when Jesus died on the cross, his blood covered the doorway to the kingdom of God—his head, his outstretched hands, and his feet. If you are inside this door, God will see the blood and pass death over you. But if you are outside the door, death will take you into eternal damnation.

Jesus said, "I am the way, the truth, and the life; no man cometh unto the Father, but by me" (John 14:6). This means everyone in heaven, on earth, and under the earth must meet the approval of Christ to enter into the kingdom of God, or to be judged, and thrown in the dark pit of hell. This is proven by two Scriptures.

- "And Jesus came and spake unto them, saying, All power is given unto me in heaven and in earth. Go ye therefore, and teach all nations, baptizing them in the name of the Father, and of the Son, and of the Holy Ghost: Teaching them to observe all things whatsoever I have commanded you: and, lo, I am with you always, even unto the end of the world. Amen." (Matthew 28:18–20)

- "And when I saw him, I fell at his feet as dead. And he laid his right hand upon me, saying unto me, Fear not; I am the first and the last: I am he that liveth, and was dead; and, behold, I am alive for evermore, Amen; and have the keys of hell and of death." (Revelation 1:17–18)

Therefore, the Passover and the cross cannot be taken lightly. They must be understood to gain eternal life; instead of eternal damnation.

Trying to explain how the Passover and Christ are intertwined is very difficult within its subject matter. Mainly because of the language sentence structure that is used throughout the Holy Bible. I find the easiest way to understand it is to read the Scripture, and then meditate on what is written; drawing on what is the thought of the writing? Therefore, bear with me as I try to unravel the law. (The complete law is presented at these notes).[508]

The First Passover

The beginning of the Jewish year starts in the month of Nisan (also called Abib), on the new moon, around March / April: because it canonized the period when the death angel of God passed over the land of Egypt. Every year, the Lord's Passover is to be memorialized and celebrated by the Jewish nation. [509]

On the tenth day of the month, every household will choose a male lamb (sheep or goat without blemish) from among the herd for the Passover sacrifice.

The elders are to kill the Passover lamb in the evening of the fourteenth day, and drain its blood for swabbing on the upper and side doorpost of the house. The lamb is to be roasted whole: with head, legs, and organs intact. None of the lamb can be eaten raw, nor can it be soaked in water, nor any of its bones broken, or any of its inner parts removed. The flesh of the lamb is to be eaten with unleavened bread and bitter herbs. All remains will be burned by fire in the morning hours.

The fifteenth day starts the Feast of Unleavened Bread. It will last seven days, until the twenty-first day of the month. The first and last days of this feast will be a "holy convocation: ye shall do no servile work therein." These two days will be observed like the seventh-day Sabbath, and is referenced by John as a "High Sabbath."[510]

Jewish Calendar

To grasp the Passover Holiday time structure, you must come to grips with the Hebrew calendar. This is not an easy task, and can be confusing at times, but given time and study you will began to see the light.

Jewish Months

- "Jewish months begin with the "new moon." That's the night in the lunar cycle when the moon is not visible in the sky. Since the new moon occurs about every 29.5 days, the Jewish year lasts 354 days. We don't know how the early Jews adjusted their calendar to make up for the missing eleven days. Later in history, though, the Jews would add an extra month (called Veadar, "second Adar") seven times in a nineteen-year period so that their months would keep pace with the years."[511]

  - "Passover and the Feast of Unleavened Bread. Passover occurs on the 14th of Nisan, and the Feast of Unleavened Bread occurs throughout the week immediately following. The purpose of these combined festivals is to remember the deliverance of the ancient Hebrews from Egypt (Exodus 12:15)."

  - "Pentecost (Feast of Weeks). This festival occurs fifty days after Passover. It is a time of joy that originally marked the harvest of the wheat crop in Israel (Leviticus 23:15-17)."[512]

- "Hebrew months were alternately 30 and 29 days long. Their year, shorter than ours, had 354 days. Therefore, about every three years (7 times in 19 years) an extra 29-day month, VEADAR, was added."[513]

- "During the 400-year period between the ending of the Old Testament and the beginning of the New Testament, some leaders tried to get Israel to change its calendar. This new calendar had twelve months of thirty days each. The last month of the year, though, had an extra five days added (for a total of 365). This calendar was more accurate than the one in use by the Jews. But the Jews did not end up accepting it."[514]

Jewish Days

Trying to fix a Jewish day to an event is grueling, but to understand Christ and the Passover is to fix our minds on the Jewish time structure. Everything that's needed to solve the mystery of Christ and the Passover Festival is recorded in the four gospels. However, without intense study you will miss the most important fact: that the time of day is founded on the first day of creation, "And the evening and the morning were the first day."

This means that a full day starts during the hours of darkness (6 pm-6 am), and ends during the hours of darkness (6 am -6 pm). The first half is called Night, and the second half is called Day.

The Jews called the nighttime "the Watch," and the daylight they counted in "hours." This way of counting days is clearly seen in the chat below:[515]

TIME CHART			
NIGHT		**DAY**	
First Watch	6 p.m. - 9 p.m.	First Hour	6 a.m. - 9 a.m.
Second Watch	9 p.m. - midnight	Third Hour	9 a.m. - noon
Third Watch	midnight - 3 a.m.	Sixth Hour	noon - 3 p.m.
Fourth Watch	3 a.m. - 6 a.m. (sunrise)	Ninth Hour	3 p.m. - 6 p.m. (sunset)

"Purge out therefore the old leaven, that ye may be a new lump, as ye are unleavened. For even Christ our Passover is sacrificed for us:" (1 Corinthians 5:7)

Jesus Celebrates the Passover

The 13th Day of the Month Nisan - It is Tuesday evening, April 3, 33 A.D, during the ninth hour (3 p.m. to 6 p.m.), and the disciples came to Jesus, and asked where he desired to eat the Passover meal. Jesus told them to go into the city of Jerusalem, and they would see a man, and they will say unto him, "The Master saith, My time is at hand; I will keep the Passover at thy house with my disciples" (Matthew 26:17–19).

The 14th Day of the Month Nisan – By the Roman calendar it is still Tuesday, but by the Jewish calendar it is the start of the Passover: Wednesday April 4, 33 A.D. This whole day will be consumed with the events leading up to the death of Christ hanging on a cross.

The First Watch (6 p.m. to 9p.m.)

When the Passover meal was ready, they all sat down and began to eat. Christ interrupted the meal, saying, "Verily I say unto you, that one of you shall betray me." This caused confusion among the disciples, "And they were exceeding sorrowful, and began every one of them to say unto him, Lord, is it I?" At this moment Judas should have confessed his sin, but he hid behind the disciples' disbelief, and his pride. After a pause, Christ said, "He that dippeth his hand with me in the dish, the same shall betray me." After another pause and then silence, Judas spoke up and said, "Master, is it I?" Jesus looking him straight in the eye said, "Thou hast said." The disciples still had no hint it was Judas who was going to betray the Lord Jesus Christ (Matthew 26:20–25).

Then Jesus pronounced a judgment toward the one who would betray him: "The Son of man indeed goeth, as it is written of him: but woe to that man by whom the Son of man is betrayed! good were it for that man if he had never been born" (Mark 14:21).

"And as they were eating, Jesus took bread, and blessed it, and brake it, and gave it to the disciples, and said, Take, eat; this is my body. And he took the cup, and gave thanks, and gave it to them, saying, Drink ye all of it; For this is my blood of the new testament, which is shed for many for the remission of sins." (Matthew 26:26–28)

When Judas partook of the bread and the wine, he doomed himself to everlasting damnation. I say this because Jesus had identified him as an unbeliever when he explained that he was the living bread that came down from heaven. (John 6:66-71) And that,

"Except ye eat the flesh of the Son of man, and drink his blood, ye have no life in you." He went on to explain three important things about communion (John 6:48-58).

- "Whoso eateth my flesh, and drinketh my blood, hath eternal life; and I will raise him up at the last day."
- "For my flesh is meat indeed, and my blood is drink indeed."
- "He that eateth my flesh, and drinketh my blood, dwelleth in me, and I in him."

In his epistle to the Corinthian church, the apostle Paul gave them a stern warning about the Lord's Supper. And I say to every believer and unbeliever, take heed to what the apostle has written:

> "Wherefore whosoever shall eat this bread, and drink this cup of the Lord, unworthily, shall be guilty of the body and blood of the Lord. But let a man examine himself, and so let him eat of that bread, and drink of that cup. For he that eateth and drinketh unworthily, eateth and drinketh damnation to himself, not discerning the Lord's body." (1 Corinthians 11:27–29)

Upon finishing the Passover meal, Jesus announced that he was going to wash the feet of his disciples. Putting a towel around his waist and filling a basin with water, he began to wash and dry the disciples' feet, including those of Judas, his betrayer. When it became Simon Peter's turn for foot washing, a conversation broke out between him and Jesus. (John 13:1–11).

> *Peter:* "Lord, dost thou wash my feet?"
> *Jesus:* "What I do thou knowest not now; but thou shalt know hereafter."
> *Peter:* "Thou shalt never wash my feet."
> *Jesus:* "If I wash thee not, thou hast no part with me."

Peter: "Lord, not my feet only, but also my hands and my head."

Jesus: "He that is washed needeth not save to wash his feet, but is clean every whit: and ye are clean, but not all. For he knew who should betray him; therefore said he, Ye are not all clean"

After Jesus washed the disciples' feet, they all sat down again around the Passover meal table. Jesus began to tell them why he washed their feet and expected the same humility to be shown among them.

Again he interrupted the table, saying, "Verily, verily, I say unto you, that one of you shall betray me." Once again the disciples looked around the table and began to doubt any of them would betray Christ. Peter tried to encourage John to subtlety wrangle the knowledge out of Jesus. John, leaning on his shoulder, asked, "Lord, who is it?" Jesus answered, "He it is, to whom I shall give a sop, when I have dipped it. And when he had dipped the sop, he gave it to Judas Iscariot, the son of Simon" (John 13:12–26).

And after the sop Satan entered into Judas. "Then said Jesus unto him, That thou doest, do quickly. Now no man at the table knew for what intent he spake this unto him. For some of them thought, because Judas had the bag, that Jesus had said unto him, Buy those things that we have need of against the feast; or, that he should give something to the poor. He then having received the sop went immediately out: and it was night." (John 13:27–30)

After Judas left, Jesus began to praise God. He said to his disciples, "Now is the Son of man glorified, and God is glorified in him." He was really jubilant about his ticket, for the trip back to heaven, had been stamped by the actions of Judas Iscariot. Jesus then told them they couldn't come with him right then, but their ticket was assured if they kept his new commandant, and the fact that he would be them through the Holy Ghost.

- A new commandment I give unto you, That ye love one another; as I have loved you, that ye also love one another. By this shall all men know that ye are my disciples, if ye have love one to another. (John 13:34–35)

- Secondly, he told them about the Holy Ghost which would come after he had ascended up into the heaven. (John Chapter's 14 -16)

The Second Watch (9 p.m. to Midnight)

Jesus and the disciples finished the Passover meal by singing a hymn. Then they removed themselves and went out into the Mount of Olives. This was an olive grove located on a mountain ridge two hundred feet above the city, on the east side of Jerusalem, separated by the valley of Kidron. In the time of Josiah, king of Judah, this valley was the common cemetery of the city.[516]

"Then saith Jesus unto them, All ye shall be offended because of me this night: for it is written, I will smite the shepherd, and the sheep of the flock shall be scattered abroad. But after I am risen again, I will go before you into Galilee."

Stepping forward, Peter bravely stated that even though the others would take flight in the time of danger, he would stay by Christ to the death. Looking Peter in the eye, Jesus told him he would deny him three times before the cock crowed announcing the beginning of morning. Again, Peter stepped up and said, "Though I should die with thee, yet will I not deny thee." This statement by Peter caused all the disciples to announce their commitment to Jesus (Matthew 26:30–35).

Then Jesus and the disciples went to a place called Gethsemane, an olive yard at the foot of the Mount of Olives, where they pressed the oil from the olive. With Peter, John, and James in tow, Christ went to pray. In great sorrow and grief, he departed from them and went off alone to pray for relief from the cross. Three times he prayed with such concentration that his sweat was like great drops of blood when it fell to the ground. During this prayer, God dispatched an angel to comfort him. Finally, Jesus accepted his plight and said, "O my Father, if this cup may not pass away from me, except I drink it, thy will be done." Approaching the disciples, Jesus said, "Sleep on now, and take your rest: behold the hour is at hand, and the Son of man is betrayed into the hand of sinners" (Matthew 26:36–46; Luke 22:39–46).

> "Gethsemane was one of the last places Jesus walked. He and his disciples walked there after their Last Supper together in the upper room. In Gethsemane, Jesus underwent a great inner struggle. He realized the hour of his betrayal was at hand (Matthew 26:36; Mark 14:32-50; Luke 22:39-53).
>
> The name Gethsemane is used only in Matthew 26:36 and Mark 14:32. It means "oil press," suggesting the presence of an olive grove. The use of the word "place" in the Gospel accounts indicates that Gethsemane was an enclosed piece of ground. It may be that the grove was privately owned and that Jesus and his disciples had special permission to enter.
>
> The Gospels of Luke and John do not mention the word Gethsemane. However, they both record Jesus' agony before his betrayal. Luke says the location was on the "Mount of Olives" (Luke 22:39). John describes the area as "across the Kidron Valley" (John 18:1); John's is the only Gospel to call the spot a garden. It is also evident that Jesus and his disciples gathered in Gethsemane often for fellowship and prayer (Luke 22:39; John 18:2). The Gospel narratives indicate that the garden was large enough for the group to separate into different parts of it."[517]

The Third Watch (Midnight to 3 a.m.)

Jesus said this because he knew Judas was on the way to betray him. Arriving with a mob consisting of chief priests, captains of the temple, and elders carrying swords and staves (sticks), Judas told them he would identify Christ with a kiss.

- *Judas:* "Hail, master; and kissed him."
- *Jesus:* "Judas, betrayest thou the Son of man with a kiss?"

Judas committed the ultimate sin by greeting Jesus as a friend with malice in his heart. When they grabbed Jesus to take him away, Peter drew his sword and cut off the ear of one of the aggressors. Jesus than calmed the whole crowd, and healed the man's ear. In the ensuing shoving match the disciples ran for their lives. One young follower broke out of his robe and "fled from them naked."[518]

The Fourth Watch (3 a.m. to Sunrise)

Then Jesus was brought before the high priest Caiaphas, and the Sanhedrin council. Many witnesses were called forth, but their stories against Jesus could not be collaborated. Finally, two witnesses testified, "This fellow said, I am able to destroy the temple of God, and to build it in three days." They were talking about the time Jesus cleansed the temple of money changers, and the Jews were upset about his actions:

- *The Jews:* "Then answered the Jews and said unto him, What sign shewest thou unto us, seeing that thou doest these things?"
- *Christ:* "Jesus answered and said unto them, Destroy this temple, and in three days I will raise it up."
- *The Jews:* "Then said the Jews, Forty and six years was this temple in building, and wilt thou rear it up in three days?"
- *Narrator:* "But he spake of the temple of his body. When therefore he was risen from the dead, his disciples remembered that he had said this unto them; and they believed the scripture, and the word which Jesus had said" (John 2:13–25).

Now it is apparent that the two witnesses lied. But that didn't matter, because the Sanhedrin council was hell-bent on committing Jesus to death. Therefore, Caiaphas tore off his robe and accused Jesus of blasphemy. He got the other members to agree that Jesus was guilty of death. Then they took turns spitting in his face, and bludgeoning him with their fists (Matthew 26:57–68).

Meanwhile, Peter, standing outside the judgment hall, was asked three times if he was a follower of Jesus. Two of the times Peter's answer was softly given. But the third time, his voice rose with a resounding shout, "I know not the man." The cock crowed immediately on his last word. Peter looked around and saw Jesus was looking him in the eye. Then Peter remembered the prophecy of Jesus and began to weep bitterly (Luke 22:54–62).

The First Hour (Sunrise to 9 a.m.)

Then they bound Jesus and delivered him to the Pontius Pilate: the Roman governor.

Overtaken by guilt, Judas returned the thirty pieces of silver to the high priests and then hanged himself.

During his questioning of Jesus, Pilate came to the conclusion that he was innocent, and should be set free. Pilate told the Jews the famous bandit Barabbas was his prisoner, and they had to choose between him and Jesus who would be freed.

While they were debating their answer, Pilate's wife said to him, "Have thou nothing to do with that just man: for I have suffered many things this day in a dream because of him?"

Working the crowd, the chief priests and elders persuaded the people to ask that only Barabbas be freed. Pilate then wanted to know, "What shall I do then with Jesus which is called Christ?" Inflamed with hatred, they cried out, "Let him be crucified." Pilate tried to convince them he found no evil cause in Christ. But they screamed even the more, "Let him be crucified."

Standing before them, Pilate took a bowl and began to wash his hands, saying, "I am innocent of the blood of this just person: see ye to it." Determined that Jesus be crucified, the crowd cried out to Pilate, "His blood be on us, and on our children" (Matthew 27:1–25).

The Third Hour (9 a.m. to Noon)

Pilate released Barabbas and had Jesus scourged before being taken to be crucified.

"Then the soldiers of the governor took Jesus into the common hall, and gathered unto him the whole band of soldiers. And they stripped him, and put on him a scarlet robe. And when they had platted a crown of thorns, they put it upon his head, and a reed in his right hand: and they bowed the knee before him, and mocked him, saying, Hail, King of the Jews! And they spit upon him, and took the reed, and smote him on the head. And after that they had mocked him, they took the robe off from him, and put his own raiment on him, and led him away to crucify him." (Matthew 27:27–31)

When the soldiers saw how weak Jesus was, they compelled Simon of Cyrene to carry his cross to the hilltop called Golgotha, "that is to say, a place of a skull."

Once the destination was reached, they tried to give Jesus vinegar to deaden the pain of being crucified, but he refused the drink. So, the Roman soldiers nailed him to a cross, putting a sign above his head that read, "JESUS OF NAZARETH THE KING OF THE JEWS." Beneath the cross the soldiers gambled for his clothing; for his, "coat was without seam, woven from the top throughout" (John 19:23).

Then the solders crucified two thieves on either side of him; who were not nailed to their crosses. This scene is a direct correlation of the atonement ritual outlined in Leviticus 16: 1-34.

The Sixth Hour (Noon to 3 p.m.)

"Now from the sixth hour there was darkness over all the land unto the ninth hour" (Matthew 27:45). It is recognized that this darkness was God coming to visit with his only begotten Son.

Who is Jesus Christ

During this period of darkness, Jesus cried out, "Eli, Eli, lamasobachthani? That is to say, My God, My God, Why has thou forsaken me?" Some believe and teach that God turned his back on Jesus while he hung on the cross. I contend God came to inspect and make sure all the conditions had been met according to the Scriptures.

> "In my distress I called upon the Lord, and cried to my God: and he did hear my voice out of his temple, and my cry did enter into his ears. Then the earth shook and trembled; the foundations of heaven moved and shook, because he was wroth. There went up a smoke out of his nostrils, and fire out of his mouth devoured: coals were kindled by it. He bowed the heavens also, and came down; and <u>darkness was under his feet</u>. And he rode upon a cherub, and did fly: and he was seen upon the wings of the wind. And he made darkness pavilions round about him, dark waters, and thick clouds of the skies. Through the brightness before him were coals of fire kindled. The Lord thundered from heaven, and the most High uttered his voice." (2 Samuel 22:714)

The Ninth Hour (3 p.m. to Sunset)

Keep in mind this is the evening of the fourteenth day of the month Nisan, (which started in the evening [6 p.m.], after the thirteenth day ended), whereby the Lamb of God (Christ) must submit to death, by crucifixion on a cross, for the atonement of the world; this also allows us to pass from death into life eternal. When Jesus died, God showed his approval by allowing certain events to happen.

(1) "And, behold, the veil of the temple was rent in twain from the top to the bottom;"
(2) "and the earth did quake, and the rocks rent;"
(3) "And the graves were opened;"

(4) "and many bodies of the saints which slept arose," (Daniel 12:2-3)

(5) "And came out of the graves after his resurrection, (Ephesians 4:7-10 / Luke 16:19-31)

(6) "and went into the holy city, and appeared unto many" (Matthew 27:51–53).

So, we see the death of Jesus caused a resurrection of the Old Testament saints. Consequently, his return will trigger a resurrection of his followers of the last days.

Prior to the ending of the ninth hour, Jesus' body was taken down from the cross and buried by Joseph of Arimathaea, and the Pharisee Nicodemus (John 19:38–42).

- John 19:30 When Jesus therefore had received the vinegar, he said, It is finished: and he bowed his head, and gave up the ghost.
- 31 The Jews therefore, because it was the preparation, that the bodies should not remain upon the cross on the sabbath day, (for that sabbath day was an high day,)
- "And when Joseph had taken the body, he wrapped it in a clean linen cloth, And laid it in his own new tomb, which he had hewn out in the rock: and he rolled a great stone to the door of the sepulchre, and departed." (Matthew 27:58–59)

First Day of the Resurrection

15th Day of the Month Nisan - By the Jewish calendar the Passover feast of the Lamb has just ended (Wednesday 6 pm), and Thursday has just begun (6:01 pm). Yet, for all practical purposes this is Thursday April 5, 33 A.D. (6 pm to 6 pm) Night and day.

This day starts the Feast of Unleavened Bread. It is designated as a holy convocation Sabbath, likened to the regular Sabbath day (the seventh day). Jesus' body had to be taken down from the cross and buried before this day began. Keep in mind this day started when the ninth hour ended on day fourteen. Now begins the task of figuring out how to reach the mathematical formula of Jesus resurrection.

- ○ Matthew 12: 40 "for as Jonas was three days and three nights in the whale's belly; so shall the Son of man be three days and three nights in the heart of the earth."

- ○ Matthew 17: 23 "He will be killed, but on the third day he will be raised from the dead."

Now here is where some mud is thrown into the game. Remember when I talked about how God's day begin in the evening?

- ○ Genesis 1:5 "And God called the light Day, and the darkness he called Night. And the evening and the morning were the first day."

Well, if you look at what is written, it is clear that the evening and the morning encompasses a day that has both Night and Day in it.

So then, why didn't Jesus just say that he was going to spend "three days in the heart of the earth?" Which would bring the whole problem to the twenty-four-hour day clock. But the way he stated his burial and resurrection, by using the biblical twelve-hour clock, and being buried in the evening (just before 6 pm), and a new day starting just after he was buried in the tomb, stretches the mathematical problem to its extreme limits.

Therefore, I'm going to say that on this first day of Jesus burial nothing happens except Jesus going down to meet with Abraham in shoal. (Luke 16:19-31)

Second Day of The Resurrection

16th Day of the Month Nisan – This is the end of Thursday (6 pm), and the beginning of Friday April 6, 33 AD. No work of any kind could be done on a designated sabbath day, but now the

Pharisees can implement their evil plan to discredit the burial of Jesus Christ.

The chief priest and the Pharisees asked Pilate to station a Roman guard at the gravesite to ensure that Jesus disciples did not come and take the body away during the night. They remembered Jesus had said, "After three days I will rise again" (Matthew 27:62-63). "So they went, and made the sepulchre sure, sealing the stone, and setting a watch" (Matthew 27:65-66). This is all took during the First Watch (6 p.m. to 9 p.m.). during this time Jesus is still with Abraham.

Third Day of The Resurrection

17th Day of the Month Nisan – This is the end of Friday (6 pm) and the beginning of Saturday (6:01 pm) April 7, 33 A.D. This is the Sabbath day that God instituted when he gave Moses the Ten Commandments on Mount Sinai (Exodus 20:1–17).

This is the last day for Jesus to spent with Abraham in shoal. After this day hell will no longer be divided into two parts put will remain singular in nature. Why? Because of the evilness of mankind's heart.

- Genesis 8: 21 And the Lord smelled a sweet savour; and the Lord said in his heart, I will not again curse the ground any more for man's sake; <u>for the imagination of man's heart is evil from his youth</u>; neither will I again smite any more every thing living, as I have done. 22 While the earth remaineth, seedtime and harvest, and cold and heat, and summer and winter, and day and night shall not cease.

- Isaiah 5: 13 "Therefore my people are gone into captivity, because they have no knowledge: and their honourable men are famished, and their multitude dried up with thirst.

- 14 Therefore hell hath enlarged herself, and opened her mouth without measure: and their glory, and their multitude, and their pomp, and he that rejoiceth, shall descend into it."

Who is Jesus Christ

The Resurrection of Christ

18th day of the Month Nisan – This is the end of the sabbath day (Saturday 6 pm), and the beginning of the first day of the week (Sunday 6:01 pm); April 8, 33 AD.

It is during this period of darkness that Jesus rose from his death bed, and the dead saints of old also rose from their captivity, and visited family, friends, and loved ones before they ascended up into the heaven.

- Matthew 27: 50 Jesus, when he had cried again with a loud voice, yielded up the ghost. 51 And, behold, the veil of the temple was rent in twain from the top to the bottom; and the earth did quake, and the rocks rent;
  52 and the graves were opened; and many bodies of the saints which slept arose,
  53 and came out of the graves after his resurrection, and went into the holy city, and appeared unto many.

Now I want to pause right here and explain why I believe this event happened at night. First, no one has ever seen a ghost, apparition, or spirit during daylight hours; they have always been seen during the time of darkness. This is also the case for dreams, and most visions. Even mediums wait until night to conjure up a spirit.

Second, the miracle and surprise are when God lets someone from the dead visit with you. Even king Saul was surprised when the witch of Endor conjured up the prophet Samuel from shoal. (1 Samuel 28:3-19)

Thirdly, all of the above events happened during the "evening and the morning." This proves that God always does things on his time; regardless of the circumstances.

Now when the "evening and the morning" had passed, on the first day of the week, just at the beginning of sunrise, Mary Magdalene and a group of women came to the tomb of Jesus to finish embalming his body. They were greeted with an earthquake and saw an angel descend from heaven, who, "rolled back the stone from the door, and sat on it." The Roman guard was so frightened by the appearance of the angel that they all fainted. The angel gave the women the following message.

- And the angel answered and said unto the women, Fear not ye: for I know that ye seek Jesus, which was crucified. He is not here: for he is risen, as he said. Come, see the place where the Lord lay. And go quickly, and tell his disciples that he is risen from the dead; and, behold, he goeth before you into Galilee; there shall ye see him: lo, I have told you. (Matthew 28:5–7)

- "And when they looked, they saw that the stone was rolled away: for it was very great. And entering into the sepulchre, they saw a young man sitting on the right side, clothed in a long white garment; and they were affrighted. And he saith unto them, Be not affrighted: Ye seek Jesus of Nazareth, which was crucified: he is risen; he is not here: behold the place where they laid him. But go your way, <u>tell his disciples and Peter</u> that he goeth before you into Galilee: there shall ye see him, as he said unto you. (Mark 16:4-7)

Full of fear and joy, the women ran to tell Peter and the disciples the resurrection news. However, before they reached the disciples, Jesus appeared in front of them and corroborated the angel's message: "Then said Jesus unto them, Be not afraid: go tell my brethren that they go into Galilee, and there shall they see me" (Matthew 28:1–10).

When those who were guarding the tomb of Jesus came to their senses, they reported to the chief priests the events that had taken place. The chief priests immediately called a council meeting, and gave a huge sum of money to the soldiers to spread the news that Jesus disciples came and stole the body while they slept. Then they assured the soldiers they would vouch for them before Pontius Pilate, because sleeping on duty was a serious military crime. So, the soldiers took the money and did as they were told, "and this saying is commonly reported among the Jews until this day" (Matthew 28:11-15).

Sadly, the Jews will have to endure great hardships until they as a nation come to the realization that Christ Jesus is truly the promised Messiah. Yet, put before them is the witness of three of the twelve disciples (Peter, the fisherman; Matthew, the tax collector; and John, the fisherman). All three men wrote about their experience with Jesus, and his work on earth. Surely, they can be trusted with telling the truth.

> "These words spake Jesus, and lifted up his eyes to heaven, and said, Father, the hour is come; glorify thy Son, that thy Son also may glorify thee: As thou hast given him power over all flesh, that he should give eternal life to as many as thou hast given him. And this is life eternal, that they might know thee the only true God, and Jesus Christ, whom thou hast sent." (John 17:1–3)

CHAPTER 25

JESUS CHRIST IS OUR RESSURECTION

Many books, videos, movies, articles, and sermons have been presented concerning the resurrection of the dead, and their travel into heavenly places or into eternal hell. The most populous has been *A Thief in the Night* and *Left Behind*.[519]

- A Thief in the Night is a 1972 evangelical Christian film written by Jim Grant directed and produced by Donald W. Thompson, and starring Patty Dunning as Patty Myers, the main character and protagonist, along with Thom Rachford, Colleen Niday and Mike Niday in supporting roles. It is the first installment in the Thief in the Night series about the Rapture, Tribulation, and Second Coming of Christ. The film is set during the near future, focusing on Patty, a young woman who was not raptured and who struggles to decide what to do in the face of the Tribulation.

- Left Behind is a series of 16 best-selling religious novels by Tim LaHaye and Jerry B. Jenkins, dealing with Christian dispensationalist End Times: the pretribulation, premillennial, Christian eschatological interpretation of the Biblical apocalypse. The primary conflict of the series is the members of the Tribulation Force, an underground network of converts, against the NWO-esque organization "Global Community" and its leader, Nicolae Carpathia, who is also the Antichrist.

The series has been adapted into four films to date. The original series of three films are Left Behind: The Movie (2000), Left Behind II: Tribulation Force (2002), and Left Behind: World at War (2005). A reboot starring Nicolas Cage, entitled simply Left Behind, was released in 2014 through Cloud Ten Pictures.

[1] The series inspired an audio drama as well as the PC game Left Behind: Eternal Forces (2006) and its several sequels.

LaHaye and Jenkins cite the influence of Russell Doughten, an Iowa-based filmmaker who directed the Thief in the Night series, a series of four low-budget but popular feature-length films in the 1970s and 80s about the Rapture and Second Coming, starting with 1972's A Thief in the Night. [9] Indeed, the title Left Behind echoes the refrain of Thief's early Christian rock theme song by Larry Norman, "I Wish We'd All Been Ready," in which he sings, "There's no time to change your mind, the Son has come and you've been left behind."

I don't want to rewrite the book on resurrection, or even debunk what has already been accepted by worldly authorities. But what I will do is outline for you the relevant Scriptures, so you can come to your own conclusions. It is imperative to understand that Christ Jesus is the one who will resurrect every created being—spirit and human—unto eternal life to live with God in the New Jerusalem. Or be forever destroyed and tormented in the lake of fire. Keep in mind I'm presenting this based on what is written in the Holy Bible.

With assurance I say the whole doctrine of the resurrection rests on the revelation revealed during a conversation between Christ Jesus and Martha, the sister of Lazarus. Jesus wanted to strengthen Martha in the belief he was going to bring Lazarus back from the dead, even though Lazarus had been dead for four days.

> "I am the resurrection, and the life: he that believeth in me, though he were dead, yet shall he live: And whosoever liveth and believeth in me shall never die. Believest thou this?" (John 11:25–26)

When the time came, Jesus stood in front of the gravesite, and with a loud voice said, "Lazarus, come forth." When Lazarus walked out of the tomb, still in his burial wrapping, Jesus told the people to "Loose him, and let him go."

When the Pharisees were told of the miracle, they hurriedly called for a special council meeting to deal with the situation: (1) for they feared that a great number of people would now began to believe in Jesus, (2) and that the Romans would get wind of his popularity and attack the nation of Israel.

The Sanhedrin Council Membership

- *Chief Priest:* Appointed leader of the council (Matthew 20:17–19).
- *Elders:* Levite priests and Jewish rulers (Matthew 16:21).
- *Pharisees:* A Jewish sect of priest that emphasized strict interpretation and observance of the Mosaic law in both its oral and written forms (Acts 23:8).
- *Sadducees:* A Jewish sect flourishing from the second century BC through the first century AD that retained the older interpretation of the written Mosaic law against the oral tradition and denied the resurrection of the dead (Mark 12:18).
- *Scribes:* Professional copyists of manuscripts and documents, and interpreters of the Scriptures (Mark 2:6–7).

- *Herodians:* Member of a political party during biblical times consisting of Jews who were apparently partisans of the Herodian house and Pharisees opposed to Christ Jesus (Mark 3:6; Matthew 22:15–22).

Christ Is Coming on the Clouds of Glory

When the council was assembled, Caiaphas the high priest suggested that only one man needed to die to save them from the supposed Roman wrath, and that man was Jesus. They also considered killing Lazarus. They reasoned he was the main cause of people believing in Jesus. (John 11: 45-57, 12:10-11).

As plotting was in the time of Christ, so it is in these last days. It seems there is a great effort to stamp out belief in the resurrection of Jesus Christ and his return to resurrect his believers from the grave. Yet, I tell you assuredly that just as a baby was born of a virgin in Bethlehem, fulfilled the prophesied Scriptures of God, died on a cross for the sins of all humankind, was resurrected from the dead on the third day, walked on this earth forty days after his resurrection, and went up into the heaven on a cloud of glory; so shall Christ Jesus return to the earth on a cloud of glory to call the dead and the living believers up into the heaven to be with him forevermore. Again, I say to you that my belief may not carry any weight, but you cannot deny the scriptural writing.

- ***Christ ascended into heaven on a cloud of glory*** - And when he had spoken these things, while they beheld, he was taken up; and a cloud received him out of their sight. And while they looked steadfastly toward heaven as he went up, behold, two men stood by them in white apparel; Which also said, Ye men of Galilee, why stand ye gazing up into heaven? this same Jesus, which is taken up from you into heaven, shall so come in like manner as ye have seen him go into heaven. (Acts 1:9–11)

- ○ ***Christ will descend from heaven on a cloud of glory*** - Behold, he cometh with clouds; and every eye shall see him, and they also which pierced him: and all kindreds of the earth shall wail because of him. Even so, Amen. I am Alpha and Omega, the beginning and the ending, saith the Lord, which is, and which was, and which is to come, the Almighty. (Revelation 1:7–8)

Significant is the point, that all those in heaven, those on the earth, and those who are dead and buried, will see him when he returns to the earth. Therefore, it is fiction to believe Christ will return to take his "church" off the face of the earth and nobody sees him, or that people will suddenly disappear without warning.

This type of thinking is fantasy and science fiction religion based on hypothetical's, and visionary prophecy designed to illuminate those possessed with a dark intelligence. And to be truthful, it sells books and movies. But it does not stand up against the written Word of God.

Christ Jesus warned the scribes and Pharisees about having this same type of thinking when he said, "Ye make the commandment of God of none effect by your tradition. Ye hypocrites, well did Esaias prophesy of you saying, this people draweth nigh unto me with their mouth, and honoureth me with their lips; but their heart is far from me. But in vain they do worship me, teaching for doctrine the commandments of men" Matthew 15: 1-9).

God also condemned the Jews in the Old Testament for preaching and believing things that were not written in his Word, or expressed by him through the prophets:

- "That this is a rebellious people, lying children, children that will not hear the law of the Lord: Which say to the seers, See not; and to the prophets, Prophesy not unto us right things, speak unto us smooth things, prophesy deceits:" (Isaiah 30:9-10)

Who is Jesus Christ

- "And I have seen folly in the prophets of Samaria; they prophesied in Baal and caused my people to Israel to err. I have seen also in the prophets of Jerusalem and horrible thing: they commit adultery, and walk in lies: they strengthen also the hand of evil doers, that none doth return from his wickedness: they are all of them unto me as Sodom, and the habitants thereof as Gomorrah" (Jeremiah 23:1-14).

Prior to his crucifixion and resurrection, Christ Jesus talked about the signs of his return to the earth and the events that would take place.

> "For as the lightning cometh out of the east, and shineth even unto the west; so shall also the coming of the Son of man be. For wheresoever the carcase is, there will the eagles be gathered together. Immediately after the tribulation of those days shall the sun be darkened, and the moon shall not give her light, and the stars shall fall from heaven, and the powers of the heavens shall be shaken: And then shall appear the sign of the Son of man in heaven: and then shall all the tribes of the earth mourn, and they shall see the Son of man coming in the clouds of heaven with power and great glory. And he shall send his angels with a great sound of a trumpet, and they shall gather together his elect from the four winds, from one end of heaven to the other. But of that day and hour knoweth no man, no, not the angels of heaven, but my Father only." (Matthew 24:27–31, 36)

The Resurrection of the Believers

First, Christ Jesus states his second coming will be like a violent storm that appears without warning. Second, that it will be right after the tribulation period. Third, the solar system will witness his coming. Fourth, there will be total panic when people see him riding on the clouds of glory. Fifth, at the sound of the trumpet, the angels will gather all God's people in heaven and from the earth (the dead and the living). And last, he warns us that only the Father knows when the time is ripe for his return. However, He did give us a hint of a clue:

- "But as the days of Noe were, so shall also the coming of the Son of man be. For as in the days that were before the flood they were eating and drinking, marrying and giving in marriage, until the day that Noe entered into the ark, and knew not until the flood came, and took them all away; so shall also the coming of the Son of man be.(Matthew 24:37-39 / Genesis 6-7)

- "Likewise also as it was in the days of Lot; they did eat, they drank, they bought, they sold, they planted, they builded; but the same day that Lot went out of Sodom it rained fire and brimstone from heaven, and destroyed them all. Even thus shall it be in the day when the Son of man is revealed." (Luke 17:28-30 / Genesis 19:1-29 / Ezekiel 16:47-52)

The apostle Paul picks up on what Christ said in his epistles to the Corinthians, and the Thessalonians.

- "Behold, I shew you a mystery; We shall not all sleep, but we shall all be changed, In a moment, in the twinkling of an eye, at the last trump: for the trumpet shall sound, and the dead shall be raised incorruptible, and we shall be changed. For this corruptible must put on incorruption, and this mortal must put on immortality. So when this corruptible shall have put on incorruption, and this mortal shall have put on immortality, then shall be brought to pass the saying that is written, Death is swallowed up in victory. O death, where is thy sting? O grave, where is thy victory? The sting of death is sin; and the strength of sin is the law. But thanks be to God, which giveth us the victory through our Lord Jesus Christ. Therefore, my beloved brethren, be ye stedfast, unmoveable, always abounding in the work of the Lord, forasmuch as ye know that your labour is not in vain in the Lord." (1 Corinthians 15:51–58)

- "But I would not have you to be ignorant, brethren, concerning them which are asleep, that ye sorrow not, even as others which have no hope. For if we believe that Jesus died and rose again, even so them also which sleep in Jesus will God bring with him. For this we say unto you by the word of the Lord, that we which are alive and remain unto the coming of the Lord shall not prevent them which are asleep. For the Lord himself shall descend from heaven with a shout, with the voice of the archangel, and with the trump of God: and the dead in Christ shall rise first: Then we which are alive and remain shall be caught up together with them in the clouds, to meet the Lord in the air: and so shall we ever be with the Lord. Wherefore comfort one another with these words." (1 Thessalonians 4:13–18)

The apostle Paul makes it clear that the Lord Jesus Christ will descend from heaven just as he prophesied in Matthew (Chapter 24:27-31). And that the whole earth will know what is happening, because they will all see him. Paul told the Galatians that he obtained all of his new found knowledge from Christ: "For do I now persuade men, or God? or do I seek to please men? for if I yet pleased men, I should not be the servant of Christ. But I certify you, brethren, that the gospel which was preached of me is not after man. For I neither received it of man, neither was I taught it, but by the revelation of Jesus Christ." (Galatians 1: 10-12)

I plead with you to closely study the Scriptures concerning his return so that you will snap out of fictional religion stories, and believe the written Word of God. Christ is secretive, but he is open to his followers. One revelation he left us is a look into the conditions of hell. This he reveals in the book of Luke, Chapter 16.

Jesus tells the story of a rich man and poor man named Lazarus. The rich man lived a life of luxury, while Lazarus was brought to his gate begging each day. The rich man refused to provide any type of food, clothing, or money to the poor man. The only comfort Lazarus received was when the dogs licked his fleshly sores.

When Lazarus died, the angels came and took his soul to where Abraham was. Sometime later, the rich man died. When he opened his eyes, he was being tormented in hell. The heat was so unbearable that he could find no relief. Then he spotted Abraham and Lazarus on the other side of hell, and noticed they were not being tormented.

In distress, the rich man began to cry out, "Father Abraham, have mercy on me, and send Lazarus, that he may dip the tip of his finger in water, and cool my tongue; for I am tormented in this flame." Abraham gave the rich man an answer that should be heeded today: "Son, remember that thou in thy lifetime receivedst thy good things, and likewise Lazarus evil things: but now he is comforted, and thou art tormented. And beside all this, between us and you there is a great gulf fixed: so that they which would pass from hence to you cannot; neither can they pass to us, that would come from thence."

The message of God is that there is a permanent force field separating good and evil, and it cannot be broached except by God. This is why Christ Jesus is so important. He is the only one who can keep you out of hell's fire.

The rich man then requested that Abraham send Lazarus to witness to his father's house. Again, Abraham let him know what he requested was not possible, and that they had at their disposal the Law of Moses and the writings prophets. If they were not persuaded by the written word or the vocal word, why would they listen to someone who came back from the dead?

Therefore, you have to choose whether to spend eternity in heaven or hell. God expends no power to cast a soul into hell, but to go up into heaven takes the power of Christ, the Holy Ghost, and the angels.

Paul describes the place where Christ will take us as the "third heaven," He was taken there but was returned to the earth. (2 Corinthians 12:1-6) The first heaven is where the birds fly; the second heaven is where the sun, moon, and stars reside. But the third heaven is far beyond anything we can imagine.

CHAPTER 26

JESUS CHRIST THE SPIRIT OF GOD BAPTIZER

Of all the things I have discussed in this book, this subject is high on the "let's get serious list." Why? Because you cannot be a follower or believer in Christ and deny the baptism of the Holy Ghost. It is Christ Jesus who performs this rite of the dual baptism. He gives all his followers—not just those ordained by religious organizations—the authority to baptize converted souls in water. (Matthew 28:18-20). I'm going to tiptoe through the Scriptures and try my best to explain to you the importance of being baptized in the Spirit of God (the Holy Ghost) by Christ Jesus.

John the Baptist Identified Christ Jesus as the Holy Ghost Baptizer

John the Baptist was commissioned by God to prepare the people for the coming of the Lord Jesus Christ; by baptizing them in water. When people asked John why he was baptizing, he said, "I indeed baptize you with water unto repentance: but he that cometh after me is mightier than I, whose shoes I am not worthy to bear: he shall baptize you with the Holy Ghost, and with fire" (Matthew 3:11).

By and by there came a day when Jesus showed up to be baptized by John. But the spirit in John recognized Jesus, just like the spirit did when John was in his mother's womb, and he said, "I need to be baptized of thee, and comest thou to me?" Jesus comforted John saying, "Suffer it to be so now: for thus it becometh us to fulfil all righteousness" (Matthew 3:15).

And it came to pass that when John had finished baptizing all the people, "Jesus also was baptized, and praying, in so much so that when he came up out of the water the heaven was opened, and the Holy Ghost descended in a bodily shape like a dove, and lighted upon him, and a voice came from heaven, which said, Thou art my beloved Son; in thee I am well pleased."[520]

The next day, John saw Jesus coming and said, "Behold the Lamb of God, which taketh away the sin of the world." John went on to say, "This is he of whom I said, After me cometh a man which is preferred before me: for he was before me. And I knew him not: but that he should be made manifest to Israel, therefore am I come baptizing with water. And John bare record, saying, I saw the Spirit descending from heaven like a dove, and it abode upon him. And I knew him not: but he that sent me to baptize with water, the same said unto me, Upon whom thou shalt see the Spirit descending, and remaining on him, the same is he which baptizeth with the Holy Ghost. And I saw, and bare record that this is the Son of God" (John 1:29-34).

Why Did John Baptize in Water?

John the Baptist was a preacher who had no fear of confrontation. When the Pharisees and Sadducees came to witness him baptizing, he cried out against them, saying, "O generation of vipers, who hath warned you to flee from the wrath to come? Bring forth therefore fruits meet for repentance: And think not to say within yourselves, We have Abraham to our father: for I say unto you, that God is able of these stones to raise up children unto Abraham. And now also the axe is laid unto the root of the trees: therefore every tree which bringeth not forth good fruit is hewn down, and cast into the fire" (Matthew 3:7-10). He spoke out against them because of their unbelief, and because they had sent priests and Levites to question his authority to baptize. (John 1:19-27)

The Pharisee priest and the Levites questioned John whether he was the Christ, Elijah, or one of the other prophets. John stated, "I am the voice of one crying in the wilderness, make straight the way of the Lord, as said the prophet Esaias" (Isaiah 40:3). John was simply telling them he was preparing them to receive the Lord Jesus Christ and the baptism of the Holy Ghost.

The People Believe John's Witness Concerning Christ Jesus

John was a great witness for Christ. Before Christ came to him, John announced his coming. And after he baptized Christ, he turned all his effort toward getting people to follow him. Under questioning, John repeatedly defended that he was not the Christ and would give good explanation to why he wasn't: "Then there arose a question between some of John's disciples and the Jews about purifying. And they came unto John, and said unto him, Rabbi, he that was with thee beyond Jordan, to whom thou barest witness, behold, the same baptizeth, and all men come to him." (John 3:26)

On the surface it seems like Jesus is also baptizing in water. However, if he did, it would make the prophecy of John concerning him baptizing in the Holy Ghost a lie. Yet, John later recorded that the disciples of Jesus went around baptizing in water, and they gave him the credit for the baptisms. "When therefore the Lord knew how the Pharisees had heard that Jesus made and baptized more disciples than John, (Though Jesus himself baptized not, but his disciples,) He left Judaea, and departed again into Galilee." (John 4:1–3)

John the Baptist was a man of great faith and integrity, and would not let the Pharisees goad him into envy or jealousy against the Lord Jesus Christ. Then John began to make bold statements about Christ.

(1) "A man can receive nothing, except it be given him from heaven. Ye yourselves bear me witness, that I said, I am not the Christ, but that I am sent before him."
(2) "He that hath the bride is the bridegroom: but the friend of the bridegroom, which standeth and heareth him, rejoiceth greatly because of the bridegroom's voice: this my joy therefore is fulfilled."
(3) "He must increase, but I must decrease."
(4) "He that cometh from above is above all: he that is of the earth is earthly, and speaketh of the earth: he that cometh from heaven is above all."
(5) "And what he hath seen and heard, that he testifieth; and no man receiveth his testimony. He that hath received his testimony hath set to his seal that God is true."
(6) "For he whom God hath sent speaketh the words of God: for God giveth not the Spirit by measure unto him. The Father loveth the Son, and hath given all things into his hand. He that believeth on the Son hath everlasting life: and he that believeth not the Son shall not see life; but the wrath of God abideth on him." (John 3:27–36)

The second time John pointed Jesus out as the Lamb of God; his disciples left him and began to follow after Christ. Andrew was first, and then his brother Simon Peter. After this came Philip, Nathanael, and many others.

John's witness of Christ was so powerful that it caused two major things to happen: (1) "And many resorted unto him, and said, John did no miracle: but all things that John spake of this man were true, and many believed on him there" (John 10:41–42), and (2)"When Jesus therefore perceived that they would come and take him by force, to make him a king, he departed again into a mountain himself alone" (John 6:15).

If the followers of Christ would be like John the Baptist, and loose themselves from the material things of this world, they, too, could bring power and glory to the newborn king. However, the prince of this world has a way of blinding humans with the deceitfulness of riches, positions of power in high places, and sexual immorality.

John Questions Whether Jesus Is the Christ

John the Baptist spoke out against Herod the tetrarch's wicked and evil reign over the Jews, and his adultery with Herodias, the wife of his brother Philip. Herod was afraid to attack John, because he feared the people would rise up and overthrow him. But he put John in prison at the request of Herodias.

While in prison, John heard of all the wonderful things Jesus was doing. He sent two of his disciples to ask him, "Art thou he that should come, or do we look for another?"

I have personally heard many a sermon decrying the faith of John in Christ Jesus. But as I got older, and wiser in my Bible studies, I came to realize John's faith did not wane at all; he just wanted to know if what he had prophesied about Christ Jesus was correct. He had said Christ would, "baptize with the Holy Ghost and with fire." And since John didn't see this happening, he brought forth a question concerning his authority to do all the other works. I believe he did this because there were many sorcerers, magicians, and false prophets in the land.

Jesus, as is true to his nature, never mentioned the Holy Ghost baptism. He sent the following message back to John: "The blind receive their sight, and the lame walk, the lepers are cleansed, and the deaf hear, the dead are raised up, and the poor have the gospel preached to them. And blessed is he, whosoever shall not be offended in me."

Then Jesus began to outline the greatness of John and ended his characterization, saying, "For all the prophets and the law prophesied until John"; "And if ye will receive it, this is Elias (Elijah), which was for to come. He that hath ears to hear, let him hear" (Matthew 11:1–15).

Did you notice that Jesus said John was the promised prophet Elijah mentioned in the book of Malachi (4:5)? This brings to mind that the angel Gabriel said John would go before the Lord Jesus Christ in the spirit and power of Elijah. Is this true? Well when we check the record, we find that John and Elijah were both alike.

- Elijah was a hairy man who wore a piece of leather to cover his loins; he was also fiery in his speech and spoke out against Ahab and Jezebel. (2 Kings 1: 1-8)

- John was a wild-looking man who came out of the desert wearing a coat of camel's hair and piece of leather warped around his loins, his food was locusts and wild honey; he was also fiery in his speech and spoke out against the religious leaders and Herod the tetrarch. (Matthew 3:1-4)

So, from the description of both men, we see John was a clone of Elijah. Yet he was not Elijah, because Elijah was alive in a glorified body, and would meet with Jesus on a mountaintop with the prophet Moses (Matthew 17:1–5).

Close to two thousand years later, human ears have still not accepted the reality of Elijah and John the Baptist. But pray that someday they will, before it's too late.

John the Baptist Is Slain by Herod the Tetrarch

By and by, Herod had a birthday party and lusted for the daughter of Herodias to dance before him. He promised to give her whatever she wanted if she fulfilled his request. At the urging of her mother Herodias, she petitioned for the head of John the Baptist to be brought to her on a platter. Herod was so full of wicked sin that he ordered it to be brought to the girl, who took the head and gave it to her mother.[521]

Christ Explains the Holy Ghost

After the death of John, the Baptist, and prior to the day of Pentecost, Jesus began to make some bold statements about the Holy Ghost, because now prophesy of him baptizing with the Holy Ghost and with fire would be fulfilled. And take into account that Jesus taught about the Holy Ghost before he began to baptize men and women in the Holy Spirit of God. This is a good marker for all preachers of the gospel of Jesus Christ to follow. The first thing he said was you must be born again to be in the presence of God.

- "Verily, verily, I say unto thee, Except a man be born again, he cannot see the kingdom of God. Nicodemus saith unto him, How can a man be born when he is old? can he enter the second time into his mother's womb, and be born?

- "Jesus answered, Verily, verily, I say unto thee, Except a man be born of water and of the Spirit, he cannot enter into the kingdom of God."

- "That which is born of the flesh is flesh; and that which is born of the Spirit is spirit. Marvel not that I said unto thee, Ye must be born again." (John 3:1–7)

Let me pause a moment here and talk about being born again. Why? Because there seems to be a great mix-up, turbulence, and confusion concerning what is meant by "being born again of the water and of the Spirit!" It seems everyone understands that being born of water equates to "water baptism." However, "being born of the Spirit" gets jumbled around because of "the baptism of the Holy Ghost." That happened on the day of Pentecost and is still being enacted by Christ Jesus in these last and evil days. So, let's walk through the Scripture steps of being born again.

- ***Believe*** – "That if thou shalt confess with thy mouth the Lord Jesus, and shalt believe in thine heart that God hath raised him from the dead, thou shalt be saved. For with the heart man believeth unto righteousness; and with the mouth confession is made unto salvation." (Romans 10:9–10)

Confession of Christ is not the "sinner's prayer," which is induced by repeating the words of a minister. This is a confession that must come forth without coercion, for words that are not sincere from the heart are meaningless, and will cause a loss of faith in Christ. Therefore, the only way you can confess Christ is by the power of the Holy Ghost who will testify through you the name of the Lord Jesus Christ.

- *The Holy Ghost will Confess Christ* – "But when the Comforter is come, whom I will send unto you from the Father, even the Spirit of truth, which proceedeth from the Father, he shall testify of me: (John 15: 26)

- No man can say that Jesus is the Lord, but by the Holy Ghost. (1 Corinthians 12:3)

- *The Spirit of God Comes into Your Life* – "And I will pray the Father, and he shall give you another Comforter, that he may abide with you for ever; Even the Spirit of truth; whom the world cannot receive, because it seeth him not, neither knoweth him: but ye know him; (1) for he dwelleth with you, (2) and shall be in you." (John 14:16–17)

When you first confess Christ as your savior, the Holy Ghost gives you the power to overcome the forces of darkness and pronounce the name of Jesus. This is when the Holy Ghost dwells with you (takes up residence). He is always with you, but often times you will not feel his presence until you are in a church worship service.

When the Lord Jesus Christ baptizes you with the Holy Ghost, it is a permanent fixture evidenced by the speaking of tongues. Just as God gave us a rainbow sign, he has also given us the sign of tongues to confirm the baptism of his Spirit with the light (soul) of human beings. And Jesus Christ is the only one that can give this Spirit or / and take it away.

Water Baptism

- "And Jesus came and spake unto them, saying, All power is given unto me in heaven and in earth. Go ye therefore, and teach all nations, baptizing them in the name of the Father, and of the Son, and of the Holy Ghost: Teaching them to observe all things whatsoever I have commanded you: and, lo, I am with you always, even unto the end of the world. Amen." (Matthew 28:18–20)

- "He that believeth and is baptized shall be saved; but he that believeth not shall be damned." (Mark 16:16)

Now it is plain to see that every believer has the authority to baptize in water, outside of a religious organization. This baptism is essential to soul saving in that it is apart from tongue speaking. The only criteria for soul saving are believing and water baptism. Yet, there may come a time when water baptism cannot be performed; such a situation was the thief on the cross who was saved by Jesus himself.

Born Again (Water and Spirit)

- "Therefore if any man be in Christ, he is a new creature: old things are passed away; behold, all things are become new." (2 Corinthians 5:17)

- "But as many as received him, to them gave he power to become the sons of God, even to them that believe on his name." (John 1: 12)

The "Born Again" experience is when a soul confesses Jesus as savior, and is then baptized in water. With the power of the Holy

Ghost they are now able to resist the temptations of the devil. But even if a believer slip, fall, or stumble into sin, the scripture assures us that "If we confess our sins, he (Christ) is faithful and just to forgive us our sins, and to cleanse us from all unrighteousness" (1 John 1:9). However, the Holy Ghost baptism is needed for power to witness for Christ.

Spirit Baptism

- "But ye shall receive power, after that the Holy Ghost is come upon you: and ye shall be witnesses unto me both in Jerusalem, and in all Judaea, and in Samaria, and unto the uttermost part of the earth." (Acts 1:8)

Make no mistake; you need the power of the Holy Ghost to witness for Christ Jesus. And that's what the Holy Ghost baptism is all about, "witnessing."

I hope you get the understanding that the Spirit of God comes and dwells with you when you first believe in Christ Jesus, and that this is the only reason you can confess Christ as your savior. He prepares you for water baptism, and at some point, will be permanently infixed in your body through Spirit baptism by the hand of Christ Jesus. The apostle Paul said it best when he stated, "Know ye not that ye are the temple of God, and that the Spirit of God dwelleth in you?"[522] "What? Know ye not that your body is the temple of the Holy Ghost which is in you, which ye have of God, and ye are not your own?" (1 Corinthians 6:19) Christ Jesus said other things about the Holy Ghost that bear learning and attention.

- ***The Holy Ghost Is the Living Water*** – "In the last day, that great day of the feast, Jesus stood and cried, saying, If any man thirst, let him come unto me, and drink. He that believeth on me, as the scripture hath said, out of his belly shall flow rivers of living water. (But this spake he of the Spirit, which they that believe on him should receive: for the Holy Ghost was not yet given; because that Jesus was not yet glorified." (John 7:37–39)

- ○ ***The Holy Ghost Is Our Teacher*** – "But the Comforter, which is the Holy Ghost, whom the Father will send in my name, he shall teach you all things, and bring all things to your remembrance, whatsoever I have said unto you." (John 14:26)

- ○ ***The Holy Ghost Will Testify of Christ through Us*** – "But when the Comforter is come, whom I will send unto you from the Father, even the Spirit of truth, which proceedeth from the Father, he shall testify of me: And ye also shall bear witness, because ye have been with me from the beginning." (John 15:26–27)

- ○ ***Jesus Must Decrease on the Earth and the Holy Ghost Must Increase*** – "Nevertheless I tell you the truth; It is expedient for you that I go away: for if I go not away, the Comforter will not come unto you; but if I depart, I will send him unto you." (John 16:7)

- ○ ***The Holy Ghost Will Convict the Heart*** – "And when he is come, he will reprove the world of sin, and of righteousness, and of judgment: Of sin, because they believe not on me; Of righteousness, because I go to my Father, and ye see me no more; Of judgment, because the prince of this world is judged." (John 16:8–11)

- ○ ***The Holy Ghost Will Show Us the Truth of Things*** – "Howbeit when he, the Spirit of truth, is come, he will guide you into all truth: for he shall not speak of himself; but whatsoever he shall hear, that shall he speak: and he will shew you things to come. He shall glorify me: for he shall receive of mine, and shall shew it unto you. All things that the Father hath are mine: therefore said I, that he shall take of mine, and shall shew it unto you." (John 16:13–14)

- ○ ***Ask Jesus to Baptize You with the Holy Ghost*** – "And I say unto you, Ask, and it shall be given you; seek, and ye shall find; knock, and it shall be opened unto you. For every one that asketh receiveth; and he that seeketh findeth; and to him that knocketh it shall be opened. If a son shall ask bread of any of you that is a father, will he give him a stone? or if he ask a fish, will he for a fish give him a serpent? Or if he shall ask an egg, will he offer him a scorpion? If ye then, being evil, know how to give good gifts unto your children: how much more shall your heavenly Father give the Holy Spirit to them that ask him?" (Luke 11:9–13)

Jesus gave the woman at the well an open request to receive the Holy Ghost when he told her "If thou knewest the gift of God, and who it is that saith to thee, Give me to drink; thou wouldest have asked of him, and he would have given thee living water." (John 4:10)

Christ Jesus told us some wonderful things concerning the Holy Ghost, and he also warned us not to take the Holy Ghost lightly. When there was brought to him a man who was possessed with a devil, and was blind and dumb, Jesus cast out the devil and healed the man. His eyes opened and he began to speak. The people who witnessed this miracle, "were amazed, and said, Is not this the son of David?" But the Pharisees who were there began to cast doubt among the people saying, "This fellow doth not cast out devils, but by Beelzebub the prince of devils." Jesus told them Satan cannot cast out Satan, because he would be divided against himself. Therefore, he gave them a stern warning about blaspheming against the working of the Holy Ghost:

- "Wherefore I say unto you, All manner of sin and blasphemy shall be forgiven unto men: but the blasphemy against the Holy Ghost shall not be forgiven unto men. And whosoever speaketh a word against the Son of man, it shall be forgiven him: but whosoever speaketh against the Holy Ghost, it shall not be forgiven him, neither in this world, neither in the world to come." (Matthew 12:31–32)

The apostle Paul also wrote tremendously about the Holy Ghost and gave the church insight into how the Holy Ghost is leading and guiding the church in these last and evil days.

- ***Nine Gifts of the Holy Ghost Given to Church Members*** – "Now there are diversities of gifts, but the same Spirit. And there are differences of administrations, but the same Lord. And there are diversities of operations, but it is the same God which worketh all in all. But the manifestation of the Spirit is given to every man to profit withal.

  - For to one is given by the Spirit the word of wisdom;
  - to another the word of knowledge by the same Spirit;
  - To another faith by the same Spirit;
  - to another the gifts of healing by the same Spirit;
  - To another the working of miracles;
  - to another prophecy;
  - to another discerning of spirits;
  - to another divers kinds of tongues;
  - to another the interpretation of tongues:
  - But all these worketh that one and the selfsame Spirit, dividing to every man severally as he will." (1 Corinthians 12:4–11)

Did you notice that each of the nine gifts is designed for the individual believer? And that no one gift is elevated above the rest; they must all work in harmony to succeed? Also take notice that wisdom, knowledge, and faith have to do with mind. The other six gifts have to do with the physical body. So, you can have a person full of the physical attributes of the Holy Ghost, but be lacking in wisdom, faith, and knowledge. This is why Paul stressed the unity of love within the church body of Christ. For one gift cannot operate alone or in isolation.

Yet, in the modern church, there seems to be a great concentration on tongue speaking, and sensational displays of power: such as blowing on crowds, and waving of hands that seemly knocks them to the ground. Surely tongues are more visible than all the other gifts, but in reality, it is a sign of Holy Ghost presence, mainly during the worshipping of God. Paul explained this his epistle to the Corinthians.

- "Wherefore tongues are for a sign, not to them that believe, but to them that believe not: but prophesying serveth not for them that believe not, but for them which believe. If therefore the whole church be come together into one place, and all speak with tongues, and there come in those that are unlearned, or unbelievers, will they not say that ye are mad? But if all prophesy, and there come in one that believeth not, or one unlearned, he is convinced of all, he is judged of all: And thus are the secrets of his heart made manifest; and so falling down on his face he will worship God, and report that God is in you of a truth." (1 Corinthians 14:22-25)

The Spirit of God will work to change the very nature of your mind and physical body. And all you have to do is accept and receive the written Word of God. The apostle Paul wrote this insight in the book of Romans (12:1-2).

- "I beseech you therefore, brethren, by the mercies of God, that ye present your bodies a living sacrifice, holy, acceptable unto God, which is your reasonable service."

- "And be not conformed to this world: but be ye transformed by the renewing of your mind, that ye may prove what is that good, and acceptable, and perfect, will of God."

Fruits of the Holy Ghost

> "But the fruit of the Spirit is love, joy, peace, longsuffering, gentleness, goodness, faith, Meekness, temperance: against such there is no law. And they that are Christ's have crucified the flesh with the affections and lusts. If we live in the Spirit, let us also walk in the Spirit. Let us not be desirous of vain glory, provoking one another, envying one another." (Galatians 5:22–26)

When Eve and Adam ate the fruit from the Tree of the Knowledge of Good and Evil, it opened their minds to an everlasting internal war within the body. This tug-of-war can drive one insane and to the point of suicide. The apostle Paul understood this when he wrote, "But I see another law in my members, warring against the law of my mind, and bringing me into captivity to the law of sin which is in my members. O wretched man that I am! Who shall deliver me from the body of death? I thank God through Jesus Christ our Lord. So then with the mind I myself serve the law of God, but with the flesh the law of sin" (Romans 7:23-25).

Paul further explains this war, and the aftereffects in the book of Galatians. (Galatians 5:16-21) In retrospect, Paul is telling us that the way out of this crisis is to believe in Christ Jesus and receive the peace given by the Holy Ghost, because without him, the war in our body and mind will continue until sin and death win in the end.

Church Leadership

> "And he gave some, apostles; and some, prophets; and some, evangelists; and some, pastors and teachers; For the perfecting of the saints, for the work of the ministry, for the edifying of the body of Christ: Till we all come in the unity of the faith, and of the knowledge of the Son of God, unto a perfect

man, unto the measure of the stature of the fulness of Christ." (Ephesians 4:11–13)

After Christ was resurrected, and prior to him taking Abraham and the saints of old into heaven, he ensured the church would have adequate leadership to complement the church members. Some believe every church should have all five leadership positions in operation, and they have named this the "Five-Fold Ministry." Yet when you look at these five titles, you come to realize that these leadership positions must be shared throughout the church body, and ingrained in one mind, body, and soul. Again, no position is greater than the other, because Christ has already said some will gain, "a hundredfold, some sixty, some thirty" (Matthew 13: 23). But in order for the church to function, all must work together for the common good!

Christ the Holy Ghost Baptizer

After Christ was resurrected from the grave, he walked among his disciples for a period of forty days, but the world won't see him again until he returns on the clouds of glory.[523] He instructed them to wait in Jerusalem for the promised baptism of the Holy Ghost, stated by John the Baptist: "And, being assembled together with them, commanded them that they should not depart from Jerusalem, but wait for the promise of the Father, which, saith he, ye have heard of me. For John truly baptized with water; but ye shall be baptized with the Holy Ghost not many days hence." (Acts 1:4-5)

Christ Jesus said this to prepare them to be baptized with the Spirit of God. This is his second time to perform this feat. The first were the seventy elders with Moses in the Sinai Desert (Numbers 11:16-30).

> **May 24, 33 AD**

The Day of Pentecost

The disciples obeyed Christ and waited in an upper room on the day of Pentecost. There were about 120 men and women, along with Mary, the mother of Jesus, and her family (Jesus' brothers and sisters).[524]

- "And when the day of Pentecost was fully come, they were all with one accord in one place. And suddenly there came a sound from heaven as of a rushing mighty wind, and it filled all the house where they were sitting. And there appeared unto them cloven tongues like as of fire, and it sat upon each of them. And they were all filled with the Holy Ghost, and began to speak with other tongues, as the Spirit gave them utterance." (Acts 2:1–4)

Now the complete list of the 120 disciples is not provided in Scripture, so I researched the Bible and came up with a list of possible men and women who were there. These are the people Christ had helped in some form or fashion during his ministry on the earth.

Who is Jesus Christ

A List of the Possible 120 Disciples

12 --**Twelve Disciples**: Peter, James, John, Andrew, Phillip, Thomas, Bartholomew, Matthew, James the son of Alphaeus, Simon Zelotes, and Judas the brother of James and Matthias (Acts 1:26)

70 - **Seventy Disciples**: These are the ones Jesus sent out to every city in Israel to minister to
Jews and Gentiles (Luke 10:1–20).

07 - **Jesus Family:** Mary, the mother of Jesus; Jesus' brothers James, Joses, Simon, Judas; Jesus'
sisters (?) (Matthew 13:54–58)

14 – **Women:** (a) Mary Magdalene and Mary, the mother of James and Salome (Mark 16:1); (b) Joanna (Luke 8:3; 24:10); (c) Susanna (Luke 8:3); (d) Martha, the sister of Lazarus (Luke 10:38–42); (e) Mary who anointed Jesus feet (John 12:1–11); (f) woman with the issue of blood (Matthew 9:20–22); (g) widow of Nain and her son (Luke 7:11–16); (h) woman who washed Jesus' feet (Luke 7:36–39); (i) the woman caught in adultery (John 8:1–11; (j) woman who anointed Jesus' head (Matthew 26:6–16); (k) Peter's mother-in-law (Matthew 8:14–17)

17 – **Men:** *Seventeen Possible Persons/Men:* (l) Lazarus (John 12:1); (m) the leper (Matthew 8:1–4); (n) one of the ten lepers (Luke 17:11–19); (o) Legion—one possessed with many devils (Luke 8:26–40); (p) the paralytic (Matthew 9:1–8); (q) two blind men (Matthew 9:27–31); (r) a father and his lunatic son (Matthew 17:14–21); (s) Jairus and his daughter (Mark 5:35–43); (t) deaf and dumb man (Mark 7:31–37); (u) blind Bartimaeus (Mark 10:46–52.); (v) man with the withered hand (Luke 6:6–11); (w) the impotent man (John 5:1–9); (x) man blind from his mother's womb (John 9:1–41; (y) dumb man possessed with a devil (Matthew 10:32–34)

Abraham Howard Jr.

The Witnesses of the Holy Ghost Baptism

The day of Pentecost is a feast celebrated fifty days after the Passover with first fruit offerings, singing, and jubilation. Besides the residents of Jerusalem and Judaea, there were gathered approximately three thousand Jews from the nations of the known world.

(1) Persia: Parthian(s), Medes (Japheth), Elam (Shem), and Mesopotamia (Babylon)
(2) Asia Minor (Turkey): Cappadocia, Pontus, Asia (Ephesus), Phrygia, and Pamphylia
(3) Africa: Egypt, Libya, and Cyrene
(4) Italy: Roman
(5) Greece: the Island of Crete
(6) Arabs: Arabia

The visiting Jews marveled that the 120 Disciples of Christ were speaking in tongues (and acting wildly). They confessed, "We do hear them speak in our tongues (our language) the wonderful works of God." This was so amazing that it stunned them with doubt as to what was happening and what it meant. Others mocked at what was going on and said, "These men (and women) are full of new wine."

If you were there, what would your reaction be? The three thousand visitors didn't hear the good news of God in their outer ears. The sound coming from the 120 disciples would no doubt sound like a bees' nest, or better yet, a buzz saw. Rather, they heard it in their inner ears, which are close to the heart. You could even say that with all that noise they received the message of God telegraphically. Therefore, I am saddened by Bible scholars who believe what was heard was a foreign language (such as Italian, Spanish, or Arabic) through the outer ears, and that God used this as a one-time delivery method to the human race. It is not feasible that with 120 people speaking that you will hear a message in your native tongue, even if they all spoke your native tongue.

Peter Explains the Holy Ghost Baptism

When Peter heard the criticism that they were drunk on new wine, he stood up and began to preach about the Lord Jesus Christ. He first told them that what had just happened was a promise God made in the book of Joel, which was sustained by John the Baptist and carried out to completion by the resurrected Jesus Christ, the son of David, the Son of God—the one who died on the cross for the remission of sins for the whole world.

When they heard this, they were convicted in their heart "and said unto Peter and to the rest of the apostles, Men and brethren, what shall we do?" "Then Peter said unto them, Repent, and be baptized every one of you in the name of Jesus Christ for the remission of sins, and ye shall receive the gift of the Holy Ghost. For the promise is unto you, and to your children, and to all that are afar off, even as many as the Lord our God shall call. And with many other words did he testify and exhort, saying, Save yourselves from this untoward generation. Then they that gladly received his word were baptized: and the same day there were added unto them about three thousand souls." (Acts 2: 14-47)

Now I want to dispel the critics who say the baptism of the Holy Ghost only happened on the day of Pentecost, for there are some who believe that tongue speaking ceased on that day. Yet Christ is not dead, but has risen from the grave, and is still baptizing in the Holy Ghost, all who ask him. So, let's review the biblical record.

The Samarians Are Baptized with the Holy Ghost

Water Baptism

After the death of Steven (Acts 7:1–60), Philip left Jerusalem, went down to Samaria, and preached Christ unto them. With great joy the people listened to him, and saw the miracles that were worked through him: "For unclean spirits, crying with a loud voice, came out of many that were possessed with them: and many taken with palsies, and that were lame, were healed. But when they believed Philip preaching the things concerning the kingdom of God, and the name of Jesus Christ, they were baptized (in water), both men and women." Also, a man named Simon, who practiced sorcery, was caught up in the moment: "Then Simon himself believed also: and when he was baptized, he continued with Philip, and wondered, beholding the miracles and signs which were done" (Acts 8:5–13, 14–17, 18–25).

Holy Ghost Baptism

When news reached the apostles at Jerusalem about what was happening in Samaria, they sent Peter and John to join Phillip. After surveying the situation, they prayed for the Samarians to receive the baptism of the Holy Ghost: "Then laid they their hands on them and they received the Holy Ghost."

However, Simon the sorcerer did not receive the baptism of the Holy Ghost; because he sought to buy the gift from Peter and was rebuked sternly. Simon the sorcerer, like Judas Iscariot pretended to believe so that he could gain power over the people.

Now this record did not say the Samarians spoke in tongues when they were baptized in the Holy Ghost. But don't be misled, for there are more Scriptures to cover. Take note that Peter and John had no power to give out the Holy Ghost, but relied on prayer and faith in the Lord Jesus Christ. And, of course, they laid their hands on them during prayer.

The Apostle Paul Is Baptized with the Holy Ghost (Acts Chapter 9)

A young Pharisee priest named Saul had put to death Stephen, a disciple of Christ, and "made havock of the church, entering into every house, and haling men and women committed them to prison. Therefore they that were scattered abroad went every where preaching the word."

He had been granted authority to do so from his superiors:

Who is Jesus Christ

"And Saul, yet breathing out threatenings and slaughter against the disciples of the Lord, went unto the high priest, And desired of him letters to Damascus to the synagogues, that if he found any of this way, whether they were men or women, he might bring them bound unto Jerusalem" (Acts 8:1–4).

Saul was drawing near Damascus when, "suddenly there shined round about him a light from heaven: And he fell to the earth, and heard a voice saying unto him, Saul, Saul, why persecutest thou me? And he said, Who art thou, Lord? And the Lord said, I am Jesus whom thou persecutest: it is hard for thee to kick against the pricks. And he trembling and astonished said, Lord, what wilt thou have me to do? And the Lord said unto him, Arise, and go into the city, and it shall be told thee what thou must do. And the men which journeyed with him stood speechless, hearing a voice, but seeing no man. And Saul arose from the earth; and when his eyes were opened, he saw no man: but they led him by the hand, and brought him into Damascus. And he was three days without sight, and neither did eat nor drink."

Take note that this is the only man the Lord Jesus Christ physically chose after his resurrection to be his disciple. He first chose twelve men from among all his disciples, and then he sent out seventy disciples into all of Israel. After Judas hanged himself, the disciples voted to replace him with Mathias. Christ put the cap on discipleship when he said, "For many are called, but few are chosen."[525]

At the end of the three days, Christ, in a vision, visited a man named Ananias. He told him to go and lay hands on Saul that he might receive his sight, and that his coming was revealed to Saul in a vision while he prayed.

Ananias tried to beg out of the mission by reminding Christ of all the evil Saul had done against the saints of God. But Christ said unto him, "Go thy way: for he is a chosen vessel unto me, to bear my name before the Gentiles, and kings, and the children of Israel: For I will shew him how great things he must suffer for my name's sake."

With the assurance of Christ, Ananias went and laid his hands on Saul. He said to him, "Brother Saul, the Lord, even Jesus, that appeared unto thee in the way as thou camest, hath sent me, that thou mightest receive thy sight, and be filled with the Holy Ghost."

Saul is Baptized in the Spirit and then in Water

- "And immediately there fell from his eyes as it had been scales: and he received sight forthwith (was filled with the Holy Ghost), and arose, and was baptized (in water). And when he had received meat, he was strengthened. Then was Saul certain days with the disciples which were at Damascus." (Acts 9:1–19)

Now when Saul (the Apostle Paul) was baptized with the Holy Ghost, the Bible doesn't say he spoke in tongues, or even prophesied as the 120 did on the day of Pentecost. However, Paul confessed in chapter 14 of his first letter to the Corinthians that he in fact did speak in tongues:

- "Wherefore let him that speaketh in an unknown tongue pray that he may interpret. For if I pray in an unknown tongue, my spirit prayeth, but my understanding is unfruitful. What is it then? I will pray with the spirit, and I will pray with the understanding also: I will sing with the spirit, and I will sing with the understanding also. Else when thou shalt bless with the spirit, how shall he that occupieth the room of the unlearned say Amen at thy giving of thanks, seeing he understandeth not what thou sayest? For thou verily givest thanks well, but the other is not edified. I thank my God, I speak with tongues more than ye all." (1 Corinthians 14:13–18)

The Roman Cornelius

This is the story of a man named Cornelius, who was a Roman centurion in charge of a group called the Italian band. He was "A devout man, and one that feared God with all his house, which gave much alms to the people, and prayed to God always."

One day, about the ninth hour of the day (3 p.m. to sunset), he saw in a vision an angel of God coming toward him, pronouncing his name. When Cornelius got past his fear, the angel said, "Thy prayers and thine alms are come up for a memorial before God. And now send men to Joppa, and call for one Simon, whose surname is Peter: He lodgeth with one Simon a tanner, whose house is by the sea side: he shall tell thee what thou oughtest to do."

When the angel departed, Cornelius called for two of his trusted house servants and a loyal fellow soldier. These three he told what had conspired between him and the angel. Then he sent them to Joppa to fetch Peter.

Unaware they were coming; Peter went up on the rooftop to pray; it was about the sixth hour of the day (noon to 3 p.m.). Suddenly, he felt very hungry. He would have eaten, but the food was not ready. Instead, he and fell into a trance. While in this state, he saw a sheet coming down from heaven with, "all manner of fourfooted beasts of the earth, and wild beasts, and creeping things, and fowls of the air." Then he heard a voice say "Rise, Peter; kill, and eat." After taking a long look at the sheet, Peter said, "Not so, Lord; for I have never eaten any thing that is common or unclean." The voice replied, "What God hath cleansed, that call not thou common." This conversation repeated itself three times. Then the sheet was called back into heaven.

While Peter was yet in deep thought, the three men from Cornelius came to Simon the tanner's house, seeking him. At that moment, "the Spirit (*the Holy Ghost*) said unto him, Behold three men seek thee. Arise therefore, and get thee down, and go with them, doubting nothing: for I have sent them."

After a short greeting, Peter took some fellow Jews and went with the three men. Once they arrived at Caesarea, they were met by Cornelius, his family, and friends. Being cautious, Peter said to, Cornelius, "Ye know how that it is an unlawful thing for a man that is a Jew to keep company, or come unto one of another nation; but God hath shewed me that I should not call any man common or unclean."

Then Cornelius began to tell Peter the story of how and why he sent for him. Peter took this opportunity to preach and tell them about the Lord Jesus Christ:

'Then Peter opened his mouth, and said, Of a truth I perceive that God is no respecter of persons: But in every nation he that feareth him, and worketh righteousness, is accepted with him. The word which God sent unto the children of Israel, preaching peace by Jesus Christ: (he is Lord of all:) That word, I say, ye know, which was published throughout all Judaea, and began from Galilee, after the baptism which John preached; How God anointed Jesus of Nazareth with the Holy Ghost and with power: who went about doing good, and healing all that were oppressed of the devil; for God was with him. And we are witnesses of all things which he did both in the land of the Jews, and in Jerusalem; whom they slew and hanged on a tree: Him God raised up the third day, and shewed him openly; Not to all the people, but unto witnesses chosen before of God, even to us, who did eat and drink with him after he rose from the dead. And he commanded us to preach unto the people, and to testify that it is he which was ordained of God to be the Judge of quick and dead. To him give all the prophets witness, that through his name whosoever believeth in him shall receive remission of sins.' (Acts 10:34–43)

Baptized in the Holy Ghost

"While Peter yet spake these words, the Holy Ghost fell on all them which heard the word. And they of the circumcision which believed were astonished, as many as came with Peter, because that on the Gentiles also was poured out the gift of the Holy Ghost. For they heard them speak with tongues, and magnify God."

Baptized in Water

"Then answered Peter, Can any man forbid water, that these

should not be baptized, which have received the Holy Ghost as well as we? And he commanded them to be baptized in the name of the Lord." (Acts 10:44–48)

Take notice here that Cornelius, his family, and friends were all baptized in the Holy Ghost before they were baptized in water. This dispels the idea that there is a sequence to follow in the baptizing formula. Normally the chain of events are (1) believe; (2) repent and confess Christ as your Savior, by the power of the Holy Ghost, who will come and dwell with you; (3) be baptized in water; (4) and then, by the grace of God and the Lord Jesus Christ, be baptized in the Holy Ghost and with fire.

Yet we see this chain is broken when the Holy Ghost is poured out and then water baptism follows. Is this possible in these modern days of the twenty-first century? I believe it is possible, but preachers have to be like Peter and preach, and proclaim Christ at every turn. And they must stay away from rhythmic oratory, exotic philosophy, and worldly doctrinal sermons.

Apollos Preaches in the Power of the Holy Ghost

- "And a certain Jew named Apollos, born at Alexandria, an eloquent man, and mighty in the scriptures, came to Ephesus. This man was instructed in the way of the Lord; and being fervent in the spirit, he spake and taught diligently the things of the Lord, knowing only the baptism of John. And he began to speak boldly in the synagogue: whom when Aquila and Priscilla had heard, they took him unto them, and expounded unto him the way of God more perfectly. And when he was disposed to pass into Achaia, the brethren wrote, exhorting the disciples to receive him: who, when he was come, helped them much which had believed through grace: For he mightily convinced the Jews, and that publickly, shewing by the scriptures that Jesus was Christ." (Acts 18:24–28)

Now the story of Apollos is a good case study for the modern church, particularly those called Pentecostals. They believe you must be baptized in the Holy Ghost in order to preach the Word of God. But we read that Apollos was a scripturally based, educated man who convincingly preached, by the Spirit of God, the Lord Jesus Christ. And all he knew was water baptism.

But by and by, his path crossed Aquila and Priscilla, friends of the apostle Paul,[526] who took him aside and explained to him the baptism of the Holy Ghost. This is the full gospel of the Lord Jesus Christ: being born again by believing in the Son of God, which brings forth the dwelling of the Holy Ghost, and the power to receive Christ as Lord; and then receiving baptism of water by the hands of man; and the baptism of the Spirit (the Holy Ghost) by the hand of Christ Jesus.

Because of Apollos, a division crept into the church and divided the believers of Christ; just as there is a division today between those who preach and believe in water baptism, but shun the baptism of the Holy Ghost; and those who preach and teach about the baptism of the Holy Ghost, with the evidence of speaking in tongues, but shun Christians who don't speak in tongues. The apostle Paul addressed this type of division when he wrote his first epistle to the Corinthian church.

- "Now I beseech you, brethren, by the name of our Lord Jesus Christ, that ye all speak the same thing, and that there be no divisions among you; but that ye be perfectly joined together in the same mind and in the same judgment. For it hath been declared unto me of you, my brethren, by them which are of the house of Chloe, that there are contentions among you. Now this I say, that every one of you saith, I am of Paul; and I of Apollos; and I of Cephas; and I of Christ. Is Christ divided? was Paul crucified for you? or were ye baptized in the name of Paul? I thank God that I baptized none of you, but Crispus and Gaius; Lest any should say that I had baptized in mine own name. And I baptized also the household of Stephanas: besides, I know not whether I baptized any other.

For Christ sent me not to baptize, but to preach the gospel: not with wisdom of words, lest the cross of Christ should be made of none effect."527

Is Apollos authorized to preach without the baptism of the Holy Ghost? The answer is yes! Christ did not send the bearers of gifts, showing great signs and wonders, to preach his Word. He sends whosoever believes he is the Son of God. It is written, "But as many as received him, to them gave he power to become the sons of God, even to them that believe on his name."

Keep in mind that the gift(s) of the Holy Ghost are given after you believe in Christ. Therefore, when we witness for Christ, we need to preach the Word of God as it is written; for the Word of God will do what we cannot do—bring a soul to Christ. I want to bring to your attention some Scriptures about the Word of God that corroborate what I'm saying.

- "I Will praise thee with my whole heart: before the gods will I sing praise unto thee. I will worship toward thy holy temple, and praise thy name for thy lovingkindness and for thy truth: <u>for thou hast magnified thy word above all thy name</u>." (Psalm 138:1–2]

- "So shall my word be that goeth forth out of my mouth: it shall not return unto me void, but it shall accomplish that which I please, and it shall prosper in the thing whereto I sent it." (Isaiah 55:11)

- "For the word of God is quick, and powerful, and sharper than any two-edged sword, piercing even to the dividing asunder of soul and spirit, and of the joints and marrow, and is a discerner of the thoughts and intents of the heart." (Hebrews 4:12)

After reviewing the above Scriptures, simple reasoning tells us the spoken Word of God has great power and is able to break through the hardest skull and cleanse the stiffest heart. " But those things which proceed out of the mouth come forth from the heart; and they defile the man. For out of the heart proceed evil thoughts, murders, adulteries, fornications, thefts, false witness, and blasphemies: These are the things which defile a man:" (Matthew 15:1-20)

And be sure that the only one that can forgive us of our sins (committed by the heart), and cleanse us from all unrighteousness is Christ Jesus. (1 John 1:8-10) I warn preachers who are carried away with their sermons, that it is not their lesson outline that excites the people when they speak; it is the spoken Word of God that they hear and obey.

Have You Heard of the Holy Ghost?

After Apollos left Ephesus, he went to Corinth. Paul then came to Ephesus and found the disciples Apollos had baptized in water: "He said unto them, Have ye received the Holy Ghost since ye believed? And they said unto him, We have not so much as heard whether there be any Holy Ghost. And he said unto them, Unto what then were ye baptized? And they said, Unto John's baptism." They spoke the truth to Paul, because Apollos only knew about the water baptism performed by John the Baptist.

- "Then said Paul, John verily baptized with the baptism of repentance, saying unto the people, that they should believe on him which should come after him, that is, on Christ Jesus. When they heard this, they were baptized in the name of the Lord Jesus. And when Paul had laid his hands upon them, the Holy Ghost came on them; and they spake with tongues, and prophesied. And all the men were about twelve." (Acts 19:1–7)

The Holy Ghost Movement in the United States of America

So far, I've presented the complete biblical evidence concerning the baptism of the Holy Ghost (the Spirit of God). Now I want to talk about the greatest outpouring of the Holy Ghost since the day of Pentecost. This happened in the United States of America, at 312 Azusa Street, Los Angles, California. The man God used to head the movement was Rev. William J. Seymour.

He was born in 1870 in St Mary's Parish, Louisiana. Around 1900, he moved to Cincinnati, Ohio, and enrolled in a "Holiness Bible School." After three years, he moved to Houston, Texas, and received extended classes under Charles F. Parham. In 1906 Seymour was called to preach in Los Angeles. It was during this time that God poured out the Holy Spirit for a period of nearly three years. From this one church movement came all of the Pentecostal and Charismatic churches: the Church of God in Christ, Assembly of God, Church of God, Apostolic and Jesus' name churches, United Pentecostals, Five-Fold Ministries, and so on. [528]

After all this evidence, you should be convinced about the baptism of the Holy Ghost that happened during the days of Moses (Numbers Chapter 11), on the day of Pentecost, and even to the present day.

Summary of the Holy Ghost Baptism

So then, if you are a believer in Christ Jesus, and have not been baptized in the Holy Ghost, do you need to be? The answer obviously is yes! For how can you follow and believe in Christ and deny him the rite of Spirit baptism? Does the baptism of the Holy Ghost save you? No! "For by grace are ye saved through faith; and that not of yourselves: it is the gift of God; and not of works, lest any man should boast" (Ephesians 2:8–9). But what it does is give you power to witness and communicate with God. See 1 Corinthians chapter fourteen for further guidance.

CHAPTER 27

JESUS CHRIST IS THE JUDGE

> "For we must all appear before the judgment seat of Christ; that every one may receive the things done in his body, according to that he hath done, whether it be good or bad. Knowing therefore the terror of the Lord, we persuade men; but we are made manifest unto God; and I trust also are made manifest in your consciences." (2 Corinthians 5:10–11)

This message from the apostle Paul is clear and understandable; Christ Jesus is the one who will judge the lives of humankind. To this end, the world has convinced itself that this is not so, and has rejected the authority of his judgeship. But it is the duty of every believer in Christ to warn the unbeliever of the horrible death that awaits those who do not embrace Jesus, the only begotten Son of the Father, as their Savior.

When the Word of God came to live among human beings, he did no judging. And to ease human minds, he said, "for I am not come to call the righteous, but sinners to repentance."[529] Many times after this statement he confirmed he would not judge humankind while walking on this earth. For example:

WHO IS JESUS CHRIST

- "For the Father judgeth no man, but hath committed all judgment unto the Son: That all men should honour the Son, even as they honour the Father. He that honoureth not the Son honoureth not the Father which hath sent him." (John 5:22–23)

- "I am come a light into the world, that whosoever believeth on me should not abide in darkness. And if any man hear my words, and believe not, I judge him not: for I came not to judge the world, but to save the world. He that rejecteth me, and receiveth not my words, hath one that judgeth him: the word that I have spoken, the same shall judge him in the last day. For I have not spoken of myself; but the Father which sent me, he gave me a commandment, what I should say, and what I should speak. And I know that his commandment is life everlasting: whatsoever I speak therefore, even as the Father said unto me, so I speak." (John 12:46–50)

It is plain to see from these Scriptures that Christ Jesus was not sent to the earth to judge humankind. Therefore, those who justify their abominable acts with claims that Christ Jesus did not condemn them during his earthly ministry are correct in their assessment of his work on earth. However, since he has resurrected from the dead, he is now the doorway to heaven or hell, and every created being—spirit and human—must be, and will be, judged by him. He claimed his "Judges chair" when he endured the crucifixion. The following Scriptures witness this claim.

- "Jesus saith unto him, I am the way, the truth, and the life: no man cometh unto the Father, but by me." (John 14:6)

- "And Jesus came and spake unto them, saying, All power is given unto me in heaven and in earth." (Matthew 28:18)

- "And I turned to see the voice that spake with me. And being turned, I saw seven golden candlesticks; And in the midst of the seven candlesticks one like unto the Son of man, clothed with a garment down to the foot, and girt about the paps with a golden girdle. His head and his hairs were white like wool, as white as snow; and his eyes were as a flame of fire; And his feet like unto fine brass, as if they burned in a furnace; and his voice as the sound of many waters. And he had in his right hand seven stars: and out of his mouth went a sharp twoedged sword: and his countenance was as the sun shineth in his strength. And when I saw him, I fell at his feet as dead. And he laid his right hand upon me, saying unto me, Fear not; I am the first and the last: I am he that liveth, and was dead; and, behold, I am alive for evermore, Amen; <u>and have the keys of hell and of death</u>." (Revelation 1:12–18)

If at this moment you are still in unbelief, and cannot except the judgeship of Christ, I plead with you to keep an open mind and realize God the Father has placed total authority in the hands of Christ Jesus. I say this to warn you—out of love—that none will escape the judgment of Christ Jesus. For just as he carried out the judgment of God in the Old Testament, when he was in the desert with Moses and the children of Israel, he will do the same in these last days; now that he has risen from the grave.

And being merciful, Christ Jesus has built a church of witnesses to warn the world that the only escape from the wrath of God (the second death and the lake of fire) is to turn from their wicked ways and believe in Him. Again, Paul said it best when he wrote, "But what saith it? The word is nigh thee, even in thy mouth, and in thy heart: that is, the word of faith, which we preach; that if thou shalt confess with thy mouth the Lord Jesus, and shalt believe in thine heart that God hath raised him from the dead, thou shalt be saved. For with the heart man believeth unto righteousness; and with the mouth confession is made unto salvation."[530]

This same mercy was extended to Solomon, when he laid down seven prayer requests concerning the sins (and uncommitted sins) of his people Israel. God answered his prayer with this message, "If my people, which are called by my name, shall humble themselves, and pray, and seek my face, and turn from their wicked ways; then will I hear from heaven, and will forgive their sin, and will heal their land."531

I cannot, and will not, believe anyone is looking forward to eternal torment, for even the devil(s) are trying their best to prolong their entry into that eternal inferno.

- "And when he was come to the other side into the country of the Gergesenes, there met him two possessed with devils, coming out of the tombs, exceeding fierce, so that no man might pass by that way. And, behold, they cried out (the devils), saying, What have we to do with thee, Jesus, thou Son of God? art thou come hither to torment us before the time?" (Matthew 8:28–29)

- "And came down to Capernaum, a city of Galilee, and taught them on the sabbath days. And they were astonished at his doctrine: for his word was with power. And in the synagogue there was a man, which had a spirit of an unclean devil, and cried out with a loud voice, Saying, Let us alone; what have we to do with thee, thou Jesus of Nazareth? art thou come to destroy us? I know thee who thou art; the Holy One of God. And Jesus rebuked him, saying, Hold thy peace, and come out of him. And when the devil had thrown him in the midst, he came out of him, and hurt him not." (Luke 4:31–35)

Now right here I have to present Scripture in its fullness, because I don't want anyone to think I am fictionalizing the judgments of God. I want people to see Christ Jesus as their Savior from the wrath of God (hell and the lake of fire).

To accept Christ Jesus as the Judge may be hard for those who can only picture him as meek and lowly of heart. This position of thinking would be correct except that the Father has placed all things into the hands of Christ Jesus until judgment day: when the works of human souls are balanced against God's Book of Life.

Keeping book on human souls is not a new concept with God. Remember when Aaron and the children of Israel made a golden calf, and began to worship it? God told Moses, "Whosoever hath sinned against me, him will I blot out of my book." Again, to open your eyes to the seriousness of the pending judgments of God, I have to present to you the Scriptures as written in the Holy Bible. So, walk carefully with me through these difficult, and in some cases, painful passages.

The Will of the Father

People often pray to God, and at the end of their prayer, they say, "Not my will, but thine will be done; or if it be thine will, let it be done." I think prayers are ended this way based upon how Jesus closed out his prayer in the Garden of Gethsemane. So, there is always a question about the will of God. But Christ Jesus had no confusion when it came to this subject, because he not only knew the will of God, but left us with the reasoning.

- And this is the Father's will which hath sent me, that of all which he hath given me I should lose nothing, but should raise it up again at the last day. And this is the will of him that sent me, that every one which seeth the Son, and believeth on him, may have everlasting life: and I will raise him up at the last day." (John 6:39–40)

It is not God's will to destroy humankind, because he made male and female for his own pleasure, and as a living vessel for the Holy Ghost.[532] Even when he judged his people Israel, he bent over backward to save them from destruction. He sent the prophets to warn them to turn from their wicked ways. And even though they didn't heed his warnings (they listened to false prophets); God gave them a ray of hope to look forward to after they received his judgment.

- "For thus saith the Lord of hosts, the God of Israel; Let not your prophets and your diviners, that be in the midst of you, deceive you, neither hearken to your dreams which ye cause to be dreamed. For they prophesy falsely unto you in my name: I have not sent them, saith the Lord. For thus saith the Lord, That after seventy years be accomplished at Babylon I will visit you, and perform my good word toward you, in causing you to return to this place. For I know the thoughts that I think toward you, saith the Lord, thoughts of peace, and not of evil, to give you an expected end. Then shall ye call upon me, and ye shall go and pray unto me, and I will hearken unto you. And ye shall seek me, and find me, when ye shall search for me with all your heart. And I will be found of you, saith the Lord: and I will turn away your captivity, and I will gather you from all the nations, and from all the places whither I have driven you, saith the Lord; and I will bring you again into the place whence I caused you to be carried away captive." (Jeremiah 29:8–14)

- "Have I any pleasure at all that the wicked should die? saith the Lord God: and not that he should return from his ways, and live?" (Ezekiel 18:23)

- "Therefore I will judge you, O house of Israel, every one according to his ways, saith the Lord God. Repent, and turn yourselves from all your transgressions; so iniquity shall not be your ruin. Cast away from you all your transgressions, whereby ye have transgressed; and make you a new heart and a new spirit: for why will ye die, O house of Israel? For I have no pleasure in the death of him that dieth, saith the Lord God: wherefore turn yourselves, and live ye." (Ezekiel 18:30–32)

- "Say unto them, As I live, saith the Lord God, I have no pleasure in the death of the wicked; but that the wicked turn from his way and live: turn ye, turn ye from your evil ways; for why will ye die, O house of Israel?" (Ezekiel 33:11)

As you can see from these Scriptures, it is clearly apparent that God wants humans to believe in Christ Jesus and live an eternal life (not eternal damnation), and through him, humankind will escape his wrath (judgment). This should not be taken lightly, because Christ had to endure being hung on a cross, and publicly humiliated as a sinner: though it could not be proven what sin he had committed. The apostle Paul waded in on this line of thinking when he said,

- Then cometh the end, when he shall have delivered up the kingdom to God, even the Father; when he shall have put down all rule and all authority and power. For he must reign, till he hath put all enemies under his feet. The last enemy that shall be destroyed is death. For he hath put all things under his feet. But when he saith, all things are put under him, it is manifest that he is excepted, which did put all things under him. And when all things shall be subdued unto him, then shall the Son also himself be subject unto him that put all things under him, that God may be all in all." (1 Corinthians 15:24–28)

- "I saw in the night visions, and, behold, one like the Son of man came with the clouds of heaven, and came to the Ancient of days, and they brought him near before him. 14 And there was given him dominion, and glory, and a kingdom, that all people, nations, and languages, should serve him: his dominion is an everlasting dominion, which shall not pass away, and his kingdom that which shall not be destroyed." (Daniel 7:13-14)

We see this being played out when Christ resurrects his followers, and reigns for a thousand years. This is when death as we know it has been abolished. After the thousand years are completed, final judgment falls, and there is only eternal life or eternal damnation (destruction of body and soul in the lake of fire).[533]

I want to delve into three categories that Christ will humbly judge: (1) corporate works, (2) church members' performances, (3) and church organizations.

The Judgment of Corporate Works

Jesus spelled out this type of judgment prior to his crucifixion. It's based on how you treat other human beings. The Scriptures that are written need not to be explained, because they are self-explanatory, clear, and to the point: Christ will judge the good and the evil.

- *__Christ will separate the Good from the evil__*: "When the Son of humanity shall come in his glory, and all the holy angels with him, then shall he sit upon the throne of his glory: And before him shall be gathered all nations: and he shall separate them one from another, as a shepherd divideth his sheep from the goats: And he shall set the sheep on his right hand, but the goats on the left " (Matthew 25:31-33).

- *__The good are judged__*: "Then shall the King say unto them on his right hand, Come, ye blessed of my Father, inherit the kingdom prepared for you from the foundation of the world: For I was an hungred, and ye gave me meat: I was thirsty, and ye gave me drink: I was a stranger, and ye took me in: Naked, and ye clothed me: I was sick, and ye visited me: I was in prison, and ye came unto me" (Matthew 25:34-36).

- *__The good question their judgment__*: "Then shall the righteous answer him, saying, Lord, when saw we thee an hungred, and fed thee? or thirsty, and gave thee drink? When saw we thee a stranger, and took thee in? or naked, and clothed thee? Or when saw we thee sick, or in prison, and came unto thee? And the King shall answer and say unto them, Verily I say unto you, Inasmuch as ye have done it unto one of the least of these my brethren, ye have done it unto me" (Matthew 25:37-40).

- *<u>The bad, the ugly, and the evil are judged</u>:* "Then shall he say also unto them on the left hand, Depart from me, ye cursed, into everlasting fire, prepared for the devil and his angels: For I was an hungred, and ye gave me no meat: I was thirsty, and ye gave me no drink: I was a stranger, and ye took me not in: naked, and ye clothed me not: sick, and in prison, and ye visited me not" (Matthew 25:41-43).

- *<u>The wicked question their judgment</u>:* "Then shall they also answer him, saying, Lord, when saw we thee an hungred, or athirst, or a stranger, or naked, or sick, or in prison, and did not minister unto thee? Then shall he answer them, saying, Verily I say unto you, Inasmuch as ye did it not to one of the least of these, ye did it not to me" (Matthew 25:44-45).

- *<u>Judgment reasoning</u>*: "And these (the bad, the ugly, the wicked and evil) shall go away into everlasting punishment: but the righteous into life eternal" (Matthew 25:46). This same concept is seen in Psalm one. Those who shun sinful ways and study God's word are rewarded with blessing; but those who are rejected as sinners are doomed to destruction.

Did you notice that hell was created for the Devil and the angels that rebelled against God? This means humankind has no business going into hell with the Devil. But Isaiah testified that hell was enlarged because of humankind's evil deeds (Isaiah 5:11–16).

Every judgment must have a firm base to rest upon, so that a precedent is sit for all further cases. In the parable of the Good Samaritan, Jesus told the story of how a priest and a Levite stepped around a wounded man who had been robbed. But a lowly Samaritan, who was considered a second-class citizen, and sinner, helped the man to recovery, and paid his food, clothing, and lodging bill. Jesus likened this type of action by the Samaritan as adhering to the great commandant, "Love the Lord thy God with all thy heart, and with all thy soul, and with all thy strength, and with all thy mind; and thy neighbor as thyself" (Luke 10:25–37).

What I'm going to present now is one of the toughest bits of Scripture to follow and commit to. It is a commandment given to those who wish to follow Christ Jesus. It concerns doing well toward those who treat you with ill will, and are your sworn enemies. What? You mean to say we are not commanded to kill our enemies? Yes, we are commanded to kill and murder our enemies, but with the "sword of love" (the Holy Bible). It is a concept hard to grasp, but if you open your mind, you'll see the reasoning of God come forward.

In Luke's version of the Beatitudes (Luke 6:20–38), he talks about blessings, time of rejoicing, warnings of woe, true love of your neighbor, walking in judgment, and the reward of God when you give—and show forth—love:

- *Blessing:* "Blessed be ye poor: for yours is the kingdom of God. Blessed are ye that hunger now: for ye shall be filled. Blessed are ye that weep now: for ye shall laugh. Blessed are ye, when men shall hate you, and when they shall separate you from their company, and shall reproach you, and cast out your name as evil, for the Son of man's sake."

- *Time to Rejoice:* "Rejoice ye in that day, and leap for joy: for, behold, your reward is great in heaven: for in the like manner did their fathers unto the prophets."

- *Time of Woe:* "But woe unto you that are rich! for ye have received your consolation. Woe unto you that are full! for ye shall hunger. Woe unto you that laugh now! for ye shall mourn and weep. Woe unto you, when all men shall speak well of you! for so did their fathers to the false prophets."

- ***True Love:*** "But I say unto you which hear, Love your enemies, do good to them which hate you, Bless them that curse you, and pray for them which despitefully use you. And unto him that smiteth thee on the one cheek offer also the other; and him that taketh away thy cloak forbid not to take thy coat also. Give to every man that asketh of thee; and of him that taketh away thy goods ask them not again. And as ye would that men should do to you, do ye also to them likewise. For if ye love them which love you, what thank have ye? for sinners also love those that love them. And if ye do good to them which do good to you, what thank have ye? for sinners also do even the same. And if ye lend to them of whom ye hope to receive, what thank have ye? for sinners also lend to sinners, to receive as much again. But love ye your enemies, and do good, and lend, hoping for nothing again; and your reward shall be great, and ye shall be the children of the Highest: for he is kind unto the unthankful and to the evil. Be ye therefore merciful, as your Father also is merciful."

- ***Don't Walk in Judgment***: "Judge not, and ye shall not be judged: condemn not, and ye shall not be condemned: forgive, and ye shall be forgiven:"

- ***The Reward of Love***: "Give, and it shall be given unto you; good measure, pressed down, and shaken together, and running over, shall men give into your bosom. For with the same measure that ye mete withal it shall be measured to you again."

As you can see Christ makes it clear that human beings must learn to help each other and to love one another; love is even extended to those who are out to do you harm. This kind of thinking may not set well with us, but it is the right attitude to have. God took Moses, a murderer, and made him a leader of a nation. He took Saul, who killed the followers of Christ, and made him a great witness to the gentle world. This same man is the beloved apostle Paul, who wrote a great number of the New Testament epistles: Romans, 1st and 2nd Corinthians, Galatians, Ephesians, Philippians, Colossians, 1st and 2nd Thessalonians, 1st and 2nd Timothy, Titus, Philemon, and Hebrews.

What more could be accomplished if we made every effort to turn our brothers and sisters away from wicked and evil ways and toward the Lord Jesus Christ? Then we would be like the western gunfighter, fast on the draw with a lot of notches on our gun grips.

But in all this, you must be, "wise as a serpent and gentle as a dove." Some evil people will take your kindness as a weakness, and think you are a sucker for helping them, because they have no intention of living righteously. But weep for them, for they are truly "the walking dead" with no hope of life.

Judgment of Church Members' Performances

> **"Not every one that saith unto me, Lord, Lord, shall enter into the kingdom of heaven; but he that doeth the will of my Father which is in heaven. Many will say to me in that day, Lord, Lord, have we not prophesied in thy name? and in thy name have cast out devils? and in thy name done many wonderful works? And then will I profess unto them, I never knew you: depart from me, ye that work iniquity."**
> (Matthew 7:21–23)

Christ Jesus makes it plain that not everyone who uses his name for the Gospels' sake will enter the kingdom of heaven. He states that many will cry out on judgment day, (when they learn that their names are not written in the Lamb's Book of Life), how they preached the gospel in his name, how they cast out devils in his name, and how, in his name, they performed many wonderful works. But then he will shock them with the news that he never knew them. This means, he knew they never believed in him, whose name they used to gain fame, fortune, and power.

There is an old quotation that says, "Some were called, some were sent, and some just jumped up and went." From my notes I'm going to present two cases I think fit within the categories specified in Mathew 7:21–23.

Judas Iscariot: He Preached and Cast Out Devils

Judas Iscariot was one of the twelve disciples Jesus called to travel with him. He gave them power to cast out unclean beings from human beings and to heal all manner of sickness and disease.

Judas was also in the group when Jesus sent them out two by two to witness to the Jews. During this mission, he gave them unlimited powers to heal the sick, cleanse the lepers, raise the dead, cast out devils, and preach the gospel by announcing as they went, "The kingdom of heaven is at hand."[534] "And they went out and preached that men should repent. And they cast out many devils and anointed with oil many that were sick, and healed them."[535]

Judas was with Christ when news came that Herod the tetrarch had jailed John the Baptist, and then had his head removed, and placed on a platter. He also heard the many parables Christ Jesus presented to the people, but in private explained the meaning to his twelve disciples.

He was there when Jesus fed about five thousand men (besides women and children) with five loaves of bread and two fishes.

He also witnessed Christ Jesus walking on water, and calling Peter out to do the same. He was in the group when Christ Jesus stopped to talk with the woman at the well in Samaria. He was standing there when Christ Jesus told a nobleman, "Go thy way; thy son liveth." And on the way home, they brought the nobleman news his son was healed.

Judas was listening when Christ Jesus stated he was the bread from heaven and then put forth a startling revelation concerning his mission to those who wanted to follow him. "I am the living bread which came down from heaven: if any man eat of this bread, he shall live for ever: and the bread that I will give is my flesh, which I will give for the life of the world. The Jews therefore strove among themselves, saying, How can this man give us his flesh to eat? Then Jesus said unto them, Verily, verily, I say unto you, Except ye eat the flesh of the Son of man, and drink his blood, ye have no life in you. Whoso eateth my flesh, and drinketh my blood, hath eternal life; and I will raise him up at the last day. For my flesh is meat indeed, and my blood is drink indeed. He that eateth my flesh, and drinketh my blood, dwelleth in me, and I in him." (John 6:51–56)

It is obvious that Christ Jesus was referring to the cross. But in the confusion, many of his disciples walked away from him in disbelief (see Luke 10:1–20). This left the twelve disciples who were his close inner circle. Now let's look at the Scriptures to see what conspired and caused Judas to fall out of fellowship with Christ Jesus. We will be examining John 6:60–71.

The Seventy Disciples: "Many therefore of his disciples, when they had heard this, said, This is a hard saying; who can hear it?"

Christ: "When Jesus knew in himself that his disciples murmured at it, he said unto them, Doth this offend you? What and if ye shall see the Son of man ascend up where he was before? It is the spirit that quickeneth; the flesh profiteth nothing: the words that I speak unto you, they are spirit, and they are life." "But there are some of you that believe not. For Jesus knew from the beginning who they were that believed not, and who should betray him. And he said, Therefore said I unto you, that no man can come unto me, except it were given unto him of my Father."

The Seventy Disciples: "From that time many of his disciples went back, and walked no more with him."

Christ: "Then said Jesus unto the twelve, Will ye also go away?"

Peter: "Then Simon Peter answered him, Lord, to whom shall we go? thou hast the words of eternal life. And we believe and are sure that thou art that Christ, the Son of the living God."

Christ: "Jesus answered them, Have not I chosen you twelve, and one of you is a devil?"

Judas Iscariot: *[John's Footnote on Jesus' Answer:]* "He spake of Judas Iscariot the son of Simon: for he it was that should betray him, being one of the twelve."

I hope you saw that Christ Jesus knew who among his disciples believed in him, and who didn't. And many times, after, he told them that one of them was going to "lift up their heel against him and betray him." The disciples never knew who it was until after Jesus was crucified.

Because Judas was pretending to be a believer in Christ Jesus, it was easy for Satan to deceive him into betraying the Son of God. He uses the same tactic on those who are using the church for personal gain, and distorting the Word of God by using beautiful oratory to tickle the ear of the weak-minded saints, and the fickle-brained sinner laden with sins and heavy burdens.

Paul also put forth a warning when he said, "Take heed therefore unto yourselves, and to all the flock, over that which the Holy Ghost hath made you overseers, to feed the church of God, which he hath purchased with his sown blood. For I know this, that after my departing shall grievous wolves enter in among you, not sparing the flock. Also of your own selves shall men arise, speaking perverse things, to draw away disciples after them."[536]

Further, "For the time will come when they (*the church*) will not endure sound doctrine; but after their own lusts shall they heap to themselves teachers, having itching ears. And shall turn away their ears from the truth, and shall be turned unto fables."[537]

This practice of saying what a church congregation wants to hear, and not addressing sin seems to be prevalent among hired preachers. Christ even commented on this when he said, "I am the good shepherd: the good shepherd giveth his life for the sheep. But he that is an hireling, and not the shepherd, whose own the sheep are not, seeth the wolf coming, and leaveth the sheep, and fleeth: and the wolf catcheth them, and scattereth the sheep. The hireling fleeth, because he is a hireling, and careth not for the sheep."538

Therefore, all preachers should check themselves against the Word of God and make sure they are called of Jesus Christ. Any fault against the Lord will cause a like judgment of Judas Iscariot, which leads to death and destruction—hell and eternal fire.

Wonderful Works in the Church

Terry Mattingly, a teacher of communications at Milligan College in Tennessee, wrote an article dated June 17, 1977, titled "Agnostics Comfy in this Church." The story is based on a book written by James Kelly, titled *Skeptic in the House of God*.539

Mattingly points out that Kelly didn't believe in God, the triune Godhead (Father, Son, and Holy Ghost), the virgin birth of Christ, and the resurrection of Christ, any of the Bible miracles, or heaven or hell. Yet he taught Sunday school, served on the church ministry board, faithfully paid his pledge, and loved his church: the incense, the stained-glass windows, the organ music, the vestments, and its rituals. Mr. Kelly said, "I don't want to give all that up, just because I don't believe in God and all."

Mr. Kelly is a prime example of someone in the church of the Lord Jesus Christ, who, from the outside, looks like a devout believer, but on the inside is wrestling with his soul, which is being tossed to and fro between flesh and spirit (Galatians 5:16–21). It is a war lost into eternal damnation, but it can be won with faith and belief in Jesus Christ.

Am I judging Mr. Kelly? No! According to the Lord Jesus Christ, humankind has already been judged: "For God sent not his Son into the world to condemn the world; but that the world through him might be saved. He that believeth on him is not condemned: but he that believeth not is condemned already, because he hath not believed in the n name of the only begotten Son of God."540

Conclusion

From these examples, I hope you can see the seriousness of representing the Lord Jesus Christ. Those who don't believe in Christ Jesus, and think they will escape the wrath of God are being deceived by none other than Satan himself. Added to this is scriptural proof that mankind's every move is being watched:

- ○ "I saw in the visions of my head upon my bed, and, behold, a watcher and an holy one came down from heaven;" (Daniel 4:13)

- ○ "Let his heart be changed from man's, and let a beast's heart be given unto him; and let seven times pass over him. This matter is by the decree of the watchers, and the demand by the word of the holy ones: to the intent that the living may know that the most High ruleth in the kingdom of men, and giveth it to whomsoever he will, and setteth up over it the basest of men." (Daniel 4:16-17)

- ○ "But I say unto you, That every idle word that men shall speak, they shall give account thereof in the day of judgment. For by thy words thou shalt be justified, and by thy words thou shalt be condemned." (Matthew 12:36–37)

- ○ "For there are three that bear record in heaven, the Father, the Word, and the Holy Ghost: and these three are one." (1 John 5:7)

Judgment of Church Organizations

"When Jesus came into the coasts of Caesarea Philippi, he asked his disciples, saying, Whom do

> men say that I the Son of man am? And they said, Some say that thou art John the Baptist: some, Elias; and others, Jeremias, or one of the prophets. He saith unto them, But whom say ye that I am? And Simon Peter answered and said, Thou art the Christ, the Son of the living God. And Jesus answered and said unto him, Blessed art thou, Simon Barjona: for flesh and blood hath not revealed it unto thee, but my Father which is in heaven. And I say also unto thee, That thou art Peter, and upon this rock I will build my church; and the gates of hell shall not prevail against it." (Matthew 16:13–18)

Jesus Christ is the founder of the church that bears the title "Christianity." He didn't give his church this name, but it was earned by Paul and Barnabas, when they preached in Antioch, the capital of a Roman province of Syria. "Then departed Barnabas to Tarsus, for to seek Saul; and when he had found him, he brought him unto Antioch. And it came to pass, that a whole year they assembled themselves with the church, and taught much people. And the disciples were called Christians first in Antioch."[541]

As founder and resurrected Lord, Christ Jesus has the authority to judge all church organizations that carry the Christianity title. Therefore, we see him sending the church denominations a stern warning on how he will judge their operation and administration by showing us seven known churches he judged after he had resurrected from the grave. Now with a little imagination, you could look at a modern-day church organization and fit it into the category of one of these ancient churches. I'm not going to name a particular church, but I do want to present how the Lord Jesus Christ will judge all churches.[542]

First, Christ lets us know that judgment against any church organization starts with the leader of the denomination. Second, he begins to unfold the good the church is doing. Next, he reveals the actions that are displeasing to him. Then he pronounces judgment. Last, he gives the church a plan to escape the wrath of God.

Judgment of the Church of Ephesus (Revelation 2:1-7)

Revelation 2: 1 Unto the angel of the church of Ephesus write; These things saith he that holdeth the seven stars in his right hand, who walketh in the midst of the seven golden candlesticks;
2 I know thy works, and thy labour, and thy patience, and how thou canst not bear them which are evil: and thou hast tried them which say they are apostles, and are not, and hast found them liars:
3 and hast borne, and hast patience, and for my name's sake hast laboured, and hast not fainted.
4 Nevertheless I have somewhat against thee, because thou hast left thy first love.
5 Remember therefore from whence thou art fallen, and repent, and do the first works; or else I will come unto thee quickly, and will remove thy candlestick out of his place, except thou repent.
6 But this thou hast, that thou hatest the deeds of the Nicolaitanes, which I also hate.
7 He that hath an ear, let him hear what the Spirit saith unto the churches; To him that overcometh will I give to eat of the tree of life, which is in the midst of the paradise of God.

TREE OF LIFE: "This tree was placed by God in the midst of the Garden of Eden (Genesis 2:8-9), a tree whose fruit could give eternal life. God told Adam and Eve that they could eat from every tree of the Garden except the tree of the knowledge of good and evil (2:16-17). When Adam and Eve disobeyed God by eating from the tree of the knowledge of good and evil, they were banished from the garden lest they "take also of the tree of life, and eat, and live for ever" (3:22).

The Genesis narrative suggests that God intended the tree of life to provide Adam and Eve with a symbol of life in fellowship with and dependence on God. Human life, as distinguished from that of the animals, is much more than merely biological existence; it is also spiritual-it finds its deepest fulfillment in fellowship with God. Life in the fullness of its physical and spiritual dimensions, however, could remain a person's possession only so long as he or she remained obedient to God's command (Genesis 2:17). Apart from Genesis, the only other Old Testament occurrences of the phrase the "tree of life" are found in Proverbs (quoted here from RSV), where it symbolizes the enrichment of life in various ways. In Proverbs 3:18 wisdom is referred to as "a tree of life to those who lay hold of her"; in 11:30 "the fruit of the righteous is a tree of life"; in 13:12 a fulfilled desire is as "a tree of life"; and in 15:4 "a gentle tongue is a tree of life."

The book of Revelation contains the only references to the tree of life in the New Testament (Revelation 2:7; Revelation 22:2 ; 22:14). The Bible begins and ends with a Paradise in the midst of which is a tree of life. The way to the tree of life, which was closed in Genesis 3, is open again for God's believing people. This was made possible by the second Adam, Jesus Christ. Those who have washed their robes in the blood of Christ (Revelation 7:14) and have sought forgiveness of their sin through the redemptive work of Christ, receive the right to the tree of life (Revelation 2:14), but the disobedient will have no access to it."[543]

The city of Ephesus was the capital of the western part of Asia Minor (modern-day Turkey). It was established by the Greeks and called, "the first and greatest metropolis of Asia," in the time of the Romans. The great Temple of Diana (called Artemis by the Greeks) was the main feature, "and was one of the seven wonders of the ancient world." It also had a theater that could contain around 50,000 spectators; who often watched gladiator and wild beast fights.[544] So there is good reason to believe this great city of riches so influenced the church that Christ had to tell them that they "had left their first love."

The greatest commandment in the Bible is "to love the Lord your God with all your heart and with all your soul, and with all your mind." Jesus added to this by saying, "He that loveth father or mother more than me is not worthy of me: and he that loveth son or daughter more than me is not worthy of me" (Matthew 10:37).

In judgment, Christ said, "Remember therefore from whence thou art fallen, and repent, and do the first works; or else I will come unto thee quickly, and will remove thy candlestick out of his place, except thou repent." And to those who heeded his message, he promised to give them the fruit from the Tree of Life to eat, "which is in the midst of the paradise of God"—the New Jerusalem (Revelation 2:1–7).

This church has been destroyed with nary a trace of its foundation stones. Therefore, the only history and location of the church is recorded in the book of Revelation.

Judgment of the Church of Smyrna (Revelation 2:8-11)

> **Revelation 2: 8 And unto the angel of the church in Smyrna write; These things saith the first and the last, which was dead, and is alive;**
> **9 I know thy works, and tribulation, and poverty, (but thou art rich) and I know the blasphemy of them which say they are Jews, and are not, but are the synagogue of Satan.**

**10 Fear none of those things which thou shalt suffer: behold, the devil shall cast some of you into prison, that ye may be tried; and ye shall have tribulation ten days: be thou faithful unto death, and I will give thee a crown of life.
11 He that hath an ear, let him hear what the Spirit saith unto the churches; He that overcometh shall not be hurt of the second death.**

The church of Smyrna was situated forty miles north of Ephesus. Today it is the major city of Anatolia, with a population of around 200,000 people, "of whom about one-third are professed Christians."[545]

Christ identified this church as having much tribulation and poverty, but they were rich in their faith in the Lord. Radio bible commentator J. Vernon McGee described their poverty as a, "congregation *of* slaves, ex-slaves, runaway slaves, freed slaves, poor people, and those who lost whatever money they had when they became Christians."[546]

Christ also knew how they were being deceived by some who called themselves Jews, but were liars like Judas Iscariot, whom Satan influenced to betray Jesus.

Christ went on to say that many of them would be thrown in jail and tortured. But they should hold onto their faith, and in the end, he would give them "the crown of life." The apostle Paul mentioned how to achieve this crown: "I have fought a good fight, I have finished my course, I have kept the faith: Henceforth there is laid up for me a crown of righteousness, which the Lord, the righteous judge, shall give me at that day: and not to me only, but unto all them also that love his appearing. (2 Timothy 4:7–8)

The bottom line is that they operated in total fear for their lives. But Christ told them, "He that overcometh shall not be hurt of the second death."

The fear of death is not something new to the Christian world. When Jesus sent his disciples out two by two, he told them he was sending them, "forth as sheep in the midst of wolves," and they would be trumped before judges and condemned for his name sake. But in all this he gave a ray of hope: "And fear not them which kill the body, but are not able to kill the soul: but rather fear him which is able to destroy both soul and body in hell" (Matthew 10:28).

I have personally experienced pastors who preach in fear. They make an apology for preaching against sin by saying, "I don't want to hurt anyone's feelings," or, "Excuse me for what I'm about to say, but I must say it, because it is written in the Bible."

Some fear the congregation will walk if they come down too hard against sin; for example: fornication (shacking up or cohabiting together), adultery (openly having an affair with thy neighbor's wife or husband), homosexuality (permitting this type of lifestyle in the church, and etc. Most of the time their cover is, "after all, God is love, so we should live, and let live; and let God be the judge."

The apostle Paul left us a record of the hardships he endured during his evangelistic travels as a gospel preacher.

> "Of the Jews five times received I forty stripes save one. Thrice was I beaten with rods, once was I stoned, thrice I suffered shipwreck, a night and a day I have been in the deep; In journeyings often, in perils of waters, in perils of robbers, in perils by mine own countrymen, in perils by the heathen, in perils in the city, in perils in the wilderness, in perils in the sea, in perils among false brethren; In weariness and painfulness, in watchings often, in hunger and thirst, in fastings often, in cold and nakedness. Beside those things that are without, that which cometh upon me daily, the care of all the churches. Who is weak, and I am not weak? who is offended, and I burn not? If I must needs glory, I will glory of the things which concern mine infirmities. The God and Father of our Lord Jesus Christ, which is blessed for evermore, knoweth that I lie not." (2 Corinthians 11:24–31)

Who is Jesus Christ

Sadly, this church has also been removed from the face of the earth, and its true origin is only known by the Lord Jesus Christ.

Judgment of the Church of Pergamos (Revelation 2:12-17)

> **Revelation 2: 12 And to the angel of the church in Pergamos write; These things saith he which hath the sharp sword with two edges;**
> **13 I know thy works and where thou dwellest, even where Satan's seat is: and thou holdest fast my name, and hast not denied my faith, even in those days wherein Antipas was my faithful martyr, who was slain among you, where Satan dwelleth. 14 But I have a few things against thee, because thou hast there them that hold the doctrine of Balaam, who taught Balac to cast a stumblingblock before the children of Israel, to eat things sacrificed unto idols, and to commit fornication.**
> **15 So hast thou also them that hold the doctrine of the Nicolaitanes, which thing I hate.**
> **16 Repent; or else I will come unto thee quickly, and will fight against them with the sword of my mouth.**
> **17 He that hath an ear, let him hear what the Spirit saith unto the churches; To him that overcometh will I give to eat of the hidden manna, and will give him a white stone, and in the stone a new name written, which no man knoweth saving he that receiveth it.**

Pergamos was a main city of Mysia, located on the banks of the Caicus River, about twenty miles from the sea coast, and sixty miles north from Smyrna, Sheep and goat skins were first produced and manufactured here for parchment. The city gained importance because it had a library that was greater than the one in Alexandria

Egypt. The Roman General Mark Anthony gave the library to Cleopatra, and she moved it to Alexandria.[547] "It is now called Bergama, and has a population of some twenty thousand of whom about two thousand profess to be Christians."[548] The main attraction in the city was a temple erected to Caesar Augustus.[549]

Christ praised this church for holding onto their faith; even after a follower named Antipas was martyred. Then he admonished them for permitting the teaching of the false prophet Balaam, for it was he who King Balak of Moab commissioned to put a curse on Israel as they traveled through his land. When Moses and the children of Israel did stop to take a rest in Moab, they were induced to sexual immorality with the women, and enticed, by lust, to bow the knee and eat food sacrificed to the god Baalpeor. This resulted in 24,000 heads being chopped off and hung up on sticks in the desert sun.[550]

Next, he chastised them for submitting to the doctrine of the Nicolaitans: "They held it lawful to eat food sacrificed to idols; to join in idolatrous worship; and that God did not create the universe. It is believed that the founder of this doctrine was the Deacon Nicolas (a proselyte of Antioch) one of the seven men selected to help the women in the daily administration of the early church."[551]

The judgment of Christ was short but powerful: "Repent; or else I will come unto thee quickly, and will fight against them with the sword of my mouth."

Christ told them he would give them a great reward if they overcame their sinful and wicked ways: "He that hath an ear, let him hear what the Spirit saith unto the churches; To him that overcometh will I give to eat of the hidden manna, and will give him a white stone, and in the stone a new name written, which no man knoweth saving he that receiveth it."

> "And he shewed me a pure river of water of life, clear as crystal, proceeding out of the throne of God and of the Lamb. In the midst of the street of it, and on either side of the river, was there the tree of life, which bare twelve manner of fruits, and yielded her fruit

every month: and the leaves of the tree were for the healing of the nations. And there shall be no more curse: but the throne of God and of the Lamb shall be in it; and his servants shall serve him: And they shall see his face; and his name shall be in their foreheads." (Revelation 22:1–4)

This church has disappeared, and is erased from the pages of history.

Judgment of the Church of Thyatira (Revelation 2:18-29)

Revelation 2: 18 And unto the angel of the church in Thyatira write; These things saith the Son of God, who hath his eyes like unto a flame of fire, and his feet are like fine brass;
19 I know thy works, and charity, and service, and faith, and thy patience, and thy works; and the last to be more than the first.
20 Notwithstanding I have a few things against thee, because thou sufferest that woman Jezebel, which calleth herself a prophetess, to teach and to seduce my servants to commit fornication, and to eat things sacrificed unto idols.
21 And I gave her space to repent of her fornication; and she repented not.
22 Behold, I will cast her into a bed, and them that commit adultery with her into great tribulation, except they repent of their deeds.
23 And I will kill her children with death; and all the churches shall know that I am he which searcheth the reins and hearts: and I will give unto every one of you according to your works.
24 But unto you I say, and unto the rest in Thyatira, as many as have not this doctrine, and which have

> **not known the depths of Satan, as they speak; I will put upon you none other burden.**
> **25 But that which ye have already hold fast till I come.**
> **26 And he that overcometh, and keepeth my works unto the end, to him will I give power over the nations:**
> **27 and he shall rule them with a rod of iron; as the vessels of a potter shall they be broken to shivers: even as I received of my Father.**
> **28 And I will give him the morning star.**
> **29 He that hath an ear, let him hear what the Spirit saith unto the churches.**

Thyatira was a city about fifty-five miles northeast of Smyrna, on a road between Pergamos and Sardis. Its modern city name is Akhisar. The gods Apollo and Artemis were worshipped there, along with many others. Security of the city was contained by a fortified Roman garrison.[552]

This city was also widely known for its clothing dyes. When the apostle Paul passed through Philippi, he met a woman named Lydia from Thyatira, who was a seller of purple dye. After her conversion and baptism, Paul and his company lived at her house (Acts 16:11–15).

Jesus said this church showed a lot of love, patience, and service to others, and it was strong in their faith in him. However, they permitted a woman named Jezebel (who called herself a prophetess) to preach the doctrine of Nicolas, "to teach and to seduce my servants to commit fornication, and to eat things sacrificed unto idols (other gods)."

Christ relayed to them that swift judgment was on the way if they didn't repent of their sins. Further, Jezebel, her children, and all those who supported her doctrine would be thrown into the bed of hell.

Now the judgment against false prophets (male or female), and all those who follow after them may seem a little harsh. But punishment

Who is Jesus Christ

against false prophets has already been established by God in the Old Testament.

- "1 If there arise among you a prophet, or a dreamer of dreams, and giveth thee a sign or a wonder, and the sign or the wonder come to pass, whereof he spake unto thee, saying, Let us go after other gods, which thou hast not known, and let us serve them; thou shalt not hearken unto the words of that prophet, or that dreamer of dreams: for the Lord your God proveth you, to know whether ye love the Lord your God with all your heart and with all your soul. Ye shall walk after the Lord your God, and fear him, and keep his commandments, and obey his voice, and ye shall serve him, and cleave unto him. And that prophet, or that dreamer of dreams, shall be put to death; because he hath spoken to turn you away from the Lord your God, which brought you out of the land of Egypt, and redeemed you out of the house of bondage, to thrust thee out of the way which the Lord thy God commanded thee to walk in. So shalt thou put the evil away from the midst of thee." (Deuteronomy 13:1-5)

- "And the word of the Lord came unto me, saying, Son of man, prophesy against the prophets of Israel that prophesy, and say thou unto them that prophesy out of their own hearts, Hear ye the word of the Lord; Thus saith the Lord God; Woe unto the foolish prophets, that follow their own spirit, and have seen nothing! Likewise, thou son of man, set thy face against the daughters of thy people, which prophesy out of their own heart; and prophesy thou against them." (Ezekiel 13:1–3, 17)

- "I have seen also in the prophets of Jerusalem a horrible thing: they commit adultery, and walk in lies: they strengthen also the hands of evildoers, that none doth return from his wickedness; they are all of them unto me as Sodom, and the inhabitants thereof as Gomorrah." (Jeremiah 23:14)

- "Therefore, behold, I am against the prophets, saith the Lord, that steal my words every one from his neighbour. Behold, I am against the prophets, saith the Lord, that use their tongues, and say, He saith. Behold, I am against them that prophesy false dreams, saith the Lord, and do tell them, and cause my people to err by their lies, and by their lightness; yet I sent them not, nor commanded them: therefore they shall not profit this people at all, saith the Lord." (Jeremiah 23:30–32)

Ultimately, this church vanished as a vapor in the wind.

Judgment of the Church of Sardis (Revelation 3:1-16)

**Revelation 3: 1 And unto the angel of the church in Sardis write; These things saith he that hath the seven Spirits of God, and the seven stars; I know thy works, that thou hast a name that thou livest, and art dead.
2 Be watchful, and strengthen the things which remain, that are ready to die: for I have not found thy works perfect before God.
3 Remember therefore how thou hast received and heard, and hold fast, and repent. If therefore thou shalt not watch, I will come on thee as a thief, and thou shalt not know what hour I will come upon thee.
4 Thou hast a few names even in Sardis which have not defiled their garments; and they shall walk with me in white: for they are worthy.
5 He that overcometh, the same shall be clothed in white raiment; and I will not blot out his name out**

of the book of life, but I will confess his name before my Father, and before his angels.
6 He that hath an ear, let him hear what the Spirit saith unto the churches.

This city was about thirty miles due south of Thyatira. It is now a ruin called Sert-Kalessi in Asiatic Turkey. It was the capital of the kingdom of Lydia. It was known for the gold that flowed from the river Pactolus. Cybele the moon goddess and Apollo the sun god were the main deities worshipped there.[553]

Christ saw this church as being dead and without life: "I know thy works, that thou hast a name that thou livest, and art dead." A dead church is one that is just going through the motions of religious worship. They spew forth a lot of programs that are pleasing to emotions and worldly living.

In his epistle to Timothy, the apostle Paul warned the church of this type of people: "Having a form of godliness, but denying the power thereof: from such turn away." [554] Jesus said "God is a Spirit: and those that worship him must worship him in spirit and in truth."[555] This means putting away sin, and living holy male and female lives.

Jesus went on to say that judgment would come upon them, "like a thief in the night," if they didn't repent of their sins. And for all those who did turn away from iniquity, "the same shall be clothed in white raiment; and I will not blot out his name out of the book of life, but I will confess his name before my Father, and before his angels."

Christ has already said, "No man can serve two masters: for either he will hate the one, and love the other, or else he will hold to the one, and despise the other. Ye cannot serve God and mammon."[556] So it should be no surprise that he calls for the church to come out of worldliness.

In the Old Testament, God told Moses, "Whosoever hath sinned against me, him will I blot out of my book" (Exodus 32:33). By the same token, there are some who strongly believe God will not take back his Spirit (the Holy Ghost) based on the doctrine of eternal security: "once you are saved you are always saved." Yet it is recorded in the book of 1 Samuel that God had the prophet Samuel anoint Saul (the first king of Israel) with oil, and the Spirit of God came upon him. But when God judged Saul for disobedience, he removed the Holy Spirit and replaced it with an unclean spirit. (1 Samuel 16:12–15)

Unfortunately, the church of Sardis and its foundation are forever lost in ancient rubble.

Judgment of the Church of Philadelphia (Revelation 3:7-13)

> **Revelation 3: 7 And to the angel of the church in Philadelphia write; These things saith he that is holy, he that is true, he that hath the key of David, he that openeth, and no man shutteth; and shutteth, and no man openeth;**
> **8 I know thy works: behold, I have set before thee an open door, and no man can shut it: for thou hast a little strength, and hast kept my word, and hast not denied my name.**
> **9 Behold, I will make them of the synagogue of Satan, which say they are Jews, and are not, but do lie; behold, I will make them to come and worship before thy feet, and to know that I have loved thee.**
> **10 Because thou hast kept the word of my patience, I also will keep thee from the hour of temptation, which shall come upon all the world, to try them that dwell upon the earth.**
> **11 Behold, I come quickly: hold that fast which thou hast, that no man take thy crown.**
> **12 Him that overcometh will I make a pillar in the temple of my God, and he shall go no more out: and I will write upon him the name of my God, and the name of the city of my God, which is new**

Jerusalem, which cometh down out of heaven from my God: and I will write upon him my new name. 13 He that hath an ear, let him hear what the Spirit saith unto the churches.

The church of Philadelphia was on a Roman road, approximately thirty miles southeast of Sardis, "in the region of Lydia in western Asia Minor" (Turkey). The modern-day name of the city is Alashehir. Its location was a vital trade link between Sardis and Pergamum to the west, and Laodicea and Hierapolis to the east. Agriculture, leather production and a textile industry were the main economic support systems.[557] Christ had only praise for this church, because they never wavered in their faith toward him.

Today there are close to fifteen churches in Philadelphia that practice Christianity. Of the 15,000 inhabitants, one-third is Greek Christians, who are allowed religious freedom in a Muslim nation. The leaders attribute this grace of freedom to the book of Revelation.[558]

A tribute to Christ is the fact the church is still active. It would behoove every disciple of Christ Jesus to study this church, and see how they measure up against it. There is an old saying, "The race is not given to the swift or the strong but to him that endures until the end." And ye shall be hated of all men for my name's sake: but he that endureth to the end shall be saved. (Matthew 10:22) And remember that one small slip could knock one out of the race, like King Saul of Israel and Judas Iscariot.

> **PHILADELPHIA:** 1. City of the Decapolis, not specifically mentioned in any NT writing. It was located on the plateau about 25 miles (40.2 kilometers) east of the Jordan River. In 63 BC Palestine came under Roman domination. Pompey, the Roman general who conquered the region, reorganized the territory. He established a league of 10 self-governing cities or city-states. Most of these were located on the eastern side of the Jordan River. Philadelphia was the

southernmost, and Damascus the northernmost, of the 10. In the Gospels this territory is referred to as the Decapolis.

2. City in western Asia Minor. It was one of the seven Asian cities to which the author of the book of Revelation addressed letters, mentioned in 1:11 and 3:7-13.

This city was founded about 140 BC by Attalus II of the city of Pergamum. Attalus II was also known as "Philadelphus"; the name of the city was derived from this royal nickname. He intended that it would serve as a center for the spread of Greek culture throughout the region, especially to the people of Phrygia. Situated on a fertile plain, it was rich with vineyards and wine production. Asian Philadelphia was heavily damaged by an earthquake in the year AD 17. For the purpose of rebuilding, it was granted disaster aid by the Roman emperor Tiberius.

When John wrote from Patmos near the end of the first century, the churches of western Asia were undergoing persecution. The church in Philadelphia was one of them. This church was enduring the persecution faithfully, and the letter to it (Revelation 3:7-13) contains no words of reproach or warning. Instead, Jesus gave them encouragement and precious promises.

Some years later, the Christian bishop and martyr Ignatius of Antioch also wrote a letter to the church in Philadelphia. He expressed appreciation for his recent visit with them, and encouraged them in Christian unity.[559]

Judgment of the Church of Laodicea (Revelation 3:14-22)

> Revelation 3: 14 And unto the angel of the church of the Laodiceans write; These things saith the Amen, the faithful and true witness, the beginning of the creation of God;
> 15 I know thy works, that thou art neither cold nor hot: I would thou wert cold or hot.
> 16 So then because thou art lukewarm, and neither cold nor hot, I will spue thee out of my mouth.
> 17 Because thou sayest, I am rich, and increased with goods, and have need of nothing; and knowest not that thou art wretched, and miserable, and poor, and blind, and naked:
> 18 I counsel thee to buy of me gold tried in the fire, that thou mayest be rich; and white raiment, that thou mayest be clothed, and that the shame of thy nakedness do not appear; and anoint thine eyes with eyesalve, that thou mayest see.
> 19 As many as I love, I rebuke and chasten: be zealous therefore, and repent.
> 20 Behold, I stand at the door, and knock: if any man hear my voice, and open the door, I will come in to him, and will sup with him, and he with me.
> 21 To him that overcometh will I grant to sit with me in my throne, even as I also overcame, and am set down with my Father in his throne.
> 22 He that hath an ear, let him hear what the Spirit saith unto the churches.

This city was forty miles east of Ephesus, near the borders of Phrygia and Lydia. It was situated on a Roman road, approximately sixty miles southeast of Philadelphia. Today it is deserted and called by the Turks Eskihissar (old castle).

Built on seven hills, the city was home to a stadium and three theaters; one which was well over 450 feet in diameter. This city was proud of its wealth, bridges, aqueducts, and gymnasium.

An archbishop and his council sit in the seat of religious power. They decreed, "that Christians should not Judaize by resting on the seventh day, but work on it as usual, and rest on the Lord's day [*Sunday*]as far as possible, like Christians," much like the majority of Christian churches today that worship and rest on Sunday.[560]

Christ was very wroth with this church: "I know thy works, that thou art neither cold nor hot: I would thou wert cold or hot." This indicates that they were drawn between two opinions on which day to worship on; even though God has not changed his Sabbath day. Nor has he given anyone the authority to make such a change.

Some believe the Lord's Day is Sunday because of the events surrounding his resurrection. But no matter what may conspire, God the Father is the one who decides changes to his Word. An example is when the angel Gabriel told Mary that the promised Immanuel would be named Jesus.[561]

Christ sent them the strong warning that if they did not repent, he would reject them from entering the kingdom of heaven: "So then because thou art lukewarm, and neither cold nor hot, I will spue thee out of my mouth." He then told them that they were arrogant and lifted up in pride: because of their riches and material processions. And pleaded with them to come back to the holiness of God.

As I have said before, I must make it clear that the gospel of Christ has nothing to do with gaining riches and goods, but of preaching against sin to turn souls back to God. All who preach the gospel for personal gain will meet the same fate as the church of Laodicea: total destruction and eternal damnation. (Philippians 1:15-18 &3:17-21 / Romans 16:17-20)

Summary Thoughts of the Seven Churches

If you thoroughly read the Scripture passages concerning the seven churches, then you are fully aware Christ Jesus knows everything there is to know about the church, and all the denominations called by his name, and those operating outside his name. Therefore, when you turn away from doing his will, you step out of his marvelous light and back into darkness.

I warn you the judgments of Christ are not isolated, but a copulation of judgments that can fall upon a church by ones, or by multiples. So, I beg you here to take heed on what he says, and pray that you not fall into the snare of O Lucifer (the great dragon, that old serpent called the Devil and Satan).

If you do keep the faith with the Lord Jesus Christ, he will bring you through and out of temptation. It is written, "There hath no temptation taken you but such as is common to man: but God is faithful, who will not suffer you to be tempted above that ye are able; but will with the temptation also make a way to escape, that ye may be able to bear it" (1 Corinthians 10:13).

CHAPTER 28

THE FINAL JUDGMENTS OF GOD

YEAR 100 AD

Revelation 1: 1 The Revelation of Jesus Christ, which God gave unto him, to shew unto his servants things which must shortly come to pass; and he sent and signified it by his angel unto his servant John: 2 who bare record of the word of God, and of the testimony of Jesus Christ, and of all things that he saw.
3 Blessed is he that readeth, and they that hear the words of this prophecy, and keep those things which are written therein: for the time is at hand.

Spirit Beings' Control of Earth

Christ revealed to us that hell was prepared for the Devil and his angels. But he also said that humankind could escape hell and the lake of fire by believing in him and the cross. Now this is a serious matter and must be addressed by the reading of Scripture. There is

Who is Jesus Christ

no other way to convince humankind except with the written Word of God.

In these last days, which started on the day of Pentecost, the spirit beings will be let loose to bring havoc, sorrow, despair, war, destruction, and tribulation upon the earth. The ones that will do this are called the "beast, the false prophet, and Satan." These three will be responsible for deceiving the world to war against the Lord Jesus Christ at Armageddon.

There are countless theories and theological positions on how the events will unfold in the book of Revelation. However, it is clear that God has put the Lord Jesus Christ in charge of monitoring the written outcomes. Again, I don't want to undermine other religious writers, but I want to present what is written for your study and evaluation.

Satan will give power to a man called the "Beast who will mark his followers with his number; his number is 666. We know this is a man, because he is thrown alive into the lake of fire with the false prophet. (Revelation 19:20)

> "And they worshipped the dragon [Satan] which gave power unto the beast: and they worshipped the beast, saying, Who is like unto the beast? who is able to make war with him? And there was given unto him a mouth speaking great things and blasphemies; and power was given unto him to continue forty and two months. And he opened his mouth in blasphemy against God, to blaspheme his name, and his tabernacle, and them that dwell in heaven." (Revelation 13:4–6)

So, there will come a time when God is truly hated, and Satan is worshipped. Looking at how the world is being shaped, it is easy to fathom how God will be replaced by Satan. Prayer and allegiance to God have been removed from the schools, and in some respects, the workplace. The right to abortion has escalated, and same-sex marriage is fast becoming an accepted national law. The death penalty has almost vanished from justice, and murder is running rampart. The love of money and materialism is consuming souls through gambling houses, lotteries, Hollywood fame and riches, and political high places. Yet there will be a small remnant that will refuse to follow the beast. And they will pay with their lives.

- "And it was given unto him [the beast and Satan] to make war with the saints, and to overcome them: and power was given him over all kindreds, and tongues, and nations. And all that dwell upon the earth shall worship him, whose names are not written in the book of life of the Lamb slain from the foundation of the world." (Revelation 13:7–8)

- "Here is the patience of the saints: here are they that keep the commandments of God, and the faith of Jesus. And I heard a voice from heaven saying unto me, Write, Blessed are the dead which die in the Lord from henceforth: Yea, saith the Spirit, that they may rest from their labours; and their works do follow them." (Revelation 14:12–13)

- "And I saw thrones, and they sat upon them, and judgment was given unto them: and I saw the souls of them that were beheaded for the witness of Jesus, and for the word of God, and which had not worshipped the beast, neither his image, neither had received his mark upon their foreheads, or in their hands; and they lived and reigned with Christ a thousand years." (Revelation 20:4)

From the above Scriptures, it is plain that the whole world will worship and follow after Satan, the beast, and the false prophet; except the followers of Christ Jesus: they will be persecuted and slain for their beliefs. So, is there a Scripture that shows how Satan will deceive the world to follow after the beast? Yes, there is.

- "And I saw three unclean spirits like frogs come out of the mouth of the dragon, and out of the mouth of the beast, and out of the mouth of the false prophet. For they are the spirits of devils, working miracles, which go forth unto the kings of the earth and of the whole world, to gather them to the battle of that great day of God Almighty." (Revelation 16:13–14)

I want to say here that, throughout the Bible, there are numerous mentions of magicians, sorcerers, astrologers, prophets, and seers who were loyal advisers to those in power. They were used to sustain reigns and kingdoms. Even the Lord Jesus Christ could not escape this kind of thinking. He was accused of using the power of Satan to heal the sick and do his miracles.[562] Yet prior to being crucified, Christ warned his disciples to be on the lookout for prophets who made an open show of power, and bragged about supernatural signs and wonders (Matthew 24:23–26).

Even though Christ gave a stern warning, people are still carried away with sensationalism, and supernatural religious worship services. Many have followed after prophesies that are not sustained by the written Word of God, but are taught as something the Bible teaches that can only be grasped through study. In these last days, people have sold all their possessions, and followed a prophet into the desert, only to be disappointed; in some cases, they have lost their lives. It seems humankind is fascinated by magic, enchantments, and supernatural miracles. However, the apostle Paul reminds the church to keep a focus on witnessing to lost souls, and not on what is physically happening around us.

- "For we wrestle not against flesh and blood, but against principalities, against powers, against the rulers of the darkness of this world, against spiritual wickedness in high places." (Ephesians 6:12)

The Wrath of God Will Fall on the Followers of the Beast

Revelation 14: 9 And the third angel followed them, saying with a loud voice, If any man worship

> the beast and his image, and receive his mark in his forehead, or in his hand, 10 the same shall drink of the wine of the wrath of God, which is poured out without mixture into the cup of his indignation; and he shall be tormented with fire and brimstone in the presence of the holy angels, and in the presence of the Lamb:
> 11 and the smoke of their torment ascendeth up for ever and ever: and they have no rest day nor night, who worship the beast and his image, and whosoever receiveth the mark of his name.
> 12 Here is the patience of the saints: here are they that keep the commandments of God, and the faith of Jesus.

There are two reasons why the followers of Christ will not accept the mark of the beast: (1) every believer is sealed by the Holy Ghost until the day of redemption, and (2) that seal is implanted in the believer's forehead.[563]

The practice of God sealing his saints in their foreheads was revealed in Ezekiel Chapters 8 and 9. This is when God took Ezekiel from Babylon to the temple in Jerusalem. On arrival, God told Ezekiel to dig a hole in the wall and walk through the exposed door. Once inside, God said, "behold the wicked abominations that they do here," for they were worshipping, "every form of creeping things, and abominable beasts, and all the idols of the house of Israel, pourtrayed upon the wall round about." There were seventy elders holding a "censer in his hand; and a thick cloud of incense went up" from them. God told Ezekiel they did this because they thought that "The Lord see us not; the Lord hath forsaken the earth." They were in disbelief and denial that God had sent Nebuchadnezzar, and his army to take away Israel into seventy years of captivity.[564]

Then God showed Ezekiel other abominations the people were committing against him. After this, God pronounced judgment: "Therefore will I also deal in fury: mine eye shall not spare, neither will I have pity and though they cry in mine ears with a loud voice, yet will I not hear them."

It seems that God has set his mind to destroy the people without mercy. Yet, just like in the days of Noah, he saved a remnant for his pleasure. This is where God will mark his believers from among the wicked, evil, and godless.

- *God his draws army to Jerusalem:* "He cried also in mine ears with a loud voice, saying, Cause them that have charge over the city to draw near, even every man with his destroying weapon in his hand. And, behold, six men came from the way of the higher gate, which lieth toward the north, and every man a slaughter weapon in his hand;"

- *God calls for the keeper of the Book of Life:* "and one man among them was clothed with linen, with a writer's inkhorn by his side: and they went in, and stood beside the brasen altar. And the glory of the God of Israel was gone up from the cherub, whereupon he was, to the threshold of the house. And he called to the man clothed with linen, which had the writer's inkhorn by his side;"

- *God gives the command to mark his people in their foreheads:* "And the Lord said unto him, Go through the midst of the city, through the midst of Jerusalem, and set a mark upon the foreheads of the men that sigh and that cry for all the abominations that be done in the midst thereof."

- *All who did not receive the mark of God were to be slain:* "And to the others he said in mine hearing, Go ye after him through the city, and smite: let not your eye spare, neither have ye pity: Slay utterly old and young, both maids, and little children, and women: but come not near any man upon whom is the mark; and begin at my sanctuary. Then they began at the ancient men which were before the house" (Ezekiel 9:1–7).

This is not the end of God marking his believers on their foreheads. This mercy is extended to New Testament believers during the time of Satan, the beast, and the false prophet. I don't want to belabor this, but I do want to give you the proof of the Scripture.

- ***The Nation of Israel:*** "And after these things I saw four angels standing on the four corners of the earth, holding the four winds of the earth, that the wind should not blow on the earth, nor on the sea, nor on any tree. And I saw another angel ascending from the east, having the seal of the living God: and he cried with a loud voice to the four angels, to whom it was given to hurt the earth and the sea, Saying, Hurt not the earth, neither the sea, nor the trees, till we have sealed the servants of our God in their foreheads. And I heard the number of them which were sealed: and there were sealed an hundred and forty and four thousand of all the tribes of the children of Israel" (Revelation 7:1–4).

- ***Believers in Christ:*** "And the fifth angel sounded, and I saw a star fall from heaven unto the earth: and to him was given the key of the bottomless pit. And he opened the bottomless pit; and there arose a smoke out of the pit, as the smoke of a great furnace; and the sun and the air were darkened by reason of the smoke of the pit. And there came out of the smoke locusts upon the earth: and unto them was given power, as the scorpions of the earth have power. And it was commanded them that they should not hurt the grass of the earth, neither any green thing, neither any tree; but only those men which have not the seal of God in their foreheads" (Revelation 9:1–4).

"And I looked, and, lo, a Lamb stood on the mount Sion, and with him an hundred forty and four thousand, having his Father's name written in their foreheads" (Revelation 14:1).

- ***The New Jerusalem***: "And he shewed me a pure river of water of life, clear as crystal, proceeding out of the throne of God and of the Lamb. In the midst of the street of it, and on either side of the river, was there the tree of life, which bare twelve manner of fruits, and yielded her fruit every month: and the leaves of the tree were for the healing of the nations. And there shall be no more curse: but the throne of God and of the Lamb shall be in it; and his servants shall serve him: And they shall see his face; and his name shall be in their foreheads" (Revelation 22:1–4).

Judgment of Spirit Beings

Revelation 19: 19 And I saw the beast, and the kings of the earth, and their armies, gathered together to make war against him that sat on the horse, and against his army.
20 And the beast was taken, and with him the false prophet that wrought miracles before him, with which he deceived them that had received the mark of the beast, and them that worshipped his image. These both were cast alive into a lake of fire burning with brimstone.
21 And the remnant were slain with the sword of him that sat upon the horse, which sword proceeded out of his mouth: and all the fowls were filled with their flesh.

Take notice here that the beast and the false prophet did not die a normal human death. They were thrown alive into the lake of fire. However, all the human beings who worshipped the beast, and followed after the false prophet died in their fleshly bodies. This is the reason Christ told his disciples, "Fear not them which kill the body, but are not able to kill the soul: but rather fear him which is able to destroy both soul and body in hell" (Matthew 10:28.)

After the battle of Armageddon, "an angel came down from heaven, having the key of the bottomless pit and a great chain in his hand. And he laid hold on the dragon, that old serpent, which is called the Devil and Satan, and bound him a thousand years." This was so Christ Jesus could reign on earth for a thousand years without any influence against him by Satan.

However, after the thousand years expired, Satan was let loose once again on the earth. And true to his nature, he went to and fro, deceiving the nations to fight against the Lord Jesus Christ. Once he got his armies in position around the holy city of Jerusalem, "fire came down from God out of heaven, and devoured them." This was the last act of Satan on planet earth, for his judgment has come; "And the devil that deceived them was cast into the lake of fire and brimstone, where the beast and the false prophet are, and shall be tormented day and night for ever and ever." (Revelation 20:10)

Some believe Satan will be the ultimate ruler of power in hell. Yet the Bible records a different view of his status in hell. For the sake of argument and verification, I ask you to read Isaiah Chapter 14, verses 10 through 17. You will see how Satan has deceived the world into thinking he has power over fleshly beings. Yet Christ has received all power in heaven and on the earth from the Father, and also has the keys to hell and death in his hands (Matthew 28:18; Revelation 1:18). Therefore, Christ boldly said, "I am the way, the truth, and the life: no man cometh unto the Father, but by me" (John 14:6).

However, it is very possible Satan will gain power and control in hell by deceiving the dead souls with the help of his allies the beast, the false prophet, and the fallen angels.

Judgment of Human and Spirit Beings

This is the final judgment of earth conducted by God with his Son (Jesus Christ) by his side. Christ is here because he is the one who will call everyone to the throne of God. This is stated in John Chapter 5: "Marvel not at this: for the hour is coming, in the which all that are in the graves shall hear his voice, And shall come forth;

they that have done good, unto the resurrection of life; and they that have done evil, unto the resurrection of damnation." Take notice that every human being and spiritual being has to come before God and his Son for final judgment. This judgment is recorded in Revelation 20:11–15.

> ***God:*** "And I saw a great white throne, and him that sat on it, from whose face the earth and the heaven fled away; and there was found no place for them."

> ***Souls:*** "And I saw the dead, small and great, stand before God;"

> ***The Judgment Books:*** "and the books were opened: and another book was opened, which is the book of life: and the dead were judged out of those things which were written in the books, according to their works."

The Book of Life needs no explanation, because names in this book are those of the faithful followers of Christ. The Old Testament saints (the followers of God whose names were written in his book) were resurrected and taken to heaven by the Lord Jesus Christ. The New Testament saints will be resurrected and caught up in the air with Christ at his second coming.

However, the book of works seems to contain the names of Old and New Testament people who were bad, ugly, and evil during their life on earth. This is confirmed by the prophet Daniel (12:2–3) and the Lord Jesus Christ (John 5:25–29).

But God will not just throw a person into the lake of fire without first giving him or her a chance to present a case before him. This is verified by Christ in Matthew 7:21-23, and 25:31-46.

The book of works are also confirmed in Matthew 12;36-37, "But I say unto you, That every idle word that men shall speak, they shall give account thereof in the day of judgment. For by thy words thou shalt be justified, and by thy words thou shalt be condemned." Lastly, a strict record is being kept by the Father, the Word, and the Holy Ghost. (1 John 5:7).

- "And the sea gave up the dead which were in it;

- and death and hell delivered up the dead which were in them: and they were judged every man according to their works."

First to be called to the throne of God were all those who died from water. I wonder, however, if the spirits that caused the swine to drown are in this group. Second, all those who are in hell, from Adam to the throwing down of Satan, are called forth. Finally, the angels that sinned during Noah's day are called before the throne of God.

When God completed his white throne judgment, he gave the order, "And death and hell were cast into the lake of fire. This is the second death. And whosoever was not found written in the book of life was cast into the lake of fire."

The Lake of Fire Judgment

Every judgment of God must be based on a written Scripture. During the great white throne judgment (Revelation 20:11–15), there is an explanation of how he will judge names written in the books, but not the Scriptures he will use to judge.

When Christ Jesus walked upon the earth, he did not judge the acts and works of humans. He stated he was not sent to judge but to present the way of salvation. Some have mistakenly taken this act of kindness by God to commit abominations that God outlawed in the Old Testament. And they use the excuse of what Christ Jesus did, or did not do, or say during his earthly ministry to justify their lustful desires. However, the book of Revelation is God's instruction to his Son, Jesus Christ, concerning the final judgment of life on the earth. Presented as a warning to the saved, and the lost, is the criteria scripture God will use to determine who will enter the New Heaven and Earth, and who will be thrown into the lake of fire.

> **"But the *fearful,* and *unbelieving,* and *abominable,* and *murderers,* and *whoremongers,* and *sorcerers,* and *idolaters,* and all *liars,* shall have their part in the lake which burneth with fire and brimstone: which is the second death."** (Revelation 21:8)

From this one Scripture it is very clear that God intends to destroy sin, and sinful ways in the lake of fire. And that he has reserved the final rite of judgment for himself. Therefore, make no mistake concerning the eight categories (types) of people listed, for they are a direct correlation of how God will conduct his final judgment of human and spirit beings when the books of judgment are opened. No "being" bearing one of those words in the heart will enter the kingdom of God. For the heart is where sin finds a home and a place of rest.

> **"But those things which proceed out of the mouth come forth from the heart; and they defile the man. For out of the heart proceed evil thoughts, murders, adulteries, fornications, thefts, false witness, blasphemies."** (Matthew 15:18–19)

This is why it is stressed in the Bible that if you "confess with your mouth the Lord Jesus Christ, and believe in your heart that God has raised him from the dead, thou shalt be saved." (Romans 10:9) After that, you must take the advice of the apostle Paul and present your body, "a living sacrifice, holy, acceptable unto God, which is your reasonable service. And be not conformed to this world: but be ye transformed by the renewing of your mind, that ye may prove what is that good, and acceptable, and perfect, will of God" (Romans 12:1–2). Be aware that repeating the "sinner's prayer" without a change of heart toward the Lord Jesus Christ will only worsen. One's plight of life.

Therefore, I will attempt to unravel the eight words for you by giving you word meanings with Scripture backup. An old proverb says, "Sticks and stones may break my bones, but words will never hurt me." This may be true, because words can be harsh and cruel. But they can't hurt the physical body. However, these judgment words have the power to destroy both body and soul in hell.

Please bear with me, and remember that souls are at stake. And that understanding must be clarified by the Word of God. Further, that Christ Jesus final judgment, at the great white throne judgment, will be based on Scripture as he stands by the right hand of the Father. You may not wholeheartedly agree with my dissertation, so I challenge you to do further research after you finish this book.

The Fearful

Fear is a normal human reaction that is induced when we are threatened, or going through a mental crisis. However, the fear that is stated in Revelation has to do with accepting or denouncing the Lord Jesus Christ. This is very serious and can be detrimental to your faith, because the fear of death is the one thing fleshly beings are threatened with by evil forces.

- Whosoever therefore shall confess me before men, him will I confess also before my Father which is in heaven. "But whosoever shall deny me before men, him will I also deny before my Father which is in heaven. (Matthew 10:32–33)

- And he said to them all, If any man will come after me, let him deny himself, and take up his cross daily, and follow me. For whosoever will save his life shall lose it: but whosoever will lose his life for my sake, the same shall save it. For what is a man advantaged, if he gain the whole world, and lose himself, or be cast away? For whosoever shall be ashamed of me and of my words, of him shall the Son of man be ashamed, when he shall come in his own glory, and in his Father's, and of the holy angels. (Luke 9:23–26)

- Also I say unto you, Whosoever shall confess me before men, him shall the Son of man also confess before the angels of God: But he that denieth me before men shall be denied before the angels of God. (Luke 12:8–9)

- Whosoever shall confess that Jesus is the Son of God, God dwelleth in him, and he in God. (1 John 4:15)

When the 120 disciples (men and women) received the power of the Holy Ghost on the day of Pentecost, they began to boldly speak and witness for Christ Jesus. For their efforts, they were brought before the Sanhedrin council, who threatened them not to continue to preach about Jesus; and they put them in jail, and beat and whipped them before they were let go. But the disciples, "departed from the presence of the council, rejoicing that they were counted worthy to suffer shame for his name."[565] And since that time, persecutions of Christians have not ceased. Solace can be taken in the words spoken by the Lord Jesus Christ and written down by the apostle Matthew: "Blessed are ye, when men shall revile you, and persecute you, and shall say all manner of evil against you falsely, for my sake Rejoice, and be exceeding glad: for great is your reward in heaven: for so persecuted they the prophets which were before you." (Matthew 5:11–12)

And Unbelieving

This word has to do with the belief that Jesus Christ is the only begotten Son of God, and the promised Messiah; and to reject him is punishable by death and destruction in the lake of fire. This is something that should not be taken lightly, because it gives you the impression that no matter what, all the other words are summed up in this one. You are confined to death, hell, and destruction if you don't believe in the Lord Jesus Christ. This is confirmed by the following three Scriptures.

- "For God sent not his Son into the world to condemn the world; but that the world through him might be saved. He that believeth on him is not condemned: but he that believeth not is condemned already, because he hath not believed in the name of the only begotten Son of God. And this is the condemnation, that light is come into the world, and men loved darkness rather than light, because their deeds were evil. For every one that doeth evil hateth the light, neither cometh to the light, lest his deeds should be reproved. But he that doeth truth cometh to the light, that his deeds may be made manifest, that they are wrought in God." (John 3:18–21)

- "Then said Jesus again unto them, I go my way, and ye shall seek me, and shall die in your sins: whither I go, ye cannot come. Then said the Jews, Will he kill himself? because he saith, Whither I go, ye cannot come. And he said unto them, Ye are from beneath; I am from above: ye are of this world; I am not of this world. I said therefore unto you, that ye shall die in your sins: for if ye believe not that I am he, ye shall die in your sins." (John 8:21–24)

- "And he said unto them, Go ye into all the world, and preach the gospel to every creature. He that believeth and is baptized shall be saved; but he that believeth not shall be damned." (Mark 16:15–16)

Based on those Scriptures, it is apparent why God put so much emphasis on teaching and learning his Word, and why he pressures parents to not only teach the children but to keep focus on their own learning. This is expressed in the Old and New Testaments.

- "Train up a child in the way he should go: and when he is old, he will not depart from it." (Proverbs 22:6)

- "Blessed is the man that walketh not in the counsel of the ungodly, nor standeth in the way of sinners, nor sitteth in the seat of the scornful. But his delight is in the law of the Lord; and in his law doth he meditate day and night. And he shall be like a tree planted by the rivers of water, that bringeth forth his fruit in his season; his leaf also shall not wither; and whatsoever he doeth shall prosper. The ungodly are not so: but are like the chaff which the wind driveth away Therefore the ungodly shall not stand in the judgment, nor sinners in the congregation of the righteous. For the Lord knoweth the way of the righteous: but the way of the ungodly shall perish." (Psalm 1:1–6)

- "Study to shew thyself approved unto God, a workman that needeth not to be ashamed, rightly dividing the word of truth. But shun profane and vain babblings: for they will increase unto more ungodliness." (2 Timothy 2:15–16)

Therefore, you should now be able to see and reason out what God is trying to tell human beings about keeping faith with him. After diagnosis, some would be like Cain who slew his brother Abel, and say, "My punishment is greater than I can bear." That is, living with the knowledge that no matter what, unbelief in Jesus Christ will cause you to end up in eternal hellfire. So, don't take this as bad news. Take this as timely news, for now you have time to reverse your life into a commitment to the Father, the Son, and the Holy Ghost.

And finally, let me say this out of love: unbelief is the one word that is the balance of all the other judgments in the book of Revelation. Therefore, the bell is tolling. Can you hear the message of its ring? "From that time Jesus began to preach, and to say, Repent: for the kingdom of heaven is at hand" (Matthew 4:17).

The Abominable

The word abominable is defined as detestable, loathsome, and thoroughly unpleasant. This word includes abominably, abomination, and abominations. All four words are used in the Bible (mostly in the Old Testament) to show God's dislike toward some of the functions, activities, and actions of humankind.

God gave the list of abominations to the nation of Israel, and they will be applied by God and the Lord Jesus Christ in the final judgment. And let me also give a warning to those who are trying desperately to qualify their abomination by assessing what the Lord Jesus Christ judged or did not judge when he came to live among humans. It is true that he did not judge during his walk among humankind, but now that he has risen from the grave, he said, "All power is given unto me in heaven and in earth." So, I beg you to turn away from evil and wicked ways, and fully commit your life to the Lord Jesus Christ before it is too late. My presented list below will be shorter than the bible list.

Uncleanness (Leviticus 15:1–33)

Romans 1: 24 Wherefore God also gave them up to uncleanness through the lusts of their own hearts, to dishonour their own bodies between themselves: 25 who changed the truth of God into a lie, and worshipped and served the creature more than the Creator, who is blessed for ever. Amen.

When God talks about "uncleanness" he's not expressing the rite of bathing dirt from the body; but filthy sexual acts. The apostle Paul explains that because of wanton lust the rules of sexual behavior were abandoned by the Romans. Therefore, sexuality transmitted disease were rampart in their society.

- *Sexually Transmitted Disease* – "When any man hath a running issue out of his flesh, because of his issue he is unclean. And this shall be his uncleanness in his issue: whether his flesh run with his issue, or his flesh be stopped from his issue, it is his uncleanness."

- *Visible Liquid of Copulation* – "And if any man's seed of copulation go out from him, then he shall wash all his flesh in water, and be unclean until the even. And every garment, and every skin, whereon is the seed of copulation, shall be washed with water, and be unclean until the even. The woman also with whom man shall lie with seed of copulation, they shall both bathe themselves in water, and be unclean until the even."

- *A Woman during her Cycle of Menstruation* – "And if a woman have an issue, and her issue in her flesh be blood, she shall be put apart seven days: and whosoever toucheth her shall be unclean until the even. And every thing that she lieth upon in her separation shall be unclean: every thing also that she sitteth upon shall be unclean. And whosoever toucheth her bed shall wash his clothes, and bathe himself in water, and be unclean until the even."

- *Copulation is forbidden during a woman's blood cycle:* "Also thou shalt not approach unto a woman to uncover her nakedness, as long as she is put apart for her uncleanness" (Leviticus 18:20).

- *If there is copulation during a woman's ministration cycle:* "And if any man lie with her at all, and her flowers be upon him, he shall be unclean seven days; and all the bed whereon he lieth shall be unclean."

- ***The penalty for disobedience:*** "And if a man shall lie with a woman having her sickness, and shall uncover her nakedness; he hath discovered her fountain, and she hath uncovered the fountain of her blood: and both of them shall be cut off from among their people" (Leviticus 20:18).

- ***When a woman's ministration cycle is abnormal:*** "And if a woman have an issue of her blood many days out of the time of her separation, or if it run beyond the time of her separation; all the days of the issue of her uncleanness shall be as the days of her separation: she shall be unclean" (Matthew 9:18–26).

- Thus shall ye separate the children of Israel from their uncleanness; that they die not in their uncleanness, when they defile my tabernacle that is among them. This is the law of him that hath an issue, and of him whose seed goeth from him, and is defiled therewith; And of her that is sick of her flowers, and of him that hath an issue, of the man, and of the woman, and of him that lieth with her that is unclean.

Incest, Pornography, Fornication, and Adultery (Leviticus 18:1–20)

- ***Incest:*** Sexual union between persons who are so closely related that their marriage is illegal or forbidden by custom. The statutory crime committed by such closely related persons who marry, cohabit, or copulate illegally.

- ***Pornography:*** Written, graphic, or other forms of communication intended to excite lascivious feelings; characterized by lust and exciting sexual desires.

- ***Fornication:*** Sexual intercourse between a man and a woman not married to each other.

- *Adultery:* Voluntary sexual intercourse between a married person and a partner other than the lawful husband or wife.

  None of you shall approach to any that is near of kin to him, to uncover their nakedness: I am the Lord.

The law made it clear that it was an abomination to view, touch, or have sexual relations with a relative, which included sexual unions outside of marriage. Further, breaking the law would, in fact, defile the seventh commandment: "Thou shalt not commit adultery" (Exodus 20:14). The penalty for disobedience was swift death, sexual diseases, and childlessness.

- "And the man that committeth adultery with another man's wife, even he that committeth adultery with his neighbour's wife, the adulterer and the adulteress shall surely be put to death."

- "And the man that lieth with his father's wife hath uncovered his father's nakedness: both of them shall surely be put to death; their blood shall be upon them."

- "And if a man lie with his daughter in law, both of them shall surely be put to death: they have wrought confusion; their blood shall be upon them."

- "And if a man take a wife and her mother, it is wickedness: they shall be burnt with fire, both he and they; that there be no wickedness among you."

- "And if a man shall take his sister, his father's daughter, or his mother's daughter, and see her nakedness, and she see his nakedness; it is a wicked thing; and they shall be cut off in the sight of their people: he hath uncovered his sister's nakedness; he shall bear his iniquity."

- "And thou shalt not uncover the nakedness of thy mother's sister, nor of thy father's sister: for he uncovereth his near kin: they shall bear their iniquity."

- "And if a man shall lie with his uncle's wife, he hath uncovered his uncle's nakedness: they shall bear their sin; they shall die childless."

- "And if a man shall take his brother's wife, it is an unclean thing: he hath uncovered his brother's nakedness; they shall be childless." (Leviticus 20:10–12, 14, 17, 19–21)

In these last days, Christ set the precedence for adultery when he stated, "Ye have heard that it was said by them of old time, Thou shalt not commit adultery: But I say unto you, That whosoever looketh on a woman to lust after her hath committed adultery with her already in his heart." (Matthew 5:27–32).

I know incest, fornication, and adultery are understood in the Old Testament. But some are asking, "How do you arrive at pornography when there was no media means in Moses' day to support the word?" Well, very simply put, porn is nothing more than the physical act of looking at, and enjoying the pleasure of naked bodies, whether they are physically present or produced through a photographic lens. The fact of the matter is that God made a law against this type of activity. Further, God put a curse on people who indulge in abominations (Deuteronomy 27:20, 22–26). The apostle Paul sums up these curses in his epistle to the Corinthians.

> **"Know ye not that the unrighteous shall not inherit the kingdom of God? Be not deceived: neither fornicators, nor idolaters, nor adulterers, nor effeminate, nor abusers of themselves with mankind, Nor thieves, nor covetous, nor drunkards, nor revilers, nor extortioners, shall inherit the kingdom of God. And such were some of you: but ye**

are washed, but ye are sanctified, but ye are justified in the name of the Lord Jesus, and by the Spirit of our God." (1 Corinthians 6:9–11)

Homosexuality and Sodomy

Several times the apostle Paul addressed abuse of the body in his epistles. And maybe what he wrote was misunderstood. But what is written above is clear and to the point: God does not want humankind to abuse the seed of reproduction, or the liquid of copulation; for its use is for procreation: and that only.

The apostle Peter even warned his readers about the epistles of Paul: "And account that the longsuffering of our Lord is salvation; even as our beloved brother Paul also according to the wisdom given unto him hath written unto you; As also in all his epistles, speaking in them of these things; in which are some things hard to be understood, which they that are unlearned and unstable wrest, as they do also the other scriptures, unto their own destruction."[566]

Now I'm going to present to you what Paul wrote to the Roman church. Again, I beg you to not only review these Scriptures but make up your mind on how you will deal with the apparent reality.

> "For the wrath of God is revealed from heaven against all ungodliness and unrighteousness of men, who hold the truth in unrighteousness; Because that which may be known of God is manifest in them; for God hath shewed it unto them. For the invisible things of him from the creation of the world are clearly seen, being understood by the things that are made, even his eternal power and Godhead; so that they are without excuse: Because that, when they knew God, they glorified him not as God, neither were thankful; but became vain in their imaginations, and their foolish heart was darkened. Professing themselves to be wise, they became fools, And changed the glory of

the uncorruptible God into an image made like to corruptible man, and to birds, and fourfooted beasts, and creeping things. Wherefore God also gave them up to uncleanness through the lusts of their own hearts, to dishonour their own bodies between themselves: Who changed the truth of God into a lie, and worshipped and served the creature more than the Creator, who is blessed for ever. Amen.

- "For this cause God gave them up unto vile affections: for even their women did change the natural use into that which is against nature:"

- "And likewise also the men, leaving the natural use of the woman, burned in their lust one toward another; men with men working that which is unseemly, and receiving in themselves that recompence of their error which was meet." (Romans 1:18–27)

The deduction from the above Scripture is that God in these last days will let you indulge in all manner of unclean, and sinful sexual acts—if that is your heart's desire. But he keeps the doors of the church open so that whenever you come to your senses, and repent of your sins through the Lord Jesus Christ, you can be saved from hellfire and eternal damnation.

But there is a stiff price to pay when you abuse the seminal fluid of copulation. For example, it is a scientific fact that venereal disease (syphilis, gonorrhea, and so on), and human immunodeficiency virus (HIV; which can lead to AIDS) are caused by filthy bacteria that is common among inappropriate sex acts; for example, oral sex and anal sex. And these scientific facts about the end result are published and are well documented; there is usually physical harm to the body and death. Again, I beg those indulging in this type of behavior to stop, and turn toward the Son of God before it is too late.

Who is Jesus Christ

- "Thou shalt not lie with mankind, as with womankind: it is abomination." (Leviticus 18:22)

- "If a man also lie with mankind, as he lieth with a woman, both of them have committed an abomination: they shall surely be put to death; their blood shall be upon them." (Leviticus 20:13)

You will not find the word "homosexuality" in the Bible. But what you will discover throughout the Old Testament is the word "sodomite." The definition of the word sodomy is (1) an inhabitant of Sodom [Genesis Chapter 19]; (2) One who practices sodomy; anal copulation of one male with another; (3) in some legal usage, anal or oral copulation with a member of the opposite sex or any copulation with an animal.

There is strong belief that God destroyed Sodom, and the inhabitants of Gomorrah, including the surrounding villages, because of homosexuality. But further research of the Bible revealed that God had other reasons to destroy them.

"As I live, saith the Lord God, Sodom thy sister hath not done, she nor her daughters, as thou hast done, thou and thy daughters. Behold, this was the iniquity of thy sister Sodom, pride, fulness of bread, and abundance of idleness was in her and in her daughters, neither did she strengthen the hand of the poor and needy. And they were haughty, and committed abomination before me: therefore I took them away as I saw good." (Ezekiel 16:48–50)

In the year 2013, there was a worldwide movement to accept the lesbian, gay, bisexual, and transgender (LGBT) lifestyle as a civil right. Many nations, and some states in the United States, have adopted laws to permit same-sex civil unions and marriages. By biblical standards, this is truly a violation of God's law and will be dealt with at the final judgment. But as a child of the King, and a believer in the Lord Jesus Christ, I again plead with you to turn back from this and all abominations, for eternal destruction awaits those who die in their sins.

Prostitution (prostitute)

The word prostitute is defined as one who solicits and accepts payment for sexual intercourse; to offer one's self, or another for sexual hire. God had strong feeling about this type of behavior.

- **Female Prostitute:** "Do not prostitute thy daughter, to cause her to be a whore; lest the land fall to whoredom, and the land become full of wickedness." (Leviticus 19:29)

- **Female and Male Prostitute:** "There shall be no whore of the daughters of Israel, nor a Sodomite of the sons of Israel. Thou shalt not bring the hire of a whore, or the price of a dog, into the house of the Lord thy God for any vow: for even both these are abomination unto the Lord thy God." (Deuteronomy 23:17–18)

    - *Whore* = Strong's Number: 6948; transliterated: *qdeshah*; phonetic: ked-ay-shaw'; Text: feminine of 6945; a female devotee (i.e., prostitute): —harlot, whore

    - *Sodomite* = Strong's Number: 6945; transliterated: *qadesh;* Phonetic: kaw-dashe'; Text: from 6942; a (quasi) sacred person, that is (technically) a (male) devotee (by prostitution) to licentious idolatry: —sodomite, unclean

    - *Dog* = Strong's Number 3611; transliterated: *keleb;* Phonetic: keh'-leb; Text: from an unused root means to yelp, or else to attack; a dog; hence (by euphemism) a male prostitute: —dog

God not only frowned on women prostitution, but likened male prostitutes as "dogs." Jesus vowed that these dogs would not enter the kingdom of heaven: "For without are dogs, and sorcerers, and whoremongers, and murderers, and idolaters, and whosoever loveth and maketh a lie. I Jesus have sent mine angel to testify unto you these things in the churches. I am the root and the offspring of David, and the bright and morning star" (Revelation 22:15–16). The apostle Paul added to this in his epistle to Timothy.

> "Knowing this, that the law is not made for a righteous man, but for the lawless and disobedient, for the ungodly and for sinners, for unholy and profane, for murderers of fathers and murderers of mothers, for manslayers, For whoremongers, for them that defile themselves with mankind, for menstealers, for liars, for perjured persons, and if there be any other thing that is contrary to sound doctrine …" (1 Timothy 1:9–10)

Wearing Opposite Gender Clothing

> "The woman shall not wear that which pertaineth unto a man, neither shall a man put on a woman's garment: for all that do so are abomination unto the Lord thy God." (Deuteronomy 22:5)

In this modern world of the twentieth century, men and women are openly wearing each other's clothing; without violation from society or national government. The attitude seems to be "what ever I want to do is alright as long as I'm not hurting anyone else." However, opposite gender's wearing each other garments is looked upon as immoral and unethical. A person may not be physically hurting anyone but many a child has been shown the open door to the world because they brought shame upon their family. Yet, let's keep in mind that this type of action is against the law of God.

Bestiality

This refers to *sexual* relations between a human being and a lower animal: sodomy. This type of activity is mentioned in four books of the law of Moses. This indicates that it was a grave problem among the children of Israel, and the world around them; for God condemned the people of the Canaan land to death and destruction for committing these abominations.

In these last days, the Internet is used as the media vehicle to exhibit sexual immorality and bestiality; which was exploited by the "Mr. Hand" video clip. The way the law is written makes you wonder if God brought the flood upon the earth because of abominations between human beings, animals, and spirit beings.

- "Whosoever lieth with a beast shall surely be put to death." (Exodus 22:19)

- "Neither shalt thou lie with any beast to defile thyself therewith: neither shall any woman stand before a beast to lie down thereto: it is confusion." (Leviticus 18:23)

- "And if a man lie with a beast, he shall surely be put to death: and ye shall slay the beast. And if a woman approach unto any beast, and lie down thereto, thou shalt kill the woman, and the beast: they shall surely be put to death; their blood shall be upon them." (Leviticus 20:15–16)

- "Cursed be he that lieth with any manner of beast. And all the people shall say, Amen." (Deuteronomy 27:21)

Killing of Babies

"And thou shalt not let any of thy seed pass through the fire to Molech, neither shalt thou profane the name of thy God: I am the Lord." Leviticus 18:21)

- *Moloch:* "The name of the national god of the Ammonites, to whom children were sacrificed by fire. He was the consuming and destroying and also at the same time the purifying fire. In Amos 5:26, 'your Moloch' of the Authorized Version is 'your king' in the Revised Version (comp. Acts 7:43). Solomon (1 Kings 11:7) erected a high place for this idol on the Mount of Olives, and from that time till the days of Josiah his worship continued (2 Kings 23:10, 13). In the days of Jehoahaz it was partially restored, but after the Captivity wholly disappeared. He is also called Molech (Lev. 18:21; 20:2–5, etc.), Milcom (1 Kings 11:5, 33, etc.), and Malcham (Zeph. 1:5). This god became Chemosh among the Moabites."[567]

- *Chemosh:* "The destroyer, subduer, or fishgod, the god of the Moabites (Num. 21: 29; Jer. 48:7, 13, 46). The worship of this god, 'the abomination of Moab,' was introduced at Jerusalem by Solomon (1 Kings 11:7), but was abolished by Josiah (2 Kings 23:13). On the 'Moabite Stone' (q.v.), Mesha (2 Kings 3:5) ascribes his victories over the king of Israel to this god, 'And Chemosh drove him before my sight.'"[568]

I know some of you have immediately grasped that there is no longer any babies being sacrificed on the altars of the gods (at least I haven't heard of any). Yet what we do have is worldwide abortion; wherein babies are sacrificed before they are born, and in some instances, being destroyed by partial birth abortions (this is where a live baby is destroyed in the mother's birth canal).

Let's keep an open mind and know that God is against any

killing of innocent babies. And if some are to die, he will determine their fate with righteous judgment.

Don't be caught up in sin like those who support abortion, and think that it is a woman's right to determine the fate of an unborn child. But I submit to you that just as God is not pleased, we human beings should rage against abortion. It is my opinion that abortion is not only insane, but a tool that depletes a nation of its youth. For example, "From A.D.1973 through A.D. 2008, nearly 50 million legal abortions have occurred in the U.S. (AGI)"[569]

For this reason, the United States is rapidly becoming a nation of senior citizens, and has turned to fill the military combat units with women. I'm all for equality, but what if young women's bodies are trained and hardened to the point that they cannot fulfill their God-given gift of producing children? This is my thinking out loud question. I guess some genius will acquire enough science fiction knowledge and produce a baby through laboratory artificial mechanical wombs. Of course, this is only seen in movies, but could become a reality some day. What a world this would be then! Whew! In a legal, biblical sense, every child who is conceived belongs to God. And He alone will decide its fate.

> *"Every thing that openeth the matrix in all flesh, which they bring unto the Lord, whether it be of men or beasts, shall be thine: nevertheless the firstborn of man shalt thou surely redeem, and the firstling of unclean beasts shalt thou redeem And those that are to be redeemed from a month old shalt thou redeem, according to thine estimation, for the money of five shekels, after the shekel of the sanctuary, which is twenty gerahs."* (Numbers 18:15–16)

Eating Blood

The restriction of eating blood was not a law first given to Moses, but a commandment established after the flood of Noah.

This commandment was reaffirmed in the law of Moses, and it is still active today. This commandment is permanent as long as there is a planet earth.

- "Every moving thing that liveth shall be meat for you; even as the green herb have I given you all things. But flesh with the life thereof, which is the blood thereof, shall ye not eat." (Genesis 9:3–4)

- "Moreover ye shall eat no manner of blood, whether it be of fowl or of beast, in any of your dwellings. Whatsoever soul it be that eateth any manner of blood, even that soul shall be cut off from his people." (Leviticus 7:26–27)

- "And whatsoever man there be of the house of Israel, or of the strangers that sojourn among you, that eateth any manner of blood; I will even set my face against that soul that eateth blood, and will cut him off from among his people. For the life of the flesh is in the blood: and I have given it to you upon the altar to make an atonement for your souls: for it is the blood that maketh an atonement for the soul. Therefore I said unto the children of Israel, No soul of you shall eat blood, neither shall any stranger that sojourneth among you eat blood"

"And whatsoever man there be of the children of Israel, or of the strangers that sojourn among you, which hunteth and catcheth any beast or fowl that may be eaten; he shall even pour out the blood thereof, and cover it with dust. For it is the life of all flesh; the blood of it is for the life thereof: therefore I said unto the children of Israel, Ye shall eat the blood of no manner of flesh: for the life of all flesh is the blood thereof: whosoever eateth it shall be cut off."

"And every soul that eateth that which died of itself, or that which was torn with beasts, whether it be one of your own country, or a stranger, he shall both wash his clothes, and bathe himself in water, and be unclean until the even: then shall he be clean. But if he wash them not, nor bathe his flesh; then he shall bear his iniquity." (Leviticus 17:10–16)

Haircuts – "Ye shall not round the corners of your heads, neither shalt thou mar the corners of thy beard." (Leviticus 19:27)

Tattoos – "Ye shall not make any cuttings in your flesh for the dead, nor print any marks upon you: I am the Lord." (Leviticus 19:28)

Cursing Father or Mother

The penalty for disrespecting father or mother was put in place through the eternal Ten Commandments: "Honour thy father and thy mother: that thy days may be long upon the land which the Lord thy God giveth thee" (Exodus 20:12).

- "For every one that curseth his father or his mother shall be surely put to death: he hath cursed his father or his mother; his blood shall be upon him." (Leviticus 20:9)

- "If a man have a stubborn and rebellious son, which will not obey the voice of his father, or the voice of his mother, and that, when they have chastened him, will not hearken unto them: Then shall his father and his mother lay hold on him, and bring him out unto the elders of his city, and unto the gate of his place; And they shall say unto the elders of his city, This our son is stubborn and rebellious, he will not obey our voice; he is a glutton, and a drunkard. And all the men of his city shall stone him with stones, that he die: so shalt thou put evil away from among you; and all Israel shall hear, and fear." (Deuteronomy 21:18–21)

God's Judgment against Abominations

It should be apparent that God's judgment toward those who commit abominations has not changed and will not change. It is written, "Jesus Christ the same yesterday, and today, and forever" (Hebrews 13:8). Therefore, I leave you with three Scriptures that reflect these modern days.

- "These six things doth the Lord hate: yea, seven are an abomination unto him: A proud look, a lying tongue, and hands that shed innocent blood, An heart that deviseth wicked imaginations, feet that be swift in running to mischief, A false witness that speaketh lies, and he that soweth discord among brethren." (Proverbs 6:16–19)

- "He that justifieth the wicked, and he that condemneth the just, even they both are abomination to the Lord." (Proverbs 17:15)

- "He that turneth away his ear from hearing the law, even his prayer shall be abomination." (Proverbs 28:9)

And Murderers

Murderer is defined as those who unlawfully kill a human being, especially with malice and forethought. This is talking about unrepented murder that has not been forgiven by the Father. God has, and can use a murderer who has repented, and sinned no more. Two good examples are Moses (Exodus 2:11–15) and the apostle Paul (Acts 7:54–60; 8:1–4; 9:1–19).

- "Whoso sheddeth man's blood, by man shall his blood be shed: for in the image of God made he man." (Genesis 9:6)

- "Thou shalt not kill" [the sixth commandment] (Exodus 20:13)

- "Whoso killeth any person, the murderer shall be put to death by the mouth of witnesses: but one witness shall not testify against any person to cause him to die. Moreover ye shall take no satisfaction for the life of a murderer, which is guilty of death: but he shall be surely put to death. And ye shall take no satisfaction for him that is fled to the city of his refuge, that he should come again to dwell in the land, until the death of the priest. So ye shall not pollute the land wherein ye are: for blood it defileth the land: and the land cannot be cleansed of the blood that is shed therein, but by the blood of him that shed it. Defile not therefore the land which ye shall inhabit, wherein I dwell: for I the Lord dwell among the children of Israel." (Numbers 35:30–34)

We need to pause here and review God's merciful national death penalty. As you can see, God made sure a person was not railroaded by an unbalanced court, and allowed those suspected of a crime to live in a city of refuge. You see, God is against murder even to satisfy the scales of justice. However, sin must be paid for by death: "For the wages of sin is death; but the gift of God is eternal life through Jesus Christ our Lord" (Romans 6:23). And this is why Christ left his followers this everlasting commandment.

> "Ye have heard that it hath been said, Thou shalt love thy neighbour, and hate thine enemy. But I say unto you, Love your enemies, bless them that curse you, do good to them that hate you, and pray for them which despitefully use you, and persecute you; That ye may be the children of your Father which is in heaven: for he maketh his sun to rise on the evil and on the good, and sendeth rain on the just and on the unjust. For if ye love them which love you, what reward have ye? do not even the publicans the same? And if ye salute your brethren only, what do ye more than others? do not even the publicans so? Be ye therefore perfect,

even as your Father which is in heaven is perfect." (Matthew 5:43–48)

So, is Christ telling his followers to let people run rampant over them with abuse? To the contrary. He justifies God as the ultimate decision maker in disputes, arguments, confrontations, and revenge.

And Whoremongers

The word whoremongers is regarded as: fornicators (sexual intercourse without marriage), including adulterers. This word has to do with "sexual immorality" and the disregard for the Word (law) of God. Before the law of Moses, there were numerous cases where the practice of sexual immorality was a common cultural practice.

- *Genesis 9:20-27:* Canaan (the youngest son of Ham) looked on the nakedness of his drunken grandfather Noah. For this one-time evil, he and his land (Canaan Land) was and is forever cursed and given to Abraham's descendants (Genesis 17:1–8).

- *Genesis 11:29:* Abraham's brother Nahor married his brother's daughter Milcah.

- *Genesis 16:1–4:* Sarah (Abraham's wife) gave her handmaiden to Abraham as a wife to have children. From this union was born Ishmael, who is called the father of the Arabs (Genesis 25:12–18).

- *Genesis 19:30–38:* Lot (the nephew of Abraham), on escaping the destruction of Sodom and Gomorrah with his two daughters, was forced (while drunk on wine) to have sexual relations with them. This resulted in the births of two sons: Moab by the eldest and Ammon by the youngest. Ruth was a Moabite who married Boaz, the father of Obed, who was the father of Jesse, who was the father of David (Ruth 4:13–17), who through the Virgin Mary, is in the genealogy of Christ Jesus (Luke 3:31–32).

- ***Genesis 20:1–12:*** Abraham confessed to Abimelech (king of Gerar) that his wife, Sarah, was also his sister, the daughter of his father, Terah (Genesis 11:26).

- ***Genesis 24:1–67****:* Isaac (the son of Abraham) married his cousin Rebekah, the daughter of Bethuel, the son of Milcah, the wife of Nahor (Abraham's brother).

- ***Genesis 28:9:*** Esau (Isaac's oldest twin son) married the daughter of his uncle Ishmael (the eldest son of Abraham, the brother of Isaac).

- ***Genesis 29:1–35:*** Jacob (the twin of Esau) married the two daughters of Laben (Leah and Rachel), the brother of his mother, Rebekah. Five sons and one daughter were the result of the union between Jacob and Leah: Reuben, Simeon, Levi, Judah, Issachar, Zebulun, and Dinah. Two sons were produced by Jacob and Rachael: Joseph and Benjamin.

- ***Genesis 30:1–8:*** Rachel gives her handmaiden, Bilhah, to Jacob as his concubine. Two sons were born from this union: Dan, and Naphtali.

- ***Genesis 30:9–13:*** Leah gave her handmaiden, Zilpah, to Jacob as his concubine. Two sons were the result of this union: Gad and Asher.

- ***Genesis 34:1–31****:* Dinah (the daughter of Jacob) was raped by Shechem the Hivite. Her brothers Simeon and Levi took revenge and killed him and all the men of their city.

- *Genesis 35:22:* Jacob discovered his eldest son, Reuben, was having sexual relations with his concubine Bilhah, the mother of his two sons Dan and Naphtali.

- *Genesis 38:1–5:* Judah married a Canaanite woman named Shuah; they had three sons: Er, Onan, and Shelah.

- *Genesis 38:1–30:* Judah (Jacob's forth son) had sexual relations with his daughter-in-law (Tamar) and twin boys were born: Pharez and Zarah. Pharez is in the genealogy of Christ Jesus (Matthew 1:3; Luke 3:33).

- *Exodus 6:20:* Amram (a Levite) married Jochebed (his father's sister) and produced three children: Aaron, Moses, and Miriam.

    - "And there went a man of the house of Levi, and took to wife a daughter of Levi. And the woman conceived, and bare a son: and when she saw him that he was a goodly child, she hid him three months." (Exodus 2:1–2)

    - "And Amram took him Jochebed his father's sister to wife; and she bare him Aaron and Moses: and the years of the life of Amram were an hundred and thirty and seven years." (Exodus 6:20)

    - "And the name of Amram's wife was Jochebed, the daughter of Levi, whom her mother bare to Levi in Egypt: and she bare unto Amram Aaron and Moses, and Miriam their sister." (Numbers 26:59)

God established his earthly priesthood (Exodus 28:1–43) through the family of Moses, which ended with John the Baptist

(Luke 1:5–13). When the high priest John died, Christ Jesus became the High Priest forever through crucifixion on the cross (Hebrews 5:5–10).

After the Law Was Given to Moses

There are a lot of questions about why God permitted certain sexual unions before the law was given to Moses. But no matter the reason, the law is clear on how God views those sexual acts today. Therefore, it behooves us to forget about the past, concentrate on the present, and let the future take care of itself.

The apostle Paul gave weight to why people are a slave to "sexual immorality" when he wrote, "And even as they did not like to retain God in their knowledge, God gave them over to a reprobate mind, to do those things which are not convenient" (Romans 1:28, 29–32).

He wrote the book of Romans sometime around AD 57. Yet in this twenty-first century (2013), we are witnessing what he wrote. We see people carried away by aggressive and inordinate sexual behaviors: including masturbation; oral sex; digital sex; phone sex; pornography; explicit sexual videos sexual books and magazines; bestiality; sadomasochism; sexual-enhancement drugs, mechanical apparatus, sexual toys, and devices; sex change operations; transvestite and transgender mind-sets (she-males); bisexual behavior, homosexuality; lesbianism; and same-sex unions (including marriage).

Like Flip Wilson (a comedy television show in the seventies), some will go so far as to say, "The Devil made me do it." But God didn't listen to excuses of sin given by Adam and Eve in the Garden of Eden; and by his Word, he will not give in to this modern-day world.

However, he did leave us with a Scripture of escape when we are drawn into temptation by the great dragon, that old serpent called the Devil and Satan. And you can be sure God will not go back on his promise to deliver us from temptation.

Who is Jesus Christ

"There hath no temptation taken you but such as is common to man: but God is faithful, who will not suffer you to be tempted above that ye are able; but will with the temptation also make a way to escape, that ye may be able to bear it." (1 Corinthians 10:13)

And Sorcerers

The word sorcerer is defined as: those who practice sorcery, claim to have supernatural powers or knowledge, use magic potions, and are considered to be in league with evil forces. In the Harry Potter movies, magic and supernatural powers are on full display.

The practice of black magic is very serious with God, because it causes the worship of false gods, and undermines the genuine miracles of the Lord Jesus Christ. One such attempt was made against Barnabas and the apostle Paul by a man named Barjesus, also called Elymas the sorcerer (for so is his name by interpretation). But Paul withstood him through the power of the Holy Ghost, and he was immediately made blind (Acts 13:6–12) Here are twelve things that I discovered about sorcerer.

- "And I will come near to you to judgment; and I will be a swift witness against the sorcerers, and against the adulterers, and against false swearers, and against those that oppress the hireling in his wages, the widow, and the fatherless, and that turn aside the stranger from his right, and fear not me, saith the Lord of hosts." (Malachi 3:5)

- *Spirit of divination:* The practice of foreseeing or foretelling future events or discovering hidden knowledge. Forbidden by God (Deuteronomy 18:10–12; Acts 16:16–18).

- *Soothsaying:* Possessing the power to foretell future events (Joshua 13:22; Jeremiah 27:9–10; Daniel 4:7).

- ***Wizards:*** Those acquainted with unseen world secrets. Male or female magicians or sorcerers (Isaiah 19:3).

- ***Familiar Spirits:*** Mediums (Leviticus 19:31; 20:6 & 27; 1 Chronicles 10:13–14).

- ***Enchantments***: Use of any form of magic. (Exodus 7:11-13)

- ***Observe times:*** Astrology, the study of stars and signs (Leviticus 19:26).

- ***Charmers:*** Enchanters, sorcerers, and magicians. (Daniel 2:1-13)

- ***Occult:*** Black supernatural secrets.

- ***Witch:*** A woman who practices black magic with the aid of a devil or familiar spirit (Exodus 22:18; 1 Samuel 28:3–25).

- ***Warlock:*** A male witch.

- ***Exorcists:*** Those who conjure or summon a devil or spirit by using charms or magic spells.

"Then certain of the vagabond Jews, exorcists, took upon them to call over them which had evil spirits the name of the Lord Jesus, saying, We adjure you by Jesus whom Paul preacheth. And there were seven sons of one Sceva, a Jew, and chief of the priests, which did so. And the evil spirit answered and said, Jesus I know, and Paul I know; but who are ye? And the man in whom the evil spirit was leaped on them, and overcame them, and prevailed against them, so that they fled out of that house naked and wounded. And this was known to all the Jews and Greeks also dwelling at Ephesus; and fear fell on them all, and the name of the Lord Jesus was magnified." (Acts 19:13–17)

And Idolaters

The word idolaters are directed at those who worship an idol or idols; anyone who blindly admires or adores another. This type of worship is widespread in entertainment, religion, and political rhetoric: the art of effective or persuasive speaking or writing, especially the use of figures of speech and other compositional techniques.

> "Thou shalt not make unto thee any graven image, or any likeness of any thing that is in heaven above, or that is in the earth beneath, or that is in the water under the earth. Thou shalt not bow down thyself to them, nor serve them: for I the Lord thy God am a jealous God, visiting the iniquity of the fathers upon the children unto the third and fourth generation of them that hate me; And shewing mercy unto thousands of them that love me, and keep my commandments." (Exodus 20:4–6)

And All Liars

Liars are people who make false statements or deliberately present a false statement as being true; anything meant to deceive or give a wrong impression.

Lying, telling fibs, and quibbling is a bad habit. But in this case, it is talking about "false prophets." That is to say, "one who lies on God." It is not human nature to tell a lie. But we do it because of the influence of O Lucifer (the great dragon, that old serpent called the Devil and Satan). Christ Jesus identified this truth when he told the Jews, "Ye are of your father the devil, and the lusts of your father ye will do. He was a murderer from the beginning, and abode not in the truth, because there is no truth in him. When he speaketh a lie, he speaketh of his own: for he is a liar, and the father of it" (John 8:44).

One thing Christians need to bear down on is proclaiming the written Word of God—not how we have studied it, but exactly how it is written, and quoted word for word, and sentence by sentence. Remember, the Lord Jesus Christ didn't defeat Satan with the philosophy of study, but by quoting the written Word of God (Matthew 4:1–11). Be reminded that Satan is a renowned student of religious organizations and their deities. (2 Corinthians 11:13-15)

So then, you lose the power of God when you think to win people with flowery sermons, that are full of catchy words and phrases. For it is written "So then faith cometh by hearing, and hearing by the word of God."

Christ Jesus and the apostle Paul wrote two stern warnings to the church about those who turn away from the written Word of God. How do you turn away from the written Word of God? Glad you asked.

First, a person can turn away from the written Word of God when they start to read other famous literature and believe they can incorporate those beliefs into the Word of God. In Matthew Chapter 23, Christ Jesus hammered the "scribes and Pharisees" for this very thing and at one point told them,

> "Why do ye also transgress the commandment of God by your tradition? For God commanded, saying, Honour thy father and mother: and, He that curseth father or mother, let him die the death. But ye say, Whosoever shall say to his father or his mother, It is a gift, by whatsoever thou mightest be profited by me; And honour not his father or his mother, he shall be free. Thus have ye made the commandment of God of none effect by your tradition. Ye hypocrites, well did Esaias prophesy of you, saying, This people draweth nigh unto me with their mouth, and honoureth me with their lips; but their heart is far from me. But in

vain they do worship me, teaching for doctrines the commandments of men." (Matthew 15:3–9)

Second, there is a stiff penalty for not following and obeying the Word of God. The children of Israel found this out when they followed the pillar of cloud across the Sinai Desert for forty years. Paul wrote about what will happen to you physically and spiritually if you fail to keep the Word of God.

> "For the mystery of iniquity doth already work: only he who now letteth will let, until he be taken out of the way. And then shall that Wicked be revealed, whom the Lord shall consume with the spirit of his mouth, and shall destroy with the brightness of his coming:
>
> Even him, whose coming is after the working of Satan with all power and signs and lying wonders, And with all deceivableness of unrighteousness in them that perish; because they received not the love of the truth, that they might be saved. And for this cause God shall send them strong delusion, that they should believe a lie: That they all might be damned who believed not the truth, but had pleasure in unrighteousness." (Thessalonians 2:7–12)

CHAPTER 29

CHRIST MESSAGE TO THE WORLD

Before Christ Jesus ascended back into the heaven, he left the world two messages; one for His followers and the other for the Jews. The question is what did he say, and where is in the bible. Well, what he said is hidden in the mystery of his parable's.

The Parable of The Wheat and The Tares

> Matthew 13: 24 Another parable put he forth unto them, saying, The kingdom of heaven is likened unto a man which sowed good seed in his field:
> 25 but while men slept, his enemy came and sowed tares among the wheat, and went his way. 26 But when the blade was sprung up, and brought forth fruit, then appeared the tares also.
> 27 So the servants of the householder came and said unto him, Sir, didst not thou sow good seed in thy field? from whence then hath it tares?
> 28 He said unto them, An enemy hath done this. The servants said unto him, Wilt thou then that we go and gather them up?

29 But he said, Nay; lest while ye gather up the tares, ye root up also the wheat with them.

30 Let both grow together until the harvest: and in the time of harvest I will say to the reapers, Gather ye together first the tares, and bind them in bundles to burn them: but gather the wheat into my barn.

Christ Jesus Explains the Parable of the Wheat and Tares

Matthew 13: 37 He answered and said unto them, He that soweth the good seed is the Son of man;

38 the field is the world; the good seed are the children of the kingdom; but the tares are the children of the wicked one;

39 the enemy that sowed them is the devil; the harvest is the end of the world; and the reapers are the angels.

40 As therefore the tares are gathered and burned in the fire; so shall it be in the end of this world.

41 The Son of man shall send forth his angels, and they shall gather out of his kingdom all things that offend, and them which do iniquity;

42 and shall cast them into a furnace of fire: there shall be wailing and gnashing of teeth. 43 Then shall the righteous shine forth as the sun in the kingdom of their Father. Who hath ears to hear, let him hear.

Now this is my understanding of what he said and explained. First the gospel will be presented in his name; but it will be buffet against by the workings of Satan. These two forces will content with one another until he returns with the holy angels. At that time the sheep will be separated from the goats; the sheep will go with Christ up to paradise, but the goats will be thrown down into the lake of fire, to be tormented forever. (Matthew 24:27-31)

The jest of this message is to encourage the saints to hold on to the faith in Christ Jesus, and be assured that God is in control of everything that happens. Therefore, a church building is not pure because it has both wheat and tares in it. Yet, the church of Jesus Christ is holy because of the righteous hearts of the believers; which is the body of the church.

The Parable of The Householder

> Matthew 21: 33 Hear another parable: There was a certain householder, which planted a vineyard, and hedged it round about, and digged a winepress in it, and built a tower, and let it out to husbandmen, and went into a far country:
> 34 and when the time of the fruit drew near, he sent his servants to the husbandmen, that they might receive the fruits of it.
> 35 And the husbandmen took his servants, and beat one, and killed another, and stoned another. 36 Again, he sent other servants more than the first: and they did unto them likewise.
> 37 But last of all he sent unto them his son, saying, They will reverence my son.
> 38 But when the husbandmen saw the son, they said among themselves, This is the heir; come, let us kill him, and let us seize on his inheritance.
> 39 And they caught him, and cast him out of the vineyard, and slew him.
> 40 When the lord therefore of the vineyard cometh, what will he do unto those husbandmen?
> 41 They say unto him, He will miserably destroy those wicked men, and will let out his vineyard unto other husbandmen, which shall render him the fruits in their seasons.
> 42 Jesus saith unto them, Did ye never read in the scriptures, The stone which the builders rejected, the

same is become the head of the corner: this is the Lord's doing, and it is marvellous in our eyes?

43 Therefore say I unto you, The kingdom of God shall be taken from you, and given to a nation bringing forth the fruits thereof.

44 And whosoever shall fall on this stone shall be broken: but on whomsoever it shall fall, it will grind him to powder.

45 And when the chief priests and Pharisees had heard his parables, they perceived that he spake of them. 46 But when they sought to lay hands on him, they feared the multitude, because they took him for a prophet.

This parable is all about the nation of Israel. When God called Abraham, Isaac and Jacob, He put a hedge around them to preserve the birth of the Hebrew nation. When the children of Israel rejected God, He lent the nation out to the reign of kings; and sent prophets to keep them in line with His law. But the people beat, killed, and stoned the prophets to death. Finally, God sent his only begotten Son; and he was not only rejected, but nailed to a cross and hung up on a hill to be viewed and mocked.

Yet, after they buried him, he rose from the grave on the third day with all power in hands: on earth, in heaven, and under the earth; to include the keys of both death and hell. In other words, he is in charge of all that happens on the realm of God.

Therefore, the blessings of God have been taken away from the nation of Israel and bestowed upon the church of the Lord Jesus Christ. However, this church consists of all nations, and kindreds, and people, and tongues; which includes Jews that believe in the only begotten Son of God. Lastly, be sure to build your house on solid ground, and not on quicksand.

Matthew 7: 24 Therefore whosoever heareth these sayings of mine, and doeth them, I will liken him unto a wise man, which built his house upon a rock: 25 and the rain descended, and the floods came, and the winds blew, and beat upon that house; and it fell not: for it was founded upon a rock.
26 And every one that heareth these sayings of mine, and doeth them not, shall be likened unto a foolish man, which built his house upon the sand:
27 and the rain descended, and the floods came, and the winds blew, and beat upon that house; and it fell: and great was the fall of it.

Parable of the Marriage feast

Matthew 22: 1 And Jesus answered and spake unto them again by parables, and said,
2 The kingdom of heaven is like unto a certain king, which made a marriage for his son,
3 and sent forth his servants to call them that were bidden to the wedding: and they would not come.
4 Again, he sent forth other servants, saying, Tell them which are bidden, Behold, I have prepared my dinner: my oxen and my fatlings are killed, and all things are ready: come unto the marriage.
5 But they made light of it, and went their ways, one to his farm, another to his merchandise: 6 and the remnant took his servants, and entreated them spitefully, and slew them.
7 But when the king heard thereof, he was wroth: and he sent forth his armies, and destroyed those murderers, and burned up their city.
8 Then saith he to his servants, The wedding is ready, but they which were bidden were not worthy.

9 Go ye therefore into the highways, and as many as ye shall find, bid to the marriage.

10 So those servants went out into the highways, and gathered together all as many as they found, both bad and good: and the wedding was furnished with guests.

11 And when the king came in to see the guests, he saw there a man which had not on a wedding garment:

12 and he saith unto him, Friend, how camest thou in hither not having a wedding garment? And he was speechless.

13 Then said the king to the servants, Bind him hand and foot, and take him away, and cast him into outer darkness; there shall be weeping and gnashing of teeth.

14 For many are called, but few are chosen.

In this parable Jesus states that the father prepared a weeding feast for His Son, and told the Jewish people to come. This feast had been prepared from before the world was, and everything was ready to be served.

But those that were called snubbed up there nose and refused to come, and entreated the Father's ambassadors harshly: some they even killed. This so enraged the king that he sent his armies to destroy the chosen people; these armies were known as the Assyrians, the Babylonians, the Greeks, and the Romans.

After this, the Father bid his servants to gathered the outcasts known as the Gentiles, and bid them to come to the weeding feast. They were instructed to bring back the good, the bad, and the ugly. Observing how the guest were overflowing the Father spotted one person who was not dressed properly for the weeding feast. Upon questioning, the stranger said that he was not invited, but just followed the crowd into the marriage chamber. The Father was wroth with anger, and ordered that the stranger be cast into the pit of darkness.

Why? Because the marriage feast of the Lamb is by invitation only. In other words, "many are called, but few are chosen."

> Revelation 19: 6 And I heard as it were the voice of a great multitude, and as the voice of many waters, and as the voice of mighty thunderings, saying, Alleluia: for the Lord God omnipotent reigneth. 7 Let us be glad and rejoice, and give honour to him: for the marriage of the Lamb is come, and his wife hath made herself ready. 8 And to her was granted that she should be arrayed in fine linen, clean and white: for the fine linen is the righteousness of saints.
> 9 And he saith unto me, Write, Blessed are they which are called unto the marriage supper of the Lamb. And he saith unto me, These are the true sayings of God. 10 And I fell at his feet to worship him. And he said unto me, See thou do it not: I am thy fellowservant, and of thy brethren that have the testimony of Jesus: worship God: for the testimony of Jesus is the spirit of prophecy.

CHAPTER 30

THE END IS THE BEGINNING

In the beginning there was God, and with him was the Word, and with them was the Holy Ghost. These three were the nebulas of the solar system. They lived in total darkness. And when questioned God said, "Remember the former things of old: for I am God, and there is none else; I am God, and there is none like me, Declaring the end from the beginning, and from ancient times the things that are not yet done, saying, My counsel shall stand, and I will do all my pleasure. (Isaiah 46:9-10) And also, "I am the Lord, and there is none else, there is no God beside me: I girded thee, though thou hast not known me: That they may know from the rising of the sun, and from the west, that there is none beside me. I am the Lord, and there is none else. I form the light, and create darkness: I make peace, and create evil: I the Lord do all these things." (Isaiah 45:5-7)

Therefore, God has brought the human race from Genesis to the book of Revelation in order from us to learn that after death there is a new beginning in the New Jerusalem. So, now it is time to compare the old with the new.

ABRAHAM HOWARD JR.

The Beginning (Genesis Chapters 1 – 3)

Genesis 1: 1 In the beginning God created the heaven and the earth. 2 And the earth was without form, and void; and darkness was upon the face of the deep. And the Spirit of God moved upon the face of the waters.
3 And God said, Let there be light: and there was light.
4 And God saw the light, that it was good: and God divided the light from the darkness. 5 And God called the light Day, and the darkness he called Night. And the evening and the morning were the first day.

- The earth is a gigantic ball of water; liken unto Jupiter which is a ball of gas and liquid.
- The Holy Ghost moved upon the water to prepare it for life.
- God separated the water above from the water below. The water above are called clouds, and the water below seas.
- God called forth dry from out of the water.
- God created vegetation on all the dry land.
- God created creatures that lived in the sea water.
- God called birds from the water that fly in the air below the clouds.
- God created animals, birds, and insects to roam on the dry land.
- God created the Sun, the moon, and the stars to give light to the earth; and to regulate years, months, weeks, days, hours, and seconds.
- God created a male and female human being in his image and likeness; and breathed into their nostrils the breath of life.
- God planted the Garden of Eden, and put in the mist of it "the tree of life," and "the tree of the knowledge of good and evil."
- God put the male and female in his Garden of Eden,, while they were yet necked, and gave them instructions to eat from every tree except "the tree of the knowledge of good and

evil." Because the day they disobeyed His instructions they would die.
- They woman listened to the wiles of "the great dragon, that old serpent, called the Devil and Satan" and they both ate from the forbidden tree. Thus, their eyes were opened to the world of sin; because they realized their nakedness.
- The man and the woman were put out of the Garden of Eden to keep them from eating from "the tree of life," and live forever in a sinful state.
- This started mankind's long painful journey back to God's new garden called "The New Jerusalem.". (**Genesis Chapter 4 – Revelation Chapter 20**)

The End (Revelation Chapters 21 – 22)

<u>The New Heaven and New Earth</u>
Revelation 21: 1 And I saw a new heaven and a new earth: for the first heaven and the first earth were passed away; and there was no more sea.

- Ecclesiastes 1:9
- Isaiah 11:6-9 / 65:17-25

<u>The New Jerusalem</u>
2 And I John saw the holy city, new Jerusalem, coming down from God out of heaven, prepared as a bride adorned for her husband.

<u>God's Tabernacle is Once Again Among Mankind</u>
3 And I heard a great voice out of heaven saying, Behold, the tabernacle of God is with men, and he will dwell with them, and they shall be his people, and God himself shall be with them, and be their God.

- Leviticus 26:11-12

Eternal Life
4 And God shall wipe away all tears from their eyes; and there shall be no more death, neither sorrow, nor crying, neither shall there be any more pain: for the former things are passed away.

- Revelation 7:9-17

God is on His Throne
5 And he that sat upon the throne said, Behold, I make all things new. And he said unto me, Write: for these words are true and faithful. (22:17)
6 And he said unto me, It is done. I am Alpha and Omega, the beginning and the end. I will give unto him that is athirst of the fountain of the water of life freely.

- Deuteronomy 4:35
- Isaiah 41:4 / 43:10-11 / 44:6-8 / 48:12-13

God is our Father
7 He that overcometh shall inherit all things; and I will be his God, and he shall be my son.

- Isaiah 33:15-17

No Sin Will Enter The New Heaven and Earth
8 But the fearful, and unbelieving, and the abominable, and murderers, and whoremongers, and sorcerers, and idolaters, and all liars, shall have their part in the lake which burneth with fire and brimstone: which is the second death.

- Leviticus 18:24-30 / 20:27
- Deuteronomy 18:9-12
- Psalm 14:2-3 / 9:17 / 135:15-18
- Isaiah 8:19-22
- John 8:24 / 14:2

- Romans 1:24-32
- 1 Corinthians 6:9-10

The New Jerusalem

9 And there came unto me one of the seven angels which had the seven vials full of the seven last plagues, and talked with me, saying, Come hither, I will shew thee the bride, the Lamb's wife.

10 And he carried me away in the spirit to a great and high mountain, and shewed me that great city, the holy Jerusalem, descending out of heaven from God,

11 having the glory of God: and her light was like unto a stone most precious, even like a jasper stone, clear as crystal;

- Ezekiel 8:1-4 / 48:35

Twelve Gates inscribed with the names of the Twelve Tribes of Israel

12 and had a wall great and high, and had twelve gates, and at the gates twelve angels, and names written thereon, which are the names of the twelve tribes of the children of Israel:

13 on the east three gates; on the north three gates; on the south three gates; and on the west three gates.

- Exodus 28:21
- Ezekiel 48:31-34

Twelve Foundations inscribed with the names of the twelve apostles

14 And the wall of the city had twelve foundations, and in them the names of the twelve apostles of the Lamb.

A Four Square City

15 And he that talked with me had a golden reed to measure the city, and the gates thereof, and the wall thereof.

16 And the city lieth foursquare, and the length is as large as the breadth: and he measured the city with the reed, twelve thousand

furlongs. The length and the breadth and the height of it are equal. ***(*1,377 miles square*)***
17 And he measured the wall thereof, an hundred and forty and four cubits, according to the measure of a man, that is, of the angel. ***(*144 x 18 = 2,592*)***

The City is Pure Gold, like Glass
18 And the building of the wall of it was of jasper: and the city was pure gold, like unto clear glass.

The Foundation of the City is made of Twelve Precious Stones
19 And the foundations of the wall of the city were garnished with all manner of precious stones. The first foundation was jasper; the second, sapphire; the third, a chalcedony; the fourth, an emerald;
20 the fifth, sardonyx; the sixth, sardius; the seventh, chrysolyte; the eighth, beryl; the ninth, a topaz; the tenth, a chrysoprasus; the eleventh, a jacinth; the twelfth, an amethyst.
21 And the twelve gates were twelve pearls: every several gate was of one pearl: and the street of the city was pure gold, as it were transparent glass.

God and the Lamb are Temple and the Light
22 And I saw no temple therein: for the Lord God Almighty and the Lamb are the temple of it. 23 And the city had no need of the sun, neither of the moon, to shine in it: for the glory of God did lighten it, and the Lamb is the light thereof.

- Genesis 1:3
- Ezekiel 41:1-4
- Matthew 17:1-5
- Acts 9:3-7 / 22:1-9 / 26:12-18
- Revelation 22:5

The Doors of the City are always Open For Worship Service

24 And the nations of them which are saved shall walk in the light of it: and the kings of the earth do bring their glory and honour into it.
25 And the gates of it shall not be shut at all by day: for there shall be no night there.
26 And they shall bring the glory and honour of the nations into it.

The City is Reserved for those whose name is written in the Lamb's book of life
27 And there shall in no wise enter into it any thing that defileth, neither whatsoever worketh abomination, or maketh a lie: but they which are written in the Lamb's book of life.

- Revelation 21:8

The River of Life
Revelation 22: 1 And he shewed me a pure river of water of life, clear as crystal, proceeding out of the throne of God and of the Lamb.

- Ezekiel 47:1-12

The Tree of Life
2 In the midst of the street of it, and on either side of the river, was there the tree of life, which bare twelve manner of fruits, and yielded her fruit every month: and the leaves of the tree were for the healing of the nations.

We Will See God
3 And there shall be no more curse: but the throne of God and of the Lamb shall be in it; and his servants shall serve him:

God's People Will Be Marked With His Name
4 and they shall see his face; and his name shall be in their foreheads.

No Twenty-four Hour Clock

5 And there shall be no night there; and they need no candle, neither light of the sun; for the Lord God giveth them light: and they shall reign for ever and ever. (Revelation 21:22-23)

6 And he said unto me, These sayings are faithful and true: and the Lord God of the holy prophets sent his angel to shew unto his servants the things which must shortly be done.

The Promise of Jesus' Return Before the End

7 Behold, I come quickly: blessed is he that keepeth the sayings of the prophecy of this book.

8 And I John saw these things, and heard them. And when I had heard and seen, I fell down to worship before the feet of the angel which shewed me these things.

9 Then saith he unto me, See thou do it not: for I am thy fellowservant, and of thy brethren the prophets, and of them which keep the sayings of this book: worship God.

10 And he saith unto me, Seal not the sayings of the prophecy of this book: for the time is at hand.

11 He that is unjust, let him be unjust still: and he which is filthy, let him be filthy still: and he that is righteous, let him be righteous still: and he that is holy, let him be holy still.

12 And, behold, I come quickly; and my reward is with me, to give every man according as his work shall be.

13 I am Alpha and Omega, the beginning and the end, the first and the last.

14 Blessed are they that do his commandments, that they may have right to the tree of life, and may enter in through the gates into the city.

- Psalm 86:8-10
- 2 Peter 3:8

Those Who Will Not Be Brought To The New Heaven and New Earth

15 For without are dogs, and sorcerers, and whoremongers, and murderers, and idolaters, and whosoever loveth and maketh a lie.

(see 21:8)

Jesus Sent His Last Message by the apostle John
16 I Jesus have sent mine angel to testify unto you these things in the churches. I am the root and the offspring of David, and the bright and morning star.
17 And the Spirit and the bride say, Come. And let him that heareth say, Come. And let him that is athirst come. And whosoever will, let him take the water of life freely.
18 For I testify unto every man that heareth the words of the prophecy of this book, If any man shall add unto these things, God shall add unto him the plagues that are written in this book:

- Deuteronomy 4:2
- Proverbs 30:6
- Galatians 1:8-9

19 and if any man shall take away from the words of the book of this prophecy, God shall take away his part out of the book of life, and out of the holy city, and from the things which are written in this book.

- Exodus 32:33
- Deuteronomy 12:32

John's Truthfulness
20 He which testifieth these things saith, Surely I come quickly. Amen. Even so, come, Lord Jesus.
21 The grace of our Lord Jesus Christ be with you all. Amen.

"I will instruct thee and teach thee in the way which thou shalt go: I will guide thee with mine eye. Be ye not as the horse, or as the mule, which have no understanding: whose mouth must bes held in with bit and bridle, lest they come near unto thee." (Palm 32: 8-9)

RESEARCH NOTES

CHAPTER 1

1 John 1: 1-2

2 1 John 5:7

3 Revelation 19:11-13

4 Matthew 28:19

5 Matthew 2:15; 3:17; 17:5; / Mark 1:11; 5:7; 9:7; 14:61; / Luke 1:35; 3:22; 8:28; 9:35; 20:13 / John 1: 4; 1:14; 3:16; 4:10; 5:19; 5:20; 5:26; 14:13; / Acts 13:33 / Romans 1:4 / 1 Corinthians 15:28 / Hebrews 1:5; 1:8; 5:5; / 1 John 5:9-10 / 2 Peter 1:17

6 John 12:28

7 Matthew 16:13-17

8 John 5:1-18

9 Daniel 9: 20 And whiles I was speaking, and praying, and confessing my sin and the sin of my people Israel, and presenting my supplication before the Lord my God for the holy mountain of my God;

21. Yea, whiles I was speaking in prayer, even the man Gabriel, whom I had seen in the vision at the beginning, being caused to fly swiftly, touched me about the time of the evening oblation.

22. And he informed me, and talked with me, and said, O Daniel, I am now come forth to give thee skill and understanding. 23. At the beginning of thy supplications the commandment came forth, and I am come to shew thee; for thou art greatly beloved: therefore understand the matter, and consider the vision.

24. Seventy weeks are determined upon thy people and upon thy holy city, to finish the transgression, and to make an end of sins, and to make reconciliation for iniquity, and to bring in everlasting righteousness, and to seal up the vision and prophecy, and to anoint the most Holy.

25. Know therefore and understand, that from the going forth of the commandment to restore and to build Jerusalem unto the Messiah the Prince shall be seven weeks, and threescore and two weeks: the street shall be built again, and the wall, even in troublous times.

26. And after threescore and two weeks shall Messiah be cut off, but not for himself: and the people of the prince that shall come shall destroy the city and the sanctuary; and the end thereof shall be with a flood, and unto the end of the war desolations are determined.

27. And he shall confirm the covenant with many for one week: and in the midst of the week he shall cause the sacrifice and the oblation to cease, and for the overspreading of abominations he shall make it desolate, even until the consummation, and that determined shall be poured upon the desolate.

10 Revelation 4:1-7 / 8-10 / 11-12 / 13-14

11 John 5:37 / John 6:46

12 The American Heritage Dictionary, page 1047

13 1 John 5:7

14 Isaiah 66:1 – "Thus saith the Lord, The heaven is my throne, and the earth is my footstool: where is the house that ye build unto me? and where is the place of my rest?"

15 Psalm 115:16

16 John 7:37-39 & 15:26

17 Exodus 19:9

18 Exodus 19:16-19

19 Exodus 20:1-17 & 18-21

20 John 14:26

21 Zechariah 4:6

22 1 Samuel 10: 6-9

23 Luke 1:67-80

24 John 16:7-15

25 Hebrews 1:3

26 John 8:12-24

27 John 1:5

28 Matthew 17: 1-5 / Mark 9:2-13 / Luke 9:28-36

29 Acts 7:51-60 / 8:1-4 "1. And Saul was consenting unto his death. And at that time there was a great persecution against the church which was at Jerusalem; and they were all scattered abroad throughout the regions of Judaea and Samaria, except the apostles.

2. And devout men carried Stephen to his burial, and made great lamentation over him.

3. As for Saul, he made havock of the church, entering into every house, and haling men and women committed them to prison.

4. Therefore they that were scattered abroad went every where preaching the word.

30 Acts 9: 1-9 / 22:1-21 / 26:1-18

31 Revelation 1:1-2

32 Revelation 21:1-27

33 Psalm 90:4

34 2 Peter 3:8

35 Matthew 12:40

36 *Dake's Annotated Reference Bible*, Large note edition, page 1, 51, and 54

37 Proverbs 8: 22-31

38 John 8:32/36

39 Psalm 118:24

40 John 14: 10-11

Abraham Howard Jr.

41 Luke 9:27-36

42 Romans 12:2

43 Revelation 21:10-23

44 Isaiah 53:8

45 Acts 8:26-40

46 Job 9:8-9 / 38:31-32

47 iLumina Gold Premium, Encyclopedia, Arcturus

48 iLumina Gold Premium, Encyclopedia, Orion

49 iLumina Gold Premium, Encyclopedia, Pleiades

50 Hebrews 1:1-3

51 John 1:4

52 (1John 5:8).

53 Ted Mooney, "Light will pass through water; and water mixed with salt will create an electrical charge." *www.Finishing.com*.

54 (Matthew 5:13).

55 Genesis 2: 16-17

56 Genesis 2:18-20

57 Genesis 2:21-25

58 Genesis 5:2

59 Genesis 2: 9/16-17; God gave mankind food to eat.

60 Genesis 3: 1:24 and Revelation 12: 7-12

61 Psalm 104:4; Who maketh his angels' spirits; his ministers a flaming fire:

62 Hebrews 1: 6-14

63 John 9:24

64 Genesis 18: 1-8; 22

65 Genesis 19: 1-29

66 Matthew 26:53

67 Psalm 68:17

68 2 Samuel 5:17-25

69 Matthew 4:5-7

70 Luke 22:39-46

71 John 10:14-18

72 Genesis 6:1-4

73 2 Peter 2:4 / Jude 6

74 Genesis 16: 1-16

75 Genesis 21: 1-21

76 Genesis 25:12-18

77 Daniel 10:2-6

78 Ezekiel 43:2

79 Colossians 1: 15-17

80 Ephesians 1: 19-23

81 Webster's Third New International Dictionary, Page 359

82 Isaiah 6:1-3; Revelation 4: 1-11

83 Ezekiel 1:1-21; 10:9-22

84 Genesis 3:22-24

85 Ezekiel 1:15-21

86 The American Heritage Desk Dictionary, Page 300,

87 Matthew 18: 1-10

88 Daniel 4:1-37

89 The American Heritage Desk Dictionary, Page 1035

90 Mark 5: 25-34

91 The American Heritage Desk Dictionary, Page 741, & Ephesians 6:12

92 Mark 5:1-13

93 The American Heritage Desk Dictionary, Page 752

94 John 16:7-11

95 Matthew 25:41

96 Ephesians 6:12

97 Daniel 10: 10-13; Revelation 12: 7-8; Jude 9

98 Revelation 1: 1-2

99 Matthew 25:41

100 Isaiah 14:9–23; Ezekiel 28:12–19.

101 Revelation 12:7–12, The war in heaven

102 Luke 10:18

103 Genesis 3:1-24

104 John 8:44

105 James 1:12–15

106 1 John 2: 16

107 Genesis 5:1–2 God called both the male and female he created Adam

108 Matthew 5: 11-12

109 Genesis 5: 1-5

110 Psalm 90:10

111 Matthew 25:41; 2 Peter 2:4; Revelation 20:10 / 11-15

112 John 3:16

113 Genesis 4:15

114 Genesis 4:17

115 iLumina Gold Premium, Encyclopedia, Lamech

116 Genesis 8:20-22 / 9:1-10

117 iLumina Gold Premium, Encyclopedia, Seth

118 iLumina Gold Premium, Encyclopedia, Enosh

119 Genesis 5:1-5 / Josephus page 27

120 Leviticus 18:1-30

121 iLumina Gold Premium, Encyclopedia, Adam

122 iLumina Gold Premium, Encyclopedia, Methuselah,

123 Genesis 21-32

124 Genesis 6:1–12.

125 2 Peter 2: 4-5

126 Jude 6

127 Genesis 6: 5-7

128 Genesis 6: 13-17

129 iLumina Gold Premium, Encyclopedia, Lamech

130 Genesis 7:2-3

131 Genesis 8:20–22.

132 Genesis 9:1–17.

133 Genesis 7; 8; 9:1–17.

134 Genesis 9: 12-16

135 Genesis 10:21-23

136 Isaiah 12:9–23.

137 Revelation 12:3-4

138 Revelation 12: 7-9

139 Luke 10:18.

140 Revelation 12:1–12; 1 Peter 5:8–9; Luke 10:18–20.

141 iLumina Gold Premium, Encyclopedia: UZ

142 Deuteronomy 13:1-3

143 1 Peter 1:5–9; 4:12.

144 Matthew 5:11–12.

145 Matthew 4:1–11; Mark 1:12; Luke 4:1–13.

146 John 14:6

147 Revelation 12:10-12

148 Numbers 1:1–50.

149 Genesis 3:5

150 Matthew 4: 8-10

151 Jeremiah 29: 10-13

152 Daniel 9:1–27.

153 Daniel 10: 1-21

154 Ephesians 6:12

155 Acts 2: 17-21

156 Revelation 13: 1-10

157 Revelation 16:13-14

158 Matthew 24:23-24

159 Matthew 8:28–34; Mark 5:1–20; Luke 8:26–40.

160 1 Corinthians 6:19

161 Luke 8:30-33

162 Matthew 8:28-34

163 Mark 16:15–19

164 Matthew 10: 1-8

165 Luke 10:1-16

166 Luke 10: 17-20

167 Matthew 12: 43-45

168 1 Corinthians 6:19

169 Romans 10: 8-10

170 John 3:16-21

171 John 10:9-10

172 1 Corinthians 7:4-5

173 Luke 8:11-12

174 1 Thessalonians 2:13-20

175 2 Corinthians 11:13-15

176 1 Peter 5:8-9

177 Proverbs 3:5-6

178 James 4:7-8

179 2 Corinthians 2:11-12

180 Ephesians 6:12-18

181 Luke 6:27-31

182 James 1:12-16

183 Matthew 10:28

184 Galatians 6:1-2

185 Leviticus 20:10 and Deuteronomy 22:22; both state that both the man and woman caught in adultery would be put to death.

186 Luke 1:39–56; Matthew 1:18–25.

187 John 1:9-10

188 Genesis 11:24

189 iLumina Gold Premium, Encyclopedia, Nahor

190 Genesis 11:26

191 iLumina Gold Premium, Encyclopedia: UR

192 Genesis 20:1-12

193 Genesis 11:26-29

194 Genesis 22:20-23 / 24:1-24

195 Genesis 11:30-32

196 iLumina Gold Premium, Encyclopedia: Haran

197 iLumina Gold Premium, Encyclopedia, Noah

198 Luke 1: 31-33

199 Romans 4:16

200 Philippians 2:10-11

201 Genesis 12:1-6

202 Genesis 12:4-8

203 iLumina Gold Premium, Encyclopedia: Bethel

204 Genesis 20:1-12

205 Genesis 12:18-20

206 Genesis 13:1-4

207 2 Samuel 5:1-10

208 Genesis 15:1-21

209 Genesis 16: 1-16

210 Genesis Chapter 18

211 Genesis 18: 16-32

212 Genesis 19: 1-29

213 The Complete Works of Josephus, page 32, Chapter VI,5.

214 Genesis 21: 1-21

215 iLumina Gold Premium, Encyclopedia: Moriah

216 iLumina Gold Premium, Encyclopedia: Beersheba

217 iLumina Gold Premium, Encyclopedia, Terah

218 The Complete Works of Josephus, page 32, Chapter VI, 5.

219 Acts 7: 4 "So Abraham left the land of the Chaldeans and lived in Haran until his father died. Then God brought him here to the land where you now live."

220 iLumina Gold Premium, Encyclopedia: Kirjatharba

221 ilumina Gold Premium, Encyclopedia: Hebron

222 iLumina Gold Premium, Encyclopedia, Heth

223 iLumina Gold Premium, Encyclopedia, Sepulchre

224 iLumina Gold Premium, encyclopedia, Shekel

225 iLumina Gold Premium, Encyclopedia, Gerah

226 iLumina Gold Premium, encyclopedia, Cave of Machpelah, Machpelah

227 Genesis 24:67 / 25:20

228 Genesis 22:20-23; 24:15 /24/29

229 Genesis 25: 1-11 / 20

230 Genesis 25: 21-26

231 Genes 25: 27-34

232 Genesis 25:1–10; 23:1–20.

233 John 6:38–40, 44, 54; 7; 11:24–25; 14:1–6.

234 Genes 26: 34-35; 36: 1-43

235 Genesis Chapters 27 – 28 – 29:1-18

236 Genesis 35: 16-19

237 Genesis 11:10

238 iLumina Gold Premium, Encyclopedia, Shem

239 Genesis 30: 1-24

240 Genesis 31: 1-41

241 Genesis 31:49

242 Genesis 32: 1-32

243 Genesis 33:1-20

244 iLumina Gold Premium, Encyclopedia, Seir

245 iLumina Gold Premium, Encyclopedia, Esau

246 Genesis 34: 1-31

247 iLumina Gold Premium, Encyclopedia, Ephrath

248 iLumina Gold Premium, Encyclopedia, Edar

249 Genesis 35: 1-22

250 Genesis 25: 12-18

251 Genesis 37: 1-36

252 Genesis 38: 1-30

253 Mathew 1: 3

254 Genesis 39: 1-23

255 Genesis Chapter's 39 & 40

256 Genesis 41: 1-46

257 Genesis 35:28-29

258 iLumina Gold Premium, Encyclopedia, Isaac

259 Genesis 41:47-53

260 Genesis 41: 54-57

261 Genesis 41:54-57

262 Genesis 15: 13-16

263 Genesis 46: 1-34 / 47: 1-26

264 Genesis 45: 1-15

265 Genesis Chapter 48 & 49 & 50:1-14

266 Genesis 50: 1-14

267 Genesis 50: 15-26

268 Exodus 1: 1-22

269 Exodus 6:19-20 / Numbers 26:59

270 Exodus 7:7

271 Exodus 2: 1-10

272 Exodus 2: 11-22

273 John 8:56-59

274 Thru the Bible, vol 1, chapter 3, page 209

275 Dake's Annotated Reference Bible, John 8: 58 -

276 Exodus 3:1-22

277 Genesis 17:1-27

278 Isaiah 1:18

279 Acts 11:19-30 / 16:36-41

280 Matthew 10:19-20

281 Ephesians 6:10-11

282 Exodus 7:7

283 Exodus 7:14 to chapter 11 / 12:29-36

284 Daniel 3:1-30

285 iLumina Gold Premium, Encyclopedia, Goshen

286 Numbers 23:19

287 The Open Bible, Page 1290, The Jewish Calendar

Abraham Howard Jr.

288 Exodus 12: 37-40

289 Genesis 17:1-27

290 John 3:16-21

291 Romans 2:25–29; John 4:19–24.

292 Exodus 14:19–20

293 Exodus 20: 21

294 1 John 5:7

295 Exodus 14:21–22

296 Joshua 3: 13-17

297 Jimmy Swaggart, *The Expositor's Study Bible*, page 132, 1 Corinthians 10:1-2, page 2016-2017

298 John 6:22-35

299 Matthew 7:13-14

300 1 Peter 1:16

301 2 Corinthians 5:17

302 Ephesians 5:23–32 and Colossians 3:5–11.

303 Psalm 1:1–6; 2 Timothy 2:15–16).

304 Galatians 5:16–26

305 John 2: 1-10

306 Numbers 20:2–29

307 John 8:23-24

308 John 4:10–14; 7: 37–39; The Living Water (the Holy Ghost)

309 Dake's Annotated Reference Bible, page 88, Exodus 23:20

310 The Expositors Study bible, page 151, Exodus 23:20

311 Thru the Bible, Vol 1, page 275, Exodus 23:20

312 1 John 3:4

313 John 5: 43-47

314 John 14:28

315 John 17:11

316 John 17:22

317 John 10:30

318 Mark 2:1-12

319 Deuteronomy 8:1-4

320 Luke 4:16-30

321 Matthew 4:23-25

322 John 15: 1-11

323 Revelation 13:7–8, 20:11–15;.Books of the Lord

324 Revelation 3:1–6; Christ controls the Book of Life

325 Matthew 12:36-37

326 1 John 5:7

327 Matthew 7:22-23

328 Revelation 21:8

329 Romans 8:28

330 1 Kings 19:1–4

331 Jeremiah 20: 7-18

332 Matthew 8:19-20

333 Acts 2: 1-4

334 Matthew 3:11

335 Luke 1:67–80, Zacharias prophesies after he is filled with the Holy Ghost

336 Isaiah 28:9-14

Abraham Howard Jr.

337 1 Corinthians 14:37-40

338 James 1:14-15

339 *Smith's Bible Dictionary*, p.16., Anak

340 Joshua 14: 6-15

341 1 Samuel 17

342 "Moreover the Philistines had yet war again with Israel; and David went down, and his servants with him, and fought against the Philistines: and David waxed faint. And Ishbibenob, which was of the sons of the giant, the weight of whose spear weighed three hundred shekels of brass in weight, he being girded with a new sword, thought to have slain David. But Abishai the son of Zeruiah succoured him, and smote the Philistine, and killed him. Then the men of David sware unto him, saying, Thou shalt go no more out with us to battle, that thou quench not the light of Israel. And it came to pass after this, that there was again a battle with the Philistines at Gob: then Sibbechai the Hushathite slew Saph, which was of the sons of the giant. And there was again a battle in Gob with the Philistines, where Elhanan the son of Jaareoregim, a Bethlehemite, slew the brother of Goliath the Gittite, the staff of whose spear was like a weaver's beam. And there was yet a battle in Gath, where was a man of great stature, that had on every hand six fingers, and on every foot six toes, four and twenty in number; and he also was born to the giant. And when he defied Israel, Jonathan the son of Shimea the brother of David slew him. These four were born to the giant in Gath, and fell by the hand of David, and by the hand of his servants. (2 Samuel 21:15-22)

343 Genesis 36:12; 10:15–20.

344 John 5:38–40

345 Matthew 10:28

346 Psalm 105:1-15)

347 Matthew 5:10–12.

348 Mathew 18:15–17

349 Luke 6:27–37

350 Ezekiel 33:11

351 "Now it came to pass in the third year of Hoshea son of Elah king of Israel, that Hezekiah the son of Ahaz king of Judah began to reign. Twenty and five

years old was he when he began to reign; and he reigned twenty and nine years in Jerusalem. His mother's name also was Abi, the daughter of Zachariah. And he did that which was right in the sight of the Lord, according to all that David his father did. He removed the high places, and brake the images, and cut down the groves, and brake in pieces the brasen serpent that Moses had made: for unto those days the children of Israel did burn incense to it: and he called it Nehushtan." (2 Kings 18: 1-4)

352 Revelation 12:7–12; 1 Peter 5:8–9; John 10:10.

353 John 3:14–15

354 And Lot went up out of Zoar, and dwelt in the mountain, and his two daughters with him; for he feared to dwell in Zoar: and he dwelt in a cave, he and his two daughters. And the firstborn said unto the younger, Our father is old, and there is not a man in the earth to come in unto us after the manner of all the earth: Come, let us make our father drink wine, and we will lie with him, that we may preserve seed of our father. And they made their father drink wine that night: and the firstborn went in, and lay with her father; and he perceived not when she lay down, nor when she arose. And it came to pass on the morrow, that the firstborn said unto the younger, Behold, I lay yesternight with my father: let us make him drink wine this night also; and go thou in, and lie with him, that we may preserve seed of our father. And they made their father drink wine that night also: and the younger arose, and lay with him; and he perceived not when she lay down, nor when she arose. Thus were both the daughters of Lot with child by their father. And the firstborn bare a son, and called his name Moab: the same is the father of the Moabites unto this day. And the younger, she also bare a son, and called his name Benammi: the same is the father of the children of Ammon unto this day. (Genesis 19:30-39)

355 1 Corinthians 6:9–10

356 Ephesians 5:3–7

357 1Timothy 1:9–11

358 Joshua 5:2-9

359 Joshua chapter 9

360 Exodus 23: 20-33

361 Joshua chapters 10 thru 24

362 Joshua 14: 6-10 / 24:29

Abraham Howard Jr.

363 Judges 2:1-5

364 Judges 2: 11-19

365 iLumina Gold Premium, Encyclopedia, Baal, Ashtaroth

366 iLumina Gold Premium, Encyclopedia, Othniel

367 iLumina Gold Premium, Encyclopedia, Eglon

368 iLumina Gold Premium, encyclopedia, Ehud

369 iLumina Gold Premium, Encyclopedia, Jabin

370 iLumina Gold Premium, Encyclopedia, Deborah

371 iLumina Gold Premium, Encyclopedia, Midian

372 iLumina Gold Premium, Encyclopedia, Ophrah

373 iLumina Gold Premium, Encyclopedia, Abimelech

374 iLumina Gold Premium, Encyclopedia, Tola, Jair, Jephthah, Elon, and Abdon

375 iLumina Gold Premium, Encyclopedia, Cush, Mizraim, Put, Phut, Canaan

376 Genesis 9: 18-27

377 iLumina Gold Premium, Encyclopedia, Ashdod, Gaza, Gath

378 iLumina Gold Premium, Encyclopedia, Heth, Jebusite, Amorite, Girgashite, Hivites, Arkite, Sinite, Arvadite, Zemarite, Hamathite

379 Judges 13: 1-25

380 iLumina Gold Premium, Encyclopedia, Samson

381 iLumina Gold Premium, Encyclopedia, Delilah

382 1 Chronicles 6:27-30

383 1 Samuel 1:9-18

384 iLimina Gold Premium, Encyclopedia: Ephod

385 Numbers chapter 18

386 1 Samuel 2:27-36

387 1 Samuel 3:1-21

388 1 Samuel 4:1-18

389 Numbers 18:7

390 1 Samuel 8:1-3

391 1 Samuel 10: 1-12

392 1 Samuel 13:8-14

393 1 Samuel 15:1s

394 iLumina Gold Premium, Encyclopedia: Amalek, Amalekites

395 1 Samuel Chapter 16

396 Matthew 20:16 / 22:14

397 Matthew 7: 13-14

398 Revelation 3:5 / Exodus 32:33 / Psalm 69:28

399 Open Bible, Page 273, Time of Samuel

400 2 Samuel 2:11

401 2 Samuel 5:1-5

402 2 Samuel chapter 7

403 2 Samuel 11:1-26

404 1 Kings 2:10-11

405 1 Chronicles 22:6–8

406 1 Kings 3:1-15 / 2 Chronicles 1:7-12

407 1 Kings 6:1

408 1 Kings 6:11–13

409 1 Kings 6:37-38

410 1 Kings 8:1-11 / 2 Chronicles 5:1-14

411 Matthew 18:20

412 2 Chronicles 6:1-42

413 2 Chronicles 7:1-3 / 12-22

414 1 Kings 10: 1-13

415 1 Kings 11:41-43

416 iLumina Gold Premium, Encyclopedia, Bethel

417 iLumina Gold Premium, Encyclopedia, Dan

418 iLumina Gold Premium, Encyclopedia; Shechem

419 1 Kings chapter 13

420 iLumina Gold Premium, Encyclopedia, Obadiah

421 iLumina Gold Premium, Encyclopedia, Jonah

422 iLumina Gold Premium, Encyclopedia, Amos

423 iLumina Gold Premium, Encyclopedia, Hosea

424 iLumina Gold Premium, Encyclopedia, Micah

425 iLumina Gold Premium, Encyclopedia, Isaiah

426 Numbers 12:6

427 Isaiah 6:1-9

428 2 Kings 18:9-12

429 The Open Bible Page 655, The Time of Isaiah

430 The Reese Chronological Bible, Page 957, B. Manasseh

431 2 Kings 21:1-18 / 2 Chronicles 33:1-20

432 The Open Bible, Page 655: The Author of Isiah,

433 iLumina Gold Premium, Encyclopedia, Nahum

434 The Open Bible, Nahum, page 876: Time of Nahum

435 2 Kings 21: 1-18 / 2 Chronicles 33:1-20

436 1 Kings 13:1-3

437 iLumina Gold Premium, Encyclopedia, Zephaniah

438 Jeremiah 1:1–11

439 iLumina Gold Premium, Encyclopedia, Anathoth

440 1 Chronicles 6:13 and 2 Kings 22:1-4

441 2 Kings 17:1–23, 24–41; 2 Kings 18:9–12.

442 iLumina Gold Premium, Encyclopedia: Grove

443 iILumina Gold Premium, Encyclopedia: Topheth

444 iLumina Gold Premium, Encyclopedia: Valley of Hinnom - Gehenna

445 2 Kings Chapter 22 & 23 / 2 Chronicles Chapter 34 & 35

446 iLumina Gold Premium, Encyclopedia, Habakkuk

447 iLumina Gold Premium, Encyclopedia, *Jehoiakim*

448 Jeremiah 52:28, Daniel 1:1-7

449 2 Chronicles 36:7

450 iLumina Gold Premium, Encyclopedia, Daniel

451 iLumina Gold Premium, Encyclopedia, Ezekiel

452 2 Kings 24:17, Josephus page 218, Chapter VII, paragraph 1

453 iLumina Gold Premium, Encyclopedia, Zedekiah

454 Revelation 11:15-19

455 iLumina Gold Premium, Encyclopedia, Cyrus the Great

456 The Open Bible, page 473

457 iLumina Gold Premium, Encyclopedia, Haggai

458 iLumina Gold Premium, Encyclopedia, Zechariah

459 iLumina Gold Premium, Encyclopedia, Esther; Mordechai

460 iLumina Gold Premium, Encyclopedia, Ezra

461 Open Bible, page 486, Nehemiah, The Time of Nehemiah / page 820, Daniel, The Christ of Daniel

462 iLumina Gold Premium, Encyclopedia, Nehemiah

463 Ezra chapters 1 through 6.

464 Luke 1:11–17; Matthew 11:1–15.

465 iLumina Gold Premium, Encyclopedia, Malachi, Malachi Book Of

466 John chapter 5.

467 Psalm 78:1-3

468 Matthew 2:18

469 John 1:14

470 Acts 17:10-12

471 Isaiah 40:3-5 / Luke 3:1-8

472 2 Kings 2:1-11

473 Matthew 11:11-15

474 Matthew 17:1-5

475 Numbers Chapter 18

476 iLumina Gold Premium, Encyclopedia, Nazareth

477 Hebrews 10:5, "Wherefore when he cometh into the world, he saith, sacrifice and offering thou wouldest not, but a body hast thou prepared me."

478 Luke 1:34-35, " Then said Mary unto the angel, How shall this be, seeing I know not a man? And the angel answered and said unto her, The Holy Ghost shall come upon thee, and the power of the highest shall overshadow thee: therefore also that holy thing which shall be born of thee shall be called the Son of God."

479 John 1:13, "Which was born, not of blood, nor of the will of the flesh, nor of the will of man, but of God."

480 Mathew 1:20, "But while he thought on these things, behold the angel of the Lord appeared unto him in a dream, saying, Joseph, thou son of David, fear

not to take unto thee Mary thy wife: for that which is conceived in her is of the Holy Ghost."

481 iLumina Gold Premium, Encyclopedia, Bethlemite, Bethlehem

482 The Reese Chronological Bible, Page 1250 / 1256, Herod's Decree

483 Dake's Annotated Bible, St Luke, Chapter 2:12, b-swaddling clothes

484 iLumina Gold Premuim, Encyclopedia, Magi

485 Smith's Bible Dictionary Page 188, Magi,

486 New Bible Dictionary, Page 478, Herod,

487 New Bible Dictionary, Page 478-479, Herod,

488 The Reese Chronological Bible, Page 1250, Herod's Decree,

489 Josephus, Page 365, Antiquities of the Jews, footnote

490 Josephus, page 379, Chapter III, 3

491 Genesis 5:18–24, The days of Enoch

492 Genesis 15:7–21, God makes a covenant with Abraham

493 Daniel 7: 9, 14, Daniel is shown the everlasting kingdom of God through Christ

494 *Easton's Bible Dictionary, Elijah.*

495 iLumina Gold Premium, Encyclopedia, Tishbe

496 Revelation 21:8 - "But the fearful, and unbelieving, and abominable, and murderers, and whoremongers, and sorcerers, and idolaters, and all liars, shall have their part in the lake which burneth with fire and brimstone: which is the second death"

497 Genesis 1:5

498 Matthew 21:12–13; Mark 11:15–19; Luke 19:45–48; John 2:13–25.

499 The Open Bible, page 820, The Christ of Daniel

500 The New Open Bible; Nehemiah 2:1–11.

501 John 8:56-57

502 The Open Bible, The Jewish Calendar, foot note

503 The American Heritage dictionary, Julian Calendar

504 The American Heritage Dictionary, Gregorian Calendar

505 iLumina Gold Premium, Encyclopedia, Calendars, Ancient and Modern, Dates, hours, and minutes

506 iLumina Gold Premium, Encyclopedia, Golgotha

507 For Passover dates, see http://judaismvschristianity.com/Passover_dates.htm Passover dates 26-34 A.D.

508 Exodus 11:47; 12:1–20; 12:21–29; 13:34; Leviticus 23:4–5; 6–8.

509 Abib: Exodus 12:2; 13:1–11; 1 Chronicles 23:24–32; 2 Chronicles 2:1–5. Nisan: Esther 3:7; Nehemiah 2:1.

510 John 19:31

511 iLumina Gold Premium, Calendars Ancient and Modern: Months and Months Names

512 iLumina Gold Premium, Calendars Ancient and Modern: Jewish Festivals

513 The Open Bible, page 272, Jewish Calendar, *foot note

514 iLumina Gold Premium, Calendars Ancient and Modern: Months and Months Names

515 The Open Bible, page 272, The Jewish Calendar

516 *Easton's Bible Dictionary, p. Gethsemane*

517 iLumina Gold Premium, Encyclopedia, Gethsemane

518 Matthew 26:47–56; Mark 14:43–52; Luke 22:47–53; John 18:1–11.

519 Wikipedia, A thief in the Night; Left Behind

520 Matthew 3:13–17; Luke 3:21–22; 1:41.

521 Matthew 14:1–12.

522 1 Corinthians 3:16–17.

523 Acts 1:9–11; Revelation 1:1–8.

524 Acts 1:1–15; Matthew 13:54–56.

525 Matthew 20:1–16; 22:1–14.

526 Acts 18:2–3; 18–22.

527 1 Corinthians 1:1–17, 18–31.

528 "William J. Seymour Biography." */azusastreet.org/WilliamJSeymour.htm.*

529 Matthew 9:1–13.

530 Romans 10:8–10.

531 2 Chronicles 5:1–14; 6:1–42; 7:1–14.

532 Revelation 4:11; Isaiah 43:7; 1 Corinthians 3:16–17; 6:19.

533 Revelation 19:17–21; 20:1–3, 4–6, 7–9, 10, 11–15.

534 Matthew 10:1–42.

535 Mark 6:7–13.

536 Acts 20:13–37.

537 2 Timothy 4:3–4.

538 John 10:11–13.

539 Abraham Howard Jr., *Searching for Jesus, A Bible Study Book* (Maitland, FL: Xulon Press, 2010), appendix P.

540 John 3:14–21.

541 Acts 11:19–29; 13:1–3.

542 *Easton's Bible Dictionary*, p.Asia; *www.revelation-today.com/Churches7.htm*; Seven Churches in Revelation-AllAboutArchaeology.org, *www.allaboutarchaeology.org/seven-churches-in-revelation.htm*

543 iLumina Gold Premium, Encyclopedia, Tree of Life

544 *Easton's Bible Dictionary*, p. Ephesus

545 *Easton's Bible Dictionary*, p. Smyrna.

546 *Thru the Bible*, with J. Vernon McGee, volume V, p.904–906.

547 *Smiths Bible Dictionary*, p.275-276

548 *Easton's Bible Dictionary*, p. Pergamos

549 *Thru the Bible*, with J. Vernon McGee, volume V, p.906

550 Numbers 22–25:1–9.

551 *Smith's Bible Dictionary*, p. 218; Acts 6:1–5; *Harper's Bible Dictionary*, p. 704.

552 *Harper's Bible Dictionary*, p. 1069; *Smith's Bible Dictionary*, p. 276.

553 *New Bible Dictionary*, p. 1073; *Thru the Bible*, with J. Vernon McGee, p. 912.

554 2 Timothy 3:1–7.

555 John 4:24.

556 Matthew 6:24; Luke 16:1–13.

557 *Harper's Bible dictionary*, p. 784

558 *Smith's Bible Dictionary*, p. 277.

559 iLumina Gold Premium, Encyclopedia, Philadelphia

560 *Smith's Bible Dictionary*, p. 277.

561 Isaiah 7:10-14, Luke 1:26-30

562 Matthew 12:22–36.

563 Ephesians 1:13–14; Ezekiel 9:1–7.

564 Jeremiah 27:6–8; 9–22.

565 Acts 4:1–37; 5:1–41.

566 2 Peter 3:15–16.

567 *Easton's Bible Dictionary*, p. Moloch

568 *Easton's Bible Dictionary*, p. Chemosh

569 Abort73.com/Abortion Unfiltered, *www.**abort73**.com* (U.S. Abortion Statistics); http://www.abort73.com/index.php?/aborttion/medical_Testimony

Bibliography

Bible Library. ValuSoft, Inc., Ellis Enterprises, Inc., 1999.

Dake's Annotated Reference Bible, Large note edition, January 1992

Easton's Bible Dictionary, Bible Library, 1999

Harper's Bible Dictionary, Harper & Row, Publishers, San Francisco, 1985

Hebrew-Greek Key Word Study Bible, King James Version. Chattanooga, TN: AMG Publishing, 1991.

Holy Bible: The New Open Bible, Study Edition. Nashville: Thomas Nelson, 1990.

iLumina Gold Premium, Tyndale House Publishers, 2006

The Complete works of Josephus, Kredel Publications, 1981

The American Heritage Desk Dictionary, Houghton Mifflin company, 1981

The Reese Chronological Bible, Bethany House Publishers, 1980

Thru The Bible, with J. Vernon McGee Thomas Nelson Publishers, Nashville, 1981

Abraham Howard Jr.

New Bible Dictionary, Second Edition, Tyndale House Publishers, Inc, 1986

Smiths Bible Dictionary, revised edition Holman Bible Publishers, Nashville, 1994

Strong's Expanded, Exhaustive, Concordance of the Bible, Red Letter Edition, Revised Edition. Nashville: Thomas Nelson, 2001.

Swaggart, Jimmy. *The Expositor's Study Bible, King James Version, Crossfire Edition.* Baton Rouge, LA: Jimmy Swaggart Ministries, 2010.

Webster's Third New International Dictionary, Unabridged). Springfield, MA: Merriam Webster Inc. 1981

Wikipedia, 2020

Who is Jesus Christ: The Complete Story?
2nd Edition

This book is the story of truths about Christ Jesus (the Word of God), who was with the Father before the world was, and his foot print through the Old Testament; to his birth, death, and resurrection in the New Testament. The following facts are prevalent:

- God created the heaven and the earth.
- The Word (Christ) is the true light of God.
- The Word created everything on the earth, the Sun, the moon, and the stars.
- The Father, the Word, and the Holy Ghost created a male human being after their image and likeness, and from him they created his female companion.
- It was O Lucifer, the great dragon, that old serpent, called the Devil and Satan, who brought sin to the earth, and caused the death of Adam & Eve.
- Year 0 is when Adam & Eve were put out of the Garden of Eden to live a life of sin and death on the earth.
- Year 1741 is about the time Satan attacked Job.
- Year 2023 is around the time that Christ and Abraham became friends.
- Year 2668 is the start of Christ guiding Moses, and the children of Israel across the Sinai desert for forty years.
- During the years of 1127 BC – 444 BC Christ walked with the prophets and the kings of Israel.
- Christ was born on April 1, 5 BC during the Passover month.
- Christ died hanging on a cross April 4, 33 AD; the first day of the eight day Passover celebration, and was resurrected from the dead after three nights and three days: in the heart of the earth.

- In the "new heaven and earth," the Word (Lamb) is the light of the New Jerusalem; which is 1377 miles square.

To prove his deity, he met with his two friends, Moses, and Elijah, up on a mountain: which was witnessed by Peter, James and John.

The Holy Bible is the only physical witness to the Lord Jesus Christ, but you can be assured that he is the one "which is, and which was, and which is to come, the Almighty."

www.ingramcontent.com/pod-product-compliance
Lightning Source LLC
Chambersburg PA
CBHW071947110526
44592CB00012B/1024